Reconstructed Portrait of Queen Tiy,
Mother of Ikhnaton

THIS MODERN PAINTING IS BASED ON THE ANCIENT SCULPTURED PORTRAITS
OF THE QUEEN. IT IS THE WORK OF MRS. WINIFRED BRUNTON,
WHOSE ARCHAEOLOGICAL KNOWLEDGE AND ARTISTIC SKILL HAVE RECREATED
FOR US IN THIS MANNER MANY OF THE OUTSTANDING PERSONALITIES
OF ANCIENT EGYPT. (COURTESY OF MRS. PERCY NEWBERRY)

HISTORY OF CIVILIZATION

EARLIER AGES

BY

JAMES HARVEY ROBINSON

JAMES HENRY BREASTED

AND

EMMA PETERS SMITH

WITH THE ASSISTANCE OF

EDITH W. WARE

GINN AND COMPANY

BOSTON · NEW YORK · CHICAGO

ATLANTA · DALLAS · PALO ALTO · TORONTO · LONDON

Preface

THIS volume presents a short survey of Western civilization from its earliest beginnings to the founding of our country. To bring the main outlines of so vast a topic within the compass of a single manual has required the utmost care in the selection, arrangement, and presentation of material. The authors have had constantly in mind the needs of young students as well as the problems of the teacher. They have tried to make the book clear, interesting, and teachable.

They have included, therefore, only topics which are vital to an understanding of the relation of the past to the present; for they believe that it is only these dynamic aspects of the past which are likely to awaken the interest and imagination of young people. Especial care has been taken not only to emphasize this bond between the past and ourselves but to show how the topic under discussion is related to and illuminates the main theme, or "frame of reference," of the book — how our civilization has grown and developed through long years of achievement.

The authors have taken advantage of the latest researches in the social sciences so that the manual may provide a sound basis for further study. They are in hearty sympathy with progressive teachers who have wished to see a closer correlation between the social studies. They have therefore freely drawn upon the various branches of the social sciences for their contributions toward a fuller understanding of the complex character of our civilization.

In the interest of clarity and force, special attention has been given to the arrangement of material so that the story may unfold logically and with accumulating interest. The current topical, or "unit," form has been adopted as the most practical in presenting the widely diverse aspects of the life of mankind. The book is divided into eight major units, or parts. Introducing each of these main divisions, a very simple statement gives in a few lines the content and significance of the part. Secondly, each part is divided into chapters which deal with the various aspects of the part, or unit. Preceding each chapter there is a short introduction which gives in brief form the key to the chapter. These forewords, or previews, not only prepare the student for what he is to find but also show him its relation to what has gone before. They thus establish continuity and show the unity of the entire narrative. If the pupil will reread the foreword after he has mastered the chapter, he will see clearly how it fits into the structure of the part as a whole. Thirdly, the paragraphs are closely knit together and arranged to carry the story forward with growing interest and emphasis toward the climax of the chapter. Fourthly, care has been taken to make the language as simple as may be and to avoid vagueness and confusion in the mind of the student by the immediate explanation of all unfamiliar and unusual terms. Thus from the vocabulary all the way to the structure of the book as a whole the authors have endeavored to make the conditions of learning as favorable as possible.

The study aids to be found at the end of each chapter are prepared with a threefold purpose: to assist the student in the interpretation and mastery of what he has read; to help him to relate his new knowledge to what he already knew, and so to broaden his intellectual outlook; and to train him to acquire scholarly methods of workmanship.

The Review Questions based on the text are designed to refresh his memory on the most important points of the chapter and to give these their proper emphasis. A list of Useful Terms is given which the student should master, to make sure that his understanding of the narrative is perfectly clear. The addition of these words to his vocabulary should enable him greatly to extend his range of general reading. Directive Questions will suggest how he can relate the special topic under consideration with other information, establish comparisons or contrasts, and follow the development of ideas and institutions. The Discussion Topics are intended to arouse critical thinking and aid the student to form independent judgments by making careful discriminations, balancing opposing ideas, and learning to sustain his position in a debate. Additional Adventures in Learning include topics and problems for further study. To train the student in forming scholarly habits of work he is asked to make constant use of dictionaries, encyclopedias, and books of reference. Above all, an early acquaintance with source materials is invaluable to the student of history. The student will get a far more vivid sense of the reality of events and personalities from these than from any second-hand or third-hand account of them. He will learn to distinguish between primary and secondary sources; he will see for himself the stuff of which history is made; he can learn something of the processes of historical scholarship, and ask himself what in our own time will form source material when its history comes to be written. Selections from the sources are given for each chapter, and the student should be encouraged to read other source material whenever it is available.

The maps have been prepared especially to illustrate the text in hand and to aid the teacher in making the topics clear. The illustrations have been carefully chosen with the purpose of giving life and reality to the narrative, as well as visual assistance to the student in his reconstruction of the past.

The Bibliography at the end of the book supplements the references following the chapters and is intended primarily for the teacher. From these references she can select assignments suitable to her particular method of teaching and the abilities of her pupils.

THE AUTHORS

PUBLISHERS' NOTE

The first part of the present volume was prepared by Dr. Breasted with the assistance of Dr. Ware, and the latter portion by Dr. Robinson and Dr. Emma P. Smith. The succeeding volume, *Our Own Age*, was prepared by Dr. Charles A. Beard, Dr. James Harvey Robinson, and Dr. Donnal V. Smith. It carries the story of civilization from the founding of our country to our own time.

THE PUBLISHERS

Contents

Earlier Ages

Contents

Contents

Earlier Ages

Contents

List of Maps

xiv

List of Maps

List of Colored Maps

Foreword

What is Civilization? Before beginning this story of our civilization we ought to get a clear idea of what is meant by civilization. It is something that surrounds us every minute of the day and night. We cannot get away from it if we would. We are so used to it that we take it for granted and as a rule hardly notice it. We become aware of it only when we have to go without some of the necessities, conveniences, or pleasures which it brings with it. There are some peoples on the earth who have very little civilization, and by comparing their condition with our own we can see what our civilization includes.

The Way the Savage Andaman Islanders Live. In the Bay of Bengal, on the other side of the globe from New York, are the Andaman Islands, where the inhabitants have as little civilization as anyone in the world. They have no houses except shelters of boughs, for they know nothing of boards, nails, bricks, or mortar ; no clothes like ours, for they cannot prepare and weave cotton, wool, linen, or silk and so cannot make cloth ; no steel knives, hammers, or axes, for they are unacquainted with metal work. They have no farms or vegetable gardens, no towns, with stores, shops, factories, schools, churches, libraries ; they have no books, for the people cannot read or write, and no one among them knows anything about geography, history, geology, chemistry, or any of our sciences or arts.

In short, the Andaman islanders manage to live without all these things which seem a natural part of our lives and make up our civilization. They have a language, however, so that they can talk to one another ; they use fire for cooking their fish, although they do not know how to make it and therefore have to be very careful not to let it go out. They make bows and arrows and weave baskets and can do a few simple things. They know too little about the looks of the stars to venture out of sight of land in their canoes, for if caught by darkness they would not be able to steer their way back. They have no money to buy anything from ships that might come from regions more advanced in civilization. For many hundreds of years they appear to have lived in much the same way they now do.

It took mankind thousands and thousands of years to learn even as much as the Andaman islanders know. If we went back far enough, we should come to a time when human beings had nothing but their bare hands with which to protect themselves and get their food. With nothing to cover their bodies, these earlier men roamed through tropical forests, gathering their daily supply of roots, seeds, and wild fruits. Later they learned to fashion weapons of wood and stone, with which they killed wild animals, using their flesh for meat and their skins for a poor kind of clothes. They gradually developed ways of talking to one another, although it was a very long time before writing was invented anywhere. We do not know when men first learned how to talk, and to make a fire so that they could cook their food and warm themselves. But speech and fire-making are perhaps the most important discoveries ever made, for without them men could not have protected themselves against the cold, fed themselves properly, or passed on to others what they themselves had learned.

Civilization made up of Discoveries and Inventions. The growth of civilization from its earliest beginnings, perhaps half a million years ago, down to our own time is largely made up of discoveries, inventions, and increasing knowledge of man and of the world in which he lives. These inventions and discoveries include not only all the comforts and conveniences which we enjoy but also our religious beliefs, our ideas of right and wrong and of government, our methods of manufacture and carrying on business, and our literature and art of every kind. All these are very important parts of civilization; but, like houses, tools, and clothes, they have developed through thousands of years and are handed down to us, from parents to children, as our heritage from the past. It is the growth of this heritage, and the way in which it developed, that form the story of our civilization.

Earliest Discoveries. In telling the long story of our civilization we have to start with men's very earliest discoveries, which they made while they were still savages wandering around in search of food. After a great many thousands of years groups of people discovered how to plant seed and raise crops and keep cattle. In order to do this they had to give up their roaming life and were led to found little villages. So long as men and women were constantly moving about from place to place there was no chance for civilization to develop on a large scale. Only when towns came into existence and great numbers of people dwelt together were conditions favorable for making discoveries and inventions and getting them adopted by the community and passed down to the following generations.

Our Civilization began in Egypt and Western Asia. One of the earliest places where men settled down and began to make rapid progress in civilization was Egypt, and it is from there and Western Asia that many of those things that we enjoy today originally came, — for example, brick and stone buildings, fine cloth, glass, metal tools, beautiful gold jewelry, our calendar, and, above all, the use of an alphabet for writing. It was in this region that the religion later accepted by western Europe also developed. It was in Western Asia that the Bible had its beginnings. So this volume begins not with Europe but with Egypt and Western Asia; for it was from there that Europeans derived the civilization which they have greatly increased and have carried with them to all parts of the earth.

The Contribution of the Greeks. The Greeks were the first European people to avail themselves of the civilization built up in Egypt and the Near East. They carried the various arts and sciences far beyond anything that had been accomplished earlier. The Greek language is still taught in our colleges, and Greek books, together with the Old Testament, are the oldest books which form a precious part of our heritage from the past. So in this volume considerable space will be devoted to a study of the way the Greek towns grew up and how they became the homes of eminent artists, scientists, philosophers, historians, and poets far superior to any that had hitherto appeared.

The Roman Period and the Middle Ages. While the Greeks were making their discoveries the Romans were building up a wide empire to the west which finally embraced the Greek cities. The Greek civilization then spread over the Roman Empire and became the basis for all later advances. For a time after the Roman government had lost its power, there was a great deal of disorder, and civilization, instead of advancing, went backward. This period is known as the Middle Ages. People forgot what had once been known, and lost some of the things which the Greeks had added to man's heritage. But after a few centuries, as we shall see, thoughtful men caught up with the past and began to find out many truths which the Greeks had not discovered and to make things never before heard of, such as compasses, printed books, gunpowder, telescopes, and microscopes. Each one of these inventions had a great effect in changing men's ways of living and their ideas of themselves and the stars and the earth and all the creatures that live on it.

How Europeans carried their Civilization across the Atlantic. About a thousand years after the break-up of the Roman Empire, Europeans began to make longer and longer voyages by sea and finally discovered two continents entirely unknown to the Greeks and Romans. These lands were claimed by Spain, England, France, Portugal, and other European countries, who sent over their officials to govern them, and settlers who were destined to build up new states which now appear on the map of the Western Hemisphere. So it came about that the civilization of Europe reached our shores. For the civilization which originated in Egypt and the Near East was adopted and greatly advanced by the Greeks. The Romans carried it westward. After a long period during which it seemed to be lost, much of the older civilization was revived. It was added to by the various European nations after the Middle Ages and was carried across the Atlantic to become the civilization of the new countries of which the United States is now the most powerful.

What may be Learned from the Story of Civilization. Except for life itself, our civilization is the most precious thing we have. It has taken mankind many thousands of years of patient labor to bring it to the degree of perfection in which we find it, and it is the chief business of us all to preserve it and do all we can to improve it. Very few of us are ingenious and original enough to make any new discovery or invention. But anyone who studies carefully the story of our civilization can learn not to oppose changes just because they are new, as many people have done in the past. We may also recognize and be on our guard against old evils which are constantly reappearing in new forms.

This volume brings the story of our civilization down to the founding of the United States and to the great movement for reform that began with the French Revolution. It shows how the evils of poverty, oppression, injustice, ignorance, and war have existed in all ages along with all the wonderful things that man has accomplished. The present volume prepares the way for the following one, called *Our Own Age,* which deals with the new knowledge and mechanical resources that have been gained in recent times, and with the plans for doing away with the ancient plagues of war and poverty and giving everyone a chance to take advantage of the wonderful opportunities offered by new discoveries and inventions which quite outrun anything known to earlier generations.

History of Civilization

EARLIER AGES

Part One

HOW MEN
MADE THEIR FIRST DISCOVERIES
AND INVENTIONS

This Part is the Shortest in the Book, but it deals with far the Longest Time. It tells how, during Thousands and Thousands of Years, Men — far more Ignorant at the Start than Any Savages on the Earth Today — made their First Discoveries and Inventions and finally settled down here and there to Cultivate Fields and Raise Cattle. In Short, how they began to Establish Homes instead of Wandering about in Search of Food All Day like Wild Animals

The Earliest Representation of Domesticated Horses (about 3000 B.C.)

An example of early picture writing showing a group of nineteen horses, each represented by the animal's head only. The other signs are numbers, and it is probable that the whole is an inventory of the horses owned by some king or nobleman. The varying positions of the manes as represented on the tablet have a meaning. The *upraised* manes doubtless indicate stallions, while those that hang down probably indicate mares. The animals without any manes are presumably foals, too young to show any mane. The signs are cut into a clay tablet, discovered by the French at Susa, the ancient capital of Elam. It dates from about 3000 B.C or possibly a century or two earlier. This evidence would therefore indicate that already at this early date the domesticated horse was found just north of the Persian Gulf, whence he gradually found his way into the Fertile Crescent during the next thousand years, so that he was common there in the Age of Hammurapi (p. 67). We now know that around 2000 B.C. the domesticated horse was in use from the Caucasus through Anatolia to the Fertile Crescent, whence he reached Egypt during or after the eighteenth century B.C. The discovery in Scania, in southern Sweden, of a horse's skull dating from about 2400 B.C., having a stone dagger driven deep into the forehead, led some archæologists to believe that the horse was domesticated in northern Europe. There is now little support for this conclusion, and the evidence from the Orient indicates that the horse was domesticated somewhere in the general region northeast of Persia. There is some uncertainty regarding the date of his arrival in the Fertile Crescent, owing to the discovery of a surprisingly large percentage of the bones of the ancient wild ass (*onager*) in the Babylonian excavations of the Oriental Institute. In Fig. 91 in Breasted's *Ancient Times*, and in our Elamite tablet above, the short ears of the animals represented have been regarded as conclusive evidence that they were horses. But the numerous bones of the wild ass in Babylonia suggest the possibility that all the horse-like animals shown in these representations might be regarded as wild asses, which we know were early used as draft animals in ancient Babylonia. If so, the domesticated horse was introduced among the most civilized peoples as late as 2000 B.C.

CHAPTER I · FROM FOOD-GATHERING TO FOOD-PRODUCTION

MAN'S EARLIEST WAYS OF LIVING · THE EARLY STONE AGES · THE EARLIEST
FOOD-PRODUCERS AND THE LATE STONE AGE

WHEN we use the word "history," we usually think of written records. Indeed, it is customary to describe the Historic Age by saying that it is the age beginning when written documents were first produced by man, — documents which tell us in written words something of man's life and career. The long period before the invention of writing has consequently been called the Prehistoric Age. Perhaps you will ask, "If there was no writing in the Prehistoric Age, how can we find out about it?" To begin with, we must ask the aid of the geologists, who study the history of the earth itself as shown by its layers, or strata. By studying fossilized vegetable remains, the positions of the rocks, and many other signs, the geologists can determine the changing kinds of climate in the Prehistoric Age, the lengths of certain geological periods, and many interesting details which furnish a background for the life of prehistoric men. Moreover, in the geological strata are found animal and human bones, together with stone tools and weapons made by man. From these finds we can tell something about the life of earliest men. For instance, if the bones of a dog and several flint arrowheads were found buried close to the skeleton of a man, we should naturally suppose that this man was a hunter, that he knew how to use a bow and arrow, and that he had domesticated the dog. We might then go farther and compare the manner of life of prehistoric men with that of primitive men today. We should find some points of similarity, and from the difficulties overcome by the ruder peoples of today we might learn something of the problems which faced prehistoric men. The description of man's earliest ways of living in Chapter I has drawn upon all these sources of information.

1. MAN'S EARLIEST WAYS OF LIVING

The Home of Earliest Civilization. Only a little more than five hundred years ago certain explorers from the Old World found a New World in which lived a race of red men whom the explorers considered savage. Yet these so-called savages had stone implements, worked with metals, lived in tents or mud houses, and some of them even planted grain. While the red

5

men of the New World therefore seemed *savage* in their way of living as compared with the people of the Old World in the fifteenth century A.D., nevertheless their life was almost *civilized* as compared with that of the earliest men who lived thousands on thousands of years ago and who were scattered over wide areas of the Old World. Scholars have nearly all agreed that the discoveries and inventions which are necessary to civilized life were first made by those earliest men who lived in the region surrounding the eastern end of the Mediterranean Sea.

We must therefore first turn our attention to the early Mediterranean world.

Early Mediterranean World; its Climate and Animals. The lands of Europe and northern Africa were very different then from what they are today. Lofty forests not only fringed the streams of Europe and clothed its wide plains but they covered also some of the Sahara Plateau, which at that time was a green and well-watered region. Huge hippopotamuses wallowed along the shores of the rivers, and many a fierce rhinoceros charged through the heavy tropical growth. Through Italy and Sicily, as well as at Gibraltar, land-bridges across the Mediterranean connected Europe and Africa. Thus most of these animals could wander by land from Africa to Europe or back again. The atmosphere was moist and warm, and the forests echoed to the notes of many tropical birds. This tropical wilderness, filled with its myriads of creatures (fish, fowl, and animals great and small), extended entirely around the Mediterranean Sea.

Life and Progress of Earliest Men. Each day the savages of this early Mediterranean world crept forth to gather their food where they could find it. They often fled in terror as they felt the thunderous tread of the giant animals of the forest, but they listened with keen and eager ear for the sound of small game which they might be able to lay low with their rough wooden clubs. At night they had no hut or shelter in which they might take refuge. They slept wherever they happened to be overtaken by darkness.

Fig. 1. *Primitive Men Hunting*

Primitive men were largely meat-eaters, and therefore hunters. Here we see the men, standing on solid ground, using their roughly-formed spears, rocks, and clubs against the large woolly mammoth caught in the soft, boggy ground. As they were physically feeble compared to the animals around them and possessed only crude weapons, it was necessary for these savages to use all their cunning against the huge beasts which they hunted. (Courtesy of Charles R. Knight)

We cannot trace all the different stages in the progress of the earliest men; but we know that they must have first discovered two important things, for without them they would have been unable to advance. These were the ability to speak and the means of kindling a fire. A third important discovery, how to shape a stone, was of the greatest help to them. They had probably sometimes found broken stones and had used the ragged edges to hack off the meat of an animal or shape their wooden clubs. After a long time they saw that they could improve the form of such a stone, and so gradually they learned to make a rude tool or weapon. At this point they entered what we now call the Stone Age, — at least several hundred thousand years ago (although no one knows exactly when). The stone weapons and tools which these savages then began to make did not rot and disappear like their bone and wooden ones, so today we can actually hold in our hands the very implements which some of these early men used in their long struggle to obtain food and to defend themselves.

2. THE EARLY STONE AGES

Archæology and the Study of Stone Implements. A stone tool or weapon made by human hands is called an *artifact*, a word of Latin origin meaning "made by art" and related to the word "artificial." Stone artifacts, lying on the ground or turned up by the plow, were noticed by our ancestors centuries ago. Since then scientific men have been carefully searching for them, especially by systematic digging (called excavation). The study of man's early works is called archæology; hence such digging is called archæological excavation, and we term a man who does such work an archæologist. The search for stone artifacts began in Europe. There the rude stone tools and weapons of the Early Stone Age hunters of Europe, and the bones of the huge animals they slew, were sometimes found lying side by side in the sand and gravel far up on the valley slopes where in prehistoric ages the rivers once flowed, before their deep modern beds had been cut out by the water. They have been found in such large numbers that great museum collections of stone implements have been established in various European countries. Recent search in North Africa has likewise revealed stone artifacts in an area stretching from Algiers to the lower Nile valley, and the same is true of Asia along the eastern shores of the Mediterranean. We are thus able to study thousands of stone weapons and implements from all the lands surrounding the Mediterranean. They reveal to us the fascinating story of man's earliest progress, after the Early Stone Age hunters had found that they could chip stones.

The Coming of the Ice. For thousands of years the life of the early hunters went on with little change. They slowly improved their rough stone tools and weapons (Fig. 2), and probably learned to make other implements out of wood. Then the air of their forest home began to lose its warmth. Geologists have not yet found out why; but as the centuries passed, the ice, which all the year round still overlies the region of the north pole and the summits of the Alps, began to spread. It pushed down across Europe, Asia, and North America.

In Europe it continued to creep farther and farther southward until it covered England as far down as the Thames, and on the Continent it covered much of Germany. In Asia the ice came down far across Siberia, and it descended from the mountains of Armenia to the upper valley of the Tigris and Euphrates rivers. On the continent of North America the southern edge of the ice is marked by lines of bowlders carried and left there by the ice sheet. Such lines of bowlders (called moraines) are found, for example, as far south as Long Island, and westward along the valleys of the Ohio and the Missouri River.

The Ice Age in the Lands North of the Mediterranean. The hunter saw the glittering blue masses of ice, with their crown of snow, pushing through the green of his forest abode and crushing down vast trees in many a sheltered glen or favorite hunting ground. Gradually the savage men of early Europe were forced to accustom themselves to a colder climate, and many of the animals familiar to the hunter retreated to the warmer south, never to return. The hunters did not know how to build themselves shelters from the cold. They therefore took refuge in rock shelters under overhanging cliffs or in the entrances of caves, where they and their descendants continued to live for thousands of years. Century after century the sand and earth continued to blow into these rock shelters or caverns, and fragments of rock fell from

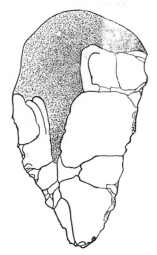

Fig. 2. *A Flint Fist Hatchet of the Early Stone Age, Found in an Ancient Bed of the Nile*

Rough flint flakes older than the fist hatchet still survive to show us man's earliest efforts at shaping stone. But the fist hatchet is the earliest well-finished type of tool produced by man. Fist hatchets have been found all around the Mediterranean, as well as in other parts of the world. The original of the above illustration is about seven and one-half inches long. This tool was usually grasped in the fist by the thicker part, and had no handle. Traces of use and wear can sometimes be noticed on fist hatchets. The above specimen was found by the Oriental Institute of the University of Chicago

the ceiling. In the masses of rubbish accumulated on the floors we find today many layers of ashes and charcoal from the fires of the prehistoric hunters, besides numerous tools, weapons, and implements which they used. The ice remained for thousands of years; then it slowly melted and retreated northward again. This forward and backward movement of the ice was repeated several times as the climate changed during a period of many thousands of years, which we call the Ice Age.

When the ice came down for the last time the European hunters had finally improved their stone implements and their manner of living. We can imagine a hunter of those days at the entrance to his cave, carefully chipping off the edges of his flint tools. By this time he had left the rude old fist hatchet (Fig. 2) far behind, and had discovered that by pressure with a hard piece of bone he could chip off a line of fine flakes along the edge of his flint tool and thus produce a much finer cutting edge than by chipping it with blows. This discovery enabled him, first, to produce a considerable variety of flint tools, — chisels, drills, hammers, polishers, and scrapers; and, second, with these improved tools, to cut and shape ivory, bone, and especially reindeer horn. The fine ivory needles found still lying in the caverns make it clear that sewing had been discovered and that the hunters were protected from cold and the brambles of the forest by clothing stitched together out of the skins of the animals which they had slain. The hunter also made sharp spear points of barbed ivory which he mounted on a long wooden shaft, and each hunter carried at his girdle a sharp flint dagger. Another clever device of horn or ivory was a throwing-stick, by which a hunter could hurl his long spear farther and with greater force than before. Such inventions made it much easier for men to procure their food and therefore much easier for them to survive; for all men were still merely food-gatherers.

Beginnings of Art. In spite of the ignorance and savagery of their daily life, these primitive hunters were standing just at the dawning of the first great light that entered the souls of men. When they lay down in their caverns at night, these savage hunters could often see mind-pictures of the great beasts they had been pursuing all day. They could recall curious trees the shapes of which might remind them of animals, or they might turn as they lay in their caverns and see a bulging mass of rock, which looked like a horse. Thus there might arise in their minds the idea of *resemblance*: the animal, and the tree that looked like it; the horse, and the rounded rock that looked like the horse. As this thought continued they began to be aware that such a resemblance might be produced by their own hands; that is, they could imitate the form of one object by shaping another like it. In this way the possibility of *imitation* awoke in their minds. In that moment, art was born. The Stone Age hunters could carve and paint with remarkable skill. They filled the caverns of France and northern Spain with pictures of the wild animals which they hunted. Similar pictures are numerous in eastern Spain, not in caverns but on the rocks under the open sky; and likewise in North Africa, where they are found from Algiers entirely across the Sahara, southward and eastward to the upper Nile. These widespread cave paintings and rock pictures, with much other evidence, reveal to us something of the ways of living of the food-gatherers on both the north and the south of the Mediterranean. But there were certain conditions of climate on the south side of the Mediterranean which affected the life of the food-gatherers of northern Africa so greatly that we must now consider them apart from the other early men of the Mediterranean world.

Early Stone Age Men South of the Mediterranean. While the invasion of the ice made life very difficult for the Early Stone Age men on the *north* side of the Mediterranean, the region *south* of the Mediterranean was never visited by the ice. The same atmospheric moisture which in frozen form built up the icy glaciers on the *north* side of the Mediterranean fell as plentiful rain on the *south* side. The Sahara Plateau therefore continued to be well watered and covered with meadows, forests, and jungle growth. At some time in the Ice Age, however, the plentiful rains in North Africa began slowly to fail. The reason for this diminished rainfall is not yet clearly understood. The rainfall in Europe also decreased. As a result of the

FIG. 3. *Examples of Stone Age Art*

The herd of reindeer sketched in *A* is carved on the wing bone of an eagle. This drawing shows that the earliest artists had some ideas about composition in art and were able to draw a group of animals so as to give an impression of a great number in an almost modern way. *B* is a hunting scene painted on a rock shelter by Stone Age man after he had invented the bow. The painting of a wolf, *C*, is from a cave in France. (After Breuil)

failing moisture the glacial ice in Europe began to shrink and to retreat toward the north, while the decreasing rainfall in North Africa caused the great Sahara Plateau slowly to change into the waterless desert which we know today.

At this period the Nile valley was of the greatest value to the plateau hunters. The valley is a gorge, or cañon, at some places more than thirty miles in width, with steep rock walls varying from a few hundred to a thousand feet in height. With its great river flowing down the gorge, the valley offered the Stone Age hunters a new home with plenty of water; for although the Nile gorge was as rainless as the desert, the river was plentifully fed from the rainy regions far south of the desert. Thus the great valley formed a *sheltered* home, where the hunters of North Africa were soon to advance in civilization much faster than the men of the same age in Europe. The stone tools and weapons which reveal this advance to us have been found buried in the rock and gravel terraces formed by the river along its shores.

3. THE EARLIEST FOOD-PRODUCERS AND THE LATE STONE AGE

The Age of Food-Production. Like the hunters, the animals of the Sahara Plateau also found it necessary to take refuge in the Nile gorge in order to find food and water. Here, however, there was not as much room for the animals as they enjoyed in Europe or as they had once found on the plateau. Thus the hunters found it easy to drive whole herds of them into the deep bays in the Nile-valley cliffs and to capture them there. At length it occurred to these hunters to close off such a bay with a stockade having only one entrance, or even to build a stockade of four sides with one gate into which the game might be driven. Wild game thus fenced in formed a very valuable source of food "on the hoof" and was always ready for use. When these captive animals lost their fear of men and learned to live with them, they became, as we say, domesticated.

After a time the Nile-gorge people discovered another new and lasting source of food. Probably for thousands of years the women had been accustomed to gather the seeds of certain wild grasses and grind them up for food. It was now discovered that such grasses could be planted and watered, so that they would grow better and produce a greater yield of eatable seed. Thus began the planting and harvesting of millet, barley, and wheat, which were once only wild grasses. After men began cultivating food in the field and raising it on the hoof, they became for the first time food-*producers*. Being therefore able to produce food *at home*, they found it less necessary to go out as hunters and kill wild animals for food. Groups of families settled down to live in one place, where it was possible to look after the tamed animals and to water the fields of grain. Most of the hunters finally became farmers and cattle-raisers, and thus began the age of agriculture and cattle-breeding, or "animal husbandry." We may call it the *Age of Food-Production.*

The Egyptian Life of the Late Stone Age. We have seen that in this new Age of Food-Production and settled life it was possible for men to make fixed homes. Their tools for this

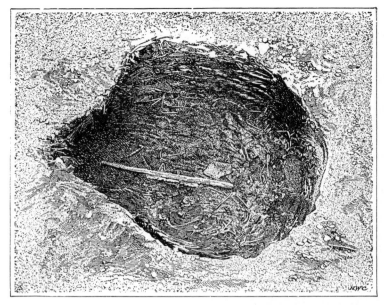

FIG. 4. *Late Stone Age Straw-lined Granary containing Wooden Sickle* (A)

This prehistoric granary was a shallow pit dug in the earth. Wet mud was smeared on the floor and sides of the pit, and then it was lined with straw. A number of such granaries were found together. Most of them were empty, but some contained quantities of wheat, barley, and other grain. The wooden sickle (A) found lying on the bottom of this granary is nearly two feet long. A dark, gluelike mass holds the three saw-toothed pieces of flint in place to serve as the cutting edge of the sickle, and they remain fixed as firmly in their groove as they were on that day thousands of years ago when the Stone Age Egyptian dropped the sickle in the pit and perhaps forgot all about it. (After Miss G. Caton-Thompson)

purpose were still made of stone, especially flint, but they now used a gritty stone upon which to sharpen or grind the edges. By this method their stone tools were so much improved that we must regard the period as another Stone Age, which we call the Late Stone Age. The homes which they made were at first only huts made of interwoven twigs and branches called "wattle," plastered with mud. Some of these early Nile-dwellers had noticed that clay will harden when heated in the fire. They began therefore to make pottery dishes and jars for the household. The useful fibers of wild plants such as flax had been discovered, and the women had learned to cultivate these plants, to spin the fibers into thread, and to weave this thread into linen for their clothing. All this happened so long ago that the little villages of wattle huts have been covered up under many feet of black soil, brought down since then by the Nile. Nevertheless, on ground high enough to be above the reach of the Nile waters, scanty traces of several of their villages have been discovered. These villagers buried their dead along the edge of the desert. The cemeteries which grew up there are often found still undisturbed, and they have yielded to the excavator's spade many objects which tell us of the life of these Late Stone Age Egyptians.

The Discovery of Metal. The articles buried with the dead in one of the graves included a copper pin. It is the oldest implement of metal ever discovered in archæological excavation. We can follow in imagination the Egyptian who must have first discovered metal as he wandered into the Peninsula of Sinai, where the oldest copper mines are found. It may have been that in this vicinity (map, p. 27) he happened to bank his camp fire with pieces of copper ore lying about on the ground. The charcoal of his wood fire would mingle with the hot fragments of ore piled around to shield the fire, and thus the ore would be "reduced," as the miner says; that is, the copper in metallic form would be released from the lumps of ore. Next morning, as the Egyptian stirred the embers, he would discover in the ashes a few shining beads of metal. We can imagine how he may have picked them up and turned them admiringly as they glittered in the sunshine. As the experience was repeated he would discover that these strange shining beads had come out of the pieces of stone around his fire.

Dawning of the Age of Metal. Without knowing it, this man stood at the dawning of a new era, the Age of Metal. The little disk of shining copper which he drew from the ashes might have reflected a vision — could the Egyptian wanderer have seen it — of what men were one day to do with metal: great steel buildings, giant bridges, huge factories roaring with the noise of thousands of machines, and vast stretches of steel railroads along which thunder hosts of rushing locomotives. Since the discovery of fire, many thousands of years earlier, man had made no conquest of the things of the earth which could compare in importance with this discovery of metal. This took place not later than about the year 5000 B.C., that is, at least some seven thousand years ago. But it was to be many centuries before copper tools and weapons came into common use. During this long period, and for some time after, the Late Stone Age life went on, just as if metal had not been discovered.

Final Retreat of the Ice; Beginning of the Late Stone Age in Europe. Meantime the hunters on the *north* side of the Mediterranean had continued to lead their food-gathering life of the Early Stone Ages. The signs left by the ice have led geologists to think that it drew back northward for the last time nearly nine thousand years ago. At this point, therefore, the men on the north side of the Mediterranean began to live under weather conditions which gradually became like those of today. Moreover, while the ice was finally retreating northward, influences from North Africa and Western Asia began to reach the European hunters. They learned how to breed cattle and grow grain. They found out how to weave linen and make pottery. And with improved ground-edged tools, they were able to build wooden houses.

Swiss Lake-Villages of the Late Stone Age. The most plentiful traces of the earliest wooden houses in Europe are to be found in Switzerland. Here groups of families of the Late Stone Age built their villages of wooden huts upon platforms stretching in long lines along the shores of the Swiss lakes. The platforms were supported by piles driven into the ground. These communities are called *lake-villages.* In a few cases they were quite large. At Wangen not less than fifty thousand piles were driven into the ground for the support of the village. The lake-villagers lived a life of peace and prosperity. Their huts were comfortable shelters, and they were supplied with wooden furnishings and pottery. The

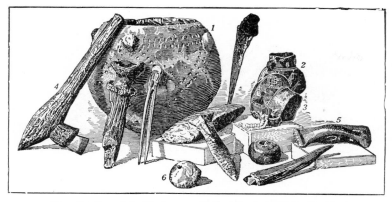

FIG. 5. *Part of the Equipment of a Late Stone Age Lake-Dweller*

This group contains the evidence for three important inventions made or received from the Near East by the men of the Late Stone Age : *first*, pottery jars, like *2* and *3*, with rude decorations — the oldest baked clay in Europe — and *1*, a large kettle in which the lake-dwellers' food was cooked ; *second*, ground-edged tools like *4*, a stone chisel mounted in a deerhorn handle like a hatchet, or *5*, a stone ax pierced with a hole for the ax handle ; and, *third*, weaving, as shown by *6*, a spinning "whorl" of baked clay, the earliest spinning wheel. When suspended by a rough thread of flax eighteen to twenty inches long, it was given a whirl which made it spin in the air like a top, thus rapidly twisting the thread by which it was hanging. The thread, when sufficiently twisted, was wound up, and another length of eighteen to twenty inches was drawn out from the unspun flax to be similarly twisted. One of these earliest spinning wheels has been found in the Swiss lakes, with the flaxen thread still attached. (Courtesy of Professor Hoernes)

hillsides looking down upon the lake-villages were green with fields of barley, wheat, and millet. At first no one person owned these fields of wheat, barley, or flax; but after a time each household gradually gained the right to cultivate a particular field, and finally they came to set up a claim to it. Thus began the ownership of land. This system of landownership established more firmly the settled agricultural life in and around the villages.

Other Late Stone Age Towns in Europe; the Rise of Government. The settled communities of the Late Stone Age at last began to build something more enduring than wooden houses and wattle huts. Toward the close of this age the more powerful chiefs learned to erect tombs, made of large blocks of stone. These tombs are still found fringing the western coast of Europe from the Mediterranean around Spain to the

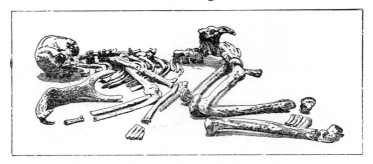

Fig. 6. *Skeleton of a Miner of the Late Stone Age*

The skeleton of this ancient miner was found lying on the floor of a flint mine in Belgium, under the rocks which had caved in and crushed him. Before him, just as it dropped from his hands at the instant of the cave-in, lies the double-pointed pick of deerhorn with which he was loosening the lumps of flint from their chalk bed

southern Scandinavian shores. Such structures are not yet of masonry, that is, of smoothly cut stone laid with mortar. They cannot, therefore, be classed as works of architecture.

Near every great group of stone tombs there must have been a town where the people lived who built the tombs. These Late Stone Age towns show us that men were learning to live together and to work together on a large scale. It required power over men and successful management of them to get together the workers who raised the earth walls of a town, or drove the fifty thousand piles supporting the lake-villages at Wangen (Switzerland), or moved great blocks of stone for a chieftain's tomb. In these works we see the beginnings of government under a leader. We may call such a government a state. Many little states, each made up of an earth-walled town with its surrounding fields, and each under a chieftain, grew up in Late Stone Age Europe. Out of such beginnings nations were later to grow.

Beginnings of Trade and Business. In this age, men were beginning to follow special trades; some men were probably wood-workers, others were potters, and still others were miners (Fig. 6). Business relations between the villages already existed, and this early commerce sometimes carried things far and wide. An example of this is an especially fine variety of French flint, which is found scattered today in many parts of Europe and is recognized by its color. Stone implements found on the islands around Europe show that men of this age lived there, and they must have had boats. Several of the dugouts of the lake-dwellers have been found lying on the lake bottom among the piles. The business of such an age was of course very simple. There were no metals and no money. Buying and selling were only exchange of one kind of wares for another kind. In all Europe there was no writing, nor did the inhabitants of the mainland of Europe *ever* invent a system of writing.

Stone Age Europe at a Standstill; Development of Civilization in the Ancient Near East. Such was the life of Stone Age men on the north side of the Mediterranean near the close of this period, about three thousand years before Christ. They were still without writing, and they did not know how to use metal. Indeed, Europe unaided never did gain these things, and without them men could go no farther. We must therefore turn away from Europe to follow the development of these and many other discoveries and inventions that help to make up our civilization. This progress was made on the other side of the Mediterranean, in Egypt and Western Asia, — in the lands which we now call the Near East.[1] As we leave Europe to follow the story of the Ancient Near East let us remember that we have been following man's *prehistoric* progress around the Mediterranean. In the Near East, beginning before 4000 B.C. and during the thousand years from 4000 to 3000 B.C., men slowly built up a high civilization, forming the beginning of the *Historic Age.*

Questions and Exercises

REVIEW OF CHAPTER

1. Where was the home of earliest civilization? What do we surmise from the geological remains about conditions in the Mediterranean world when man first appeared there?

[1] The term "Far East" is used today to include Japan, China, and India. The term "Near East" became very common during the World War, and is now the most convenient name for the lands grouped about the eastern end of the Mediterranean, although the word "Orient" is still a correct designation of the same region.

2. What is archæology? What is meant by "Ice Age"? From what materials did the men of the Early Stone Ages make their tools and weapons? How do we know that Stone Age men were artists?

3. What is meant by the term "Age of Food-Production"? What industries did the Late Stone Age Egyptians have? the Late Stone Age Europeans? How do archæologists find out about prehistoric man?

USEFUL TERMS

See how much meaning you can give to the following: *prehistory, civilization, fossilized, geological, savages, food-gathering, domestication of animals, landownership, government.*

DIRECTIVE QUESTIONS

1. In what different ways has the prehistory of man been revealed to modern archæologists?

2. Have you ever found any evidence of the existence of prehistoric man?

3. In what ways did the men of the Early Stone Ages find use for the animals apart from eating them?

4. Can you show why men had to learn to work together before they could advance in civilization?

DISCUSSION TOPICS

1. Food-gathering peoples cannot stop long in one place.

2. Would it pay to excavate in the Sahara?

3. There are various ways by which animals may be domesticated.

4. Man conceived the idea of navigation from watching floating logs.

ADDITIONAL ADVENTURES IN LEARNING

1. **Topical Studies.** What proofs have we that the Sahara Plateau was once a well-watered region where man was able to live? (See page 6.) BREASTED, *Ancient Times*, p. 48, Note. List the animals painted or drawn by Stone Age men. BREASTED, *Ancient Times*, Figs. 7–10; BURKITT, *Old Stone Age*, pp. 158–228; *Our Forerunners*, chap. ix; GARDNER, *Art through the Ages*, chap. i; MACALISTER, *Textbook of European Archæology*, Vol. I, pp. 62–87; OSBORN, *Man rises to Parnassus*, chap. iii; PEAKE and FLEURE, *Hunters and Artists*, chap. 6.

2. Look up in an encyclopedia: *archæology, glacier, glacial period, wheat, flax, reindeer, copper, Sinai.*

Part Two

HOW DURING THREE THOUSAND YEARS PEOPLES IN THE NEAR EAST LAID THE FOUNDATIONS OF OUR CIVILIZATION

One of the Places where Men settled down Earliest was the Nile Valley, called Egypt. There they learned how to write, construct and decorate Imposing Buildings, navigate Ships, and organize Powerful Governments. East of the Mediterranean Other Peoples progressed in an Astonishing Manner and made Many Discoveries which are Still a Part of Our Civilization Today

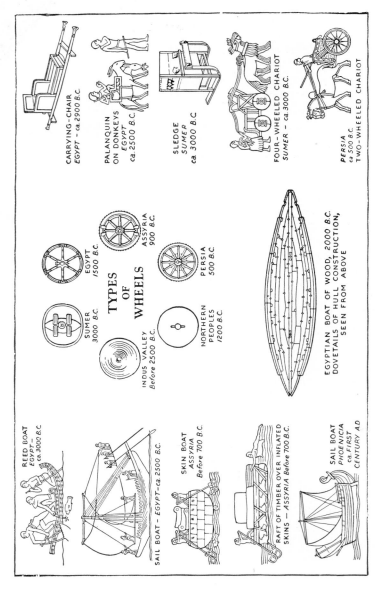

CARRYING-CHAIR
EGYPT - ca.2900 B.C.

PALANQUIN
ON DONKEYS
EGYPT
ca.2500 B.C.

SLEDGE
SUMER
ca.3000 B.C

FOUR-WHEELED CHARIOT
SUMER - ca.3000 B.C.

PERSIA
ca.500 B.C.
TWO-WHEELED CHARIOT

SUMER
3000 B.C.

EGYPT
1500 B.C.

ASSYRIA
900 B.C.

TYPES OF WHEELS

INDUS VALLEY
Before 2500 B.C.

NORTHERN
PEOPLES
1200 B.C.

PERSIA
500 B.C.

EGYPTIAN BOAT OF WOOD, 2000 B.C.
DOVETAILS OF HULL CONSTRUCTION,
SEEN FROM ABOVE

REED BOAT
EGYPT -
ca.3000 B.C.

SAIL BOAT - EGYPT-ca.2500 B.C.

SKIN BOAT
ASSYRIA
Before 700 B.C.

RAFT OF TIMBER OVER INFLATED
SKINS — ASSYRIA Before 700 B.C.

SAIL BOAT
PHOENICIA
ca.FIRST
CENTURY A.D

Transportation in the Ancient Near East

CHAPTER II · THE STORY

THE FIRST UNION OF EGYPT AND THE RISE OF CIVILIZⱭ
(THIRTIETH TO TWENTY-FIFTH CENTURY B.C.) · THE Ⱥ
EMPIRE · CIVILIZATION OF THE Eᴎ

I N THE previous chapter we traced the begiᴜ
made by earliest man during hundreds of thousands of years. ᴏᴜᴍᴜ ᴜᴜ
thousand years ago, that is, about 4000 ʙ.ᴄ., mankind had gradually reached
nearly the same stage of progress all around the Mediterranean, — in North
Africa, Europe, and, as we shall see, Western Asia. The drying up of
northern Africa led numbers of people to take refuge in the Nile valley, which
lies in the temperate zone and extends from the African tropics to the
Mediterranean Sea. In this deep, sheltered retreat a supply of food was
insured by the discovery of methods of raising crops and breeding animals.
In this way began farming, or agriculture, which has ever since played a great
part in civilization. The Egyptians, however, went much farther. They
learned to make tools of copper, which enabled them to do far better work
than they could with the old stone implements and to create many new
and beautiful things. They also developed the use of pictures and letters to
represent the sounds which make up speech. In this way phonetic, or
"sound," *writing* was invented, which we now use constantly. Under
these favorable circumstances the population of the valley increased to
several millions, who were gradually brought together into the first great
people, or nation. In this chapter we shall follow the development of the
Egyptian state and see how various discoveries were added to those already
known to the men who first found safety in the Nile valley.

1. THE FIRST UNION OF EGYPT AND THE
RISE OF CIVILIZATION

Irrigation and the Soil of Egypt. As we take up our study
of the Ancient Near East we start with Egypt. We followed
the hunters of North Africa from the drying plateau down
to the well-watered floor of the Nile valley, where they
learned to feed herds of once wild cattle in stockades and to
plant fields of grain. Grain, of course, cannot grow without
water, and these early Egyptians, living in a country without
rain, had to make a simple machine for lifting water to the
fields from the river or from canals filled by the river. The

tians of today still continue to use the ancient water-
ing machine (Fig. 7), and our ancestors inherited it in

Fig. 7. *An Egyptian Shadoof, the Oldest
of Well Sweeps, Irrigating the Fields*

The man below stands in the water, holding his leather bucket (*A*). The pole (*B*)
of the sweep is above him, with a large
ball of dried Nile mud on its lower end (*C*)
as a lifting weight, or counterpoise, seen
just behind the supporting post (*D*). This
man lifts the water into a mud basin (*E*).
A second man (in the middle) lifts it from
this first basin (*E*) to a second basin (*F*).
A third man (*G*) lifts the water from the
middle basin (*F*) to the uppermost basin
(*H*) on the top of the bank, where it runs
off to the left into trenches spreading over
the fields. The low water makes necessary three successive lifts (to *E*, to *F*, to
H), continued without ceasing, night and
day, for one hundred days. The weird and
plaintive songs of the shadoof-worker are
heard day and night along the Nile

the well sweep once com-
mon in New England.

The soil of Egypt is very
fertile, for it is enriched
each year by the overflow
of the river. The muddy
waters rise above the river
banks every summer, then
spread far over the flats,
and lie there long enough
to deposit a very thin layer
of rich earth. The mud
carried down the valley
for centuries has filled a
large bay at the mouth of
the river and formed what
we now call the Nile Delta.
At the present day the
Delta and the valley above,
as far as the First Cata-
ract, contain together over
twelve thousand square
miles of fertile farm land,
— about the area of Mas-
sachusetts and Connecti-
cut.

*The Delta and the Rise
of Government.* In the Late
Stone Age, however, the
area which could be cul-
tivated must have been
much smaller than it is
today; for at that time
the valley above the Delta
was still largely occupied by extensive marshes, and only
here and there between the marshes was it possible to plant

and harvest a crop. But in the Delta, where the river branched out into smaller streams with slower currents, the marshes were easier to drain for cultivation. Gradually, therefore, the people of the Delta outstripped the dwellers on the upper river and became more advanced in their manner of living. This advance led to the first regulations of community life, which finally became *government*.

It came about in this way. The overflow of the river (called the inundation) often clogged the canals with mud, so that the men of a whole group of villages would have to go out together to clear the canals. They knew that if they did not do so there would be no water for the grain fields, no harvest, and finally no bread. The leader of one of these groups of Delta villages probably became in time a local chieftain who controlled the irrigation trenches and canals of the district. To him the people of the district were obliged to carry every season a share of the grain or flax which they gathered from their fields. These shares of grain or flax were the earliest taxes, and the chieftain's control of the canals and collection of the taxes formed the earliest government.

The Two Kingdoms and the First Union. Eventually some one of these Delta chieftains conquered the rival chieftains in the other districts and united all the Delta into a kingdom which we call Lower Egypt, for although higher on the map, it was *lower* on the river. In the same way there also arose another kingdom, extending up the Nile valley from the southern apex of the Delta to the region of the First Cataract. This kingdom we call Upper Egypt; for it is on the *upper* course of the river, although lower on the map. There must have been much traffic between the two kingdoms, as they were, of course, connected by the Nile. Finally, perhaps in the forty-third century B.C. (although we are not sure about the date), a powerful king of Lower Egypt, whose name we do not know, marched southward out of the Delta and conquered his rival, the king of Upper Egypt. In this manner the two kingdoms were united under one king, who became king of Upper and Lower Egypt. We shall call this first kingdom of Upper and Lower Egypt the First Union as

a matter of convenience, although this was not its ancient
name. The history of the First Union is the most important
chapter in the entire human story, because civilization really
began in this age.

Hoe Culture Changed into Plow Culture. We have seen
that agriculture greatly improved human conditions and
made it possible for men to give up the hunting life and to
live in villages surrounded by little grain fields. But those
grain fields had, up to the time of the First Union, been *cultivated by hand with the hoe.* This was a slow and laborious
method of work, and limited the amount of land which could
be cultivated. Finally it occurred to some clever Egyptian
that he might lengthen the handle of his hoe so that it could
be fastened to a yoke resting on the foreheads of two oxen.
Thus the old hoe handle became the beam of the plow, and
the hoe blade became the plowshare. The oxen could then
drag the plowshare (old hoe blade) through the soil; and in
order to guide the plow, the farmer attached handles at the
point where beam and share met.

This invention of the first agricultural machinery marked a
new epoch; for it enabled man to begin the use of animal
power, that is, power other than the strength of man or
woman. As this power was applied to the work of cultivating
the fields, Egypt was able to farm the largest area that had
ever been prepared for the raising of crops. Thus there arose
in the Nile valley the first great agricultural nation. The
annual income in grain was not only a source of increased
wealth to the people and the government but it was the first
portable wealth. Because it could be carried about, loans
could be made with it, taxes paid, and business debts settled.
This was in an age before there was any money, and it therefore made an enormous difference, and aided in carrying the
Egyptians forward in their civilization.

The Egyptian Origin of Our Calendar. The important
place occupied by agriculture in the government of the Egyptians may be seen in the names which were adopted for the
different seasons of the year. There were three seasons in

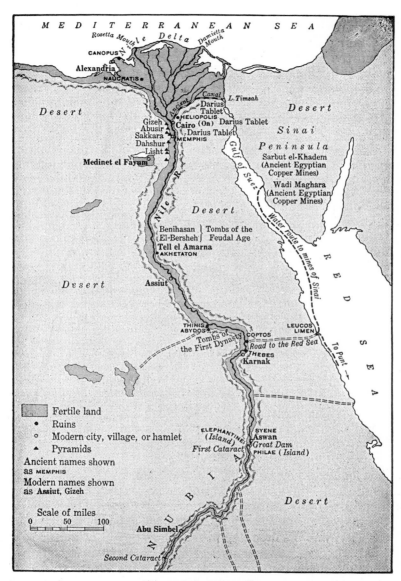

MEDITERRANEAN SEA

Rosetta Mouth *e Delta* Damietta Mouth

CANOPUS

Alexandria

NAUCRATIS

Desert

Canal
L. Timsah
Darius Tablet
HELIOPOLIS
Gizeh
Abusir
Cairo (On) Darius Tablet
Sakkara
Dahshur
MEMPHIS Darius Tablet
Lisht
Medinet el Fayum

Desert

Sinai

Peninsula

Sarbut el-Khadem
(Ancient Egyptian
Copper Mines)

Wadi Maghara
(Ancient Egyptian
Copper Mines)

Gulf of Suez

Desert

Benihasan ⎰ Tombs of the
El-Bersheh ⎱ Feudal Age
Tell el Amarna
AKHETATON

Water route to mines of Sinai

Desert Assiut

R
E
D

THINIS
ABYDOS
LEUCOS
LIMEN
Tombs of
the First Dynasty COPTOS
Road to the Red Sea
THEBES
Karnak

To Punt

S
E
A

Fertile land
• Ruins
○ Modern city, village, or hamlet
▲ Pyramids
Ancient names shown
as MEMPHIS
Modern names shown
as Assiut, Gizeh

ELEPHANTINE
(Island) SYENE
Aswan
First Cataract Great Dam
PHILAE (Island)

N
U
B
I
A

Desert

Scale of miles
0   50   100

Abu Simbel

Second Cataract

Egypt and the Nile Valley

their first calendar, and they bore the names "Inundation," "Coming Forth" (meaning the coming forth of the fields from the inundation which had covered them), and "Harvest." Each of these three seasons was four months long, and months were measured from new moon to new moon. The moon-month varies in length from twenty-nine to thirty days, and it does not evenly divide the three hundred and sixty-five days of the year. In time the Egyptians made a calendar which disregarded the moon, and divided the year into twelve months of thirty days each. At the end of the year they celebrated five feast days, a kind of holiday week. This gave them a year of three hundred and sixty-five days. They did not yet know that every four years they ought to have a leap year of three hundred and sixty-six days, although they discovered this fact later. Astronomical calculations show that this convenient Egyptian calendar was introduced in 4241 B.C., and its introduction is the *earliest dated event in history*. It is the same calendar that has descended to us, after more than six thousand years, although the length of the months was changed in later times.

Invention of Writing. The months in the Egyptian calendar were numbered. It was thus easy to identify any particular month in a single year, but there was no way of identifying a particular year. In order to have some means of identifying a certain year when it was long past, the Egyptians gave each year a name after some important event which had happened in it. Lists of these year names began to be kept long before the First Union. As the Egyptians did not yet know how to *write*, the year-names were indicated by pictures of the important events in them. Such picture records were used also in the business of government and in the market place. These pictures were not real writing, but their use was the first step in the development of writing.

All writing, whether it developed in Egypt, or in Babylonia, or, later, in China, is derived from such pictures. As time went on, each picture came to represent a *sound* as well as the object for which it originally stood. Let us imagine for convenience that the Egyptian words were the same as

English. The word "leaf" might be written thus: 🖊. This sign might come to stand for the sound "leaf" wherever it occurred. So the sign 🖊 might come to stand for the sound "be." But when these two sounds are combined they form a word, "belief." The sound signs could be used in many combinations. The sign for "man," 🖊, could be used in "manifold," "manifest," "manufacture," "mankind," and any other word in which the sound "man" occurs. Writing came in this way to represent the sounds we make when we speak.

If the writing of the Egyptians had remained merely a series of pictures, such words as "belief," "hate," "love,' "beauty," and the like could never have been written. But when a large number of their pictures had become phonetic signs, each representing a syllable, it was possible for the Egyptians to write any word, whether that word meant a thing of which they could draw a picture or not. This use of *phonetic* signs was what made the first real writing. It began among these Nile-dwellers earlier than anywhere else in the ancient world.

The Egyptian Alphabet. The Egyptians went still further and devised an alphabet, or series of signs, each one representing only one letter. There were twenty-four letters in this alphabet, which was used by the thirty-fifth century B.C. It is the earliest alphabet known and the one from which our own has probably descended.

Invention of Writing Materials. Early in their efforts to write, the Egyptians found out that they could make an excellent paint or ink by thickening water with a little vegetable gum and then mixing in a little soot from the blackened pots over the fire. By dipping a pointed reed into this mixture they could write very well. They learned also that they could split a kind of river reed, called *papyrus*, into thin strips and make large sheets by pasting the strips together with overlapping edges. This gave them a very thin sheet. By pasting *two* such sheets together "two-ply," with the grain crossing at right angles, and removing all unevenness by pounding and rubbing, they produced a smooth, tough, pale-yellow paper. The Egyptians had thus made the discovery that a thin vegetable membrane offers a most practical surface on which to write, and the world has since discovered nothing better. In this way pen, ink, and paper first came into use (Fig. 9). The word *papyrus* gave us our word "paper," by the loss of the ending *us* and the change of *y* to *e*. With the invention of writing and of writing materials, civilization had made a great advance, for written records of what man did and thought could now be made. And we must not forget that this advance was made under the First Union.

The Second Union and the Age of Metal. The consolidation of the North and South, which we have called the First Union, did not endure. In time the two kingdoms fell apart and for a period existed independently side by side. Then there arose in Upper Egypt a strong leader named Menes, who succeeded in permanently uniting the two kingdoms (about 3100 B.C.). Just as the power and prosperity of the First Union were based on plow culture and the production of plentiful grain, so the progress of the Second Union grew out of the earliest mining on a large scale and the possession of plentiful copper.

The graves of the cemeteries of the First Union had contained many more tools and implements of copper than those of the previous two kingdoms. There was some trade in copper axes and chisels, and a few workmen used them. The First Union had therefore brought the Age of Metal much nearer. With the Second Union the Age of Metal actually began. The early kings of the Second Union were very proud of their ability to send mining expeditions into the mountains of the neighboring Peninsula of Sinai, and there we still find the mining tunnels which they drove into the mountains. As a result of the possession of many varied copper tools the Egyptian kings were able to erect hewn stone tombs and stone temples, beginning about 2800 B.C. In these great stone buildings we may read records of the history of Egypt.

2. THE PYRAMID AGE
(TWENTY-NINTH TO TWENTY-FOURTH CENTURY B.C.)

The Pyramids as Royal Tombs. In order to see the first chapter of this history in stone, we must turn our attention to the royal cemetery at Gizeh. Here we find first the pyramids — the tombs of the kings — and then, clustering about the pyramids, great numbers of much smaller tombs of stone masonry. In these smaller tombs were buried the relatives of the king, and the great men of his court who assisted him in the government of the land. These tombs reveal many things about the men who built them. In the first place, they show that the Egyptians believed in a life after death and that to obtain such life they thought it necessary to preserve the body from destruction. They built these tombs to protect the body after death. From this belief came also the practice of "embalming," by which the body was preserved as a mummy.

The Gods of Egypt: Re and Osiris. The Egyptians had many gods, but there were two whom they worshiped above all others. The Sun, which shines so gloriously in the cloudless Egyptian sky, was their greatest god, and their most splendid temples were erected for his worship. Indeed, the pyramid was a symbol sacred to the Sun-god. They called him Re (pronounced "ray"). The other great power which they revered as a god was the shining Nile. The mighty river and the fertile soil it refreshes, and the green life which it brings forth, — all these the Egyptian thought of together as a single god, Osiris, the wondrous life of the earth which revives and fades every year with the changes of the seasons.

Rapid Progress from the Earliest Stone Masonry to the Great Pyramid. But the pyramid cemetery of Gizeh — not far from the modern city of Cairo — tells us of many other things besides the religion of the Egyptians. As we look up at the lofty pyramids behind the Sphinx we marvel at the progress made by the Egyptians since the days when they were buried with their flint knives in a pit scooped out on the margin of the desert. It was chiefly the skillful use of metal tools which carried them so far. Complete mastery of stone building was a step taken very quickly, but we have seen that it was preceded by a slow and gradual change from stone tools to those of metal. That Egyptian in Sinai who noticed the first bit of metal (p. 15) probably lived over two thousand years before these pyramids were built. He was buried in a pit like that of the earliest Egyptian peasant. By the thirty-fourth century B.C. the Egyptians had learned to build tombs of sun-baked brick for their kings. Such a royal tomb was merely a chamber in the ground, roofed with wood and covered with a mound of sand and gravel. Tombs of this kind continued to be built for hundreds of years.

It was probably about 2800 B.C. that some skillful workmen found out that with their copper tools they could cut blocks of limestone and line the burial chamber with these stone blocks in place of the soft bricks. This was the first piece of *stone* masonry ever put together, so far as we know. During the next hundred years or so tombs began to be built in the form of a pyramid, and not very long after 2650 B.C. the architect of King Khufu was constructing the Great Pyramid of Gizeh. Most of this amazing progress was made between 2800 and 2500 B.C.

Vast Size of the Great Pyramid. We can appreciate this achievement of the Egyptians when we realize that the Great Pyramid covers thirteen acres. It is a solid mass of masonry containing two million, three hundred thousand blocks of limestone, each weighing, on an average, two and a half tons; that is, each block is as heavy as a large wagonload of coal. The sides of the pyramid at the base are seven hundred and fifty-six feet long, and the building was originally nearly five hundred feet high. Herodotus (p. 208) tells us that a hundred thousand men worked on this tomb for twenty years.

Length of the Pyramid Age. From the summit of the Great Pyramid there is a grand view southward, down a long line of lesser pyramids rising dimly as far as one can see on the

Fig. 8. *Airplane View over the Royal Cemetery at Gizeh*

The three large pyramids are tombs of Fourth Dynasty kings, the one farthest away being the Great Pyramid, of King Khufu. In the smaller pyramids and tombs are buried members of the royal family and prominent courtiers. The cultivated plain and the modern Egyptian town in the background form an interesting contrast to the sand-covered desert plateau on which stand the ruins of the ancient city of the dead. (Courtesy of Lieutenant Commander Noel F. Wheeler and the editor of *Antiquity*)

southern horizon. Each pyramid was a royal tomb, and each tomb means therefore that a king lived, ruled, and died. The line is over sixty miles long, and its oldest pyramids represent the glorious age of Egyptian civilization after the land was united for the second time under one king. We may call it the Pyramid Age. It lasted about five hundred years, — from the end of the twenty-ninth to the end of the twenty-fourth century B.C., according to recent research.

Government in the Pyramid Age. Building operations such as those involved in the erection of the pyramids show that there was a firmly established *government*. It must have required a very skillful ruler and a large body of officials to manage and to feed a hundred thousand workmen around the Great Pyramid. The king who was able to undertake such vast works was the most powerful human being that the world had ever seen. He was so reverenced that the people did not mention him by name, but instead they spoke of the palace in which he lived, that is, *Pharaoh*, a word made up of two Egyptian words which mean "Great House." The Pharaoh had two kinds of officials to aid him in carrying on his government. There were the *local* officials, who were scattered about through all Egypt, and the *central* officials, who lived at the capital near the king. It was the duty of the *local* officials to collect taxes all over Egypt. It was also their business to try the law cases which arose, and every judge had before him the *written law*[1] which bade him judge justly.

The taxes received from the people were not in coined money, since this did not yet exist, but in produce, such as live stock, grain, wine, honey, linen, and the like. These were kept in cattle yards, granaries, and storehouses, — a large group of buildings, which formed the treasury and central offices of the king, where hundreds of clerks, with their reed pens and their rolls of papyrus, were daily keeping the king's records and accounts. The clerks had lists of the taxpayers' names and how much they owed, and they issued receipts when the taxes were paid, just as at the present day. Such arrangements as these are not found in Europe until the time of the Roman Empire.

The Royal City. The residences and gardens of the officials who assisted the king in all this business of government formed a large part of the royal city. The chief quarter, however, was occupied by the palace of the king and the luxurious parks and gardens which surrounded it. The royal palace and its grounds, the houses of the officials, and the various government offices made up the capital of Egypt, which once extended along the foot of the Gizeh pyramid cemetery and stretched far to the south over the valley plain. It was later called Memphis. Built entirely of sun-baked brick and wood, it has long since vanished.

---

[1] This Egyptian code of laws has unfortunately been lost.

Earliest Seagoing Ships. The earliest Pharaohs of the Second Union had not only made use of the copper mines of Sinai but also dispatched expeditions northward by sea to Byblos, on the coast of Syria. Byblos was very important because of the forests that lay behind it ; and here the timber which Egypt needed was cut and loaded on the Egyptian ships, to be sent back to the Nile. This commerce across the southeastern corner of the Mediterranean was the earliest sea-borne trade of which we have any record. Later during the Pyramid Age communication between Egypt and Asia was most active. Blocks from a pyramid-temple south of Gizeh show carved and painted reliefs of the Egyptian ships of this period. These may be dated to the middle of the twenty-sixth century B.C., and are the oldest known *pictures* of seagoing ships.

Agriculture and Cattle-Raising. A stroll among the tombs clustering so thickly around the pyramids of Gizeh is almost like a walk among the busy communities of the Nile valley during the days of the pyramid-builders ; for the stone walls are often covered from floor to ceiling with carved scenes, beautifully painted, picturing the daily life on the great estate of which the buried noble had been lord (Figs. 9 and 10). The tallest figure in all these scenes on the walls is that of the noble. He stands looking out over his fields and inspecting the work that is going on there. These fields where the oxen draw the plow and the sowers scatter the seed are the oldest scenes of farming known to us. Here too are the herds, long lines of sleek, fat cattle. While they graze in the pasture, the cows are led up and tied to be milked. These cattle are also beasts of burden. We have noticed the oxen drawing the plow, and the donkey too is everywhere, for it would be difficult to harvest the grain without him. But we find no pictures of horses carved on the walls of these tombs of the Pyramid Age, for the horse was then unknown to the Egyptians.

The Coppersmith. On a neighboring wall we find again the tall figure of the noble overseeing the booths and yards

FIG. 9. *Scene from the Chapel of a Nobleman's Tomb in the Pyramid Age*

The tall figure of the noble stands at the right. A piece has fallen out of the wall, immediately before his face and figure. He is inspecting three rows of cattle and some fowl brought to him. Note the two scribes who head the two middle rows. Each is writing with a pen on a sheet of papyrus, and one carries two pens behind his ear. Such carvings were colored in bright hues by the painter

where his skilled workmen are busily occupied. The copper-smith could make excellent copper tools [1] of all sorts. The tool which demanded the greatest skill was the long, flat ripsaw, which the smith knew how to hammer into shape out of a broad strip of copper sometimes five or six feet long. A saw of this kind may be seen in use in *Ancient Times*, Fig. 46.

The Goldsmith and Jeweler. On the same wall we see the booth of the goldsmith filled with workmen and apprentices weighing gold and costly stones, hammering and casting, soldering and fitting together richly wrought jewelry which can hardly be surpassed by the best goldsmiths and jewelers of today (see *Ancient Times*, Figs. 48–49). A workman is

---

[1] Before the end of the Pyramid Age the coppersmiths had learned how to *harden* their tools by melting a small amount of tin with the copper. This produced a mixture of metals called bronze, which is much harder than copper

holding up for the noble's admiration splendid stone bowls cut from diorite. Although this kind of stone is as hard as steel, the bowl is ground to such thinness that the sunlight glows through its dark-gray sides.

The Potter's Wheel and Furnace; Earliest Glass. In the next space on this wall we find that the potter does not mold his jars and bowls with his fingers, as in the Stone Age. He now sits before a small horizontal *wheel*, upon which he skillfully shapes the vessel as it whirls round and round under his fingers. When the soft clay vessels are ready, they are no longer unevenly baked in an open fire, as among the Late Stone Age potters in the Swiss lake-villages (Fig. 5), but in closed furnaces.

Here we also find the craftsmen making *glass*. This art the Egyptians had discovered centuries earlier. They spread the glass on tiles in gorgeous glazes for adorning house and palace walls. Later they learned to make charming many-colored glass bottles and vases, which were widely exported.

Weaving. On another wall the women are weaving a fabric of linen. Although the picture cannot show how delicate are its threads, fortunately pieces of such material have been found wrapped around the royal mummies of the time. They are so fine that it requires a magnifying glass to distinguish them from silk, and the best work of the modern *machine* loom is coarse in comparison with this fabric of the ancient Egyptian *hand* loom.

In the next space on the wall we find huge bundles of papyrus reeds, which barelegged men are gathering along the edge of the Nile marsh. These reeds furnish piles of pale-yellow paper in long sheets (p. 30). Egyptian ships on the Mediterranean (p. 35) added bales of this Nile paper to their cargoes and carried it to Syria and Europe. Egypt thus came to be the world's paper mill for three thousand years.

Shipbuilders and Cabinetmakers. We seem almost to hear the hubbub of hammers and mallets as we approach the next section of wall, where we find the shipbuilders busily at work finishing the hulls of some ships. Beside them are

cabinetmakers fashioning luxurious furniture for the nobleman's house. The chairs and couches for the king or the
rich were very handsomely overlaid with gold and silver, or
inlaid with ebony and ivory, and were upholstered with soft
leather cushions.

Business and Money. Here on the wall is a picture of
the market place. We can watch the cobbler offering the
baker a pair of sandals as payment for a cake, or the carpenter's wife giving the fisherman a little wooden box to pay
for a fish. We learn therefore that the people have *no coined
money* to use, and that in the market place business is carried
on by actual exchange of goods, commonly called barter. If
we could see the larger dealings taking place in the palace,
we should find that they used heavy rings of gold of a standard weight, as we use money. Rings of copper served the
same purpose. Therefore rings of gold and sometimes of
copper were the forerunners of the earliest coins (Fig. 39).

Three Classes of Society in the Pyramid Age. These people
in the market place painted on the wall of the tomb are the
common folk of Egypt in the Pyramid Age. Some of them
were *free men*, following their own business or industry.
Others were *slaves*, working the fields on the great estates.
Neither of these lower classes owned any land. Over them
were the *landowners*, the Pharaoh and his great lords and
officials, such as the owner of the tomb (Fig. 9) which we have
been describing.

Life and Art in the Pyramid Age. Here on this chapel
wall, again, we see its owner seated at ease in his carrying
chair, a kind of wheelless carriage borne upon the shoulders
of slaves. He is returning from the inspection of his estate,
where we have been following him. His bearers carry him
into the shady garden before his house, where they set down
the carrying-chair and cease their song. Here the nobleman
may remain for an hour of leisure with his family and friends,
playing with gaming pieces on a draughtboard, listening to
the music of harp, pipe, and lute, watching the women in the
slow and stately dances of the time, while his children are

Fig. 10. *Market Scene in the Pyramid Age*

At the right we see the Egyptian "shopper" entering the market place, where he is immediately set upon by men with goods for sale. The vender who has been able to get to him first is trying to sell staves, concerning which he cries, "Look at the very beautiful staff!" These staves, which in the ancient world served much the same purpose as our canes, or walking sticks, are being examined by the prospective purchaser, who remarks, "How pleasing is its head!" The men standing behind the vender of staves encourage the purchaser by exclaiming about the low price of the wares. In the center two men are bargaining over an exchange of sandals and cloth. Behind them a man holds out a jar of oil and calls out concerning the excellence of his product. At the extreme left a man boring a cylinder seal (cf. Fig. 20) is approached by another man, for whom he is perhaps making the seal

Fig. 11. *Portrait of King Khafre, the Builder of the Second Pyramid of Gizeh*

This portrait statue was found in his valley temple (see *Ancient Times*, Fig. 54). It is carved in very hard stone, called diorite. The falcon, with protecting wings outstretched, is a symbol of the great god Horus (c. twenty-sixth century B.C.)

Fig. 12. *Head of Portrait Statue of King Mernere as a Child*

The metal statues of the little prince and of his father, Pepi I (see *Ancient Times*, Fig. 52), were found together. They were apparently hammered into shape over a wooden form. Although the metal is incrusted with rust, the eyes, of inlaid rock crystal, make the portraits very lifelike

splashing in the pool, or playing with ball, doll, and jumping jack, or teasing the tame monkey, which takes refuge under their father's ivory-legged stool.

The portrait sculptor was the greatest artist of this age. His statues were carved in stone or wood and painted in lifelike colors; the eyes were inlaid with rock crystal (Fig. 12). Few more lifelike portraits have ever been produced by any age, although they are the earliest portraits in the history of art. The statues of the kings, the best of which were set up in the Pharaoh's pyramid-temple, are often superb (Fig. 11). In size the most striking statue of the Pyramid Age is the Great Sphinx, in the cemetery of Gizeh. This gigantic figure was carved from a promontory of rock overlooking the royal city. The head is a portrait of Khafre, the king who built the second pyramid of Gizeh; it is the largest portrait ever made.

About 2800 B.C., the famous royal architect Imhotep
created the first architecture in stone. He built for the king
a tomb, around which he erected a wonderful group of beautiful buildings, including other tombs for the royal family.
The fronts of these tombs were adorned with stone supports
so gracefully fluted that they look like the slender Greek
columns of twenty-five hundred years later. A second stage
of architecture in stone is to be found in the massive granite
piers and walls of Khafre's valley temple beside the Sphinx.
This hall was lighted by a series of oblique slits which occupied the difference in level between a higher roof over the
middle aisle of the hall and a lower roof on each side of the
middle. Such an arrangement of roof and windows, called
a clerestory (clearstory), passed from Egypt over to Greece
and Rome and was finally used by builders of Christian
churches and cathedrals.

The weight and massiveness of the piers or pillars in
Khafre's hall make it a place of grandeur, but less than a
century later the Egyptian architects sought gracefulness.
Instead of these heavy *square* supports they began to erect
slender and graceful *round* columns with beautiful capitals.
Each column represented a plant, often a palm, the capital
of the column being the crown of foliage. These shafts, when
ranged in rows, formed the earliest known colonnades in the
history of architecture (Fig. 69).

3. THE AGE OF THE NOBLES

Rise of the Nobles. The Pyramid Age lasted until about
2300 B.C. (p. 44, note 1). It was not the end of civilization on
the Nile; other great periods were to follow. But the leadership of Egypt now passed farther to the south. If we should
voyage upriver by steamer from Gizeh, we should discover
that after a time the great stone pyramids disappear altogether; but far away in the south we should find other buildings, tombs, and monuments which tell us of two more great
ages on the Nile, — the Feudal Age [1] and the Empire. By

---

[1] Since the nobles resembled in some ways those of medieval times in Europe.
this period is called the *Feudal Age.*

2000 B.C. a class of powerful lords had grown up, who owned vast tracts of land which had been granted to them by the Pharaoh in return for promises to aid him in various ways, especially when he wished to go to war. These landowners, or barons, became very wealthy, and lived like kings themselves on their great estates. The Age of the Nobles, or the Feudal Age, lasted for several centuries.

Tombs and Libraries of the Feudal Age. It is in the cliffs back of the fertile valley estates that the tombs of these nobles are built, and from the scenes painted on the tomb walls we may reconstruct the life of the times. Fragments from the libraries of these feudal barons — the oldest libraries in the world — have also been found, and from these papyrus rolls we actually learn what these people *thought*, as well as how they lived! These oldest of all surviving books are in the form of rolls of papyrus. Here are the most ancient storybooks in the world: tales of wanderings and adventures in Asia, tales of shipwreck at the gate of the unknown ocean beyond the Red Sea, the earliest "Sindbad the Sailor"; and tales of wonders wrought by ancient wise men and magicians. Some of these stories set forth the sufferings of the poor and the humble and seek to stir the rulers to be just and kind in their treatment of these unfortunate people.

There are also rolls containing songs and poems. A papyrus dating from the eighteenth or nineteenth century B.C. contains a drama in the form of a pageant, with stage directions accompanied by pictures of the action. This is probably the oldest illustrated book in the world. It is a surprising fact that even at this early date it took a number of rolls to describe what was known about science. The most valuable roll of all tells what had been learned about surgery and the organs of the human body. This book gives the earliest known mention of the human brain and the earliest notice of the fact that the brain controls the limbs and hence when the brain suffers an injury the limbs are paralyzed. There are also rolls containing many of the recognized rules of arithmetic, based on the decimal system which we still use; others treat the beginnings of geometry.

Fig. 13. *An Egyptian Nobleman of Four Thousand Years ago Counting his Cattle*

This entire group is made of wood, brightly painted, and about six feet long. Such miniature representations of Egyptian life were placed in the tomb to furnish the dead man with all the necessities and luxuries in the next world, where these models were believed to become real. This group and many others were discovered at Thebes by the Metropolitan Museum of New York in 1920. (Courtesy of the Metropolitan Museum of Art)

Pharaoh's Interest in Foreign Trade. While the Egyptians were thus making great progress in higher things *at home,* the Pharaohs reached out to secure the wealth of *other lands.* Their fleets sailed among the Ægean Islands and it may be that they got control of the island of Crete (map, p. 47). It was in this period that a canal was dug from the eastern branch of the Nile across the Delta to the northern end of the Red Sea. So the Pharaoh's ships could then sail up the Nile, pass through the canal, and enter the Red Sea. This was the forerunner of the great Suez Canal completed in 1869. The wise rule of the Pharaohs of the Feudal Age did much to prepare the way for Egyptian leadership in the early world. Three of these kings bore the name "Sesostris," which became one of the illustrious names in Egyptian history. But not long after 1800 B.C. the power of the Pharaohs of the Feudal Age suddenly declined. Their final fall was due to an invasion of a foreign people called Hyksos, who entered Egypt from Asia. The Hyksos kings established themselves in the Delta and ruled Egypt from there. In the south there were many local native princes, who probably rebelled frequently against the hated invaders. But not until the sixteenth century B.C. did there arise a native ruler strong enough to drive the Hyksos out of Egypt.

4. THE EMPIRE

The Monuments of Thebes. The tombs and pyramids along the river banks have thus far told us the story of two of the three periods, or ages,[1] into which the career of this great Nile people falls. After the modern traveler on the Nile has passed the tombs of the Age of the Nobles and has continued his journey over four hundred miles southward from Cairo, he sees mighty masses of stone masonry and rows of tall columns rising among the palms on the east side of the river. They are the ruins of the great city of Thebes, which will tell us the story of the third period, that of the Empire.

Here we find not only a large cemetery but also great temples. A walk around the colossal temple of Karnak[2] at Thebes is as instructive in studying the Empire as the cemetery at Gizeh in studying the Pyramid Age. The walls of the Karnak temple are covered with enormous sculptures in relief, depicting the wars of the Egyptians in all directions but especially in Asia, whither they drove back the Hyksos. In these pictures we see the giant figure of the Pharaoh — who is given all the credit — as he stands in his war chariot, scattering the enemy before his plunging horses. The Pharaohs of the Pyramid Age had never seen a horse (p. 35), and this is the first time we have found horses portrayed on the ancient monuments. After the close of the Age of the Nobles, horses began to be imported from Asia; the chariot, the first wheeled vehicle in Africa, came with them, and Egypt, having learned how to carry on warfare on a scale unknown before, became a military empire.

The Empire (1580–1150 B.C.). The Pharaohs were now great generals, with a well-organized standing army. With

---

[1] These three ages into which Egyptian history seems to fall are (1) the Pyramid Age, about 2815–2294 B.C.; (2) the Age of the Nobles, flourishing about 2000 B.C.; (3) the Empire, about 1580–1150 B.C.

[2] A view of the great temple of Karnak taken from an airplane will be found in *Ancient Times*, Fig. 66. Karnak is a tiny modern village near the temple.

The Story of Egypt

45

these forces the Pharaohs conquered an empire which extended from the Euphrates in Asia to the Fourth Cataract of the Nile in Africa (map, p. 47). By an "empire" we mean a group of nations which have been conquered and are ruled by some more powerful nation. The earliest form of government seems to have been the little city-states, independent of each other. Then a group of such city-states would gradually unite into a nation. With the formation of the Egyptian Empire we have for the first time a great state made up of *many nations* which have been combined into an empire and forced to accept the government of a conquering ruler. The period of the Empire, during which the Pharaohs were really emperors, lasted from the early sixteenth century to the twelfth century B.C., — somewhat over four hundred years.

Fig. 14. *Portrait of Thutmose III (Fifteenth Century B.C.)*

Carved in granite and showing the great conqueror wearing the tall crown of Upper Egypt, with the sacred asp forming a serpent crest above his forehead. Such portraits in the Empire can be compared with the actual faces of these Egyptian emperors as we have them in their mummies, and they are thus shown to be good likenesses (see *Ancient Times*, Fig. 65)

Campaigns of Thutmose III. The greatest of the Egyptian emperors as a soldier and leader was Thutmose III, who ruled for over fifty years, beginning about 1500 B.C. He was the first great general in history. On the temple walls at Karnak we can read the story of nearly twenty years of warfare, during which Thutmose crushed the cities and kingdoms of Syria and Palestine and united them into an empire. He also built up the largest fleet of war vessels that Egypt had so far had and with it extended his power even to the Ægean Sea.

5. CIVILIZATION OF THE EMPIRE

The Empire Temples. The wealth which the Pharaohs plundered from the peoples they conquered in Asia and Nubia brought them great power and enabled them to build their capital city at Thebes on a scale of magnificence unknown to the world before. Vast and splendid buildings were erected, and a new period in the history of art and architecture began. The temple of Karnak contains the greatest colonnaded hall ever erected by man. The columns of the central aisle are seventy-nine feet high. The capital forming the summit of *each* column is large enough to hold as many as a hundred men standing crowded upon it. European architects later borrowed from these buildings of Egypt many ideas which are familiar to us (see columns as they are today, Fig. 16).

Such temples as these at Thebes were seen through the deep green of clustering palms, among towering obelisks and colossal statues of the Pharaohs. The whole scene was bright with color, flashing at many a point with bands of sheet gold and silver. Mirrored in the unruffled surface of the temple lake, these monumental buildings made a picture of marvelous beauty and splendor.

Painting and Sculpture in the Temples. Much of the grandeur of Egyptian architecture was due to the sculptor and the painter. The colonnades, with flower capitals, were colored to suggest the plants they represented. The vast battle scenes, carved on the temple wall, were painted in bright colors. The portrait statues of the Pharaohs, set up before these temples, were often higher than the buildings themselves and could be seen for miles around.

The sculptors could cut these colossal figures from a single block, although they were sometimes eighty or ninety feet high and weighed as much as a thousand tons. This is equal to the load drawn by a modern freight train of twenty-five cars, but, unlike the trainload, it was not cut up into small units of weight light enough for convenient handling and loading. Nevertheless, the engineers of the Empire moved many such vast figures for hundreds of

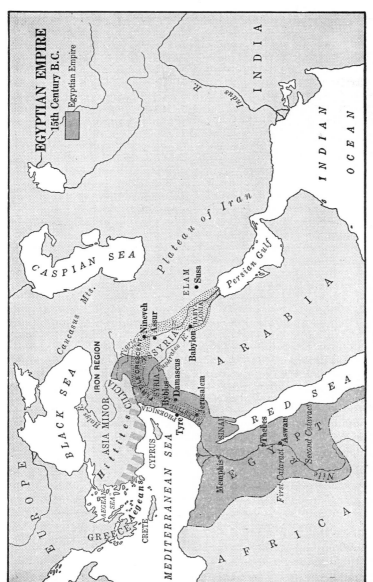

The Egyptian Empire

Fig. 15. *Restoration of the Great Hall of Karnak, Ancient Thebes — Largest Building of the Egyptian Empire*

This vast and imposing building is three hundred and thirty-eight feet wide and one hundred and seventy feet deep. There are one hundred and thirty-four columns, in sixteen rows. The central aisles (nave) were made higher than the rest, so as to permit tall windows to be placed at the sides

miles. It was in works of this massive, monumental character that the art of Egypt excelled.

Life and Art of the Empire. Just as at Gizeh, the cemetery of Thebes tells us much of the life of the people who lie buried there. In the majestic western cliffs across the Nile from Karnak are cut hundreds of tomb-chapels belonging to the great men of the Empire. Here were buried the able generals who marched with the Pharaohs on their campaigns in Asia and in Nubia. Here lay the gifted artists and architects who built the vast monuments we have just visited. Here in these tomb-chapels we may read their names and often long accounts of their lives. Here, for example, is the story of the general who saved Thutmose III's life in an elephant hunt in Asia by rushing in and cutting off the trunk of an enraged elephant which was pursuing the king.

These tombs are wonderful treasuries of Egyptian art, for the very furniture which these rich men used in their houses was put into their tombs. Many beautiful things, like chairs covered with gold and silver and provided with soft cushions of leather, bedsteads of exquisite workmanship, jewel boxes and perfume caskets of the ladies, and even the gold-covered

FIG. 16. *The Colossal Columns of the Nave in the Great Hall of Karnak*

These are the columns of the middle two rows in the nave (Fig. 15). On the top of the capital of each one of these columns a hundred men can stand at once. The human figures below show by contrast the vast dimensions of the columns towering above them

chariot in which the Theban noble took his afternoon outing thirty-three or thirty-four hundred years ago, have been found in these tombs. These works of art may now be seen in the National Museum at Cairo, and there is also a fine collection in the Metropolitan Museum of Art, New York. The discovery in 1922 of the tomb of Tutenkhamon, a young king who ruled after 1360 B.C., has added greatly to our knowledge of the art of Egypt at its height. The great importance of this discovery lies in the fact that archæologists were able for the first time to study a royal tomb whose inner chamber, where the mummy rests, had never been disturbed since the king was buried, some three thousand two hundred and seventy years ago.

Religion of the Empire. These tombs, like those of the earlier periods, tell us much of the religion of the time. The Egyptians of the Empire had developed some important new religious ideas. Each of the men buried in the Theban cemetery looked forward to a judgment in the next world, where Osiris (p. 31) was the judge and king. Every good man might rise from the dead as Osiris had done, but in the presence of Osiris he would be obliged to see his soul weighed in the balances over against the symbol of truth and justice. The dead man's friends put into his coffin a roll of papyrus containing prayers and magic charms intended to aid him in the hereafter. This magical guidebook for the next world, with its varied contents, we now call the Book of the Dead.

Some of the leading Egyptians of the Empire finally came to believe that there was only one God. Such a belief we call monotheism (p. 88). Ikhnaton (about 1375–1358 B.C.), the most unique of their kings, endeavored to make this belief in one god the religion of the whole Empire; but the opposition of the priests and the people was too strong, and he perished in the attempt.

Decline and Fall of the Egyptian Empire (1150 B.C.). Serious religious conflicts at home had greatly weakened Egypt by the middle of the fourteenth century (1350) B.C. After it had recovered somewhat, the great Pharaohs Seti I

Fig. 17. *Model of an Egyptian Nobleman's Villa (about 1350 B.C.)*

The reconstruction of this house is based upon the plans of an actual house excavated at Tell el-Amarna by Dr. Henri Frankfort in 1929. The model was made for exhibition at the Oriental Institute of The University of Chicago. In the foreground, by the nearest corner, an avenue of trees leads from the main entrance, with its small porter's lodge, to a little square private chapel. To the right of the chapel is the entrance to an inner courtyard, from which the house can be entered through a projecting porch. The house consists of a central room with clerestory lighting, and low outer rooms lit from the side. A tradesmen's entrance (on the right of the main entrance) leads from the street to the granary courtyard, with four beehive-shaped granaries. The chariot room, horse stables, servants' quarters, kitchens, cattle pens, and dog kennels are to be seen on the right and center in the background. A simple formal garden with trees is at the left, and in a small courtyard between this garden and the little pens is a shallow well with a spiral staircase leading into it

and his son Ramses II partially restored the old splendor. Their two reigns covered almost a century (ending about 1225 B.C.). They fought great wars in Asia, but they were unable to restore the Empire to its former extent and power. Their most powerful enemies were at first the Hittites of Asia Minor (pp. 94–98).

Then more dangerous foes arose. We find them pictured in the temple reliefs, and it is interesting to discover that these new enemies were many of them Europeans from the northern Mediterranean lands, where we left them in the Late Stone Age. These northerners finally entered Egypt in such large numbers after 1200 B.C. that the weakened Egyptian Empire fell (about 1150 B.C.). Egypt was never again to recover her old power and leadership.

Significance of Egyptian History and Civilization. Thus ends the story of the Empire at Thebes. The pyramids, tombs, and temples along the Nile have told us the history of early Egypt in three epochs: the pyramids of Gizeh and the neighboring cemeteries have disclosed to us the Pyramid Age; the cliff tombs and the papyrus-roll libraries have revealed the history and civilization of the Age of the Nobles; and the temples and cliff tombs of Thebes have given us the story of the Empire. The ruins along the Nile have thus become for us a great volume of history. Let us remember, however, that, preceding these three great chapters of civilization on the Nile, we also found here the earlier story of how man passed from Stone Age barbarism to a civilization possessed of metal, writing, and government.

We should remember, moreover, that the three great ages did not end the story; for the influence of Egyptian ideas and civilization continued far down into the Christian age and greatly affected the history of Europe. Later, Egypt became subject to many different powers, but is today once more an independent nation.

Decipherment of Egyptian. In this summary of the story of ancient Egypt we have gained our knowledge from the monuments and the written records. However, only a little

FIG. 18. *Tutenkhamon and his Queen in a Garden Pavilion*

The young queen presents bouquets of lotus and papyrus to Tutenkhamon. Below, in the garden, ladies of the court gather fruit and flowers for the royal pair. This scene is carved on an ivory panel set in the lid of a box found in the tomb of Tutenkhamon. (Courtesy of Howard Carter)

over a hundred years ago no one knew what these written records meant; for the last men who could read Egyptian hieroglyphs had been dead for over a thousand years, and after their time there was no one who understood the curious writing which travelers found covering the ancient Egyptian monuments. It was not until 1822 that the ability to read Egyptian hieroglyphics was recovered. In that year a young French scholar named Champollion announced that he had learned how to read the old Egyptian writing. Since that time scholars in other countries have also mastered the Egyptian language and so have been able to interpret for us the story written in Egypt's tombs and temples.

Development of Civilization in Asia. In a similar way the inscriptions on monuments discovered along the Tigris and Euphrates rivers in Asia have been deciphered and made to tell their story. From them we learn that, following the Egyptians, the peoples of Asia emerged from barbarism, developed industries, learned the use of metals, devised a system of writing, and finally rose to the leading position of power in the ancient world. We must therefore turn, in the next chapter, to the story of the early Near East in Asia.

Questions and Exercises

REVIEW OF CHAPTER

1. Explain the necessity of irrigation in Egypt. What led to the rise of government? Explain the importance of the invention of the plow. Trace the development of Egyptian picture writing. To what country were the earliest mining expeditions sent, and who sent them?

2. Describe the effect of the use of metal on architecture. Describe the government of the Pyramid Age. What industries are shown in the Egyptian tomb-chapel pictures? What three architectural arrangements were first used by the Egyptians?

3. Why do we call the Age of the Nobles in Egypt the "Feudal Age"? What kinds of books did the Egyptians have? What great commercial link between two seas was created in the Feudal Age of Egypt? What is the name of this canal today?

4. What are the dates of the Egyptian Empire? How did Thutmose III strengthen the Egyptian Empire?

5. What did the Egyptian emperors do with the wealth gained from subject peoples? Give an account of the Theban cemetery and what it contains. What is monotheism? What peoples helped to destroy the Egyptian Empire? How long have modern archæologists known how to read the old Egyptian writing?

USEFUL TERMS

See how much meaning you can give to the following: *irrigation, portable wealth, seasons of the year, picture writing, mummy, stone masonry, Pharaoh, taxes, clerestory. nave, obelisk, drama, empire.*

DIRECTIVE QUESTIONS

1. Name three mechanical labor-saving devices invented by the ancient Egyptians which are still used today.

2. What department of the Egyptian government was operated in the Pyramid Age much as modern states carry on the same governmental activity?

3. What form of monuments today is copied from the Egyptian? Can you give any examples?

4. What Egyptian Pharaohs had you heard of before you studied this textbook?

5. Discuss the importance of the discovery of the tomb of Tutenkhamon.

DISCUSSION TOPICS

1. The Nile valley provided perfect surroundings for man's progress from barbarism to civilization.

2. The Egyptians built the pyramids by use of man power, not machine power.

3. When people begin to consider the sufferings of the poor, they have a tendency to *write* about them.

4. Is it of any significance that the Egyptians conquered an empire *after* they began to use the horse?

5. The mummies of the emperors of ancient Egypt have been placed in a tomb and are no longer on exhibition in a museum.

ADDITIONAL ADVENTURES IN LEARNING

1. Studies in Source Materials. ERMAN, *Literature of the Ancient Egyptians*: (1) Complaints of the peasant, pp. 116–131; (2) Instructions to schoolboys, pp. 188–198.

2. Supplementary. Describe the articles found in the tomb of Hetep-heres, the mother of King Khufu. BREASTED, *Ancient Times*, Figs. 47–49, § 103; *Bulletin of the Boston Museum of Fine Arts*, Vol. XXV (May, 1927), Supplement; Vol. XXVI (1928), pp. 76–88; Vol. XXVII (1929), pp. 83–90; Vol. XXX (1932), pp. 55–60. Also name the crafts employed in their manufacture.

3. Look up in an encyclopedia: *Egypt, inundation, shadoof, plow, hoe, calendar, hieroglyphics, Cheops (Khufu), pyramid, papyrus, paper manufacture, obelisk.*

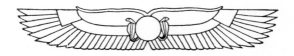

CHAPTER III · DEVELOPMENT
OF CIVILIZATION IN WESTERN ASIA:
BABYLONIA, ASSYRIA, CHALDEA,
AND THE HEBREWS

THE FERTILE CRESCENT AND ITS PEOPLES · THE EARLIEST CIVILIZATION IN BABY-
LONIA : THE SUMERIANS · THE AGE OF HAMMURAPI AND AFTER · THE ASSYRIAN
EMPIRE (ABOUT 750 TO 612 B.C.) · THE CHALDEAN EMPIRE : THE LAST SEMITIC
EMPIRE · THE HEBREWS

WE HAVE followed the rise and progress of civilization south of the
Mediterranean in northeastern Africa, particularly in Egypt, and we
must now trace the beginnings and the spread of civilization in Asia, especially around the eastern end of the great sea. A study of the map of
Western Asia will show that the north consists chiefly of mountain ranges
stretching from west to east and southeast, while the south is a vast desert
of sands and rocks extending to the sea.

Between the mountains on the north and the desert on the south, however,
we find a borderland of rich soil. Here Stone Age men early began to cultivate grain and to breed cattle and sheep. This manner of life left them time
to turn to other things. They developed a group of the great civilizations
of the ancient world — Babylonian, Assyrian, Chaldean, and Hebrew —
civilizations of which we have heard ever since we could remember.

Archaeologists who have unearthed the remains of these long-past civilizations, and who have read the writing they found, have been able to tell
us much concerning the life of these early peoples. In that distant past there
already existed the beginnings of things with which we are familiar today.
We shall find, for instance, that the peoples of Western Asia had learned
how to tame wild horses, to make wheels for their carts, to carry on business, and to use *shekels*, or money, in their transactions. We shall learn how
the days of the week came to be named as they are, how people began
to collect libraries, and how the Bible came into existence.

In modern times poems have been written and pictures have been painted
to illustrate the greatness of the Assyrian Empire. The learning of the
Chaldeans and the wonders of their city of Babylon will never be forgotten.
The beauties of the Hebrew religion are set forth each Sunday in our churches.
The story of the peoples of Western Asia is therefore being constantly re-
called to us in many phases of our life today.

57

1. The Fertile Crescent and its Peoples

The Fertile Crescent. The most important early home of
men in Western Asia was the borderland between the mountains on the north and the desert on the south. This borderland, which has very rich soil for farming, is a kind of fringe
of the desert, — a Fertile Crescent [1] having the mountains
on one side and the desert on the other (map, p. 47). It
forms roughly a semicircle, with the open side toward the
south. Its western end is at the southeastern corner of the
Mediterranean, the center lies directly north of Arabia, and
the eastern end is at the northern part of the Persian Gulf.
The end of the western side is Palestine, Assyria makes up
a large part of the center, while the end of the eastern side
is Babylonia. Historically man's life in this region of Western Asia may be described as an age-long struggle between
the mountain peoples of the north and the desert wanderers
of the south — a struggle which is still going on — for the
possession of the Fertile Crescent.

The Arabian Desert and the Semitic Nomads. There are
no rivers in Arabia, and it rains there only during a few weeks
in the winter. There is therefore very little vegetation for
either man or beast. The inhabitants of the desert have been
from the earliest times a white people called Semites, made
up of many tribes. We are familiar with the names of two of
the ancient Semitic peoples, — the Arabs and especially the
Hebrews, of whom we read in the Bible. For ages the desert
people have been compelled to move up and down the vast
barren plain in search of water and pasturage for their flocks
and herds. These wandering herdsmen we call *nomads.* In
the springtime they pressed northward, for after the short
winter rains a portion of the northern desert is thinly covered
with grass. The herdsmen were now and then tempted to
forsake the sandy waste altogether and push farther north
into the more promising region of the Fertile Crescent. If

---

[1] There is no name, either geographical or political, which includes all of this
great semicircle. Hence in the first edition of *Ancient Times* (1916) the author was
obliged to coin a term for it. He accordingly called it the Fertile Crescent. The
term has since become current and is now widely used.

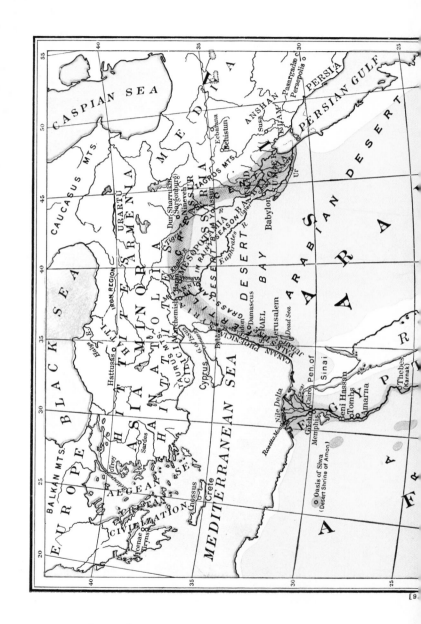

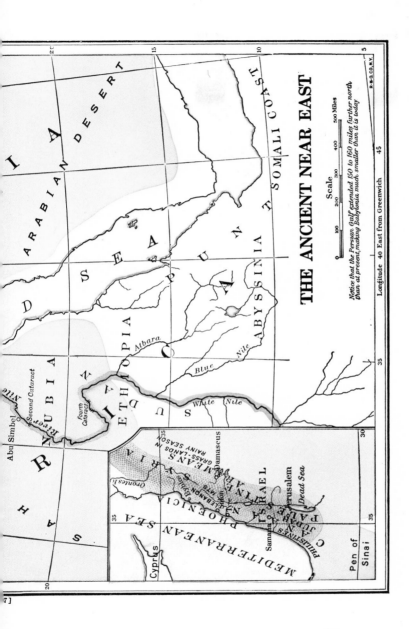

THE ANCIENT NEAR EAST

Scale

|0 100 200 300 400 500 Miles|

Notice that the Persian Gulf extended 150 to 160 miles further north than at present, making Babylonia much smaller than it is today

Longitude 40 East from Greenwich

they were fortunate enough to find a place where they could settle, many of them gave up their wandering life. They then had food at hand, and no longer needed to roam from place to place. They could become farmers and raise crops for themselves and their flocks.

Life of the Semitic Nomads. Out on the wide reaches of the desert the tribesmen led a life of complete freedom. There were no boundaries; for no man owned land, and pasturage belonged to the first comer. The few possessions which the herdsmen had besides their flocks they carried with them as they moved from place to place. They were unable to write and were subject to few laws. When they were in need of something, they would seek out a little village in which to do their trading, and they often carried goods for merchants from one of these little settlements to another. They led their caravans back and forth across the great desert, especially between Syria-Palestine and Babylonia.

The vast and lonely stretches of wilderness affected the religion of the nomads. Their imagination peopled the far reaches of the desert with invisible and uncanny beings. They fancied that the utterance of magic charms — the earliest prayers — would either make these gods help them or render the gods powerless to do them injury. Each tribe had a favorite, or tribal, god, who, as they believed, journeyed with them from pasture to pasture. The thoughts of the desert wanderer about such a god were crude and barbarous. But the nomads had a dawning sense of justice and of right, and they felt toward their fellows some obligations of kindness which they believed to be the commands of their god.

The Semites at the West End of the Fertile Crescent. As early as 3000 B.C., Semite wanderers were drifting in from the desert and settling at the *western* end of the Fertile Crescent, in what was later called Palestine. By 2500 B.C. they were living in walled towns. These people, who were the predecessors of the Hebrews, were called Canaanites. Farther north settled a powerful tribe known as Amorites. Later came the Arameans, who grew to be the most successful merchants throughout Western Asia.[1] Some of these one-time desert wanderers — the Phœnicians, who found their way to the shores of northern Syria — took to the sea and became great traders among the countries bordering the Mediterranean (pp. 126–127). By 2000 B.C. all these settled communities of the Semites had made considerable progress in civilization; for they had learned much from both Egypt and Babylonia.

The East End of the Fertile Crescent. At the same time we can watch similar movements of the nomads at the *eastern* end of the Fertile Crescent, along the lower course of the Tigris and Euphrates, which we shall often speak of as the "Two Rivers." Rising in the northern mountains (map, p. 47), these streams flow in a southeasterly direction across the Fertile Crescent and the northern end of the desert. On these two great rivers of Western Asia developed the earliest civilization anywhere known in Asia.

The Plain of Shinar (or Babylonia). On the Tigris and Euphrates, as on the Nile, the earliest progress was made in the lower valley, near the rivers' mouths. As the Two Rivers approach most closely to each other (originally about a hundred and sixty or seventy miles from the Persian Gulf[2]) they leave the desert and enter a low plain of fertile soil, formerly brought down by the rivers. This plain, at the eastern end of the Fertile Crescent, is generally known as Babylonia. But during the first thousand years of its history it was called the Plain of Shinar. It was hardly more than forty miles wide at any point and contained probably less than eight thousand square miles of farm land, — roughly equal to the state of New Jersey. It lies in the Mediterranean belt of rainy winter and dry summer, but the rainfall is nevertheless so slight (less than seven inches a year) that the fields must be irrigated in order to ripen the grain. When properly irrigated, however, the Plain of Shinar is very fertile, and so

---

[1] On the remarkable achievements of the Arameans, especially as to how they spread the alphabet, see Breasted's *Ancient Times*, §§ 241–244.

[2] This was the distance in ancient Babylonian and Assyrian times. But the mud carried down by the rivers has since then filled up the Persian Gulf, extending the land one hundred and fifty to sixty miles (see note under scale on map, p. 58).

the chief source of wealth in ancient Shinar was farming. This plain was the scene of the most important and long-continued of those frequent struggles between the mountaineer and the nomad, of which we have spoken.

2. THE EARLIEST CIVILIZATION IN BABYLONIA: THE SUMERIANS

The Sumerians. At the time when the Egyptians were building up their civilization, a people of uncertain race, called Sumerians, from the highlands of the north and east, wandered into the Plain of Shinar and drained the marshes around the head of the Persian Gulf. The southern part of the Plain of Shinar came to be called, after them, Sumer. It is clear from recent excavations at their ancient city of Ur, southeast of Babylon, that the Sumerians had reached a high degree of civilization by the year 3000 B.C.

These people learned to control the spring freshets by means of dikes, to guide the waters into irrigation trenches, and to reap large harvests of grain. They were already cultivating barley and wheat, which were the two chief grains in Western Asia as they were in Egypt. They owned cattle, used the ox for plowing, and had donkeys to pull their *wheeled* carts and chariots. They were very skillful in making copper tools; the examples of their carving and gold and silver ornaments which have been discovered show astonishing ability. Recent excavation has revealed that they were also able to erect imposing buildings.

The Sumerians began to keep their business accounts by scratching pictures on soft clay with the tip of a reed. In trying to make these pictures simpler the ancient scribes gradually came to use strokes or lines, each of which was a *wedge-shaped* mark. Hence these signs are called *cuneiform,* a word of Latin origin meaning "wedge-form." The use and knowledge of this writing ceased some two thousand years ago; but it was deciphered about 1850, and modern scholars are able to read the clay tablets which have been found buried in the mounds of ancient towns. In this way we learn much of what we know of these and other early peoples.

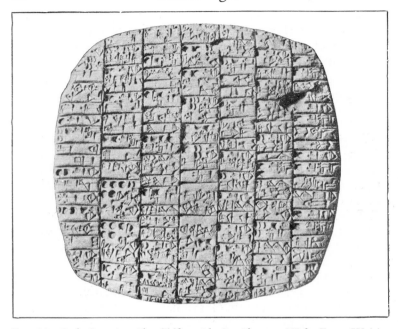

FIG. 19. *Early Sumerian Clay Tablet with Cuneiform, or Wedge-Form, Writing*

This tablet was written in the twenty-eighth century B.C., toward the close of the early period of the city-kings. It contains business accounts. The scribe's writing reed, or *stylus*, was usually square-tipped. He pressed a corner of this square tip into the soft clay for *each line* of the picture sign. Lines so produced tended to be broad at one end and pointed at the other, that is, wedge-shaped. Each picture sign thus became a group of wedges (see *Ancient Times*, § 177). When the clay dried, it was hard enough to make the tablet a fairly permanent record. Such tablets were sometimes baked and thus became as hard as pottery. (By permission of Dr. Hussey)

The Sumerian system of numbers was not based on tens, as is ours — twenty, thirty, forty, fifty, and so forth — but had sixty as a basis. A large number was given as so many sixties; that is, 120 would be two sixties. From this unit of sixty has descended our division of the hour into sixty minutes and the minute into sixty seconds.

The Sumerian Temples, Houses, and Towns. The most important portion of the Sumerian town was the temple inclosure. Surrounded and protected by a massive wall were

Fig. 20. *Early Babylonian Cylinder Seal (about Twenty-fifth Century* B.C.)

Instead of signing his *name* to a clay-tablet document the early Sumerian rolled over the soft clay a little stone roller, or cylinder, engraved with beautiful pictures and sometimes also bearing the owner's name, as here. The impression left by the roller in the soft clay served as a signature. These seals have been found in great numbers, showing the growth and decline of Babylonian art for some three thousand years. The picture above shows a side view of the cylinder (right) and the impression made by rolling it on soft clay (left). The subject of the seal is the story of Gilgamesh, the Sumerian ancestor of Hercules. He is seen slaying a wild bull (center). His friend Engidu, half man, half bull, wrestles with a lion (at left and right). We can appreciate the excellence of the carving when we realize that this seal is only a little over one inch high. A hole was bored lengthwise through the seal so that it might be worn on a string of some sort. See an Egyptian boring a hole through a cylinder seal in Fig. 10

places of worship, storehouses, and business offices. Rising high above the other buildings in the temple inclosure was the tower-temple, which was in general shape almost a cube, though it tapered slightly in a series of steps toward the top. In front were three lofty flights of stairs, rising nearly a hundred and fifty feet, which met at a door about half-way up the front of the building. In the upper part of the tower was a square temple, with a court open to the sky and with a holy place behind it. Probably the first of such tower-temples was built at Nippur, as a sanctuary to Enlil, the Sumerian god of the air. Alongside the tower-temple was a low building which served as the temple proper.

Around the temple inclosure were the houses of the towns-people. They were bare rectangular dwellings of sun-dried brick. The towns were small and usually stood upon an artificial mound. Today nothing is left but mounds of earth and crumbled brick, in which lie buried the clay-tablet records, household articles, or sculptures of the ancient people who once lived there. When we dig out such a mound, we therefore find it a rich storehouse of things which tell us much regarding this ancient civilization.

Fig. 21. *Sculpture once Adorning the Entrance of the Temple of the Cow-Goddess near Ur*

In the middle is a lion-headed eagle hovering over the figures of two stags. This balanced arrangement of animal figures is one of the great creations of Sumerian art. The entire monument is seven feet nine inches long. It was probably mounted over the door of the temple, although it had long since fallen down when found by the excavator, Dr. H. R. Hall. It is the largest sculpture in copper of so early a date ever yet found in Western Asia. The eagle is the divine bird which the Sumerians called "Im-dugud," a malicious creature perhaps placed over the door of the temple to frighten away evil powers and protect the place. Such symbols, made up of balanced pairs of animal figures, later passed over into Europe, where they are still used in decorative art and in the heraldic symbols or arms of kings and nations. The eagle still appears in the arms of Austria, Prussia, and other European nations, and finally reached the West as the "American" eagle, — really the Sumerian eagle of five thousand years ago. (Courtesy of the British Museum)

Sumerian City-Kingdoms (about 2900 to 2350 B.C.). The clay tablets tell us about a class of free, landholding citizens, working their lands with slaves and trading with caravans and small boats up and down the river. Over both these classes, free and slave, there was a large body of officials and priests, — the aristocrats of the town. They were ruled, along with all the rest, by a priest-king. Such a community owned the fields for a few miles round about the town. The whole — that is, the town and its fields — formed a *city-kingdom.* Sumer consisted of a number of such small city-kingdoms, and this earliest Sumerian period may be called the Age of the City-Kingdoms. These little states were not united under one king, and the early history of Sumer was largely made up of the ever-changing fortunes of the city-kingdoms in war with each other.

© *The Illustrated London News*

FIG. 22. *Household of a Prince of Ur Awaiting Death at the Door of his Tomb*

The Anglo-American Expedition under C. L. Woolley, which excavated Ur, discovered the bodies of these men, women, and animals, with their equipment, lying at the door of the burial chamber of the prince's tomb. Directed by the archæologists, the modern artist has here raised the dead by depicting them in the positions which they occupied at the last fatal moment before they were slain. Their slaughter was thought to insure their passing on into the next world with their ruler and continuing to serve him there

The Civilization of Ur. The earliest city to gain the leadership was Ur,[1] a city of the extreme south, and the earliest known king in Western Asia was Mes-anni-padda, who ruled at Ur about 2900 B.C. Recent excavations at the ancient city have resulted in the most surprising discoveries. Far beneath the accumulated rubbish of fallen buildings were found the tombs of the princes and nobles who were buried there at this time. The magnificent equipment of these very early burials rivals that of the tombs of Egypt. Objects of personal adornment wrought in gold show remarkable skill and craftsmanship, as well as beauty of design. Impressive figures in copper, and sculptured bands of decoration, were recovered from the ruins of a neighboring temple of the cow-goddess (Fig. 21).

[1] The power and splendor of Ur were never forgotten, and later, when Hebrew civilization had developed in Palestine, the Hebrews were very proud to trace back their ancestry to Abraham, believed by them to have been a citizen of Ur.

These works of the Sumerian goldsmiths and sculptors at Ur show how far the life of Western Asia had risen above the Stone Age savagery which had once existed in this region. But this civilization was not permitted to continue its growth undisturbed. Ur was eventually overwhelmed by a neighboring city-kingdom. After this, the leadership passed from town to town according to the military strength of the contestants.

FIG. 23. *Jeweled Headdress and Other Ornaments of a Sumerian Woman*

These objects of gold and silver set and inlaid with lapis lazuli and carnelian belonged to one of the ladies shown in the restoration, Fig. 22. The gold hair ribbon, the wreath of gold triple willow leaves, the silver comb with inlaid flowers, the dog collar of gold and lapis lazuli, and all the other beautiful ornaments were found in such a position in the tomb that they could be restrung and placed correctly on the model head as here shown. This head was modeled by Mrs. C. L. Woolley over the cast of a female Sumerian skull. The result is thought to be something very like the physical type of the woman who once wore this headdress. (Courtesy of The University Museum, Philadelphia, and the British Museum)

Sargon and his Kingdom of Akkad (about 2350 B.C.). While the city-kingdoms of Sumer were thus fighting among themselves, they were also called upon to meet an enemy from the outside. The Semitic tribesmen from the desert had early begun to migrate into the Plain of Shinar, north of Sumer. By the end of the twenty-fifth century B.C. they had established a kingdom there known as Akkad. This region comprised the narrow strip of land where the Two Rivers approach each other most closely (map, p. 71). The men of Akkad, or Akkadians, under a bold and able leader named Sargon, descended the Euphrates and conquered the Sumerians. Thus arose the first *Semitic* kingdom of importance in history, and Sargon, its founder, is the first great name in the history of the Semitic race.

The Semitic Akkadians adopt Sumerian Civilization. Sargon's conquests forced his nomad tribesmen (the Akkadians) to make a complete change in their manner of life. They gave up living in their desert tents and built houses of sun-dried brick, which they could not pick up each morning and pitch, like a tent, somewhere else at night. At first they did not even know how to write, and they had no industries. Some of them now learned to write their Semitic tongue by using the Sumerian wedge-form signs for the purpose. And so a *Semitic language* began to be written for the first time. The Akkadians imitated the art of the Sumerians, especially sculpture (Fig. 24), in which they later far surpassed their Sumerian teachers. The beautiful art of seal-cutting (Fig. 20) was now carried to a wonderful degree of perfection. Thus the Akkadians took over the civilization of the Sumerians, whom they had conquered, and the life of the desert Semites mingled with that of the non-Semitic townsmen.

3. The Age of Hammurapi and After

Hammurapi and the Second Great Semite Kingdom. Centuries of struggle between the Sumerians and Semites followed. About 1800 B.C. a tribe of Amorites (p. 59) came in from the west and seized the little town of Babylon, on the Euphrates River. Hammurapi, one of their later kings, after thirty years of fighting conquered the entire region of Shinar (about 1700 B.C.). Again the desert people won, as this *second great Semitic ruler*, Hammurapi, made Babylon, thus far a small and unimportant town, the leading city in the Plain of Shinar. Beginning with Hammurapi, we may more properly call the plain Babylonia.

Hammurapi created order and system where all had formerly been confusion. He collected all the older laws and customs which related to business and to social life and had these written out. He had these laws engraved upon a stone tablet nearly eight feet high, which has survived to our day, — the oldest code of ancient law that we have. On the whole, the laws are very just and show much consideration for the poor and defenseless classes.

Expansion of Babylonian Commerce. Under her wise ruler Babylonia prospered as never before. Her merchants traveled far and wide into the surrounding countries. The Babylonian writing of the clay-tablet bills which accompanied the heavily loaded caravans had to be read by many a merchant in the towns of Syria and behind the northern mountains. Thus the wedge writing of Babylonia gradually spread through Western Asia. There was as yet no coined money, but the Babylonians early began to use pieces of silver each weighing a *shekel*, or the sixtieth part of a pound (*mina*). When a silver shekel was shaped into a disk, it might be no larger than a dime. It was now possible to fix prices and values in weights of silver. Lending of money was common, and the rate of interest was 20 per cent. Business was the chief occupation and was carried on even in the temples.

Higher Life of Babylonia. A journey through Babylonia today could not tell us such a story as we found among the monuments on our voyage up the Nile, for the Babylon of Hammurapi has entirely disappeared. There seems to have been no painting; the sculpture of the Semites was in one instance, at least (Fig. 24), powerful and dramatic, but the portrait sculptor was scarcely able to make one individual look different from another. Of architecture little remains. Although columns were known, the colonnade played no important part in architecture. The main lines were all *straight* (verticals and horizontals), but the *arch* was used over doorways. All buildings were of brick, as Babylonia had no stone. There were schools where boys could learn to write cuneiform, and the ruins of a schoolhouse of Hammurapi's time may still be seen.

End of First Chapter of the History of the Two Rivers. Not long after Hammurapi's death his successors found themselves unable to drive from the northern mountains the

Fig. 24. A King of Akkad Storming a Fortress, — the Earliest Great Semitic Work of Art (about Twenty-third Century B.C.)

King Naram-Sin of Akkad, grandson of Sargon (p. 66), has pursued the enemy into a mountain stronghold. His heroic figure towers above his enemies, each one of whom has fixed his eyes on the conqueror, awaiting his signal of mercy. The sculptor, with fine insight, has depicted the dramatic instant when the king lowers his weapon as the sign that he grants the conquered their lives. The king's enemies are made much smaller than he, to indicate their inferiority

barbarians, who now began to invade the Babylonian plain. The city of Babylon itself was captured, and the last of the great king's family was overthrown. Thereupon the uncivilized highland peoples made themselves masters of Babylonia, and for a long time all progress in civilization in Babylonia stopped.

As we look back over the first age of human progress along the Two Rivers we find that it lasted over a thousand years (from the century following 3000 B.C. to the century following 1800 B.C.). During this time the Sumerians laid the foundations of civilization in Shinar and began their long struggle with the Semites of the desert. The Semites triumphed twice: first under the leadership of Sargon (about 2350 B.C.) and second under that of Hammurapi (1700 B.C.). The Sumerians then disappeared, and the language of Babylonia became Semitic. With the coming of the barbarians after the reign of Hammurapi the first great chapter of the history of the Two Rivers came to an end.

4. THE ASSYRIAN EMPIRE (ABOUT 750 TO 612 B.C.)

The Beginnings of Assur. The *second chapter of history along the Two Rivers* carries us up the river valley from Babylonia to the northeast corner of the desert (map, p. 71). Here was an easily defended elevation overlooking the river Tigris and possessing a natural strength unknown to the towns in the flat Plain of Shinar. The place was known as Assur, which later gave its name to the land of Assyria. Being in a highland region, Assur enjoyed a climate much more invigorating than that of the hot Babylonian plain. It also possessed quarries of limestone, alabaster, and other harder stones. In this respect too Assyria differed from Babylonia, which had no building stone and had therefore developed its architecture in brick.

Assur was a fertile land and had a farming population. By 2900 B.C. there was already living at Assur a small settlement of Sumerians. At the same time the men whom we call Assyrians were there. It is not wholly certain whence they came or whether they were of pure Semitic race, but they

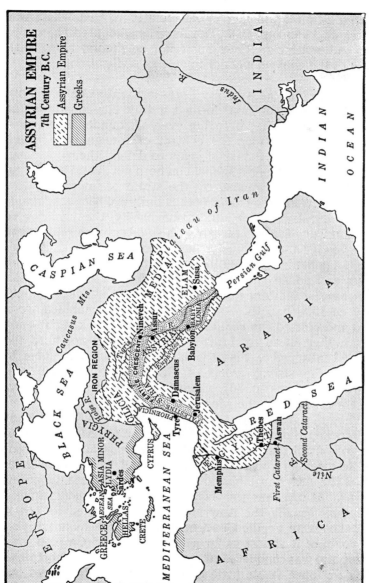

Assyrian Empire

spoke a Semitic language closely related to that which was spoken at Akkad (p. 66). The Assyrians adopted the sculpture and writing of their Sumerian neighbors, along with many of the conveniences of Sumerian civilization.

Foundation of the Assyrian Empire (Eighth Century B.C.). The men of Assur first formed a tiny city-kingdom like those of Sumer. They were, however, surrounded by enemies and were often under the control of foreign conquerors. Obliged for over a thousand years to defend their uncertain frontiers against their neighbors on both north and south, the Assyrians were toughened by the strain of unceasing war. The military state, which was thus built up, became a stable and powerful organization, unshaken by the rivalries of city-kingdoms such as those which so often weakened Babylonia. Assyria could muster her undivided strength and direct it against her foreign foes. Her kings early made use of horses and added chariots to their army. They finally had the strongest military force the early world had yet seen. As early as 1300 B.C. the Assyrian armies had marched westward and crossed the Euphrates. They had looked out upon the Mediterranean by 1100 B.C.; but it was not until the eighth century B.C. that the kings of Assur were able to conquer the strong group of Aramean, Phœnician, and Hebrew kingdoms (p. 86), which had blocked Assyria's permanent advance to the Mediterranean.

While the great object of the Assyrians was the conquest of the west, in order to gain a foothold on the Mediterranean and to control the trade routes between east and west, their hostile neighbors on the north, east, and south often compelled the Assyrian kings to send armies in these directions as well. At one time the Assyrians even captured and ruled Babylon. Finally the Assyrian Empire extended its power over the entire Fertile Crescent, and over the mountains on the north of it almost as far as the Black and Caspian seas. Egypt also was conquered (670 B.C.) and held for a short time. Thus the once feeble little city of Assur finally gained the lordship over Western Asia, as head of the largest empire which had thus far arisen in the ancient world.

Sargon II of Assyria. In the midst of the great western campaigns there succeeded to the Assyrian kingship a prince who took the name of Sargon, the first great Semite of Babylonia, who had reigned eighteen hundred years earlier. The new Sargon, whom we call Sargon II, raised Assyria to the height of her grandeur and power as a military empire. His descendants were the great emperors of Assyria.[1] On the northeast of Nineveh (map, p. 71) he built a new royal residence, which was on a vaster scale and more magnificent than any that had ever been constructed in Asia. Babylonia in her greatest days had never possessed a capital like this.

Sennacherib; Nineveh, the Capital. The grandeur of Sargon II was even surpassed by his son Sennacherib, one of the great statesmen of the early Orient. He devoted himself to the city of Nineveh, north of Assur, and it now became the far-famed capital of Assyria. To secure for the city a sufficient water supply Sennacherib connected it with the streams of the northern mountains by a canal with a magnificent aqueduct, the oldest aqueduct known. Along the Tigris the vast palaces and high tower-temples of the Assyrian emperors arose during reign after reign. The lofty and massive walls of Nineveh which Sennacherib built stretched two miles and a half along the banks of the Tigris. Here, in his gorgeous palace, he ruled the Western Asiatic world with a firm hand and collected tribute from all the subject peoples.

Organization of the Assyrian Empire. The government of the king's great empire was centered in his business office. He had a system of royal messengers who were sent to and fro on business for the state. The Assyrian ruler received letters and reports from some sixty governors under him, as well as reports from the subject kings who were allowed to continue their rule under Assyrian control. The most im-

---

[1] The leading Assyrian emperors of the dynasty of Sargon II are as follows:

Sargon II	722–705 B.C.
Sennacherib	705–681 B.C.
Esarhaddon	681–668 B.C.
Assurbanipal (called Sardanapalus by the Greeks)	668–626 B.C.

Fig. 25. *Scene in an Assyrian Camp*

In contrast to the impressive fortifications in the background the peaceful, every-day pursuits of camp life in the foreground offer an interesting study. In the center we are shown the tent of some officer of importance. A man who is apparently an orderly is straightening the bed, while a comrade is serving the officer food and drink. The tent at the right appears to be a sort of storeroom containing jars of food and haunches of meat. Scattered here and there in the landscape are animals which were no doubt used in transportation or to provide food. (Courtesy of the Berlin Museum)

portant work of the state, however, was to keep up the army; for the state was a vast military organization, more powerful and more terrible than any we have met before.

The Assyrian Army. The Assyrians learned the use of iron from the Hittites (p. 97), and the Assyrian forces were *the first large armies completely equipped with weapons of iron.* The bulk of the Assyrian army was composed of archers, spearmen, and shield-bearers. Besides these, the famous horsemen and chariots of Nineveh became the scourge of the East. For the first time, too, the Assyrians employed powerful siege machinery, especially the battering-ram. This machine was the earliest "tank," for it ran on wheels and carried men. The sun-dried brick walls of the Asiatic cities could easily be battered down, and no fortified place could long withstand the assaults of the fierce Assyrian infantry. The Assyrian soldiers, moreover, showed a ferocity which held all Western Asia in terror. Wherever the Assyrian armies swept through the land, they left a trail of ruin and desolation behind, and there were few towns which escaped being plundered.

Civilization of the Assyrian Empire. While this plundered wealth was used for the support of the army, it also served higher purposes. As we have seen, the Assyrian palaces were now fine buildings, suggesting by their size and splendor the far-reaching power of their builders. The Assyrian architects made the arch, inherited from Babylonia, for the first time an important feature in building. The impressive triple arches of the Assyrian palace entrance were the forerunners of the Roman triumphal arches. They were faced with glazed brick in brilliant colors, and on either side were vast human-headed bulls carved out of alabaster.

Within the palace were hundreds of feet of pictures sculptured in alabaster. They portray especially the great deeds of the emperor in war and in hunting wild beasts. The human figures are very much alike. The faces show no trace of feeling, — neither joy nor sorrow, pleasure nor pain. The Assyrian sculptor's wild beasts, however, are sometimes magnificent in the animal ferocity which they suggest (Fig. 26).

Assurbanipal's Library. Assurbanipal, the last great Assyrian emperor and the grandson of Sennacherib, boasted that his father had instructed him not only in riding and in shooting with bow and arrow but also in writing on clay tablets and in all the wisdom of his time. A great collection of twenty-two thousand clay tablets was discovered in the ruins of Assurbanipal's library rooms at Nineveh, where they had been lying on the floor covered with rubbish for twenty-five hundred years. They are now in the British Museum. In this library the religious, scientific, and literary works of past ages had been carefully collected by the emperor's orders.

These collections of tablets, begun under Sargon **II**, formed the earliest library known in Asia.

Economic and Agricultural Decline. Like many later rulers, however, the Assyrian emperors made a great mistake in their method of governing their empire. The industries were destroyed and the farms left idle in order to supply men for the army. Even so, the empire had grown so large that the army was unable to defend it. As reports of foreign invasions and continual revolts came in, the king forced the subjects of his foreign kingdoms to enter the army. With an army made up of so many foreigners, with the business of the country also in the hands of foreigners, with no industries, and with untilled fields, the Assyrian nation rapidly lost its strength.

Fall of Assyria; Destruction of Nineveh (612 B.C.). In addition to such weakness within, there were the threatening dangers from without. These came, as of old, from both sides of the Fertile Crescent. Especially dangerous was a desert tribe whom we know as the Chaldeans. They had been for centuries spreading slowly around the head of the Persian Gulf and settling along its shores at the foot of the eastern mountains. The Chaldeans mastered Babylonia, and then, in combination with the Median hosts from the northeastern mountains, marched against Nineveh itself.

Weakened by a generation of decline within, and struggling vainly against its combined enemies from without, the mighty city of the Assyrian emperors fell (612 B.C.). In the voice of the Hebrew prophet Nahum [1] we hear an echo of the glad shout which resounded from the Caspian to the Nile as the nations learned that the terrible scourge of the East had at last been laid low. The second great chapter of history on the Two Rivers was ended, having lasted hardly a century and a half (about 750 to 612 B.C.).

Summary of Progress of the Assyrian Empire. The Empire of Assyria had greatly altered the nations of Western Asia. The rule of a single sovereign had been forced upon the

---

[1] Nahum ii, 8, 13, and iii.

FIG. 26. *Stone Relief of Lioness in an Assyrian Park*

Such representations of a wild animal in repose are rare in Assyrian art. The composition of trees, vines, and flowers contrasting with the long, graceful lines of the beast furnishes us one of the most interesting pieces of relief sculpture from the ancient world. (Courtesy of the British Museum)

FIG. 27. *Glazed Brick Lion from Wall of Nebuchadnezzar's Palace*

This splendid example of Chaldean art in glazed brick offers an excellent contrast to the Assyrian art in stone as shown in Fig. 26. (Courtesy of the Berlin Museum)

whole great group of nations around the eastern end of the Mediterranean, and the methods of organizing such an empire had been much improved. In spite of its often ferocious harshness, the Assyrian rule had furthered civilization. We have seen that the building of the magnificent palaces in and near Nineveh formed the first chapter in great architecture in Asia. At the same time Nineveh also possessed the first libraries as yet known in Asia.

5. THE CHALDEAN EMPIRE : THE LAST SEMITIC EMPIRE

Rise of the Chaldean Empire (612 B.C.). After the fall of Assyria the brief career of the Chaldean Empire formed the *third* great chapter of history on the Two Rivers.[1] The Chaldeans made their capital at Babylon and gave their name to the land, so that we now speak of it as Chaldea. They were the last Semitic lords of Babylonia in ancient times.

Reign of Nebuchadnezzar (604–561 B.C.). At Babylon, Nebuchadnezzar, the greatest of the Chaldean emperors, began a reign of over forty years, — a reign of such power and magnificence, especially as described in the Bible, that he has become one of the great figures of Oriental history. It was he who carried away many Hebrews from Palestine to Babylonia as captives and destroyed Jerusalem, their capital (586 B.C.).

Copying much from Assyria, Nebuchadnezzar was able to surpass even the Assyrians in the splendor of the great buildings which he now erected at Babylon. High over all towered the lofty building which rose, like a veritable Tower of Babel, in the temple precinct of Marduk, their greatest god. Masses of rich tropical foliage, rising in successive terraces

---

[1] The three great chapters of history on the Two Rivers are :

1. *Early Babylonia*, about 2900–1750 B.C. (Sargon I, about 2500 B.C.; Hammurapi, about 1948–1905 B.C.).

2. *The Assyrian Empire*, about 750 to 612 B.C.

3. *The Chaldean Empire*, about 612 to 538 B.C.

With the exception of parts of the first, these three epochs were periods of *Semitic* power. To these we might in later times add a *fourth* period of Semitic supremacy : the triumph of Islam, in the seventh century of our era, after the death of Mohammed (pp. 410–415).

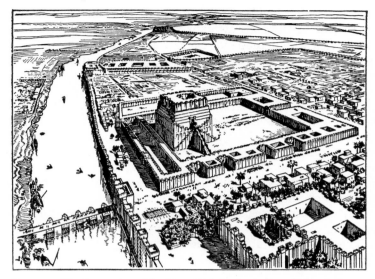

FIG. 28. *The Restoration of the City of Babylon in the Age of Nebuchadnezzar*

The tower (cf. page 78) in the foreground shows the position of the great temple of Marduk, surrounded by other buildings and temples of the sacred quarter in the southern section of the city. The group of buildings in the background, by the first bend in the river, is the palace of Nebuchadnezzar, with its Hanging Gardens. On the east (right) side of the temple quarter the Procession Street runs northward to connect with the palace and the Ishtar Gate on the east (right) side of the palace (see *Ancient Times*, Plate II). The Euphrates, flowing along the west (left) side of the city, is crossed by a bridge, the oldest passenger bridge known to us, dating from the sixth century B.C. Its ruinous piers still stand in the now dry bed of the Euphrates. A campaign of over eighteen years' excavation by the Germans under Koldewey has made this restoration possible. (Drawing after Koldewey)

and forming lofty roof gardens, crowned the roof of the emperor's gorgeous palace. Here, in the cool shade of palms and ferns, the great king might enjoy his idle hours, looking down upon the splendors of his city. These roof gardens were the mysterious "Hanging Gardens of Babylon," whose fame spread far into the West until they were numbered by the Greeks among the Seven Wonders of the World. The city was immensely extended by Nebuchadnezzar, and enormous fortified walls were built to protect it. It was this Babylon of Nebuchadnezzar whose marvels more than a century later so impressed the Greek historian Herodotus. This too is the

Babylon which has become familiar to all Christian peoples as the city of the Hebrew captivity. So little survives of all the glories which made it world-renowned in its time that nearly twenty years of excavation have discovered almost no buildings still standing.

Civilization of Chaldean Babylon: Astrology. The Chaldeans seem to have absorbed the civilization of Babylonia in much the same way as earlier Semitic invaders of this ancient plain. Science made progress in one important branch — astronomy. This was at first only what we call astrology, namely, a study of the movements of the heavenly bodies with a view to forecasting the future. But the art of astrology was slowly developing into the science of astronomy.

The five planets then known (which we call Mercury, Venus, Mars, Jupiter, and Saturn) were regarded as the powers especially controlling the fortunes of men, and as such the five leading Babylonian divinities were identified with these five heavenly bodies. The names of these Babylonian divinities have come down to us as the names of the planets. But on their way to us through Europe the ancient Babylonian names were translated into Roman forms. So the planet of Ishtar, the goddess of love, became Venus, while that of Marduk, the great god of Babylon, became Jupiter, and so on.

Chaldean astrology has also left an indelible mark on our calendar in the names which we apply to the days of the week. The five planets just mentioned, together with the sun and the moon, make up a group of seven celestial bodies, each of which was an important divinity. As Chaldean temple worship spread into Syria it became customary finally to recite the ritual and sing the praise of each god on a certain particular day. Thus the worship of each one of these seven divinities came around every seventh day. The name of the god worshiped on that day was finally transferred to the day itself. In this way the day which was devoted to the Sun-god became Sun-day, the day sacred to the Moon became Mon-day, and so on through the week, until the last day, sacred to Saturn, was called Satur-day. As our language

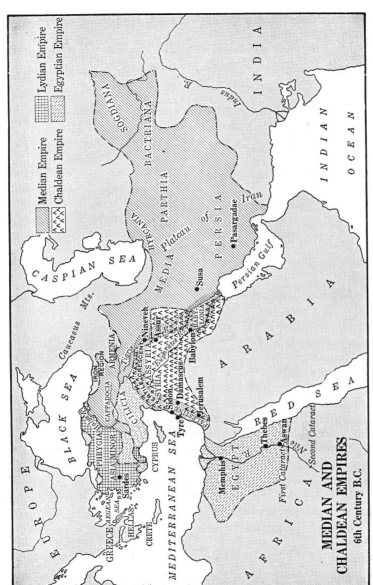

Map legend

Median Empire

Chaldean Empire

Lydian Empire

Egyptian Empire

Map labels

EUROPE

ASIA MINOR

GREECE

HELLAS

CRETE

CYPRUS

PHRYGIA

CAPPADOCIA

CILICIA

ARMENIA

IRON REGION

Sardes

AEGEAN SEA

BLACK SEA

Caucasus Mts.

CASPIAN SEA

SOGDIANA

BACTRIANA

HYRCANIA

PARTHIA

MEDIA

Plateau of Iran

PERSIA

Pasargadae

Susa

Persian Gulf

ARABIA

INDIA

Indus

INDIAN OCEAN

RED SEA

AFRICA

EGYPT

Memphis

Thebes

Aswan

First Cataract

Second Cataract

Nile

Nineveh

ASSUR

ASSYRIA

FERTILE CRESCENT

Tigris

Euphrates

Babylon

BABYLONIA

Damascus

Sidon

Tyre

Jerusalem

MEDITERRANEAN SEA

MEDIAN AND CHALDEAN EMPIRES
6th Century B.C.

Median and Chaldean Empires

came to us along a Northern route, and there are consequently Norse elements in it, the names of several of our week
days have reached us in a Northern form, like "Wednesday"
(Woden's-day) and "Thursday" (Thor's-day).

Civilization of Chaldean Babylon: Astronomy. Much more
important than these remains of Babylonian astrology were
the services the Chaldeans performed in gradually improving
the observations of the skies till they became something
more than aids to fortune-telling. As far back as the twenty-
third century B.C. the astrologers had observed an eclipse of
the moon, but such observations were only occasional and
very inaccurate. Gradually observations became more frequent, until in 747 B.C. they became continuous and a record
of them was kept on file. These records of the Chaldean
astronomers continued for over three hundred and sixty
years. Modern astronomers have so far never made such a
long-continued and uninterrupted series of observations.

More remarkable than this great body of observations was
the use to which the ablest Chaldean astronomers put these
records. Around 500 B.C., when the files of records had been
accumulating for about two hundred and fifty years, a
Chaldean named *Nabu-rimannu* used them to compile tables,
in which he calculated the time of the revolution of the
moon around the earth and the apparent annual revolution
of the sun in the heavens. He was able also exactly to date
the eclipses. The length of the year as computed by Nabu-
rimannu was only 26 minutes and 55 seconds too long. This
is the earliest known close calculation as to the length of a
year. A little over a century later another Chaldean astronomer named *Kidinnu* made a similar group of tables
which were even more accurate. Of these two Chaldeans
a modern astronomer has said that they "are entitled to a
place among the greatest of astronomers."

Decline of the Old Oriental Lands. While the Chaldeans
thus surpassed in science anything accomplished by their
predecessors on the Two Rivers, in other fields they were
content merely to copy the ancient Babylonians or Assyr-

ians. Indeed, after the death of Nebuchadnezzar (561 B.C.),
whose reign marks the height of Chaldean civilization, the
old civilized lands of the Orient seem to have lost most of
their former ability to progress in their civilization. The
leadership of the Semitic peoples in the early world was
drawing near its close, and they were about to give way before the advance of new peoples of the Indo-European race.
But before we take up the movements of these new peoples,
let us glance briefly at the little Hebrew kingdom, which was
destined to influence the history of man more profoundly
than any of the great empires of the early world.

6. THE HEBREWS

Hebrews settle in Palestine (about 1400 to 1200 B.C.). The
Hebrews were originally wandering shepherds of the Arabian
Desert (p. 58). As early as 1400 B.C. some of them were
slowly drifting over into Palestine, which became their
permanent home. When they entered it the Hebrews were
still nomad shepherds and had made very little progress
in civilization. A southern group of their tribes had been
slaves in Egypt, but with the help of their leader, Moses,
had managed to escape.

When the Hebrews came into Palestine they found another
people, the Canaanites (p. 59), already living there in towns
which were surrounded by walls. The Canaanites, whose
country lay on the road between Egypt and Babylonia, had
learned much from these centers of civilization. They lived
in houses, had their own government, carried on valuable
industries, and used the cuneiform writing of the Babylonian
merchants, who brought in their bills and lists written on
clay tablets. The Hebrews settled around the towns of the
Canaanites and slowly mingled with them until the two
peoples became one. In this way the Hebrews gradually
adopted the civilization of the Canaanites.

The Rise of the Hebrew Kingdom (about 1025 to 930 B.C.).
Even after the Hebrews had set up a king, the old nomad
customs still persisted; for Saul, their first king (about

1025 B.C.), had no fixed home, but lived in a tent. His successor, David, saw the importance of a strong castle as the king's permanent home. He therefore seized the old Canaanite fortress of Jerusalem. From this new capital David extended his power far and wide and made the Hebrews a strong nation. His people never forgot his heroic deeds as a warrior nor his skill as a poet and singer. Centuries later they revered him as the author of many of their religious songs, or "psalms."

Solomon and the Division of the Kingdom (about 930 B.C.). David's son, Solomon, delighted in Oriental luxury and display. To pay for his palace and finery he weighed down the Hebrews with heavy taxes. The discontent was so great that when Solomon died the Northern tribes withdrew from the nation and set up a king of their own. In this way the Hebrew nation was divided into two kingdoms before it was a century old.

There was much hard feeling between the two Hebrew kingdoms, and sometimes fighting. Israel, as we call the Northern Kingdom, was rich and prosperous; its market places were very busy, and its fertile fields produced plentiful crops. Israel enjoyed the wealth and luxury of town life. On the other hand, Judah, the Southern Kingdom, was poor, and its land was barren. Besides Jerusalem, the capital, it had no large and prosperous towns. Many of the people still led the wandering life of shepherds.

The contrast between the townspeople and the old-fashioned shepherds was shown in their ideas of God. Every Canaanite town had for centuries worshiped its "baal," or lord, as its local god was called. The Hebrew townsmen found it very natural to worship these gods of their neighbors, and so they were unfaithful to their old Hebrew God, Yahveh (or Jehovah).[1] To some devout Hebrews, therefore, and especially to those in the South, the Canaanite gods seemed to be the protectors of the wealthy people of the towns, who

---

[1] The Hebrews pronounced the name of their God "Yahveh." The pronunciation "Jehovah" began less than six hundred years ago and was due to a misunderstanding of the pronunciation of the word "Yahveh."

were hard on the poor. On the other hand, Yahveh appeared to be the guardian of the simpler shepherd life of the desert, and therefore the protector of the poor and needy.

The Earliest Historical Writings among the Hebrews. Many thoughtful Hebrews began to see the injustice of a civilization where the rich had fine houses and clothes and led a life of ease but were cruel to those who were unfortunate. They remembered the grand old days of their shepherd wanderings on the broad reaches of the desert, where no man "ground the faces of the poor." The Old Testament pictures very vividly the simple shepherd life of the Hebrews in the accounts of Abraham, Isaac, Jacob, and Joseph.[1]

Amos and the Prophets. Other men were not content merely to tell tales of the good old days. Amos, a simple herdsman clad in sheepskin, came from the South to the towns of the wealthy North and denounced the showy clothes, fine houses, and beautiful furniture of the inhabitants, and, above all, their corrupt lives and their hard-heartedness toward the poor among their fellow Hebrews, whose lands they seized for debt and whose labor they gained by enslaving them. By such attacks as these Amos, of course, endangered his life, but he became the first social reformer known in Asia. These great Hebrew teachers, who tried to persuade men to trust in Yahveh and to show more kindness to their fellow men, we call "prophets."

The Hebrews learn to Write. The peoples of Western Asia were now giving up the clay tablet and beginning to write on papyrus, with the Egyptian pen and ink. The Hebrews adopted the alphabet of their neighbors and began to write down the stories of their past, and their laws. The rolls containing the tales of the patriarchs or the teachings of such men as Amos were the first books which the Hebrews produced (*Ancient Times*, Fig. 122). Those portions of the Hebrew literature which form the Old Testament are the great contribution of this people to Western thought and religion.

[1] The student should read the accounts, especially Genesis xxiv, xxvii, xxviii, xxxvii, xxxix–xlvii, 12.

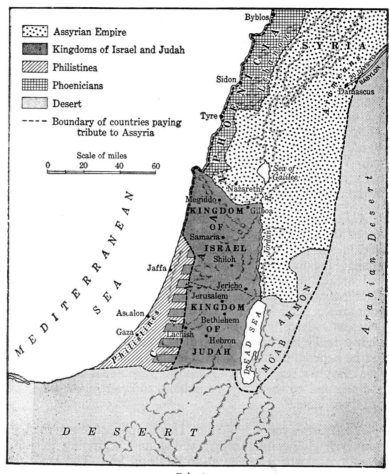

Palestine

Destruction of the Northern Kingdom by Assyria (722 B.C.).
While the Hebrews had been deeply stirred by their own
conflicts *at home*, such men as Amos had also seen and proclaimed the dangers coming from *abroad*, from beyond the
borders of Palestine, especially from Assyria. As Amos had
foreseen, the Assyrians crushed the kingdom of Israel, and
Samaria, its capital, was captured by them in 722 B.C. Many

of the unhappy Northern Hebrews were carried away as captives, and Israel was destroyed after having existed as a separate kingdom for a little over two centuries.

The hopes of the Hebrews as a nation were now centered in the helpless little kingdom of Judah (map, p. 86), which still struggled on for over a century and a quarter. Judah was soon entangled in a great world conflict, in which Assyria was the most dangerous power. Thus far the Hebrews had been accustomed to think of their God as dwelling and ruling in Palestine only. Did he have power also, they asked themselves, over the vast world where all the great nations were fighting? But even if so, was not Assur, the great god of victorious Assyria, stronger than Yahveh, the God of the Hebrews? A wonderful deliverance of Jerusalem from the cruel Assyrian army of Sennacherib (701 B.C.) enabled the great prophet Isaiah to proclaim to the Hebrews that Yahveh, their God, controlled the great world arena, where *He*, and not Assur, was their triumphant champion.

Destruction of the Southern Kingdom by Chaldea (586 B.C.). Nearly a century later Jerusalem was able to rejoice over the fall of Assyria and the destruction of Nineveh (612 B.C.). But it had only exchanged one foreign lord for another, for Chaldea followed Assyria in control of Palestine. The people of Judah now shared the same fate which their kindred of Israel had suffered. In 586 B.C. Nebuchadnezzar, the Chaldean king of Babylonia, destroyed Jerusalem and carried away the people to exile in Babylonia. The Hebrew nation had existed only about four and a half centuries.

A Great Prophet answers Hebrew Doubts. Forced to dwell in a strange land, the Hebrews were more than ever faced by the hard question Was Isaiah right? Or did Yahveh dwell and rule in Palestine only? We hear the echo of their grief and their uncertainty in some of their songs.

> By the rivers of Babylon,
> There we sat down, yea, we wept,
> When we remembered Zion [Jerusalem].
> We hanged our harps
> Upon the willows in the midst thereof. (Psalms cxxxvii. 1–2)

Had they not left Yahveh behind in Palestine? And then arose the greatest prophet[1] among the Hebrew exiles, — one who in their affliction gave them the answer they longed for, that Yahveh was the creator and the sole God of the universe.

Monotheism of the Hebrews in Exile. Thus had the Hebrew idea of Yahveh slowly grown from the days of their shepherd life. Then they had thought of him only as the fierce war god of their tribe, having no power beyond the corner of the desert where they lived. But now they had come to regard him as a kindly father and a righteous ruler of all the earth. This was *monotheism*, which is a Greek word meaning "one-god-ism." They had reached it only through a long development, which carried them through suffering and disaster. It had been a discipline lasting many centuries.

Restoration of Exiled Hebrews by Persian Kings. When the victorious Persian king Cyrus entered Babylon (p. 101), the Hebrew exiles there greeted him as their deliverer. His triumph gave the Hebrews a Persian ruler. With great humanity the Persian kings allowed the exiles to return to their native land. Some had prospered in Babylonia and did not care to return. But at different times enough of them went back to Jerusalem to rebuild the city on a very modest scale and to restore the Temple.

The Old Testament. These returned exiles arranged and copied the ancient writings of their fathers, such as the accounts of the patriarchs or the speeches of Amos (p. 85). They added also other writings of their own. All these writings form the Sacred Scriptures of the Jews and the first part of the Christian Bible, called the Old Testament. It is the most precious inheritance which we have from the Ancient Near East before the coming of Christ. It tells the story of how a rude shepherd folk issued from the wilds of the Arabian Desert to live in Palestine and to go through experiences there which made them the religious teachers of later times. And

---

[1] A great poet-preacher, a prophet of the Exile, whose addresses to his fellow exiles are preserved in sixteen chapters embedded in the Old Testament book of Isaiah (chaps. xl–lv, inclusive).

we should further remember that, crowning all their history, there came forth from them in due time the founder of the Christian religion (p. 349). One of the great things that we owe to the Persians, therefore, was their restoration of the Hebrews to Palestine. The Persians thus saved and aided in transmitting to us the precious legacy from Hebrew life which we have in the Old Testament and in the life of the founder of Christianity. Let us now consider the invasion of Western Asia by the new peoples of the Indo-European race, of whom the Persians were the most important.

Questions and Exercises

REVIEW OF CHAPTER

1. What is meant by "Fertile Crescent"? Describe the life of the Semitic nomads. Name the Semitic tribes who played parts in the history of the Fertile Crescent.

2. Were Sumerian agricultural methods unlike the Egyptian? Were the early Sumerians united in one kingdom? Who conquered the Sumerians?

3. Why may we call Hammurapi a great king? What city first became famous in the time of Hammurapi? What contribution did the people of the Two Rivers make to architecture?

4. Locate Assyria on the Fertile Crescent. Whence did its people receive their civilization? What did the Assyrian Empire at its greatest extent chiefly include? What were some of the causes of the fall of Assyria?

5. Who was Nebuchadnezzar? Describe Chaldean Babylon. What did the Chaldeans learn in their study of astronomy?

6. Where was the *original* home of the Hebrews? What was the result of their living among the Canaanites? Why was the Hebrew kingdom divided after Solomon? Contrast the two Hebrew kingdoms. What were the first books of the Hebrews? What happened to the two Hebrew kingdoms? What conception of God did the Hebrews attain while in exile?

USEFUL TERMS

See how much meaning you can give to the following: *nomads, Semites, language, writing, code of laws, medium of exchange, astrology, astronomical observations, planets, science, psalms, baal, Hebrew prophets.*

DIRECTIVE QUESTIONS

1. Are there Semitic nomads today?

2. What contribution did the Sumerians make to the history of transportation?

3. How does the history of the Two Rivers illustrate the often close connection between the spread of commerce and the advance of civilization?

4. Were the Assyrian emperors progressive?

5. Were the Chaldean astronomers scientific in their method of work?

6. Is the Old Testament valuable solely from a religious point of view?

DISCUSSION TOPICS

1. The governments holding Arabia today are powerless to control the wandering Arabs.

2. Although the Sumerian city-kingdoms were constantly at war, they developed a high degree of civilization.

3. Precious metals have proved to be the most convenient form of money.

4. The animal sculpture of Assyria was never surpassed, if ever equaled, by any other ancient people.

5. Many modern hotels have "hanging gardens."

6. The Hebrew exiles rendered a great service to civilization.

ADDITIONAL ADVENTURES IN LEARNING

1. Studies in Source Materials. BOTSFORD, *Source-book*: (1) Laws of Hammurapi, pp. 29–31; (2) The Babylon of Nebuchadnezzar, pp. 32–33; (3) Solomon's temple, pp. 50–53.

2. Supplementary. BREASTED, *Ancient Times*: Money and business credit in Western Asia, §§ 202–203, 224, 238.

3. Write a paragraph on the handicrafts of the Sumerians, especially their work in gold. Figs. 20–21, 23; BREASTED, *Ancient Times*, Figs. 92–93, § 192; GADD, *History and Monuments of Ur*, pp. 27–40; *Museum Journal of the University of Pennsylvania*, Vol. 19 (1928), pp. 5–34; WOOLLEY, *Sumerians*, pp. 35–40; *Ur of the Chaldees*, pp. 17–89.

4. Look up in an encyclopedia: *cuneiform, brick, the Bible, alabaster, chariots, Babylonia, Nineveh, Semites.*

CHAPTER IV · DEVELOPMENT OF CIVILIZATION IN WESTERN ASIA: THE COMING OF THE INDO–EUROPEANS

THE INDO-EUROPEAN PEOPLES · THE HITTITES · THE ARYAN PEOPLES: ZOROASTER · THE RISE OF THE PERSIAN EMPIRE: CYRUS THE GREAT · THE CIVILIZATION OF THE PERSIAN EMPIRE (530 TO 330 B.C.)

THE early Indo-Europeans were the ancestors of the leading peoples of Europe today. As our forefathers came from Europe, the Indo-European nomads were also our own ancestors. It is very important for us, therefore, to study their origin and history. Moreover, with the appearance of the Indo-Europeans the history of the ancient world tends to become a history of the struggle between the Semitic peoples, who had lived in the Arabian Desert, and the Indo-European peoples, who now moved down from the grasslands of northern and northeastern Asia. At their easternmost point some of the Indo-Europeans wandered down into India. We shall find that certain groups established themselves in Asia Minor, while others drew near the Fertile Crescent and confronted the older Semitic civilizations there. Many Indo-European tribes spread out in various directions over Europe, and some of them finally reached as far west as Britain. In the south the Semites extended from Babylonia on the east, through Phoenicia and the Hebrew kingdoms, westward to Carthage and similar Semitic settlements of Phoenicia in the Western Mediterranean. The two great races thus faced each other across the Mediterranean like two vast armies stretching from Western Asia westward to the Atlantic. The result of the long conflict was the complete triumph of the Indo-European line, which conquered along the center and both wings and finally, as represented by the Greeks and Romans, gained unchallenged supremacy throughout the Mediterranean world. This triumph was accompanied by a long struggle for the mastery between the Indo-Europeans themselves. Among them the victory moved from east to west as first the Persians, then the Greeks, and finally the Romans gained control of the Mediterranean and Oriental world. In Chapter IV we shall watch the first appearance of the Indo-Europeans in the east; the development of their civilizations, especially of the two groups known to us as Hittites and Persians; and the beginning of the contest between Indo-Europeans and Semites.

1. THE INDO-EUROPEAN PEOPLES [1]

The Northern Grasslands. We have seen how the Semitic shepherds who wandered toward the grasslands of the Arabian Desert often pushed on into the Fertile Crescent. In the north there were peoples of a different race who found pasture for their flocks in the great stretch of grassland which extends north and east of the Caspian Sea and westward, across what is now Russia, to the lower Danube. These northern peoples also led a wandering shepherd life and during thousands of years pushed into Europe and Western Asia from time to time, just as the Semites of the south penetrated the Fertile Crescent.

Origin of the Indo-European Peoples. Among these nomads of the north there was, in very early times, an important branch of the white race which we call *Indo-European.* They began to migrate in very ancient times, moving out along diverging routes until they extended at last in a long line from the frontiers of India, on the east, westward across all Europe to the Atlantic, as they do today; hence their name, "Indo-Europeans." These peoples were finally to conquer the older kingdoms of the Semites and to raise civilization to a far higher point than it had ever before reached.

Recent investigations show that the parent people from which these Indo-Europeans sprang was probably occupying the pasture lands on the east and northeast of the Caspian Sea about 3000 B.C. Some of the tribes had settled down and farmed a little, but their civilization was still that of the Stone Age except for some slight use of copper. Besides cattle and sheep they had *horses,* which they rode and which they also used to pull their wheeled carts. They could not write and had little in the way of government, but they were the most gifted and imaginative people of the ancient world.

[1] Pages 92–94 should be carefully worked over by the teacher with the class before the class is permitted to study this section alone. The diagram (Fig. 29) should be put on the blackboard and explained in detail by the teacher, and the class should then be prepared to put the diagram on the board from memory. This should be done again when the study of the Greeks is begun (p. 111), and a third time when Italy and the Romans are taken up.

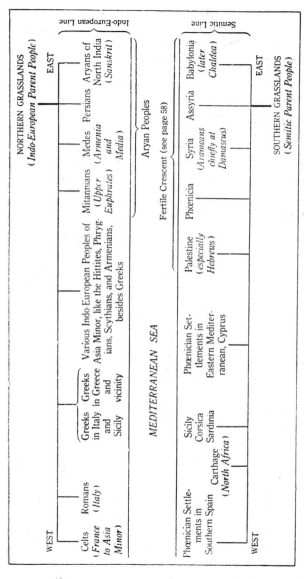

FIG. 29. *Diagram Suggesting the Two Lines of Semitic and Indo-European Dispersion*

In this explanation the word "line" means much the same as "row." The geographic lines along which these peoples lie are of course not straight. The racial lines sometimes overlie the southern line, as in Sicily, and are mentioned in both lines. The Egyptians, who physically belong to the southern line, have been omitted because they are not purely Semitic, although physically and in language closely related to the Semites. Notice also that in the West the two races face each other for the most part across the Mediterranean; in the East they confront each other along the Fertile Crescent

The Indo-European Languages. As the tribes wandered farther and farther apart they lost contact with each other. Although they all at first spoke the same language, differences in speech gradually arose, and these finally became so great that the widely scattered tribes, if they had happened to meet, could no longer have understood one another. At last they lost all knowledge of their original relationship. But the principal languages of modern Europe, having sprung from the same Indo-European parent language, are therefore related to each other; so that, beginning with our own language and going eastward across Europe into India, we can trace a number of common words from people to people.

WEST			EAST		
English	German	Latin	Greek	Old Persian and Avestan	East Indian (Sanskrit)
brother	*bruder*	*fräter*	*phrätēr*	*brätar*	*bhrätar*
mother	*mutter*	*mäter*	*mētēr*	*mätar*	*mätar*
father	*vater*	*pater*	*patēr*	*pitar*	*pitar*

2. THE HITTITES

The First Appearance of Indo-Europeans in Western Asia. The earliest known group of these wanderers from the northern grasslands had entered Asia Minor by 2500 B.C. These were the invaders who founded the First Hittite Empire. Another Indo-European group pushed into the Fertile Crescent and easily subdued the population in the great western bend of the Euphrates, where they became the ruling class of a new nation called Mitanni. The Mitannians later threatened to block the westward advance of Assyria, but were eventually crushed in the conflict between the Egyptians and the Hittites (pp. 52 and 96). This invasion was the first of those vast movements of Indo-European migration in Western Asia which, as we shall see later, resulted finally in the conquest of the Fertile Crescent and the whole Near East by the Indo-European Medes and Persians.

Rise of Hittite Civilization and the First Hittite Empire.
When they entered Asia Minor, or Anatolia,[1] the Hittites
were barbarians. The rise of the civilization which we may
call Hittite was at first due to influence from the Fertile
Crescent. In times past, Babylonian caravans had traded in
Asia Minor, and later Assyrian merchants had settled there.
These business communities from the Fertile Crescent made
the Hittites acquainted with commercial transactions. In
carrying on their business the Hittites themselves gradually
learned to read clay-tablet bills and invoices written in cuneiform. Excavations have even uncovered fragments of their
clay-tablet dictionaries with three columns, the first Sumerian, the second Babylonian, or Akkadian, and the third
Hittite. Thus they learned to write their own Hittite words
in cuneiform.[2] The clay tablet became common in the
Hittite world, and it was probably through the Hittites
that the use of clay tablets passed over into Crete (p. 116).
After the introduction of writing the Hittites made noticeable progress, and by 2000 B.C. they had become a highly
civilized people.

It is quite clear that the Hittites did not at first form a
single nation, but lived in a number of kingdoms which, like
the later Greek kingdoms, were often at war with one another.
The leadership was finally gained by the kingdom of Hatti,[3]
which lay inside the great bend of the river Halys in central
Asia Minor. Its capital was called Hattusas. The kings of
Hatti were able to conquer neighboring kingdoms and build
up a small empire. About 1600 B.C. the Hittite king Mursil I
even captured Babylon. This First Hittite Empire lasted
from about 1800 to 1590 B.C.

---

[1] "Anatolia" is a Greek word equivalent to the Latin "Orient"; but usage has
given it a much more limited meaning, for it is used to designate only Asia Minor
as far east as the upper Euphrates. It has now been discovered that the earliest
peoples of this region were not identical with the historic Hittites. Before the
incoming of the Hittites we may therefore call the peoples of Asia Minor Anato-
lians, a term which implies nothing regarding their race or nationality.

[2] The Hittite tablets contained so many Babylonian word signs that during the
World War the Czechoslovakian scholar Bedřich Hrozný succeeded in deciphering
the Hittite cuneiform.

[3] The name *Khatti*, or *Hatti*, is of course the origin of our modern name "Hittite." The closeness of the resemblance will be evident when the modern ending
tle is removed, leaving *Hitt.*

Second [1] Hittite Empire, the Leader of Western Asia. After a period of decline there arose, about 1400 B.C., the Second Hittite Empire, which remained for two centuries the greatest power in Western Asia. Its founder bore the long name Suppilulyuma.[1] He was the ablest soldier that Western Asia had seen since the campaigns of Thutmose III (p. 45). But now there was no Thutmose III to turn back the powerful Hittite soldiers. Weakened by the religious revolutions of Ikhnaton, the Egyptians could only helplessly watch the advance of the Hittites as they conquered all Syria and made it Hittite territory. Suppilulyuma next crossed the Euphrates and crushed the power of Mitanni. Feeble Assyria was at that time the vassal of Mitanni, and the Hittite conqueror of Mitanni was therefore lord over the greater part of Western Asia.

Egypto-Hittite Rivalry; Fall of Hittite Empire. But Egypt still held Palestine. Thus the two empires, Egyptian and Hittite, were now rivals for the leadership of the world. It was a rivalry which was fought out for over a quarter of a century between the grandsons of Suppilulyuma and the great Pharaohs Seti I and Ramses II. As the war went on, especially after 1300 B.C., the rise of Assyria gave the Hittite emperors increasing uneasiness. They made treaties with their vassal kings in Syria which pledged them to act as enemies of Assyria. Then, as dissensions arose among the Hittites themselves, Suppilulyuma's grandson, Hattusil, arranged a treaty of peace with Ramses II, who received the treaty from the Hittite king engraved upon a silver tablet. This is the earliest known important attempt made by nations to settle their difficulties by diplomacy rather than by war.

A little over a century later the whole of Asia Minor was overrun by another wave of Indo-European migration like that of the Hittites and Mitannians more than a thousand years earlier. These new Indo-Europeans crossed the Hellespont into Asia Minor from Europe. The most important of

---

[1] Historians now believe there was only one Hittite Empire. For a fascinating account of this research, see C. Ceram, *The Secret of the Hittites.*

them were the Phrygians and Armenians. The Hittite Empire, lying directly in their path, was so completely crushed that after 1200 B.C. it entirely disappeared.

Introduction of Iron in Second Hittite Empire. Iron was already known to man in prehistoric days, but it remained scarce for several thousand years. For centuries it was a precious metal, which kings hoarded and the rich wore as ornaments. In the thirteenth century B.C., however, iron became better known throughout the Near East. This seems to have been due to its distribution by the Hittites, who were now working iron and who may have actually mined it in the iron region east of the Halys River (map, p. 71). A clay-tablet letter has been found from a Hittite king to Ramses II. It was an answer to a request of the Egyptian

FIG. 30. *Figure of Hittite Warrior Carved in Relief on a Gate at Hattusas*

king for a supply of "pure [meaning *smelted*] iron." The Hittite king appears to have put off Ramses by saying that there was no smelted iron at hand, but that he would later send a shipment and in the meantime was forwarding an iron dagger. By 1000 B.C. the Iron Age was beginning in the Ægean. This letter, written in the thirteenth century B.C., is therefore most important as indicating the source from which the metal first became common in the Eastern Mediterranean.

Hittite Civilization. The civilization of the Second Hittite Empire attained a high level and had a far-reaching influence. It had a good government and wise laws which even the king himself was bound to obey. After the peace with Egypt the Hittite king, perhaps Hattusil, issued a revised code of these laws which was much more humane than the savage laws of Assyria, and more so, indeed, than the codes of Babylonia or Egypt.

The character of the Hittite kings was doubtless partly responsible for the remarkable development among the Hittites along lines other than government. The earliest impressive stone architecture in Asia was the work of the Hittite builders. The powerful walled city of Hattusas which they erected was the first really large city ever built in Asia. It far surpassed the Babylon of that day in size, and the Nineveh of the Assyrian emperors was still some six centuries in the future. As the Hittite emperors began to erect stone buildings they felt the need of a larger monumental style of writing which would make it possible to decorate a building with historical records, as the Egyptians did. They therefore invented a system of writing made up of picture signs. With these new hieroglyphic signs [1] they engraved great stone records like those of Egypt.

The clay-tablet cuneiform records of the Hittite emperors are the earliest historical narratives which have a literary prose style. Besides historical compositions we find special treatises, such as an essay on horse-breeding. Unlike the scribes of other great civilizations, the Hittite writers were interested in being known as authors and attached their names to their writings. They were therefore the earliest professional authors of whom we know.

Lying between southeastern Europe and the great civilizations of the Near East, Hittite civilization served as a link connecting the two, and the Oriental influences which it passed on to the early Ægean world were of permanent importance. At the same time, as we have seen, the Hittite Empire made significant original contributions to the cultures of the Ancient Near East. These influences were passed on by Assyria to the Persians, that other great Indo-European people of Western Asia, whom we shall now study.

---

[1] Unfortunately, this *hieroglyphic* writing of the Hittites has not yet been fully deciphered, and we are still unable to read more than parts of it.

3. THE ARYAN PEOPLES: ZOROASTER

The Aryans and their Descendants. The easternmost tribes of the Indo-Europeans, having left the parent people, were pasturing their herds in the great steppe on the east of the Caspian by about 2000 B.C. Here they formed a people called the Aryans.[1] They had no writing, and have left no monuments.

About 1800 B.C. the Aryan tribes separated, and some of them wandered southeastward and eventually reached India. In their sacred books, which we call the *Vedas*, written in Sanskrit, we find many references to their earlier, less civilized life on the east of the Caspian.

Other tribes, who kept the name "Aryan" in the form "Iran," when they left the region of the Caspian pushed westward and southwestward into the mountains bordering the Fertile Crescent. We call them Iranians, and among them were two powerful tribes, the Medes and the Persians.

The Empire of the Medes. By 700 B.C. the Medes had established a powerful Iranian empire in the mountains east of the Tigris. It extended from the Persian Gulf, where it included the Persians, northwestward in the general line of the mountains to the Black Sea region. As their capital the Medes founded the city of Ecbatana, which lay directly opposite the pass that led through the Zagros Mountains to the Fertile Crescent and to the city of Babylon itself. A century later Nebuchadnezzar and his successors at Babylon looked, therefore, with anxious eyes at this dangerous Median power, recalling no doubt how in 612 B.C. (p. 76) these same people had so willingly united in the assault against Nineveh.

The Religion of the Iranians and the Spread of Zoroastrianism. Though the Medes and the Persians at this time

---

[1] The term "Aryan" is often popularly applied to the *parent* Indo-European people and, indeed. to the Indo-European races collectively; but this use of the word is incorrect. "Aryan" (from which "Iran" and "Iranian" are derived) designates a group of tribes which detached themselves from the parent people and found a home just east of the Caspian Sea. The Aryans, then, were *Eastern* descendants, as we are *Western* descendants, of the Indo-European parent people. The Aryans are our distant cousins, — not our ancestors.

had not reached the degree of civilization of the Semites, in one respect they had made a great advance. A generation or so after the fall of Nineveh [1] a religious teacher, Zoroaster, appeared among them, who had thought out a religion which he believed was well fitted to meet the needs of man. He watched the ceaseless struggle between Good and Evil which met him wherever he turned. The Good became to him a divine person, whom he called Mazda, or Ahuramazda (which means "Lord of Wisdom"), and whom he regarded as God. Ahuramazda was surrounded by a group of helpers much like angels, of whom one of the greatest was the Light, called "Mithras." Opposed to Ahuramazda and his helpers was an evil group led by a great Spirit of Evil named Ahriman.

The new religion of Zoroaster called upon every man to stand on one side or the other, — to fill his soul with the Good and the Light or to dwell in the Evil and the Darkness. Whatever course a man pursued, he must expect a judgment hereafter. This was the earliest appearance in Asia of belief in a last judgment. Zoroaster kept the old Aryan veneration of fire as a symbol of the Good and the Light. The new faith had gained a firm footing before the prophet's death. Indeed, before 500 B.C. it was the leading religion of the Iranians and accepted by the Persian emperors. It is even possible that King Darius erected the prophet's tomb. Hymns and fragments of Zoroaster's teaching have descended to us in writings put together in the early Christian Era, many centuries after the prophet's death. All together these sacred writings form a book known as the *Avesta*. This we may call the Bible of the Persians.

4. THE RISE OF THE PERSIAN EMPIRE: CYRUS THE GREAT

The Rise of the Persians. No people were more zealous followers of Zoroaster than the group of Iranian tribes known as the Persians. At the time of the fall of Nineveh they had already been long settled in the region at the southeastern

---

[1] There has been much difference of opinion about the date of Zoroaster. Several earlier dates formerly seemed possible, but the evidence now seems to favor the sixth century B.C.

end of the Zagros Mountains, just north of the Persian Gulf. Here the Persians occupied a district some four hundred miles long. They were a hardy mountain folk who led a simple farming life and had no writing, art, or literature, and very little government.

Cyrus and his Conquests. One of their tribes dwelling in the mountains of Elam (map, p. 58) was organized as a little kingdom called Anshan. About fifty years after the fall of Nineveh, Anshan was ruled over by a Persian named Cyrus, who united the other tribes of his kindred Persians into a nation. He then rebelled against the rule of the Medes. Cyrus was very energetic and skillful. He made good soldiers of his peasants, and trained his army to fight like the Assyrians. Within three years he completely defeated the Median king and made himself master of the Median territory (p. 99). The success of Cyrus was now so great as to fill the peoples to the west with wonder and alarm.

With a powerful Persian army Cyrus marched far to the west, into Asia Minor, and conquered the kingdom of Lydia, which with other states had dared to rise against him. He captured its capital, Sardes, and took prisoner its king, the wealthy and powerful Crœsus. Within five years the power of the little Persian kingdom in the mountains of Elam had swept across Asia Minor to the Mediterranean and had made Persia the leading state in the Oriental world. Turning eastward again, Cyrus had no trouble in defeating the Chaldean army led by the young crown prince Belshazzar, whose name we find in the Book of Daniel (see Daniel v). In spite of the strong walls erected by Nebuchadnezzar to protect Babylon, the Persians entered the great city in 538 B.C., seemingly without resistance.

Persia Supreme; Death of Cyrus. Thus the Semitic East completely collapsed before the advance of the Indo-European power, only seventy-four years after the Chaldean conquest of Nineveh. Some nine years later Cyrus fell in battle (529 B.C.). He was buried in a massive but simple tomb which may still be seen by the traveler today. Thus passed away the first great conqueror of Indo-European blood.

As a result of the brilliant victories of Cyrus all Western Asia was subject to Persia. Four years after his death his son Cambyses conquered Egypt (in 525 B.C.). The Persian Empire now included the whole civilized East from the Nile Delta around the entire eastern end of the Mediterranean to the Ægean Sea, and from this western boundary eastward almost to India (map, p. 103). The great task had consumed just twenty-five years since the overthrow of the Medes by Cyrus.

5. THE CIVILIZATION OF THE PERSIAN EMPIRE (530 TO 330 B.C.)

Civilization of Conquered Lands adopted by the Persians. The Persians found in the lands they had conquered great cities with impressive monuments. In spite of its remoteness the Persian kings tried to live in their old Persian home. There they began to build palaces copied after those of the older civilized peoples. The enormous terraces on which the Persian palaces stood were imitated from Babylonia. The winged bulls at the palace gates, like the magnificent stairways leading up to them, were copies of those in Assyria and the west. The vast colonnades stretching along the front and filling the enormous halls — the earliest colonnades of Asia — were like those of over two thousand years earlier on the Nile. Likewise the idea of having gorgeously colored palace walls of enameled brick reached Persia from the Nile by way of Assyria and the west.

Popularity of Aramaic. Aramaic, the speech of the Aramean merchants (p. 59), had by this time become the language of the whole Fertile Crescent. Business papers were now written in Aramaic, with pen and ink, on papyrus. The clay tablets, in cuneiform writing, were slowly being given up. The Persian officials were therefore obliged to carry on their government business, such as the collection of taxes, in the Aramaic language throughout the western half of the Persian Empire, and probably also in much of the eastern half. The government of the Persian kings thus employed two languages: Aramaic and the old Persian tongue.

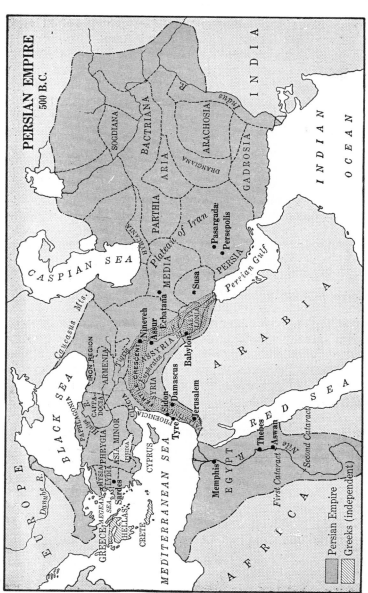

The Persian Empire

But even in writing Persian, Aramaic letters were often used, just as we write English with Roman letters. However, the Persians already possessed a cuneiform *alphabet* of thirty-nine cuneiform signs, which was probably devised by the Medes. These cuneiform records of the Persians have proved very important, for it was through the decipherment of Persian cuneiform that the archæologists were able to decipher Babylonian cuneiform.

Organization of the Persian Empire by Darius. The organization of the vast empire, stretching from the Indus River to the Ægean Sea (almost as long as the United States from east to west) and from the Indian Ocean to the Caspian Sea, was an enormous task. Though begun by Cyrus, it was carried through by Darius the Great (521–485 B.C.). His organization remains one of the most remarkable achievements in the history of the ancient Orient.

Darius did not wish to make further conquests, but he planned to maintain the empire as he had inherited it. He had himself made actual king in Egypt and in Babylonia, but the rest of the empire he divided into twenty provinces, each called a satrapy. Each province was under the control of a governor called a satrap, who was appointed by the "Great King," as the Persian sovereign came to be called. The subject nations, or provinces, enjoyed a good deal of independence as long as they paid regular tribute and furnished soldiers for the Great King's army.

In the east the tribute was paid, as of old, in produce. In the west, chiefly in Lydia and the Greek settlements in western Asia Minor, the use of money was common by 600 B.C. (p. 141), and there this tribute was paid in *coined money*. Darius now began in Persia the coinage of gold and permitted his satraps to coin silver. Thus this great convenience in business — coined money issued by the state — became more common in the Near East during the Persian period.

Darius makes Persia the Earliest Great Sea Power in Asia. Nothing shows the wise statesmanship of Darius the Great more clearly than his remarkable efforts to make Persia a mighty sea power. He sent a skillful Mediterranean sailor

Fig. 31. *The Ruins of the Palace of Darius the Great at Persepolis*
Each door in this palace is topped with a *horizontal* block of stone, called a lintel.
This architectural device was copied from Egypt

by the name of Scylax to explore the course of the great
river Indus in India, and then to follow along the coast of
Asia from the mouth of the Indus westward to the Isthmus
of Suez. Scylax was the first Western mariner to explore this
south coast of Asia, so little known to Western peoples at that
time (about 500 B.C.). At Suez, Darius cleared out the ancient
but long filled-up canal of the Egyptians connecting the Nile
with the Red Sea (p. 43). This gave him a sea route all the
way from the Persian coast to the Mediterranean. Unlike the
Assyrians, Darius treated the Phœnician cities (p. 60) with
kindness, and he succeeded in organizing a great Phœnician
war fleet in the eastern Mediterranean. Thus the more enlightened Persian kings accomplished what the Assyrian emperors never achieved, and Persia became the first great sea
power in Asia. From end to end of the vast empire the Persian
emperors laid out a system of excellent roads, on which royal
messengers maintained a regular postal system.

Decline of Empire; Results of Persian Rule. For the
Oriental world as a whole, Persian rule meant about two
hundred years of peaceful prosperity (ending about 330 B.C.).

FIG. 32. *Envoys from Subject Nations Bringing Gifts and Tribute on New Year's Day to the Persian King*

Upper left, Ionian Greeks bringing woolens and pottery vessels; upper right, Cappadocians bringing clothing; lower left, a Scythian bringing a thoroughbred horse; lower right, Babylonians bringing humped cattle. These reliefs are found on the side walls and balustrades of one of the great stairways leading to the audience hall of King Darius. (Photographs from the Oriental Institute)

The later Persian kings, however, were no longer so strong and skillful as Cyrus and Darius had been. They loved luxury and ease, and left much of the task of ruling to their governors and officials. This meant that the government became corrupt and was badly managed. As a result Persian power and influence declined.

The later world, especially the Greeks, often represented the Persian rulers as cruel and barbarous Oriental tyrants. This unfavorable opinion is not wholly justified. For there can be no doubt that the Persian Empire, the largest the ancient world had thus far seen, enjoyed a government far more just and humane than any that had preceded it in the East.

Persian rule showed men how a vast group of nations might be forced to yield to the power of a single sovereign and to accept his rule as if it were his permanent right. Moreover, such a union of all the civilizations of the Ancient Near East produced a new situation, and one of tremendous importance for the history of Europe. Cyrus had carried his victories westward to the shores of the Ægean Sea, and the Greek cities of western Asia Minor fell under Persian sway. Thus the Oriental colossus rose directly alongside southeastern Europe. If we look at the map (p. 103) and observe how the western advance of the great empire finally extended, under Darius, to include European territory as far as the Danube, we shall understand that a hostile collision with Greece was unavoidable. This situation was yet to bring about a more complete commingling of the civilizations of the Near East with the life of Europe than had ever been possible before. These wars between Europe and Persia were not of much importance to Persia, but they meant a great deal to little European nations like the Greeks. It will therefore be more fitting to consider the conflict between Persia and the Greeks in the discussion of the development of civilization on the continent of Europe, to which we must now turn.

Questions and Exercises

REVIEW OF CHAPTER

1. What is meant by the term "northern grasslands"? Name the Indo-European peoples. What animals had the Indo-European parent people domesticated?

2. What Indo-European groups first entered Western Asia? What form of writing and what kind of writing material did the Hittites use? What languages are found in the Hittite dictionaries? What is the origin of our modern name "Hittite"? Discuss the difficulties leading up to the earliest known treaty of peace. What part did the Hittite Empire play in the progress of civilization?

3. To what part of the world did the Aryans migrate? What Indo-Europeans took part in the conquest of Nineveh? What were some of the differences between the Zoroastrian religion and the other religions of the Ancient Near East?

4. Who were the Persians? What nations did Cyrus conquer?

5. Make a list of things which the Persians borrowed from the peoples they conquered. How did Darius make Persia a sea power?

USEFUL TERMS

See how much meaning you can give to the following: *Indo-Europeans, Anatolia, diplomacy, Aryans, satrap, Great King, postal system, sea power, tribute.*

DIRECTIVE QUESTIONS

1. Is English an Indo-European language?

2. As Hittite hieroglyphs have not been deciphered, but Hittite cuneiform has, what would be the advantage of finding a tablet with the same inscription written in Hittite cuneiform and Hittite hieroglyphs?

3. Does the religion of Zoroaster have any ideas resembling those of the Christian religion?

4. What race did Cyrus subdue in the Fertile Crescent?

5. Why have so many governments desirous of sea power turned their attention to what is now called the Suez Canal?

DISCUSSION TOPICS

1. The Semites taught the Indo-Europeans how to write.

2. Why do you suppose the Hittite king would not send Ramses II a shipment of iron?

3. The Medes and Persians could organize but could not originate.

4. Cyrus was a conqueror because he had no great adversaries.

5. Is a common language necessary in the governing of a large empire?

ADDITIONAL ADVENTURES IN LEARNING

1. Studies in Source Materials. BOTSFORD, *Source-book*: (1) Behistun monument of Darius I, pp. 57–59, (2) Persian customs according to Herodotus, pp. 59-63.

2. Supplementary. Read CHARLES BREASTED, "Exploring the Secrets of Persepolis," in the *National Geographic Magazine*, Vol. LXIV (1933), pp. 381–420, and examine the pictures. What scientific and mechanical devices are used by modern archæologists in excavating? The Behistun monument of Darius I has been called the "Rosetta Stone of Asia." Why is that? BREASTED, *Ancient Times*, §§ 351–352, Fig. 133; ROGERS, *A History of Ancient Persia*, pp. 95–98.

3. Look up in an encyclopedia: *Mithras, Avesta, Asia Minor, iron, Crœsus, Vedic literature, Scylax, fire worship, Suez Canal, coinage.*

Part Three

HOW THE GREEKS DID MORE TO ENRICH OUR CIVILIZATION THAN ANY OTHER ANCIENT PEOPLE

Formerly Historians supposed that a Great Part of our Civilization began with the Greeks. We know Better now, and the Previous Chapters have made Clear what a Good Start Mankind had before the Greeks appeared. Nevertheless, we owe a Great Debt to the Greeks, especially to the Wonderful Books they wrote on a Great Many Subjects and to the Buildings they planned, and the Statues they carved, which are still Admired and Imitated

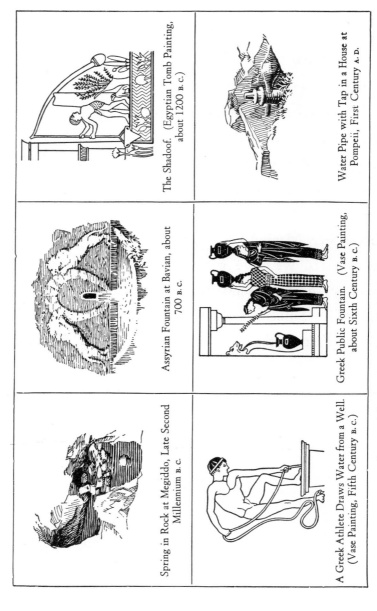

Spring in Rock at Megiddo, Late Second Millennium B. C.

Assyrian Fountain at Bavian, about 700 B. C.

The Shadoof. (Egyptian Tomb Painting, about 1200 B. C.)

A Greek Athlete Draws Water from a Well. (Vase Painting, Fifth Century B. C.)

Greek Public Fountain. (Vase Painting, about Sixth Century B. C.)

Water Pipe with Tap in a House at Pompeii, First Century A. D.

Sources of Community and Household Water Supply in the Ancient World

CHAPTER V
THE EASTERN MEDITERRANEAN WORLD
AND THE GREEK CONQUEST

THE AEGEAN WORLD: THE ISLANDS · AEGEAN CIVILIZATION: CRETE · THE AEGEAN
WORLD: THE MAINLAND · THE GREEKS TAKE POSSESSION OF THE AEGEAN WORLD ·
THE WANDERING GREEKS SETTLE DOWN · GREEK CIVILIZATION IN THE AGE OF KINGS

AS WE have seen, Persia was the last great power of the Ancient Near East. We now turn westward, therefore, to watch the further advance of civilization in Europe. But first let us see what Oriental civilization had accomplished. The Ancient Near East had made for the first time a whole group of inventions, which have since been surpassed only by those of the modern world. The Oriental peoples were the first to build up art, architecture, literature, and science. They had the earliest known written laws and had also developed the earliest belief in One God and his fatherly care for all men. On the other hand, the East had always accepted as a matter of course the rule of a king. It had never occurred to anyone there that the people should have anything to say about how they should be governed. Liberty as we understand it was unknown, and the rule of the people, which we call democracy, was hardly dreamed of. Just as the Orientals accepted the rule of kings without question, so they believed in the rule of the gods. This limited their ideas of the world about them. They thought that every storm was due to the interference of some god, and that every eclipse must be the act of an angry god or demon. Hence the Orientals made little inquiry into the natural causes of things. Under these circumstances natural science could not go very far, and religion was much darkened by superstition. There was therefore much more for mankind to do, and great progress was still possible. It is important that in Chapter V we follow the course of rising civilization as it passed from the Ancient Near East to our European forefathers from four to three thousand years ago.

1. THE ÆGEAN WORLD: THE ISLANDS

Dawn of European Civilization in the Ægean World. We have already studied the life of the earliest men in Europe, where we followed their progress from the savagery of the earliest Stone Age hunters to the time when they introduced farming from the Near East, and were able to shift from the wandering life of the hunter to the settled life of agri-

culture and cattle-breeding. At that point we were obliged
to turn to the Near East, to watch there the first appearance
and the gradual growth of civilization, while Europe still
remained in the barbarism of the Late Stone Age. Civilization first appeared in Europe at its southeastern corner.

The most important center of this civilization was the
Ægean Sea. This sea is like a large lake, almost completely
encircled by the surrounding shores of Europe and Asia
Minor, while the long island of Crete on the south lies like a
breakwater shutting off the Mediterranean. From north to
south this lakelike sea is at no point more than four hundred
miles in length; its width varies greatly. Its coast is deeply
indented with many bays and harbors, and it is so thickly
sprinkled with hundreds of islands that it is often possible
to sail from one island to another in an hour or two. The
Ægean Sea, with its islands and the fringe of shores around
it, formed a region by itself, which we may call the Ægean
world. It enjoys a mild and sunny climate; and its fertile
valleys and plains yield rich harvests of wheat, barley,
grapes, and olives. In the wet season the uplands are clothed
with rich green pastures, where the shepherds may graze the
flocks which dot the hillsides far and near. Few regions of
the world are better suited to be the home of happy and
prosperous communities.

Nearness of the Ægean World to the Near East. We can see
from a map of the Mediterranean (p. 137) that the Ægean
islands are not far distant from the mouths of the Nile, and
that Asia and Europe face each other across the waters of the
Ægean. Mariners sailing out of the Nile and steering northwest would come in sight of the Cretan mountains in a few
days. Traders pushing westward overland from the Fertile
Crescent would come to the shores of the Ægean. The older
Oriental civilizations were thus connected with the Ægean
by two routes: first, by ship across the Mediterranean from
Egypt; second, by land through Asia Minor from the world
of the Tigris and Euphrates rivers. So the Ægean islands
formed, as it were, a bridge over which the older civilizations
slowly passed to the West.

2. Ægean Civilization: Crete

Rise of Cretan Civilization. Because of their location the Ægean islands had, as early as the Late Stone Age, felt the influence of the great Oriental civilizations which we have found so early on the Nile and the Euphrates. It was on the Ægean *islands*, therefore, and not on the *mainland* of Europe that the earliest high civilization on the north side of the Mediterranean grew up. From the beginning the leader among the islands was Crete. The little sun-dried brick villages of the Late Stone Age settlements of Crete probably received copper from the ships of the Nile by 3000 B.C. Somewhat later the Cretans learned to mix copper with tin, producing bronze, which they found would make better tools and utensils than those they were using. At the time when the great pyramids of Egypt were being built, the Cretan craftsmen learned from their Egyptian neighbors the use of the potter's wheel and the closed oven. They could then shape and bake much finer clay jars and vases. They learned also how to hollow out hard varieties of stone and to make stone vases, bowls, and jars. In the system of writing, which the Cretans then developed, they used picture signs, or hieroglyphs.

By 2000 B.C. the Cretans had become a highly civilized people. At Cnossus, not far from the middle of the northern coast (map, p. 137), there grew up a kingdom which finally included a large part of the island. Here the progressive Cretan kings built a fine palace arranged in the Egyptian manner, with a large number of rooms clustered around a central court. This palace was not a fortified castle, but the Cretan kings were not without means of defense. In the ruins of the armory rooms of the palace have been found hundreds of bronze arrowheads and the charred shafts of the arrows, along with written lists of weapons and armor and chariots. Moreover, the Cretan kings early began to build ships, both for warfare and for commerce. Indeed, it has become the modern custom to call the rulers of Crete the "sea-kings of Crete." The Cretan ships, the earliest which Europeans ever sailed, carried to other countries the pottery and metal work produced by the Cretan craftsmen. The many-colored Cretan vases were so highly prized by the Egyptian noblemen of the Feudal Age that they even placed them in their tombs for use in the next world. In these Egyptian tombs modern excavators have recovered them, to tell us the story of the wide popularity of the beautiful Cretan products in the twentieth and nineteenth centuries B.C.

The Grand Age in Crete (1600–1400 B.C.), *and its Art.* Beginning in the seventeenth century B.C., Cretan civilization rose to its highest level, and the Cretans entered upon what we may call their Grand Age. The older palace of Cnossus had been succeeded by a larger and more splendid building, with colonnaded hall, fine stairways, and great open courts. The palace walls were painted with fresh and beautiful scenes from daily life, full of movement and action; or were adorned with

Fig. 33. *Restoration of North Entrance Passage in a Cretan Palace of the Grand Age at Cnossus*

In the foreground may be seen the inner gateway before which the sentinel stands. On the other side of the gate the passage rises toward the central court. Overlooking the ascending passage on either side are porticoes, upon the walls of which were painted scenes of bull-catching and bull-grappling. This restoration was made by Sir Arthur Evans, whose remarkable excavations at Cnossus not only have uncovered the royal palaces but have revealed the whole development of Cretan civilization beginning back with the Stone Age settlement over which the palaces were built. (After Sir Arthur Evans)

glazed figures, for the Cretans had learned from the Egyptians the art of making glass. The pottery-painters had by this time given up the use of many colors. They now employed one dark tone on a light background, or they modeled

FIG. 34. *Bathroom of Queen's Apartment in the Cretan Palace of the Grand Age at Cnossus*

A restored view with the bathtub in place. A frieze of running spirals with rosettes above the gypsum wall slabs, together with the charming decoration of conventionalized papyrus plants on the terra-cotta tub, makes this ancient bathroom quite as attractive as one of ours today. The tub was probably filled at a cistern in a room at the back and emptied, after the bath, into a sink with drain found in the same place. (After Sir Arthur Evans)

the design in relief. Noble vases were thus painted in grand designs drawn from plant life or often from the life of the sea, where the Cretans were now more and more at home. This wonderful pottery of the Cretans, as well as their carvings in ivory and their work in gold and bronze, ranks with the finest examples of decorative art ever produced by any people.

Crete's Commercial Expansion: Cretan Linear Writing.
From the palace of Cnossus the Cretan king could issue at the
North Gate and, mounting his chariot, ride in half an hour
to the harbor, three and a half miles away. At the harbor he
looked out northward, where the nearest islands of the Ægean
could be clearly seen on the horizon (map, p. 163). Here the
trading galleys of the Cretan kings were carrying Cretan art
and industries far and wide through the Mediterranean. The
works of Cretan craftsmen are found as far east as Cyprus.
In the West, excavation has uncovered Cretan products in
Sicily and also on the Mediterranean coast of Spain.

The growth of Cretan business began to require greater
speed and convenience in writing than was possible in using
the old picture signs. As a result, just as in Egypt and
Babylonia, these picture signs were gradually reduced to
simpler forms, each picture becoming only a few strokes. In
this more rapid hand, called *linear* writing, the pictures had
mostly disappeared, and the number of signs seems to have
been less than a hundred. Crete had no papyrus marshes and
therefore could not manufacture papyrus paper. Cretan
ships, however, had brought back clay-tablet bills of merchandise from the ports of Asia, and thus the Cretans learned
to write their new linear hand on clay tablets. Masses of
such tablets have been found covered by the rubbish and
ruins of the fallen palace. In spite of much study, scholars
are not yet able to read these precious records, the earliest
known writing on the borders of the European world.

Crete the Third Great Civilization in the Ancient World. Besides the two older centers of civilization on the Nile and
the Two Rivers in this age, there thus grew up here in the
Eastern Mediterranean, as a *third* great center, this splendid
civilization of Crete and the Ægean Sea. This third civilization formed the chief link between the cultural achievements of the Ancient Near East and the later progress of
man in Greece and western Europe. As we have already
seen, Asia Minor was also a very important link between the
Near East and Europe. To the mainland, therefore, we
must now turn, first in Europe and then in Asia Minor.

3. The Ægean World: the Mainland

Cretan Civilization on the European Mainland; Mycenæan Age (about 1500 to 1200 B.C.). Up to this time civilization on the mainland, around the Ægean, had lagged behind that of the islands. But the fleets of Egypt and Crete traded with the mainland of Greece, and about 1500 B.C. certain chieftains, probably Ægeans, had built, in the plain of Argos, the great strongholds of Tiryns and Mycenæ. They imported works of art in pottery and metal from Egypt and Crete. Some of these have been found in modern times in the ruins of palaces and in tombs. They are the earliest evidence we have of a life of higher refinement on the continent of Europe. This period is commonly known as the Mycenæan Age, after Mycenæ, where this civilization was first discovered.

Europe remains in Late Stone Age Barbarism. But civilization was confined to a narrow fringe along the coast. For a thousand years after the rise of the brilliant Cretan civilization the towns and villages of the Late Stone Age men beyond Thessaly (map, p. 163) still stretched northward and westward across Europe. Their settlements were thickly strewn far up the winding valleys of the rivers into inner Europe. It was therefore the rivers which furnished the natural routes along which the products of Near Eastern civilization were carried by the traders into the interior of Europe. The most important of these routes was the valley of the Danube, for the lower course of this stream is nearer to Asia Minor and the Near East than any other great river of Europe. Moving up the Danube, the trade from the Near East now passed down the Rhine to the North Sea, or, turning southward, followed the Rhone to the Western Mediterranean and the coasts of Spain (map, p. 137).

The Introduction and Spread of Metal in Europe. The visits of the traders who traveled these river routes from the coast were welcome events. Their wares were eagerly purchased. The Late Stone Age villagers bargained for decorated jars of pottery, necklaces of glittering blue-glaze beads, and shining beads or neck rings of a strange, heavy, gleaming reddish substance. Most desired of all, however, was the dagger or ax head made of the same unfamiliar substance. Such ax heads, although they were much thinner than the stone axes, did not break so easily, and could be ground to a better edge. So Europe slowly learned the use of metal. Having reached the islands of southeastern Europe about 3000 B.C., metal passed by slow stages, in the course of a thousand years, into northern and western Europe. It long continued to be used side by side with stone, and it was nearly 2000 B.C. before it became the chief material for tools and weapons. In the beginning the metal used was copper, but some time before 2000 B.C. *tin* was discovered in Bohemia. After they became familiar with tin the farmers along the Danube learned to produce bronze, and so developed the earliest independent Bronze Age culture on the continent of Europe about 1800 B.C. Thence it spread widely, especially westward and northward, up the Danube valley.

Civilization on the Asiatic Mainland: Troy (about 3000 to 1200 B.C.). Along the Asiatic side of the Ægean Sea there was much earlier progress than on the European side. In the days when metal was first introduced into Crete there grew up at the northwest corner of Asia Minor a shabby little Late Stone Age village known to us as Troy. By 2500 B.C. the rulers of Troy were wealthy commercial kings, and their castle was the earliest fortress in the Ægean world. Though several times destroyed, Troy was rebuilt and continued to prosper, — probably because of the development of a profitable industry in bronze, — until it finally controlled a kingdom of considerable size in northwestern Asia Minor. By about 1500 B.C. the splendid and cultivated city had grown into a powerful stronghold which now became a northern rival of Cnossus, the center of Cretan civilization in the south. We have already learned (pp. 94–98) that inland from Troy and the Ægean world the greater part of Asia Minor had been settled by that group of the Indo-Europeans who developed the highly civilized Hittite Empire.

Fig. 35. *The Mound Containing the Nine Cities of Ancient Troy (Ilium)*

When Heinrich Schliemann, the excavator, first visited this mound in 1868, it was about 125 feet high, and the Turks were cultivating grain on its summit. Schliemann, having won a large fortune, set out to fulfill his boyhood dream of discovering Troy. In 1870 he excavated a pit like a crater in the top of the hill, passing downward in the course of four years through nine successive cities built each on the ruins of its predecessors. At the bottom of his pit Schliemann found the original once bare hilltop, about 75 feet high, on which the men of the Late Stone Age had established a small settlement of sun-baked brick houses about 3000 B.C. Above the scanty ruins of this Late Stone Age settlement rose, in layer after layer, the ruins of the later cities, with the Roman buildings at the top. The entire depth of 50 feet of ruins represented a period of about thirty-five hundred years from the First (Stone Age) City to the Ninth (or Roman) City. The Second City contained the earliest copper found and a splendid treasure of golden jewelry. This Schliemann believed to be the Troy of Homer's Greek heroes, but we now know that this Second City was built a thousand years before Homer's Troy, which was the Sixth City (see *Ancient Times*, Fig. 151). Schliemann never saw the walls of the Sixth City, because as he dug down in the middle of the mound, inside the ancient walls, he covered the walls of the Sixth City with the rubbish he dug out. An American expedition from the University of Cincinnati has resumed excavation here

The Eastern Mediterranean World. It is very clear that after the middle of the second millennium B.C. the Ægean islands, together with Troy, central Asia Minor, and the plain of Argos, formed a civilized region on the north of the Mediterranean. We have now followed the rise and early history of civilization around the eastern end of the Mediterranean from the lower Nile valley, through the nations of the Fertile Crescent, to Asia Minor and the Ægean Sea. We can see that there was thus created a civilized world of the Eastern Mediterranean. We recall that our first glimpse of this Eastern Mediterranean world was gained from the pictures of the Egyptian ships which crossed the Eastern Mediterranean nearly three thousand years before the Christian Era (p. 35). But now we have studied the peoples on the east and north of the Mediterranean and have seen how, at the close of the Grand Age in Crete, the splendid Ægean civilization had been mingling for centuries with the older Near Eastern civilizations, especially with that of the Nile but also with that of Hittite Asia Minor, and through it with the civilization of the Fertile Crescent.

The Northern Intruders. We have learned how the successive Indo-European migrations penetrated the Fertile Crescent and Asia Minor. We are now to see these Indo-European invasions entering likewise the Eastern Mediterranean, where arts and industries and far-reaching commerce were so active. It was into such a highly civilized Eastern Mediterranean world that the uncivilized Indo-Europeans of the north, from behind the Balkan Mountains and the Black Sea, were beginning to intrude. These uncivilized northern Indo-Europeans included, besides others, the earliest Greeks. They were soon to overwhelm the Eastern Mediterranean, and with these northern intruders we must begin not only a new chapter in the history of the Eastern Mediterranean world but an entirely new epoch in the history of our civilization.

4. THE GREEKS TAKE POSSESSION OF THE ÆGEAN WORLD

Southward Advance of the Indo-European Line in Europe. The people whom we call the Greeks were a large group of tribes belonging to the Indo-European race. We have already followed the migrations of the Indo-European peoples, whose wanderings finally scattered them from the Atlantic Ocean to northern India (p. 92 and Fig. 29). While their Eastern kindred were drifting southward on the east side of the Caspian, the Greeks on the west side of the Black Sea were likewise moving southward from their pasture lands perhaps along the lower Danube (map, p. 137).

Driving their herds before them, with their families in rough carts drawn by horses, the rude Greek tribesmen must have come in sight of the fair lands of northern Greece, the snowy summit of Olympus, and the blue waters of the Ægean about the year 2000 B.C. Unable to write and possessing only the crudest beginnings of civilization, the Greeks thus entered

FIG. 36. *Battle between a Fleet of Northern Invaders and an Egyptian Fleet*

This scene, sculptured on the wall of an Egyptian temple, is the earliest surviving picture of a naval battle. It represents the defeat of the invading northern Mediterranean peoples by Ramses III not long after 1200 B.C., somewhere along the Syrian coast. Of the nine ships engaged, the four with oars and with a lion's head on the prow are Egyptian. The remaining five (with a goose head on the prow) are ships of the invaders. They carry round shields, and spears or two-edged swords, but no bows. The Egyptians, being chiefly archers, were thus able to overwhelm the enemy with their storm of arrows at long range. They then closed in, boarding the enemy ships and taking many prisoners, some of whom may be seen standing bound in the Egyptian ships

the highly civilized Eastern Mediterranean world. As the newcomers looked out across the waters they could dimly see the Ægean islands, where flourishing towns were carrying on industries in pottery and metal the products of which the ships of Egypt and the Ægeans were distributing far and wide. Had the gaze of the Greek nomads been able to penetrate beyond the Ægean isles, they would have seen a vast panorama of great and flourishing Oriental states. Here on the borders of the Near Eastern world, and under its influences, the Greeks were now to go forward toward the development of a civilization higher than any the Near East had yet produced, — the highest, indeed, to which man ever attained before our times.

The Greeks take Possession of the Ægean World. Gradually the Greeks pushed southward into the southernmost part of Greece, called the Peloponnesus, and doubtless some of them mingled with the dwellers in the villages settled near the walls of Tiryns and Mycenæ. Our knowledge of the Greek invasions is very meager ; for the Greeks could not yet write and therefore have left no account of their wanderings. It is evident, however, that the various Greek tribes kept on pushing southward until by 1500 B.C. they were established in the Peloponnesus and had conquered the earlier inhabitants of the region. A century later one of the Greek tribes, having learned to sail ships, passed over to Crete. This must have been about 1400 B.C. Cnossus, unfortified as it was, undoubtedly fell an easy prey to the invaders, who conquered the island and seized the other southern islands of the Ægean. Between 1300 and 1000 B.C. the Greek tribes took possession of the remaining islands, as well as the coast of Asia Minor, — the Dorian Greeks in the south, the Ionian Greeks in the middle, and the Æolians in the north. A famous Greek expedition in the twelfth century B.C., after a long siege, captured and burned the prosperous city of Troy, a feat which the Greeks never afterward forgot (p. 129). Thus during the thousand years between 2000 and 1000 B.C. the Greeks took possession not only of the whole Greek peninsula but also of the entire Ægean world.

GREECE

IN THE FIFTH CENTURY B.C.

Scale of miles
40 10   20   40   60   80

Ionians

Dorians

Other Greeks

Barbarians

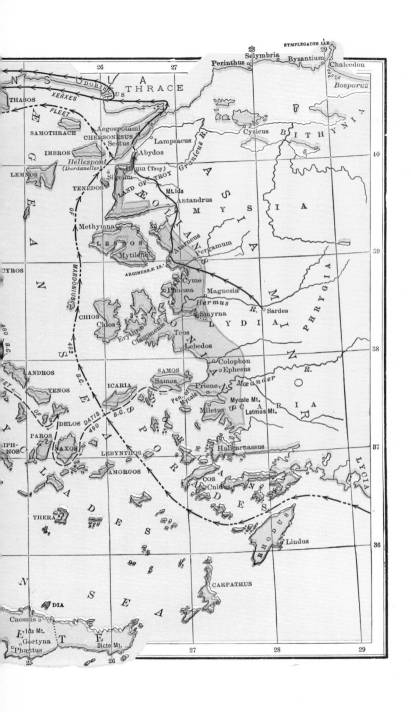

Effects of the Indo-European Migration on the Eastern Mediterranean World. Not only the Ægeans but also the peoples of Asia Minor fled in terror before the invading Indo-Europeans. In the attempt to find new homes these fugitives began to descend upon the eastern and southeastern shores of the Mediterranean from the Nile Delta to the harbors of Phœnicia (map, p. 137). Ramses III of Egypt defeated these invaders not long af⁺er 1200 B.C. It was necessary to fight them on both land and sea ; for some of the northerners approached the Asiatic frontier in a great caravan of bullock carts, while others had collected a fleet and advanced by sea. Repulsed by Egypt, the fugitives were compelled to take again to their ships, and many probably led a sea-roving life in the eastern Mediterranean. It was perhaps at this time that such peoples as the Etruscans and Sardinians sailed westward to settle in Italy and Sardinia. A group of the fleeing Cretans called Philistines had already settled on the coast of Palestine. There they established a nation and gave their name to the country, for our word "Palestine" is simply another form of the word "Philistine." Thus for two or three centuries around 1200 B.C. the easterɲ Mediterranean world was seething with the movements of the dispossessed peoples of the Ægean world as they wandered here and there seeking a new home. The Indo-Europeans meanwhile were settling down to enjoy the lands which they had conquered until other invaders should come to disturb *them* in their turn.

Fall of Ægean Civilization. The Indo-European invaders, including the Greeks, were still in the barbarian stage. Their coming, therefore, had broken up the prosperous and civilized communities which we have seen growing up on the north side of the Mediterranean. The collapse of civilization in the Ægean world was complete. It gave way to northern barbarism, little better than the Late Stone Age life which we have already seen in Europe. At least for a time, writing disappeared in the Ægean world after the Greek invasion. Enough of Ægean industries survived, however, to form an essential part of the foundation upon which the barbarian Greeks were later to build up the highest civilization of the ancient world. Such of the Ægean population as had not fled before the incoming Greeks now began to mingle with their Greek conquerors. The result was, of course, a mixed race, — the people known to us as the Greeks of history. Greek, the language of the conquerors, became the speech of this mixed race, and so it has remained to this day.

5. The Wandering Greeks Settle Down

Earliest Government among the Greeks. Long after the Greeks had taken possession of the Ægean world they remained a simple people tending their flocks and herds. Like the wandering tribesmen along the Fertile Crescent, they had very little government; for there was no public business to attend to. They continued their old organization of the people into tribes. Each tribe was composed of groups of families which considered themselves related and were called brotherhoods. A "council" of the old men ("elders") occasionally decided matters in dispute or questions of importance to the tribe. Probably once a year, or at some important feast, an "assembly" of all the weapon-bearing men of the tribe might be held, that they might express their opinion as to a proposed war or migration.

After the Greeks had learned about government by kings, such as they saw in the Ægean cities like Mycenæ, they too began to have kings. In this way the old-time chieftains who had acted as the leaders of their tribes not only in war but in religion, and who had settled matters of dispute which arose among the people, became rude shepherd kings of the tribes.

The Greeks Learn to Farm. Meantime the Greek shepherds slowly began to learn to cultivate the land. They gave up their wandering life and built houses in which to live. But nomad instincts and nomad customs were not easily rooted out. The Greeks were still influenced by their old life, and we find that their flocks and herds continued to be their chief wealth for centuries after they had turned to farming.

As the Greek tribes settled down, and their little communities grew into villages, the surrounding land was divided among the families of the village. After the people came to own the land, there arose from time to time disputes about boundaries, the inheritance of property, and other questions not easily settled. So the need developed for some kind of government which would make laws concerning property and other matters, and see that these laws were obeyed. During the four centuries from 1000 to 600 B.C. we find the Greeks struggling with the problems of learning how to transact the business of settled landholding communities and how to control the ever-growing strife between the rich and the poor, the social classes created by the holding of land.

Rise of Greek City-States. In course of time a group of villages would grow together and merge at last into a city. This was the most important step in the development of government among the Greeks; for the *organized city* became the only nation which the Greeks ever knew. Each city-state was a nation; each had its own laws, its own army and gods, and each citizen felt a patriotic duty toward his own city and no other. On a high, rocky hill around which the Greeks built their towns was the king's residence, which was called the "citadel" or "acropolis." Later the houses and the market below were protected by a wall. The king had now become a strong and respected ruler of the city and a guardian of the worship of the city gods. King and council sat all day in the market place, to carry on the business of government and settle disputes between the people. For the first time the Greeks, previously wandering shepherds and warriors, had a state and a form of government managed by a king and by a council of leading citizens. There were soon hundreds of such Greek city-states. Indeed, the entire Ægean world came to be made up of these tiny nations. It was while the Greeks were living in these little city-states under the rulership of kings that a higher Greek civilization arose, especially during the last two and a half centuries of this period.

6. Greek Civilization in the Age of the Kings

The Iron Age, and the Dawn of Greek Civilization. In one very important matter the Greek invaders were more fortunate than their Ægean predecessors. The use of iron which we have seen spreading in the Near East from the Hittite country (p. 97) had at the same time (the thirteenth century B.C.) also begun to reach the Greeks. It was, of course, a matter of some centuries before iron tools and weapons entirely displaced those of bronze, but by 1000 B.C. iron was common in Greece. The Bronze Age had therefore lasted about a thousand years. We may say that the period of Ægean civilization coincided with the Copper Age and the Bronze Age together (3000–1000 B.C.), while the civilization of the Greeks arose at the incoming of the Iron Age.

Long after 1000 B.C. the life of the Greeks continued to be crude and uncivilized. Here and there memories of the old Ægean civilization still lingered, especially in the plain of Argos. Above the Greek village at Mycenæ still towered the massive stone walls of the ancient Ægean princes, who had long before passed away. To these huge walls the Greeks looked up with wonder, and thought that they must have been built by vanished giants called Cyclopes. Without any skill in workmanship, the Greek shepherds and peasants were slow to take up building, industries, and manufacturing on their own account. They made a beginning at pottery, imitating the methods used by the Ægean potters in Crete a thousand years earlier.

Influence of the Phœnician Merchants on the Greeks. The Greeks were able, however, to buy many beautiful objects of Oriental craftsmanship from the Phœnician traders who brought their ships laden with merchandise to Greek shores. Before the longing eyes of the Greek men and women were displayed glass or alabaster perfume bottles from Egypt and rich-blue porcelain dishes. If the women did not bid for these, they were quite unable to resist the handsome ivory combs carved in openwork, and polished till they shone in the sun. Wealthy Greeks were attracted by furniture elaborately inlaid with ivory, and by the magnificent large, round platters of bronze or even of silver, richly engraved. Splendid purple robes enriched the display of golden jewelry with flashes of brilliant color. Here too were the *ketons*, the Phœnician shirtlike garments of woven wool, which the Greeks were beginning to wear.

The Expansion of Phœnician Commerce. After the fall of the Egyptian Empire and the destruction of the Ægean towns the ships of both the Egyptians and the Ægeans, who had been the first traders in the Mediterranean, had disappeared. The Phœnicians at the west end of the Fertile Crescent, along the Syrian coast, were now taking advantage of this opportunity. They became the greatest merchants of the Mediterranean for several centuries after 1000 B.C. They even pushed westward beyond the Ægean and were the discoverers of the Western Mediterranean. Their colony of Carthage, in North Africa (map, p. 137), became the most important commercial state in the Western Mediterranean. They planted settlements as far away as the Atlantic coast of Spain, and so carried the art and industries of the Orient throughout the Mediterranean.

Phœnicians carry the First Alphabet to Europe. But the Phœnicians brought to the Greeks a gift of far more value than manufactured goods. Not later than about 1800 to 1600 B.C. the western Semites near Egypt had devised an alphabet of twenty-two signs adapted from Egyptian hieroglyphics. It was the first system of writing that used letters exclusively, instead of word signs or syllable signs (cf. page 29). The Phœnicians adopted this system. At the same time they gave up the inconvenient clay tablet and began to write on Egyptian papyrus paper (twelfth century B.C.). The Greeks soon became familiar with the Phœnician tradesman's papyrus, used for his bills and receipts, and at last they began to write Greek words by using the Phœnician letters. In this way an alphabet reached Europe for the first time about 1000 B.C., — possibly as early as 1200 B.C. By 700 B.C. even the Greek potters had begun to write their

FIG. 37. *Vase Painting Containing the Earliest Example of Greek Writing*

Aristonothos, the artist who made this vase painting, has inserted his name over the standard at the right, in the lower row, where the letters run to the right and drop down. It reads, "Aristonothos made it." This is not only the earliest signed vase but also the earliest signed work of art, crude though it may be, in Europe

names on the jars which they painted (Fig. 37), and writing was shortly afterwards common among the Greeks. From the alphabet which the Phœnicians brought to the Greeks, all the alphabets of the Western world have been derived, including our own. Along with the alphabet, pen, ink, and paper (papyrus) came into Europe for the first time.

Warfare and Weapons. The Greek nobles of this age loved war and spent much time in fighting and plundering. Their shields, like the armor that they wore, were of bronze, but their weapons were usually made of iron. Only wealthy men possessed a fighting outfit like this and served as warriors. As the ordinary troops had no armor, they were of little use in warfare. Battles consisted of a series of single combats between two warriors representing the opposing sides, and were decided by the skill and daring of the hero chosen to fight for his people rather than by the strength of masses of soldiers, as in later times.

Hero Songs. Long before the Greeks could write they loved to sing of the deeds of their mighty heroes or of the feats of the gods who dwelt on Mount Olympus. Into these songs were woven also vague memories of remote wars which had actually occurred, especially the war in which the Greeks had captured and destroyed the splendid city of Troy. Probably as early as 1000 B.C. some of these songs had found their way to the coasts and islands of Ionia, on the Asiatic side of the Ægean Sea.

Here arose a class of professional bards, or singers, who recited tales of battle and adventure to the music of the harp.[1] Gradually the songs of the bards grew into story-poems, or *epics,* centering about the siege and burning of Troy. They were not the work of one man, but were added to during several centuries, and were finally written down after 700 B.C.

Homer. Among these ancient singers there seems to have been one of great fame whose name was Homer. He was supposed to have been the author of two great series of songs: the *Iliad,*[2] the story of the Greek expedition against Troy; and the *Odyssey,* or the tale of the wanderings of the hero Odysseus on his return from Troy. These are the only two series of songs that have come down to us in complete form.

Homeric Songs and Greek Religion. Homer became the great religious teacher of the Greeks. In the Homeric songs and in the tales about the gods, which we call myths, the Greeks learned how the gods dwelt among the clouds on the summit of Mount Olympus. There, in his cloud palace, Zeus, the Sky-god, with the lightning in his hand, ruled the gods like an earthly king. Apollo was the Sun-god, whose beams were golden arrows. He protected the flocks of the shepherds and the fields of the plowman, and he was a wondrous musician. Above all, he knew the future; and when he was properly consulted at his shrine at Delphi (Fig. 43), he could tell anxious inquirers what the future had in store for them. He was the best-beloved god of the Greek world.

---

[1] These were in hexameter; that is, six feet to a line. This Greek verse is the oldest literary form in Europe.

[2] So named after *Ilium,* the Greek name of Troy.

Athena, the greatest goddess of the Greeks, seems to have been a warrior goddess, and the Greeks loved to think of her standing with shining weapons, protecting the Greek cities. But they believed she held out her protecting hand over them also in times of peace, as the potters shaped their jars, the smiths wrought their metal, and the women wove their wool. Thus she became the wise and gracious protectress of the peaceful life of industry and art. Of all the goddesses she was the wisest, and an ancient tale told how she had been born in the very brain of her father Zeus, from whose head she sprang forth full-armed. These three — Zeus, Apollo, and Athena — became the leading divinities of the Greek world.

There were other great gods, each of whom controlled some special realm. In a brazen palace deep under the waters Poseidon ruled the sea. The ancient Earth Mother, whom they called Demeter, brought forth the produce of the soil. At the same time they looked also to another earth-god, Dionysus, for the fruit of the grapevine, and they rejoiced in the wine which he gave them. Hermes was the messenger of the gods, doing their bidding with winged feet; he was also the god of trade and commerce. The goddess of love the Greeks called Aphrodite.

The Greek Gods, their Conduct and Worship. All these divinities the Greeks pictured in human form, and they thought of them as possessing human traits, both good and bad. Homer pictures to us the family quarrels between the majestic Zeus and his wife Hera, just as such things must have occurred in the household life of the Greeks. Such gods were not likely to require anything better in the conduct of men. Religion was therefore not yet an influence leading to good conduct and right living.

One reason why the Greeks did not yet think that the gods required good conduct of men was their notion of life after death. They believed that at death all men passed into a gloomy kingdom beneath the earth (Hades), where the fate of good men did not differ from that of the wicked. As a special favor of the gods, the heroes, men of mighty and godlike deeds, were permitted to enjoy a life of endless bliss in the beautiful Elysian Fields or in the Islands of the Blest, somewhere far to the west, toward the unexplored ocean.

The symbols of the great gods were set up in every house, and in the dwelling of the king there was a special room which served as a kind of shrine for them. There was also an altar in the forecourt, where sacrifices could be offered under the open sky. In so far as the gods had any dwellings at all, we see that they were in the houses of men, for there were probably as yet no temples.

Questions and Exercises

REVIEW OF CHAPTER

1. What do we mean by "Ægean world"? By what two ways was the Ægean world connected with the Ancient Near East?

2. Can you mention some evidences of Egyptian influences in Crete? What evidences of the extent of Cretan commerce have been found by modern archæologists? What is *linear* writing? Has the Cretan writing been deciphered?

3. What is meant by "Mycenæan Age"? What products of Near Eastern civilization reached the Late Stone Age Europeans? How? Where was Troy? Was it ever an important city? What is meant by the term "Eastern Mediterranean world"?

4. To what race did the Greeks belong? Describe their settlement and spread in the Ægean world. What was the effect upon the predecessors of the Greeks in the Ægean? in Asia Minor? Describe the attempts of the fleeing northerners to find new homes. What happened to Ægean civilization?

5. Describe the transition of the Greeks from nomad to settled life. Describe their government and its different institutions. What problems did their new settled life create?

6. When did the Iron Age begin? To what civilized influences were the Greeks exposed after settling in the Ægean? What people succeeded the Egyptians and Ægeans as merchants of the Mediterranean? What was the greatest thing the Phœnicians brought to the Greeks? Describe early Greek arms and warfare. What was the relation of valiant deeds and song? Tell of Homer and the poems attributed to him. How did the Homeric songs affect religion? Name the leading Greek divinities and tell something of each. Discuss Greek beliefs about the dead.

USEFUL TERMS

See how much meaning you can give to the following: *industrial art, pottery, barbarism, migrations, council, assembly, social classes, acropolis, Iron Age, epics.*

DIRECTIVE QUESTIONS

1. Why was it to be expected that civilization should appear first in Europe at its southeastern corner?

2. Name the various materials in which the Cretan craftsmen and sculptors worked. Where do you suppose these materials came from?

3. Explain how traders are carriers of civilization.

4. Why do people migrate?

5. What can you say of the social effects of agriculture and landownership?

6. What place has the epic in modern literature? Is Benét's *John Brown's Body* an epic?

DISCUSSION TOPICS

1. The wonderful development of Grecian civilization proves that climate affects history.

2. The Cretans made a mistake when they did not adopt a policy of "preparedness" and erect fortifications.

3. River valleys furnish natural routes by which civilization is spread.

4. There will probably be no more great migrations of peoples.

5. Was the Greek assembly a *representative* body like the House of Representatives in the United States?

6. The Greek children who memorized the Homeric poems were not uneducated.

ADDITIONAL ADVENTURES IN LEARNING

1. **Studies in Source Materials.** THALLON, *Readings in Greek History*: (1) The shield of Achilles, pp. 24–27; (2) Odysseus in Scheria, pp. 21–23.

2. **Supplementary.** The Hebrews found the Philistines a formidable enemy. What advantage did the Philistines have over the Hebrews? BREASTED, *Ancient Times*, §§ 288–289, 392–396, 414; BURN, *Minoans, Philistines, and Greeks*, pp. 147–148, 160; *Judges* xv, 9–11; 1 *Samuel* xiii, xxxi.

3. Look up in an encyclopedia: *Heinrich Schliemann, tin, Olympus, Cyclopes, Mycenæ, Tiryns, Phœnicia, Carthage, alphabet.*

CHAPTER VI · THE GROWTH
OF THE GREEK CITY-STATES
AND THE REPULSE OF THE PERSIANS

THE DISAPPEARANCE OF THE KINGS AND THE RISE OF THE NOBLES · GREEK COLONIZA-
TION AND THE DEVELOPMENT OF GREEK COMMERCE · RISE OF DEMOCRACY AND THE
AGE OF THE TYRANTS · THE PERSIAN INVASIONS OF EUROPE

THE ANCIENT states about which we have studied were all monarchies. However oppressed the common people might be, the best they
could hope for was the overthrow of one king and the substitution of another. It was in the Greek cities that the people first gained control of the
government. Very early the Greek nobles became so powerful that they
were able to take away the powers of the kings, and monarchy disappeared
from Greece. Then, in the eighth century B.C., a struggle began between the
nobles and the common people which ended finally in the triumph of the
people and in what we call a *democratic* form of government.

In the midst of these struggles the Greeks had to face an invasion of the
Persians. For a time the Greek cities put aside their differences and united
to drive back the mighty forces of the Eastern monarch. Although the Persians had reached a high degree of civilization, they had many traditions and
superstitions which would have interfered with the progress of Greek
genius. The triumph of the Greek states over the Persian Empire was therefore one of the great crises in the development of our civilization.

1. THE DISAPPEARANCE OF THE KINGS AND THE
RISE OF THE NOBLES

The Geography of Greece. Although the Greeks owed their
early progress to what they had learned from the Near East,
they remained quite independent in their ideas of government. In the Near East, as we have seen, the cities were
joined into a powerful empire, like Egypt or Babylonia. In
Greece, however, the city-states never united into one great
nation which included all the Greek people. One reason for
this was the character of the land itself; for the country was
broken up by mountain ridges and deep bays of the sea, so
that the different communities were cut off from one another.
Moreover, the people on the mainland were separated from

their kindred on the Ægean Islands and in Asia Minor. So the various Greek settlements developed not only quite different habits but also many differences in language.

The Four Chief City-States. There were four distinct regions on the mainland of Greece, each forming a pretty clearly outlined geographical section, like the peninsula of Laconia or that of Attica (map, p. 122). Each of these regions permitted the union of its city-states into a larger nation. The oldest of them seems to have been *Argos.* The town of Argos gradually gained control of the ancient strongholds of Mycenæ and Tiryns, and others in the neighborhood, and became the nation of Argos, giving its name to the plain. In the same way the kings of *Sparta* conquered the two peninsulas to the south of them and finally also the land of the Messenians, to the west. The two kingdoms of Argos and Sparta thus held a large part of the Peloponnesus.

In the Attic peninsula *Athens* slowly took possession of the little city-kingdoms and at last gained control of the entire region. On the northern borders of Attica the region called *Bœotia* fell under the leadership of Thebes, which finally succeeded in uniting the other cities in a federation called the Bœotian League. Elsewhere no large and permanent unions were formed. Sparta and Athens led the two most important unions among the Greeks. Let it be borne in mind that *such a nation remained a city-state* in spite of its enlarged territory. The nation occupying the Attic peninsula was called Athens, for it was ruled by the city government at Athens; and every peasant in Attica was called an Athenian.

The Greek State and the Struggle toward Democracy. The governments of the little city-states entered upon a new stage of their development about 750 B.C., when the common people began the struggle to better their lot. As we shall see, this long and bitter struggle finally resulted in giving the people in some Greek states so large a share in governing that the form of the government might be called *democracy.* This is a word of Greek origin, meaning "the rule of the people," and the Greeks were the first people of the ancient world to gain such a privilege.

The cause of this struggle was not only the unjust rule of the kings but also oppression by the wealthy *nobles*. These powerful men had been able, by trickery, by unlawful seizure of property, or by marrying into families which already owned land, to get vast tracts under their control. There had arisen in this way a class of nobles whom we call *hereditary* because their wealth and rank were handed down to them by their parents, who had held these privileges before them.

Their fields stretched for some miles around the city and its neighboring villages. In order to be near the king or secure membership in the Council, and thus control the government, these men often left their lands in the care of others and lived in the city. They finally grew so powerful that they gained entire control of the Council and permitted no one but their own class to have membership in it. Moreover, as they were wealthy and had leisure for continual practice in the use of arms, they became skilled soldiers, forming the chief protection of the state in time of war.

Misery and Helplessness of the Peasants. There grew up a sharp distinction between the city community and the peasants living in the country. The country peasant was obliged to divide the family lands with his brothers. His fields were therefore small, and he was poor. He went about clad in a goatskin, and his labors never ceased. He had no leisure to learn the use of arms, nor any money to buy them. Hence he and his neighbors were of small account in war. Indeed, he was fortunate if he could struggle on and support himself and family on his scanty crops. Many of his neighbors sank into debt and had to give up their lands to the nobles. They became day laborers, working for more fortunate men, or, still worse, sold themselves to pay their debts and thus became slaves. These day laborers and slaves had no rights in the government and could not vote in the Assembly.

Browbeaten by the powerful nobles, the meager Assembly, which had once included all the weapon-bearing men of the tribe, became a feeble gathering of a few peasants and unimportant townsmen who had little influence. Hence the peasant was less and less likely to attend the Assembly at all.

Triumph of the Nobles; Fall of the Kings (800–650 B.C.). Between 750 and 650 B.C. the office of the king disappeared. While the king was in some cases violently overthrown, in most states the nobles chose from among themselves certain elective officers to take charge of matters formerly controlled by the king. Thus in Athens they appointed a noble to be leader in war, while another noble was chosen *archon,* or ruler, to assist the king in attending to the increasing business of the state. The Athenian king was gradually but peacefully deprived of his powers until he became nothing more than the leader of the people in religious matters. In Sparta the power of the king was checked by the appointment of a second king, and on this plan Sparta continued to retain her kings. Elsewhere the nobles came into complete control of the state, and the office of king disappeared entirely.

2. GREEK COLONIZATION AND THE DEVELOPMENT OF GREEK COMMERCE

Greek Colonies in the Eastern Mediterranean. The oppressive rule of the nobles and the resulting poverty of the peasants drove many Greek farmers to seek new homes and new lands beyond the Ægean world. Not only were Greek merchants trading with the northern Ægean, but their vessels had even entered the great northern sea which they called the Pontus and which is known to us as the Black Sea. Their trading stations among the descendants of the Stone Age peoples in these distant regions offered to the discontented farmers of Greece plenty of land with which to begin life over again. Before 600 B.C. Greek colonists girdled the Black Sea with their towns and settlements, reaching the broad grain fields along the lower Danube and the iron mines of the old Hittite country on the southeastern coast of the Black Sea.

Along the southern coasts of Asia Minor, Greek expansion was stopped by the Assyrian Sennacherib when he defeated a body of Greeks in Cilicia about 700 B.C. This was the earliest collision between the Hellenes and a great power of the Oriental world. The Greek colonies of Cyprus long

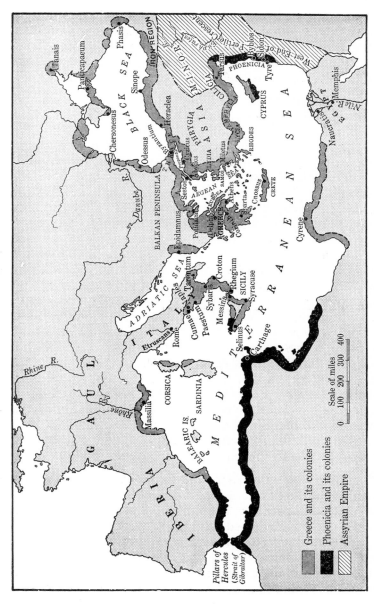

Colonial Expansion of the Greeks and Phoenicians down to the Sixth Century B.C.

remained the easternmost outposts of the Greek world. In
the south they found a friendly reception in Egypt, and there
in the Nile Delta they were permitted to establish a trading city at Naucratis, the predecessor of Alexandria. West
of the Delta they eventually founded Cyrene also.

Greek Colonies in the Western Mediterranean. It was the
unknown West, however, which became the America of the
early Greek colonists. Many a Columbus pushed his ship
into this strange region of mysterious dangers on the distant
borders of the world, where the heroes were believed to live
in the Islands of the Blest. Looking westward from the
Greek coast, the seamen could discover the shores of the
heel of Italy, only fifty miles distant. When they had once
crossed to it, they coasted around Sicily and far to the west.

By 750 B.C. colonies appeared in this new Western world,
and within a century they fringed southern Italy from the
heel to a point well above the instep north of Naples, where
they were stopped by the settlements of the Etruscans. This
region of the Greek colonies of southern Italy came to be
known as Great Greece. The Greek colonists likewise crossed
over to Sicily and drove out the Phœnician traders there,
except at the western end of the island, where the Phœnicians
held their own. Syracuse, at the southeast corner of the
island, soon became the most cultured as well as the most
powerful city of the Greek world. At Massilia (Marseilles),
on the coast of later France, the western Greeks founded a
town which controlled the trade up the Rhone valley, and,
attracted by the silver mines of Tartessus, they reached over
even to the Mediterranean coasts of Spain.

Growth of Greek Commerce and Industry. The remarkable
spread of the Greek colonies led to a great increase of business
and manufacturing for the Greek home cities. The new
colonies not only had needs of their own but also had dealings
with settlements farther inland, and so a large market was
opened up for Greek wares. Ere long the merchant ships of
Greece were making their way along the coasts of the Mediterranean, bearing to distant towns Greek metal work, woven
goods, and beautiful pottery.

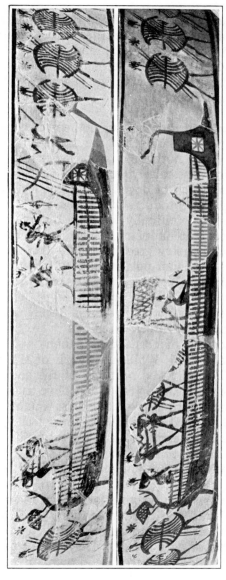

Fig. 38. *Two Sea Battles Pictured on an Athenian Vase of about 700 B.C.*

The upper boat is represented as beached, and thus there is no one at the rudder; the lower boat is at sea, and a man stands at the rudder. Both boats have a half deck at each end. A ram at the prow indicates that these are battleships and not merchant vessels. In both boats there are men engaged in hand-to-hand fighting. In the bow of the upper boat one man is throwing a spear, and another is shooting an arrow at one of the enemy, who is about to throw a pike and who, with his left hand, is grabbing another pike from the boat. In the stern of the lower boat two men are fighting with swords. It is difficult to know whether the man sitting in the middle of the lower boat is wounded or is tending the sail. (Courtesy of the Metropolitan Museum of Art)

They brought back either raw materials and foodstuffs, such as grain, fish, and amber, or finished products like the magnificent objects of bronze from the cities of the Etruscans in northern Italy. At the yearly feast and market on the island of Delos the Greek householder found the Etruscan bronzes of the West side by side with the gay rugs and rich silver vessels from the Orient.

The Economic Development of Athens. Athens became important commercially much later than the Ionian cities, because at first the city had nothing of value to export. The land of Attica was not particularly fertile except the inland region east of Athens, which belonged to the nobles. Hence there were no agricultural products which could be shipped out in exchange for imports. Finally, however, Athens began to develop one important industry, the manufacture of pottery. In time this industry grew to such an extent that the workshops of the Athenian potters filled a large section of the city. By examining the signed Attic vases which have been found, we may trace the rise and spread of Athenian commerce from the earliest beginnings until Athens became the commercial leader of the Greek cities.

Agriculture was so well managed that Athens was prosperous for several centuries. While nearly all of the farm products were not allowed to be sent out of the state but were kept to feed the people, the grapes and olive trees were so plentiful that farmers were allowed to export wine and oil. These products were shipped out in Athenian pottery vases to all the ports of the Mediterranean, and the returning ships brought the cattle, hides, timber, wax, pickled and dried fish, salt, and drugs which Athens might need.

Improvement of Ships. The growing foreign trade encouraged shipbuilders to build craft far larger than the old fifty-oar galleys. The new merchantmen were still driven by sails, an Egyptian invention of ages before. They were so large, however, that they could no longer be drawn up on the strand. Hence sheltered harbors were necessary, and the anchor was now invented. The protection of these merchant ships demanded more effective warships, and the distinction arose between a man-of-war, or battleship, and a merchantman. Corinth boasted the production of the first decked warships, — a great improvement, giving the warriors above more room and better footing, and at the same time protecting the oarsmen who were below. Warships, which must be independent of the wind, were propelled by oars. The oarsmen were arranged in three rows, one above the other, each man sitting behind the one below him. Thus the power of an old "fifty-oar" could be multiplied by three without increasing the size of the craft. These ships were called *triremes* and were in use by 500 B.C. With superior equipment on the sea and the marked growth of their industries, the Hellenes were soon surpassing the Phœnicians (p. 127) in the Mediterranean markets.

The Greeks begin to use Coins (Early Seventh Century B.C.). Meantime Greek business was greatly simplified by the introduction of coined money. Not long after 700 B.C. the kings of Lydia, in Asia Minor, following an Oriental custom (p. 68), began to have silver cut into lumps of a fixed weight. These were stamped with some symbol of the king or state, to show that the state guaranteed their value, and were the earliest known coins.

This great convenience was quickly appreciated by Greek merchants and adopted by them. The coin most used by the Athenians was a lump of silver worth from eighteen to twenty cents. It was called a *drachma*. The buying power of a drachma was very much greater then than it would be in our day. For example, a sheep cost one drachma, an ox five drachmas, and a landowner with an income of five hundred drachmas (approximately one hundred dollars) a year was considered a wealthy man.

Rise of a Moneyed Class. Greek wealth had formerly consisted of lands and flocks, but now men began to accumulate wealth in *money*. Loans were made, and the custom of charging interest for lending money came in from the Orient. Interest rates were high, sometimes as much as 18 per cent. Men who could never have hoped for wealth as farmers were growing rich. There now arose a class of people who made a great deal of money in business and trade, — a *middle class*, neither nobles nor peasants. These prosperous men demanded that they be given some share in the government. They refused to be considered as unimportant any longer and insisted that their wishes in the management of public affairs should be considered. They soon managed to gain much influence and compelled the nobles to consult them.

3. Rise of Democracy and the Age of the Tyrants

Condition of the Small Farmer. While a prosperous moneyed or capitalistic class was thus arising, the condition of the farmer on his lands grew steadily worse. His fields were dotted with stones, each the sign of a mortgage, which the Greeks were accustomed to mark in this way. The wealthy creditors were foreclosing these mortgages and taking possession of the lands, and the unhappy owners were being sold into slavery or were fleeing abroad to escape such bonds. The nobles in control did little to improve the situation. Moreover, the wealthy merchants were buying their way into the nobility. The plight of the poorer classes was becoming so hopeless that revolt was threatened in many cities.

The Rise of Tyrants (650–500 B.C.) There were in ancient Greece, just as there are in modern America, men who liked the idea of controlling the city government. Such men are usually born leaders, and in Greece they came from the noble class, which was accustomed to leadership. These nobles, by championing the cause of the people, obtained a large following and sometimes gained control of the state.

This new type of leader differed from the kings of old in that he had no royal ancestors and had seized the control of the state by force. The people did not revere him as of ancient royal descent; so his position always remained insecure. The Greeks called such a man a "tyrant," which was not at that time a term of reproach, as it is with us. The word "tyranny" was merely a term for the high office held by this ruler. Nevertheless, the Greeks felt that they were no longer free under a ruler of this kind, and the slayer of a "tyrant" was regarded as a hero and a savior of the state. In spite of prejudice against tyrants, they were the first champions of the rights of the people. They also gave much attention to public monuments, art, music, and literature.

Earliest Written Greek Codes of Law. Up to this time the Greek laws had not been written out but had been handed down by word of mouth. It was very easy for a judge to twist the law to favor the man who gave him the largest present. The people were now demanding that the laws be put into writing. After a long struggle the Athenians secured such a written code, arranged by a man named Draco, about 624 B.C. It was an exceedingly severe code; hence our adjectives "Draconian" and "Draconic," meaning "harsh."

The Reforms of Solon. But writing down the law did not meet all needs nor quiet unrest in Athens. In 594 B.C. a noble named Solon was chosen as archon (p. 136) and was given full power to improve the unhappy condition of the poor. He declared void all mortgages on land and all large claims of creditors which endangered the liberty of a citizen, and he also set a limit to the amount of land which a noble might hold. All men who had become slaves on account of their debts were given their freedom. Furthermore, it was made unlawful to accept the body of a man as security for his indebtedness.

Solon also made a law that anyone who had lost a lawsuit could appeal the case to a jury of citizens. Such improvements in the laws greatly increased a citizen's chance of securing justice. Solon's laws were all written, and they formed the first Greek code of laws by which all free men were given equal rights in the courts. Some of these laws have come down to our own time and are still in force.

Furthermore, Solon proclaimed a new constitution which gave to all a voice in the control of the state. It recognized four classes of citizens, graded according to the amount of their income. The wealthy nobles were the only ones who could hold the highest offices, and the peasants were permitted to hold only the lower offices. Although the government remained in the hands of the nobles, the humblest free citizen could now be assured of the right to vote in the Assembly of the people. As a guide in the proceedings of the Assembly there was created a Council of four hundred members. This new council existed along with the Council of Elders, called the Areopagus, which now acted as an adviser and devoted itself to maintaining and enforcing the laws.

The Tyrants at Athens. In spite of Solon's fine work, Pisistratus, a member of one of the powerful noble families, finally gained control of the Athenian state as tyrant. He ruled with great wisdom, and many of the Athenians gave him their loyal support. Pisistratus saw that there was not enough grain raised in Attica to feed the growing population, and realized the necessity of gaining for Athens some means of access to the grain harvests which were shipped from the northern and western ports of the Black Sea. Having built a small war fleet, therefore, he seized Sigeum, a city at the mouth of the Hellespont (Dardanelles). Pisistratus made many public improvements at Athens and encouraged skilled craftsmen from other cities to come to Athens, thus greatly stimulating industrial art. Athenian manufactures and commerce flourished as never before, and when Pisistratus died he had laid the foundation on which much of the later greatness of Athens was built. The sons of Pisistratus, however, in spite of their ability, were unable to win the support of the Athenians. One of them was killed, and the other was finally obliged to flee. Thus, shortly before 500 B.C., Athens was freed from her tyrants.

The Reforms of Clisthenes. The cause of the people was now taken up by a noble named Clisthenes, who introduced many reforms which improved the system of voting and gave the people a greater opportunity to share in the running of the government.

In order to prevent the rise of a new tyrant, Clisthenes established a law that once a year the people might by vote declare any prominent citizen dangerous to the state and banish him for ten years. To cast his vote against a man, a citizen had only to pick up one of the pieces of broken pottery lying about the market place, write upon it the name of the citizen to be banished, and deposit it in the voting urn. Such a bit of pottery was called an *ostrakon*, and to "ostracize" a man (literally, to "potsherd" him) meant to banish him. In this and other ways the people were able to take an active part in the government, and so, to a large extent, Athens became a democracy.

Expansion of Sparta. Meantime Sparta also had greatly increased in power. The Spartans had pushed their military successes until they held over a third of the Peloponnesian peninsula. The result was that long before 500 B.C. the Spartans had forced the neighboring states into a combination, the Spartan League, which included nearly the whole of the Peloponnesus.

The Spartans did no farming and did not occupy themselves with the crafts. They had reduced the peoples in their immediate vicinity to the condition of serfs, and these serfs tilled the soil and manufactured the few iron implements needed. Wealth was measured in terms of land and serfs. As the serfs greatly outnumbered the Spartan landholding aristocracy, the latter lived in constant fear of a serf uprising and had turned their city into an armed camp. The Spartans had become the greatest soldiers of Greece and consequently enjoyed a prestige which permitted Sparta to impose her will on the Greek states many times during the next century.

4. THE PERSIAN INVASIONS OF EUROPE

The Persian Advance to the Ægean (546 B.C.). While the Greek cities were developing their trade and founding colonies throughout the Western Mediterranean, the Medes and Persians were building up a powerful empire in the East. The Persians kept extending their conquests westward until the Greek cities of Asia Minor, in the midst of their remarkable progress in civilization (pp. 220–224), suddenly lost their liberty and actually found themselves forced to become subjects of Persia. There seemed little prospect that the tiny Greek states, even if united, could successfully resist the vast Oriental empire which held control of all the countries of the ancient East. Nevertheless, the Ionian cities dared to revolt against their Persian lords.

FIG. 39. *Coins from the Foundation Deposit of King Darius at Persepolis*

A is one of the gold coins struck by Crœsus, king of Lydia (561–546 B.C.). The obverse has two animal heads face to face, — a lion on the left (facing right) and a bull on the right (facing left) ; the reverse has two incuse (that is, stamped-in) squares. They are the impress left by the upper of the two dies (blocks) between which the lump of metal was placed for stamping the coin. *B* is a so-called "tortoise" issued by Ægina, which was probably the first European town to strike coins. The obverse bears the figure of a sea turtle. The reverse has an incuse square divided into eight parts. This coin is very primitive and may be dated as early as the beginning of the seventh century B.C. It is most interesting to find that Darius placed, among other coins in the *foundation deposit of his great audience hall*, a coin which came from the country said to have been the first to issue coins, and a coin of the type thought to be the first ever struck in Europe. This foundation deposit was discovered by the Oriental Institute of The University of Chicago

First Persian Invasion of Europe. During the struggle which followed this revolt the Athenians sent twenty ships to aid their Ionian kindred. This act furnished an excuse to the Persian monarch, Darius, for bringing an army into Europe. The long march of the Persians across the Hellespont and through Thrace cost them many men, and the fleet which accompanied the Persian army was wrecked in trying to round the high promontory of Mount Athos (492 B.C.). This advance into Greece was therefore given up for a plan to invade Greece by water across the Ægean.

The Second Persian Invasion ended by Battle of Marathon. In the early summer of 490 B.C. a large fleet of transports and

Ewing Galloway

FIG. 40. *Mound Raised as a Monument to the Fallen Greeks at Marathon*

The mound is nearly fifty feet high. Excavations undertaken in 1890 disclosed beneath it the bodies of the one hundred and ninety-two Athenian citizens who fell in the battle. Some of their weapons and the funeral vases buried with them were also recovered and are now in the National Museum at Athens

warships carrying the Persian forces put out from the island of Samos, sailed across the Ægean, and entered the straits between Eubœa and Attica. The Persians finally landed on the shores of Attica, in the Bay of Marathon (map, p. 154), intending to march directly on Athens.

There was great excitement and confusion among the Greek states. The defeat of the revolting Ionian cities, and especially the sack of Miletus by the Persians, had aroused the fears of the Greeks. After sending messengers in desperate haste to seek aid from Sparta the Athenian citizens tried to save their beloved city. Thinking to find the Athenians unprepared, Darius had not sent a large army. The Persian forces probably numbered no more than twenty thousand men, but at the utmost the Athenians could not put more than half this number into the field. Fortunately for them, there was among their generals a skilled commander named Miltiades. He was able to induce the Athenians not to await the assault of the Persians at Athens but to march across the peninsula and block the Persian advance. When the Persians, encamped in the plain of Marathon, attempted to march along the road to Athens, they were met by the Attic army. The battle that followed was a contest between bow and spear; the Persian bow was useless at close range, while the Greek spear everywhere spread death and terror. As the Persians fled to their ships they left over six thousand dead upon the field, while the Athenians lost less than two hundred men. When the Persian commander sailed around the Attic peninsula and appeared with his fleet before the port of Athens, he found it useless to attempt a landing, for the victorious Athenian army was already encamped beside the city. The Persians therefore retired, and we can imagine with what joyous feelings the Athenian citizens watched the great Asiatic fleet of Darius as it finally disappeared.

Accession of Xerxes; Leadership and Plans of Themistocles. Darius the Great (p. 104) died without having avenged the defeat of his army at Marathon. His son and successor, Xerxes, therefore planned a far-reaching assault on all the Greek settlements along the line from Greece to Sicily with the aid of the Phœnicians. Meanwhile the Greeks made ready to meet the new Persian attack. They soon found that Xerxes' commanders were having a canal cut behind the promontory of Athos to secure a short cut and thus avoid all risk of such a disaster as had overtaken their former fleet in rounding this dangerous point. When Themistocles discovered their plan, he persuaded the Athenian Assembly to build a great fleet of about a hundred and eighty triremes. So the Greeks were prepared for the first time to meet the Persian advance by both sea and land.

The masterly plan of action now devised by Themistocles corresponded exactly to that of the Persian advance. The Asiatics were coming with combined land and sea forces, the army and fleet moving together down the east coast of the Greek mainland. The plan of Themistocles, therefore, was to meet the Persian fleet *first*, with full force, and fight a decisive naval battle as soon as possible. If victorious, the Greek fleet would then be able to sail up the eastern coast of Greece and cut off the supplies of the Persian army. There

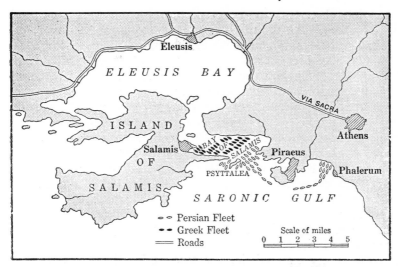

The Battle of Salamis

The island of Salamis is separated from Attica by a narrow channel leading into the Bay of Eleusis. This channel is divided in two at its entrance by the low rocky island of Psyttalea. The Persian fleet sailed in from the right (south) and was drawn up in a line facing north between the harbor of Piræus and the island of Salamis. However, when the order was given to enter the straits, because of the position of Psyttalea the Persian ships could not advance in a long front so as to enfold the Greek fleet. Instead, the Persians passed on either side of the obstructing island in columns, and so were exposed to flank attack from the Greeks, who came into action from the left (northwest of Psyttalea). Persian troops stationed by Xerxes on Psyttalea were all slain by the Greeks

must be no attempt of the small Greek army to fight the vast land forces of the Persians. On the contrary, they must delay them as long as possible at the narrow northern passes, which could be defended with a few men. An effort to persuade *all* the Greek states to act together in fighting the Persians was not successful. Indeed, it was only by giving Sparta command of the allied Greek fleets that Themistocles was able to induce the Spartans to join with Athens and to accept his plan for the campaign.

The Persian Advance into Attica and the Battle of Salamis. In the summer of 480 B.C. the Asiatic army approached the pass of Thermopylæ, just opposite the westernmost point of the island of Eubœa (map, p. 154). Their fleet advanced with them. The Asiatic host must have numbered over two hundred thousand men, while the enormous fleet consisted of perhaps a thousand vessels, two thirds of which were warships. The Spartan king Leonidas led some five thousand men to check the Persians at the pass of Thermopylæ, while the Greek fleet of less than three hundred triremes was trying to engage the Persian navy at Artemisium, on the northern coast of Eubœa. The Persians now attempted two flank movements, by land and by sea, — one over the mountains, to strike the little army of Leonidas in the rear and the other around the island of Eubœa, to take the Greek fleet likewise from behind. A storm destroyed the flanking Persian ships, but the Persian troops succeeded in climbing around the pass and completely wiped out the forces of Leonidas.

The main army of the Spartans and their allies was now drawn up on the Isthmus of Corinth, the only point at which the Greek land forces could hope to make another defensive stand. As the Persian army moved southward from Thermopylæ the undaunted Themistocles gathered together the Athenian population and had them carried in ships to the little islands of Salamis and Ægina and the shores of Argolis. Meantime the Persians entered Attica and advanced on Athens, burning and pillaging as they came. With masterly skill Themistocles held together the irresolute Greek leaders, while he induced Xerxes to attack by means of a false message that the Greek fleet was about to slip out of the bay. The Greek navy had cleverly taken up its position in the narrow waters between the island of Salamis and the Attic mainland, where the Persian ships found it impossible to maneuver for lack of space. The huge Asiatic fleet soon fell into confusion.

The combat lasted throughout the entire day, and when darkness settled on the Bay of Salamis the Persian fleet had been almost completely destroyed. Xerxes was now troubled lest he and his army should be cut off from Asia by the victorious Greek fleet. He therefore retreated to the Hellespont and withdrew into Asia.

Final Defeat of the Persians. Although Xerxes himself withdrew from Greece, he left an army of perhaps fifty thousand men to winter in Thessaly. The following spring the united armies of Athens, Sparta, and other allies, under the leadership of the Spartan king, met the enemies' forces at Platæa, where the Persians were overwhelmingly defeated. Not only European Greece but Ionia too was saved from Asiatic despotism; for the Greek triremes, having meantime crossed over to Asia Minor, drove out or destroyed the remnants of the Persian fleet. The Athenians now got control of the Hellespont, and thus closed the crossing from Asia into Europe against further Persian invasion. No Persian army ever set foot in European Greece again.

Questions and Exercises

REVIEW OF CHAPTER

1. Were the geographical influences in Greece favorable to a political union of all Greeks? How did the political development of the Near East differ from that of Greece? What is a democracy?

2. What were the reasons for Greek colonization? Why were the Greek colonies on the Black Sea of particular importance to the cities of Greece? Explain how colonization affected Greek trade and industry. Why did Athens prohibit the exportation of agricultural products?

3. What happened when the Greek farmer could not "pay off" the mortgage? How did a Greek become a "tyrant"? Which of Solon's reforms was, in your opinion, of the most importance to the people? How did the people benefit by the reforms of Clisthenes?

4. Why did Darius and Xerxes want to conquer Greece?

USEFUL TERMS

See how much meaning you can give to the following: *city-state, colonization, exports, raw materials, merchantmen, triremes, capitalistic class, tyrant, jury, democratization, ostracism, rights of the people.*

DIRECTIVE QUESTIONS

1. What influence did colonization have on the rise of the Greek capitalistic class?

2. Why do people demand written laws?

3. How did the tyrants promote the welfare of the people?

4. What was the importance of the battles of Salamis and Platæa? What effect might a Persian victory have had on the Greek experiment with democracy?

DISCUSSION TOPICS

1. Compare the Greek farmer and the American "share-cropper."

2. One of the early instances of government regulation of trade was the prohibition by Athens of the exportation of agricultural products.

3. How did the Greek "tyrant" differ from the modern "dictator"?

4. Patriotism might have *prevented* the Greeks from uniting against the Persians.

ADDITIONAL ADVENTURES IN LEARNING

1. **Studies in Source Materials.** THALLON, *Readings in Greek History*: (1) Development of Greek commerce, pp. 46–47; (2) The Spartan serfs, pp. 90–93, 96–97; (3) The Ionian revolt against Persia, pp. 154–163; (4) Pheidippides, the runner, pp. 169–170.

2. **Supplementary.** Greek industries: BRITISH MUSEUM, *Guide to Greek and Roman Life*, pp. 132–178; GLOTZ, *Ancient Greece at Work*, pp. 127–143; MCCLEES, *Daily Life of the Greeks and Romans*, pp. 109–120.

3. Look up in an encyclopedia: *amber, Marseilles, olive oil, code, Dardanelles (Hellespont), Xerxes I, Laurion (Laurium)*.

CHAPTER VII · THE STRUGGLE FOR LEADERSHIP AMONG THE GREEK STATES

THE RISE OF THE ATHENIAN EMPIRE · THE DEVELOPMENT OF THE DEMOCRACY IN ATHENS · THE COALITION AGAINST ATHENS AND THE PELOPONNESIAN WARS · THE FINAL CONFLICTS AMONG THE GREEK STATES · GREEK POLITICAL PROBLEMS BECOME WORLD PROBLEMS

THE GREEK city-states had combined valiantly to drive off their common enemy, Persia, but when the war was over they soon fell apart. Athens succeeded in forming a defensive league with the Ionian cities and the Aegean Islands, which were directly exposed to attack from the East; but most of the Greek city-states were not inclined to put themselves under her control. Moreover, when they saw her prospering and transforming the league into an empire, they were so aroused that a long series of civil wars followed which ended in the downfall of the Athenian Empire. The Greeks would never tolerate for long the supremacy of any one city-state, and so Greece could never develop into a strong, unified nation.

It will be interesting to see that, while Athens was creating an empire by autocratic methods, she was at the same time developing within her own borders a democratic form of government.

1. THE RISE OF THE ATHENIAN EMPIRE

Athens forms the Delian League. Although the Greeks had three times defeated the Persians, they nevertheless still feared the vengeance of the powerful Eastern monarch. Under the wise leadership of Themistocles the Athenians had built up a strong navy and constructed a naval base at the Piræus. Themistocles now determined to fortify the city and seaport, to protect Athens in case of siege. When the Spartans therefore refused to continue longer to command the combined Greek navies, the great Athenian fleet became mistress of the Ægean.

It was easy for Athens to persuade the Ionian cities and the Ægean Islands, which were exposed to attack from Persia, to join her in a defensive league. The wealthier of these cities agreed to contribute ships, while others were to pay a sum of money each year into the treasury of the league.

Central Greece

Athens was to have command of the fleet and collect the money. The treasury was placed for protection in the temple of Apollo on the island of Delos, and the federation was therefore known as the Delian League. The transformation of such a league into an empire made up of states subject to Athens was but a matter of time. In the meanwhile the Athenian fleet prevented Persian ships from making use of the Ægean. It also cleared the waters of pirate ships which had long sailed forth from the island of Scyros, so that Greek trade in the East flourished as never before. All this was viewed with increasing jealousy by Sparta.

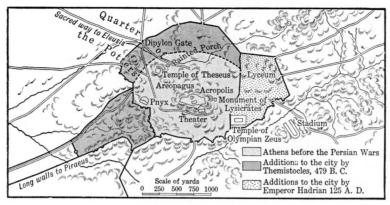

The Growth of Athens

The Dangerous Position of Athens. Under three great leaders — Themistocles, Cimon, and Pericles — Athens became the most prosperous and powerful city of Greece. But there were dangerous elements in her situation. The Ægean Islands and the cities of Asia Minor which had joined the Delian League were at first glad to be free from danger of attack by Persia, but they soon began to resent the domination of Athens. They seemed to forget that Athens was assuming the responsibility of keeping the seas free and safe, while Athens on her part began to treat her allies as if they were her subjects. When some of the island states wished to withdraw, Athens would not permit them to do so. She sent out her war fleet, conquered them, and forced them to pay money tribute instead of contributing ships. Sometimes their citizens were driven out, and their lands were divided among Athenian settlers. In time a section of the Athenian fleet was on constant duty, sailing about in the Ægean and collecting the tribute money by force. These funds were used by Athens as she pleased, even to beautify her own city.

The Tyranny of Athens; the League transformed into an Empire. Besides forcing her allies to remain in the League, Athens was finally guilty of interference in the local affairs of the allied peoples. The time came when she would permit none of her allies to have any but a democratic constitution. In addition, the judicial power of the allies was greatly restricted, for certain legal cases had to be taken to Athens for trial. As none of these allied peoples were admitted to Athenian citizenship, Athens failed to gain many citizens whose loyal support and devotion she might otherwise have enjoyed. There was no feeling of unity within the League, for the council of representatives from the states of the League, which at first guided its affairs, after a time held no more meetings. In the end Athens gained complete control and governed the allied states as she liked. The Delian League had become an Athenian Empire. Many of the allies revolted or refused to pay tribute. These were reduced to the position of "subject allies." Some of the seceding states appealed to Sparta for help, and some even went so far as to ask aid of the Persian governors in the near-by provinces. Forty years of so-called Athenian tyranny were to pass by, however, before Sparta would agree to become the champion of the Athenian allies.

2. The Development of the Democracy in Athens

Fall of Themistocles. Although Themistocles had saved Greece from the Persians and had later done much to make Athens supreme in Greece, he nevertheless lost the confidence of the citizens and was ostracized (472–471 B.C.). His downfall was partly due to his policy of hostility to Sparta, which finally accused him of treasonable relations with Persia, and he was obliged to flee for his life. He spent the remainder of his life in the service of the Persian king. In the meantime Cimon, a member of the noble class who had become a popular hero in the last years of the Persian Wars, had risen to leadership and was the chief of the opposing party, who favored an alliance with Sparta. When, however, after furnishing troops to aid Sparta in an uprising of the serfs, Cimon was rebuffed by her and the troops were sent home, the Athenians were so humiliated that the people's party gained in strength, and Cimon lost favor and was ostracized (461 B.C.).

Fig. 41. *Excavations being Carried on in the Athenian Market Place (Agora) by the American School at Athens*

We look southward directly through the houses of modern Athens which had to be bought up before the clearance could begin. The excavated area was covered by such houses. Just out of range on the right (west) is the temple of Theseus (Fig. 42), while far back and entirely invisible on the left is the Acropolis. The ruined walls which we see in the excavated area are almost all parts of buildings much later than ancient Athens, although this extensive clearance has revealed facts concerning the civilization of the Attic peninsula for over three thousand years. beginning with the contents of a Mycenæan burial and concluding with the frescoes of a Byzantine chapel of the seventeenth century A.D. Many important works of art, including interesting examples of Roman portrait heads, have been uncovered, and over a thousand new inscriptions have been found. (Courtesy of Professor Edward Capps)

Growing Power of the People. As Cimon was a noble, his overthrow was really a victory of the people's party over that of the nobles. This was followed by an attack on the Areopagus, or Council of Elders, once made up only of nobles. The people now passed new laws limiting the duties of the Areopagus to the trial of murder cases and the settlement of questions of state religion, and so taking from it all political power. The citizen juries introduced by Solon as a court of appeal (p. 143) had been greatly enlarged. To enable the poorest citizens to serve on these juries, laws were now passed granting pay for jury service. These juries, or citizen courts, finally became so important that they formed a kind of judicial body which formed and interpreted the laws made by the popular assembly. The people were indeed in control of the government. In addition to this the right to hold office was greatly extended. All citizens were permitted to hold the office of archon except members of the laboring class who owned no property. In order to permit citizens of small means to serve as state officials, all officials were paid salaries. With one exception there was no longer any *election* of the higher officers, but they were now all *chosen by lot* from the whole body of eligible citizens.

How Pericles became the Leader in Athens. There was one kind of officer whom it was impossible to choose by lot, and that was the military commander, the general (*strategus*). There were ten of these generals. They not only led the army in war but also managed the war department and had large control of the treasury and of the government of the empire, including its foreign affairs. The leader, or president, of this body of generals was the most powerful man in the state, and his office was elective. It thus became more and more possible for a noble with military training to make himself a strong and influential leader and, if he had a gift for public speaking, he could propose a series of plans for the nation and by his eloquence persuade the Assembly to accept them.

After the fall of Cimon there came forward a handsome and brilliant young Athenian named Pericles. He desired to build up the splendid Athenian Empire of which Themistocles had dreamed. He became the head of the progressive party, which favored the increase of power for the people. He kept their support year after year and finally became the actual head of the state. As we might say, he was the political "boss" of Athens from about 460 B.C. until his death over thirty years later.

The Meaning of Athenian Citizenship: Duties. The Athenians held a high ideal of citizenship. In the funeral oration which Pericles delivered on the Athenian citizens who had been killed in the First Peloponnesian War, he said. "We alone regard a man who takes no interest in public affairs not as a harmless but as a useless person." In the opinion of the Athenians, citizenship included not only *privileges* but *duties*. There was a feeling that the state should not do anything for the citizens which the citizens could do for themselves. The result was that the Athenian citizens became more self-reliant and independent than any other people in the history of the world.

All Athenian citizens had to serve in some branch of the army or navy. The citizens who were able had to render certain services which involved the spending of large sums of money and which were in some ways like our taxes. But these payments were made in a more gracious spirit than that in which our taxes are paid. This, of course, was largely due to the fact that citizens who gave the money were permitted to direct the spending of it. Even citizens of moderate means often made small voluntary gifts to the state. Other public services of the Athenian citizens included holding of offices, serving on the jury, and attending the Assembly. As there was pay for such services as these, the people benefited as much as the state. Moreover, constant share in public affairs gave the Athenians experience and training which sharpened their wits and made them self-sufficient.

The Meaning of Athenian Citizenship: Privileges. While the Athenian citizens had many duties, they also enjoyed many privileges. All citizens were permitted to sit in the Assembly. Any citizen could obtain a state office. Justice was assured because the citizens themselves were the jurors. The state also provided public entertainments, — as "relaxations from toil," said Pericles. Every spring, at the ancient Feast of Dionysus, the greatest play-writers submitted dramas to be played in the theater for a prize given by the state. All Athens streamed to the theater to see them, and poor citizens were given free tickets. Many other state festivals, celebrated with music and gayety, filled the year with holidays so numerous that one fell every six or seven days.

Every man of Athens shared in both the duties and the privileges of citizenship. Perhaps no other people have enjoyed such a degree of freedom and equality as did the Athenians. Pericles admirably summed up the situation in the following phrases: "It is true that we are called a democracy, for the administration is in the hands of the many and not of the few. But while the law secures equal justice to all alike in their private disputes, the claim of excellence is also recognized; and when a citizen is in any way distinguished, he is preferred for the public service, not as a matter of privilege but as a reward of merit. Neither is poverty a bar, but a man may benefit his country whatever be the obscurity of his condition."

3. THE COALITION AGAINST ATHENS AND THE PELOPONNESIAN WARS

Superior Wealth and Power of Athens. The new Athens of which Pericles had become the head was rapidly becoming the leader of the Greek world. In this leadership, business and money were coming to play a very large part.[1] A period of business prosperity followed the Persian Wars. The population of Attica rose to probably over two hundred thousand, of whom over half lived at Athens. The state needed far more money than formerly. It required a hundred thousand dollars a year to pay the salaries of the jurymen and officials (p. 158). Large sums were needed for the new temples of marble; but the greatest expense was for war. The war fleet required nearly a hundred and twenty thousand dollars a month for the wages of the sailors alone. The task of securing enough money to run the government was a serious one.

The yearly income of the Athenian state at this time hardly reached three quarters of a million dollars. Small as this seems to us in modern times, no other Greek state could raise anything like so large an amount. Sparta, clinging to her old-fashioned ways, without manufactures or trade and using only her old-time *iron* money, could not compete in wealth with Athens. This was very important, for Sparta could not

[1] A fuller statement of the growing importance of business and finance in the life of the Greek states will be found in Breasted's *Ancient Times*, §§ 569–577.

Fig. 42. *The So-called Temple of Theseus (foreground at left) and the Acropolis of Athens*

afford to keep her full army in the field more than a few weeks at a time because of the expense. In so far as war was a matter of money, the business prosperity of Athens was giving her a growing superiority over all the other Greek states.

Growing Hostility to Athens. Pericles had won favor by advising a policy of hostility to Sparta. Athens now began to increase the feeling of distrust toward herself by making alliances on the mainland. She established an understanding with Argos; and when she secured Megara as an ally, she brought upon herself the hatred of Corinth, who had hoped to annex portions of her neighbor's territory. An Athenian alliance with Thessaly caused Sparta to turn to Thebes and the Bœotians. The commercial success of the small island of Ægina had aroused the jealousy of Athenian merchants; and when Ægina placed itself under the protection of Sparta, Athens landed troops on the island and laid siege to the city by land and sea. Moreover, Pericles used the Athenian navy for years in blockading the merchant fleets of Corinth, and this brought financial ruin on its merchants.

This activity on the part of Athens aroused a general fear that the Athenians wished to build up a land empire in addition to their supremacy in the Ægean.

The First Peloponnesian War (459–446 B.C.). Not long after Pericles became leader, war with Sparta broke out. It lasted nearly fifteen years, until both sides were exhausted. When peace was made, all that Athens was able to hold was Ægina. It was agreed that peace should be observed for thirty years. This was the first of what are called the Peloponnesian Wars. Pericles had shown that he was neither a great military nor a great naval commander.

The Second Peloponnesian War (431–421 B.C.). The peace was badly kept. Not only Sparta but Corinth was at enmity with Athens because she had given aid to one of Corinth's revolting colonies and had also endeavored to seize the trade of Corinth in the west. Indeed, it seemed as if all Greece had united against Athens. Sparta controlled the

Greece at the Beginning of the Second Peloponnesian War

entire Peloponnesus except Argos. Though Athens began the struggle with a large war fund and a fine fleet, she could not hope to defeat the united land forces arrayed against her. Pericles planned to throw all the resources of Athens into naval enterprises and make no effort to defend Attica by land. When the Peloponnesian army entered Attica, the country people were directed by Pericles to leave their homes and take refuge in the open markets and squares of Athens, in the temples, and especially between the fortified walls (called the Long Walls) which had been built to connect Athens with the Piræus. Here they were safe behind the strong defenses of Athens and her seaport. While the Spartan army was spreading ruin throughout Attica, all that Athens could do was either to make sea raids and inflict as much damage as possible along the coasts of the Peloponnesus or to blockade and destroy Corinthian commerce.

The masses of people crowded within the walls of Athens had none of the ordinary comforts of life, so that many of them fell ill, and a plague, brought in from the Orient, raged during several seasons. Probably a third of the population died from it, and from this unforeseen disaster Athens never recovered. Constantly under arms for the defense of the walls, deprived of any opportunity to strike the enemy, the Athenian citizens finally revolted against Pericles and his policies. Pericles was removed from office and emissaries were sent to sue for peace. The peace negotiations were, however, unsuccessful.

The empire was in a sad plight. There were no leaders who could win the respect of the people or save the state from disaster. The war dragged on until 421 B.C., when a peace was arranged by Nicias, an Athenian leader. The peace was to last fifty years, but it was not faithfully kept by either side, and war between Sparta and Athens continued off and on for nearly twenty years longer.

Alcibiades and the Expedition to Syracuse. After the peace of Nicias, Athens needed more than ever the guidance of a statesman like Pericles. Instead, she was obliged to depend for leadership upon the uncertain Nicias and a reckless, self-seeking young Athenian named Alcibiades, a relative of Pericles. Alcibiades might have become the savior of Athens and Greece. As it happened, he was more largely responsible than anyone else for the destruction of the Athenian Empire and the downfall of Greece. He did all he could to excite the war party in Athens to renew the war. He was elected strategus and finally persuaded the Athenians to send a joint expedition of army and navy to Sicily, especially against the mighty city of Syracuse, which had been founded as a colony of Corinth. Just as the fleet was about to sail, certain sacred images in Athens were found to have been mysteriously defaced, and Alcibiades was blamed for this. When Alcibiades was recalled to Athens for trial, he deserted to the Spartans, and greatly aided them with his advice. Nicias, who was now left in sole command of the Sicilian expedition, was so incompetent that after he had maneuvered the

Athenian ships into the harbor at Syracuse, he permitted the Syracusans to blockade the channel to the sea and thus bottle up the Athenian fleet. When the desperate Athenian army attempted to escape into the interior of the island of Sicily, they were overtaken and forced to surrender. The commanding officers were executed, and the other Athenians were either sold into slavery or thrown into the stone quarries of the city.

The Fall of the Athenian Empire. After these disasters the Athenian Empire began to show signs of breaking up. In spite of some success at sea, Athens now suffered more than ever before for lack of competent commanders. As a result, the final disaster could not be long averted. The Attic fleet of a hundred and eighty triremes, as it lay drawn up on the beach in the Hellespont, was surprised by the able Spartan commander Lysander and captured almost intact. The entrance to the Black Sea, whence came the grain to feed Athens, was now in the hands of the enemy.

Not a man slept on the night when the terrible news of final ruin reached Athens. It was soon confirmed by the appearance of Lysander's fleet blockading the Piræus. Starvation finally forced the stubborn democratic leaders to submit, and the city surrendered. The Long Walls and the harbor fortifications were torn down, the remnant of the fleet was handed over to Sparta, all foreign possessions were given up, and Athens was forced to enter the Spartan League.

4. THE FINAL CONFLICTS AMONG THE GREEK STATES

Spartan Rule and the King's Peace. With the overthrow of the Athenian Empire, Sparta assumed the leadership of the Greek world. The Greek cities were not long in perceiving that the rule of the victorious Spartans was to be much more offensive than the old tyranny of Athens. Sparta's policy was to rule by force. Garrisons of soldiers commanded by Spartan officers were stationed in many of the Greek towns. The government was placed in the hands of a small group of men from the noble, or upper, class. With the soldiers to support them, these men could run things as they chose. The rulership of a small group is called an *oligarchy*, a Greek term meaning "rule of a few." The oligarchs in many cases were guilty of great cruelty, killing their political opponents or driving them from the cities and taking their property for themselves.

The rule of Sparta finally caused such dissatisfaction that the Greeks, led by Athens, formed a league against Sparta. Behind this combination was Persia, whose agents had brought it about in order to weaken Sparta. The success of the Athenians, however, led the Persians at length to fear lest Athens should again be strong enough to endanger Persian control in Asia Minor. So the Spartans were able to make peace with Persia and even won back the Greek states opposed to them. When peace was at last established in Greece, it was under the humiliating conditions of a treaty accepted by the Greeks at the hands of a Persian king. It is known as the King's Peace (387 B.C.). It did not end the leadership of Sparta over the Greek states, and the Greek cities of Asia Minor were shamefully abandoned to Persia.

Anti-Spartan Alliance; the Peace Conference of 371 B.C. Sparta was finally more hated than Athens had ever been. At Thebes a group of fearless and patriotic citizens succeeded in slaying the oligarchs. The Spartan garrison at Thebes surrendered, and a democracy was set up which gained the leadership of all Bœotia. Athens and Thebes then led another alliance against Sparta. The Spartans met disaster on land; and when this was followed by the defeat of their fleet by Athens they were ready for peace.

To arrange this peace all the Greek states met at Sparta. By giving every state equal rights, Sparta might still have finally united the Greeks into a great nation. But this she would not do. When the conditions of peace were being decided upon, Sparta refused to allow Thebes to speak for all Bœotia, although she herself demanded the right to act for her own allies. The Thebans rejected these unequal terms, and the treaty was made without them. This left Sparta and Thebes still in a state of war.

Epaminondas and the Leadership of Thebes. All Greece now expected to see the Thebans crushed by the heavy Spartan phalanx, which had so long proved irresistible. But owing to the military skill of the Theban commander, a gifted and patriotic citizen named Epaminondas, the Thebans were victorious in the decisive conflict which took place at Leuctra, in southern Bœotia. Over half of the Spartan forces were slain, and with them their king. The long-invincible Spartan army was at last defeated. After more than thirty years of leadership Spartan power was ended.

A third Greek state was now victorious on land, and it remained to be seen whether Thebes could accomplish what Athens and Sparta had failed in doing, — create a Greek nation. But Theban supremacy was based upon the genius of a single man; and when Epaminondas fell in a final battle with Sparta at Mantinea (362 B.C.), the power of Thebes collapsed. Thus the only Greek states which might have developed a federation of the Hellenic world had crushed each other, and Hellas was ready to fall before any conqueror from the outside. The Greek world, whose civilization was everywhere supreme, had failed to create a strong government for itself.

5. GREEK POLITICAL PROBLEMS BECOME WORLD PROBLEMS

Greek Political Problems at the Beginning of the Fourth Century B.C. The political collapse of Greece was due *first* to the inability of the Greek city-states to lay aside their local prejudices and form a strong protective alliance, and *second* to the interference of the Persians. For the hundred years after the Persian Wars the Greeks never ceased to think about and discuss the advantages or disadvantages of federation. They had learned of the advantages of union when, under the leadership of Sparta, they had been able to thrust back the invasions of Darius and Xerxes. They had learned of the disadvantages of union from the action of the Delian League, and from the Spartan rule after the Peloponnesian Wars. When the leadership passed to Thebes, that city soon found itself surrounded by enemies. Although the Greeks saw the desirability of federation, no Greek state was willing to submit to the rule of another. The result was a mad scramble among the states for Persian financial support, in order to attack any Greek city which seemed to be gaining power.

The conflicts among the Greek states had become so frequent by the end of the Peloponnesian Wars that the Persians realized that long, difficult, and expensive expeditions such as those of Darius and Xerxes were no longer necessary. The amount of Persian gold needed to finance the campaign of one Greek state against another was very small compared with the cost of a great Persian invasion of Europe. Until the fall of the Persian Empire, therefore, the Persians continuously fought the Greeks with Persian gold *darics* and not with armies. This was much easier for them because the Persian Empire in its efforts to hold its distant provinces had weakened its army until it had finally come to be made up largely of hired soldiers (mercenaries), who were chiefly Greeks.

Greeks in Persia; the March of the Ten Thousand. As a result of the political failures of the Greeks, men had become more interested in their own careers and were no longer devoted to the state. This was especially true in the matter of military service. The Peloponnesian Wars had kept large numbers of Greeks so long in the army that many of them remained in military life and became *professional* soldiers. The Greek youths who could find no opportunities to make a living at home therefore enlisted as soldiers in Egypt, in Asia Minor, and in Persia, and the best young blood of Greece was being spent to strengthen foreign states instead of to build up the power of the Greeks.

When, in 401 B.C., Cyrus "the Younger" determined to become king of Persia in place of his brother Artaxerxes, who held the throne, he took with him a body of Greek troops on his expedition. Cyrus was killed, and his Asiatic forces fled from the field; but the Greeks were able to defeat the great army of the Persian monarch. The Greeks now found themselves without a leader in a foreign country surrounded by enemies. Courageously they chose new generals, one of whom was Xenophon, an adventurous young Athenian, and began the long retreat homeward. The little army of ten thousand endured every kind of hardship on their weary march. Though they lost many of their original number, they reached home at last after a journey of a thousand miles. The story of this famous retreat is told by Xenophon in the *Anabasis*, one of the great books that have come down to us from ancient times.

Growth of a Grecized World. Boundary lines cannot separate nations; their life overlaps and interfuses with the life round about them. It was so within Greece, and it was so far beyond the borders of Greek territory. There had grown up a *civilized world* which was reading Greek books, fitting up its houses with Greek furniture and decorating them with Greek paintings, building Greek theaters, learning Greek tactics in war, — a great Mediterranean and Oriental world bound together by lines of commerce, travel, and common business interests. To this world, once dominated by Oriental culture, the Greeks had given the noblest ideas yet attained by the mind of civilized man, and to this world likewise the Greeks might have given political leadership. The Greeks were now, however, to be subjected to a foreign people. The Greek city-states were to be engulfed in a larger world-state, but Greek genius was to go on to many future triumphs.

Questions and Exercises

REVIEW OF CHAPTER

1. What services did Themistocles render in the establishment of Athenian supremacy? What combination did Athens make with the Greek cities of Asia and the Ægean Islands? How did Athens treat her allies in the Delian League?

2. What new victories did the people gain after the ostracism of Cimon? How was it made possible for poor Athenians to serve the state? How could a statesman gain the leadership in Athens?

3. What were the chief expenses of the Athenian state? What were Sparta's exact feelings toward Athens?

4. Was Spartan leadership of the Greeks successful? What were the final results of the peace of 371 B.C.?

5. What were the two great political problems of the Greeks in the fourth century B.C.?

Useful Terms

See how much meaning you can give to the following: *progress, league, treason, people's party, allies, conservative party, citizenship, equality, demagogue, federation.*

Directive Questions

1. Do you agree with the following estimate of Themistocles given by Thucydides, the Greek historian? "Themistocles gave the strongest proof of force of genius. . . . He was an admirable judge of an emergency on a moment's consideration, and could forecast with rare insight the most distant future." Give your reasons.

2. Why might the wealthy Athenian have been more willing to make gifts to the Athenian state than the wealthy American is to pay an income tax?

3. Compare the peace conference of 371 B.C. with modern peace conferences.

4. What problems connected with federation have been met by modern states?

Discussion Topics

1. The Athenian fleet policed the Ægean Sea and made it safe for Greek trade; therefore the Athenian allies gained rather than suffered from association with Athens.

2. The payment of citizens for service on the jury and in the state offices was the strongest influence for democracy in the Athenian state.

3. The wars among the Greek states were for the most part commercial wars.

4. In the first part of the fourth century B.C. Greek greed outweighed Greek patriotism.

5. Could the Greeks have used the inscription *E pluribus unum*?

Additional Adventures in Learning

1. **Studies in Source Materials.** THALLON, *Readings in Greek History*: (1) Relations between Athens and the allies, pp. 250–253; (2) Cimon, pp. 255–263; (3) Pericles, pp. 268–270, 293–294; (4) The Funeral Oration, pp. 294–302; (5) Peace of Nicias, pp. 357–363.

2. Look up in an encyclopedia: *democracy, Piræus, Sparta, Pericles, treaties, Triple Alliance, plague, oligarchy, Xenophon.*

CHAPTER VIII · GREEK LIFE

THE HELLENES · ATHENS AND THE ATHENIANS · GREEK HOME LIFE · THE TRAINING OF
THE YOUNG CITIZEN AT ATHENS · THE ATHENIAN WAY OF LIVING

THE GREEKS, in spite of rivalry among the city-states, had a certain sense of race unity, which was increased by the possession of a common language and by a common interest in religious affairs and public festivals. Moreover, the Greeks were conscious of a difference between their civilization and that of either the barbarians on the north or the civilized Near Eastern countries on the south and east. The Greeks came, therefore, to call themselves Hellenes, and the group of Greek city-states Hellas. Yet this feeling of unity did not lead to the formation of a great Hellenic federation. Indeed, the Delian League (p. 153) was the most powerful federation of Greek city-states ever established. As leader of the Delian League, Athens gained prestige and riches. By the middle of the fifth century B.C. she had become the " school of Greece," and Greek life and thought were patterned to a large extent after Athenian life and thought. Some contrasts with the civilization of Sparta — which was distinctly unlike all other Greek states — will help to bring out the lights and shadows in this picture of life among the most highly civilized of the Greeks.

1. THE HELLENES

Bonds of Unity among the Greeks. Although the jealousies between the Greek states kept them from uniting to form a single nation, there were certain things which gave the Greek people a sense of kinship. As early as 776 B.C. they began to hold athletic contests at Olympia every year in honor of the gods, and in these games all the Greeks had a chance to take part.[1] Religion also served as a bond between the Greeks, for there were some gods at whose temples all the Greeks worshiped. Committees of representatives from the various city-states met together from time to time for the management of these temples. There were also councils which had charge of the Olympic games, the sanctuary of Apollo at Delphi, and the great annual feast of Apollo on the island of Delos.

[1] The Olympic games have been revived in modern times as an international project.

171

Greek Unity furthered by Language. These representatives spoke various Greek dialects at their meetings. They could understand each other, however, just as a Scot can make himself understood in southern England, or a citizen from Maine understands another from Louisiana, though they may laugh at each other's oddities of speech. Their common language helped to bind together the people of the many different Greek cities. Another bond was the Homeric songs, with which every Greek was familiar, — a common inheritance depicting all the Greeks united against the Asiatic city of Troy.

Barbarians and Hellenes. Thus bound together by ties of custom, religion, language, and common traditions, the Greeks gained a feeling of race unity which set them apart from other races. They called all men not of Greek blood "barbarians," which was not originally a term of reproach for the non-Greeks. Then the Greek sense of unity found expression in the first all-inclusive term for *themselves.* They gradually came to call themselves Hellenes, and found pleasure in the belief that they all descended from a common ancestor called Hellen. But it should be clearly understood that this new name did not represent a Greek *nation,* or state, but only the group of Greek-speaking peoples or states, often at war with one another.

Greek Unity and Trade. The lack of coöperation among the Greek cities was also very noticeable in their business relations. A merchant of one city had no legal rights in another city where he was not a citizen. Even his life was not safe, for there were no laws protecting strangers. He could secure protection only by appealing to the old nomad custom of "hospitality," after he had been received by a friendly citizen as a guest. If a stranger had no such friend to be his host, a city might appoint a citizen to act as its official host. There is in the British Museum, for instance, a bronze tablet bearing a Greek inscription which certifies to the appointment of such a host. A man named Dionysius was supposed to give hospitality and assistance to citizens of Corcyra

Fig. 43. *A Detail from a Model of the Sanctuary of Apollo at Delphi*

This model was made by Hans Schleif for the Hall of Architectural Casts of the Metropolitan Museum of Art. In the center is the temple of Apollo, surrounded by the treasuries of the city-states and the votive offerings of the Greeks to the great god, — the statues and victorious trophies, many of them of gold and silver, presented by states, kings, and individuals. Higher up the slope on the left-hand side is the theater, the only model of a Greek theater made to scale. In studying the model of Delphi it is useful to consult the description of Pausanias, a Greek traveler and writer of the second century of our era, as a guidebook to locate the many objects of interest. Universal reverence for this famous sanctuary failed to protect it, for it was finally plundered by the Romans. Although the Roman emperor Nero (A.D. 54–68) removed five hundred statues, there were still three thousand left when Pliny (p. 346) visited Delphi some years later. (Courtesy of the Metropolitan Museum of Art)

(modern Corfu) when they were in Athens. He was expected, furthermore, to receive any ambassadors sent to Athens from Corcyra and to give some attention to the commercial interests of Corcyra in Athens. In return he was granted the right to possess land and house property in Corcyra. The Greek official host (*proxenos*) thus corresponded to the *consul* of modern nations. These arrangements show clearly how strong was the *local* prejudice of each Greek city. The most fatal defect in Greek character was the inability of the various states to forget their local differences and jealousies and to unite into a common federation or great nation including all Greeks.[1]

2. ATHENS AND THE ATHENIANS

Great Importance of Athens. As we have seen (pp. 153 f.), the strongest federation of Greek states was that formed after the Persian Wars (480 B.C.) by Athens with the Ionian Greek cities of Asia Minor and the Ægean Islands. Down to the middle of the sixth century B.C. the cities of Asia Minor and the Ægean were leaders among the Greeks in trade and commerce as well as in art, literature, and the different branches of learning. But the Greeks of Asia Minor eventually lost their liberty and became the subjects of Persia. So when Athens assumed the leadership of the Delian League, she seemed at the same time to have assumed the leadership of the Ionian Greeks and to have fallen heir to the position of power and intellectual supremacy which her kindred of Asia Minor had once held.

Solon and Pisistratus had laid the foundations of Athenian prosperity. The laws of Solon had provided Attica with an agricultural policy which developed a strong race of peasants, poor but decidedly happy, and, above all, free. Pisistratus had encouraged the best craftsmen from all Greece to come to Athens. This open door for the foreign skilled laborer was part of the Periclean policy also. As a result, in the fifth century B.C., experts in all the crafts congregated at Athens and helped to make her the business center of the Mediterranean world.

Athens, the School of Greece. Pericles succeeded in making Athens the center of Greek intellectual life, so that it became customary for all men of learning and culture throughout the Mediterranean world to visit Athens at some time in their careers. As Pericles himself said, Athens was "the

---

[1] We may recall here how local and sectional differences long prevented the union of Great Britain and also how slow were the thirteen colonies of America to suppress local pride sufficiently to adopt a constitution uniting all thirteen into a nation. It was local differences similar to those among the Greeks which afterward caused the American Civil War.

school of Greece." The Athens which thus molded the opinions and lives of the other Greeks in the fifth and fourth centuries B.C. is considered by the modern student the foremost city of the Greeks, and the picture of life in the Athens of that period is the fullest and best picture of ancient Greek life obtainable. In the following paragraphs, therefore, we shall be thinking usually of the Athenian Greeks.

The Athenian People. The population of Attica was made up of citizens, resident aliens, and slaves. A large group of wealthy citizens lived in Athens on the income from their lands. They continued to be the aristocracy of the nation, for land was still the most respectable form of wealth. The wealthy manufacturer hastened to buy land and join the landed aristocracy. The social position of his family might thus become an influential one, but it could not compare with that of a noble. On the other hand, anyone who actually performed manual labor was looked down upon as without social station. Athens was a great beehive of skilled craftsmen and small shopkeepers. These classes were beginning to organize into guilds of masons, carpenters, potters, jewelers, and many others, — organizations somewhat like our labor unions. Below them was an army of unskilled laborers, free men but little better than slaves. All these classes contained many citizens. Nevertheless, the majority of the Athenian citizens were still the farmers and peasants throughout Attica, although the Persian invasion had seriously reduced the amount of land cultivated.

The City of Athens. The houses of Athens clustered around the Acropolis (p. 125). In prehistoric times the Athenian Acropolis was the citadel hill, on which stood the castle of the kings. With the disappearance of the kings the royal castle was of course vacated. As it fell into decay the shrines and holy places which it contained were still preserved as religious buildings. After the Persian Wars, Pericles erected the famous temples which now stand in ruins on the Acropolis.

Though not laid out in blocks, the city surrounding the Acropolis was about ten modern city blocks wide and several more in length. The streets were merely lanes or alleys, narrow and crooked, winding between the bare mud-brick walls of the low houses standing wall to wall. There was neither pavement, nor sidewalk, and a stroll through the town after a rain meant wading through the mud. All household rubbish and garbage were thrown directly into the street, and there was no system of sewage. When a person passed a two-story house he might hear a warning cry and spring out of the way barely in time to escape being deluged with sweepings or filth thrown from a second-story window. The few wells and fountains fed by city water pipes did not furnish enough water to flush the streets, and there was no system of street cleaning. During the hot summers of the south, therefore, Athens was not a healthful place in which to live.

Public Improvements in Athens after the Persian Wars. When, after the Persian Wars, the Athenians returned to look over the ashes of what had once been Athens, amid which rose the smoke-blackened heights of the naked Acropolis, their hearts must have been heavy. Nevertheless, they set about to construct a new and greater Athens. First, they fortified the new city by erecting watchtowers on the great city wall, and gates which opened onto all important highways. From each gate a road led inside to the market place, or *agora* (Fig. 41), which was the central point of the life of the city.

The open square in the center of the market place, shaded by plane and poplar trees, was a favorite gathering place of the Athenians. In time elegant colonnaded porches (*stoas*), to which the loungers might withdraw in case of rain or when the sun was too hot, almost entirely surrounded the market.

It was not until Pericles came into power that the restoration of the ancient shrines on the Acropolis (pp. 212–215) was undertaken. It was Pericles also who erected the music hall in which were held the musical contests during the Panathenaic festival (p. 186). This building joined the theater (Fig. 47), at the foot of the Acropolis. The temples, the music hall, and the theater were the only important buildings at Athens until a much later period.

3. Greek Home Life

The Greek Houses. There were few luxurious private houses in Greece. The one-story front of even a wealthy man's house at Athens was simply a blank wall, usually of sun-dried brick, rarely of stone. It had no windows, and the door, the only opening in the front, led into a court open to the sky and surrounded by a porch with columns. Here in the mild climate of Greece the family could spend much of their time as in a sitting-room. In the middle stood an altar of the household Zeus, the protector of the family, while around the court opened a number of doors leading to a living-room, sleeping-rooms, dining-room, storerooms, and also a tiny kitchen.

This Greek house had no conveniences. There was no chimney, and the smoke from the kitchen fire, though intended to drift up through a hole in the roof, choked the room or floated out of the door. In winter gusty drafts filled the house; for many entrances were without doors, and glass in the form of flat panes for the windows was still unknown. In this mild climate, however, a pan of burning charcoal, called a brazier, furnished enough heat to temper the chilly air of a room. The ground-floor rooms depended entirely on the doors opening on the court for light. At night the dim light of an olive-oil lamp was all that the household had. There was no plumbing or piping of any kind in the house, no drainage, and hence no sanitary arrangements. The water supply was brought in jars by slaves from the nearest well or spring.

The floors were simply of earth, with a surface of pebbles tramped and beaten hard. There was no oil paint, but a plain water-color wash, such as we call calcimine, might be used on the inside. If used on the outside, however, it would soon wash off, exposing the mud brick.

The simplicity and bareness of the house itself were in marked contrast with its rich furnishings. These consisted of beautiful furniture made by the skilled Greek craftsmen, as well as metal utensils and lovely pottery — painted jars, vases, and dishes.

The Position of Women. The Athenian women of the better class lived shut up in their houses in almost Oriental seclusion. They had no share in the intellectual life or athletic contests of the men and could not appear at their social meetings. This attitude toward women was not, however, characteristic of all Greeks. The position of women in the age of Homer is represented as being comparatively free and pleasant. In many of the Greek states, indeed, women seem to have had social and intellectual freedom and to have been respected by men throughout the whole period of high Greek civilization. In the seventh and sixth centuries B.C. some Greek women were evidently given an education equal to that of the men. Of the several successful poetesses of this period the most famous was Sappho. In Sparta the girls, until they were married, were always given athletic training similar to that given the boys. After marriage the men lived in barracks, but the women lived at home, free from care and in comparative luxury. As the husbands were away most of the time and the boys were taken from them at seven years of age, the women had a great deal of leisure. They used this leisure wisely, and were, as a whole, much more intellectual than the Spartan men. They had, moreover, in time acquired by inheritance or dowry a great part of the Spartan land.

The Greek attitude toward women grew steadily more liberal throughout the fourth century B.C., until the free-moving, free-thinking wives of the Macedonians put an end to any old ideas of woman's inferiority. Finally Greek girls were admitted to private schools, and Greek women even produced works of literature or made investigations in the field of science.

The Athenian Home. In all Greece there was no home life such as we know. There was, however, family loyalty, and a recognition of the obligations involved in family relationships. The Athenian home was particularly the province of the women. The Athenian men used their homes only for sleeping and eating. Household slaves cared for and disciplined the Athenian boy under the direction of his mother.

In his earliest years there was the nurse who spoiled him outrageously, and then frightened him with bugaboos or paddled him with a slipper to make him obey. When he grew older and started for school, the boy was placed in charge of a man slave called a pedagogue (*paidagogos*), which really means "leader of a child." The pedagogue accompanied him everywhere he went, and was supposed to supervise his conduct and give him lessons in deportment. The Athenian youth slept on soft cushions, ate three meals a day, played ball and blind man's buff, or harnessed the pet goat to a cart. In time he might go to a private school and learn to play the flute, recite Homer, or throw the discus; but all these things he learned as an individual, not as one of a group.

The Spartan Camp. The conditions under which the Spartan boy grew up were very different. He was taken from his mother and his home at seven years and placed with other boys of his age in groups, or "herds" as they were called. Officers were appointed to train them, and to these officers the boys had to give unquestioned obedience. If the Spartan boy did not obey, he was brutally punished. Often he had to steal his food, in order that he might be able to forage for food in time of war. He slept on the ground, he wore no shoes, he bathed in the river winter and summer. He sang choruses, danced war dances, and took part in public whipping contests, — always in company with other lads.

Contrast between Athens and Sparta. The Spartan system of education was devised by the *state* in order to prepare the youth for service to the *state*. In Athens *each Athenian father* gave his boy the training which he as a father felt was necessary, or which the boy as an *individual* seemed to demand. In short, the Spartan system emphasized the group and resulted in what the educators of today call "regimentation." The training at Athens emphasized the individual.

4. THE TRAINING OF THE YOUNG CITIZEN AT ATHENS

School-teachers. The Athenian children were under the care of the mother and a nurse until they were about seven or eight years old. At that time the boy was usually started in school, and the girl retired to the seclusion of the women's quarters to learn housekeeping. There are Greek reliefs, statuettes, and vase paintings, however, which show little girls carrying wax tablets, or sitting with tablets spread out and a stylus in the hand ready for writing. Perhaps some Athenian girls therefore did receive instruction in reading and writing. As school began at sunrise, the boy was started off soon after daybreak. There are interesting statuettes and paintings showing the departing youngster accompanied by his pedagogue, who carries the boy's books, flute or lyre, and writing tablet. In certain other charming statuettes the old slave appears with his charge on his shoulder and a lantern in his hand; these may represent the pedagogue's return from school with the weary boy, for the school day did not end till sundown. There were no schools maintained by the state, and no schoolhouses. Usually some poor citizen, perhaps an old soldier or even a foreigner, conducted school in his own house.

The Lessons of Greek Boys. The teachers were much looked down upon. They received their pay from the parents, but there was a board of state officials appointed to look after the schools and to see that nothing improper was taught. With no special education for his work, the teacher merely taught without change the old-time subjects he had learned in his own youth. Proficiency in music was regarded very seriously by the Greeks, not merely for entertainment but chiefly as an influence toward good conduct. Besides learning to read and write, as of old, the pupil learned by heart many passages from the poets, and here and there a boy with a good memory could repeat the entire Iliad and Odyssey. A few simple problems in arithmetic were solved with the aid of a counting board; for the Greek system of writing numbers was clumsier even than the Roman, which we, being accustomed to Arabic (really Hindu) numerals, find most inconvenient.

At intervals during the day the boys were taken by their pedagogues to the wrestling school (*palæstra*), which was owned or rented by the schoolmaster. The palæstra was often little better equipped than grade-school playgrounds and gymnasiums in small towns today and served pretty much the same purpose. Here the boys probably played games, were given certain gymnastic exercises, were taught wrestling as a sort of drill, and perhaps mastered the movements used in throwing the discus or the javelin. The training in the palæstra simply prepared the boys for later work in the athletic field, or gymnasium.

Attainment of Citizenship. When the Athenian lad reached the age of eighteen years and left school, he became a citizen, provided that both his parents were of Athenian citizenship. The oath which he took was a solemn reminder of the obligations he now assumed. It had been composed by Solon, and it called upon the youth "never to disgrace his sacred arms; never to forsake his comrade in the ranks, but to fight for the sacred temples and the common welfare, whether alone or with others; to leave his country not in a worse but in a better state than he found it; to obey the magistrates and the laws and to defend them against attack; finally, to hold in honor the religion of his country."

The youth then spent a year in garrison duty at the harbor of Piræus, where he was put through military drill. Then at nineteen the young recruits received spear and shield, given to each by the state. Thereupon they marched to the theater and entered the orchestra circle, where they were presented to the citizens of Athens assembled in the theater before the play. Another year of garrison service on the frontier of Attica usually completed the young man's military service, although some of the recruits, whose means permitted, joined the small body of select Athenian cavalry.

Athletics in Greek Life. On the completion of his military service, if the wealth and station of his family permitted, the Athenian youth spent a great deal of his time on the athletic fields in the beautiful open country outside of

FIG. 44. *The Discus-Thrower*

A copy (in the Vatican) of a statue by the Greek sculptor Myron, who lived in the time of Pericles

the city walls. On the north of Athens, outside the Dipylon Gate, was the field known as the Academy. It had been adorned with olive groves; and its shady walks and seats for loungers made it a place where the Athenians loved to spend their idle hours. On the east of the city there was a similar athletic ground known as the Lyceum. The later custom of holding courses of instructive lectures in these places finally resulted in giving to the words "academy" and "lyceum" the meanings which they now have.

The chief athletic events were boxing, wrestling, running, jumping, casting the javelin, and throwing the discus. These events, with the exception of boxing, formed a fivefold match called the *pentathlon*, which it was a great honor to win at Olympia. The earliest contest established at Olympia seems to have been a two-hundred-yard dash, which the Greeks called a *stadion*, that is, six hundred Greek feet. Many other contests were added to this, and in the Age of Pericles boxing, or boxing and wrestling combined, the pentathlon, chariot racing, and horseback races made up a program in which all Greek youths were anxious to gain distinction. A generation later some of the philosophers severely criticized the Greeks for giving so much time and attention to athletic pursuits.

5. The Athenian Way of Living

Daily Life of the Athenian Citizen. All Athens lived out of doors. For most Athenian *citizens* the daily routine consisted partly in devoting oneself to affairs of state, such as service in the Council, the Assembly, and the jury, and partly in merely lounging or chatting. As the Athenian democracy developed, the citizens were engaged less and less in trade, and they had thus more leisure for discussion and recreation. Every Athenian spent some part of each day in the market place. Here were located certain government buildings and all the retail shops. In the northern section, which was given over to the tradespeople, the merchants set out their wares on tables protected by awnings. Many of the commodities displayed had been bought from the importers at the great merchandise market in the Piræus.

In the morning the Athenians did their shopping and attended to their business — if they had any; but the afternoons were likely to be spent in social chatter, discussion of politics, or philosophical speculation. As the Roman writers so often and disgustedly observed, the Greeks were always talking and arguing. Some citizens would gather in the center of the market place, under the trees, or sit around on the colonnaded porches. Others would wander through the beautiful public gardens surrounding the athletic fields on the outskirts of the city. Many a group of argumentative Greeks was also to be found on the stone benches of some palæstra.

As the afternoon drew to a close, preparations for the evening banquet might be made at the public baths. The correct costume consisted of the keton (p. 127), with a cloak above. Much stress was laid on the proper adjustment of clothing, and gentlemen were supposed to be able to arrange the folds with elegant carelessness. After the bath, visits to the perfumery shops and barber shops were usual; for here one not only could get personal service but might also hear the latest news. Just before sundown those men who had secured invitations to dinner made their way to the homes of their hosts; those who had nowhere else to dine went to their own homes.

Great Importance of Banquets. The only way in which the
Athenian gentleman could amuse himself in the evening was
to give a dinner or to attend a dinner. These dinners varied
from simple, pleasant gatherings, where serious-minded men
engaged in delightful conversation on such subjects as art,
literature, music, or personal conduct, to elaborate banquets
where hired entertainers performed for the amusement of
the guests. Among the entertainers were musicians, clowns,
tumblers, acrobats, dancers, jugglers, and marionette play-
ers. But the entertainment and conversation were a part of
the so-called "symposium," and before the symposium came
the meal.

The food was served in beautiful, painted pottery dishes,
which were as thin and light as our finest china. The dipper,
the pitcher, the lamp, and the vinegar cruet might be made
of highly polished bronzed ware. The guests reclined on
couches overlaid with silver or gold, while the parts of wood
were inlaid with ivory, precious metals, or tortoise shell.
Before the couches were tables laden with food. There was
no soup, and the food was already cut in pieces ready to eat,
for there were as yet no forks or spoons. When the guests
finished, they wiped their fingers on bits of bread, and afterwards tossed the soiled crumbs to the dogs squatting anxiously on the floor. Among these highly civilized Greeks
some of our necessities of life were not so necessary. For the
symposium the large tables were replaced by small tables
which held dried fruits and nuts. Wine was served, and the
rest of the evening was given over to amusement and recreation. Many essential elements in our civilization arose in
connection with the banquet, and the word "symposium"
has been taken over into our language and come to refer to
certain round-table discussions or to collections of published
articles on special subjects.

Various Forms of Amusement. There was no limit to the
number of banquets which one might attend, but it was
possible to have plays in the theater, musical competitions,
and national sports events only at certain periods. Such
institutions were connected with religion. In Athens, for

© British Museum

FIG. 45. *Parts of the Parthenon Frieze of Phidias, Showing Scenes from the Panathenaic Festival*

The relief above shows two young men riding in the great procession. This procession and the other festivities of the day are probably being discussed by the group of citizens who, leaning on their staves, stand at ease in the scene below

instance, drama was produced once a year at the Festival of Dionysus. Many activities and competitions were associated with the great state feast, called the *Panathenæa*, which occurred every four years. A brilliant procession, made up of the smart young Athenian cavalry, groups of dignified government officials, priests, and sacrificial animals, marched with music and rejoicing across the market place, carrying a beautiful new robe embroidered by the women of Athens for the goddess Athena. The procession marched to the Acropolis, where the robe was delivered to the goddess amid splendid sacrifices and impressive ceremonies. Contests in music and in athletic games, war dances, and a regatta in the channel off Salamis served to furnish entertainment for the multitude which flocked to Athens for the great feast. In this celebration every Athenian, rich or poor, citizen or resident alien, might participate.

Resident Aliens. By the end of the fifth century B.C. the foreign craftsmen and merchants, who had been encouraged to come to Athens by the great political leaders, had become a very important part of Athenian society. Some of the greatest sculptors, vase-painters, and metal-workers in Athens were not citizens but resident aliens. After the Peloponnesian Wars, Athenian money was almost entirely in the hands of these foreigners. The real estate was, of course, still held only by Athenian citizens, and the resident aliens were rarely admitted to citizenship. The contribution to the cultural life of Athens made by these resident aliens was beyond measure. The philosopher Aristotle, the painter Zeuxis, the historian Herodotus, the speech-writer Lysias — all were born outside of Athens.

Business in Athens. Merchants from all the known world came to sell their goods at Athens and to buy those made in her factories. These factories were usually only small shops in which the owner and a few employees — or, more likely, slaves — worked. They plied their craft in the open or in open-front shops; thus all who passed could watch them. Certain sections or streets were set aside for the use of potters, tanners, or box-makers. All wholesale business was done in the Piræus, and the market place at Athens was given over to the retail merchants, who displayed their wares in open booths and called to those who passed to buy. Here the Athenians could find all the necessities and luxuries of life for sale. Among these booths and stalls were also the tables of the money-changers and money-lenders. Called upon to carry on an increasingly large number of money transactions, they finally developed a function very similar to that of the modern bank, receiving money on deposit to be loaned out at interest for business purposes. Athens thus became not only the greatest city and the leading business center in the Mediterranean world but also the financial center of the ancient world, as New York and London are the financial centers of the modern world, and her bankers were the wealthiest men of the time. This was the Athens that remained great even though she lost political power at the end of the Peloponnesian Wars.

Questions and Exercises

REVIEW OF CHAPTER

1. Discuss athletic games as an influence toward unity. How did language favor Greek unity? What was the attitude of Greek cities toward Greeks who were not their own citizens?

2. In what ways was Periclean Athens superior to the other Greek cities? What three classes, divided according to legal status, were found in Attica in the Periclean Age? Which of these classes contributed most to Athenian economic supremacy?

3. Describe the Athenian house. Contrast the position of women in Sparta and Athens. Describe the Spartan training.

4. Describe the usual Athenian school and its teacher. What oath of citizenship did an Athenian boy take? Tell about his military service; his athletic training. What was the Academy? the Lyceum? What were the chief events in Greek athletics?

5. Write a paragraph describing a morning in the market place at Athens.

USEFUL TERMS

See how much meaning you can give to the following: *unity, dialect, representative government, resident aliens, agora, lyceum.*

Directive Questions

1. Resident aliens had almost a monopoly of Athenian crafts. What would be the result of such a situation in a modern state?

2. What common bonds united the Greeks? What divided them?

3. The Greek system of numerical notation was alphabetic. Show how this was true also of the Roman system.

4. How is the intellectual character of the Greek symposium further evidenced by the present-day use of the word?

Discussion Topics

1. The modern Olympic games have had an influence on world peace.

2. Was the absence of garbage-collectors, street-sweepers, and street lamps in Athens due to the policy of the Athenian state of doing nothing for the citizens which the citizens could do for themselves?

3. Compare the standard of living in ancient Athens with our own standards.

4. Does modern citizenship mean as much as did citizenship in a Greek city-state?

5. The life of the resident alien of Athens was more interesting than the life of the Athenian citizen.

Additional Adventures in Learning

1. Studies in Source Materials. Botsford, *Source-book*: (1) The Greek wife, pp. 283–288; (2) Education, pp. 231–233, 294–295; (3) A young man of Athens, pp. 223–227.

2. Supplementary. Compare American athletics with fifth-century Athenian athletics. British Museum, *Greek and Roman Life*, pp. 55–60; Gardiner, *Athletics of the Ancient World*, pp. 90–93, 99–103; Rostovtzeff, *Out of the Past of Greece and Rome*, pp. 33–44. Gulick, *Modern Traits*, p. 43, says, "Civilization has tended to postpone the chief meal of the day from an earlier to a later hour," and shows how this was true in Athens. Has it been true in the United States?

3. Look up in an encyclopedia: *Olympic games, Amphictyonic Council, Hellenes, Delphi, slavery, Delos, wax, stadium, Sappho, Lysias.*

CHAPTER IX · THE BOOKS
WHICH THE GREEKS HAVE LEFT US

GREEK INTELLECTUAL LIFE AND GREEK LITERATURE BEFORE THE SIXTH CENTURY
B.C. · THE BEGINNINGS OF SCIENCE · GREEK LYRIC POETRY AND DRAMA · HIGHER
EDUCATION AND SCIENCE IN FIFTH-CENTURY GREECE · HOW THE GREEKS DISCUSSED
OLD IDEAS AND NEW · CELEBRATED GREEK ORATORS AND HISTORIANS: PLATO

THE highest achievements of the Greeks were in art, — architecture, sculpture, and painting, — in literature, and in original thought in philosophy, science, and politics. In the present chapter we shall trace the progress of new ideas in philosophy and science as set forth in Greek writings; and we shall, furthermore, investigate the style and contents of Greek literature, which was the first literature of the West. If we should read the writings of Greek thinkers and teachers and compare them with the writings of modern thinkers and teachers, we should find that much of the progressive thought in philosophy and science during the last two centuries seems to continue ways of thinking discovered by the ancient Greeks. In literature the Greeks invented drama and many forms of poetry which we still use, and they developed a prose style which has been studied as a model down through the centuries.

1. GREEK INTELLECTUAL LIFE AND GREEK LITERATURE
BEFORE THE SIXTH CENTURY B.C.

The Written Documents of the Greeks. Much of our knowledge of the life and ideas of ancient peoples has come down to us in their writings. These may be state archives, business papers, inscriptions, personal records, chronicles, or various kinds of literary works. As early as the eighth century B.C. a few Greek city-states had developed their governments to such an extent that there was a need for written records. From this period there remain lists of city-state magistrates and of the victors at Olympia. During the next three centuries the recording of governmental business affairs was considered by the Greeks more and more necessary. By the fourth century B.C. some Greek states required even the registration of private deeds of sale. All these records were engraved on stone, bronze, wood, or lead, or written on papyrus or even scratched on potsherds.[1] Such records add much to our knowledge of Greek thought and custom; but in order that the richness and fullness of the Greek genius may be shown to us, we must consider especially those Greek writings which may strictly be called *literature*.

Early Greek Literature in Verse. For several centuries after the Greeks began to write, prose was used only for records of business and government. This seems strange to us, for the reading public of today is interested principally in prose. Until the fifth century B.C. there were in Greece, however, only a few men who *could* read; hence there was no reading public in earliest Greece. There was, on the other hand, a listening public, and the commonest form of literature was recited in poetry, such as the hero songs (p. 129). In this early period, therefore, there were poems dealing not only with romantic subjects but also with every phase of Greek life. But most of this poetry has disappeared; only some long poems, a few short ones, and a collection of fragments remain. In this limited material we can follow to some extent the development of Greek thought and spirit while Hellas was yet young.

Hesiod: Earliest Cry for Social Justice in Europe (750–700 B.C.). We learn, among other things, that about the middle of the eighth century B.C. the Greeks began to be interested in the life of their own time. The old Homeric singers (p. 129) never referred to themselves; they never spoke of their *own* lives; they described the valiant deeds of their heroes, who had died long before. Now men heard the first voice raised in Europe on behalf of the poor and the humble. Hesiod, an obscure farmer under the shadow of Mount Helicon, in Bœotia, described the oppression of the weak by the strong, and the dreary and hopeless life of the peasant. All this he put in a poem which we call *Works and Days*; for in it the poet points out the reward of unceasing

---

[1] The fragments of broken pots were like bits of a modern flower pot on which one could scratch a few words with any hard substance. There were no convenient bits of paper in those days.

work, and gives a list of *days* that are lucky or unlucky for certain undertakings. The period in which Hesiod lives, he says, is an age of hard work and hard-heartedness.

Interest in Human Conduct: the Fables. The Greeks were thus beginning to think about human conduct. The old Greek word for virtue no longer meant merely valor in war but also kindly and unselfish conduct toward others. Men told their children quaint fables, representing animals acting like human creatures, and by means of these tales with a moral made it clear what a man ought or ought not to do.

Of all the inventors of fables the most famous was Æsop, who is supposed to have lived somewhere around the year 600 B.C. The stories of "sour grapes," of the fox who lost his tail, of the dog in the manger, of the tortoise who caught up with the hare, of the greedy dog who lost his bone, and many other familiar moral tales are to be found in Æsop's *Fables.*

Growing Sense of Right and Wrong. By the middle of the seventh century the Greeks were much interested in the distinction between right and wrong. Men could no longer believe that the gods led the evil lives pictured in the Homeric songs. Hades became a place of torment for the wicked, guarded by Cerberus, a monstrous dog. Likewise it was believed that there must be a place of blessedness in the next world for the good. Accordingly, in the temple of Eleusis, west of Athens, scenes from the mysterious earth life of Demeter and Dionysus, to whom men owed the fruits of the earth, were presented by the priests in dramatic form before the initiated, and in some mysterious way those who viewed them received immortal life. They were promised admission to the Islands of the Blest, where it had formerly been believed none but the ancient heroes could be received. Even the poorest slave was permitted to enter this fellowship and be initiated into the "mysteries," as they were called.

Oracles. Men also turned to the gods for a knowledge of the future. It was believed that men heard the voice of Apollo when his priestess was consulted on the success of some plan or asked to answer some serious question. Her utterances were called "oracles." Apollo's shrine at Delphi (Fig. 43) became a national religious center, to which the whole Greek world resorted.

2. THE BEGINNINGS OF SCIENCE

Thales Predicts an Eclipse. At the opening of the sixth century, while some of the Greeks were finding comfort in religious myths and mysteries, other Greeks were rejecting the beliefs of older times, especially those regarding the world and its control by the gods. The Ionian cities, long the commercial leaders of the Ægean, were the first to turn their attention to these new problems. In constant contact with Egypt and the Phœnician cities, they had learned the beginnings of mathematics and astronomy as known in the Near East, and one of the Ionian thinkers had even set up an Egyptian shadow clock. At Miletus, the most important of these Ionian cities, there was an able statesman named Thales, who had traveled widely and had received from Babylonia a list of observations of the heavenly bodies. From such lists the Babylonians had already learned that eclipses of the sun occur at regular intervals. With these lists in his hands, Thales could calculate when the next eclipse would occur. He therefore told the people of Miletus that they might expect an eclipse of the sun before the end of a certain year. When the promised eclipse (585 B.C.) actually occurred as he had predicted, the fame of Thales spread far and wide.

Natural Law versus the Interference of the Gods. The foretelling of an eclipse, a feat already accomplished by the Babylonians, was not so important as the conclusions which Thales drew from it. Hitherto men had believed that when the sun was darkened or other strange things happened in the skies, they were the result of the anger of some god. Now, however, Thales boldly proclaimed that the movements of the heavenly bodies were not caused by the gods but were made in accordance with fixed laws. The gods were thus banished from control of the sky, where the eagle of Zeus had once ruled.

Ionian Geography and History. Another citizen of Miletus, perhaps a pupil of Thales, explained the origin of animals by assuming a develop-
ment of higher forms from the lower ones, in a manner which reminds us of the modern theory of evolution. He studied the forms of the seas and the countries, and made a map of the world. It is the earliest world map known to us, although maps of a limited region were already in use in Egypt and Babylonia. A little later another geographer of Miletus, named Hecatæus, traveled widely, made a journey up the Nile, and wrote a geography of the world. In this book, as in the map just mentioned, the Mediterranean Sea was the center, and the lands about it for a short distance back from its shores were all that were known to the author. Hecatæus also put together a history made up of the mythical stories of early Greece and the

Fig. 46. *Greek Physician Reading from a Roll*

It will be seen that the physician holds the roll so that he rolls up a portion of it with one hand as he unrolls another portion with the other. He soon has a roll in each hand, while he holds, smoothly stretched out between the two rolls, the exposed portion, from which he reads a column of writing. Such a column formed for him a page; but when it was read, instead of turning a page as we do, he rolled it away to the left side and brought into view a new column from the other roll on the right side. The physician has taken the roll from a cabinet, the upper shelf of which still holds eight other rolls arranged in a pyramid-like pile. From the cases of surgical instruments standing open on the top of the cabinet we may assume that these rolls contained informative medical material, perhaps discussions of the parts and operations of the human body and suggestions for treatments of injuries such as may be found in the rolls of the Egyptian and Greek surgeons. (After Birt)

tales of the past which he had heard in the Near East. He is the first historical writer since the Hebrew historians (p. 85).

Ionian Mathematics and Natural Science. Pythagoras, an Ionian, was interested in mathematics and natural science. He and his pupils made important mathematical discoveries; for example, that the square of the hypotenuse of a right-angled triangle equals the sum of the squares of the other two sides. They also found out that if the thickness and tension of a musical string remain the same, its length is in exact mathematical relation to its pitch. They likewise discovered that the earth is a sphere which moves. Another Ionian scientist called attention to the presence of petrified sea plants and fish in the rocks, to prove that the sea had at one time covered the land.

Great Step taken by Ionian Thinkers. Thus these Ionian thinkers became the forerunners of natural scientists and philosophers, for they strove to discover the *natural* laws which in the beginning had brought the world into existence and still continued to control it. In explaining the world in terms of natural law rather than of religion they entered upon a new world of thought, which we call *science* and *philosophy*, — a world which had never dawned upon the greatest minds of the early East. This step, taken by Thales and the great men of the Ionian cities, remains and will forever remain the greatest achievement of the human intellect.

3. Greek Lyric Poetry and Drama

Relation of Greek Literature to Music. Early Greek poetry was always recited with music. The epic was sung or recited to the music of the iyre. A later kind of poems called "elegies" were, however, usually sung with flute accompaniment. The flute had been brought from Egypt to Crete in early times, and from the Cretans the Greeks had adopted it. Long a favorite instrument, it was used even more after the eighth century B.C., and one musician even wrote a composition for the flute which was intended to tell the story of Apollo's fight with the dragon of Delphi. The lyre, a kind of harp, which formerly had but four strings, was finally made with seven, and compositions for the lyre alone were popular. Either or

FIG. 47. *The Theater of Athens*

This theater was the center of the growth and development of Greek drama, which began as a part of the celebration of the spring feast of Dionysus, god of the vine and the fruitfulness of the earth. The temple of the god stood here, just at the left. Long before anyone knew of such a thing as a theater, the people gathered at this place to watch the celebration of the god's spring feast, where they formed a circle about the chorus, which narrated in song the stories of the gods. This circle (called the orchestra) was finally marked out permanently, and seats of wood (later stone) for the spectators were erected in a semicircle on one side; but the singing and action all took place in the circle on the level of the ground. On the side opposite the public was a booth or tent (Greek *skēnē*, "scene") for the actors, and out of this finally developed the stage. From the seats, accommodating possibly seventeen thousand people, the citizens had a grand view of the sea, with the island of Ægina; for orchestra and seats had no roof, and a Greek theater was always open to the sky

both of these instruments might be played as the accompaniment of song with choruses. Here we have the beginnings of orchestral music as the accompaniment of choral singing.

Lyric Poetry: Pindar and Sappho. Greek lyric poetry — that is, poetry accompanied by the lyre — expressed various moods, — longings, dreams, hopes, and fiery storms of passion. Each poet found a wondrous world within *himself*, which he thus pictured in short songs. As every Greek lyric poem was composed to be sung to music, it was necessary that all Greek lyric poets should also be musicians. Probably the greatest of these poets was Pindar of Thebes. Another great lyric singer of the age was the poetess Sappho, the earliest woman to gain undying fame in literature.

Festival Choruses became Drama. A favorite form of song was the chorus with which the country folk loved to celebrate their picnics. The poet Stesichorus, who lived in Sicily, began to write "choruses" which told the stories of the gods found in the old myths. The singers, who came to be called a chorus, marched in procession, wore goatskins, and concealed their faces with masks. Some of the songs were sung responsively by the chorus and their leader. For the entertainment of the listening peasants the leader would illustrate with gestures the story told in the song. He thus became to some extent an actor, the forerunner of the actors on our own stage. When, later, a second actor was introduced, dialogue between the two was possible, though the chorus continued to recite most of the narrative. Thus arose a form of musical play, or *drama*, the action, or story, of which was carried on by the chorus and two actors. The Greeks called such a play a *tragedy*, which means "goat's play," probably because the members of the chorus had always disguised themselves as goats.

The grassy circle where the chorus danced and sang was usually on a slope in the hills, from which the spectators had a fine view of the country and the sea beyond.

The Drama: Æschylus (525–456 B.C.). The Greek theater would seem strange to us now; for although it had a stage, it had little or no scenery, and the actors, who were always men, wore grotesque masks, as in the old days. The play was largely carried on in song by the chorus, but this was varied by the dialogue of the actors, and the whole was not unlike an opera. It was said that the dramatist Æschylus was the first tragedian to attempt to give importance to the dialogue of the actors as well as to the songs of the chorus. In his seven surviving plays we can trace a development which makes clear to us why Æschylus has been considered the first great master of drama. The work of Æschylus was

FIG. 48. *Relief Showing Euripides Seated before a Statue of the God Dionysus*

The dramatist is handing a mask to the laurel-crowned actor on the left, who serves here as a sort of personification of the play. (Courtesy of Dr. Arif Müfid, Musées des Antiquités d'Istanbul)

the culmination of all the Greek poetry that had been produced before him. He retold the stories of Homer in an epic manner, but used the meter and spirit of the lyrists as well. The plays of Æschylus usually dealt with the struggle of man against his destiny. He employed a sort of grandiose language of which the Athenians themselves later tired, but the magnificence and sweep of his themes demanded a lofty style.

Sophocles. Sophocles (497–405 B.C.) was the greatest of the Greek dramatists. He was an Athenian, and probably therefore the playwright whom the Athenians most admired. His plays were based on the old stories of the Greek heroes and heroines, — Ajax, Œdipus, Heracles, Antigone, and Electra. They concerned revenge, sorrow for sin, and wounded pride, and made a deep impression on the people. The plays of Sophocles are perfect in structure as well as language. For this reason Sophocles is held to have contributed more to the Greek drama than either Æschylus or their younger contemporary Euripides. It was Sophocles, for instance, who introduced a *third* actor into the plays, which made them more interesting and full of action.

Euripides (480–406 B.C.). Sophocles still believed in the gods, but his later rival Euripides was what we should call a skeptic. His questioning of the old beliefs in the gods troubled many of the old-fashioned citizens. Sophocles suited them much better, and it was very rarely that Euripides, in spite of his great ability, was able to carry off a prize. The Athenian citizen felt some anxiety that his own son and most of the other young men of his set were enthusiastic admirers of Euripides and read his plays and talked them over with the Sophists. Although the structure of Euripides' plays is so complicated that the modern reader is often sorely puzzled by them, the characters are human and understandable. Euripides was the last of the great Greek writers of tragedy ; and it was not until Shakespeare appeared, at the end of the sixteenth century, in Queen Elizabeth's time, that dramas of such grandeur and power were again created.

Comedies. The great Greek tragedies were given in the morning, and in the afternoon the people were ready for less serious plays, such as the comedies. In these plays leading politicians (even Pericles), writers, and philosophers were made fun of while the audiences roared with laughter. The best-known comedy-writer was Aristophanes (446?–385 B.C.), who gave up the old themes, and wrote such plays as *The Frogs*, in which he made fun of Euripides, or *The Clouds*, in which he represented the great philosopher Socrates as a dirty old impostor. After Aristophanes this sort of comedy, which dealt with questions and personalities of the day, went out of fashion, and there developed a new style of comedy which did not make sport of definite individuals but rather of typical characters. It is this later form of comedy which has most influenced modern drama.

4. HIGHER EDUCATION AND SCIENCE IN FIFTH-CENTURY GREECE

Higher Education Offered by Sophists. The Ionian thinkers and their followers raised a great many questions in regard to education. It became necessary for the educated man to know more than how to read, to write, and to perform on some musical instrument. This new learning was furnished by the Sophists, a group of clever-witted lecturers who wandered from city to city. Many a bright youth who had finished his music, reading, and writing at the old-fashioned private school demanded money to pay for a course of lectures delivered by one of these new teachers.

For the first time a higher education was thus open to young men who had hitherto thought of little more than a victory in the Olympic games or a fine appearance when parading with the crack cavalry of Athens. The appearance of these new teachers therefore marked a new age in the history of the Greeks, but especially in that of Athens. In the first place, the Sophists recognized the importance of effective public speaking in addressing the large citizen juries or in speaking before the assembly of the people. They therefore taught rhetoric and oratory with great success, and many a father who had no gift of speech had the pleasure of seeing his son a practiced public speaker. It was through the teaching of the Sophists, also, that the first successful writing of Greek prose began. At the same time they founded the study of language, which was to become grammar. They also taught mathematics and astronomy, and the young men of Athens for the first time began to learn a little natural science. Thus the truths which Greek philosophers had begun to observe in the days of Thales were, after a century and a half, beginning to spread among the people.

The Sophists and the New Teachings. In these new ideas the fathers were unable to follow their sons. When a father of that day found his son with a book by one of the great Sophists, which began with a statement doubting the existence of the gods, the new teachings seemed impious. The old-fashioned citizen could at least vote for the banishment of such teachers and the burning of their books, although he heard that they were read aloud in the houses of the greatest men of Athens. Indeed, some of the leading Sophists were friends of Pericles, who stepped in and tried to help them when they were prosecuted for their teachings. The revolution which had taken place in the mind of Thales was now taking place in the minds of ever-increasing numbers of Greeks, and the situation was yet to grow decidedly worse in the opinion of old-fashioned folk.

Limited Knowledge of Science shown in Time Measurement. In spite of the spread of knowledge due to the Sophists, the average Athenian's acquaintance with science was still very limited. This gave him great trouble in the measurement of time. He continued to call the middle of the forenoon the "time of full market," and the Egyptian shadow clock in the market place had not yet led him to speak of an hour of the day by *number*, as the Egyptians had been doing for a thousand years. When it was necessary to limit the length of a citizen's speech before the law court, it was done by allowing him to speak as long as it took a certain amount of water to run out of a jar with a small hole in it. The Greeks still used the moon-months, and they were accustomed to insert an extra month every third, fifth, and eighth year.

Astronomy and Geography. Scientists, however, continued to make important discoveries. One of them now taught that the sun was a glowing mass of stone "larger than the Peloponnesus." He maintained also that the moon received its light from the sun, that it had mountains and valleys like the earth, and that it was inhabited by living creatures.

Travel was difficult, for there were no passenger ships. Except for rough carts or wagons, there were no conveyances by land. The roads were bad, and the traveler went on foot or rode a horse. Nevertheless, Greeks who could afford to were now beginning to travel more frequently. This, however, was for the purpose of gathering information; travel for pleasure was still a century and a half in the future. From long journeys in Egypt and other Eastern countries the historian Herodotus (p. 208) returned with much information regarding these lands. His map showed that the Red Sea connected with the Indian Ocean, a fact unknown to his predecessor Hecatæus (p. 193). The scientists were still much puzzled by the cold of the north and the warmth of the south, a curious difference which they could not yet explain.

Progress in Medicine. Herodotus must have seen in Egypt the earliest known government medical school, which had been restored and endowed by Darius only a generation earlier. Although without the microscope or the assistance of chemistry, medicine nevertheless had made progress. In the first place, the Greek physicians completely rejected the older belief that disease was caused by evil demons, and, like the great unknown Egyptian surgeon (p. 42), endeavored to find the *natural causes* of the ailment. To do this they sought to understand the organs of the body. Following the Egyptian surgeon's discovery that the brain was the source both of the nervous control and also of the paralysis of the limbs, the Greek physicians had now discovered that the brain was the organ of thought. But the arterial system, the circulation of the blood, and the nervous system as a whole were still entirely unknown. Without a knowledge of the circulation of the blood, surgery was unable to attempt amputation, but otherwise it made much progress. The greatest physician of the time was Hippocrates, who became the founder of scientific medicine. The fame of Greek medicine was such that the Persian king called a Greek physician to his court.

5. How the Greeks Discussed Old Ideas and New

Age of Uncertainty after Death of Pericles. Any young Athenian born at about the time of Pericles' death found himself in an age of conflict and uncertainty wherever he went, — an age of conflict *abroad* on the field of battle as he stood with spear and shield in the Athenian ranks in the long years of warfare between Athens, Sparta, and Thebes; an age of conflict *at home* in Athens amid the excited shouting and applause of the turbulent Assembly or the tumult and even bloodshed of the streets and markets of the city as the common people, the democracy, struggled with the nobles for the leadership of the state; and, finally, an age of uncertainty *in himself* as he felt his faith in old beliefs struggling to maintain itself against new views.

Religion and Conduct. Greeks grew up with little religious instruction, for there was nothing like a church, a clergy, or any religious teachers. There was no sacred book revered by all, like our Bible. Boys were not taught that the gods had any interest in them or their conduct, or that they required men to be either good or bad. As long as one did not neglect any of the ceremonies desired by the gods, he knew he need have no fear of them. At the same time, he realized that if he lived an evil life he might be condemned to enter at death a dark and gruesome dwelling place beneath the earth. On the other hand, a good life might bring him at last to the beautiful Elysian Fields.

Religion of the Multitude. One of the ways of reaching this place of blessedness was by initiation into the mysteries of Eleusis. Another way was to follow the teachings of the beggar-priests and soothsayers of Orpheus. These wandering teachers went about in all Greece, followed by hordes of the poor and ignorant, who eagerly accepted their mysterious teachings as they promised every blessing to those who listened and obeyed. The more mysterious it all was, the better the multitude liked it. These teachings were recorded in the wonderful book of Orpheus, which finally gained wide circulation among the common people. It came nearer to being the sacred book of the Greeks than any other that they ever had. All the lower classes believed in magic and were deeply impressed by the mysterious tricks of the magicians and soothsayers, whom they consulted on all the ordinary acts of life.

Foreign Gods from the Near East. Down at the Piræus the Athenian citizen found the busy streets crowded with foreign merchants from Egypt, Phœnicia, and Asia Minor. They too had their assurances of divine help and blessedness, and they brought with them their strange gods: the Great Mother from Asia Minor; Isis from her lovely temple at Philæ, above the First Cataract of the Nile; and the Egyptian Amon from his mysterious shrine far away in the Sahara, behind the Greek city of Cyrene. The famous Greek poet Pindar had written a poem in his honor and had erected a statue of the great Egyptian god. As a deliverer of oracles revealing the future, Amon had now become as great a favorite among the Greeks as Apollo of Delphi. There was an Athenian ship which sailed regularly between the Piræus and Cyrene, carrying the Greeks to Amon's distant Sahara shrine. Egyptian symbols too were common on Greek tombstones.

Growth of Religious Doubts. Some of these foreign beliefs had once greatly impressed our Greek citizen in his younger days. Then, when he left his boyhood teachers behind him and went to hear the lectures of a noted Sophist, he found that no one knew with any certainty whether the gods even existed; much less did anyone know what they were like. A philosopher, Xenophanes, who had lived before the coming of the Persians, said, "There is one god, supreme among gods and men, resembling mortals neither in form nor in mind." But ignorant men, he said, make the gods in their own likeness and "fancy that gods are born, and wear clothes, and have a voice and form like themselves." If our young man heard this opinion of Xenophanes, it would greatly disturb him. He began to look with some pity at the crowds of pilgrims who followed the sacred road leading to the hall of the mysteries at Eleusis. He had only contempt for the mob which filled the processions of the strange Oriental gods and almost every day marched with tumult and flute-playing through the streets of Athens. While he could not accept such superstitions of the ignorant poor, he found, nevertheless, that he was not yet quite ready to give up his belief in the gods and reject them altogether, as some of his educated neighbors were doing.

Victory of Doubt: Euripides. He recalled the days of his youth, when he had scoffed at these very doubts which now overwhelmed him. He had once enjoyed the caricatures of Aristophanes, the greatest of the comedy-writers. His fellow citizens had shouted with delight at Aristophanes' mockery of the religious questionings of Euripides (p. 198) or at the ridicule which the clever comedy heaped upon the Sophists. Since then, however, had come the new light which he himself had gained from the Sophists. Whatever the gods might be like, he was sure that they were not such beings as were described aiding and opposing his heroic forefathers in the Homeric poems. He had long since cast aside his Homer. In spite of Aristophanes he and his educated friends were all reading the splendid tragedies of Euripides, with their conflicts and doubts about life and the gods. Euripides, the victim of Aristophanes' ridicule, to whom the Athenians had rarely voted a victory during his lifetime, had now triumphed; but his triumph meant the overthrow of the old beliefs in the gods, and the incoming of a new age of thought.

The Great Questioner. The citizen remembered well another comedy of Aristophanes, which had likewise found a ready response from the Athenian audience. It had placed upon the stage the rude and comical figure of a poor Athenian named Socrates, whom Aristophanes had represented as a dangerous man, to be shunned or even chastised by good Athenians. He was the son of a stonecutter, or humble sculptor. The ill-clothed figure and ugly face of Socrates had become familiar in the streets to all the folk of Athens since the outbreak of the second war with Sparta. He was accustomed to stand about the market place all day long, talking to anyone he met and asking a great many questions. Our citizen recalled that Socrates' questions left him in a very confused state of mind; for he seemed to call in question everything which the citizen had once regarded as settled. Yet this familiar and homely figure of the stonecutter's son was the personification of the best and highest in Greek genius. Without desire for office or a political career, Socrates' supreme interest nevertheless was the state. He believed that the state, made up as it was of citizens, could be purified and saved only by the improvement of the individual citizen through the education of his mind to recognize virtue and right.

"*The Socratic Method.*" Socrates did not write anything, and we have to rely on the reports of his admirers, especially Plato and Xenophon, for our impressions of his beliefs and methods of getting at the truth. Instead of relying on books, he thought that discussion — asking questions and trying to answer them — was the best way to see one's mistakes and reach the truth. This is still called the "Socratic method." His ardent follower, Plato, as we shall see later (p. 209), wrote many dialogues in which Socrates is the chief character. Friends and acquaintances would meet together in the market place or at someone's house, and, after some light talk, serious questions would be raised in regard to the real nature of justice, virtue, beauty, or as to how the state should be organized for the greatest good of all. The teachings of the Sophists might be taken up, and the value of studying natural science. Socrates appears to have believed that there were eternal standards of the perfect Good, True, and Beautiful. All the imperfect things in life were good, true, and beautiful only in so far as they approached these everlasting standards. By careful thought and discussion and argument the nature of these "master ideas" could be discovered and men could use them as guides in trying to lead a good life.

Fig. 49. *Portrait of Socrates*

This is not the best of the numerous surviving portraits of Socrates, but it is especially interesting because it bears beneath the philosopher's name nine inscribed lines containing a portion of a conversation of Socrates with one of his friends as reported by Plato in his *Crito*

Socrates made no appeal to religion as a help in right living. Nevertheless, he had a devout faith in the gods, although he did not share the old beliefs about their nature and conduct. He even felt, like the Hebrew prophets, that he could hear a voice within him guiding him and warning him against evil acts.

Trial and Death of Socrates. A group of pupils gathered about Socrates, of whom the most famous was Plato. But Socrates was not generally understood. His keen questions seemed to throw doubt upon the old beliefs. So he was summoned to trial for corrupting the youth with all sorts of impious teachings. Such an example as Alcibiades (p. 164), who had been his pupil, seemed a convincing illustration of the evil effects of his teaching. The comedy of Aristophanes in which the great teacher was stupidly misrepresented and held up to contempt may have prejudiced the people a good deal. Socrates might easily have left Athens when the complaint was lodged against him. Nevertheless, he appeared for trial and made a powerful and dignified defense; but the court voted the death penalty, which consisted in taking poison. He passed his last days in tranquil conversation with his friends and pupils, in whose presence he then quietly drank the fatal hemlock (399 B.C.). Thus the Athenian democracy, which had so fatally mismanaged the affairs of the nation in war, brought upon itself much greater reproach in condemning to death, even though in accordance with law, the greatest and purest soul among its citizens.

The undisturbed serenity of Socrates in his last hours, as pictured to us in Plato's idealized description of the scene (in the *Phædo*), profoundly affected the whole Greek world and still forms one of the most precious possessions of humanity. Socrates was the greatest Greek, and in him Greek civilization reached its highest level. But the glorified figure of Socrates as he appears in the writings of his pupils was to prove more powerful even than the living teacher.

6. CELEBRATED GREEK ORATORS AND HISTORIANS: PLATO

The Final Development of Prose Writing. The books written by the pupils of Socrates belong to that period in which Greek prose achieved a smooth and finished style. During the fifth century B.C. prose writing had been becoming more and more of an art, particularly in the hands of the philosophers, the historians, and the speech-writers. As we remember, prose had been used by some of the Ionian philosophers as far back as the sixth century to set forth their theories and principles, and also by the early historians who prepared chronicles and collections of myths. We shall now find that the speeches of the leading Greek orators must also be considered as examples of great Greek prose. We moderns do not think of speeches as literature; but the situation in Greece was somewhat different, for the art of public speaking had been esteemed even in Homeric times. In democratic Athens, where a political career depended much on the speeches made before the Assembly or Council, and where the citizen juries were often swayed by eloquence, there were produced great masterpieces of oratory. Some of the speeches, moreover, were not delivered publicly but were written as a sort of essay and distributed to the people as we distribute pamphlets today.

Speeches and the Speech-writers. Many speeches were intended for delivery by other men than those who wrote them. This might easily be true of the addresses given before the Assembly; it was especially true of those made in the Athenian law courts, where plaintiff or defendant was required to present his own case. The position of the speech-writer in ancient Greece was very like that of the "ghost writer" for radio stars in modern America. Of course, there were scores of professional speech-writers, and some were very bad; but from the pens of the really excellent ones there have come down to us examples of eloquence which are to be placed with the world's best literature.

The most celebrated Greek orator was Demosthenes. He spoke with eloquence, but did not disturb himself greatly over laws of rhetoric. As he grew older his style became smoother, but he liked always to insert into his speeches impressive metaphors, similes, and sayings of his day, and now and then an oath. Demosthenes was, however, the most inspired of the speech-writers and has been recognized ever since as one of the world's foremost orators. The orators of the fifth and fourth centuries B.C. were trained by the Sophists and their successors, the teachers of rhetoric.

The Historians: Herodotus. The first great Greek historian, Herodotus of Halicarnassus (about 484–424 B.C.), published his entertaining record just at the close of Pericles' life, in the midst of national calamities. It was a history of the world so told that the glorious leadership of Athens would be clear to all Greeks and would make plain that to her the Hellenes owed their deliverance from Persia. Throughout Greece it created a deep impression, and so tremendous was its effect in Athens that in spite of the heavy expenses of war the Athenians voted Herodotus a reward of ten talents, some twelve thousand dollars. In this earliest history of the world which has come down to us, Herodotus traced the course of events as he believed them to be directed by the will of the gods and as prophesied in their divine oracles. There was little or no effort to explain historical events as the result of natural processes.

Thucydides writes on his Own Times. The first scientific writer of history was Thucydides, born in Athens near the middle of the fifth century B.C. A generation earlier Herodotus's history had ascribed the fortunes of nations to the will of the gods; but Thucydides, like modern historians, traced historical events to their *earthly* causes in the world of men where they occur. There were only thirty years or so between them; but how different the beliefs and style of the two historians, the old and the new! Thucydides was one of the greatest writers of prose that ever lived. His work was received by the Greeks with enthusiastic approval, and it has been one of the world's great classics ever since.

Another writer of contemporary history was the Athenian Xenophon. He wrote of the period after the fall of the Athenian Empire. Xenophon's *Anabasis* (p. 169) is one of the great contributions to military history, because it describes the most remarkable retreat of all times. His histories are romantic rather than scientific.

The Dialogues of Plato. Greek literature, as well as Greek prose, reached its height in the writings of Plato, who is easily the greatest author of the ancient world. He is, furthermore, the only great Greek writer whose complete works we probably still have. Until the death of Socrates, Plato seems to have lived the leisurely life of the average young man about Athens. Greatly shaken by the death of his beloved master, Plato left Athens and traveled extensively in Egypt and also to the West. Upon his return home he set up his school in the grove of the Academy (p. 182).

The literary form known as the "dialogue," which was used so successfully by Plato, was probably inspired by the method of question and answer which Socrates employed in his teaching. Plato, in his dialogues, supposedly reproduced the discussions of his great teacher, and it is to these writings that we owe our knowledge of the philosophy of Socrates. Often, however, it is difficult to determine whether it is the teaching of Socrates or Plato's own beliefs which are being expressed. Plato writes with delicacy and charm as well as with grandeur and austerity. He was a man of science and at the same time a man of remarkable imagination.

Questions and Exercises

REVIEW OF CHAPTER

1. What was the earliest form of Greek literature? In what literary forms were moral lessons presented by the Greeks? Discuss the Greek ideas of the hereafter.

2. What was the importance of the prediction of an eclipse by Thales? Was he the first person to do this? List some of the accomplishments of the Ionian thinkers.

3. What was lyric poetry? How did festal choruses lead to drama? Contrast the plays of Æschylus, Sophocles, and Euripides.

4. What was the contribution of the Sophists to the history of education? How much scientific knowledge had the average Athenian of the fifth century B.C.? What did the Greek physicians of Pericles' time know about the human body?

5. In what respects was the age following Pericles one of doubt? What were the various beliefs concerning the gods? Can you sum up the teaching of Socrates?

6. Greek prose was used to present what three subjects? Name some of the great Greek prose writers.

USEFUL TERMS

See how much meaning you can give to the following: *chronicles, literature, reading public, social justice, didactic poetry, natural laws.*

DIRECTIVE QUESTIONS

1. If you wanted to write a history of your town, what documents would you try to get hold of?

2. Were there any scientific theories of the Ionian thinkers which we accept today?

3. Greek music was merely the accompaniment of Greek poetry. What is the comparative importance of American music and American poetry?

4. Can you give the scientific explanation of some natural phenomenon which puzzled the Greeks? Who first advanced this explanation?

5. What religious doubts arose in the time of Pericles?

6. Is the dialogue often used by modern writers?

DISCUSSION TOPICS

1. No finer epics than the Iliad and Odyssey have ever been written.

2. Why was the prediction of an eclipse by Thales a more important matter than such a prediction by the Babylonians?

3. Music is the one great art which has been developed almost wholly in modern times; few new poetic forms have been invented since the time of the Greeks.

4. In what ways is our own calendar inconvenient? Are we as non-progressive in the matter of time measurement as were the Greeks?

5. Socrates *did*, in a sense, corrupt the youth of Athens.

ADDITIONAL ADVENTURES IN LEARNING

1. Studies in Source Materials. THALLON, *Readings in Greek History*: (1) Tales from Herodotus, pp. 80–82, 132–133, 153–154; (2) The plans of Pericles, from the history of Thucydides, pp. 315–318; (3) Battle of Leuctra, from Xenophon's *Hellenica*, pp. 493–495; (4) Isocrates on Pan-Hellenic unity, pp. 520–521.

2. Look up in an encyclopedia: *eclipse, arteries, Euripides, drama, pageant, dialogue, oratory, musical instruments.*

CHAPTER X · THE ARTS AND CRAFTS
OF THE GREEKS

GREEK BUILDINGS · GREEK SCULPTURE · THE BEAUTIFUL PRODUCTS OF GREEK HANDI-
CRAFT · THE DISCOVERIES MADE BY GREEK PAINTERS

IN THE previous chapter we saw how Greek thinkers and writers got away from older ideas and thought of new things and new ways of saying them in prose and verse. They questioned the beliefs of their ancestors and raised new problems and tried to solve them. This is what is called "originality," as contrasted with men's tendency to revere the past and regard the sayings of sages of old as true and binding on them. The greatness of the Greeks consisted largely in their originality and in the beauty of their writings. They made more progress in a couple of centuries than has been made, in a similar period, by any other people of which we know, unless it be the vast increase of knowledge and inventions which has come in the last two hundred years.

In this chapter we shall take up the various forms of art in which the Greeks showed marked originality. They created wondrous buildings, carvings, and household utensils, and discovered ways of painting hitherto unknown. We still copy their buildings and venerate their statuary. The works wrought either by the Greeks or by their imitators are collected in the art galleries of the world. In order to follow what is said in this chapter it will be necessary to look carefully at the illustrations and visit, if possible, a museum or collection in which there are examples of Greek art or copies of them.

1. GREEK BUILDINGS

The First Greek Temples. The earliest Greek temples were erected on the citadel, where former shrines attached to the royal palace had stood. These, like the houses in the city below, were built of sun-dried brick. They were probably rectangular in shape, and all had a "peaked" roof with a triangular gable at each end. Many of these buildings had a porch with a row of wooden posts.

The Earliest Greek Architecture in Stone. Architecture made very important advances in the Age of the Tyrants (p. 142); for many of the tyrants built harbors, aqueducts, and temples. The Greek cities were still simply groups of sun-dried brick structures. Great stone buildings such as we have seen on the Nile had been unknown in Europe since the time of the Ægeans, but now the rough Greek temples were rebuilt in limestone. Indeed, the front of the temple of Apollo at Delphi was even built of marble. At no other time before or after were so many temples erected as in the Greek world during the sixth century B.C. In Sicily and southern Italy a number of the noble temples of this age still stand, revealing the beauty and simplicity of Greek architecture even at that early stage. Instead of the wooden posts of the earlier period, rows of plain *stone* columns (colonnades), in a style which we call Doric (Fig. 50), surrounded these temples. Although the architects borrowed the idea and the *form* of these colonnades from Egypt, they improved them until they made them the most beautiful columns ever designed by early builders. Like the temples on the Nile, those of Greece were painted in bright colors.

Athens, the Monumental City. The greatest political leaders of Athens had all developed a public-works program for their city. One had interested himself in fortifications and harbor works. Another turned his attention to beautifying those places where the people congregated daily. It was also at this time that the Athenians began to enlarge the area of the Acropolis by grading and embankments. Thus was prepared the way for Pericles, the celebrated builder, by whose efforts Athens became known throughout the ancient world for its architectural triumphs.

The Acropolis in the Age of Pericles. Above Athens towered the height of the Acropolis. It was about one thousand feet in length, — two of our average city blocks. There, on its summit, had always been the dwelling place of Athena, whose arm was ever stretched out in protection over her beloved Athens. But for years after the repulse of the Persians the Acropolis rose smoke-blackened over the rebuilt houses of the city, and no temple of Athena appeared to replace the old building, which the Persians had burned. At last Pericles

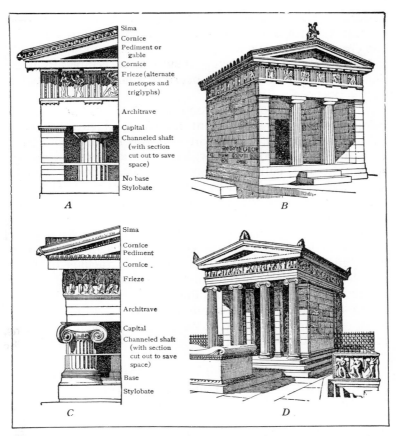

Sima
Cornice
Pediment or
  gable
Cornice
Frieze (alternate
  metopes and
  triglyphs)

Architrave

Capital
Channeled shaft
  (with section
  cut out to save
  space)

No base
Stylobate

A

B

Sima

Cornice
Pediment
Cornice

Frieze

Architrave

Capital
Channeled shaft
  (with section
  cut out to save
  space)

Base

Stylobate

C

D

Fig. 50. *The Two Leading Styles of Greek Architecture, the Doric* (A and B)
and the Ionic (C and D)

The little Doric building *B* is the treasury of the Athenians at Delphi (Fig. 43),
containing their offerings of gratitude to Apollo. On the low base at the left side
of the building were placed the trophies from the battle of Marathon. Over them
on the walls are carved hymns to Apollo, with music attached, one of the oldest
Greek musical notations surviving. The beautiful Ionic building *D* is a restoration
of the temple of Victory on the Athenian Acropolis. Contrast its slender columns
with the sturdier shafts of the Doric order, and it will be seen that the Ionic is a
more delicate and graceful style. *A* and *C* show details of both styles. (After
Luckenbach)

undertook the restoration of the ancient shrines on a scale of magnificence and beauty before unknown anywhere in the Greek world. His sumptuous plans cost about two and a quarter millions of dollars — a sum far exceeding any public outlay that had ever been heard of among the Greeks for such a purpose.

At the west end of the Acropolis rose the imposing marble colonnades of the magnificent monumental entrance hall, called the *Propylæa*. The architect of this building combined with the stately Doric a new, lighter, and more decorative style of column called the Ionic (Fig. 50). The old, simple Doric was, however, used by the architect of the Parthenon, a noble temple dedicated to Athena (Fig. 51). The beauty of the Doric colonnades of the Parthenon is awe-inspiring even today, as it stands roofless and mutilated. What must have been the effect upon the Greeks, long ago, when it was first finished, — a temple beautiful and gracious of form and decorated with colored bands of sculptured relief carved under the supervision of Phidias, the greatest sculptor of his time! It was in these wondrous Greek buildings that the architect and the sculptor, working hand in hand, produced marvelously harmonious results.

Architecture in Athens during the Wars between the City-states. When the long wars and the expenses of the democracy had swallowed up the wealth of Athens, the great and splendid public works of the Age of Pericles were no longer possible. Athens was obliged to rebuild her fortifications, erect war arsenals, and build sheds for her battleships. The maintenance of art and architecture during this period was therefore largely in the hands of individual artists, who were not supported by the state but were producing works of art for private buyers.

A notable exception was the Erechtheum, one of the most beautiful buildings that was ever erected. This temple had been begun before the death of Pericles and largely completed during the unhappy days of the last Peloponnesian War. It was built in the Ionic style, adorned with colonnades of wonderful refinement and beauty; and at one

Fɪɢ. 51. *Restoration of the Parthenon as it Was in the Fifth Century* ʙ.ᴄ.

The gable ends of the temple each contained a triangular group of sculpture depicting the birth of Athena and her struggle with Poseidon, god of the sea, for possession of Attica. The wonderful frieze of Phidias extended around the building, inside the colonnades, at the top of the wall. (After Thiersch and Michaelis)

corner was an exquisite porch, with its roof supported by lovely marble figures of Athenian maidens.

Rise of the Corinthian Style of Architecture. Egyptian artists, as we remember, had long before crowned their columns with a capital representing growing flowers or palm-tree tops. Perceiving the great beauty of their own acanthus plant, the Greek architects designed a capital adorned with a double row of acanthus leaves. This new capital was richer and more ornate than the simpler Doric and Ionic forms. Columns with these capitals are now called Corinthian, although one of the earliest examples of such columns still survives at Athens.

Greek Architecture after the Fifth Century ʙ.ᴄ. While Athens no longer had the money to erect great state temples, other Greek states were not so financially exhausted. New temples, chiefly in the Doric style, were erected at Delphi and in the Peloponnesus. Architecture in the Ionic style was at the same time being further developed in the cities of Asia Minor. At Halicarnassus the Mausoleum, a huge marble tomb, was erected for King Mausolus of Caria. It was, when built (in the middle of the fourth century B.C.), the most magnificent tomb on the north side of the Mediterranean; and it is because of its wide-spread fame that its name has been preserved, for we now call any stately tomb a mausoleum. While imposing as an example of ancient architecture, the Mausoleum was also renowned because of the rich and remarkable sculpture with which it was adorned by the leading sculptors of Greece. Indeed, the splendor of all the great architectural achievements of the Greeks was increased by their sculptured decorations.

2. GREEK SCULPTURE

The Beginnings of Greek Sculpture. The Greek temples were usually adorned, in the triangular gable end, with sculptured relief figures of the gods, grouped in scenes from old stories, the *myths*. Although at first very much influenced by earlier Oriental reliefs, the sculptors soon produced works of real beauty and independence.

Although we possess many of the original Greek sculptures of the early period (seventh to sixth century B.C.), — especially fragments from the earlier temples on the Athenian Acropolis, which were burnt by the Persians, — we have few original pieces of statuary from the early fifth century. We do have, however, copies of these sculptures. There are for instance, some particularly fine copies of statues wrought by Myron, who is considered by some scholars as probably the very first Greek sculptor to free his work entirely from the restraint and rigidity of the old ways and to create in bronze true representations of the human body. Particularly interesting were Myron's statues of victorious athletes (Fig. 44). He was also proficient as a sculptor of animals. Most of the existing marble copies of Greek sculpture were made later, in Roman times. When a wealthy Roman collector could not persuade the Greeks to sell some certain statue which he fancied, he usually employed a sculptor to

FIG. 52. *Monument of the Tyrant-Slayers of Athens, Harmodius and Aristogiton*

On the slopes of the Areopagus, overlooking the market place, the Athenians set up these statues, depicting at the moment of attack the two heroic youths who lost their lives in an attempt to slay the two sons of Pisistratus and to free Athens from the tyrants (514 B.C.). Our illustration is an ancient copy in marble, the lost original having been made in bronze

make a copy of the original for him. We know that these copies were generally good reproductions; for many of the Greek writers who saw the original statues have described them for us. Fortunately, when we come to the period of Athenian greatness, during the Age of Pericles, we find on the Acropolis a splendid collection of original sculpture, consisting not only of relief decorations on buildings[1] still standing but also of many beautiful fragments of statuary and relief which have been placed in the modern Acropolis Museum.

Phidias and the Sculptures of the Parthenon. Phidias was the greatest of the sculptors at Athens during the Periclean Age. In a long band of carved marble extending entirely around the four sides of the Parthenon at the top, inside the colonnades, Phidias and his pupils portrayed, as in a glorified vision, the people of Athens moving in the stately proces-

[1] It should be remembered that nearly half of the original frieze of the Parthenon is now in the British Museum.

sion (Fig. 45) of the Panathenaic festival. To be sure, these were not individual portraits of actual Athenian folk, but only types which lived in the exalted vision of the sculptor. Inside the new temple was placed a tall figure of Athena, wrought by the cunning hand of Phidias in gold and ivory. Out in the open area behind the colonnaded entrance rose another great work of Phidias, a colossal *bronze* statue of Athena, seventy feet high including its tall base. With shield and spear the goddess stood, the gracious protectress of Athens, and the glittering point of her gilded spear could be seen shining like a beacon far across the land, even by the sailors as they rounded the promontory of Mt. Hymettus (map, p. 154) homeward-bound.

It should be noted with what wisdom Phidias chose his materials for his two statues of Athena : the gleaming bronze to catch and reflect the sun's rays out of doors; the soft, mellow ivory and sparkle of gold for the shaded temple interior. Both of the Athenas disappeared in antiquity, as did that other Phidian masterpiece, the gold and ivory statue of Zeus at Olympia. There exist today only the representations of the Zeus on some Roman coins and the descriptions of Greek and Roman writers who were awed by its beauty.

The Sculpture of Praxiteles. Phidias and his pupils thus depicted the gods — whom they wrought in stone or metal, or overlaid with gold and ivory — as lofty, majestic, unapproachable beings, lifted high above human weaknesses and human feeling. Even the *human* figures of Phidias did not look like the everyday men and women, youths and maidens, whom one might have met on the streets of Athens. When Phidias and his pupils had passed away, the sculptors who followed them made their figures look more human. Among them we must give perhaps the highest place to the eminent Athenian sculptor Praxiteles, who lived after the Peloponnesian Wars.

As his native city had no money for great monumental works, Praxiteles made individual figures of life size, mostly for foreign states. The gods of Praxiteles seem less remote than the majestic and exalted figures of Phidias. They at

A B

Fig. 53. *Two Greek Gods as Sculptured by Praxiteles*

Notice the wonderful ease and grace with which these figures in repose are poised. In a country where lizards were darting along every sunny wall, a lad with a stone ready to throw was a frequent sight. This common human action is the one which Praxiteles chose for his Apollo (*B*), and he has depicted the satyr (*A*) in an equally natural posture, with drinking horn and a bunch of grapes. These very human gods are quite different from those of Phidias

once appeal to us as being human like ourselves, interested in a life like our own. As they stand at ease in attitudes of repose the grace and balance of the flowing lines give them a splendor and beauty unattained by any earlier sculpture of the Greeks (Fig. 53).

Scopas and the Sculpture of Violent Action and Emotion. In marked contrast to the work of Praxiteles was that of Scopas, who did much of the sculpture of the Mausoleum. He loved to fashion figures not in tranquil moods but in violent action, in moments of excitement, like that of warriors in battle. The figures are intense and dramatic with their large heads, deep-set eyes, and straining bodies. They mark the beginning of the transition from the serene and restful composition of the fifth-century Greeks to the more passionate and tempestuous monuments of the Hellenistic Age (pp. 244–245). The influence of Scopas was shown even in the work of the stonecutters on the fourth-century tombstone reliefs at Athens. In the fifth century the artist-craftsmen had carved on the tombstones representations of the deceased as tranquil, resigned men and women of the Parthenon type. But now the reliefs were done with a soft and melancholy beauty that displayed the wistful uncertainty with which the Greeks of this age were beginning to regard the world beyond the grave.

3. The Beautiful Products of Greek Handicraft

The Importance of Greek Crafts. No people have ever enjoyed more than the Greeks the use, in everyday life, of things which showed beauty and artistic merit. Indeed, the Greeks developed the crafts into arts in a manner seldom equaled by modern peoples; for few modern craftsmen have possessed such joy in workmanship and pride in achievement. Although craftsmen occupied an inferior social position in the Greek states, yet the Hellenes respected both good craftsmanship and the skilled craftsman. The names of successful engravers, lapidaries, and tapestry weavers live on today in Greek literature. Men boasted of drinking from golden cups engraved by the great Thericles of Corinth or from bowls of beechwood carved with twining ivy by Alcon of Mylæ. It was said that Alexander the Great always wore in battle a cape that had been woven by that master weaver Helicon of Cyprus. Athenian leaders invited skilled craftsmen to Athens, and a Greek city was pleased when any particular craft carried on within its gates became renowned. Corinth was proud to be the home of the master bronzeworkers; from Colophon in Ionia came the finest goldsmiths; the Greek artist-craftsmen of Cyprus designed the most exquisite tapestry.

Oriental Influences on Early Greek Industrial Art. As the Greeks of Cyprus were so close to the Orient, it was to be expected that they would excel in the art of weaving; for the most beautiful rugs, hangings, and draperies came from the East in ancient times, as they do today. As a matter of fact, all Greek industrial art owed much in its origins to the craftsmen of the ancient East. The shepherds and peasants who entered Greece around 1000 B.C. had no skill in craftsmanship and were slow to take up industries and manufacturing. When they did make a beginning with pottery, the crude paintings with which they decorated their rough ware show an attempt to imitate methods employed by the Ægean potters in Crete a thousand years earlier.

On the metal platters and the furniture of carved ivory landed from the Phœnician ships (p. 126), however, the Greek craftsmen found designs of palm trees, lotus flowers, hunting scenes along the Nile, the Assyrian tree of life, and especially those strange winged creatures of Oriental fancy, the sphinx, the gryphon, the winged horse. The Greeks therefore began to use these designs in their own work.

During the seventh century Greek industries were still unequal to those of the Orient, but after 600 B.C. the Greeks began to surpass their Oriental teachers. In Samos they learned to make *hollow* bronze castings like those of the Egyptians. They decorated pottery with *their own* original designs, and so freed themselves from the domination of the Orient.

Greek Crafts and Greek Industry. The earliest Greek craftsmen worked, for the most part, in metal, wood, clay, and leather. At this time the craftsman had no regular home or workshop, but journeyed from place to place and became the guest of his customer, who furnished the raw material for the job in hand. By the sixth century B.C. the industrial situation had changed greatly. Factories and workshops were opened, and the manufacturer or craftsman generally furnished the raw material. The finished product was then sent from the shop to the customer. Under these conditions specialization arose to such an extent that even among the cabinetmakers there was one group which made chairs, another which made chests, and still another which made beds.

Development of the Greek Crafts. A further factor in the revolutionizing of Greek industry in the sixth century was the invention or rediscovery of improvements in craft technique. The craftsmen in metal had learned not only how to make hollow bronze castings, a process discovered in the East, but also how to weld iron. At length the Greek metalworkers could cast either solid or hollow, weld, solder, engrave, beat out designs in relief, cut and inlay, and cut into filigree, — in short, they could do most of the things metalworkers do today. Much of the technique had been employed by earlier peoples, but they had never produced metal objects of such perfect and artistic workmanship. The armor worn in war was decorated with marvelous designs; the toilet accessories of bronze were as exquisitely cut as a modern copperplate engraving; and the tableware in the homes of the well-to-do might be embossed or even inlaid with costly stones.

Indeed, every plain surface seemed to tempt the Greek craftsman. There was much carving on wood, and tables, chairs, and beds were inlaid. The truth of the descriptions by ancient writers of the magnificently decorated cedar chests, in which clothing was stored, is proved by the examples of exquisite woodwork found on fragments of coffins.

The Story of Greek Pottery. We must pay especial honor to the Greek potters, who made the most wonderful vessels of clay that the world has ever seen. Other potters made pots, bowls, cups, and jugs of more or less pleasing form, but the Greeks made vases beautiful in shape and decoration. The Greek vases which we still have are, moreover, very valuable in tracing the history of art; for no other original Greek paintings have ever been found, and the steps by which the Greek painters improved their work may be followed to some extent in the vase paintings which reflected the methods used in painting on walls and panels.

Growth of Trade in Greek Vases. On an early terra-cotta plaque from Corinth appears a drawing of a ship loaded with pottery jars, for the Greeks began very early to ship earthen-

A. Mixing vessel (*krater*)
Metropolitan Museum of Art

B. Wine jug (*oinochoë*)
Museum of Fine Arts, Boston

C. Provision jar (*amphora*)
Metropolitan Museum of Art

D. Drinking cup (*kylix*)
Metropolitan Museum of Art

E. Wine jar (*stamnos*)
Metropolitan Museum of Art

F. Water jar (*hydria*)
Metropolitan Museum of Art

G. Oil jug (*lekythos*)
Museum of Fine Arts, Boston

Fig. 54. *Examples of the Skill of Early Athenian Potters*

ware vases and pots. The making of pottery soon became the leading industry of Greece. Some of it was used for household dishes, some as storage vessels for wine, olive oil, or honey, while other, more valuable, jars and vases were used as display pieces at the banquets of the rich, or as offerings to the dead. A great deal of pottery was needed to supply the demand, and nearly every Greek city went into the business. The first decorated Greek pottery of any degree of excellence was produced during the eighth century B.C. The earliest Greek vase-painters employed bands of geometrical designs to decorate their pottery. They painted triangles, circles, zigzag lines, swastikas, dots, and stars running parallel to bands which contained human and animal figures more or less in silhouette (see mixing vessel, *A*, Fig. 54). The patterns are not unpleasing, but the whole effect is cold and stiff. It is therefore a relief to turn to the vases with Oriental decorative patterns, consisting usually of rosettes and rows of animals arranged to suggest tapestry (jug, *B*, Fig. 54).

Attic Vase Paintings, Black-Figured Style. The earliest pottery style perfected by the Athenians — although used earlier by the Corinthians — is known as black-figured, because the technique consisted in applying *black-glazed* silhouette figures on a red-clay ground. Incised markings were made within the figures to indicate eyes, hair, muscles, folds of clothing, trappings on horses, and the like (provision jar, *C*, Fig. 54). As these incised marks pierced through the black glaze down to the original clay, the lines produced were a yellowish white. The lines were sometimes filled with white paint in order to give emphasis to them. The vases were no longer decorated with rows of animals, geometrical designs, or rosettes, but with scenes from the lives of gods and heroes or from everyday life. They were a great deal more lifelike than the old, queerly shaped animals and human beings with triangles for bodies. The skill required for perfection in the black-figured style was, however, the skill of the engraver rather than that of the painter. Figures could be made with mechanical precision, but the soft contour lines which may be achieved with the painter's brush were absent.

Red-Figured Vases. It is not known when the *red-figured* style was worked out by the Attic vase-painters, but they seem to have used it rather shyly at first. Sometimes one side of a vase would be painted in the black-figured style and the other side in the red-figured. The advantages of the technique to the craftsmen must, however, have been apparent from the first. In producing the red-figured ware, the Athenian vase-painter first covered the surface of the clay with a red-ocher wash to make it darker. Then the outlines of the figures were sketched in with some blunt instrument. This sketch was then traced around again by one or two painted lines. The figures were thus left on the red of the surface clay, but the details of eyes, muscles, draperies, and so on were afterwards painted in with black glaze. Finally the entire background was filled in with black glaze applied with a brush (drinking cup, *D*, Fig. 54).

Of course this type of work required more skill and at the same time gave the artist a better chance to improve his drawing. Instead of reducing the human figure to a silhouette, the vase-painters could give more attention to the presentation of anatomical details, folds of clothing, and similar matters. At first they obtained some strange results. In an attempt to draw the eyes in profile, instead of in front view as had always been done before, they produced a few cross-eyed gods and heroes. But eventually the Greek vase-painters solved most of the problems of foreshortening and perspective (wine jar, *E*, and water jar, *F*, Fig. 54).

4. THE DISCOVERIES MADE BY GREEK PAINTERS

Early Greek Painting. Mural decorators made vast paintings on the walls of temples, stoas, clubrooms, and sometimes even private houses. None of these have survived, and we have to depend for our knowledge of them upon descriptions by ancient writers, as we did in the case of certain Greek statues.

It is generally agreed that Polygnotus was the first Greek artist to produce real paintings and not colored drawings. The ancients praised this artist particularly for giving some facial expression to the men and women he painted, instead of representing them with stiff, set features as former artists had done. His achievements in composition and use of color also were noted. Like others before him, Polygnotus painted only with white, red, yellow, and black, but his use of black was said to be exceptionally striking. The white oil jars of this period (*G*, Fig. 54) were also painted in four colors, and from them we can gain some idea of the manner in which the major artists handled the several colors.

The masterpieces of the period seem to have been principally wall decorations. The technique was probably that of the fresco, which means that the colored paintings were put on the plastered walls while the plaster was still wet.

Use of Portable Paintings. The introduction of portable paintings on canvas or panels of wood, ivory, or marble freed the painters from the necessity of painting large scenes on the walls of state buildings. As no oil colors were known in the ancient world, the Greek painters either employed some material like white of egg, honey, or a gluey substance to hold the colors together for application to a dry surface or else adopted the Egyptian method of mixing colors in melted wax and then applying the fluid wax, with a brush and palette knife, to the picture. The painter could now work in his own studio to please his own fancy, and could sell his paintings to any private purchaser who wished to buy. It thus became customary for people of wealth to set up paintings in their own houses, and in this way the private support of art increased and painting was greatly stimulated.

Discovery of how to paint Light, Shadow, and Perspective. An Athenian painter named Apollodorus, who worked in the latter half of the fifth century B.C., seems to have been one of the first to notice that the light usually fell on an object from *one side*, leaving the unlighted side so dark that but little color showed on that side, while on the lighted side the colors came out very brightly. When he painted a woman's arm in this way, it looked round and seemed to stand out from the surface of the painting; whereas in the Painted Porch all the human limbs in the old painting of "The Battle

FIG. 55. *Marble Panel Painting of Women Playing Knucklebones*

This painting from the ruins of Herculaneum is thought to be a copy of a late fifth-century work, for the technique is typical of that period. It displays the beginnings of shading. Just as young people of today play jackstones (or "jacks"), the young people of ancient Greece played a similar game, using the knucklebones of sheep as playing pieces. Two of the group in the rear have apparently not been good sports but have quarreled over the game, and the third is attempting to act as peacemaker

of Marathon" looked perfectly flat. By representing figures in the background of his paintings as smaller than those in front, Apollodorus also introduced what we now call perspective. As a result his paintings had an appearance of depth; and when he painted the interior of a house, one seemed to be looking into the very room itself. He was called by the Athenians the "shadow-painter," and the good old-fashioned folk shook their heads at his work, preferring the old style. Even the great philosopher Plato condemned this new method of painting as employing devices and creating illusions of depth which were really deception.

Triumph of New Method of Painting. Nevertheless the new method triumphed, and the younger painters who adopted it produced work which was the talk of the town. People gossiped about it and told how a painter named Zeuxis, in order to outdo his rival Parrhasius, had painted some grapes so naturally that birds flew up to the painting and pecked at them. Thereupon Parrhasius invited Zeuxis over to his studio to inspect a painting of his. Zeuxis found it covered with a curtain, which he attempted to draw aside; but his hand fell on a painted surface, and he discovered to his confusion that the curtain was no more real than his own painted grapes had been. Such artists as Polygnotus, Apollodorus, Zeuxis, and Parrhasius may be considered as pioneers in the art of painting. Their discoveries and improvements with regard to technique, use of color and shade, or relation of objects in space have prepared the way for all those painters who have come after them.

Achievements of Greek Genius in Spite of Constant Wars. The rivalries of the city-states which proved fatal to the independence of the Greeks had constantly spurred them all on, as each city strove to surpass the others in art and literature and all the finest things in civilization. The tiny Athenian state alone, having at most twenty-five or thirty thousand citizens, had furnished a group of great names unsurpassed in many lines of human achievement.

Questions and Exercises

REVIEW OF CHAPTER

1. Why was Athens called " the Monumental City "? Describe the two earliest styles, or orders, of Greek architecture. Why do we call an imposing tomb a "mausoleum"?

2. How do we know about the work of the Greek sculptors of the fifth and fourth centuries B.C.? What materials did the Greek sculptors work in? Contrast the work of Praxiteles with that of Scopas.

3. Give an estimate of Greek craftsmanship. What is the difference between Attic black-figured vases and Attic red-figured vases?

4. List the innovations made by the Greek painters of the fifth and fourth centuries B.C. How did the Greek painters mix their colors?

USEFUL TERMS

See how much meaning you can give the following: *symmetry, gable, colonnade, rubble, monumental city, frieze, industrialism, filigree, monopoly, technique, foreshortening, fresco.*

DIRECTIVE QUESTIONS

1. Can you name some building in your neighborhood for which one of the Greek architectural styles has been used?

2. Many modern sculptors are making statues of athletes. Do you suppose that these will differ greatly from those of the Greek sculptors?

3. Have you ever heard of people in modern times who, like the potters of Corinth, have tried to make and sell the most and not the best products?

4. What great ambition of the Greek sculptor and painter led to the rise of such stories as those concerning Zeuxis' grapes or Parrhasius' curtain?

DISCUSSION TOPICS

1. The individuality of the Greeks prevented their combining to form a good government, but the same quality was a valuable one in creative art.

2. Many of our public buildings are in the Greek style. Use illustrations.

3. Americans are becoming more and more interested in buying for everyday use objects which are beautiful and show artistic merit.

4. Naturalness is not such an important thing in modern art as it was in Greek art.

ADDITIONAL ADVENTURES IN LEARNING

1. Studies in Source Materials. THALLON, *Readings in Greek History*: (1) The public works of Pericles, pp. 275–279; (2) The temple of Apollo at Delphi and the gifts of Crœsus, pp. 57–59.

2. Supplementary. Read R. T. McKENZIE, "The Athlete in Sculpture," in *Art and Archæology*, Vol. 33, No. 3 (May–June, 1932), pp. 115–125, and write a paragraph comparing the sculpture illustrated with the Greek statues of athletes.

3. Look up in an encyclopedia: *classical temples, Phidias, perspective, Tanagra, Ceramicus, paints, pigment.*

CHAPTER XI · ALEXANDER THE GREAT
AND THE HELLENISTIC AGE

THE RISE OF MACEDONIA · CAMPAIGNS OF ALEXANDER THE GREAT · AMBITIOUS
PLANS OF ALEXANDER · THE HEIRS OF ALEXANDER'S EMPIRE · THE CIVILIZATION OF
THE HELLENISTIC AGE

SINCE the Greeks would not unite to form a strong nation, they were bound to fall victim to a foreign invader. Fortunately their conqueror, Philip of Macedon, appreciated the civilization of Greece. His son and successor, Alexander, had as his tutor the great Greek philosopher Aristotle; so the youth early learned to love and revere the marvelous achievements of the Greek people. When, later, Alexander the Great brought the whole Mediterranean world under his control, Greek learning and art were carried far and wide. So instead of being destroyed, as were many early civilizations, the knowledge which the Greeks had gained was preserved and furnished a basis for still further progress.

We call this period the Hellenistic Age; for during these centuries Hellenic civilization dominated the ancient world.

1. THE RISE OF MACEDONIA

Uncultured States of the Balkan Peninsula. The backward and barbarous northern peoples in Thrace and Macedonia spoke Indo-European tongues akin to Greek, but their Greek kindred of the south could not understand them. A little Greek civilization began here and there to improve somewhat the rough and simple life of the people of Macedonia. The Macedonian kings commenced to cultivate Greek literature and art, and the mother of Philip, king of Macedon, was grateful that she had been able to learn to read and write Greek in her old age.

Philip of Macedon and his New Army. Philip himself had had a Greek education and admired the Greeks, but he also knew how weak and disunited they were and how unable to resist a foreign power. Philip was a skillful statesman and a good soldier; and when he became ruler of Macedonia, in 359 B.C., he planned to make himself master of the Greeks.

He formed a permanent, or standing, army of professional soldiers out of the peasant population of his kingdom. The infantrymen soon became famous as the "Macedonian phalanx." Heretofore horsemen had played but a small part in war in Europe. Philip now drilled a large body of riders to move about *together* and to attack in *a single mass*, either alone or with the phalanx of foot soldiers, so that the whole combined force, infantry and cavalry, moved as one great unit, making a powerful fighting machine.

Philip becomes Leader of the Greeks. Philip then steadily extended the territory of his kingdom eastward and northward until it reached the Danube and the Hellespont. His progress on the north of the Ægean soon brought him into conflict with the Greek states which had colonies in this region. Two parties then arose at Athens. One of them proposed to accept Philip's friendship and recognized in him the savior of the Greek world. The other denounced Philip as a barbarous tyrant who was trying to enslave the free Greek cities. The leader of this group was the great orator Demosthenes. His *Philippics*, as his public speeches denouncing King Philip are called, are probably the finest example of Greek oratory.

After a long series of conflicts Philip defeated the Greek forces in a final battle at Chæronea (338 B.C.) and firmly established himself as head of a league of all the Greek states except Sparta, which still held out against him. Two years later he was stabbed by enemies during the revelries at the wedding of his daughter (336 B.C.).

Education and Character of Alexander the Great. The kingship passed into the hands of Philip's son Alexander, a youth of only twenty years. Seven years before, when Alexander was thirteen years of age, his father had summoned to the Macedonian court the great philosopher Aristotle (p. 250), a former pupil of Plato, to be the teacher of the young prince. Under his instruction Alexander learned to know and love the masterpieces of Greek literature, especially the Homeric songs. The deeds of the ancient heroes kindled his youthful imagination and lent a heroic tinge to his whole character. As he grew older he came to be a great admirer of Greek genius and culture.

2. CAMPAIGNS OF ALEXANDER THE GREAT

Alexander conquers the Greek States. The Greek states were still unwilling to submit to Macedonian leadership, and fancied they could easily overthrow so youthful a ruler as Alexander. They were soon to learn how shrewd a head there was on his young shoulders. When Thebes revolted against Macedonia for the second time after Philip's death, Alexander captured and completely destroyed the ancient city, sparing only the house of the great poet Pindar. This example taught the Greeks to acknowledge and fear his power. The Greek states, thereupon, with the exception of Sparta, elected Alexander as their leader.

Alexander, the Champion of Hellas against Asia. The Asiatic campaign which Alexander now planned was to make it clear that he was the champion of Hellas against Asia. Marching his army into Asia Minor, he stopped at Troy and camped upon the plain (map, p. 233) where the Greek heroes of the Homeric songs had once fought. Here he worshiped in the temple of Athena and prayed for the success of his cause against Persia. He thus contrived to throw around himself the heroic atmosphere of the Trojan War, till all Hellas beheld the dauntless figure of the Macedonian youth as if he had stepped out of that glorious age in which they believed the Greeks had united against Asia.

Battle of the Granicus (334 B.C.) *and the Conquest of Asia Minor.* Meantime the Persian king had hired thousands of Greek heavy-armed infantry, who were now to fight against their own countrymen. At the river Granicus, in his first important battle, Alexander had no difficulty in scattering his enemies. Marching southward he took the Greek cities one by one and freed all western Asia Minor forever from the Persian yoke.

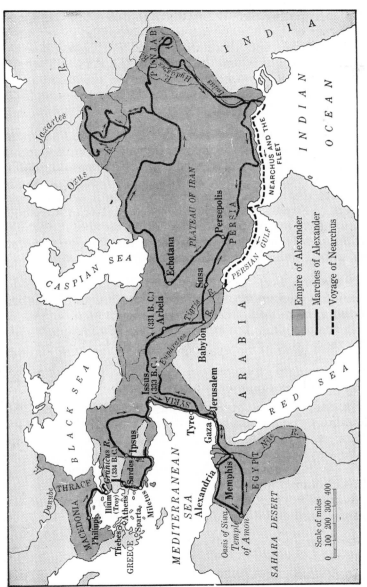

The Empire of Alexander the Great

He then pushed boldly eastward and rounded the northeast corner of the Mediterranean. Here, as he looked upon the Fertile Crescent, there was spread out before him the vast Asiatic realms where the family of the Persian king had been supreme for two hundred years. In this great arena Alexander was to be the champion for the next ten years (333–323 B.C.).

Defeat of Darius III at the Battle of Issus (333 B.C.). At Issus, Alexander met the main army of Persia, under the command of Darius III, the last of the Persian line. The Macedonians swept the Asiatics from the field, and the disorderly retreat of Darius never stopped until his army had crossed the Euphrates. Darius then sent a letter to Alexander requesting terms of peace and offering to accept the Euphrates as a boundary between them, all Asia west of that river to be handed over to the Macedonians.

Alexander's Decision; Conquest of Phœnicia and Egypt. Alexander's advisers urged him to accept these terms, fearing lest the Persian fleet should stir up the cities of Greece to revolt against him; but before the eyes of the young Alexander there arose a vision of vast empire through which Greek civilization should spread. He waved aside his father's old counselors and decided to advance to the conquest of the whole Persian Empire.

The danger from the Persian fleet he now carefully and deliberately met by a march southward along the shore of the eastern end of the Mediterranean. All the Phœnician seaports on the way were captured. Egypt, which had been for so long a Persian province (p. 102), then fell an easy victim to the Macedonian army. The Persian fleet, thus deprived of all its home harbors and cut off from its home government, soon scattered and disappeared.

Alexander Lord of the Ancient East. Having thus cut off the fleet of the enemy in his rear, Alexander returned from Egypt to Asia, and, marching eastward along the Fertile Crescent, crossed the Tigris close by the mounds which had long covered the ruins of Nineveh. Here, near Arbela, Darius had gathered his forces for a last stand (map, p. 233). Although greatly outnumbered, the Macedonians crushed the Asiatic army and forced the Persians into disgraceful flight. In a few days Alexander was living in the winter palace of the Persian king in Babylon.

As Darius III fled into the eastern mountains he was stabbed by his own treacherous attendants (330 B.C.). Alexander rode up with a few of his officers in time to look upon the body of the last of the Persian emperors, the lord of Asia, whose vast realm had now passed into his hands. Thus both the valley of the Nile and the Fertile Crescent, the homes of the two earliest civilizations, were finally in the hands of a *European* power. Alexander continued eastward through the original little kingdom of the Persians, whence Cyrus had victoriously come forth over two hundred years before.

The Campaigns of Alexander in the Distant East (330–324 B.C.) *and his Return to Babylon* (323 B.C.). During the next five years the young Macedonian seemed to disappear in the mists on the far-off eastern fringes of the known world. He marched his army in one vast loop after another through the heart of the Iranian Plateau (map, p. 233), northward across the Oxus and Jaxartes rivers, southward across the Indus and the frontiers of India, where at last the complaints of his weary troops forced him to turn back.

He descended the Indus and even sailed the waters of the Indian Ocean. Then he began his westward march again along the shores of the Indian Ocean, accompanied by a fleet which he had built on the Indus. The return march through desert wastes cost many lives as the thirsty and ill-fed troops dropped by the way. Over seven years after he had left the great city of Babylon, Alexander entered it again. He had been less than twelve years in Asia, and he had carried Greek civilization into the very heart of the continent. At important points along his line of march he had founded Greek cities and had set up kingdoms which were to be centers of Greek civilization on the frontiers of India. Never before had East and West been so closely brought together as in these amazing marches and campaigns of Alexander.

3. Ambitious Plans of Alexander

Alexander's Attempt to merge European and Asiatic Civilization. Meantime Alexander had not neglected to organize and provide the proper government for his vast conquests. He was convinced of the superiority of Greek civilization and was determined to Hellenize the world and to unite Asia with Europe by settling colonies of Greeks and Macedonians in the East. On the other hand, he realized that he could not successfully rule the Orient as if it were Macedonia, but must permit the Persians to retain their familiar habits and forms of government. He therefore appointed Persians to high offices and set them over provinces as satraps.

Alexander's Plans to conquer the Western Mediterranean. Alexander carefully worked out a plan of campaign for the conquest of the *Western* Mediterranean. A fleet of a thousand battleships was to be built, with which to subdue Italy, Sicily, and Carthage. A roadway was also to be laid along the northern coast of Africa, to be built at enormous expense, to furnish a highway for his army from Egypt to Carthage and the Atlantic.

Deification of Alexander. What was to be Alexander's own position in this colossal world-state of which he dreamed? Many a great Greek had come to be recognized as a god, and there was in Greek belief no sharp line dividing gods from men. It had been customary to regard the king as divine in Egypt, where he was a son of the Sun-god, and the idea was a common one in the ancient East. Alexander found in this general attitude the solution of the question of his own position. He would have himself lifted to a place among the gods. As a god he might impose his will upon the Greek cities without offense.

Early in his conquest of Egypt, therefore, he had taken the time to march with a small following far out into the Sahara Desert to the Oasis of Siwa, where there was a famous shrine of Amon. The oracle of Amon at Siwa enjoyed the respect

Fig. 56. *Sculpture on the So-Called Sarcophagus of Alexander*

This deep relief on one side of the sarcophagus of Alexander represents Persians and Greeks joining in a lion hunt. The Persians can be distinguished by their headdress and tight breeches, the Greeks being bareheaded and barelegged. This sarcophagus probably never contained the body of Alexander but receives its name from the magnificent sculptured reliefs representing Alexander in battle and hunt. His figure is probably the rider at the left charging with leveled spear which has been broken away

of the whole Greek world. Here, in the vast solitude, Alexander entered the holy place alone. No one knew what took place there, but when he came out Alexander was greeted by the high priest of the temple as the son of the god Amon. All Greece soon heard of this remarkable occurrence.

After a time the young king found that this divinity which he claimed lacked outward signs. Hence he adopted Oriental customs, among which was the requirement that all who approached him on official occasions should bow down to the earth and kiss his feet. He also sent formal notice to all the Greek cities that he was henceforth to be officially numbered among the gods of each city, and that as such he was to receive the state offerings which each city presented. Thus Alexander introduced into Europe as early as the third century B.C. *absolute monarchy* and the *divine right of kings*, of which we shall hear later.

Effects of Power on Alexander. This godlike position which Alexander assumed was gained at tragic cost. For his old friends and followers could not understand the necessity for actions which strained or broke entirely those bonds of friendship which had linked together comrades in arms for so many years. The Persians were given high offices and treated like the equals of his personal friends (Fig. 56) or even placed over them! Disagreements caused the estrangement and even the execution of some of Alexander's old-time friends and supporters. Indeed, in a fit of rage, he himself murdered Clitus, who in the battle of the Granicus had saved his life, and who now had dared to reproach him openly. As we see the king in abject remorse sitting for three days in his tent, speechless with grief, refusing all food, and restrained only by his officers from taking his own life, we gather some slight impression of the terrible personal cost of Alexander's policy as a monarch.

Death of Alexander. After Alexander's return to Babylon, as he was preparing for an expedition to subjugate the Arabian peninsula and thus be free to carry out his great plans for the conquest of the Western Mediterranean, he fell sick, probably of a malarial fever, which after a few days caused his death (June, 323 B.C.). He was thirty-three years of age and had reigned thirteen years. Although so short, his life was without doubt the most influential and impressive in history. In many ways his influence was felt throughout the entire world of that day from Rome to China, especially in science, art, commerce, and statesmanship.

4. THE HEIRS OF ALEXANDER'S EMPIRE

Division of Alexander's Realm; the Ptolemies in Egypt. After a generation of exhausting wars by land and sea, Alexander's vast empire fell into three main parts — in Europe, Asia, and Africa — with one of his generals, or one of their successors, at the head of each. In Europe, Macedonia passed finally into the hands of Antigonus Gonatas, grandson of one of Alexander's commanders. In Asia most of the territory of the former Persian Empire was under the rule of Alexander's general Seleucus. In Africa, Egypt was held by Ptolemy, one of the cleverest of Alexander's Macedonian leaders. He succeeded in making himself king and became the founder of a dynasty, or family, of kings whom we call the Ptolemies. Ptolemy at once saw that he would be constantly obliged to depend upon mercenary troops from Greece. With statesmanlike judgment he therefore built up a fleet which gave him the mastery of the Mediterranean. He chose as his residence the great harbor city of Alexandria, which Alexander had founded in the western Nile Delta. For nearly a century (roughly, the third century B.C.) the Eastern Mediterranean, from Greece to Syria and from the Ægean to the Nile Delta, was an Egyptian sea. The new Hellenistic rulers of Egypt did not set up a Greek form of state, but regarded themselves as the successors of the ancient Pharaohs. Thus the Macedonians ruling on the Nile were continuing an ancient Oriental absolute monarchy. The example of this form of state, thus preserved, was of far-reaching influence throughout the Mediterranean world and finally displaced the democracies of the Greeks and Romans.

The Asiatic Empire of the Seleucids. The Seleucids, as we call Seleucus and his descendants, were the chief heirs of Alexander; for they held the larger part of his empire, extending from the Ægean to the frontiers of India. The fleet of the Ptolemies, however, interfered with the business development and prosperity of the Seleucids, who found it difficult to reach Greece for trade, troops, or colonists. They therefore gave special attention to the region around the northeast corner of the Mediterranean extending to the Euphrates, and here the Seleucids determined to develop another Macedonia. Their empire is often called *Syria*, after this region. Antioch (named after Seleucus's father, Antiochus), on the lower Orontes, finally became the business rival of Alexandria and the greatest seat of commerce in the northern Mediterranean.

The Macedonian Empire of the Antigonids. Compared with her two great rivals in Egypt and Asia, Macedonia, in Europe, seemed small indeed. Antigonus Gonatas determined to make himself lord of the Macedonians and the Greeks. Having defeated the barbarians who, in 280 B.C., broke through the northern mountains and devastated Macedonia, he was proclaimed king (277 B.C.). He at once took up the problem of restoring his kingdom in Macedonia and establishing his power among the Greek cities. The Egyptian fleet held complete command of the Ægean and thwarted him in every effort to control Greece. The energetic Antigonus, however, built a war fleet at vast expense, and in a long naval war with the Ptolemies he twice defeated the Egyptian fleet, thereby freeing the Eastern Mediterranean from the former control of Egypt.

Decline of Greece. The victories of Alexander the Great had opened up the vast Persian Empire to Greek business men, who poured into all the favorable centers of trade. Not only did Greece decline in population but the leadership in business and trade which she had enjoyed passed to Alexandria and Antioch. As the Greek cities lost their wealth they could no longer support fleets or armies of soldiers, and they

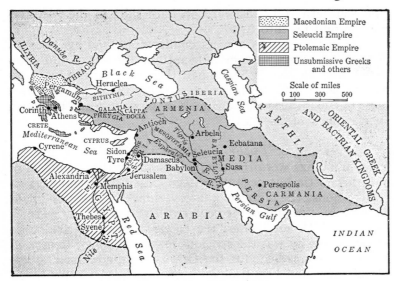

The Division of Alexander's Empire

soon became unable to protect themselves. Although they began to combine in alliances or federations for protection, they could not throw off the Macedonian control. Nevertheless, in spite of the weakness of the government of the Greeks in this age, their civilization continued to advance.

5. THE CIVILIZATION OF THE HELLENISTIC AGE

The Hellenistic Age; Supremacy of the Greek Language. The three centuries following the death of Alexander are called the Hellenistic Age, because during this period Greek civilization spread throughout the ancient world, especially the Orient. The people of Egypt and Western Asia now had Greek-speaking rulers who conducted the government in the Greek language. This was in the main the Greek spoken in Attica. The Orientals were also constantly transacting business with Greek merchants; they found many Greek books to read, and Greek plays to attend. Attic Greek thus gradually became the daily language of the great cities and of an enormous area stretching from Sicily (Fig. 76) and southern Italy eastward on both sides of the Mediterranean and far into Asia.

Life in the cities was more comfortable than ever before. The better houses were more beautifully furnished and decorated, and for the first time had their own water pipes connected with the town water supply. The streets were equipped with drainage channels or pipes, a thing unknown in the days of Pericles.

Construction of Public Buildings. In Pericles' time the great buildings were the temples, but now the architects of the Hellenistic Age began to design large and splendid buildings to house the offices of the government. These fine public buildings occupied the center of the city, where in early Greek and Oriental cities the castle of the king had once stood. Close by was the spacious market square, surrounded by long colonnades; for the Greeks were now making use of this airy and beautiful form of architecture contributed by Egypt. Here the citizens transacted much of their business. There was, furthermore, a handsome building containing an audience room with seats arranged like a theater. The Assembly no longer met in the open air but held its sessions here, as did the Council. There were also gymnasiums and baths, a race track, and a theater. Even a small city of only four thousand people, like Priene in Asia Minor, possessed all these buildings, besides several temples, one of which was erected by the order of Alexander himself.

Alexandria: Capital of the Hellenistic World. If a little city like Priene possessed such splendid public buildings, an imperial capital and great commercial city like Alexandria was correspondingly more magnificent. In population, wealth, commerce, power, and all the arts of civilization Alexandria was now the greatest city of the ancient world. Along the harbors stretched extensive docks, where ships which had braved the Atlantic storms off the coasts of Spain and Africa moored beside Oriental craft which had sailed as far as the Indian Ocean and brought back the wares of the vast Oriental world beyond. Far out at sea the mariners

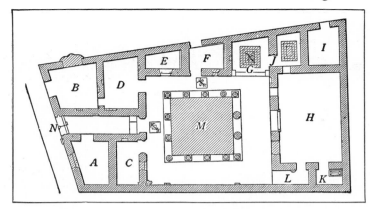

Fig. 57. *Ground Plan of the House of a Wealthy Greek in the Hellenistic Age*

The rooms are arranged around a central court (*M*), which is open to the sky. A roofed porch with columns (called a peristyle) surrounds the court (cf. Fig. 68). The main entrance is at *N*, with the room of the doorkeeper on the right (*A*). At the corner is a shop (*B*). *C*, *D*, and *E* are for storage and housekeeping. *F* is a back-door entry through which supplies were delivered ; it contained a stairway to the second floor. *G* was used as a small living-room, with an inner living-room (*J*) beside it. It had a built-in divan, and the entire side toward the peristyle was open. The finest room in the house was *H*, measuring about sixteen by twenty-six feet, with a mosaic floor, in seven colors, and richly decorated walls. It was lighted by a large door and two windows, and could be reached by the passage *L*. *K* was a little bathroom with a large marble bathtub. The sleeping-rooms were all on the second floor, which cannot now be reconstructed. *I* was a second tiny shop. This house was excavated by the French on the island of Delos

were guided at night by the light of a lofty beacon shining from a gigantic lighthouse tower which marked the entrance of the harbor of Alexandria.

From the deck of a great merchant ship of over four thousand tons the incoming traveler might look past the lighthouse and beyond the great war fleet of the Ptolemies and see, surrounded by rich masses of tropical foliage, the magnificent marble buildings of Alexandria and the fine houses of the wealthy citizens. Unfortunately, not one of these splendid buildings still stands.

Pergamum and its Sculpture. We are more fortunate in the case of Pergamum (map, p. 241), another famous city of this age which grew up under Athenian influences. One of the kings of Pergamum defeated and beat off the hordes

FIG. 58. *Corner of the Altar of Zeus in the Pergamon Museum at Berlin*

The treasures excavated at Pergamum for the Berlin State Museum have been placed in a separate building, which is called the Pergamon Museum. Here has been built a reconstruction of the great Zeus altar, with the sculptured reliefs placed as they were originally. (Courtesy of Pergamon Museum, Berlin)

of Gauls (or Galatians) who had come in from Europe. This achievement greatly affected the sculptors who were employed by the kings of Pergamum. They carved heroic marble figures of the northern barbarians in the tragic moment of death in battle (Fig. 59). It was probably this same struggle with the Gauls that was commemorated in an enormous band of sculpture representing the mythical battle between

FIG. 59. *Statue Commonly Known as the Dying Gaul*
This statue is a copy of the bronze original (now lost), which was made at Pergamum. It represents a Gallic trumpeter as he sinks in death with his trumpet at his feet

the gods and the giants. This extended almost entirely around a colossal altar (Fig. 58) erected by the kings of Pergamum in honor of Zeus, to adorn the market place of the city. Among the best works of the sculptors of this age were the reliefs on a wonderful marble sarcophagus, which depicted hunting and battle scenes from the life of Alexander the Great (Fig. 56).

Painting and Mosaic. The great Greek painters of this age also loved to portray intensely dramatic and tragic incidents. Their original works have all perished; but copies of some of them have been found in the Italian city of Pompeii, painted on the walls as interior decorations of fine houses or worked out in mosaic as floor pavement.

Mechanical Progress; Archimedes. The keen intelligence of this wonderful age was everywhere apparent, but especially in the application of science to the work and needs of daily life. It was an age of inventions, like our own. An up-to-date man would install an automatic door-opener for the doorkeeper of his house, and a washing machine which delivered water and mineral soap as needed. On his estate olive oil was produced by a press operating with *screw* pressure, for it was at this time that the screw as a mechanical device was invented. Outside the temples the priests set up automatic dispensers of holy water, while a water sprinkler operated by water pressure reduced the danger of fire. The application of levers, cranks, screws, and cogwheels to daily work brought forth cable roads for use in lowering stone from lofty quarries, and water wheels for drawing water on a large scale.

The most remarkable inventor and scientist of the time was probably Archimedes. He lived in Syracuse, and one of his famous feats was the arrangement of a series of pulleys and levers which so multiplied power that the king was able, by turning a light crank, to move a large three-masted ship standing fully loaded on the dock, and to launch it into the water. After witnessing such feats as this the people easily believed Archimedes' proud boast, "Give me a place to stand on and I will move the earth." But Archimedes was far more than an inventor of practical appliances. He was a scientific investigator of the first rank, the discoverer of what science now calls specific gravity. Besides his skill in physics he was also the greatest of ancient mathematicians.

The Alexandrian Scientists. Archimedes was in close correspondence with his friends in Alexandria, who formed the greatest body of scientists in the ancient world. They lived together at the *Museum*, a sort of university, where they were paid salaries and supported by the Ptolemies. With the exception of an Egyptian hospital, or medical school, endowed by King Darius of Persia, this organization was, so far as we yet know, the first scientific institution founded and supported by a government. The scientists of the Hellenistic Age, especially this remarkable group at Alexandria, were the forerunners of systematic scientific research, and their books were regarded as authorities for nearly two thousand years, until the revival of science in modern times.

Among the famous mathematicians at the Museum was Euclid, whose geometry is still used as a textbook in England. Along with mathematics much progress was also made in

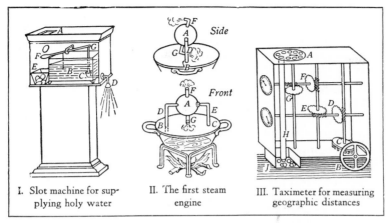

| I. Slot machine for sup-
plying holy water | II. The first steam
engine | III. Taximeter for measuring
geographic distances |

FIG. 60. *Mechanical Devices and Inventions of the Hellenistic Age*

The above machines, invented in the Hellenistic Age, are found described in books written somewhere around the first century A.D. by Hero of Alexandria and the Roman Vitruvius. **I** illustrates the principle of the lever. An inner vessel B contains holy water, which flows out through the vent C and the outside tube D. The vent C is kept closed by the lower end of a vertical rod CG. This rod is raised and lowered by a lever FG, flattened into a small disk at F. The rod CG is heavy enough by its own weight to keep the vent C closed; but when a coin is dropped through the slot A it falls upon F, where it rests long enough to depress the lever at F, thus raising the other end at G and lifting the rod CG. This opens the vent through which the holy water flows into the worshiper's hand at D until the coin falls off at F and drops into the money box E. Such boxes at the doors of the Hellenistic temples enabled the priesthood to sell holy water without an attendant. **II** shows how heat energy may be changed into mechanical energy and motion. A cauldron B–C of boiling water has a steam-tight cover. Above it a hollow ball A is supported by the tube D and the rod E, which does not penetrate either the ball or the top of the cauldron. The ball A is pivoted on the rod E. The tube D enters both the ball and the top of the cauldron, and therefore conducts the accumulating steam from the cauldron into the hollow ball, where it escapes with a roar through the small bent pipes F and G. The recoil of this escaping steam causes the ball to rotate. **III** illustrates two principles of the *toothed*, or *cog*, wheel: (1) when the teeth of two such wheels catch in each other, the wheels always rotate in opposite directions; (2) by making one wheel large and one small, power may be multiplied. The wheel B, which rolls on the surface of the road, has attached to its axle a peg fitting into the cogs of the wheel C, which is thus rotated. Its rotation is transmitted upward through the gears D, E, F, and G. On the top of the vertical shaft G is attached a flat disk A, which is perforated with a circular line of holes. Pebbles are placed in these holes, where they rest on the top of the box. As the disk A revolves it drags the pebbles along; and when a pebble comes over the top of the tube H, it falls down through the tube into the box J. The machine is so geared that for every mile that is traveled one pebble falls into the box J, where the number of pebbles indicates the distance traveled

astronomy. The Ptolemies built an astronomical observatory at Alexandria; and although it was, of course, without telescopes, important observations and discoveries were made. An astronomer of little fame named Aristarchus, who lived on the island of Samos, even discovered that the planets revolve around the sun, though few people would believe him, and his discovery was for a long time forgotten.

Astronomy greatly aided in the progress of geography. Eratosthenes, a mathematical astronomer of Alexandria, very cleverly computed the size of the earth within fifty miles of its true diameter. Much new information had also been gained regarding the extent and the character of the new regions reached by navigation and exploration in this age from the eastern coast of India to the British Isles. Eratosthenes was therefore able to write a more accurate geography than anyone before his time. It contained the first map having a cross-net of lines indicating latitude and longitude. This enabled him to show the location of any spot on the earth far more exactly than had been possible before. He thus became the founder of scientific geography.

Development of the Biological Sciences. In the study of animal and vegetable life Aristotle and his pupils remained the leaders, and the ancient world never progressed beyond their teachings. While their knowledge of botany, acquired without a microscope, was of course limited and contained errors, a large mass of new facts was observed and arranged. The medical men of the Museum at Alexandria were the first Greeks to undertake the dissection of the human body. They discovered the nerves and showed that the lines of connection between the whole body and the brain were the nerves. Herophilus, one of the greatest of these Alexandrian anatomists, discovered the optic nerve and traced it from the eye to the brain. In this way the brain was shown to be the center of a great system of sensation and control which we call the nervous system. Although such research came very near to discovering the circulation of the blood, the arteries were still thought to be channels for the circulation of air from the lungs. Alexandria became the greatest center of

Fig. 61. *A Greek Teacher Instructing Pupils in Writing (Left)*
and Reading (Right)

medical research in the ancient world, and here young men
went through long periods of study to train themselves as
physicians, just as medical students do at the present day.

The Alexandrian Library and Book-Publishing. Besides
the interest taken in the natural sciences, the study of literature made much progress. The great library of the Ptolemies at Alexandria far surpassed all other libraries of the
time, finally containing over half a million rolls. It required
an immense amount of editing and copying by hand to make
from old and often badly written manuscripts of famous works
the perfect editions needed for this great collection. In order
to correct these older texts a knowledge of the changes which
had taken place in languages was necessary, and so Alexandrian scholars began to compile Greek dictionaries and to
write the first grammars.

Hellenistic Literature. The writers of this age no longer
chose great and dramatic subjects, like war and fate, but

loved to picture peaceful scenes, such as the shepherd at the spring, listening to the music of the overhanging boughs or lazily watching his flocks. These charming scenes of country life, described in melodious verse, delighted the cultivated people of Alexandria more than the classics of former days. Their favorite writer was a Sicilian named Theocritus.

Education: Elementary Schools and Gymnasiums. In such a cultivated world, education had made much progress. The elementary schools, once *private*, were now often *supported by the state.* When the lad had finished at the elementary school, his father allowed him to attend lectures on rhetoric, science, philosophy, and mathematics in the lecture rooms of the gymnasium building. Such was the interest in learning that often a youth spent a few years of study at the Museum or in the schools of philosophy at Athens.

Moreover, special training had now become absolutely necessary to a young man's success in the pursuit of a profession. Like the medical student, the architect studied his profession. He bent industriously over books that told him how to erect an arch that would be safe and secure, and what were the proper proportions for a column. Young fellows who wished to become engineers studied many things in mechanics, like bridge-building and devices for moving heavy bodies. It was an age of technical training. The specialization in the professions was also to be found among the scientists, who now devoted their attention to a particular branch, like astronomy or mathematics or geography.

The Schools of the University at Athens; Aristotle. Athens, not Alexandria, was the leading home of philosophy. The youth who went there to take up philosophical studies found the successors of Plato still continuing his teaching in the quiet grove of the Academy, where his memory was still greatly revered. Plato's pupil Aristotle, however, had not been able to accept his master's teachings. After completing the education of the young Alexander, Aristotle had returned to Athens and established a school of his own at the famous Lyceum. With the help of groups of his more advanced stu-

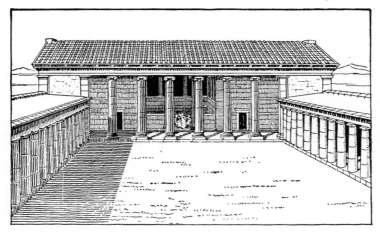

FIG. 62. *Hellenistic Gymnasium at Miletus, Third Century* B.C.

The Hellenistic *gymnasium* was not only a gymnasium in our modern sense but also a school. Here the boys attended elementary school, and the older men, standing among the colonnades, would discuss scientific or philosophic theories while they watched the athletic exercises and contests of the boys and young men. Miletus was one of the few ancient states to recognize its responsibility in education. We know that at least two large gifts, which corresponded to modern educational endowments, were given to the city for educational purposes. (After Krischen)

dents, Aristotle put together a kind of encyclopedia containing old and new facts in the different natural sciences, besides writing many treatises on other subjects, like logic, ethics, psychology, the drama, government, etc. The work was never completed, and many of the essays and treatises which it included have been lost. When Aristotle died, soon after the death of Alexander, his school declined. Aristotle's works, however, formed the greatest attempt ever made in ancient times to collect and to state clearly the whole mass of human knowledge. No writer ever enjoyed such widespread and unquestioned authority as did Aristotle for hundreds of years.

Stoics and Epicureans. But many Greeks desired, in addition to knowledge about the world, some teaching which would give them a happy and contented frame of mind and guide men in their attempts to live a good life. To meet this desire two more schools of philosophy arose at Athens. The first, the *Stoic* School, taught that man's chief aim should be to learn to face misfortune bravely by rising superior to both pleasure and pain. Its followers were famous for their fortitude, and hence our common use of the word "stoicism" to indicate indifference to suffering. The Stoic School was very popular, and finally became the greatest of the schools of philosophy. The second, the *Epicurean* School, founded by Epicurus in his garden at Athens, taught that the highest good was pleasure both of body and of mind. However, as Epicurus tells us in his letters, one cannot experience pleasure unless one lives "wisely, nobly, and justly," for life which is not so lived is not pleasant. Thus Epicurus sought to instill in his followers certain ideals of serenity and self-sufficiency. It is indeed a tragedy that later men, particularly the Romans, distorted this teaching into a justification for a life of sensual pleasure. The Oriental proverb "Eat, drink, and be merry, for tomorrow we die" has therefore been commonly applied to the Epicureans. Hence we still call a man devoted to pleasure, especially in eating, an epicure.

The Fall of the Old Greek Gods; Popularity of Oriental Religions. For highly educated men the beliefs of Stoicism or Epicureanism served as their religion. They often rejected the old beliefs about the gods. Moreover, they did not have to keep silent about their beliefs. The teachings of Socrates would no longer have caused his condemnation by his Athenian neighbors.

The great multitude of the common people, however, had not the education to understand philosophy nor the money to attend the philosophical schools. With the decline of their faith in the old Greek gods many Greeks adopted the religions of the Near East, and the Oriental gods became more and more popular. The Orient exerted a steady influence upon the life of the Eastern Mediterranean, in commerce, government, customs, industry, art, literature, and religion. So when Christianity issued from Palestine, it found itself but one among many influences from the Orient which were passing westward. Thus, while Greek civilization, with its language, its art, its literature, its theaters and gymnasiums, was Hellenizing the Orient, the Orient in the same way was exercising a powerful influence on the West and was Orientalizing the Eastern Mediterranean world. In this way there was gradually formed an Eastern Mediterranean world of Hellenic-Oriental civilization.

The Larger World of the Hellenistic Age. In this larger world the old Greek city-citizen, who had made Greek civilization what it was, played but a small part. The city-citizen had no share in guiding the affairs of the great nation or empire of which his city-state was a part. It was as if a citizen of Chicago might vote at the election of a mayor of his own city but had no right to vote at the election of a president of the United States. There was not even a name for the empire of the Seleucids, and their subjects, wherever they went, bore the names of their home cities or countries. The conception of "native land" in our sense was wanting, and patriotism did not exist.

A larger world had thus swallowed up the old Greek city-states; but this world of the Eastern Mediterranean, with its mixed Hellenic-Oriental civilization, had by 200 B.C. reached a point where it was to feel the iron hand of a great new military power from the distant world of the Western Mediterranean. We shall therefore be unable to understand the further story of the Eastern Mediterranean until we have turned back and taken up the career of the Western Mediterranean world. There in the West, for some three centuries, the city of Rome had been developing a power which was to unite both the East and the West into a vast empire including the *whole Mediterranean.*

Questions and Exercises

REVIEW OF CHAPTER

1. Who were the Macedonians? Describe the new military arrangements of Philip of Macedon. What did the Athenians think about Philip's plans? What was the outcome of Philip's struggle with the Greeks?

2. Discuss Alexander's relations with the Greeks. What decision did Alexander make after his conquest of Asia Minor? What battle ended the rule of the Great King?

3. What was Alexander's policy regarding the relations of Asia and Europe? What further conquests did he plan? Discuss the consequences of Alexander's death. What three empires resulted from the wars after Alexander's death? What was the policy of the first Ptolemy?

4. How did the scientists of the Hellenistic Age differ from those of Pericles' day? What state-supported scientific foundation was established in the Hellenistic Age? What advances were made in biological knowledge?

USEFUL TERMS

See how much meaning you can give to the following: *a philippic, the Ptolemies, cosmopolitan, hygiene, applied science, specific gravity.*

DIRECTIVE QUESTIONS

1. Who was the last advocate of the Greek city-state and Greek independence? Could Athens have withstood the Macedonians?

2. How did the Athenians, the Ten Thousand, and others prepare the way for the Macedonians?

3. What is Alexander's place in world history?

4. Who succeeded Athens as "policeman" of the Mediterranean?

DISCUSSION TOPICS

1. Was Alexander a genius or was he merely fortunate?

2. If Alexander had carried out his plans to conquer the Western Mediterranean, there would have been no Roman Empire.

3. The decline of the city-states was a tragedy from the standpoint of progress in civilization.

ADDITIONAL ADVENTURES IN LEARNING

1. **Studies in Source Materials.** THALLON, *Readings in Greek History*: (1) Philip's preparation for conquest, pp. 562–565; (2) Speeches of Isocrates addressed to Philip, pp. 570–573.

2. **Supplementary.** When Alexander conquered the Persian Empire, he found in the palaces of the Great King quantities of silver and gold. What was the effect of these on business? CARY, *Legacy of Alexander*, pp. 299–302; FRANK, *Economic History of Rome*, pp. 74–75; GLOTZ, *Ancient Greece at Work*, pp. 325–331.

3. Look up in an encyclopedia: *Macedonia, Antioch, Galatia, mosaic.*

Part Four

HOW THE ROMANS ESTABLISHED
A GREAT EMPIRE AND BROUGHT
GREEK CIVILIZATION NEARER US

We shall now see how a Little Latin Village in Italy,
Roma, became the Center of a Vast Empire, including
the Greek Cities which the Romans conquered. But
the Conquered Greeks became the Teachers of their
Conquerors, who enthusiastically imitated their Writings and Buildings and Art, and carried them into the
Uttermost Parts of their Vast Empire. The Romans
handed down the Greek Civilization to Coming Generations, with Various Additions of their Own. Later
it will be shown, in Part Five, how for Centuries Men
venerated the Roman Empire, and tried to keep it
Alive, at Least in Name

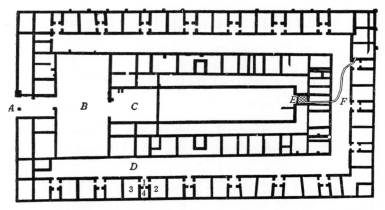

The Roman Military Hospital at Novaesium (near Neuss, in the Prussian Rhine Province), about A.D. 100

While the scientific progress made in medicine after the sixth century B.C. was of Greek origin, yet it was during the Roman Empire that the Greek and Greek-trained physicians made certain improvements in the *practice* of medicine. These improvements were principally in organization, in development of surgical implements, and in sanitation. The greatest physician of Roman times was the Greek Galen, from Asia Minor. It seems evident from his books that the ideas of sanitation which Rome developed made the doctors of the Roman Empire perhaps the cleanest group of doctors in antiquity. The ground plans of the hospital excavated at Novæsium well illustrate the above three points in the progress of medicine in the Roman Empire. The Empire was very particular about the health of the soldiers. Indeed, the doctors of such a well-regulated Roman military hospital as that at Novæsium, around the end of the first century A.D., would have been shocked at the horrors which Florence Nightingale found at the Scutari barrack hospital in the Crimean War in 1854. The hospital at Novæsium was about 165 feet wide by 295 feet long. The arrangement, as may be seen from the diagram above, was very similar to the corridor system in modern hospitals. The entrance corridor, beginning at *A*, led into the court *B*, which probably held a reservoir for rain water. Room *C* was perhaps the dining-hall. There are some seventeen suites distributed along the main corridor, like the one at *D*. Apparently one entered the anteroom 1, opening off the corridor, and could immediately shut the door to keep drafts and noise from the sickrooms 2 and 3. In the small room 4 the attendant probably sat, and clothes and supplies could also be stored there. The room *E* was apparently for the disposal of waste, as it contains a brick tile covering under which begins the channel *F*, which seems to have continued on to the outside of the building. Many surgical implements were found scattered throughout the ruins of the building. (After Meyer-Steinig)

CHAPTER XII · THE WESTERN MEDITERRANEAN WORLD AND ROME'S CONQUEST OF ITALY

OF ALL the great cities of Europe today, Rome has had the longest and most fascinating history. Starting as a tiny market place on the Tiber, it became the first great city of western Europe, and finally ruled an empire which reached from Britain on the north to the Persian Gulf and the Indian Ocean, and from the Atlantic to the Caspian Sea.

How greatly the Roman Empire influenced the development of the Western world we shall realize as we read the story of European history. Scattered from England to Palestine are remains of its wonderful buildings, and automobiles now traverse roads which were first laid out by engineers of the Roman Empire. Many of our handsome public buildings are modeled upon Roman buildings.

Latin, the language of the Romans, is studied in our schools; and from it are descended not only the French, Italian, and Spanish languages but many English words. Latin terms are also used today in scientific studies.

Scholars have regarded the contribution of the Romans to the development of law as their greatest achievement; and law students today are usually required to learn something of Roman law.

It took many centuries for the Romans to learn to found cities, build fine buildings, improve their language, develop their law and government, and reach their highest development in the days of the Roman Empire. In order to appreciate the greatness of this achievement it will be necessary first to trace their progress from their appearance as wandering tribesmen to the establishment of the Roman Republic as mistress of all Italy.

1. THE WESTERN MEDITERRANEAN WORLD

The Division of the Mediterranean into an Eastern and a Western Basin. The Mediterranean is not a single compact body of water, like the North Sea or one of the American Great Lakes. A land-bridge made up of Italy and Sicily extends across a large part of this great sea and almost divides it into two parts, an eastern and a western basin.

257

There are no accepted geographical names for these two basins, but we may call them, for convenience, the Eastern and Western Mediterranean worlds. The story of civilization began very early in the Eastern Mediterranean world (p. 23), but civilization was much slower in reaching and improving the life of the Western Mediterranean peoples.

Italy. its Geography and Climate. The most important land in the Western Mediterranean world in early times was Italy. It slopes westward in the main, and thus it faces and belongs to the Western Mediterranean world. The Italian peninsula, thrusting far out into the sea, is nearly six hundred miles long. The main chain of the Apennines, though crossing the peninsula obliquely in the north, is nearly parallel with the coasts. There are more extensive plains for the cultivation of grain than we find anywhere in Greece; at the same time there is much more room for upland pasturage of flocks and herds. A considerably larger population can be supported in the plains of Italy than in Greece. And since there are few good harbors, agriculture and live stock developed much earlier than trade.

Bronze Age Civilization in Italy. The Late Stone Age has left comparatively few traces in the Italian peninsula; but with the coming of metal many more remains of this early civilization have survived. Northern Italy was the first to feel the influence of the Bronze Age civilization which had developed on the north side of the Alps in the Danube valley. The fertile plains and forest-clad slopes of Italy have always attracted the peoples of northern Europe to forsake their own bleak and wintry lands and migrate to this warm and sunny peninsula in the southern sea. Perhaps as early as 2000 B.C. a people from the north side of the Alps pushed southward through the Alpine passes and settled around the lakes of northern Italy. The remains of over a hundred of their pile-supported settlements have also been found under the soil of the Po valley, once a vast morass, which these people reclaimed by erecting their dwellings farther and farther out in it. The city of Venice — still standing on piles,

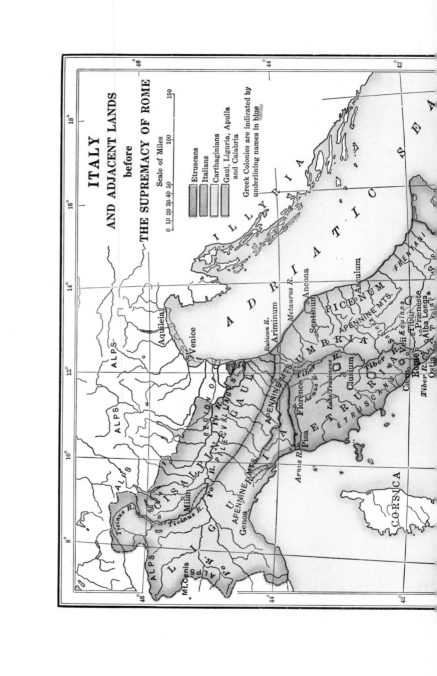

ITALY
AND ADJACENT LANDS
before
THE SUPREMACY OF ROME

Scale of Miles

0 10 20 30 40 50   100   150

Etruscans
Italians
Carthaginians
Gaul, Liguria, Apulia
and Calabria

Greek Colonies are indicated by
underlining names in blue

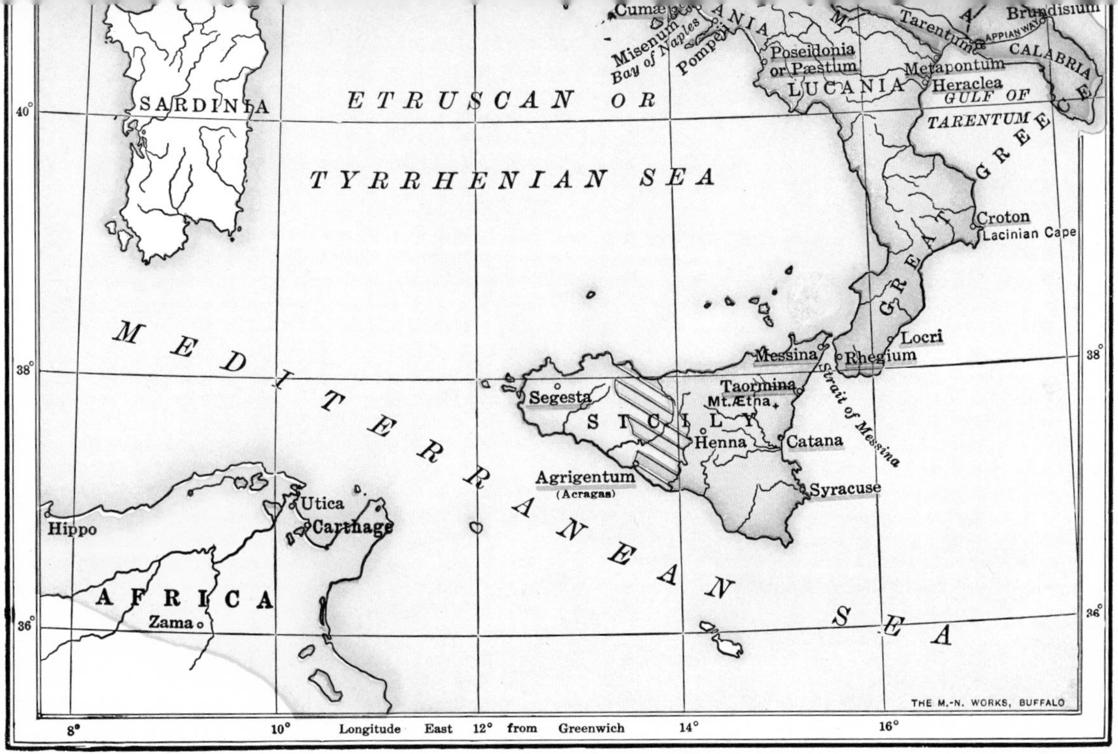

SARDINIA
ETRUSCAN OR
TYRRHENIAN SEA
MEDITERRANEAN SEA
Cumae
Misenum
Bay of Naples
Pompeii
Poseidonia
or Pæstum
LUCANIA
Tarentum
APPIAN WAY
Brundisium
CALABRIA
Metapontum
Heraclea
GULF OF
TARENTUM
GREAT GREECE
Croton
Lacinian Cape
Locri
Rhegium
Messina
Strait of Messina
Taormina
Mt. Ætna
SICILY
Segesta
Henna
Catana
Syracuse
Agrigentum
(Acragas)
Utica
Carthage
Hippo
AFRICA
Zama
40°
38°
36°
8°
10°
Longitude East 12° from Greenwich
14°
16°
THE M.-N. WORKS, BUFFALO

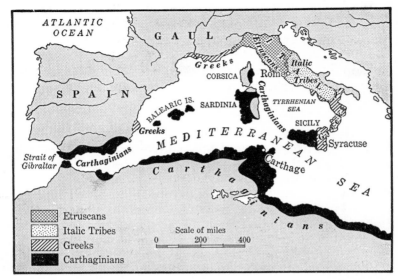

The Four Rival Peoples of the Western Mediterranean: Etruscans, Italic Tribes, Greeks, and Carthaginians

although it is now built mostly of stone — is an example of the way the lake-dwellers once built their little wooden houses on piles in the same region. This kind of building was copied by the later Romans, who made their military camps on a plan exactly like that of the Po-valley pile-villages.

The Western Wing of the Indo-Europeans enters Italy. While the pile-villagers were settling in the Po valley the tribes forming the western end of the Indo-European migration (Fig. 29) began to feel the attractiveness of the warm and verdant hills of Italy. Probably not long after the Greeks had pushed southward into the Greek peninsula (p. 120), other Western tribes of Indo-European blood crossed the Balkan peninsula and, moving westward, entered the beautiful Western Mediterranean world. They came in successive migrations, but the most important group that settled in the central and southern parts of the Italian peninsula were the *Italic* tribes, the earliest Italians.

We remember that the Greeks, in conquering the Ægean, took possession of a highly civilized region. This was not the case with the Indo-European invaders of Italy. They found the Western Mediterranean world without civilization. It had no fine buildings, no fortified cities, only the simplest arts and industries, no writing, no literature, and no organized governments.

Three Western Rivals of the Italic Invaders. The Italic invaders were plain peasant folk, cultivating their little fields and pasturing their flocks. As illiterate peasants they seemed to have slight prospect of advancement. Their chief qualities were a certain steadfastness of purpose, undaunted courage, and a hardihood which nothing seemed to weaken. The Italic tribes were to find these traits very useful; for, besides the pile-village folk, they were after a time confronted in Italy by three strong rivals who came from the Eastern Mediterranean world, where they had had the advantage of the wealth and weapons, military discipline, and governmental organization which we have seen growing up in the great imperial civilizations of the East. It did not seem probable that the tiny groups of Italic villagers could ever hope to oppose successfully these more fortunate rivals, who soon extended their commerce to the West and began to occupy a strong position on the shores of the Western Mediterranean. From north to south the three rivals of the Italic tribes were the Etruscans, the Greeks, and the Phœnicians.

The Etruscans settled on the western coast of Italy north of the Tiber, and in the course of several centuries took possession of north-central Italy from the Tiber to the Arnus River. The leading Etruscans became industrial and commercial princes who did not give up the seafaring life. The triangular basin inclosed by Italy and the three islands of Corsica, Sardinia, and Sicily finally came to be called the Tyrrhenian — that is, Etruscan — Sea. From these waters the Etruscans marketed their wares far and wide throughout the Mediterranean.

Before 1000 B.C. the Phœnicians had already established trading posts in Spain. At about the same time they settled on the African coast opposite Sicily and founded there the city of Carthage, which was before long the chief harbor in the Western Mediterranean. The Carthaginians soon held the northern coast of Africa westward to the Atlantic. Besides gaining southern Spain, they were also taking possession of the islands of the Western Mediterranean, especially Sicily. While the Carthaginians were endeavoring to make the Western Mediterranean their own, the *third* rival of the Italic peoples invaded the West. They were the Greeks.

Let us now turn back to follow the career of the barbarous Italic tribes of central Italy under the leadership of Rome, and watch them slowly gaining territory and, finally, adopting the civilization of the Etruscans on their *north* and then of the Greeks to the *south* of them.

2. Earliest Rome and the Etruscans

The Tribes of Latium. On the south bank of the river Tiber there was a group of Italic tribes known as the Latins. In the days when the Etruscan sea raiders were still landing on the shores north of the Tiber, these Latin tribes had occupied a plain less than thirty by forty miles in area. They called it Latium; whence their own name, "Latins." Like their Italic neighbors, they lived in small, scattered communities, cultivating grain and pasturing flocks. Their land was not very fertile, and the struggle for existence developed a strong and hardy people. A small town called Alba Longa was the leader of the Latin tribes when they were obliged to unite to drive off their hostile neighbors. They watched very anxiously the growth of the flourishing Etruscan towns on the other side of the Tiber, and did what they could to keep the Etruscans from crossing to the Latin side.

The Beginnings of Rome. When the Latin peasants needed weapons or tools they were obliged to take their grain or oxen to a trading post on the south side of the Tiber, ten or twelve miles from its mouth. On the neighboring hills there were several straggling villages, and on a hill called the Palatine there was a stronghold, or fortification. On the low,

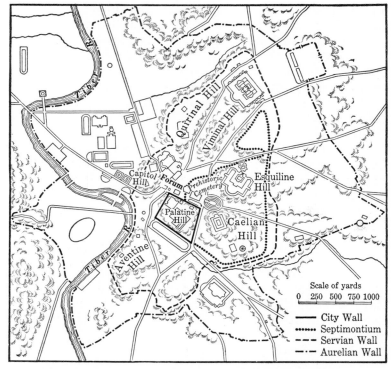

Map of Early Rome Showing Successive Stages of its Growth

marshy plain, encircled by the hills, was an open-air market called the Forum, where the Latin peasants could meet the Etruscan traders and exchange grain or oxen for the metal tools or weapons they needed. Such must have been the condition about 1000 B.C. of the group of villages which were to become Rome.

Rome seized by Etruscans (about 750 B.C.). An Etruscan invasion, which the Latin tribes had always feared, finally took place. Perhaps as early as 750 B.C., one of the Etruscan princes crossed the Tiber with an army, drove out the last of the line of Latin chieftains, and took possession of the stronghold on the Palatine. He then gained control of the villages on the hills above the Tiber, which gradually merged into the city of Rome. The Etruscan kings soon extended their power over the Latin tribes of the plain of Latium. The town of Alba Longa, which had once led the Latins, disappeared. Thus Rome became a city-kingdom under an Etruscan king, like the other Etruscan cities which stretched from Capua far north to the harbor of Genoa (map, p. 259). Although Rome was ruled by Etruscan kings for probably two centuries and a half, the people of Latium, whom the Etruscan kings governed, continued to be Latin and to speak the Latin tongue.[1]

FIG. 63. *Bronze Wolf from the Capitol at Rome*

The wolf (sixth century B.C.) was made by Etruscan artists under Greek influence in Italy. The two infants nourished by the she-wolf are later additions, put there in accordance with the tradition at Rome that the city was founded by these twin brothers, named Romulus and Remus. Their ancestor, so said the tradition, was Æneas, one of the Trojan heroes, who had fled from Troy after its destruction and, after many adventures, had arrived in Italy. His son founded and became king of Alba Longa. In the midst of a family feud among his descendants these twin boys, the sons of the war-god, Mars, were born; and after they had been set adrift in the Tiber by the ruling king, their boat gently ran aground at the base of the Palatine Hill, where a she-wolf found and nourished the babes. When they grew up they founded Rome. Similar legends formed all that the Romans knew of their early history, through the period of the kings and far down into the Republic

Etruscan Influences in Rome. Nevertheless, the civilization of Rome became essentially Etruscan, and with the Etruscan kings began a much more civilized

---

[1] This presentation makes the line of early kings at Rome (about 750 to about 500 B.C.) exclusively Etruscan. The traditional founding of Rome not long before 750 B.C. would then correspond to its capture and establishment as a strong kingdom by the Etruscans. We possess no written documents of Rome for this early period. Our conclusions are based on a study of archæological remains. If these remains had formed our only evidence, no one could ever have reached any other conclusion than that the kings of Rome were Etruscan. The later Romans themselves, however, with evident disinclination to believe that their early kings had been outsiders, cherished a tradition that their kings were native Romans. This tradition has found a place in literature and is still widely believed.

life than the city had ever seen before. They introduced important improvements. The Forum, the low market valley, was often flooded in the rainy season by stagnant water, which formed malaria-breeding pools. The Etruscan kings therefore built a massive masonry drain, which carried off the excess water and conducted it into the river. This made the city more healthful. This ancient sewer drain built by the Etruscans still remains. The earliest architecture in Rome was Etruscan.

Etruscan ships had, however, sailed Greek waters since Mycenæan days, and the Etruscans were constantly trading in the Greek harbors. Etruscan civilization, therefore, finally became a mixture of old Eastern-Mediterranean culture and Greek civilization. It was this Etruscan civilization, influenced by the Greeks, which shaped the life of Rome after 600 B.C.

Expulsion of Etruscan Kings of Rome (about 500 B.C.). While the Etruscan rulers did much for Rome, their tyranny finally caused a revolt, led probably by the Etruscan nobles themselves, and the kings of Rome were driven out. The fugitive king and his followers fled northward to their kinsmen, to the city of Cære. Thus about 500 B.C. the career of Rome under kings came to an end; but the two and a half centuries of Etruscan rule had left their mark on Roman civilization, religion, tribal organization, art, and industry.

3. The Early Roman Republic

Origin of the Latin Alphabet; Coins. As we have seen, during the Etruscan period Greek influences were equally important in Latium. At the dock below the Tiber ford, ships from the Greek cities of southern Italy were becoming more and more common. Long before the Etruscan kings were driven out, the Roman traders had gradually learned to scribble memoranda of their own, using the alphabet employed by the Greek merchants. Greek letters became likewise the Roman alphabet, slightly changed to suit the Latin language. Thus the Oriental alphabet was carried one step farther in the long westward journey which finally made it the alphabet with which this book is printed.

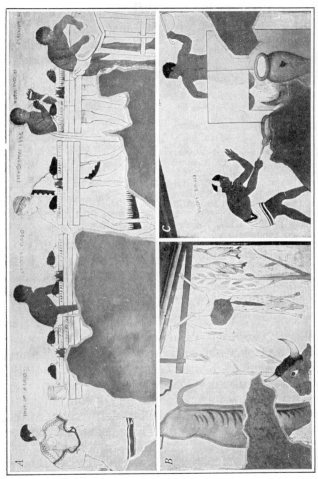

FIG. 64. *Wall Paintings from an Etruscan Tomb*

These scenes give us some idea of the domestic arrangements of the Etruscans. In the first scene (*A*) we see servants preparing food for cooking, cheered by the music of a double pipe. Beef, venison, hare, and fowl are indicated in the painting of the pantry (*B*). An irritable cook and a frightened kitchen boy in the kitchen scene (*C*) add a touch of humor. The inscriptions are in Etruscan, written with Greek letters

The Romans used letters instead of figures for writing numbers. We still use this old system, as may be seen at the beginning of this chapter: "Chapter XII." The page is, however, 257 instead of CCLVII, as it would have been in Latin. Men originally counted on their ten fingers, as ignorant people still do. The numbers from 1 to 10 were written by the Romans I, II, III, IV, V, VI, VII, VIII, IX, X. V meant a whole hand; X, both hands. IV was the whole hand less one finger; IX was both hands less one finger. L meant fifty, C a hundred, D five hundred, and M a thousand. The year 1937 could be written MCMXXXVII. We *continue* to use this way of numbering, with letters instead of figures, in books, on clock faces, and over the entrances to public buildings. Our convenient "Arabic" figures began to be used in Italy, France, and England about seven hundred years ago.

FIG. 65. *Early Roman Bronze Coin, Called an As*

In the time of Alexander the Great (second half of the fourth century B.C.) the Romans found it too inconvenient to continue paying their debts in goods and cattle. That cattle were used very frequently for money is shown by the fact that the Roman word for cattle (*pecus*) was the origin of one of their common words for property (*pecunia*) and has descended to us in our common word "pecuniary." The Romans probably learned from the Etruscans how to use large disks of bronze as money. The coin shown above weighed about a pound. It was minted at Rome and stamped on the obverse (*A*) with the head of Janus (god of gates and doors) and on the reverse (*B*) with a ship's prow

As Roman trade grew it was found very inconvenient to pay bills with grain and oxen while the Greek merchant at the dock paid his bills with copper and silver coins. At length, over a hundred and fifty years after the Etruscan kings had been driven out, the Romans began to issue copper or bronze coins (Fig. 65).

The Romans adopt the Greek Gods. But the Greeks influenced other things besides Roman business. For the Roman heard of strange gods of the Greeks, and he was told that they were the originals of his own gods. He was told that Venus was the Greek Aphrodite, Mercury was Hermes, Ceres was Demeter, and so on. For the Roman there was a god over every natural thing and for all human actions: Jupiter was the great Sky-god and king of all the gods; Mars, the patron of all warriors; Venus, the queen of love; Juno, an ancient Sky-goddess, was protectress of women, of birth and marriage, while Vesta too watched over the household life; Ceres was the goddess who maintained the fruitfulness of the earth, and especially the grainfields (compare English "cereal"); and Mercury was the messenger of the gods, who protected business and *merc*handising, as his name shows.

Roman Lack of Imagination. The practical and hardheaded Romans did not have the vivid imagination of the Greeks which had created the beautiful Greek mythology. The Romans were better fitted for success in war and government than for making any original contributions to religion, art, or literature, or for making discoveries in science. Let us now see how the practical gifts of the Romans aided them in developing the Roman state.

Establishment of the Roman Republic. When the Etruscan kings were driven out of Rome, about 500 B.C., the nobles, called *patricians*, came into control of the government. The patricians agreed that two of their number should be *elected* as heads of the state. These two magistrates, called *consuls*, were to have the same powers, were to serve for a year only, and were then to give way to two others. Annual elections were held in an assembly composed of the weapon-bearing men. This assembly was largely under the control of the patricians. Nevertheless, we must call this new state a republic, of which the consuls were the presidents; for the people had a voice in electing them. But as only patricians could serve as consuls, the people were not satisfied. As the government of the nobles became oppressive, the people, called the *plebs* (compare our "plebeian"), finally revolted and left the city. They refused to come back until the patricians had granted some of their demands.

The Tribunes Defenders of the People. The patricians were unable to get on without the help of the people as soldiers in their frequent wars. They therefore agreed to give the people a larger share in the government, by allowing them in their own assembly to elect a group of new officials, called *tribunes*. The tribunes had the right to veto the action of any officer of the government, even that of the consuls themselves. When any citizen was treated unjustly by a consul, he might appeal to one of the tribunes for aid.

Growing Body of Government Officials. It gradually became necessary to create new officers for various kinds of business. To take care of the government funds, treasury officials called *quæstors* were appointed. Officials called *censors* were required to keep lists (a census) of the people, and to look after their daily conduct and see that nothing improper was permitted. Our own use of the word "censor" is derived from these Roman officials. A judge called a *prætor* was appointed to assist the consuls in deciding legal cases. In times of great national danger it was customary to appoint some revered and trustworthy leader as the supreme ruler of the state. He was called the *dictator,* and he could hold his office for only a brief period.

The Senate, and the Struggle of Plebs and Patricians. The consuls had great power and influence in all government matters, but they were much influenced by a council of patricians called the *Senate* (from Latin *senex,* meaning "old man"). The patricians enjoyed the exclusive right to serve as consuls, to sit in the Senate, and to hold almost all the offices created to carry on the business of government.

The tribunes, as we have seen, could protect the people from some injustices, but they could not secure to the plebeian citizen the right to be elected as consul, or to become a senator, or to marry into a patrician family. The struggle of the common people to win equal rights from the wealthy and powerful therefore continued. It was a struggle like those of earlier times in Athens and the other Greek states; but at Rome it resulted in a much wiser and more successful settlement. The citizens of Rome gained their rights, without civil war or bloodshed, to a large extent during the first two centuries after the founding of the Republic.

The People gain Written Laws. The people now demanded that the existing laws be put *in writing,* in order that they might know by what laws they were being judged. About fifty years after the establishment of the Republic the earliest Roman laws were set down in writing and engraved upon twelve tablets of bronze (450 B.C.). The people then demanded the right to share in the making of *new* laws and to have an assembly of the people, which might pass new laws.

Growing Power of the People. Having shaken off the legal power of the Senate to control their action, the assemblies of the people became the lawmaking bodies of the Roman state. In this way the people gradually were able to secure a fairer share of the public lands. Most important of all, these new laws increased the rights of the people to hold office. In the end Roman citizens elected their plebeian neighbors as censors and quæstors, as judges, and at last even as consuls, and they saw men of the people sitting in the Senate.

New Nobility made up of Former Magistrates. Roman citizens had a deep respect for government and for its officials. There soon grew up a group of once-plebeian families respected by the Roman citizens on account of their public service to the state when they held office. When the voters were called upon to select their candidates for government officials, they preferred members of these eminent families, especially for the consulship. A new nobility was thus formed, made up of these illustrious families of plebeians and the old patricians.

As a result of these changes this new nobility found its way into the Senate, which was thus composed of the three hundred men of Rome who had had the most experience in government and in public affairs. Their combined influence was finally stronger than that of the consuls themselves. The consuls were then obliged to carry on the government according to instructions from the Senate.

The Roman Senate rules the State. By far the larger part of the Roman citizens lived too far away to come to the city and vote. Knowing, too, their own ignorance of public affairs, the Roman citizens were willing that important public questions should be settled by the Senate. In this way the Roman Senate became a large committee of experienced statesmen, guiding and controlling the Roman state. They formed the greatest council of rulers which ever grew up in the ancient world. They were a body of aristocrats, and their control of Rome made it an aristocratic state, in spite of its republican form. We are now to watch the steady development and progress of Roman power under the able leadership of the Senate. We should bear in mind, however, that the Senate's power was a slow growth, developing during the wars and conquests which we are now to follow.

4. The Expansion of the Roman Republic and the Conquest of Italy

Early Struggles of the Republic. It was a tiny nation which began its uncertain career after the expulsion of the Etruscan kings about 500 B.C. The territory of the Roman Republic thus far included only the city, with the neighboring fields for a very few miles around. On the other side of the Tiber lived the dreaded Etruscans, and on the Roman side of the river, all around the little republic, lay the lands of the Latin tribes, only loosely united with Rome by treaty.

For two generations the new republic struggled to maintain its mere existence. Fortunately for the Romans, within a generation after the foundation of the Republic the Greek fleet of Syracuse utterly destroyed the Etruscan fleet (474 B.C.). Later the Etruscans were attacked by the Gauls, who were at this time pouring over the Alpine passes into the valley of the Po and destroying the Etruscan cities of the north. This weakening of the Etruscans probably saved Rome from destruction. By 400 B.C., or a little after, the Romans were able to conquer and take possession of a fringe of new territory on all sides, which served as a protection against their enemies.

Roman Policy of Expansion. In this new territory the Romans planted colonies of citizens, or granted citizenship or other valuable privileges to the conquered people. Roman peasants, who were under obligation to fight for Rome and who had a voice in the government, thus pushed out into the new and enlarging Roman territory. So Rome grew not only in size but in strength, for she had an ever-increasing body of hardy and loyal citizen-soldiers. The Roman policy was thus in striking contrast with the narrow methods of the Greek republics, which jealously prevented outsiders from gaining citizenship. It was the steady growth of Rome under this plan which in a little over two centuries after the driving out of the Etruscan kings made the little republic on the Tiber mistress of all Italy.

Capture of Rome by the Gauls. The second century of Roman expansion opened with a fearful catastrophe, which very nearly caused the complete destruction of the nation. In the first two decades around 400 B.C. the barbarian Gauls of the north, who had been overrunning the territory of the Etruscans, finally reached the lower Tiber, defeated the Roman army, and entered the city. Unable, however, to capture the citadel on the Capitol Hill, the Gauls at length agreed to accept a payment of gold and to return northward, where they settled in the valley of the Po. But they still remained a serious danger to the Romans.

Rome achieves the Leadership of the Latin Tribes. As Rome recovered from this disaster it was evident that the city needed fortifications, and for the first time stone walls (the so-called Servian Wall; plan, p. 262) were built around it. Alarmed at the growing power of Rome, the Latin tribes now endeavored to break away from the control of the powerful walled city. In the two years' war which followed, Rome completely subdued the Latin tribes, who in time were to help her to gain the leadership of Italy.

The year 338 B.C., in which this important conquest was completed, is a date to be remembered, for it was also the year that the Greek cities were defeated by Philip of Macedon. In the same year, therefore, both the Greeks and the Latins came under the leadership of a single state,—the Greeks, under that of Macedonia; the Latins, under that of Rome.

Samnite Wars (325–290 B.C.) *and the Battle of Sentinum* (295 B.C.). Meantime another dangerous foe, a group of Italic tribes called the Samnites, had been taking possession of the mountains inland from Rome. These people were able to muster a large army of hardy peasants who were good fighters. By 325 B.C. a fierce war broke out between the Romans and the Samnites. It lasted with interruptions for a generation. The Romans lost several battles, and the Samnites succeeded in moving their army northward and joining forces with Rome's enemies, the Etruscans and the Gauls. In the mountains midway between the upper Tiber and the eastern shores of Italy the Roman army met and crushed the combined forces of the allies in a terrible battle at Sentinum. This victory not only gave the Romans possession of central Italy but made them the leading power in the whole peninsula.

Rome Mistress of Central and Northern Italy. After this the Etruscans were no longer dangerous. One by one their cities either were taken by the Romans or entered into alliance with Rome. The Gallic invaders were beaten off, though the Gauls, who had already settled there, continued to hold the Po valley. The northern boundary of the Roman conquests was therefore along the Arnus River, south of the Apennines. The Romans then controlled the peninsula from the Arnus to the Greek cities of southern Italy (maps, p. 273).

The War with Pyrrhus (280–275 B.C.): *the Greek Cities come under Roman Control.* The two remaining rivals of the Romans in the Western Mediterranean world were now the Greeks and the Carthaginians. Four centuries of conflict among themselves had left the western Greek colonies still a disunited group of cities fringing southern Italy and Sicily. Alarmed at the threatening expansion of Roman power, they endeavored to unite, and sent an appeal for help to Pyrrhus, the energetic and able king of Epirus, just across from lower Italy (map I, p. 284).

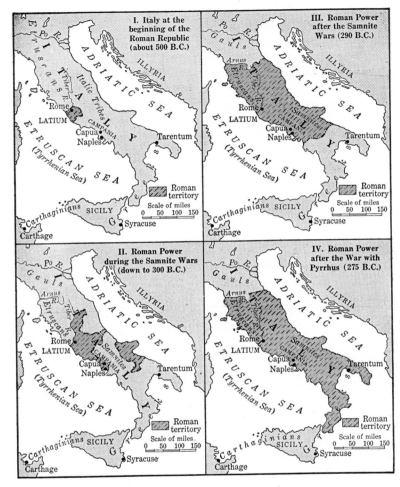

Expansion of Roman Power in Italy

With his strong army Pyrrhus was a highly dangerous foe. His purpose was to form a great nation of the western Greeks in Sicily and Italy. He completely defeated the Romans in two battles, and gained practically the whole island of Sicily. But the Carthaginians, when they saw this powerful rival rising only a few hours' sail from their home harbor, sent a fleet to assist the Romans against Pyrrhus. With a friendly Carthaginian fleet at the mouth of the Tiber, the Roman Senate refused to make peace with the Greeks so long as the army of Pyrrhus occupied Italian soil. Moreover, the Greeks disagreed among themselves, as they usually did at critical times. Pyrrhus, thus poorly supported, found himself unable to gain a decisive victory over the Romans, and returned to Epirus. One by one the helpless Greek cities of Italy then surrendered to the Roman army and had no choice but to accept alliance with the Romans. Thus ended all hope of a great Greek nation in the West.

Questions and Exercises

REVIEW OF CHAPTER

1. Into what divisions does the Mediterranean fall? What Indo-European tribes first came into Italy? What other peoples settled in the Western Mediterranean?

2. Who were the Latins? Describe Latium. What were the results of Etruscan rule at Rome?

3. How did the western Greek colonies influence the Romans? Who took the place of the expelled Etruscan kings? What form did the government of Rome take? How did the people gain power? Why did the Senate gain such power and importance?

4. Describe the Roman policy of expansion. Sketch the history of the Roman conquest of Italy.

USEFUL TERMS

See how much meaning you can give to the following: *Carthaginians, Italians, Romans, Latin, drainage, dictator, Roman consul, American consul, republic.*

DIRECTIVE QUESTIONS

1. The Etruscans, Carthaginians, and Greeks exploited the lands of the Western Mediterranean. Could this have had any influence on the final outcome in the struggle for supremacy?

2. The Etruscan inscriptions are written with an alphabet related to our alphabet; therefore the words and letters may be read, but no one knows the meaning. How does the problem of deciphering the Etruscan language differ from the problem of deciphering the Cretan language?

3. How did the situation of the Roman plebeian in the fifth century B.C. differ from that of the Greek peasant in the seventh century B.C.?

4. What great mistake did the Carthaginians make when Pyrrhus invaded Italy?

DISCUSSION TOPICS

1. Rome was victorious over her rivals because the Latins were an agricultural people.

2. The civilization of Rome was more greatly influenced by Etruscan culture than by Greek culture.

3. The Romans were too materialistic to understand fully what Greek culture meant.

4. The rivalry in the Western Mediterranean helped to make Rome powerful.

ADDITIONAL ADVENTURES IN LEARNING

1. Studies in Source Materials. BOTSFORD, *Source-book*: (1) Growth of plebeian rights, pp. 350–360; (2) Sack of Rome by Gauls, pp. 362–365; (3) Pyrrhus, pp. 365–369; (4) The Appian Way, p. 376.

2. Look up in an encyclopedia: *Palatine Hill, Forum, Capua, Etruria, plebeians, censor, census, Pyrrhus, Venice, malaria.*

CHAPTER XIII · THE ROMAN CONQUEST OF THE WESTERN MEDITERRANEAN WORLD

ITALY UNDER THE EARLY ROMAN REPUBLIC · THE GROWING RIVALRY BETWEEN ROME AND CARTHAGE · THE STRUGGLE WITH CARTHAGE: THE SICILIAN WAR, OR FIRST PUNIC WAR · THE WAR WITH HANNIBAL (SECOND PUNIC WAR); THE DESTRUC-TION OF CARTHAGE

IN THE previous chapter we followed the fortunes of Rome beginning with the earliest settlements near the mouth of the Tiber. We watched the development of the city-state under the rule of Etruscan kings. Then we saw how, having freed itself from the tyranny of its kings, the new Roman Republic about 500 B.C. found itself faced by three dangerous rival peoples, the Etruscans, Carthaginians, and Greeks. Meanwhile the Romans were developing their government so that Rome was guided by a great council of her most experienced men, called the Senate. By settling farmer colonists on the territory seized in war, the tiny republic on the Tiber grad-ually gained the mastery of the entire Italian peninsula south of the Po valley, and thus absorbed two of its Western rivals, the Etruscans and the Greeks. It now remains, first, to discuss the Roman attitude toward the conquered peoples of Italy, and, second, to follow the relations between Rome and Carthage, after the Carthaginians were left the only rivals of the Romans in the Western Mediterranean world.

1. ITALY UNDER THE EARLY ROMAN REPUBLIC

The Problem of making Italy a Nation. After Rome had gained the leadership of Italy, there were men still living who could remember the Latin War (ended 338 B.C.), when Rome had for a time lost even the surrounding fields of little Latium. Now, sixty-five years later, the city on the Tiber was mistress of all Italy. The new power over a large group of cities and states, thus gained within a single life-time, was exercised by the Roman Senate with the greatest skill and success. The problem was to make Italy a nation, controlled by Rome. But if Rome had *annexed* all the con-quered lands and endeavored to rule them from Rome as mere subjects, the people of Italy would have been dissatis-fied, and constant revolts would have followed.

The Romans accordingly granted the defeated cities a kind of citizenship, which entitled them to all the protection of the Roman state in the courts and in carrying on business but did not entitle them to vote. In distant communities, however, no one felt the lack of this privilege, for in order to vote it was necessary to go to Rome. Cities and communities controlled by Rome in this way were called "allies." Enjoying the protection of the powerful Roman state, the allies were willing to place their troops entirely at the disposal of Rome.

Rome had also gradually taken over a good deal of territory to pay her war expenses and to supply her increasing numbers of citizens with land. Her own full citizens thus occupied about a sixth of the territory of Italy. Rome, moreover, continued her policy of establishing Roman colonies throughout the territory of her allies until all Italy was more or less dotted with such communities made up of Roman citizens.

Lack of National Unity in Italy. Roman methods of organization had in this way created a kind of union of the states of Italy, which might in the course of time become merged into a nation. Many of these peoples, however, had no feeling of patriotism toward Rome. Having no common traditions, like those of the Trojan War among the Greeks (p. 129), and speaking many different languages, they remained for a long time quite distinct from each other and from Rome. Italy was therefore still far from being a *nation.*

Italy to become Latin in Speech but Greek in Civilization. The language of the future nation was to be Latin, the tongue of the ruling city, and its government Roman. Its civilization, however, was to become more and more Greek. In the Greek settlements of southern Italy the Roman soldiers for the first time had beheld with wonder and admiration the beautiful Greek temples of such cities as Pæstum and Tarentum. They had also seen fine theaters, and they must have attended Greek plays, although they understood little or nothing of what was said on the stage. But the races and athletic games in the handsome stadium of such a Greek city required no interpretation in order to be understood

FIG. 66. A Roman Denarius of Silver

After the capture of the Greek cities of southern Italy the Romans began the coinage of silver (268 B.C.). The large and inconvenient bronze coin (Fig. 65) was then displaced by silver for all large transactions. The value of this coin, called a *denarius*, was about twenty cents, like the Athenian drachma. (Courtesy of the American Numismatic Society)

by the sturdy Roman soldiers who had fought Pyrrhus in the south.

In southern Italy the Romans had taken possession of the western fringe of the great Hellenistic world, whose wonderful civilization we have already studied (pp. 241–253). The Romans at once appreciated the superiority of this new world of cultivated life, which they had entered in the Greek south. It was as yet chiefly in commerce and in business that Greek influences were most felt. Greek silver money appeared in greater quantities after the capture of the Greek cities; and not long after the war with Pyrrhus, Rome minted her first silver coin (Fig. 66). Like Athens several centuries earlier (p. 141), Rome now began to have a moneyed class, made up largely of merchants. They were not manufacturers, as at Athens, for Rome never became a great manufacturing center.

2. THE GROWING RIVALRY BETWEEN ROME AND CARTHAGE

Growth of Roman Commerce. A policy of *agricultural* expansion had slowly brought Rome the leadership *within* Italy (p. 271). A new policy of *commercial* expansion was to bring her into conflict with the Mediterranean world *outside of* Italy. Roman ships issuing from the Tiber entered the triangular inclosure of the Mediterranean called the Tyrrhenian Sea. A glance at the map (I, p. 284) shows us how Rome and Carthage faced each other across this triangular sea, where both cities were now carrying on extensive business.

Carthaginian Business Expansion in Africa. As the trade of Carthage increased she had gradually gained control over the North African coast from the frontiers of the Greek city of Cyrene westward to the Atlantic. She had become the leading commercial power in the Western Mediterranean world. Her merchants seized southern Spain, with its rich silver mines, and also gained control of the import of British tin by way of the Strait of Gibraltar. Outside of this strait their settlements extended both northward and southward far along the Atlantic coast. Moreover, it was only the incoming of the Greeks which had prevented the Carthaginians from taking possession of all the western Mediterranean islands upon which their splendid harbor looked out, especially the island of Sicily. They closed the ports of the islands and the Strait of Gibraltar *to ships from all other cities.* Ships of other nations sailing into these waters were promptly rammed and sunk by Carthaginian warships.

Carthaginian Army and State. Unlike Rome, Carthage had built up her military power entirely on a basis of money, with which she supported a large army of mercenaries or foreign soldiers. She had no farmers cultivating their own land, from whom she could draw an army of citizen-soldiers as did Rome. This was a serious weakness. The rulers of the city never trusted the army, made up as it was of hired foreigners. Carthage was governed by a group of merchant nobles, a wealthy aristocracy whose members formed a council which had complete control. They were energetic and statesmanlike rulers. Centuries of shrewd guidance on their part made Carthage a great state, far exceeding in power any of the Greek states, not excepting Athens. The city of Carthage itself was luxurious and splendid, and in area it was three times as large as Rome.

Early Relations between Carthage and Rome. In the fourth century B.C., before Rome had gained the leadership of Italy, when the Roman merchants were still doing only a small business and the Roman nobility was contemptuous of trade, the Senate had made a treaty with Carthage.[1] By this

---

[1] The historian Polybius writes of a similar treaty made with Carthage about one hundred and fifty years earlier.

treaty all ports in the Western Mediterranean of which the Carthaginians had complete control were closed to Roman trade. With increasing vexation the merchants of Italy realized that Rome had gained the supremacy of Italy and pushed her frontiers to the southernmost tip of the peninsula, only to look across and find that the merchant princes of Carthage held the markets of Sicily and had made the Western Mediterranean a Carthaginian sea. Indeed, Carthage was gaining a position which might cut off Rome from communication by sea with her allies on the southern and Adriatic coasts of Italy. To reach them, Roman ships must pass through the Strait of Messina, between Italy and Sicily. The advance of Carthage in Sicily might enable her at any time to seize the Sicilian city of Messina and close this strait to Roman ships.

War Strength of the Romans. The Romans could put a *citizen*-army of about three hundred thousand men into the field. Besides the troops made up of Roman citizens an army included also about an equal number of troops drawn from the *allies*. This plan doubled the number of troops. The Roman army consequently was far greater in size than any army ever organized before in the Mediterranean world.

The Romans had been able to make several improvements on the Hellenistic methods of fighting. After hurling spears into the ranks of the enemy, the Romans fought with short swords, which were much more easily handled at close range than long spears. At the same time the Romans had likewise improved the phalanx, which had thus far been a long, solid line with an average depth of eight men. This was difficult to manage. The Romans devised a means of making it easier to move quickly by dividing it into small groups. As the Romans gradually learned to shift these smaller units more and more rapidly and skillfully, the art of war entered upon a new stage. For purposes of mustering and feeding its army the Romans divided it into *legions*, each containing from forty-two hundred to five thousand men.

3. THE STRUGGLE WITH CARTHAGE: THE SICILIAN WAR, OR FIRST PUNIC WAR

Opening of the Sicilian War (264 B.C.). The Romans soon discovered that the struggle with Carthage could not be avoided. A local war in Sicily gave a Carthaginian garrison opportunity to occupy the citadel of Messina, and the Carthaginians were then in command of the Strait of Messina (map, p. 258). A Roman army now left the soil of Italy, crossed the sea for the first time in Roman history, and entered Sicily. The struggle with Carthage had begun.

Naval Operations of the Romans. An alliance with Syracuse soon gave the Romans possession of eastern Sicily, but they were long hampered by lack of a fleet. In the fifth year of the war, however, the new Roman warships, which the Senate had caused to be built, put to sea for the first time. They numbered a hundred and twenty battleships.

In spite of inexperience, the Roman fleet was at first victorious. Then one newly built Roman fleet after another was destroyed by heavy storms at sea, and one of them was badly defeated by the Carthaginians. Year after year the struggle dragged on, while Hamilcar Barca, the Carthaginian commander, was plundering the coasts of Italy with his fleet. The treasury at Rome was empty, and the Romans were at the end of their resources; but by private contributions they succeeded in building still another fleet, which put to sea in 242 B.C. with two hundred battleships of five banks of oars. The Carthaginian fleet was defeated and broken up (241 B.C.), and as a result the Carthaginians found themselves unable to send aid across the sea to their army in Sicily.

Peace after the Sicilian War. The Carthaginians were therefore at last obliged to accept hard terms of peace at the hands of the Romans. They were to give up Sicily and the neighboring islands to Rome and to pay the Romans as war damages the sum of thirty-two hundred talents (over three and a half million dollars) within ten years. Thus in 241 B.C., after more than twenty-three years of fighting, the first period of the struggle between Rome and Carthage ended with the victory of Rome.[1] For the first time Rome held territory outside the Italian peninsula.

4. The War with Hannibal (Second Punic War); the Destruction of Carthage

New Conquests of Rome and Carthage. Both the rivals now devoted themselves to increasing their strength. In spite of protests from Carthage, only three years after the settlement of peace Rome took possession of both Sardinia and Corsica (238 B.C.). She now held three island outposts against Carthage. At the same time the Romans conquered the Gauls and seized their territory in the Po valley. Roman power thus was extended northward to the Alps, and the entire peninsula was now held by Rome.

To offset this increase of Roman power the Carthaginian leaders turned toward Spain. There Hamilcar's gifted son Hannibal took possession of the country as far north as the river Ebro (map II, p. 284), to which point Rome also extended her claims. Although only twenty-four years of age, Hannibal was planning to surprise Rome by boldly invading her territory and crushing Roman power in Italy.

Opening of the War with Hannibal (218–202 B.C.). Hannibal quickly found opportunity for a quarrel with Rome over the frontier in Spain (219 B.C.). With a strong and well-drilled army of about forty thousand men, he was soon marching along the east coast of Spain with the purpose of crossing southern Gaul and invading Italy. While the Roman Senate was planning to invade Spain and Africa, Rome found her own land suddenly threatened from the north.

It was late autumn when Hannibal reached the Alps (218 B.C.). Overwhelmed by snowstorms, struggling over a steep and dangerous trail (sometimes so narrow that the rocks had to be cut away to make room for his elephants), looking down over dizzy precipices, or up to snow-covered heights where

---

[1] This is commonly called the First Punic War. "Punic" is a Latin form of the word "Phœnician," the name of the race to which the Carthaginians belonged.

hostile natives rolled great stones down upon the troops, the discouraged army of Hannibal toiled on day after day, exhausted, cold, and hungry. At every point along the straggling line where help was most needed the young Carthaginian was always present, encouraging and guiding his men. But when they issued from the Alpine pass and entered Italy in the upper valley of the Po, they had suffered such losses that they were reduced to some thirty-four thousand men.

With this little army the fearless Carthaginian youth had entered the territory of the strongest military power of the time, — a nation which could now call to her defense about seven hundred thousand men (citizens and allies). Hannibal, however, was thoroughly acquainted with the most highly improved methods of warfare, and the deeds of Alexander a century earlier were familiar to him. On the other hand, the Roman consuls, commanding the Roman armies, were simply magistrates, like our mayors, often without much more knowledge of handling an army than has a city mayor in our time. They were no match for the crafty young Carthaginian.

By skillful use of his cavalry, in which the Romans were weak, Hannibal easily won two battles in the Po valley. The Gauls of the region at once began to join Hannibal, but they were raw, undisciplined troops. Having successfully passed the Roman fortresses guarding the roads through the Apennines, Hannibal surprised the army of the unsuspecting Roman consul Flaminius on the march. On the shores of Lake Trasimene he suddenly attacked the Roman legions in both front and rear and cut to pieces the entire Roman army. The consul himself fell. Being only a few days' march from Rome, Hannibal might now have advanced directly against the city; but he had no siege machinery, and his forces were not numerous enough to besiege so strong a fortress. He therefore desired a further victory, in the hope that the allies of Rome would desert her and join him in attacking the city.

A Year of Delay and Preparation (217–216 B.C.). At this dangerous crisis the Romans appointed a dictator, a stable old citizen named Fabius, whose plan was to wear out Han-

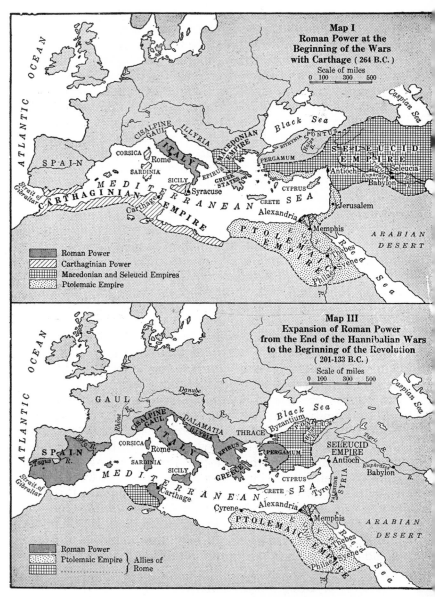

**Map I
Roman Power at the
Beginning of the Wars
with Carthage** (264 B.C.)

Scale of miles
0   100   300   500

Roman Power
Carthaginian Power
Macedonian and Seleucid Empires
Ptolemaic Empire

**Map III
Expansion of Roman Power
from the End of the Hannibalian Wars
to the Beginning of the Revolution**
(201-133 B.C.)

Scale of miles
0   100   300   500

Roman Power
Ptolemaic Empire } Allies of
} Rome

Sequence Maps Showing the Expansion of the Roman Power from

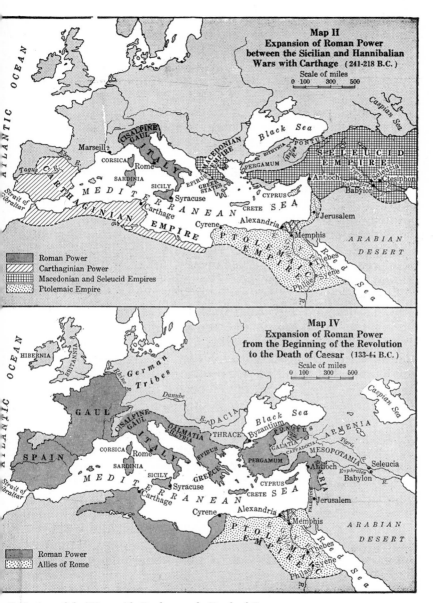

Map II
Expansion of Roman Power between the Sicilian and Hannibalian Wars with Carthage (241-218 B.C.)

Scale of miles
0 100   300   500

- Roman Power
- Carthaginian Power
- Macedonian and Seleucid Empires
- Ptolemaic Empire

ATLANTIC OCEAN
Marseilles
CISALPINE GAUL
ITALY
CORSICA
Rome
SARDINIA
SICILY
Syracuse
Carthage
MEDITERRANEAN SEA
CARTHAGINIAN EMPIRE
Ebro R.
Tagus R.
Strait of Gibraltar
Cyrene
Alexandria
Memphis
Thebes
Philae
Syene
PTOLEMAIC EMPIRE
ARABIAN DESERT
Black Sea
MACEDONIAN EMPIRE
EPIRUS
GREEK STATES
CRETE
CYPRUS
BITHYNIA
PONTUS
PERGAMUM
SELEUCID EMPIRE
Antioch
Euphrates
Seleucia
Ctesiphon
Babylon
Jerusalem
Caspian Sea
Red Sea

Map IV
Expansion of Roman Power from the Beginning of the Revolution to the Death of Caesar (133-44 B.C.)

Scale of miles
0 100   300   500

- Roman Power
- Allies of Rome

ATLANTIC OCEAN
HIBERNIA
BRITANNIA
German Tribes
Rhine R.
Danube
GAUL
CISALPINE GAUL
ITALY
SPAIN
CORSICA
Rome
SARDINIA
SICILY
Syracuse
Carthage
MEDITERRANEAN SEA
Strait of Gibraltar
DALMATIA
ILLYRIA
DACIA
THRACE
Byzantium
EPIRUS
GREECE
CRETE
CYPRUS
PERGAMUM
GALATIA
CAPPADOCIA
PONTUS
ARMENIA
MESOPOTAMIA
Antioch
Seleucia
Babylon
Euphrates
Tigris
Jerusalem
PALESTINE
Cyrene
Alexandria
Memphis
Thebes
Philae
Syene
PTOLEMAIC EMPIRE
ARABIAN DESERT
Black Sea
Caspian Sea
Red Sea

Beginnings of the Wars with Carthage to the Death of Caesar

nibal by delaying battle and by using every opportunity to harass the Carthaginians. This policy of caution and waiting did not meet with popular favor at Rome. The people called Fabius "the Laggard" (*Cunctator*), a name which ever afterward clung to him. The new consuls elected for 216 B.C. therefore prepared an army of nearly seventy thousand men and pushed southward to fight Hannibal. The battle took place at Cannæ (map, p. 273).

The Battle of Cannæ (216 B.C.). Hannibal's stronger cavalry put to flight the horsemen of the Romans. Then they turned back to attack the heavy mass of the Roman center in the rear, and the Romans were caught between the Carthaginian army before them and the Carthaginian cavalry behind them. Two bodies of African reserves which Hannibal had kept waiting now pushed quietly forward till they closed in on both sides of the fifty-five thousand brave soldiers of the Romans. What followed was simply a slaughter of the doomed Romans, lasting all the rest of the day. When night came, the Roman army was annihilated. Ex-consuls, senators, nobles — thousands of the best citizens of Rome — had fallen in this frightful battle. Every family in Rome was in mourning. Of the gold rings worn by Roman knights as a sign of their rank Hannibal is reported to have sent a bushel to Carthage.

Hannibal's Statesmanship. Thus this masterful young Carthaginian, the greatest of Semite generals, within two years after his arrival in Italy and before he was thirty years of age, had defeated his powerful enemy in four battles and destroyed three of the armies sent against him. He might now count upon a revolt among the Roman allies. Within a few years southern Italy, including the Greek cities, and even Syracuse (in Sicily), forsook Rome and joined Hannibal. Only some of the southern Latin colonies held out against him. To make matters worse for Rome, immediately after Cannæ, Hannibal arranged an alliance with Macedonia.

In all that he did Hannibal showed the judgment of a great statesman combined with amazing ability as a general. But opposing him were the dogged resolution, the statesmanship, the organization, and the seemingly inexhaustible numbers of the Romans. It was a battle of giants; for the victor in this struggle would without any question be the greatest power in the Mediterranean. In spite of Hannibal's victories, the steadiness and fine leadership of the Roman Senate held central Italy loyal to Rome. Although the Romans were finally compelled to place arms in the hands of slaves and mere boys, new armies were formed. With these forces the Romans proceeded to besiege and capture, one after another, the allied cities which had revolted against Rome.

Decline of Hannibal's Power. When Hannibal had finally been ten years in Italy, he realized that unless a large force came to his assistance his cause was hopeless. His brother Hasdrubal, in Spain, had gathered an army and was now marching into Italy to aid him. But Hasdrubal was met by a Roman army, completely defeated, and himself slain (207 B.C.). To the senators, waiting eagerly at Rome, the news of the victory meant the salvation of Italy and the final defeat of an enemy who had all but accomplished the destruction of Roman power.

Defeat of Hannibal by Scipio (202 B.C.). For a few years more Hannibal struggled on in southern Italy. Meantime the Romans, taught by the defeat of their consuls, who were not soldiers, had given the command of their forces in Spain to Scipio, one of the ablest of their younger leaders and a trained warrior. Scipio drove the Carthaginians entirely out of Spain, and so cut off their chief supply both of money and of troops. The Romans had at last found a great military leader. He demanded of the Senate that he be sent to Africa to invade the territory of Carthage, as Hannibal had invaded that of Rome.

By 203 B.C. Scipio had twice defeated the Carthaginian forces in Africa, and Carthage was forced to call Hannibal home. He had spent fifteen years on the soil of Italy, and the great struggle between the almost exhausted rivals was now to be decided in Africa. At Zama the final battle of the war took place. The great Carthaginian was at last met by an equally great Roman, and Scipio won the battle.

Treaty ending the War (201 B.C.) ; *the Fate of Hannibal.* The victory over Carthage made Rome the leading power in the whole ancient world. In the treaty which followed the battle of Zama the Romans forced Carthage to pay ten thousand talents (over $11,000,000) in fifty years and to surrender all her warships but ten triremes. But, what was worse, Carthage lost her independence as a nation, and according to the treaty she could not make war anywhere without the consent of the Romans.

Hannibal escaped after his lost battle at Zama. He was one of the most gifted leaders in all history — a lion-hearted man, so strong of purpose that only a great nation like Rome could have crushed him. Rome still feared Hannibal and compelled the Carthaginians to send him far away ; so as a man of fifty he went into exile in the East, where he was continuously stirring up the successors of Alexander to combine against Rome (p. 292).

Destruction of Carthage (146 B.C.) : *Third Punic War.* Such was the business ability of the Carthaginians that they continued to prosper even while paying the heavy tribute with which Rome had burdened them. As a result Cato, a famous old-fashioned senator, was so convinced that Carthage was still a danger to Rome that he concluded all his speeches in the Senate with the words, "Carthage must be destroyed." For over fifty years more the merchants of Carthage were permitted to trade in the Western Mediterranean, and then the iron hand of Rome was laid upon the city for the last time. It happened in this way. To defend herself against the Numidians, a troublesome people living close by, Carthage was finally obliged to begin war against them. This step, which the Romans had secretly been desiring, was a violation of the treaty with Rome which forbade the Carthaginians to go to war without her consent. The Senate seized the opportunity at once, and Carthage was called to account. In the three years' war (Third Punic

War) which followed, the beautiful city was captured and completely destroyed (146 B.C.). Its territory was taken by Rome and called the Province of Africa. A struggle of nearly one hundred and twenty years had resulted in the annihilation of Rome's only remaining rival in the Western Mediterranean world.

Questions and Exercises

REVIEW OF CHAPTER

1. How did Rome govern the defeated cities of Italy? Was Italy now a unified nation?

2. What was the result of Roman commercial expansion? What was the trade policy of the Carthaginians in the Western Mediterranean? Why was the Strait of Messina so important to Rome?

3. Why did Rome organize a navy? What was the first territory outside the Italian peninsula held by Rome?

4. What are the evidences of Hannibal's greatness? Why was Hannibal not able to conquer the Romans? What became of Carthage?

USEFUL TERMS

See how much meaning you can give to the following: *nation, Italian allies, agricultural expansion, mare clausum, legionaries, munitions, statesmanship.*

DIRECTIVE QUESTIONS

1. Why was Rome able to unite the cities of Italy, whereas the Greek city-states could secure neither union nor peaceful relations with each other?

2. Did the policy of closing the Western seas to trade (*mare clausum*) prove of lasting benefit to the Carthaginians?

3. Name some other states besides Rome which have been *forced* into organizing navies and developing naval power.

4. Hannibal spent the best years of his life in an enterprise that failed. What part did he play in the development of civilization?

DISCUSSION TOPICS

1. The Roman bronze coins grew smaller in the third century B.C. because copper became scarce and the conquests of Alexander the Great had released the Persian gold and silver hoards.

2. Rome won the first war with Carthage because the Carthaginians had made no improvements in their ships.

3. Scipio was a greater man than Hannibal.

4. Scipio Nasica thought it would have been a good thing for Rome to have a strong rival in the Western Mediterranean, and therefore that it would have been to the advantage of Rome not to destroy Carthage.

ADDITIONAL ADVENTURES IN LEARNING

1. Studies in Source Materials. BOTSFORD, *Source-book*: (1) The story of Regulus, pp. 379–380; (2) The manufacture of munitions in Syracuse, pp. 241–243.

2. Supplementary. SHOWERMAN, *Rome and the Romans*: (1) The Roman army, pp. 453–468; (2) Rome as a sea power, pp. 474–484.

3. Look up in an encyclopedia: *republic, legion, Hannibal, strategy, Scipio Africanus Major, Hamilcar.*

CHAPTER XIV · HOW ROME WAS CHANGED BY HER CONQUESTS

THE ROMAN CONQUEST OF THE EASTERN MEDITERRANEAN WORLD · ROME'S GOV-
ERNMENT AND CIVILIZATION AFTER HER CONQUESTS · EFFECTS OF WEALTH IN CITY
AND COUNTRY

IN THE preceding chapter we have seen how the fourfold rivalry in the Western Mediterranean, which had long included the Etruscans and Carthaginians, the Greeks and the Romans, had ended with the triumph of the once insignificant group of villages above the prehistoric market on the Tiber. The Western Mediterranean world was at last under the leadership of a single great nation, the Romans, as the Eastern Mediterranean world had once been under the leadership of the Macedonians. It was now evident that Roman supremacy could not be maintained if confined to the Western Mediterranean. Hannibal's effort to secure help from the East had shown the Roman Senate that they could not safely permit any other state on the Mediterranean to develop such strength as to endanger Rome in the way Carthage had done during the war with Hannibal. The Romans could not forget how the Carthaginian general had induced Macedonia to combine with him against Rome. Thus we shall find that Rome was drawn into a struggle with the Hellenistic nations in which the Romans were able to gain the leadership of the East also. The question which the Roman Senate then faced was the organization of this vast conquered territory. In Italy there were, moreover, serious economic and social problems caused by the long wars and the new wealth and power that she had acquired.

1. THE ROMAN CONQUEST OF THE EASTERN MEDITERRANEAN WORLD

Alexander's Successors become Subject to Rome (200–168 B.C.). While the heirs of Alexander were carrying on their wars and making alliances in the Eastern Mediterranean (down to about 200 B.C.) (pp. 239–241), the power of Rome had been slowly growing in the West. Hannibal had persuaded Macedonia into an alliance with him against Rome. This hostile step could not be overlooked by the Romans; and so, a year after the close of the war with Hannibal, the king of Macedon found himself face to face with a Roman army. Shortly after, on the field of Cynoscephalæ, in 197 B.C., the Macedonian army was disastrously defeated, and the ancient realm of Alexander the Great became a subject state under Rome. The Greek cities which had been brought under Macedonian control by Philip and Alexander the Great were now granted their freedom as *allies*, but Rome continued to keep a strict watch on them.

This war with Macedonia brought the Romans into conflict with Antiochus the Great, the Seleucid king, who held in Asia a large part of the vast empire of Persia. A war with this powerful Asiatic empire was not a matter which the Romans could view without great anxiety. Moreover, Hannibal, who had fled eastward from Carthage (p. 288), was now with Antiochus, giving him the benefit of his long experience in fighting the Romans. Nevertheless, at Magnesia, in Asia Minor, Rome was able to defeat the forces of Antiochus (190 B.C.), and the lands of Asia Minor eastward to the river Halys were ceded by him to Roman control.

Roman Provinces in the Eastern Mediterranean. The Romans were at first opposed to ruling directly the territory conquered in the East. They preferred to establish for the peoples of Asia Minor, Macedonia, and Greece some sort of local self-government, under the protection of Rome. But pretenders to kingship would arise, and the little city-states kept up their continuous quarreling. It finally became necessary for the Romans to take harsh measures. The Greek cities were reorganized so as not to give further trouble, and, as an object lesson, Corinth was burned in 146 B.C. Macedonia was made a tribute-paying Roman province with a Roman governor in 147 B.C. It was not, however, until 133 B.C. that Rome organized a province in Asia Minor. From 168 B.C. on, Rome interfered in Egyptian affairs in order to save Egypt from the ambitions of the Seleucids (p. 240).

2. ROME'S GOVERNMENT AND CIVILIZATION
AFTER HER CONQUESTS

Misgovernment of Roman Provinces. The Romans were now faced by the problem of governing wisely the wide realms which they had conquered. Most of the newly acquired countries were organized as provinces, each under a Roman governor who possessed almost unlimited power. He had complete control of all the taxes of the province, and could demand as much money as he pleased from its people for the expenses of government and troops. These governors were very often inexperienced in ruling, but were eager to make a fortune during their short term of office (usually a single year); and their rule frequently became a mere system of looting and robbery. The Senate found it necessary to have laws passed for the punishment of such evils, but these laws were of little use in improving the condition.

The provinces were soon filled with Roman businessmen whom we should call "loan sharks." There were men called *publicans* who were allowed to collect the taxes for the state at a great profit. We remember the common references to the publicans in the New Testament, where they are regularly classed with "sinners." These grafters plundered the provinces worse than the greedy Roman governors themselves.

Rise of a Wealthy Class at Rome. As these people returned to Italy, there grew up a wealthy class such as had been unknown there before. Their demand for luxuries resulted in a great increase in foreign trade. From the Bay of Naples to the mouth of the Tiber the sea was white with the sails of Roman ships going and coming to and from the docks of Rome. The men who carried on this trade became wealthy merchants. To handle all the money that was now being used, banks were required. The banks at Rome occupied a line of booths on each side of the Forum. With the great increase of wealth the appearance of Rome and the life of the people changed greatly.

When a returned governor of Africa put up a showy new house, the citizen across the way who still lived in his father's old house began to be dissatisfied. This house was built of sun-dried brick, and, like the old settler's cabin of early America, it had but one room; this was called the *atrium* (Fig. 67). The Roman citizen of the new age had long before become familiar with the comfort, luxury, and beauty with which the Greek houses of southern Italy were filled. He therefore soon added a colonnaded Hellenistic court, with adjoining dining-room, bedrooms, library, rest rooms, and kitchen.

Fig. 67. *An Old Roman Atrium House*

There was no attempt at beautiful architecture, and the bare front showed no adornment whatever. The opening in the roof, which lighted the atrium, received the rainfall of a section of the roof sloping toward it, and this water collected in a pool built to receive it in the floor of the atrium below (Fig. 68, *B*). The tiny area, or garden, shown in the rear was not common. It was here that the later Romans added the Hellenistic peristyle (Fig. 69)

The New Luxury at Rome. Not long before the Carthaginian wars an ex-consul had been fined for having more than ten pounds' weight of silverware in his house. A generation later a wealthy Roman was using, in his household, silverware which weighed some ten thousand pounds.

The original atrium in the finer houses was now converted into a large and stately reception hall where the master of the house could display statues, paintings, and other works of art seized in Eastern cities. One of the Roman conquerors of Macedonia entered Rome with two hundred and fifty wagonloads of Greek statues and paintings. Even in so small a city as Pompeii a citizen of wealth paved a handsome dining alcove with a magnificent mosaic picture of Alexander in battle, which had once been a floor in a splendid Hellenistic residence in Alexandria.

The finest residences sometimes had pipes for running water, baths, and other sanitary conveniences. Some of the houses had a system of heating by means of tile pipes which conducted into the rooms the hot air from a furnace. This was a great improvement on the charcoal brazier, which was all the Romans had once had. The kitchen was furnished with bronze utensils far better than those commonly found in our own homes.

The rich had a great number of household servants. There was a doorkeeper at the front door (he was called "janitor," from the Latin word *janua*, meaning "door"), and within the house there was a servant for every small duty. Almost all these servants were slaves.

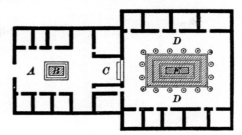

Fig. 68. *Plan of a Roman House with Peristyle*

The earliest Roman house had consisted of a single room, the atrium (A), with the pool for the rain water (B). Then a small alcove, or lean-to, was erected at the rear (C) as a room for the master of the house. Later the bedrooms on each side of the atrium were added. Finally, under the influence of Greek life, the garden court (D and Fig. 69), with its surrounding colonnaded porch (peristyle) and a fountain in the middle (E), was built at the rear. Then a dining-room, a sitting-room, and bedrooms were added, which opened on this court, and, being without windows, they were lighted from the court through the doors. In town houses it was quite easy to partition off a shop, or even a whole row of shops, along the front or side of the house, as in the Hellenistic house (Fig. 57). The houses of Pompeii were almost all built in this way

Influence of Greek Art and Literature in Rome. The cultivated Romans appreciated the beautiful Greek works of art, which some of their artists tried to imitate and copy. The Greek theater too became popular, and Roman playwrights, such as Plautus and Terence, adapted Greek comedies to suit the taste of Roman audiences, who laughed heartily at the old Greek jokes. Hellenistic buildings were beginning to appear in Rome, and it was not long before a Greek theater was erected, improved by the Romans with awnings, a stage curtain, and seats in the orchestra circle.

FIG. 69. *Peristyle of a Pompeian House (Below) compared with the Colonnades in the Court of an Egyptian Pyramid Temple*

We must imagine ourselves standing in the Pompeian house (below), with our backs toward the atrium, having immediately behind us the room *C* in Fig. 68. We look out into the court, the garden of the house (Fig. 68, *D*). The marble tables and statues and the marble fountain basin in the middle (Fig. 68, *E*), just as we see them in the drawing, were found by the excavators in their places, as they were covered by volcanic ashes over eighteen hundred years ago. Here centered the family life, and here the children played about the court, which was brightened with flowers and the tinkling music of the fountains

The Romans had been accustomed to do very little in the way of educating their children. There were no schools at first, but gradually parents began to send their children to the schools which the freed Greek slaves at Rome were beginning to open. Here and there a household possessed an educated Greek slave, like one named Andronicus, who became the tutor of the children, teaching his pupils to read from his new "primer," as we may call the Latin translation which he had made of Homer.

Rise of Latin Literature. Poets and writers of history now arose in Italy under the influence of Greek literature. Educated Romans could read of the great deeds of their ancestors in long epic poems modeled on those of Homer. In such literature were gradually being recorded the picturesque legends of early Rome, — the story of Romulus and Remus and similar tales (Fig. 63). Imitating the Greek comedies, Latin playwrights also were producing very clever comedies which made fun of the society of Rome and to which the Romans listened with delight.

As the new Latin literature grew, papyrus rolls containing Latin works were more and more common in Rome. One of the Roman conquerors of Macedon brought back the books of the Macedonian king and founded the first private library in Rome. Wealthy educated Romans were now providing library rooms in their houses, and they often spoke Greek almost as well as Latin.

3. Effects of Wealth in City and Country

Evil Effects of the New Luxury. The new life of Greek culture and luxury shocked those who admired the old ways. Even the younger Scipio, an ardent admirer of Greek litera- ture and art, expressed his pained surprise at finding Roman boys in a Greek dancing school. Laws were passed to check expensive habits, such as wearing showy jewelry and the use of carriages; but they amounted to little. The old simplicity of Roman family life was disappearing. The greatest days of old-fashioned Roman character were past, and Roman power was to go on growing without the restraining influence of the old Roman virtue.

During the wars with Carthage there had been introduced an ancient Etruscan custom of single combats between slaves or condemned criminals, who were forced to fight to give added importance to the funeral of some great man. These fighters came to be called gladiators, from a Latin word *gladius*, meaning "sword." Officials in charge of the various public feasts, without waiting for a funeral, used to arrange a long program of such combats, sure of pleasing the people, gaining their votes, and thus securing election to higher offices. These barbarous and bloody entertainments took place in a great stone structure called an amphitheater, because it was formed by placing two (*amphi*) theaters face to face. Soon afterward combats between gladiators and wild beasts were introduced. The Romans began also to build enormous courses for chariot races, surrounded by seats for vast numbers of spectators. Such a building was called a *circus*.

Corruption in the Government. The Roman politician now sought office chiefly with the hope of finally gaining the governorship of a province. There he might hope to make himself rich for life. When he wished to be elected, therefore, the politician at first naturally took advantage of the habit that had grown up of distributing free grain and bread among the poorer people; and then, in order to make himself more popular with the voters, he arranged programs of gladiatorial games and other spectacles. Bribery of this sort became common, and laws passed to prevent it had little effect. If the politician finally won the governorship of a rich province, he more than covered all his expenses. When a retired provincial governor returned to Rome, he was no longer the simple Roman of the old days. He was rich enough to live like a prince and surround himself with every kind of luxury.

Growth of Great Estates; Decline of Small Farms. The evils of the desire for new wealth were not less evident outside of Rome. It was not thought proper for a Roman senator or noble to engage in any business. The most respectable form of wealth was land. Hence the successful Roman noble or wealthy citizen bought farm after farm, which he combined into a great estate or plantation. Only here and there were still to be found groups of little farms of the old Roman days. The small farm seemed in a fair way to disappear.

Slave Revolts and Disorders. It was impossible for a wealthy landowner to work these great estates with free, hired labor. Nor was he obliged to do so. From the close of the war with Hannibal onward, the Roman conquests had brought to Italy great numbers of captives of war. These unhappy prisoners were sold as slaves. The estates of Italy were now filled with them. The life of such slaves on the great plantations which they worked was little better than that of beasts. When the supply of captives from the wars failed, slave pirates for many years carried on wholesale kidnaping in the Ægean and Eastern Mediterranean.

Thus Italy and Sicily were fairly flooded with slaves. The brutal treatment which they received was so unbearable that at various places in Italy they finally rose against their masters. In central and southern Sicily the revolting slaves, some sixty thousand in number, united and slew their masters, captured towns, and set up a kingdom. It required a Roman consul at the head of an army, and a war lasting several years, to subdue them.

Destruction of Farm Life in Italy by War. Slave labor and the great wars were meantime further ruining the small farmers of Italy. Never has there been an age in which the terrible and desolating results of war have so tragically shown the awful cost of military glory. Fathers and elder sons had been absent from home for years holding their posts in the legions, fighting the battles which had brought Rome her great position as mistress of the world. Home life and wholesome country influences were undermined and broken up. The mothers, left to bring up the younger children alone, saw the family scattered and drifting away from the little farm, till it was left forsaken.

Decline of Agriculture in Italy. Too often, as the returning soldier approached the spot where he was born, he no longer found the house that had sheltered his childhood. His family was gone, and his little farm, sold for debt, had been bought up by some wealthy Roman of the city and had become part of a great plantation. There was nothing left for him to do but wander up to the great city to look for free bread from the government, to enjoy the games and circuses, and to increase the poor class already there.

Or if he found his home and his little farm uninjured, he was soon aware that the hordes of slaves now cultivating the great plantations around him were raising grain more cheaply than he. When he sold his harvest, he did not receive enough for it to enable him and his family to live. Forced to sell the little farm at last, he too wandered into Rome, where he found thousands upon thousands of his kind homeless, miserable, and dependent upon the state for food. These once sturdy farmer-citizens who were now destitute had made up the bulk of the citizenship of Rome, from whose ranks she had formerly drawn her splendid armies.

Decline of Hellenistic Civilization. Nor was the situation any better in the most civilized portions of the empire outside Italy, particularly in Greece. Under the large plantation system the Greek farmers had also been crowded out by large landholders. Besides, the Greeks suffered from the robberies and extortions of the Roman taxgatherers and governors; from the raids of the Ægean pirates, whose pillaging and kidnaping the Roman Republic criminally failed to prevent (p. 299); and from the loss of their trade (p. 240). These were reasons enough for the destruction of business, agriculture, and prosperity in the Greek world. At the same time, that wondrous development of higher civilization which we found in the Hellenistic world was also showing signs of decline.

Failure of Roman Government of the Mediterranean World. The failure of the Roman Senate to organize a successful government for the empire they had conquered — a government even as good as that of Persia under Darius — had brought the whole world of Mediterranean civilization dangerously near destruction. In the European background beyond the Alpine frontiers there were the beginnings of vast movements among the northern barbarians, who threatened to descend as of old and completely overwhelm the civilization which for over three thousand years had been slowly built up by Orientals and Greeks and Romans in the Mediterranean world. It now looked very much as if the Roman state were about to perish, and with it the civilization which had been growing for so many centuries. Rome was a city-state. Among the Greeks this very form of state had outlived its usefulness and had over and over again proved its inability to organize and control successfully a larger world, that is, an empire. Would the Roman Republic be able to transform itself into a great imperial state, with all the many offices necessary to give successful government to the peoples and nations surrounding the Mediterranean?

Questions and Exercises

REVIEW OF CHAPTER

1. Why did the Romans think it necessary to extend their conquests to the Eastern Mediterranean? Why were Macedonia and Asia Minor not organized into provinces until some fifty years after they were conquered?

2. What success had the Roman Senate in controlling the provincial governors? Who were the publicans? Contrast Roman living conditions before the foreign wars with those that prevailed afterwards. What elements of Greek civilization now began to influence Roman culture?

3. What was the effect of the new luxury and culture on Roman character? Discuss Roman political corruption. Why was farming in Italy no longer profitable?

USEFUL TERMS

See how much meaning you can give to the following: *comedies, amphitheater, politician, slave pirates, Hellenistic civilization, Roman Republic.*

DIRECTIVE QUESTIONS

1. Compare the attitude of the Roman Republic, from about 200 B.C. to 150 B.C., toward the conquered territory in the Eastern Mediterranean with the attitude of the United States toward the Philippines.

2. Have the mistakes made by the Roman Republic in the government of the provinces been repeated by any modern nations?

3. Describe some of the tactics of the Roman vote-getters.

Discussion Topics

1. The burning of Corinth by the Romans was necessary in order to maintain peace in Greece.

2. Cato was justified in his dislike of Greek civilization because of its effects on Roman character.

3. Conditions in post-war Italy in the second century B.C. were typical of post-war conditions in any country at any time.

Additional Adventures in Learning

1. **Studies in Source Materials.** BOTSFORD, *Source-book*: (1) The subjection of the Greeks, pp. 394–395; (2) Cato the Censor, pp. 411–415; (3) Agriculture, pp. 404–408.

2. **Supplementary.** SHOWERMAN, *Rome and the Romans*: (1) The Roman house, pp. 76–88; (2) Roman games and pastimes, pp. 141, 299–382; (3) Roman women, pp. 112–123.

3. Look up in an encyclopedia: *Antiochus III (the Great), Corinth, province, banks and banking, architecture, Rome, circus, Spartacus*

CHAPTER XV · A CENTURY
OF REVOLUTION AND THE END
OF THE ROMAN REPUBLIC

THE LAND SITUATION, AND THE BEGINNING OF THE STRUGGLE BETWEEN SENATE
AND PEOPLE · THE RISE OF ONE-MAN POWER: MARIUS AND SULLA · THE OVER-
THROW OF THE REPUBLIC: POMPEY AND CAESAR · THE TRIUMPH OF OCTAVIAN AND
THE END OF THE CIVIL WAR

WE STAND at the point where the civilization of the Hellenistic
world began to decline, after the destruction of Carthage and Corinth
(146 B.C.). We are now to watch the Roman people struggling with three
difficult and dangerous problems at the same time: first, the deadly hostility which we have seen growing up between rich and poor; second, the
organization of successful Roman government of the Mediterranean world;
and third, the invasions of the barbarian hordes of the north. We shall see
that during a century of revolution and bloodshed, there gradually developed
a feeling that these problems could not be solved by a republic, — that
they could be settled only by uniting the Mediterranean world under the
power of a single ruler. In the conflict between rich and poor and in the
attempt to maintain order in the possessions outside of Italy, various leaders arose, each steadily gaining in control of the state, especially by using
military power, until about 30 B.C., when the stage was set for Octavian,
who became Augustus, the first emperor of Rome.

1. THE LAND SITUATION, AND THE BEGINNING OF THE
STRUGGLE BETWEEN SENATE AND PEOPLE

The Dangerous Situation to be met by the Senate. We must
now take up the difficult problems demanding settlement
by the Roman Senate. *In Italy* there was, above all, the
growing poverty of the small farmer and finally the disappearance of large numbers of farms, which became part of
the vast estates of rich landowners. This meant the increase
of the poor and unemployed as the poor farmers drifted into
the cities. Then there was the discontent of the Italian allies,
who had never been given the vote or the right to hold office
(p. 277). The problems *outside Italy* were not less serious.
There was, first, the need of a complete reform of government

in the provinces, and the creation of a system of honest and successful management of the great Roman state. And, second, there was the settlement of the frontier boundaries and the driving back of the invading barbarians who were threatening to overwhelm the Mediterranean world and its civilization, as the early Greek tribes had crushed Ægean civilization.

Reforms of the Gracchi (133–121 B.C.). The crying needs of the farming class in Italy failed to produce any effect upon the selfish aristocrats of the Senate. The patriot who undertook to become the leader of the people against the Senate and to save Italy from destruction by restoring the farmer class was a noble, however, named Tiberius Gracchus. He was a grandson of Scipio, the hero of Zama. After he was made tribune, he used to address the people with great feeling and tell them of the wrongs they suffered. "The beasts that prowl about Italy have holes and lurking places, where they may make their beds. You who fight and die for Italy enjoy only the blessings of air and light. These alone are your heritage. Homeless, unsettled, you wander to and fro with your wives and children. . . . You fight and die to give wealth and luxury to others. You are called the masters of the world; yet there is no clod of earth that you can call your own."

Tiberius Gracchus brought before the Assembly a law for the redistribution of public lands and the protection and support of the farming class. It was a statesmanlike and moderate law. Finally Gracchus succeeded in passing his law; but in the effort to secure reëlection, so that he might insure *enforcement* of the law, Gracchus was slain by a mob of senators who rushed out of the Senate-house and attacked him and his supporters. This was the first murderous deed introducing a century of revolution and civil war (133–30 B.C.), which ended in the destruction of the Roman Republic.

Ten years after the tribunate of Tiberius Gracchus his younger brother Gaius was elected to the same office (123 B.C.). He tried not only to secure some reforms to better the lot of the landless farmers but also to reduce the power of the Senate, which he believed was the cause of many of the troubles of the state. At the same time he proposed to give to the Italian allies the full citizenship which they had so long desired. This proposal angered the people as much as it did the Senate. His efforts finally resulted in a riot in which he was killed (121 B.C.), as his brother had been.

2. THE RISE OF ONE-MAN POWER: MARIUS AND SULLA

The People turn to Army Leaders to help them. The work of the Gracchus brothers had taught the people to look up to a leader. This was the beginning of one-man power. But the leader to whom the people now turned was not a city official, as the Gracchus brothers had been, but a *military commander*. The misrule of the Senate abroad had become increasingly serious. In a war between Rome and Jugurtha, ruler of the great kingdom of Numidia in North Africa, the African king succeeded first in bribing one of the Roman consuls and then in inflicting a crushing defeat on the Roman army. These events greatly angered the Romans, and in spite of the fact that the Senate's commander at this time was an able and honest consul who had defeated Jugurtha, the Assembly appointed Marius, a newly elected consul, to command the army in North Africa. As the Senate had the right to select the commander by lot, this act signified that the people, through the Assembly, had taken the matter out of the Senate's hands and themselves assumed charge of a great foreign enterprise. What was more important, *the people by this action seized control of the army.*

Services of Marius, the People's Commander. Marius, the commander whom the people selected, was himself a man of the people, who had once been a rough plowboy and was now an able soldier. He was quickly victorious in North Africa and returned to Rome in triumph. Meantime two powerful tribes of German barbarians, the Cimbrians and the Teutons, together with some Gauls, had been shifting southward and crossing the northern frontiers of the Roman possessions. Six Roman armies which opposed them, one after another, had been disastrously defeated. There was great anxiety in Rome. The people repeatedly reëlected Marius consul and sent him against the terrible northern barbarians. In two great battles in the north the people's hero not only defeated but almost destroyed the German hosts (101 B.C.). A soldier of the people had saved Rome.

Marius was not only a good soldier but also a great organizer. In order to secure sufficient men for the legions, he abolished the old custom of drafting citizens to serve in the army, and took volunteers from among the poor and the penniless. These men became professional soldiers, and it was clear that the old days when Rome could rely merely on her *citizens* to defend her had passed.

Struggle between Rome and her Italian Allies (90–88 B.C.). While the struggle between Senate and people was going on, there was increasing discontent among the Italian allies. They had furnished as many troops for the conquering armies as had Rome herself, and yet they were refused any voice in the control of the conquered territory or any just share in the immense wealth which they saw the Romans drawing from it.

There were, fortunately, some statesmanlike Roman leaders who realized that this was unfair and who urged that the Italian allies should be granted citizenship. Among them was a wealthy and popular noble named Drusus, who was elected tribune (91 B.C.) and who tried to secure this privilege for the allies. But so fierce was the opposition his efforts aroused, both in the Senate and among the people, that Drusus was assassinated. Thereupon the leading Italian communities of central and southern Italy finally revolted in protest against this treatment and formed a new state of their own, with a capital which they named Italica (90 B.C.).

Unable to win the war which followed (90–88 B.C.), the Romans finally granted the desired citizenship. The Italian communities then rejoined the Roman state. But the citizens living in distant communities could not vote or take any part in the government unless they journeyed to Rome to do so.

Sulla defies the People's Laws with an Army. At the head of an army which he had been leading against the Italian allies was a former officer of Marius, a very successful soldier named Sulla. The Senate now selected him to command in a war in Asia Minor. But the leaders of the people would not accept the Senate's appointment, and passed a law electing Marius to this command. Marius, however, had no army at the moment; so Sulla marched with his troops on Rome. For the first time a Roman took possession of the city *by force.* The *Senate* was now carrying out its will with the assistance of an army, as the *Assembly* had formerly done. Sulla forced through a new law requiring the Assembly to get the consent of the Senate before voting on any measure. Having thus destroyed the power of the people lawfully to oppose the Senate, Sulla marched off to the war in Asia Minor.

Revenge of Marius, and his Death. The Senate had triumphed, but with the departure of Sulla and his legions the people refused to submit. Marius, having entered Rome with troops, began a frightful massacre of the leading men of the senatorial party. The Senate, the first to use violence in the murder of Tiberius Gracchus, was now repaid. Marius was elected consul for the seventh time, but he died a few days after his election (86 B.C.). Meantime the leaders of the people ruled in Rome until the return of Sulla.

Sulla gives the Senate Supreme Power (82–79 B.C.). Having finished a victorious campaign in Asia Minor, Sulla returned. On the way back the Roman army of Sulla defeated the Roman armies of the people, one after another, and entered Rome as master of the state. With the help of his soldiers he forced his own appointment as dictator. His first action was to begin the slaughter of the leaders of the people's party and to take away their property. Then he forced the passage of a whole series of new laws which deprived the Assembly and the tribunes of their power and gave the supreme leadership of the state to the Senate. To Sulla's great credit, he made no attempt to gain permanent control of the state himself but on the completion of his legislation retired to private life.

3. THE OVERTHROW OF THE REPUBLIC:
POMPEY AND CÆSAR

People elect Pompey as their Leader (70 B.C.). After the
death of Sulla the people began an agitation for the repeal
of the laws which deprived them and their tribunes of all
control over the government. They selected Pompey, a
former officer of Sulla's, as their leader. Pompey was elected
consul (70 B.C.) and managed to get the hated laws of Sulla
repealed.

Achievements of Pompey (67–62 B.C.). Pompey made a
great name for himself by attacking and destroying the
pirates who preyed on Roman trading ships and dared even
to come as far as the Tiber, robbing and burning. He gained
also important victories in Asia Minor and Syria, where he
crushed the remnant of the kingdom of the Seleucids (p. 240)
and made Syria a Roman province. He entered Jerusalem
and brought the new Jewish kingdom under Roman control.
Before he turned back, the legions under his leadership had
marched along the Euphrates and had looked down upon the
Caspian. There had been no such conquests in the Orient
since Alexander had marched in triumph through the East.

Rise of Cæsar; his Election as Consul (59 B.C.). Meantime a new hero had arisen at Rome. He was a nephew of
Marius, named Julius Cæsar, born in the year 100 B.C. He
took up the cause of Marius and quickly gained a prominent
place among the leaders of the people.

When Pompey returned to Italy, hailed as the great conqueror of the Orient, he needed influence to secure the
Senate's approval of his actions in Asia Minor, and a grant
of land for his troops. For two years the Senate refused Pompey these demands. Then Cæsar, to gain the help of Pompey,
stepped forward in Pompey's support, and the two secured
the backing of a very wealthy Roman noble named Crassus.
This alliance of these three powerful men (called a "triumvirate") gave them the control of the situation. As a result
Cæsar was elected consul for the year 59 B.C.

Cæsar's Achievements in Gaul (58–50 B.C.). The consulship was but a step in Cæsar's plans. Having fearlessly put through new land laws for the benefit of the people, Cæsar then provided for his own future career. It was clear to him that he must have an important military command in order to gain an army. He saw a great opportunity in the West, in the vast country a part of which is now France but which was then occupied by the Gauls (map IV, p. 285). He had no difficulty in securing the appointment as governor of Gaul on both sides of the Alps for five years.

Cæsar took charge of his new province early in 58 B.C. and at once showed himself a military commander of great skill. In eight years he subdued the Gauls and got possession of their territory from the ocean and the English Channel eastward to the Rhine. He even crossed the Channel and invaded Britain as far as the Thames. He added to the Roman state a vast realm comprising in general the territory of modern France and Belgium. We should not forget that his conquest brought into France the Latin language, from which French speech has descended.

Cæsar as a Statesman. Cæsar had shown himself a successful politician at Rome. In Gaul he proved his ability as a brilliant soldier. He was now to show that he was also a great statesman. Cæsar believed that Rome needed an able commander, with an army behind him, who would make himself the permanent master of the government. He therefore steadily pursued this aim. One of his cleverest moves was the publication of a history of his campaigns in Gaul, which he had found time to write even in the midst of dangerous marches and critical battles. Although it is one of the greatest works of Latin prose, the book was really a political pamphlet, intended to tell the Roman people the story of the vast conquests which they owed to their governor in Gaul. It did not fail of its purpose. At present it is the best-known Latin reading book for beginners in that language.

Pompey supports the Senate. The senators dreaded Cæsar's return to Italy and his probable election as consul, for they wished to have another leader like Sulla who would keep the Senate in control of the state. Some of the senators therefore made offers to Pompey, in spite of the fact that thus far he had been at the head of the people's party. He was no statesman and was simply looking for a position as a general. The result was that he undertook to defend the cause of the Senate. What should have been a lawful political contest between two parties, the Senate and the people, thus again became a military struggle between two generals, Cæsar and Pompey, like that of Marius and Sulla a generation earlier.

Cæsar manages to get Pompey out of Italy; is elected Consul (49 B.C.). Cæsar endeavored to make terms with the Senate, but on receiving as their reply a summons to give up his military command he had no hesitation as to his future action. The professional soldiers who now made up a Roman army felt little responsibility as citizens to the government, but were usually greatly attached to their commanding general. The veterans of Cæsar's campaigns in Gaul were loyally devoted to him. Before the Senate's message had been in his hands an hour, Cæsar and his troops had crossed the Rubicon, the little stream which formed the boundary of his province toward Rome (49 B.C.). Beyond this boundary Cæsar had no right under the law to lead his forces. In crossing it he had taken a step which became so memorable that we still speak of any great decision as a crossing of the Rubicon.

The swiftness of Cæsar's blows was always one of the greatest reasons for his success. Totally unprepared for so swift a response on Cæsar's part, the Senate turned to Pompey, who informed them that the forces at his command could not hold Rome against Cæsar. As Pompey retreated the majority of the senators and a large number of nobles fled with him and his army. By skillful maneuvers Cæsar forced Pompey and his followers to leave Italy and cross over to Greece. Being now in possession of Rome, Cæsar, after a brief dictatorship, was elected consul, and could then assume the rôle of lawful defender of Rome against the Senate and the army of Pompey.

Cæsar defeats Pompey and the Armies of the Senate. Pompey had the advantage in the struggle, for he could draw men and supplies from the kingdoms he had conquered in the East. Moreover, he still held the great fleet with which he had overcome the pirates, and he was thus master of the sea. He was now using every moment to collect and train an army with which to crush Cæsar. Furthermore, some of Pompey's officers held Spain. Cæsar was therefore obliged to reckon with the followers of Pompey on both sides, east and west. He determined to deal with the west first. With his customary swiftness he was in Spain by June (49 B.C.). Here, by cutting off their supplies, he forced Pompey's commanders to surrender without fighting a battle.

Having heard of Cæsar's departure into Spain, Pompey was preparing to cross over and again take possession of Italy. Before he could even begin the crossing, Cæsar had returned from Spain victorious, slipped past Pompey's warships, and landed his army on the coast of Epirus (map IV, p. 285). Though his army was smaller than that of Pompey, Cæsar met his enemy on the field of Pharsalus, in Thessaly (48 B.C.), and crushingly defeated him. Pompey's forces now surrendered to the victorious Cæsar.

Cæsar completes the Conquest of the Mediterranean World (48-45 B.C.). Pompey then escaped into Egypt, where he was basely murdered. Cæsar, following Pompey to Egypt, found ruling there Cleopatra, the last of the Ptolemies (p. 239). The charms of this remarkable queen seem to have captivated the great Roman. Her realms had long been under the protection of Rome (p. 292). We know little of the campaign by which Cæsar next overthrew his opponents in Asia Minor. It was from there that he sent his famous report to the Senate: "I came, I saw, I conquered" (*veni, vidi, vici*). The only other obstacles to Cæsar's complete control of the Mediterranean world were all disposed of by March, 45 B.C., a little over four years after he had first taken possession of Italy with his army (map, IV, p. 285). The speed and thoroughness of this memorable campaign have probably never been excelled in military history.

Cæsar's Reorganization of the State and Empire. Cæsar used his power with moderation and humanity. From the first he had taken great pains to show that his methods were not those of the bloody Sulla. It is clear that he intended his own position to be that of a sovereign like Alexander the Great. Nevertheless, he was too wise a statesman to abolish at once the outward forms of the Republic. He had himself made dictator for life, and he took over also the powers of the other leading offices of the state.

Cæsar lived only five years after getting control of Italy. Of this period, as we have seen, four years were almost wholly occupied by campaigns. Little time was therefore left him for the immense task of organizing the vast Roman dominions, the task in which the Roman Senate had so completely failed. Cæsar did not abolish the Senate, but he greatly increased its numbers and filled it with his own friends and supporters, some of them from the provinces. He began far-reaching reforms of the corrupt Roman government. In all this he was laying the foundations for the Roman Empire. He was, in fact, its first emperor, and only his untimely death prolonged the last struggles of the Republic.

Cæsar's Vast Plans and his Death (44 B.C.). Cæsar sketched vast plans for the rebuilding of Rome; he laid out great roads along the important lines of communication; and he completely reformed the government of cities. He put an end to centuries of inconvenience with the Greco-Roman moon calendar by introducing the Egyptian calendar, which we are still using in a somewhat altered form.

But there were still men in Rome who were not ready to submit to the rule of one man. On the fifteenth of March, 44 B.C., three days before the date arranged for his departure on a great campaign beyond the Euphrates, these men struck down the great leader of the Romans. If some of his murderers fancied themselves patriots overthrowing a tyrant, they little understood how vain were all such efforts to restore the ancient Republic. World conquests and military power had destroyed forever the Roman Republic, and the murder of Cæsar again plunged Italy into civil war.

4. THE TRIUMPH OF OCTAVIAN AND THE END OF THE CIVIL WAR

Early Career of Cæsar's Nephew, Octavian (Augustus). Over in Illyria the terrible news from Rome found Cæsar's grand-nephew Octavian (Fig. 70), a youth of eighteen, quietly pursuing his studies. A letter from his mother, brought by a secret messenger, bade him flee far away eastward without delay, in order to escape all danger at the hands of his uncle's murderers. The youth's reply was to proceed instead without a moment's hesitation to Rome. This statesmanlike decision reveals the quality of the young man.

On his arrival in Italy, Octavian learned that he had been legally adopted by Cæsar and

Fig. 70. *Portrait of Augustus (now in the Museum of Fine Arts, Boston)*

also made his sole heir. He was too young to be regarded as dangerous by Cæsar's enemies. But his young shoulders carried a wise head. In spite of his youth and inexperience he managed to find supporters and secure a military command, so that two years later he was able to defeat his enemies, including Cæsar's assassins, in the battle of Philippi (42 B.C.). During the following ten years he made his position stronger and stronger, and at the age of twenty-eight he had gained almost complete control over both the eastern and the western portion of the Roman realms.

Octavian ends a Century of Revolution and Civil War (133– 30 B.C.). Octavian's last struggle was with his former friend and supporter Mark Antony, who had become infatuated with the Egyptian queen Cleopatra and was in Alexandria. It was reported to Octavian that Antony and Cleopatra were planning to make themselves rulers of Rome. Octavian persuaded the Senate to declare war on Cleopatra, and he was accordingly able to advance against Antony. They met in battle at Actium, on the west coast of Greece, and Antony was defeated (31 B.C.).

The next year Octavian landed in Egypt. Antony, probably forsaken by Cleopatra, took his own life. The proud queen too, unwilling to be displayed at Octavian's triumph at Rome, died by her own hand. She was the last of the Ptolemies, the rulers of Egypt for nearly three hundred years. Octavian now made Egypt Roman territory. To the West, which he already controlled, Octavian had added the East. The entire Mediterranean world was at last under the power of a single ruler.

Questions and Exercises

REVIEW OF CHAPTER

1. What were the causes of the acute labor situation in Italy in the second century B.C.? Why were the Italian allies discontented? What problems of empire occupied the attention of the Roman Senate in the second century B.C.? Outline the political platforms of the Gracchi.

2. Give an estimate of the services of Marius to the Roman Republic. Did the Italian allies gain greatly by being admitted to citizenship?

3. Contrast Pompey and Cæsar. Was Cæsar far-sighted in wishing to be governor of Gaul rather than of one of the rich Oriental provinces? How did Cæsar show himself to be a constructive statesman?

4. How did Octavian become ruler of Rome?

USEFUL TERMS

See how much meaning you can give to the following: *public lands, paternalistic government, the Roman people, volunteers, Roman city government, moon calendar, a month.*

DIRECTIVE QUESTIONS

1. Discuss the unemployment situation in Italy during the second century B.C. with reference to the recent unemployment situation in the United States.

2. Compare the military leaders of the last century of the Roman Republic with the leaders of the Athenian democracy with special reference to patriotism.

3. What action of Pompey's and Cæsar's might be compared to "pork-barrel rolling" in our own government?

4. Have modern legislative bodies ever been dealt with as Cæsar dealt with the Roman Senate?

DISCUSSION TOPICS

1. The reforms of the Gracchi were paternalistic.

2. The services of the military leaders of the Republic to the state outweighed the evil effects on the Romans of a century of revolution.

3. Cæsar was a greater politician than soldier.

4. Extensive building programs, such as Cæsar contemplated, are usually initiated by dictators to appease the people.

ADDITIONAL ADVENTURES IN LEARNING

1. Studies in Source Materials. BOTSFORD, *Source-book*: (1) Pompey, pp. 433–437; (2) Cæsar's municipal reforms, pp. 450–454.

2. Supplementary. Cæsar's calendar: American Council on Education, *Story of Our Calendar*, pp. 14–18; SHOWERMAN, *Rome and the Romans*, pp. 304–307.

3. Look up in an encyclopedia: *Numidia, Gaius Marius, Lucius Cornelius Sulla, Senate, Pompey, triumvirate, Britain, Gaul, Marcus Antonius.*

CHAPTER XVI · THE AGE OF AUGUSTUS; HIS SUCCESSORS

THE RULE OF AUGUSTUS (27 B.C.—A.D. 14) AND THE BEGINNING OF TWO CENTURIES OF PEACE · THE CIVILIZATION OF THE AUGUSTAN AGE · THE LINE OF AUGUSTUS AND THE END OF THE FIRST CENTURY OF PEACE (A.D. 14–68)

JULIUS CAESAR was not permitted to realize his dream of creating a vast Mediterranean empire, with Rome as its capital. But those who struck him down at the height of his power did not succeed in crushing his plans. For his nephew, Octavian, quickly conquered his enemies in the East and West and became the first ruler over a *Roman Empire*. The new ruler had many titles conferred upon him, but the most important were *Augustus*, by which name he is known in history, and the title of *imperator*, from which our word " emperor " is derived.

Augustus was not only the first Roman emperor but one of the wisest rulers the empire ever had; for he was able to organize the many peoples within his realms into one great *unified* state. He provided the new empire, moreover, with good and efficient government by appointing honest of- ficials in the provinces, and these officials were made directly responsible to the emperor himself. Moreover, in assuming control of the government Augustus respected the customs and traditions of the people of Italy and of the provinces as well, and was able by his wise management to awaken in all a sense of pride and loyalty to the empire.

With the accession of Augustus the Roman world entered on a long era of peace. The great capital at Rome was beautified with stately build- ings, and the people prospered. The reign of Augustus is sometimes called the Golden Age of Latin literature ; for it was during this period that Latin poetry reached a high degree of perfection in the works of Horace, Virgil, Livy, and Ovid.

1. THE RULE OF AUGUSTUS (27 B.C.–A.D. 14) AND THE BEGINNING OF TWO CENTURIES OF PEACE

Octavian's Wise Policy. When Octavian returned to Italy the people rejoiced ; for they felt that peace had come at last, after the long years of civil war and disorder. The great majority of Romans now believed that one supreme ruler was necessary for the control of the vast Roman domin- ions. There was therefore no further opposition to Octavian, and he devoted the remaining forty-four years of his life to giving the Empire the efficient organization and good government which it had so long lacked. His most difficult task was to alter the old form of the state so as to make legal the position in the government which he had taken by military force. Unlike Cæsar, Octavian felt a sincere respect for the older institutions of the Roman Republic and did not wish to destroy them or to gain a throne for himself.

Organization of the Roman Empire by Octavian (Augustus). Accordingly, on returning to Rome, Octavian voluntarily handed over his powers to the Senate and the Roman people in January, 27 B.C. The Senate thereupon gave him *officially* the command of the army and the control of the most important frontier provinces. Besides these vast powers he held also the important rights of a tribune, and it was chiefly on this last office that he based his right to power.

At the same time the Senate conferred upon him the title of *Augustus*, that is, "the August"; but his chief official title was *Princeps*, that is, "the First," meaning the first of the citizens. Another title given the head of the Roman Empire was an old word for commander or general; namely, *Imperator*, from which our word "emperor" is derived. Augustus, as we may now call Octavian, regarded his position as that of an official of the Roman Republic, appointed by the Senate.

The Roman Empire was thus organized under a double government of the Senate and of the Princeps, whom we commonly call the emperor. But this double power could not remain well balanced. The old authority of the Senate could not be maintained reign after reign when the Senate controlled no army. The Princeps held too much power to remain a mere appointed official. He was the real ruler, because the legions were behind him; and the so-called republican state created by Augustus tended, as we shall see, to become a military monarchy.

Peace Policy of Augustus. The empire which Rome now ruled consisted of the entire Mediterranean world, or a fringe of states extending entirely around the Mediterranean

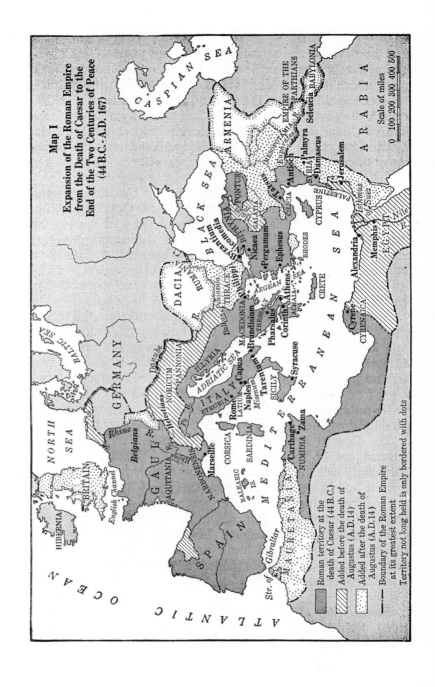

Map I

**Expansion of the Roman Empire
from the Death of Caesar to the
End of the Two Centuries of Peace
(44 B.C.-A.D. 167)**

Scale of miles
0 100 200 300 400 500

Roman territory at the
death of Caesar (44 B.C.)

Added before the death of
Augustus (A.D.14)

Added after the death of
Augustus (A.D.14)

Boundary of the Roman Empire
at its greatest extent

Territory not long held is only bordered with dots

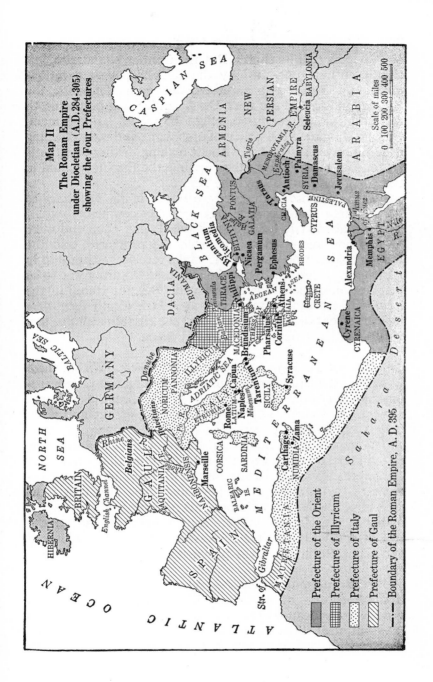

Map II

The Roman Empire
under Diocletian (A.D. 284-305)
showing the Four Prefectures

Scale of miles
0 100 200 300 400 500

CASPIAN SEA

ATLANTIC OCEAN

NORTH SEA

BALTIC SEA

HIBERNIA

BRITAIN

English Channel

GERMANY

GAUL

Belgians

Rhine R.

AQUITANIA R.

Rhône

NARBONENSIS

Marseille

SPAIN

Str. of Gibraltar

MAURETANIA

NUMIDIA

Zama

Carthage

Sahara Desert

CORSICA

SARDINIA

BALEARIC IS.

ITALY

ETRURIA

LATIUM

Rome

Capua

Naples

Misenum

Tarentum

Brundisium

SICILY

Syracuse

MEDITERRANEAN SEA

NORICUM

PANNONIA

ILLYRICUM

ADRIATIC SEA

Danube R.

RUMELIA R.

DACIA

VINDIA

THRACE

MACEDONIA

Philippi

Pharsalus

THESSALY

Corinth

Athens

ACHAIA

AEGEAN SEA

CRETE

Cyrene

CYRENAICA

BLACK SEA

Byzantium

BITHYNIA

Nicomedia

Nicaea

PONTUS

GALATIA

Pergamum

Ephesus

RHODES

CYPRUS

Tarsus

CILICIA

ARMENIA

Tigris R.

NEW PERSIAN EMPIRE

MESOPOTAMIA R.

Euphrates R.

SYRIA

Antioch

Palmyra

Damascus

Jerusalem

PALESTINE

Seleucia BABYLONIA

ARABIA

Alexandria

Memphis

EGYPT

Nile R.

Isthmus of Suez

Prefecture of the Orient

Prefecture of Illyricum

Prefecture of Italy

Prefecture of Gaul

Boundary of the Roman Empire, A.D. 395

and including all its shores. But the frontier boundaries, left almost entirely unsettled by the Republic, were a serious question. There was a natural boundary in the south, the Sahara, and also in the west, the Atlantic; but on the north and east further conquests might be made. In the main, Augustus adopted the policy of organizing and strengthening the Empire *as he found it*, without making further conquests. In the east his boundary thus became the Euphrates, and in the north the Danube and the Rhine.

For the defense of these vast frontiers it was necessary to keep a large standing army. It probably contained, on the average, about two hundred and twenty-five thousand men. It was now recruited chiefly from the provinces, and the foreign soldier who entered the ranks received citizenship in return for his service. Thus the idea that the army was to be made up of citizens was maintained. But the tramp of the legions was heard no more in Italy. Henceforth they were posted far out on the frontiers, and the citizens at home saw nothing of the troops who defended them.

The Great Task of Organizing the Provinces. Within these frontiers Augustus now undertook to organize a government for the entire Mediterranean world. Great peoples and nations had to be provided for in the huge empire and given honest and efficient government.

The appointment of the governors of the provinces now rested almost wholly with the emperor, and they knew that they were responsible to him for the wise and honest management of their territory. A governor knew also that if he proved successful he could hold his post for years or be promoted to a better one. There thus grew up under the control of Augustus and his successors a body of experienced and capable officials in the provinces (contrast page 293).

The Mediterranean World becoming a Mediterranean Nation. A process of unification began which was to make the Mediterranean *world* a Mediterranean *nation*. The separate national threads of our story have heretofore been numerous, as we have followed the history of the various

Oriental nations, of Athens, Sparta, Macedonia, Rome, Carthage, and others. For a long time we have followed these stories separately, like individual strands; but now they are to be twisted together into a single thread of national history, that of the Roman Empire.

2. THE CIVILIZATION OF THE AUGUSTAN AGE

Augustus rebuilds Rome. In the new Mediterranean nation which Augustus proposed to form it was his purpose that Italy should occupy the leading position. He wished to revive the old Roman customs and the beliefs of the fathers. He undertook also to rebuild Rome and make it the leading art center of the ancient world. On the Palatine Hill he had several dwelling-houses remodeled into a palace for himself.

The palace looked down upon a splendid array of new marble buildings surrounding the ancient Forum (p. 262). The finest of these was the handsome business hall (basilica) begun by Cæsar, left unfinished, and later damaged by fire. It was now restored and completed by Augustus (Fig. 72, *E*). On the north of the old Forum, Cæsar had constructed another, called the Forum of Cæsar (Fig. 72, *N*); but the growing business of the city led Augustus to build a third forum, known as the Forum of Augustus (Fig. 72, *O*), which he placed next to that of Cæsar. The first stone theater in Rome had been built by Pompey. Augustus now erected a larger and more magnificent one, which he named the Theater of Marcellus.

Architecture and Painting in the Augustan Age. In the new architecture Greek and Oriental ideas were combined. The arch, long used in the Orient, and the colonnade were the leading features of the new buildings. It was through these Roman buildings that the arch gained its important place in our own modern architecture. Not only in Rome but throughout Italy may be found ruins of arches and arcaded buildings surviving from the Augustan period.

Painting, for the Romans, had become largely wall decoration. Our room walls dotted with hanging pictures would

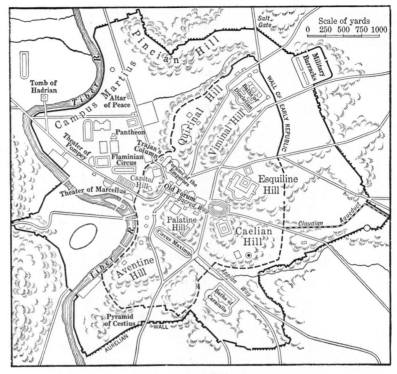

Rome under the Emperors

have been considered by the Romans as rather poor taste.
Like the Greeks, the Romans desired to arrange the decorations of a room so as to give a feeling of space, — a tendency
now shown by many of our most modern interior decorators.
This attitude of the Romans explains the character of the
wall paintings which have been uncovered in Roman ruins,
as in the houses of Pompeii. In these we find great sweeping
landscapes, as though we were looking out from a balcony
or a window; or buildings are painted in such a manner as
to give depth, as if the observer saw before him colonnades,
gardens, and distant villas.

The decoration of their house interiors became exceedingly
important to the wealthy Romans. And so great was their

appreciation of the Greek genius that if they could not have in their houses the originals of the great pieces of Greek sculpture and painting, they were willing to buy copies. Indeed, it seemed as though every Greek who could handle a sculptor's chisel or a painter's brush sat down to make copies of Greek statuary or rushed off to Rome to secure a commission to copy some Greek or Hellenistic painting on the wall of a Roman villa. Many copies were made in mosaic.

Fig. 71. *Detail from Sculptured Frieze of the Altar of Peace*

The Augustan Altar of Peace was built by the Senate in honor of the Augustan peace and formed a part of the great state thanksgiving for the safe return of Augustus from an expedition against German tribes. At the right are two men belonging to the senatorial group; at the left are citizens, evidently representing the lower classes. One of the latter holds a small child by the hand. The first sympathetic treatment of children in art is shown in the sculpture of this age. The citizens face left, the senatorial group right; thus they are carefully distinguished. (Courtesy of the German Archæological Institute in Rome)

Science in the Augustan Age. If Rome was a borrower in art, she was even more indebted to Greek and Hellenistic civilization for her science. Rome had no such men as Archimedes and Eratosthenes (p. 248). When Agrippa, the minister of Augustus, drew up a great map of the world, all he had in view was the practical use of the map by Roman governors going to their provinces or by merchants traveling with goods. Hence the roads were elaborately laid out, not on a fixed scale, but so that there would be space enough along each road for the names of all the towns situated along it and for all the distances in miles between towns, which were inserted in figures on the map. Such a map was without doubt convenient; but it entirely lacked the network of latitude and longitude so carefully worked out by Eratosthenes. The leading geography of the time was written by a Greek living in Rome, named Strabo. It was a delightful narrative of wide travels mingled with history; and although lacking in scientific method, it was for many centuries the world's standard geography, and may still be read with great pleasure and profit as an ancient book of travel.

Writers of Augustus's Time: Cicero. Indifference to science at Rome was in marked contrast with Roman interest in literature. It was during the reign of Augustus that the writing of Latin reached its highest perfection. Educated Romans showed great devotion to literary studies. Often these men had studied in Athens or Rhodes and were well acquainted with Greek learning and literature. They spoke Greek every day among themselves, perhaps more than they did Latin. Cæsar put together a treatise on Latin speech while crossing the Alps when his mind must have been filled with the problems of his great wars in Gaul.

One of the most cultivated men that Rome ever produced was Cicero. In the struggle to save the Republic, Cicero had failed as a statesman. Thereupon he devoted himself to his literary studies. As the greatest orator (or public speaker) in Roman history he had already done much to perfect and beautify Latin prose in the speeches which he delivered in the course of his career as a lawyer and a statesman. After his

---

* The Sacred Way (plan, p. 322) passed the little circular temple of Vesta (A) and reached the Forum at the Arch of Augustus (B) and the Temple of the deified Julius Cæsar (C). On the right was the oldest basilica in the Forum (D), and on the left the magnificent new Basilica of Julius Cæsar (E). Opposite this, across the old Forum market place (F), was the new Senate-house (G) planned by Julius Cæsar. At the upper end of the Forum was the new speaker's platform (H); near it Septimius Severus later erected his crude arch (I). Beyond rises the Capitol, with the Temple of Saturn (J) and the Temple of Concord (K) at its base; above, on its slope, is the Tabularium (L), a place for public records; and on the summit of the Capitol the Temple of Jupiter (M). Julius Cæsar extended the Forum northward by laying out his new Forum (N) behind his Senate-house (G). The later growth of the emperors' forums on this side may be seen in Breasted's *Ancient Times*, Fig. 242, where the same lettering is repeated and continued.

Fig. 72. *The Roman Forum and its Public Buildings in the Early Empire* *

We look across the ancient market place (*F*) to the Tiber with ships moored in the river. On each side of the market place, where we see the buildings *E*, *J*, and *D*, *G*, *I*, were once rows of little wooden booths for selling meat, fish, and other merchandise. Especially after the beginning of the Carthaginian wars these were displaced by fine buildings like the basilica hall *D*, built not long after 200 B.C. Note the Attic roofs and colonnades and the clerestory windows of the basilicas (*D*, *E*), copied from the Hellenistic cities and originally from the Orient (Fig. 15). This style was soon to be adopted as a form for Christian church buildings. See complete key on opposite page, footnote.
(After Luckenbach)

retirement he wrote a group of remarkable essays (based on Greek models) on duty, the gods, friendship, old age, and the like, and he left behind also several hundred letters which were preserved by his friends. As one of the last sacrifices of the civil wars, Cicero had fallen by the hands of Antony's brutal soldiers; but his writings were to have an undying influence. His works were so beautifully and elegantly expressed that they became models of Latin style. They were used in teaching Latin in the Middle Ages and are still read in schools and colleges wherever Latin is studied.

Poetry in the Augustan Age: Horace and Virgil. In the last days of the Republic, in spite of disorder and civil war, Cicero and the men of his time had perfected Latin *prose*. On the other hand, the greatest of Latin *poetry* arose under the inspiration of the early Empire and the universal peace established by Augustus. Horace, the foremost poet cf the time, although the son of a freedman of unknown race, had studied in Greece. He knew the old Greek lyric poets who had suffered danger and disaster as he himself had done in the long civil war. With the haunting echoes of old Greek poetry in his soul, he began to write of the men and the life of his own time.

Virgil, the other great poet of the Augustan Age, spent much of his time in the quiet of his farm under the shadow of the Alps in the north. Here, as he looked out upon his own fields, the poet began to write verses like those of Theocritus (p. 250), reflecting in poetic beauty the rustic life of his day on the green hillsides of Italy. As time passed he was filled with an exalted vision of the mission of Rome, and especially of Augustus, as the restorer of world peace. Virgil then undertook the creation of a great epic poem, in which he pictured the wanderings of the Trojan hero Æneas after the fall of Troy. He represented Æneas as having finally reached Italy, where he founded the royal line of Latium (Fig. 63). From Æneas, according to the story, were descended the Julian family, the Cæsars, whose latest leader, Augustus, had saved Rome and established a world peace. The Æneid (as this poem is called after Æneas) is one of the greatest Roman classics.

Death of Augustus and his Account of his Deeds. Augustus himself, when he was over seventy-five years old and felt his death approaching, put together an account of his life, which was engraved on bronze tablets and set up before his tomb. In this simple story the career of Augustus is unfolded with such grandeur as to make the document the most impressive brief record of a great man's life which has survived to us from the ancient world. Almost in his last hours Augustus penned the closing lines of this remarkable record, and on the nineteenth of August, the month which bears his name, in the fourteenth year of the Christian Era, the first and most famous of the Roman emperors died.

3. The Line of Augustus and the End of the First Century of Peace (A.D. 14–68)

The Four Successors of the Line of Augustus. Augustus had been in supreme control of the great Roman world for nearly half a century. Four descendants of his family, either by blood or adoption, were to rule for more than another fifty years and thus to fill out the first century of peace. Augustus had made a law providing for the appointment of his successors. Any prominent Roman citizen might have aspired to the office. Augustus left no son, and one after another his male heirs had died. He had finally been obliged to ask the Senate to associate with him in the government his stepson Tiberius, his wife's son by an earlier marriage.

Tiberius (A.D. 14–37) *and Caligula* (A.D. 37–41). At the death of Augustus the Senate therefore immediately appointed Tiberius to all his stepfather's powers, without any limit as to time. He was an able soldier and an experienced man of affairs. He gave the provinces wise and efficient governors and showed himself a skilled and successful ruler. Tiberius no longer allowed the Roman rabble to go through the farce of voting on what the emperor had already decided, and even the appearance of a government by the Roman people thus finally disappeared forever.

As Tiberius had lost his son, the choice for his successor fell upon Gaius Cæsar, a great-grandson of Augustus, nicknamed

Caligula ("Little Boot") by the soldiers among whom he was brought up. After a mad career of drunkenness and debauchery this mockery of a reign was brought to a sudden close by Caligula's own officers, who put an end to his life in his palace on the Palatine, when he had reigned only four years.

Claudius (A.D. 41–54). The imperial guards, ransacking the palace after the death of Caligula, found in hiding the trembling figure of a nephew of Tiberius and uncle of the dead Caligula, named Claudius. Though now fifty years old, Claudius had had no position of great responsibility. He had always been merely tolerated by his family as a man both physically and mentally inferior. But the guards hailed him as emperor, nevertheless, and the Senate was obliged to consent.

Claudius, however, accomplished much for the Empire and devoted himself to its affairs. He conducted in person a successful campaign in Britain and for the first time made its southern portion a province of the Empire, to which Britain was to remain subject for three and a half centuries. It was this conquest which probably introduced the first elements of Latin speech into the English language. At Rome, Claudius was greatly interested in buildings and practical improvements. He built two vast new aqueducts, together nearly a hundred miles in length. In order to make safe the supply and storage of grain, he began the construction of new harbor works and granaries at Ostia, the port of Rome. At the same time his own officials, chiefly able Greek freedmen who were aiding him in his duties, were beginning to form a kind of cabinet destined finally to give the Empire for the first time a group of efficient ministers whom we should call the Secretary of the Treasury, the Secretary of State, and so on.

The Infamy of Nero (A.D. 54–68). Agrippina, the last wife of Claudius, was able to push aside his son, Britannicus, and to obtain succession to the throne for her own son, Nero. Not only on his mother's side but also on his father's Nero was descended from the family of Augustus. His mother had intrusted his education to the philosopher Seneca, and for the first five years of his reign, while Seneca was his chief minister, the rule of Nero was wise and successful. Then palace intrigues removed this able minister from the court. Nero's strong-minded mother, Agrippina, was also banished. Thereafter he cast aside all restraint and followed his own evil nature in a career of such vice and cruelty that the name of Nero has ever since been regarded as one of the blackest in all history.

Nero, however, was devoted to art and wished personally to follow it. He even made a tour of Greece as a musician and composer. In his admiration for Greek civilization he tried to interest young Romans of the upper classes in athletic contests as well as in competitions in literature and music. But he was suspicious and ruthless, and he caused the assassination of the manly young son of Claudius as well as of many other innocent people. He was persuaded even to take the life of his wife, and, to crown his infamy, he had his own mother assassinated.

A great disaster, meantime, took place in Rome. A huge fire broke out and destroyed a large portion of the city. Dark rumors ran through the streets that Nero himself had set fire to the city that he might rebuild it more splendidly, and gossip told how he sat watching the city burn while he recited to the accompaniment of the lyre a poem of his own on the destruction of Troy. There is no evidence to support these rumors. But under the circumstances Nero was glad to accuse a new religious sect — called Christians — of having started the fire, and he executed a large number of them.

Death of Nero and End of the First Century of Peace. The dissatisfaction at Rome, and Nero's treatment of the only able men around him, deprived him of support there. Then the provinces began to protest against heavy taxation. This discontent finally broke out in open revolt, and rebellious troops marched on Rome from several points. The cowardly Nero went into hiding, and on hearing that the Senate had voted his death he theatrically stabbed himself and passed away uttering the words, "What an artist dies in me!" Thus ended (A.D. 68) the last ruler of the line of Augustus, and with him closed the first century of peace (27 B.C.–A.D. 68).

Questions and Exercises

REVIEW OF CHAPTER

1. Why did Augustus succeed, where Cæsar failed, in organizing the Roman Empire? What was the real position of Augustus in the newly organized Roman Empire? Discuss the peace policy of Augustus. How did the Roman provincial governors under Augustus differ from those before the time of Cæsar?

2. Explain the building program of Augustus. What distinctive features in Roman art were essentially Roman? Give an estimate of Roman geography and map-making. Where did Augustus place his autobiography?

3. Why did Tiberius become so unpopular with the Roman people? Discuss the public-works program of Claudius.

USEFUL TERMS

See how much meaning you can give to the following: "*Roman peace*," *Mediterranean world, Augustus, peace policy, basilica, Christian Era, Roman Empire.*

DIRECTIVE QUESTIONS

1. What was the policy of Augustus in regard to the boundaries of the Empire? Do you know of any boundary disputes now in progress?

2. How did the Roman idea of interior decoration differ from ours?

3. What part did Augustus and the successors of his line play in the history of our civilization?

DISCUSSION TOPICS

1. The "Roman peace" was the gift of Augustus to civilization.

2. The Romans were peaceful and prosperous during the Augustan Age, and were therefore able to produce more and better literature.

3. Because Claudius was a comical figure in the eyes of the Romans, succeeding generations have not appreciated his real ability.

ADDITIONAL ADVENTURES IN LEARNING

1. **Studies in Source Materials.** BOTSFORD, *Source-book*: (1) Augustus as emperor, pp. 464–467, 472–473; (2) Claudius, pp. 480–482.

2. **Supplementary.** FRANK, *History of Rome*: (1) Augustan literature, pp. 362–368; (2) Business life of Rome, pp. 375–405.

3. Look up in an encyclopedia: *Strabo, Marcus Vipsanius Agrippa, Æneid, Tiberius, aqueducts, Ostia, cabinet, Lucius Annæus Seneca. map.*

CHAPTER XVII · THE CIVILIZATION
OF THE ROMAN EMPIRE

FOR two centuries after the Roman dominions came under one ruler, there was peace within the Empire — the so-called *Pax Romana*; and during this period Roman civilization reached its height.

The Roman Empire, through the ability of its able rulers, acquired a well-organized government and built up a magnificent standing army. It also enjoyed the justice of a body of clear and efficient laws. Excellent roads were laid out connecting all parts of the Empire, and a navy protected its shipping. Under these favorable conditions men began to travel about both for business and for pleasure, and so became acquainted with the civilization of other peoples and other lands. All this exchange of ideas had a profound influence on the people of the Empire. Wealth and luxury increased, and learning spread more widely.

The ruins of many of the fine Roman buildings may be seen today, not only in Italy but in lands that once formed part of the Empire — silent witnesses to a highly developed civilization which reached from England to the Tigris-Euphrates. We must now see what the Romans gained from earlier civilizations and what were their own contributions to the progress of mankind.

1. THE EMPERORS OF THE SECOND CENTURY OF PEACE
(BEGINNING A.D. 69)

Vespasian and the Second Century of Peace. For about a year after the death of Nero the struggle among the leading military commanders for the throne of the Cæsars continued. Fortunately, Vespasian, a very able general who commanded troops in the East, was finally victorious, and was declared emperor by the Senate. Under Vespasian, who was followed by a line of able emperors, began the second century of peace, which brought to the Empire its greatest period of prosperity.

THE ROMAN EMPIRE
AT ITS GREATEST EXTENT

Scale of miles
0   100   200   300   400   500

The Roman Emp

DACIA

Danube R.

OESIA

THRACE

MACEDONIA

GREECE

AEGEAN SEA

Corinth Athens

ACHAEA

CRETE

Cyrene

CYRENAICA

Heraclea

BLACK SEA

Byzantium
Nicomedia

BITHYNIA AND PONTUS

ASIA

CAPPADOCIA

PAMPHYLIA

CILICIA

CYPRUS

N SEA

Alexandria

EGYPT

Nile R.

Caesarea

PALESTINE

Jerusalem

Petra

Sarmatians

Huns

Alans

COLCHIS IBERIA ALBANIA

CASPIAN SEA

Artaxata
ARMENIA

Nisibis
Edessa Nineveh
MESOPOTAMIA ASSYRIA

Antioch

SYRIA

EMPIRE OF THE
PARTHIANS

Emesa Palmyra

Euphrates Seleucia

Babylon

R.

Tigris

A R A B I A

ts *Greatest Extent*

Need of Protection of the Empire. The main task of the emperors of this period was that of strengthening the defenses on the frontiers. On the south the Empire was protected by the Sahara Desert and on the west by the Atlantic, but on the north and east it was open to attack. The shifting German tribes constantly threatened its northern frontiers, and in the east the boundary on the Euphrates was continually made unsafe by the Parthians, the only civilized power still unconquered by Rome (map I, p. 318). Owing to the pressure of the barbarians from the north, Mediterranean civilization was in grave danger.

The Flavian Emperors strengthen the Northern Frontiers (A.D. 69–96). The Flavian family, as we call Vespasian and his two sons, Titus and Domitian, did much to make the northern boundary safe by building walls and fortifications. But on the lower Danube they were unable to crush the growing power of the Dacians (map I, p. 318). Domitian even sent gifts to the Dacian king, intended to keep him quiet and satisfied. Instead, Domitian created a difficult problem in this region, which had to be solved by his successors.

Trajan and his Wars. The brief and quiet reign of the senator Nerva, who was selected by the Senate to succeed Domitian (A.D. 96), left the whole dangerous situation on the lower Danube to be met by the brilliant soldier Trajan, who followed Nerva as emperor in A.D. 98. He quickly realized that there would be no safety for the Empire along the Danube frontier until the Dacian kingdom was crushed. Bridging the Danube with boats and hewing his way through wild forests, Trajan captured one stronghold of the Dacians after another and finally destroyed their capital. He built a massive stone bridge across the Danube, made Dacia a Roman province, and settled numerous Roman colonies on the north side of the river. The descendants of these colonies still call themselves *Rumanians* and their land *Rumania,* both names being forms of the word "Roman."

Trajan then turned his attention to the eastern frontier, where a large portion of the boundary was formed by the

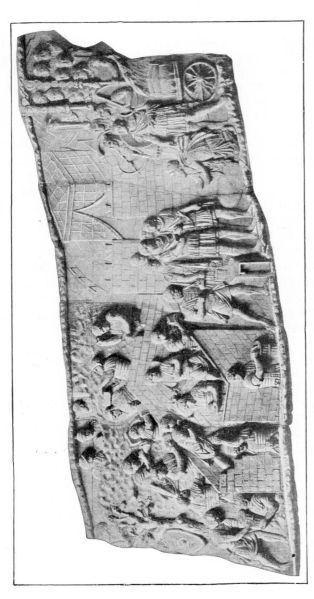

FIG. 73. *Relief Showing Scene from Trajan's Campaign against the Dacians*

The Romans have set up camp, and legionaries are finishing the fortifications. In accordance with the strict system maintained in all their operations it was the invariable practice of a Roman army, when it halted, to construct a fortified camp. The emperor is the foremost figure of the group in the central foreground. Before him kneels a messenger sent by the Dacian king to beg that Roman envoys be dispatched to treat with him. Officers and legionaries bearing the eagle, standards, and other emblems of a Roman legion are lined up behind the Dacian. (Cichorius, *Die Reliefs der Traianssäule*, plate XLII)

upper Euphrates River. While Rome held the western half
of the Fertile Crescent, it had never conquered the eastern
half, the region of the ancient Babylonian and Assyrian
empires, which was now held by the powerful kingdom of the
Parthians. Trajan attempted, like Alexander the Great, to
add this territory to his empire; but he failed, and died a
bitterly disappointed man (A.D. 117).

Hadrian (A.D. 117–138) *completes the Frontier Defenses.*
Trajan's successor, Hadrian, was a good soldier, but he had
also the judgment of a statesman. He made no effort to
continue Trajan's conquests in the East. On the contrary,
he wisely brought the frontier back to the Euphrates. But he
kept Dacia and strengthened the whole northern frontier,
especially the long barrier reaching from the Rhine to the
Danube, where the completion of a continuous wall was
largely due to him. He built a similar wall along the northern
boundary across Britain (map, p. 332). The line of both
these walls can still be seen. As a result of these wise
measures and the victories of Trajan, the frontiers of the
Empire were safe and quiet for a long time.

The Army under Trajan and Hadrian. Under Trajan
and Hadrian the army which defended these frontiers was
the greatest and most skillfully managed organization of the
kind which the ancient world had ever seen. Drawn from all
parts of the Empire, the army now consisted of many different
nationalities, like the British army in the World War. A
legion of Spaniards might be stationed on the Euphrates, or
a group of youths from the Nile might spend many years in
sentry duty on the wall that barred out the Germans. We
are able to hold in our hands the actual letters written from
a northern army post by a young Egyptian recruit in the
Roman army to his father and sister in a distant little village
on the Nile.[1] Such posts were equipped with fine barracks
and living-quarters for officers and men, and the discipline
necessary to keep the troops always ready to meet the barbarians outside the walls was never relaxed.

[1] See Breasted's *Ancient Times*, Fig. 248 and p. 709, footnote.

Improvements in Government. Meantime the Empire had been undergoing important changes within. Hadrian perfected the organization of government into departments, each headed by an efficient minister. With the control of these departments entirely in his own hands, the power of the emperor was much increased.

Among many changes, one of the most important was the abolition of the system of "farming" taxes; that is, allowing them to be collected by private individuals for profit, — a system which had caused both the Greeks and the Romans much trouble. Government tax collectors, called *procuratores*, now gathered in the taxes of the great Mediterranean world. This method, which had been favored by Cæsar and Augustus, was fully developed by Hadrian.

Rise of a System of Law for the Whole Empire. Not only did the subjects of this vast state pay their taxes into the same treasury but they were also controlled by the same laws. The lawyers of Rome were now the most able that the world had ever seen. They altered the narrow *city* law of Rome that it might meet the needs of the whole Mediterranean world. In spirit these laws of the Empire were most fair, just, and humane. Antoninus Pius (A.D. 138–161), the kindly emperor who followed Hadrian, maintained that an accused person must be held innocent until proved guilty, — a principle of law which has descended to us and is still part of our own law. These laws did much to unify the peoples of the Mediterranean world into a single nation; for these peoples were now regarded legally not as belonging to different nations but as subjects of the same great state, which extended to them all the same protection of justice, law, and order.

Close Attention to the Provinces by the Emperors. Able and conscientious governors were now controlling affairs all over the Empire. Emperors like Trajan and Hadrian took over a greater share of the government of the provinces than formerly, and so relieved the communities of much responsibility for their own affairs. Hadrian traveled for years among the provinces and became very familiar with their needs. However, as the provinces depended more and more on the emperor and were governed from Rome, their interest in public affairs and their ability to manage them declined.

2. THE CIVILIZATION OF THE EARLY ROMAN EMPIRE : THE PROVINCES

The Peoples of the Roman Empire. The vast Roman Empire, which circled the entire Mediterranean, is supposed to have had a population of somewhere between sixty-five and one hundred million inhabitants, made up of the most varied peoples. We might have stood at the Strait of Gibraltar, and, if we had been able to see so far, we might have surveyed these peoples as our eyes swept along the Mediterranean coast of Africa and around through Asia and Europe to the strait again. On our right, in Africa, would have been Moors, North Africans, and Egyptians; in the eastern background, Arabs, Jews, Phœnicians, Syrians, Armenians, and Hittites; and, as our eyes followed the European coast, Greeks, Italians, Gauls, and Iberians (Spaniards); while north of these were the Britons and some Germans within the frontier lines. All these people were, of course, very different from one another in native manners, clothing, and customs, but they all enjoyed Roman protection and rejoiced in the far-reaching Roman peace. For the most part, as we have seen, they lived in cities, and the life of the age was in general that of the city, even though many of the cities were small.

Pompeii. Fortunately one of the provincial cities has been preserved to us with much that we might have seen there if we could have visited it nearly two thousand years ago. The little city of Pompeii, which was covered with volcanic ashes in the reign of Titus (A.D. 79), still shows us the very streets and houses, the forum and the public buildings, the shops and the markets, as they were in the days when they were suddenly overwhelmed by the eruption of the volcano

Fig. 74. *A Street in Ancient Pompeii as it Appears Today*

The pavement and sidewalk are in perfect condition, as when they were first covered by the falling ashes. At the left is a public fountain. Of the buildings on this street only half a story still stands, except at the left, where we see the entrances of two shops, with the tops of the doors in position and with the walls preserved to the level of the second floor above

of Vesuvius. Pompeii was not far from the Greek cities of southern Italy, and we at once discover that the place was essentially Hellenistic in its life and art.

Roman Roads Great progress had been made throughout the Empire in the means of communication between one part and another. Everywhere the magnificent Roman roads, massively paved with smooth stone, like a town street, led straight over the hills, crossing the rivers by great bridges. Some of these bridges still stand and are in use today (Fig. 77). The speed of travel and communication was fully as high as that maintained in Europe and America before the introduction of the steam railway; and the roads were better.

By sea, however, the chief difference was the freedom from the old-time pirates, and therefore the resulting regularity of

FIG. 75. A Victim of the Eruption of Vesuvius, A.D. 79

This man was one of those who were unable to make their escape from the doomed
city of Pompeii. The fine volcanic ashes settled around the man's body, and these
rain-soaked ashes made a cast of his figure before it had perished. After the body
had decayed, it left in the hardened mass of ashes a hollow mold, which the modern excavators poured full of plaster and thus secured a cast of the figure of the
unfortunate man just as he lay smothered by the deadly ashes which overwhelmed him over eighteen hundred years ago

over-sea travel. For example, a Roman merchant could send
a letter to his agent in Alexandria in ten days. The huge
government corn ships that sailed between the Roman harbors and Alexandria were stately vessels carrying several
thousand tons. Good harbors had everywhere been provided
with docks, and lighthouses modeled on the Pharos at Alexandria guided the mariners into every harbor.

Wide Extent of Commerce. Under these circumstances
business flourished as never before. The good roads led merchants to trade beyond the frontiers and to find new markets.
Great fleets sailed regularly across the Indian Ocean between
the Red Sea and the harbors of India. The wares that they
brought were shipped west from the docks of Alexandria,
which still remained the greatest commercial city on the
Mediterranean. There was a saying that you could get
everything at Alexandria except snow. A vast network of

trade thus covered the ancient world from the frontiers of China and the coast of India on the east to Britain and the harbors of the Atlantic on the west.

Travel and Life in the Provinces. Both business and pleasure now made travel very common. The Roman citizen of means and education made his tour of the Mediterranean much as the modern sight-seer does. As he passed through the towns of the provinces, he found public buildings and monuments everywhere. There were fountains, theaters, music halls, baths, gymnasiums, and schools, erected by men of wealth and given to the community. The boys and the girls of these towns had schools, with teachers paid by the government, where all the ordinary branches of study which we have found in the Hellenistic Age were taught. The boy who turned to business could engage a stenographer to teach him shorthand, and

Fig. 76. *Scribblings of Sicilian Schoolboys on a Brick in the Days of the Roman Empire*

In passing a brickyard these schoolboys of 1700 years ago amused themselves by scribbling school exercises in *Greek* on soft clay bricks before these were baked. At the top a little boy who was still making capitals carefully wrote the letter *S* (the Greek Σ) ten times, and under it the similar letter *K*, also ten times. Then he wrote "turtle" (ΧΕΛΩΝΑ), "mill" (ΜΥΛΑ), and "pail" (ΚΑΔΟΣ), all in capitals. An older boy then pushed the little chap aside and proudly showed his superiority by writing in two lines an exercise in tongue gymnastics (like "Peter Piper picked a peck of pickled peppers," etc.) which in our letters is as follows:

Nai neai nea naia neoi temon, hōs neoi ha naus

This means: "Boys cut new planks for a new ship, that the ship might float." A third boy then added two lines at the bottom. The brick illustrates the spread of Greek as well as provincial education under the Roman Empire

the young man who wished higher instruction could still find university teachers at Alexandria and Athens and also at a number of younger universities in both the East and the West.

The Roman Traveler in Greece and the Orient. To an intelligent Roman traveler wandering in Greece, the Greece
of the time of Pericles — some six hundred years earlier —
seemed to belong to a distant and ancient world, of which he
had read in the histories of Thucydides and Herodotus. As
the Roman visitor strolled through Athens or Delphi he noticed many an empty pedestal, and he recalled how the villas
of his friends at home were now adorned with the statues
which had once occupied those empty pedestals. The Greek
cities which had brought forth such works of art were now
poor and unimportant.

When the traveler visited the flourishing cities of Asia
Minor and Syria, he might feel proud of what Roman rule
was accomplishing. In the western half of the Fertile Crescent, especially just east of the Jordan, where there had
formerly been only a wilderness, there were now prosperous
towns, with long aqueducts for their water supply, and with
baths, theaters, basilicas, and fine public buildings, of which
the ruins even at the present day are astonishing. All these
towns were linked together by fine roads and were also connected with Rome by other fine roads leading entirely
across Asia Minor and the Balkan peninsula. Beyond the
desert behind these towns lay the former empires of Babylonia, Assyria, and Persia, with their great cities reduced to
mounds of rubbish. The traveler could now take a great
Roman galley at Antioch and cross over to Alexandria, where
a still more ancient world awaited him. Here our traveler
found himself among a group of wealthy Greek and Roman
tourists on the Nile. As they left the magnificent buildings
of Hellenistic Alexandria, their voyage up the river carried
them at once into the midst of an earlier world, — the earliest
world of which they knew. At Memphis and Thebes were
buildings which were thousands of years old before Rome
was founded. On these monuments we still find the tourists'
scribblings at the present day.

Widely Distributed Remains of Roman Buildings. The
Eastern Mediterranean was regarded by the Romans as *their*
ancient world. There the Roman traveler found Greek used

FIG. 77. *Roman Bridge and Aqueduct near Nîmes, France*

This structure was built by the Romans about A.D. 20 to supply the Roman colony of Nemausus (now called Nîmes), in southern France, with water from two excellent springs twenty-five miles distant. It is nearly nine hundred feet long and one hundred and sixty feet high, and carried the water over the valley of the river Gard. The channel for the water is at the very top, and one can still walk through it. The miles of aqueduct on either side of this bridge and leading up to it have almost disappeared

everywhere as far west as Sicily (Fig. 76). But when he entered the Western Mediterranean he found that there the language used was Latin, — the language of Rome. In the Western Mediterranean, civilization was a recent matter, just as it is in America. In that age western Europe had for the first time been building cities; but it was under the guidance of Roman architects, and their buildings looked like those at Rome. We can still see the remains of massive bridges, spacious theaters, imposing public monuments, fine villas, and luxurious public baths — a line of Roman ruins stretching from Britain through southern France and Germany to the northern Balkans. Similarly in North Africa, west of Carthage, the ruins of whole cities with magnificent public buildings still survive and show us how Roman civilization developed there.

The Whole Mediterranean World highly Civilized. All these Roman buildings reveal to us the fact that as a result of all the ages of human progress which we have studied, the whole Mediterranean world had now gained a high civilization. The Roman legions and their military stations stretched, on the north of the Mediterranean, from Britain to Jerusalem, and, on its south, from Jerusalem to Morocco, like a great dike holding back the stormy sea of barbarians outside, which would otherwise have poured in and destroyed the results of centuries of civilization and progress.

3. THE CIVILIZATION OF THE ROMAN EMPIRE: ROME

New Public Buildings of Rome. As for Rome itself, a visitor at the close of the reign of Hadrian found it the most magnificent city in the world of that day. It had by that time quite surpassed Alexandria in size and in the number and splendor of its public buildings. It was especially in and alongside the old Forum that the grandest structures of the Empire had grown up. There Vespasian erected a vast amphitheater for gladiatorial combats, now known as the Colosseum. Along the north side of the old Forum the emperors built three beautiful new forums.

The buildings erected during the reigns of Trajan and Hadrian represent the highest level of splendor and beauty reached by Roman architects. In the Hellenistic Age builders had learned to use larger and larger quantities of cement concrete. The domed roof of Hadrian's Pantheon is an enormous concrete cast, over a hundred and forty feet across. The Romans, therefore, eighteen hundred years ago were employing concrete on a scale which we have only recently learned to imitate, and after all this lapse of time the roof of the Pantheon seems to be as solid and safe as it was when Hadrian's architects first knocked away the posts which supported the wooden form for the great cast.

Roman Sculpture and Painting. The sculpture adorning all these monuments reveals Roman art at its best. The relief sculpture of this period shows increased skill in method.

As the reliefs were made in order to illustrate the military triumphs or events in the careers of the emperors, the sculptors attempted to make their works appear lifelike. This was achieved by copying from painting certain devices of perspective which produced the effect of depth and atmosphere. Houses and cities are shown in the distance; leaves of plants seem to move gently; and human bodies so stand out that it is startling to realize that they are attached to the stone background. The reliefs still covering Trajan's column thus form a sort of picture book of his campaigns (Fig. 73). The *portrait* busts of leading Romans are, moreover, among the finest of such works that have ever been done, and give us a lively notion how the people of the time looked.

Not much painting has survived from the reigns of the emperors following Vespasian. But European museums have many fine mosaics of the period, which were evidently copied for the most part from paintings. A number of mosaics, and some few fragments of paintings, come from the ruins of the villa of Hadrian at Tivoli. Portrait-painting became increasingly popular, and the hack portrait artist at the street corner, who painted your picture quickly for you on a tablet of wood, finally came to be almost as common as our own portrait photographer.

Decline of Literature. There was now a larger educated public at Rome than ever before, and the splendid libraries maintained by the state were open to all. Authors and literary men were also liberally supported by the emperors. Even under these favorable circumstances, however, the literature was inferior to that of the Age of Augustus, for writers were less original. They used old themes over and over again, but freshened them up, as they thought, with conceits, epigrams, and other forms of literary artifice. Educational methods, social customs, and political conditions tended to stifle thought and to encourage the development of this artificial and unnatural style.

The emperors during the greater part of the first century, moreover, strictly censored all writings concerning events in the past, lest something should be said which would affect the attitude of the people toward the imperial government. This put an end for a time to the writing of history. It was therefore not until after the death of Domitian (A.D. 96), and the rise of the new freedom of speech under Nerva and Trajan, that Tacitus, one of the great masters of Latin prose, was able to produce a frank history of the early Empire. Among his other writings was a brief account of Germany, which furnishes us our first full glimpse into the life of the peoples of northern Europe. The letters which at this time passed between the younger Pliny and the emperor Trajan are among the most interesting literature of the ancient world. With these writers in Latin we should also mention the Greek Plutarch, who at this time wrote his remarkable series of lives of the greatest men of Greece and Rome, placing them in pairs, a Greek and a Roman together, and comparing them. The "Lives" contain much that belongs in the world of romance, but they form an imperishable gallery of heroes which has held the interest and the admiration of the world for eighteen centuries.

Lack of Scientific Progress. In science the Romans continued to be collectors of the knowledge gained by the Greeks. During a long and successful official career the elder Pliny devoted himself with amazing industry to scientific studies. He made a vast collection of the facts, then known to science, to be found in books, chiefly Greek. He put them all together in a huge work which he called *Natural History,* — really an encyclopedia. He was so deeply interested in science that he lost his life in the great eruption of Vesuvius as he was trying both to study the tremendous event at short range and (as admiral of the fleet) to save the fleeing people of Pompeii. But Pliny's *Natural History* did not contain any new facts of importance discovered by the author himself, and it was marred by many errors in matters which Pliny misunderstood. Nevertheless, for hundreds of years, until the revival of science in modern times, Pliny's work was, next to Aristotle, the standard authority referred to by all educated Europeans. Thus men fell into an indolent attitude of mind and were satisfied merely to learn what earlier discoverers had found out. This attitude never would have led to the discovery of the size of the earth as determined by Eratosthenes, or in modern times to X-ray photographs or wireless telegraphy.

The Ptolemaic System. A great astronomer and geographer of Alexandria, named Ptolemy, who flourished under Hadrian and the Antonines, was the last of the famous scientists of the ancient world. He wrote, among other works, a handbook on astronomy, for the most part a compilation from the works of earlier astronomers. In it he unfortunately adopted the conclusion that the sun revolved around the earth as a center. His book became a standard work, and hence this mistaken view of the solar system, called the Ptolemaic system, was everywhere accepted by the later world. It was not until four hundred years ago that the real truth, already long before discovered by the Greek astronomer Aristarchus (p. 248), was rediscovered by the Polish astronomer Copernicus. Knowledge of the spherical form of the earth as shown by Ptolemy and earlier Greek astronomers reached the travelers and navigators of later Europe, and finally led Columbus to undertake the voyage to India and the East westward, — the voyage which resulted in the discovery of America.

Cosmopolitan Life of Rome. Educated men from the provinces were now holding important positions at Rome, either in the government or as teachers and professors paid by the government. The city was no longer Roman or Italian. Men from all parts of the Empire elbowed each other and talked business in the banks and countinghouses of the magnificent new forums; they filled the public offices and administrative departments of the government, and discussed the hand-copied daily paper published by the state; they sat in the libraries and lecture halls of the Roman university; and they crowded the lounging-places of the public baths and the vast amphitheater. We call such all-inclusive, widely representative life "cosmopolitan," — a word of Greek origin meaning "worldcitylike."

This inflow of all the world at Rome was shown in the luxuries now enjoyed by the rich. Roman ladies were adorned with diamonds, pearls, and rubies from India, and dressed in shining silks from China. On the tables of the rich were new rare fruits, — peaches, which they called "Persian apples," and apricots. Roman cooks learned to prepare rice, formerly a delicacy prescribed for the sick. Instead of sweetening their dishes with honey, as formerly, Roman households began to use a new product known as "sakari"; for so the report of a sailor of the first century of our era calls the sirup of sugar cane, which for the first time he brought by sea from India into the Mediterranean. This is the earliest mention of sugar in history. These new things from the Orient were beginning to appear in Roman life just as the potatoes, tobacco, and Indian corn of America found their way into Europe after the voyages of Columbus had disclosed a new Western world in the fifteenth century.

4. POPULARITY OF ORIENTAL RELIGIONS AND THE EARLY SPREAD OF CHRISTIANITY

Decline of the Old Roman Religion. Many thoughtful Romans read the Greek philosophy of the Stoics and Epicureans in the charming treatises of Cicero or the discussions of Seneca (p. 328). They had given up their belief in the old Roman gods and accepted as their religion the teachings of the Stoic or Epicurean philosophy. But such teaching was only for the highly educated and the intellectual class.

Oriental Religions in Europe. Multitudes, including even the educated, were attracted to the mysterious religions coming in from the East. Many took up the faith of the Egyptian Isis, and temples of Isis were to be found in all the larger cities. Today tiny statuettes and other symbols of the Egyptian goddess are found even along the Seine, the Rhine, and the Danube.

In the army the Persian Mithras, a god of light (p. 100), was a great favorite, and many a Roman legion had its underground chapel where its members celebrated his triumph over darkness and evil. These and other Oriental faiths all had their "mysteries," which were a kind of drama representing the life of the god, especially his submission to death, his triumph over it, and his ascent to everlasting blessedness. It was believed that to see these things and to undergo certain holy ceremonies of initiation would enable one to share in the pure and endless life of the god and to dwell with him forever.

The old Roman religion, like the early Greek beliefs, had little to do with conduct and held out to the worshiper no hopes of happiness in the next world, as did the Oriental religions. Little wonder, then, that the multitudes were attracted by the comforting promises of these Eastern faiths and by the blessed future to be gained in their "mysteries."

The Jews also, since their temple in Jerusalem had been destroyed by the Romans (A.D. 70), were to be found in increasing numbers in all the larger cities. Strabo, the geographer, said of them, "This people has already made its way into every city, and it would be hard to find a place in the habitable world which has not admitted this race and been dominated by it." The Roman world was becoming accustomed to their synagogues; but the Jews refused to acknowledge any god besides their own, and this brought them into disfavor and trouble with the government.

Rise of Christianity. Among all these faiths of the Orient the common people were more and more inclining toward that of the Christian missionaries, who told how their Master, Jesus, a Jew born in Palestine in the days of Augustus, had preached his faith, of human brotherhood and of divine fatherhood, till in the reign of Tiberius he was accused of trying to make himself king of the Jews and was put to death. A Jewish tentmaker of Tarsus named Paul became the leading Christian missionary. He preached the new gospel in the cities of Asia Minor and Greece and finally in Rome itself, and Christian churches began to spring up. Some of Paul's letters to the churches he had founded were widely circulated. There were, finally, four accounts in Greek of the life and teachings of Jesus that came to be accepted as true. These were the accounts of Matthew, Mark, Luke, and John, which we call the Four Gospels. These, with Paul's letters and some other early Christian writings, were brought together to form the New Testament

The Appeal of Christianity. The other Oriental faiths, in spite of their attractiveness, did not seem to offer to their followers the consolation and fellowship of a life so exalted and beautiful, so full of brotherly appeal and human sympathy, as that of the new Hebrew teacher. The slave and the freedman, the simple workman, the humble, the despised, and the poor eagerly listened to this new "mystery" from the East, as they thought it to be. As time passed, multitudes learned of the new gospel and found joy in the hopes which it awakened. In the second century of peace, Christianity was rapidly outstripping the other religions of the Roman Empire.

Roman Persecution of the Early Christians. The government officials often found these early converts, like the Jews, not only refusing to sacrifice to the emperor as a god, as all good Roman citizens were expected to do, but also openly prophesying the downfall of the Roman state Their religion seemed to interfere with good citizenship, since it forbade them to show the usual respect for the emperor and the government. While the Roman government was usually very tolerant in matters of religion, the early Christians were looked upon as enemies of the state and were frequently cruelly persecuted. Nevertheless, their numbers steadily grew.

5. MARCUS AURELIUS AND THE END OF THE SECOND CENTURY OF PEACE

End of the Second Century of Peace (about A.D. 167). In spite of outward prosperity, Mediterranean civilization was declining in the second century of peace. The efforts of Trajan and Hadrian could not permanently protect the Empire against the barbarians. The noble emperor Marcus Aurelius (A.D. 161–180), when he took charge of the government, was called upon to face a very serious situation. He had to fight the troublesome Parthians, who had long threatened the eastern boundary of the Empire. Then bar-

barian hordes of Germans in the north broke through the
frontier defenses, and for the first time in two centuries
poured down into Italy (A.D. 167). The two centuries of
peace were ended. During the rest of his reign Marcus Aurelius struggled against the barbarian invaders, but he was unable to expel them entirely from the northern part of the
Empire. He finally took the very dangerous step of allowing
some of them to settle within the frontier on condition that
they would help defend it from their fellow Germans. Marcus Aurelius was a Stoic and an able and high-minded ruler.
During his campaigns he found time to write in Greek a
little book called *Meditations*, which we may still read with
pleasure and profit. It is really a diary in which he set down,
day by day, his good resolutions. He regarded his high
office as a sacred trust to which he must be true. But no
ruler, however pure and unselfish his purposes, could stop
the processes of decline going on in the midst of the great
Roman world. Following the two centuries of peace, therefore, was to come a fearful century of revolution, civil war,
and anarchy, from which a very different Roman world was
to emerge.

Questions and Exercises

REVIEW OF CHAPTER

1. Describe conditions on the frontiers of the Roman Empire
during the first and second centuries A.D. How did the Flavian em-
perors deal with the problem of the frontiers? By what steps did
Trajan and Hadrian make the northern frontiers comparatively safe?
What can you say of the Roman army under Trajan and Hadrian?
How was the management of the government improved?

2. Give an imaginary bird's-eye view of the Roman Empire from
Gibraltar to the Euphrates. Where did the Roman's ancient world lie?

3. What was the Colosseum? What advances were made in the
art of sculpture during this period? How did the imperial policy of
allowing freedom of speech after Domitian affect the writing of
history? What great Greek biographer wrote in the first century A.D.?

4. Describe the rise of Christianity and the work of Paul. What
practical difficulty did the Christians meet in their relations with
the Roman government?

5. Give an estimate of the mind and character of Marcus Aurelius.

Useful Terms

See how much meaning you can give to the following: *public welfare, state ownership of utilities, social legislation, cement, concrete, freedom of speech, Ptolemaic system, Roman religion, Stoic philosophy.*

Directive Questions

1. Discuss the Roman experiment in paternalism during the second century B.C. and compare it with certain attempts of modern nations to solve their social problems in a like manner.

2. List some of the consequences resulting from the increase in transportation facilities under the Roman Empire.

3. Do we employ sculptured reliefs to commemorate historical events?

4. What did Christianity have to offer to the Roman citizen?

5. What did Stoicism have to offer to the Roman citizen?

Discussion Topics

1. The paternalistic attitude of Hadrian was necessary for the safety and peace of the Roman Empire.

2. The Romans Hellenized the world.

3. Collections of letters, such as those of the younger Pliny, must be used carefully if studied as historical material.

4. The growth of the Christian sect was one of the causes of the fall of the Roman Empire.

5. The Romans should have withdrawn from Asia and should not have attempted to hold the Asiatic frontier in A.D. 167.

Additional Adventures in Learning

1. Studies in Source Materials. BOTSFORD, *Source-book* : (1) Destruction of Pompeii, pp. 488–490; (2) Trajan's correspondence with Pliny, pp. 502–505, 523–525; (3) Hadrian, pp. 505–510.

2. Supplementary. SHOWERMAN, *Rome and the Romans* : (1) Travel in the Roman Empire, pp. 485–502; (2) The coming of Christianity, pp. 572–582.

3. Look up in an encyclopedia : *Vespasian, Parthia, Dacia, Hadrian's wall, Antoninus Pius, Pompeii, Colosseum, Publius Cornelius Tacitus.*

CHAPTER XVIII · A CENTURY OF REVOLUTION AND THE DIVISION OF THE EMPIRE

WITH THE invasion of the northern barbarians in the reign of Marcus Aurelius (about A.D. 167) the two centuries of peace ended. We shall see in the next century the power seized by one military leader after another, until, in A.D. 285, Diocletian, a prefect of the guard born probably in Dalmatia, subdued other claimants and set up an Oriental despotism as his ideal of government. He divided the Empire into East and West, and, by taking up his residence in the East, turned the attention of the Mediterranean world away from Rome and toward the East. Diocletian's choice of a residence was dictated, moreover, by the rise in the Fertile Crescent of a vigorous new state, a New Persia. This state threatened to become a rival for the empire of the world. From this time on, the center of Roman government activity is found in the East. In the West, on the other hand, after Christianity was legalized (A.D. 311), it was the Church which offered new opportunities for the abilities of men of action. But the development of the Christian Church belongs to the next period in the world's history; and so with Chapter XVIII we come to the end of the history of civilization in the ancient world.

1. The Decline of the Roman Empire

The Empire in the Second Century of Peace. We have seen good government, fine buildings, education, and other signs of civilization more widespread in the second century of peace than ever before. Nevertheless, the great empire was really degenerating in many ways. In the first place, the decline of farming, so noticeable before the fall of the Republic, had gone steadily on. This was partly due to the exhaustion of the soil and to bad cultivation; that is, the soil was in such poor condition that it no longer yielded good crops.

Decline of Farming; Cities Overcrowded with Poor. Most of the land which should have been farmed, to feed the people of Italy, continued to pass into the hands of the rich. A rich man's estate was called a *villa,* and villa estates, having ruined the small farmers of Italy, were now causing the same trouble in the provinces. Villas covered not only Italy but also Africa, Gaul, Britain, Spain, and other provinces.

Most of the small farmers gave up the struggle to keep their little bit of land, for the taxes had become unbearable. A discouraged farmer would often become the *colonus* of some wealthy villa-owner. By this arrangement the farmer and his descendants were assured the right to farm the land, and in this way they got a small portion of the produce and made at least a poor living. On the other hand, they were forever bound by law to the land which they worked, and they passed with it from owner to owner when it changed hands. The owner profited by this arrangement, since he received the largest part of what the farm yielded. While not actually slaves, the *coloni* (plural of *colonus*) were not free to go where they pleased. The great villas which had once been worked by slaves were now cultivated chiefly by these *coloni,* the forerunners of the medieval serfs (p. 433), while slaves had steadily diminished in numbers.

Multitudes of the country people, unwilling to become *coloni,* forsook their fields and flocked to the city for relief. Great stretches of unworked and weed-grown fields were a common sight. As the amount of land under cultivation decreased, the ancient world was no longer raising enough food to feed itself properly. The scarcity was felt most severely in the cities like Rome, where prices had rapidly gone up. Our own generation is not the first to complain of the "high cost of living." Rome was filled with the unemployed, who were supported by the state with money which had been raised by taxing more heavily the few remaining farmers. The same situation was, in the main, to be found in all the leading cities.

Decline of Population. The Latin population declined because of a decrease in birth rates, and thus the citizenship contained a larger and larger percentage of non-Latin peoples, especially Orientals. Men who had served in the army were given citizenship. Moreover, slaves were constantly gaining their freedom, and they frequently retained slave ideas of conduct even after they were freedmen. This change in the nationality of the citizens, and the subsequent change in ideals, conduct, and government, were perhaps the chief causes of the downfall of Rome.

Decline of Business   At the same time the business in the cities fell off. The country communities, which were poor, could no longer afford to buy; so the manufacturers were unable to dispose of their goods and had to discharge their workmen. This, in turn, increased the number of poor and unemployed in the city.

For a number of reasons the government was unable to secure enough precious metals to coin the money necessary to carry on business. The state was obliged to begin mixing with silver some less valuable metals and coining this cheaper alloy. A *denarius*, the small coin worth (when made of pure silver) about twenty cents (Fig. 66), a century after the death of Marcus Aurelius was worth only half a cent.

Decline of the Army.   As it became impossible to collect taxes *in money*, the government was obliged to accept grain and produce as payment of taxes. Here and there the army was paid in grain. On the frontiers, for lack of other pay, the troops were given land, which of course did them no good unless they could cultivate it. So they were allowed to marry and to live with their families in little huts on their lands near the frontier. As was to be expected, they soon lost all army discipline and became merely a feeble militia.

Lack of a Law of Succession.   One very serious defect in the organization of the Roman state was that there had never been a legal method established for choosing a new emperor and thus maintaining from reign to reign the supreme authority in the state. The various divisions of the army found that they had the power to set up an emperor and also to depose him if he displeased them. They had very little respect for an emperor chosen in this way; and if he attempted to enforce discipline or did not heed their wishes, they put him out of the way and selected another. Crude and barbarous soldiers became the chief controlling power in the state. There were often several of these "barrack" candidates for the imperial throne fighting among themselves.

2. A CENTURY OF DISORDER

Beginning of a Century of Revolution (A.D. 180). These forces of decline were swiftly bringing on a century of revolution which was to shipwreck the civilization of the Roman Empire. This fatal period began with the death of Marcus Aurelius (A.D. 180). The assassination of his unworthy son Commodus was the opportunity for a struggle among a group of military usurpers. From this struggle a rough but successful soldier named Septimius Severus came out triumphant. He filled the highest offices in the government with military leaders of low class. Thus, both in the army and in the government, the ignorant and often foreign masses were gaining control.

When the line of Severus ended (A.D. 235), the storm broke. The barbaric troops in one province after another set up their own emperors to fight among themselves for the throne of the Mediterranean world. The proclamation of a new emperor would be followed again and again by news of his assassination. From the leaders of the barbaric soldier class, after the death of Commodus, the Roman Empire had eighty claimants to imperial power in ninety years. Most of these so-called emperors were not unlike the revolutionary bandits who have sometimes proclaimed themselves presidents of the small republics of South and Central America.

Fifty Years of Anarchy; Collapse of Higher Civilization. For fifty years there was no public order, as the plundering troops tossed the scepter of Rome from one soldier-emperor to another. Life and property were nowhere safe ; robbery and murder were everywhere. The disorder and fighting between rival emperors hastened the ruin of all business, till national bankruptcy resulted. In this tempest of anarchy during the third century of our era the civilization of the ancient world fell into final ruin. The intelligence and scien-

Fig. 78. *Relief Scene Showing the Roman Emperor Valerian Kneeling before Shapur, the Victorious King of New Persia*

Shapur defeated and captured Valerian in A.D. 258. This sculpture is the eastern-most representation of a Roman emperor. As sovereign of a new and revived Persia, Shapur showed a fine realization that his triumph was the renewal of ancient Persian glory; for he sent his sculptors to Persepolis, and there they carved this monument of Oriental triumph at the foot of the cliff, under the splendid tomb where Darius the Great had been buried almost seven hundred and fifty years earlier (see *Ancient Times*, Fig. 136). Shapur's victory and his monument were the Oriental reply to Alexander the Great, a Western conqueror, who had burned Persepolis nearly six centuries before

tific knowledge which had been achieved were overwhelmed by the ignorance and superstition that prevailed in the anarchy of the *third century of the Christian Era.*

Such turmoil ruined the Roman army. The northern barbarians were quick to realize the helplessness of the Empire. They crossed the frontiers almost without opposition and penetrated far into Greece and Italy; in the West they over-ran Gaul and Spain, and some of them even crossed to Africa.

Rise of New Persia (A.D. 226) *under Sassanian Kings.* At the same time a new danger had arisen in the East. An outburst of patriotism among the people of Persia, coupled with a religious revival, had resulted in great enthusiasm for their country. The leaders of this movement, a family called

Sassanians (or Sassanids), overthrew the Parthians (A.D. 226) and furnished a new line of enlightened Persian kings. As they took possession of the Fertile Crescent and established their capital at Ctesiphon, on the Tigris, close to Babylon, a new Orient arose on the ruins of seemingly dead and forgotten ages. The Sassanian kings organized a much more powerful state than that of the Parthians which they overthrew, and regarded themselves as the rivals of the Romans for the control of the world. The old rivalry between the Orient and the West, as in the days of the conflict between Greece and Persia, was now continued, with Rome as the champion of the West and with this New Persia as the leader of the East.

Aurelian (A.D. 270–275) *and Diocletian* (A.D. 284–305) *restore Order.* It now looked as if the Roman Empire were about to fall to pieces, when one of the soldier-emperors, named Aurelian, defeated all his rivals and restored some measure of order and safety. But in order to protect Rome from the future raids of the barbarians, he built entirely around the great city the massive wall which still stands, — a witness to the decline of Rome in the third century A.D. It was a little over a century after the death of Marcus Aurelius when the emperor Diocletian restored what for the moment seemed a lasting peace (A.D. 284).

3. THE ROMAN EMPIRE AN ORIENTAL DESPOTISM

Diocletian (A.D. 284–305) ; *the Roman Empire an Oriental Despotism.* The Roman world under Diocletian was a totally different one from that which Augustus and the Roman Senate had ruled three centuries before. Diocletian deprived the feeble Senate of all power except that of governing the city of Rome. Reduced to a mere city council, or board of aldermen, it then disappeared from the stage of history. The emperor thus became an absolute monarch, with none to limit his authority. With the absolute power of an Oriental despot the emperor now assumed also its outward symbols, — the diadem, the gorgeous robe embroidered with pearls and precious stones, the throne and footstool, before which all who came into his presence must bow.

Long regarded as a divinity, the emperor had now become an Oriental sun-god, and he was officially called the Invincible Sun. His "birthday" was on the twenty-fifth of December, — when the sun begins to rise higher again in the winter sky. All were obliged as good citizens to join in the official sacrifices to the head of the state as a god. With the incoming of this Oriental attitude toward the emperor, the long struggle for democracy, which we have followed through so many centuries of the history of early man, ended for a time in the triumph of Oriental despotism.

Division of the Empire by Diocletian. War with New Persia took the emperor much to the East. The result was that Diocletian lived most of the time at Nicomedia, in Asia Minor, and so was unable to give close attention to the West. Diocletian therefore appointed another emperor to rule jointly with himself, whose business it was to watch over the western part of the Empire. It was not Diocletian's purpose to *divide* the Roman Empire, any more than the Republic had been divided when, long before, two consuls were elected. But the division of authority nevertheless led in time to its separation into East and West.

The provinces of the Empire were by this time over a hundred in number. Diocletian and his successors organized the business of each province in the hands of a great number of local officials graded into many ranks and classes from high to low. The expense of this vast organization, together with the luxurious Oriental court of the emperor, was enormous; for this multitude of government and court officials and the clamorous army had all to be supported by ever-increasing taxation.

Interference of the State in Business. The scarcity of money (p. 355) had forced the government to accept grain and produce from the taxpayers. The Roman Empire thus relapsed into a primitive system of taxation already thousands of years old in the Orient. It became customary to oblige a group of wealthy men in each city, mainly the members of the city councils and their families, to become responsible for the payment of the entire taxes of the district each year. If sufficient money was not raised, these men were obliged to make up the balance out of their own income. The penalty of wealth seemed to be ruin, and there was no incentive to hard work when success in business meant ruinous over-taxation. As the Roman Empire had already lost its prosperous *farming class*, it now lost also its energetic and successful *business men*. Diocletian, therefore, chiefly to insure the payment of taxes, tried to *force* these classes to continue their occupations. He forbade any man to leave his lands or change his occupation, and even tried to make business hereditary by demanding that sons follow the same occupation as their father.

Disappearance of Liberty and Free Citizenship. Thus, under this Oriental despotism, liberty disappeared, and the once free Roman citizen lost his independence. Even the citizen's wages and the prices of the goods he bought or sold were, as far as possible, fixed for him by the state. The emperor's countless officials, who were little better than spies, kept an eye upon even the humblest citizen. They watched the grain dealers, butchers, and bakers, and saw to it that they properly supplied the public and never deserted their occupation. In a word, the Roman government now attempted to regulate almost every interest in life, and wherever the citizen turned he felt the irksome interference and oppression of the state.

Staggering under his burden of taxes, in a state which was practically bankrupt, the citizen now seemed like a mere cog in the vast machinery of the government. His whole life consisted of toil for the state, for he had to pay so much in taxes that he was fortunate if he could live on what was left. As a mere toiler for the state he was finally just where the peasant on the Nile had been for thousands of years.

4. THE DIVISION OF THE EMPIRE AND THE TRIUMPH OF CHRISTIANITY

Constantine (A.D. 324–337) *and the Shift of Power from Italy to the Balkan Peninsula.* Under Diocletian, Italy had been reduced to the position of a taxed province and had thus lost all her former superiority over the other provinces of the Empire. During the century of revolution the soldiers of the Balkan peninsula had provided the army with the best troops and furnished more than one emperor, among them Diocletian himself. An emperor who had thus risen from the ranks of provincial troops in the Balkans felt little attachment to Rome. Not only had Rome ceased to be the capital and residence of the emperor, but the center of power had clearly shifted from Italy to the Balkan peninsula.

Out of the struggles for the throne following Diocletian's death the emperor Constantine the Great emerged victorious (A.D. 324). He did not hesitate to turn to the eastern edge of the Balkan peninsula and establish there a New Rome as his capital. He chose the ancient Greek town of Byzantium, on the European side of the Bosporus, a situation overlooking both Europe and Asia and well fitted to be a center of power in both. The emperor stripped many an ancient city of its great monuments in order to secure materials for beautifying his splendid residence. By A.D. 330 the new capital on the Bosporus was a magnificent city, worthy to be the successor of Rome as the seat of the Mediterranean empire. It was named Constantinople ("Constantine's city") after its founder.[1]

The Separation of East and West. The transfer of the capital of the Roman Empire to the east side of the Balkan peninsula meant the separation of East and West, — the cutting of the Roman Empire in two. Although the separation did not take place abruptly, yet within a generation after Constantinople was founded the Roman Empire had in fact, if not in name, become two states. The ideal of the Empire

[1] The Arabic form of this name is *Stambul,* from which the official Turkish form *Istanbul* is derived.

as a single great state remained, but it was never more than temporarily realized thereafter.

Growth of Christian Churches. Meantime the Christian churches had steadily increased in numbers. The management of the great Christian communities and their churches needed men of ability and experience. The Church thus gave a new opportunity for the development of statesmanship, and ecclesiastical statesmen were, as we shall see, soon to be the most influential men of the age.

These officers of the Church came to be distinguished from the other members and were called the *clergy*, while the people who made up the membership of the churches were called the *laymen*, or the *laity*. The old men who cared for the smaller country congregations were called *presbyters*, a Greek word meaning "old men," and our word "priest" is derived from this Greek term. Over the group of churches in each city a leading priest was given authority as *bishop*. In the larger cities these bishops had such influence that they became *archbishops*, or head bishops, having authority over the bishops in the surrounding cities of the province. Thus the Christian Church, once weak and despised, became a powerful organization, strong enough to cope with the government.

Christianity placed on a Legal Basis with Other Religions (A.D. 311). The Roman government therefore began to see the uselessness of persecuting the Christians as Diocletian had done. After his retirement his associate Galerius, realizing the dangers threatening Rome from *without* and the uselessness of the struggle against the Christians *within*, issued a decree (A.D. 311) by which Christianity was recognized in his territories by law. Its followers received the same rights under the law as the worshipers of the old gods. This decree was later maintained by Constantine for the whole Empire. Constantine and succeeding emperors went even further in their favor toward the Christians. They gradually abolished all other religions; they gave their whole support to the Christian Church; they granted its officials many important privileges, such as freedom from taxation and the right of having their own church law and courts.

Fig. 79. *Newly Uncovered Mosaics in the Church of St. Sophia Showing the Emperor of the Eastern (or Byzantine) Empire Kneeling in Adoration before Christ*

This scene is one of the Christian mosaics recently uncovered by the Byzantine Institute of America in the mosque-church of St. Sophia, at Istanbul (p. 361, note). The emperor is probably Leo VI (A.D. 886–912), identified by the likeness of the face to his image as found on coins, as well as by his costume, a description of which, made by his own son, is still extant. The book in the hand of the Christ is represented as open and facing us. The inscription reads: "Peace be with you. I am the Light of the World." The magnificent throne shows clearly its descent from New Persian originals. The beautiful coloring of the mosaics, as well as the artistic excellence of the composition, suggests the importance of this contribution to the history of art resulting from the baring of the Byzantine mosaics in St. Sophia. (Courtesy of Mr. Thomas Whittemore and the Byzantine Institute)

Ancient Civilization at a Standstill. The century of revolution which ended in the despotic government set up by Diocletian completely destroyed the creative ability of earlier times in art and literature, as it likewise stopped all progress in business and affairs. In so far as the ancient world was one of *progress in civilization,* its history was ended with Diocletian. Besides the increasing invasions of the barbarians, the other outstanding events of the age were the founding of an Eastern capital at Constantinople, the passing of the importance of Rome as the head of the state, and the triumph of Christianity. As the barbarians came in and the power of the Roman Empire waned, it had still a great task before it to preserve at least something of the heritage of civilization, which it was to hand down through centuries of strife and trouble to us today.

5. RETROSPECT

Summary of Ancient History. Besides the decline of the Roman Empire and the triumph of the Christian Church, the other great outstanding feature of the last centuries of the Roman Empire was the incoming of the barbarians, with the result that while civilization steadily declined in the Mediterranean world it slowly spread northward, especially under the influence of the Church, till it transformed the ruder life of the north. There, in the region of western and northern Europe, among the crumbling monuments of the Stone Age, Christian churches now began to rise. Books and civilized government, once found only along the Mediterranean Sea, reached the northern shores of Europe, where grass and great forest trees were growing over the graves of Stone Age Norsemen.

The Long Struggle of Civilization and Barbarism. We have watched early man all around the Mediterranean slowly progressing through thousands of years of Stone Age barbarism, while toward the end of that long period civilization was arising in Egypt. Then, on the borders of the Orient, we saw the Stone Age Europeans of the Ægean receiving civilization from the Nile and thus beginning to develop a wonderful civilized world of their own. This remarkable Ægean civilization, the earliest in Europe, was overwhelmed and destroyed by the incoming of those Indo-European barbarians whom we call the *Greeks*. Writing, art, architecture, and shipbuilding were destroyed for a time by the Greek nomads from the north. Civilization would have been lost entirely had not the Orient still preserved it. The Greeks were therefore able to make another start, and from the Orient again received writing, art, architecture, shipbuilding, and many other things which make up civilization. After having thus halted civilization in Europe for over a thousand years, the Greeks outgrew their early barbarism and, developing a culture of their own, carried civilization to the highest level it had attained. However, as the Indo-European barbarians (this time the *Germans*) again descended to the Mediterranean, Roman organization, as we shall see, prevented civilization from being destroyed for the second time. Thus enough of the civilization which the Orient and the Greeks had built up was preserved so that after a long period it rose again in Europe to become what we find it today.

The Trail which we have Followed. Today, marking the various stages in the long career of ancient man, the stone fist hatchets lie deep in the river gravels all around the Mediterranean world; the furniture of the pile-villages rests at the bottom of the Swiss lakes; the majestic pyramids and temples announcing the dawn of civilization rise along the Nile; the silent and deserted city mounds by the Tigris and Euphrates shelter their myriads of clay tablets; the palaces of Crete look out toward the sea they once ruled; the noble temples and sculptures of Greece still reveal the new world of beauty and freedom first discovered by the Greeks; the splendid Roman roads and aqueducts show the supremacy and organized control of Rome; and the Christian churches proclaim a new ideal of human brotherhood. These things still reveal the trail along which our ancestors came, and we can now appreciate how wonderful were the achievements of *ancient times.*

Questions and Exercises

REVIEW OF CHAPTER

1. Describe the system of *coloni.* What can you say of the extent of cultivated lands and of the food supply? List all the signs of inner decay in the later Roman Empire and tell what you think was the most important single cause of the fall of Rome.

2. Describe briefly conditions in the Empire in the years between the reigns of Marcus Aurelius and Diocletian. What do we mean by New Persia?

3. How did Diocletian treat the Roman Senate? Discuss the administrative organization of Diocletian.

4. To what part of the Empire did the center of power shift under Diocletian? How did Christianity gain legal recognition?

5. Sketch briefly the struggle of civilization and barbarism from its earliest beginnings.

USEFUL TERMS

See how much meaning you can give to the following: *villa estates, debasement of coinage, tax in kind, militia, standing army, law of succession, fixed prices.*

DIRECTIVE QUESTIONS

1. If the condition of the farmers is bad, they move to the city for relief. If the farmers cannot afford to buy goods, production is lower and the industrial system is affected. Explain these statements in regard to Rome at this time. Has this also been true in the United States since 1921?

2. Why did the Roman army cease to be efficient?

3. Russia, Germany, the United States, and other countries are experimenting in governmental control of trades and business. Compare the experiment in Rome with that in one of the countries today.

4. Why did the later Roman emperors give their whole support to the Christian Church?

DISCUSSION TOPICS

1. The racial change which took place in the population was the greatest single cause of the downfall of Rome.

2. In the third century A.D. only a despot could have restored peace throughout the Empire.

3. The paternalistic legislation of Diocletian hastened the disintegration of the Roman Empire.

4. Roman civilization influenced the organization of the Christian Church.

ADDITIONAL ADVENTURES IN LEARNING

1. Studies in Source Materials. BOTSFORD, *Source-book*: The rule of Diocletian, pp. 527–532, 537–539.

2. Supplementary. Roman law: FRANK, *History of Rome*, pp. 584–585; SHOWERMAN, *Rome and the Romans*, pp. 503–522.

3. Look up in an encyclopedia: *Lucius Septimius Severus, Sassanidæ (Sassanids), Diocletian, Constantine I, bishop, Lucius Domitius Aurelianus. Nicomedia.*

Part Five

HOW BARBAROUS PEOPLES
INVADED THE ROMAN EMPIRE
AND CREATED SUCH DISORDER
THAT FOR SEVERAL HUNDRED YEARS
OUR FOREFATHERS FORGOT MUCH
THAT THE GREEKS AND ROMANS
HAD KNOWN

During the Dark Ages following the Break-up of the Roman Empire, Men were so Poor or Busy Fighting that they had No Time to Interest themselves in Learning, Art, Science, or Inventions. Even Business almost Disappeared. There was scarcely Any Money, and Wealth consisted in Land, for which Kings and Nobles Fought. Our Forefathers in Europe fell into Two Sharply Defined Classes, the Fighters, led by the Nobles, and the Farmers, who lived much like Wretched Slaves. This Period created the Problem of Recovering the Old Knowledge, and also the Task of Reducing the Power of the Fighting Class and Improving the Condition of the Farmers

The Ceremony of Homage
See page 428

CHAPTER XIX · BARBAROUS TRIBES
BREAK UP THE ROMAN EMPIRE

HOW PEOPLES MOVED ABOUT · GERMAN CHIEFS SET UP KINGDOMS WITHIN THE
ROMAN EMPIRE · THE FRANKS SETTLE IN GAUL · EFFECTS OF THE INVASIONS ON
CIVILIZATION

I T IS customary to divide the story of civilization into three parts:
Ancient Times, the Middle Ages, and Modern Times. We have seen
that Ancient Times includes the history not only of the Greeks and Romans
but of all the peoples who for thousands of years before had been building
up civilization. The "Middle Ages" is the name usually given to about a
thousand years between the break-up of the Roman Empire and the discovery of America. The first half of this period, described in Part Five, may
be called "the Dark Ages" or "the Age of Disorder." The second half,
called "the Later Middle Ages" (treated in Part Six), was a period of
recovery of what had been lost during the first half and of fresh additions to
our civilization. Of course, there are no clear divisions between these so-
called "periods," because human habits usually change very gradually and
much that is old continues to go on even though new things may come.

In this chapter we shall see how peoples much less civilized than the
Romans wandered into the Empire, headed by chieftains who founded kingdoms of their own. This caused great disorder, and much that had formerly
been known was lost for a time. The European nations which were later to
develop our civilization and spread it throughout the earth gradually grew
up not from the Roman Empire directly but from the kingdoms which the
invaders established.

1. How Peoples Moved About

Invasions very Common. The study of the Middle Ages
usually opens with the story of the "barbarian invasions";
it tells how German tribes pushed into the Empire, fought one
another, plundered Roman towns and villages, and established governments of their own. The "barbarian invasions"
have often been featured as an unusual series of misfortunes
which resulted in the downfall of the Roman Empire and the
setback of European civilization for many centuries. Only
part of this is true.

As a matter of fact, there was nothing new in a "barbarian invasion." Indeed, there is no more common event in the whole history of mankind than the migrations, or shiftings, of peoples from one part of the earth to another. It is a habit not only of man but of many other living creatures — birds and animals — as well. It has gone on since primitive times and continues to go on today. Its primary cause — one which in early times was most important — was the search for food or sunshine. Whenever food was scarce or the climate too severe, men moved about looking for better farmlands, where they could grow crops and find pasturage for their cattle, or a climate in which they could live more easily.

Examples of Ancient Invasions. We have only to recall the story of Ancient Times in this volume to find many illustrations. The wandering (nomad) tribes of the Arabian Desert were always searching for a more fertile region and fighting with those who had reached it before them. The downfall of Egypt was hastened by peoples pressing in from the north. The Sumerians were overcome by the more primitive Akkadians. When their kingdom became prosperous, it was conquered by the Babylonians, who, in turn, were overwhelmed by the Assyrians, and they in their turn by the Chaldeans, and so on. One could also follow the wide dispersion of the Indo-European peoples all the way from India to the Atlantic. The story of the Ancient World was a succession of invasions, the building up of civilizations, and their overthrow by less civilized newcomers.

Causes of Migrations. Migrations or invasions may be *forced* or *voluntary,* or both. Men may be driven by starvation to seek new living conditions, but they may also be tempted by the lands and goods of others and try to take them for themselves. In later times other reasons led people to move about, but it was generally land or loot which spurred them to seek adventure or new homes. Religious faith and a spirit of conquest combined to drive the Mohammedans across northern Africa to the Atlantic. Much later we shall find that the geographical discoveries of the fifteenth century which opened up vast continents across the seas tempted Europeans to seek trade and new homes in far lands. The story of the development of the British Empire, with her colonies scattered throughout the world, is a striking example of how peoples sometimes peaceably, sometimes in a warlike manner, have shifted across the face of the earth. We must note, however, that in modern times the character of migrations has changed in one respect. With the development of the means of transportation it is not backward peoples only who seek other lands; advanced peoples also penetrate undeveloped regions and establish business agencies and permanent homes.

Migration to America. One of the most astonishing examples of migration is that of European peoples to North America. Before their coming the vast region north of Mexico was inhabited by a few hundred thousand savages, mostly in a low state of civilization. Since the time when Europeans discovered lands across the Atlantic, a constant invasion of various nationalities has been going on. The earliest settlers brought over their customs and language, and it happened that the English-speaking peoples spread their speech throughout the whole region north of Mexico. The civilization of the Western Hemisphere is therefore European in origin and, as we have seen, can be traced back through Rome and Greece to various peoples who preceded them. With these facts in mind we may follow the German invasions of the Roman Empire with more interest than we might otherwise do; for they are part of the story of the civilization of all English-speaking peoples.

Who the Barbarians Were. While the peoples living within the Roman Empire were enjoying a high degree of civilization, the life of the people who lived in the forest lands of northern and eastern Europe had not improved much since the Stone Age (p. 19). Yet these German tribes — or "barbarians," as the Romans called them — belonged to the same great group of peoples to which the Persians, Greeks, and Romans themselves belonged — the Indo-Europeans (p. 92). Like their earlier kinsmen they also showed a disposition to wander about and seize the lands and possessions of others. They too loved to fight. Just as the Greek tribes had overwhelmed the Ægean world, and the Etruscans had overcome the settlers of Latium, so now German tribes from central and eastern Europe pushed their way into the Empire and managed to stay there.

What the Germans were Like. The Germans must have seemed like a race of giants to the Romans, for they were tall and strong. Skeletons have been found which measure seven feet in height. The Germans had fierce blue eyes and fair hair, which they sometimes dyed red. This fashion, it is said, was later adopted by Roman ladies.

In their native forests each German tribe or nation occupied a very small area, probably not over forty miles across. The Germans lived in villages, of about a hundred families each, and there was a head man over each village. Their houses were huts of rough timber plastered with mud. They did not like farming, which requires a settled life, but preferred to get their living by hunting and to shift their homes often. Sometimes they kept cattle or raised a few crops. They did not know how to write, made very few things, and did little trading. Most of the men's time was spent in fighting or plundering other tribes.

How the Germans Fought. Hardened to wind and weather in their raw Northern climate, their fearlessness and love of war and plunder often led them to wander about, followed by their wives and families in heavy wagons. An entire people might include some fifty villages, but each village group remained together, protected by its body of about a hundred warriors, the heads of the village families. When combined, these hundreds made up an army of five to six thousand men. Each hundred held together in battle as a fighting body. They all knew each other: the village head man, the leader of the group, had always lived with them; the warrior in the midst of battle saw all around him his

FIG. 80. *Teutonic Warriors Awaiting the Approach of the Enemy*
From a drawing by A. Forestier

friends and relatives, the sons of his brothers, the husbands of his daughters. Although untrained, these bands of relatives and neighbors were as terrible as any groups of warriors ever seen in the ancient world. Their eager joy in battle and the untamed fierceness of their onset made them almost impossible to defeat.

Long-standing Trouble with Barbarians. The danger from the northern barbarian tribes was not a new one; it had existed for centuries. Marius had marched against the advancing Cimbri and Teutons and saved Rome in 101 B.C. (p. 306). Julius Cæsar had carried on his "Gallic wars" to protect the Empire against German invaders. In Hadrian's time a fortified wall was built across the German frontier (A.D. 117). Emperor Marcus Aurelius was unable to drive out the barbarians who had pushed across the boundaries. He finally consented to let some of them remain within the

Empire and gave them lands for homes in return for military service. This was a fatal mistake; for in the following centuries the barbarians continued to find their way into the Empire and obtain places in the armies. The lack of men for the Roman legions forced the emperors to hire the Germans as soldiers. Finally *entire* German peoples were allowed to settle within the Empire and keep their old customs. While the men fought in the Roman army, they remained under their own German leaders and fought in their own village unit. The highly trained Roman legions were now no more, and the rude strength of the barbarian soldiers gave the army what power it had.

Germans and Romans learn to Live Together. This constant mingling of the Germans with the civilized peoples of the Empire was bound to have an effect on their manners and customs. Their leaders, who held office under the Roman government, came to have friends among highborn Romans. German generals sometimes married educated Roman women of high rank, even relatives of the emperors. Some of them, too, were converted to Christianity. An educated German named Ulfilas translated portions of the Bible into Gothic, a tongue related to German. As the Germanic peoples had no writing, he was obliged to make up an alphabet from Greek and Latin for writing Gothic. His New Testament, which was used in converting the Northern peoples to Christianity, is the earliest example of a written Germanic tongue that we know of.

2. German Chiefs set up Kingdoms within the Roman Empire

The Huns force the Goths into the Empire. There were already many Germans living within the Empire when suddenly the Huns, a Mongolian folk from central Asia, swept down upon the Goths, a German tribe settled upon the Danube, and forced a part of them to seek shelter across the river, within the limits of the Empire.

The Goths had hitherto only dared to make occasional raids across the frontier. Now they begged the emperor for

Fig. 81. Alaric's Soldiers Looting a Goldsmith's Shop in Rome

protection within his boundaries. An arrangement was made by which the Goths, in return for food and land, should serve in the army. But the Roman officials broke their word, and a battle was fought at Adrianople in 378 in which the Goths defeated and slew the Roman emperor, Valens. The Germans had now not only pushed through the boundaries of the Empire but also learned that they could defeat the troops on which the Empire relied for protection. The battle of Adrianople may therefore be said to mark the beginning of the conquest of the western part of the Empire by the Germans. For some years, however, after the battle of Adrianople the various bands of West Goths — or *Visigoths*, as they are often called — were persuaded to live on the terms of peace offered by the emperor's officials, and some of the Goths agreed to serve as soldiers in the Roman armies.

Alaric takes Rome (A.D. 410). Among the Germans who succeeded in getting an important position in the Roman army was Alaric, but he appears to have become dissatisfied with the treatment he received from the emperor. He therefore collected an army, — of which his countrymen, the West Goths, formed a large part, — set out for Italy, and finally decided to march on Rome itself. The Eternal City fell into his hands in A.D. 410 and was plundered by his followers.

West Goths settle in Southern Gaul and Spain; the Vandals. Alaric died before he could find a satisfactory spot for his people to settle upon permanently. After his death the West Goths wandered into Gaul and then into Spain. Here they found the Vandals, another German tribe, who had crossed the Rhine four years before Alaric had captured Rome. For three years they had devastated Gaul and then had moved down into Spain. After the arrival in Spain of the West Goths there was war for a time between them and the Vandals. The West Goths seem to have got the best of their rivals; for the Vandals determined to move on across the Strait of Gibraltar into northern Africa, where they established a kingdom and conquered the neighboring islands in the Mediterranean (map, p. 377).

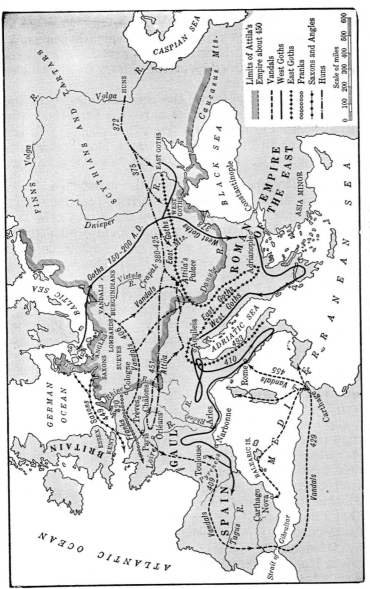

The Migrations of the Germans in the Fifth Century

Having rid themselves of the Vandals, the West Goths took possession of a great part of the Spanish peninsula; and this they added to their conquests across the Pyrenees in Gaul, so that their kingdom extended from the river Loire to the Strait of Gibraltar.

It is unnecessary to follow the confused history of the movements of the countless bands of restless barbarians who wandered about Europe during the fifth century. Scarcely any part of western Europe was left untroubled; even Britain was conquered by German tribes, the Angles and Saxons.

Attila and the Huns. To add to the general confusion caused by the inpouring of the German tribes, the Huns (the Mongolian people who had first pushed the West Goths into the Empire) now began to fill all western Europe with terror. Under their chief, Attila, this savage people invaded Gaul. But the Romans and the German inhabitants joined together against the invaders and defeated them in the battle of Châlons, in A.D. 451. After this setback in Gaul, Attila turned to Italy; but Pope Leo the Great succeeded in persuading him to give up his plan of marching upon Rome. Within a year Attila died, and with him perished the power of the Huns, who never troubled Europe again.

The Fall of the Empire in the West (A.D. 476). The year 476 has commonly been taken as the date of the "fall" of the Western Empire and of the beginning of the Middle Ages. What happened in that year was this. Most of the Roman emperors in the West had proved weak and lazy rulers. So the barbarians wandered hither and thither pretty much at their pleasure, and the German troops in the service of the Empire became accustomed to set up and remove emperors to suit their own special interest, very much in the same way that a boss in an American city often succeeds in securing the election of a mayor who will carry out his wishes. Finally Odoacer, the most powerful among the German generals in Italy, declared himself *king* and banished the last of the emperors of the West.[1]

---

[1] The common misapprehensions in regard to the events of the year 476 are discussed in James Harvey Robinson's *New History*, pp. 154 ff.

Map of Europe in the Time of Theodoric

It will be noticed that Theodoric's kingdom of the East Goths included a much larger area than the present kingdom of Italy, and that the West Gothic realms extended into southern France. The Vandals held northern Africa and the neighboring islands. The Burgundians lay in between the East Goths and the Franks. The Lombards, who were later to move down into Italy, were in Theodoric's time east of the Bavarians after whom modern Bavaria is named. Some of the Saxons invaded England but many stayed in Germany, as indicated on the map. The Eastern Empire, which was all that remained of the Roman Empire, included the Balkan Peninsula, Asia Minor, and the eastern portion of the Mediterranean. The Britons in Wales, the Picts in Scotland, and the Scots in Ireland were Celts; consequently Welsh, Gaelic, and Irish are closely related and belong to the Celtic group of languages

Theodoric establishes the Kingdom of the East Goths in Italy. Odoacer was unable to establish a permanent kingdom in Italy; for in A.D. 493 he was conquered by Theodoric, king of the East Goths (or Ostrogoths), who had long been eager to gain a foothold in some part of the Empire. After the death of Attila had freed the Ostrogoths from fear of the Huns, they had established themselves in the Empire and chosen Theodoric for their leader. Theodoric had spent part of his youth in Constantinople as a hostage and had grown to admire Roman life and customs. The Ostrogoths had at first threatened Constantinople, but Theodoric was now on friendly terms with the emperor. Hoping to regain more direct control over Italy, the emperor sent Theodoric to conquer Odoacer and take possession of his kingdom. He doubtless also thought that this would be a good way of ridding himself of a too powerful neighbor. The Ostrogoths therefore set out for Italy, and the struggle between Theodoric and Odoacer was carried on for several years. Finally Odoacer was shut up in Ravenna and surrendered. A few days later, however, he was treacherously slain by Theodoric.

Theodoric put the name of the emperor at Constantinople on the coins which he issued and did everything to gain the emperor's approval of the new kingdom. He adopted Roman laws and customs. He kept old offices and titles, and Goth and Roman lived together under the same Roman law. Order was maintained and learning was encouraged. In Ravenna, which Theodoric chose for his capital, beautiful buildings still exist that were erected during his reign.

Franks and Burgundians. The Burgundians, a Teutonic tribe who had been given lands on the upper Rhine, moved south and established themselves between the Franks and the East Goths. Their kingdom lasted for about a century, until A.D. 534, when they were conquered by their powerful neighbors the Franks, of whom we shall speak later.

Justinian tries to Regain Part of the Western Empire. The year after Theodoric's death one of the greatest emperors of the East, Justinian (A.D. 527–565), came to the throne at Constantinople. Justinian attempted to win back for his empire the provinces in Africa and Italy that had been occupied by the Vandals and East Goths. His general, Belisarius, overthrew the Vandal kingdom in northern Africa in 534, but it was a more difficult task to destroy the Gothic rule in Italy. However, after a struggle lasting twenty years the Goths were so completely defeated by A.D. 553 that they agreed to leave Italy with all their movable possessions. What became of the remnants of the race we do not know.

FIG. 82. *The Church of St. Sophia at Constantinople (Istanbul)*

This famous church was built by Justinian from 532 to 537. The gigantic dome is one hundred and eighty-three feet high at the center. Justinian is said to have expended eighteen tons of gold and used the labor of ten thousand men in the erection of the building. After the capture of Constantinople by the Turks in 1453 the vast church served as a Mohammedan mosque. The Turks whitewashed the gorgeous mosaics and hung large circular shields, bearing the monogram of the Sultan, against the walls. Under the enlightened rule of Ghazi Mustafa Kemal permission has been granted for cleaning these Christian mosaics, and the work is now being carried on by American archæologists, with very important results

Justinian's Work at Home. The new emperor did not use all his energies in war but did much to beautify his capital. Justinian was an ardent Christian and spent vast sums in building beautiful churches. St. Sophia, in Constantinople, still stands today, the most magnificent of the early churches in the East. The worship of the old gods had long before been prohibited by Christian emperors, and the beautiful old temples along the shores of the Mediterranean had been neglected or destroyed. Justinian now struck the last blow to what the Church regarded as the heathen religion of the Greeks by closing the schools of philosophy at Athens, established centuries earlier by the followers of Plato and Aristotle and by the Stoics and Epicureans. These, as we have seen (p. 250), formed a sort of university attended by scholars from all parts of the Empire.

The Justinian Code of Law. Justinian employed a lawyer named Tribonian to gather together all the many laws which had grown up since the age of the Twelve Tablets (p. 269), a thousand years before. He was the Hammurapi (p. 67) of the Roman Empire, and the great body of laws which he collected were intended to teach the people to live peaceably together and to deal with one another fairly in all things. The collection of decisions of famous Roman judges brought together in Justinian's *Digest* became the foundation of law for later ages and still greatly influences the laws of civilized peoples of today.

The Lombards occupy Italy. The destruction of the Gothic kingdom was a disaster for Italy, for the Goths would have helped to defend it against later and far more barbarous invaders. Immediately after the death of Justinian the country was overrun by the Lombards, the last of the great German peoples to establish themselves within the bounds of the former Empire. They were a savage race, a large part of which was still pagan. The newcomers first occupied the region north of the Po (which has ever since been called "Lombardy" after them) and then extended their conquests southward. Instead of settling themselves peaceably under a wise ruler, as had the East Goths, the Lombards moved about the peninsula pillaging and massacring. They were unable, however, to conquer all of Italy. Rome, Ravenna, and southern Italy continued to be held by the emperors who succeeded Justinian at Constantinople. As time went on, the Lombards lost their wildness and adopted the habits and religion of the people among whom they lived. Their kingdom lasted over two hundred years, until it was conquered by Charlemagne (p. 420).

The Later Roman Empire, called Eastern or Byzantine. Although the western portion of the Empire fell into the hands of many chieftains, the Eastern, or Byzantine, Empire, as it came to be called, lasted for nearly a thousand years. Constantinople was admirably situated to resist the attacks of invaders. The peninsula on which it was built was approached on three sides by water. The approach from north and south was through a narrow channel which could easily be defended with a small force. Across the peninsula to the west was built a strong wall to protect the city from attack by land.

Many peoples lived within the boundaries of the Eastern Empire, but the tradition of the glorious days of the old Roman Empire helped to unite them under one rule. The business of government was largely carried on by a system of well-organized departments with permanent officials; so emperors might rise and fall and yet the affairs of the state remain undisturbed. The Eastern Empire was also strengthened by its excellent body of laws, which provided the same treatment for all nationalities. Justinian's Code, with some later additions, remained in force. While the Greeks formed but a small part of the population, Greek displaced Latin as the official language of the realm. Justinian was the last emperor to speak Latin as his mother tongue. Greek not only was the language of the government but was used also in the services of the Church.

The Empire suffered much violence and loss of territory (p. 514). Nevertheless, in spite of all dangers, it was able to maintain itself until 1453, when Constantinople was captured by the Turks and the Eastern Roman Empire came to an end.

Permanent Kingdoms of the Angles, Saxons, and Franks. Most of the kingdoms established by German chieftains were not permanent. As we have already seen, the Vandals in northern Africa and the Ostrogoths in Italy were overcome by Justinian's armies. In A.D. 534 the Franks added the lands of the Burgundians to their own growing territory. The West Goths were driven out of Gaul into Spain and fell before the Mohammedans in the year 711. Lombardy became a part of the Frankish realms in 774.

There were, however, three Teutonic tribes whose settlements were destined to endure; for they laid the foundations of our modern states of England and France. These tribes were the Angles and Saxons, who invaded Britain, and the Franks, who conquered Gaul.

Angles and Saxons conquer Britain. Rome's far province of Britain shared the same fate as the rest of the Western Empire. For centuries it was a prey to barbarian tribes who raided its coasts and sometimes succeeded in making settlements on its shores. In A.D. 409 the emperor, no longer able to spare troops to garrison the island, recalled the Roman legions and practically abandoned the former province. A period of great confusion followed. Although we have no reliable accounts of just what happened, we know that the unorganized, untrained inhabitants were not able to protect themselves against the invaders, who made a determined effort to conquer the island. The most important of the newcomers were the Angles, Saxons, and Jutes, from northern Europe. These fierce sea-roving folk soon managed to gain a firm foothold in Britain, and shortly after the year 500 half the island was under their control.

It is important to notice that it is from these Teutonic ancestors rather than from the Latins that the English derive their laws, customs, and much of their language. Anglo-Saxon (the name of the early form of the English language) replaced the Latin language, and the names of the present counties of Essex and Sussex indicate the location of two of the early Saxon settlements. The name "England" (Angle-land) finally came to be the common name adopted for the early kingdom of Britain.

3. The Franks Settle in Gaul

How the Franks extended their Dominion. The Franks were originally settled along the Rhine, from Cologne to the North Sea. Their way of getting a foothold in the Empire was entirely different from that of the Goths, Lombards, and Vandals. Instead of cutting themselves off from Germany, they conquered little by little the territory round about them. However far they might extend their control, they remained in constant touch with their fellow barbarians behind them. In this way they kept the warlike energy that was gradually given up by the races who were completely surrounded by the refinements of Roman civilization.

In the early part of the fifth century the Franks had occupied the district that forms today the kingdom of Belgium, as well

Fig. 83. A Frankish Warrior

From a model in the Musée de l'Armée, Paris

as the regions to the east of it. In A.D. 486, they went forth under their great king, Clovis (whose name later grew into "Louis"), and defeated the Roman general who opposed them. They extended their control over Gaul as far south as the Loire, which at that time formed the northern boundary of the kingdom of the West Goths. Clovis next enlarged his empire on the east by the conquest of the Alemanni, a German people living in the region of the Black Forest and north of the Lake of Constance.

The Dominions of the Franks under the Merovingians

This map shows how the Frankish kingdom grew up. Clovis, while still a young man, defeated the Roman general Syagrius in 486, near Soissons, and so added the region around Paris to his possessions. He added Alemannia, on the east, in 496. In 507 he made Paris his capital and conquered Aquitania, previously held by the West Goths. He also made a beginning in adding the kingdom of the Burgundians to his realms. He died in 511. His successors in the next half-century completed the conquest of Burgundy and added Provence, Bavaria, and Gascony. There were many divisions of the Frankish realms after the time of Clovis, and the eastern and western portions, called Austrasia and Neustria, were often ruled by different branches of the *Merovingians*, as Clovis's family was called

The Franks become Christians (A.D. 496).

The battle in which the Alemanni were defeated (496) is in one respect important above all the other battles of Clovis. Although still a pagan himself, his wife had been converted to Christianity. In the midst of the battle, seeing that his troops were losing, he called upon Jesus Christ and promised to be baptized in his name if he would help the Franks to victory over their enemies. When he won the battle he kept his word and was baptized, together with three thousand of his warriors.

Clovis and his Successors build up the Frankish Kingdom.
To the south of Clovis's new possessions in Gaul lay the
kingdom of the West Goths; to the southeast that of another German people, the Burgundians. Clovis speedily
extended his power to the Pyrenees and forced the West
Goths to confine themselves to the Spanish portion of their
realm, while the Burgundians soon fell completely under the
rule of the Franks. Then Clovis, by committing a number
of murders, brought under his control parts of the Frankish
nation itself that had previously been independent of him.

Clovis had made Paris his capital, and it was there that
he died in 511. His four sons divided his possessions among
them. Wars between rival brothers, together with the most
horrible murders, fill the record of the Frankish kingdom
for over a hundred years after the death of Clovis. Yet the
nation continued to develop in spite of the wicked deeds of
its rulers.

The Frankish kings who followed Clovis succeeded in
extending their power over pretty nearly all the territory
that is included today in France, Belgium, and the Netherlands, as well as over a goodly portion of western Germany.
Half a century after the death of Clovis their dominions
extended from the Bay of Biscay on the west to a point east
of Salzburg.

4. Effects of the Invasions on Civilization

How the Barbarians became Part of the Roman Peoples. As
one looks back over the German invasions it is natural to
ask in what manner the newcomers lived among the old inhabitants of the Empire, how far they adopted the ways of
those among whom they settled, and how far they clung to
their old habits. These questions cannot be answered very
satisfactorily. So little is known of the confused period of
which we have been speaking that it is impossible to follow
closely the mixing of the two races.

In the first place, we must be careful not to exaggerate
the numbers in the various bodies of invaders. The readiness with which the Germans appear to have adopted the

language and customs of the Romans would seem to prove that the invaders formed, after all, but a small part of the population. Moreover, since many thousands of barbarians had already settled in the Empire during the previous five centuries, the newcomers of the *fifth* century probably did not make a sudden change in the character of the population. We can get some idea of the situation when we reflect that thousands of immigrants have come to our country who have learned English, accustomed themselves to our ways of living, and become part of our people.

Contrast between Spoken and Written Latin. The barbarians within the old Empire were soon speaking the same Latin which the Romans around them used. This was much simpler than the language used by the classical writers, which we find so hard to learn nowadays. In the various countries of southern Europe the speech of the common people was gradually becoming more and more unlike written Latin and finally grew into French, Spanish, Italian, and Portuguese.

The northern Franks, who did not push very far into the Empire, and the Germans who remained in what is now Germany and in Scandinavia, did not come in contact with the Latin-speaking peoples and so had no reason for giving up their native speech; the Angles and Saxons in Britain also kept theirs. These Germanic languages in time became Dutch, English, German, Danish, Swedish, and so on. Of this matter something will be said later (pp. 580–581).

The Roman and the German Law. The Germans and the older inhabitants of the Roman Empire appear to have had no dislike for one another except when there was a difference in religion.[1] When there was no religious difficulty, the two races intermarried freely from the first. The Frankish kings appointed Romans to important positions in the government and army, just as the Romans had employed the barbarians as generals and officials. In only one respect did the two races differ for a time — each had its own separate law.

---

[1] The West and East Goths and the Burgundians had been converted to Christianity by missionaries who bitterly disagreed with the Catholic Church on certain important points.

The West Goths were probably the first to write down their ancient laws, using the Latin language for the purpose. Their example was followed by the Franks, the Burgundians, and later by the Lombards and other peoples. These codes make up the "Laws of the Barbarians," and from them we get our knowledge of the habits and ideas of the Germans at the time of the invasions. For several centuries following the barbarian conquests the members of the various German tribes preferred to be judged by the laws of the people to which they belonged. The older inhabitants of the Empire, on the contrary, continued to have their lawsuits decided according to the Roman law.

Medieval Trials. The German laws did not provide for trials, as we are familiar with them today. There was no attempt to gather and weigh evidence and base the decision upon it. All this was far too elaborate for the simple-minded Germans. Instead of a regular trial, one of the parties to the case was required to prove that his side of the case was right in one of the following ways:

1. He might solemnly swear that he was telling the truth, and get as many other persons of his own class as the court required, to swear that they believed he was telling the truth. This was called *compurgation*. It was believed that God would punish those who swore falsely.

2. On the other hand, the parties to the case, or persons representing them, might fight one another; for it was believed that Heaven would grant victory to the right. This was the so-called *wager of battle.*

3. Lastly, one or other of the parties might be required to submit to the *ordeal* in one of its various forms: He might plunge his arm into hot water or carry a bit of hot iron for some distance, and if at the end of three days he showed no ill effects the case was decided in his favor. Or he might be ordered to walk over hot plowshares, and if he was not burned it was believed that God had performed a miracle to show who was right. This method of trial is but one example of the crude ways which displaced the refined and advanced civilization of the Romans.

The Ignorance and Disorder of the Early Middle Ages. We are now in a position to see why the early Middle Ages were a time of ignorance and disorder. The German tribes, no doubt, differed from one another a good deal in their habits and character, but they were all alike in knowing nothing of the art, literature, and science which had been developed by the Greeks and adopted by the Romans. The invaders were ignorant, simple, hardy people, with no taste for anything except fighting, eating, and drinking. Their coming produced so much disorder that the declining civilization of the Empire pretty nearly disappeared. The libraries, buildings, and works of art were destroyed or neglected, and there was no one to see that they were restored.

The loss was, however, for a time only. The great heritage of skill and invention which had been slowly accumulated in Egypt and Greece, and which formed a part of the civilization that the Romans had adopted and spread abroad throughout their great empire, did not wholly perish. It is true that the break-up of the Roman Empire, and the centuries of turmoil which followed, set everything back; but we shall see how the barbarian nations gradually developed into our modern European states, and how universities were established in which the books of the Greeks and Romans were studied. In time architects arose, who imitated the old buildings and also erected a new kind of their own as beautiful as those of the Romans; and men of science made discoveries far beyond anything known to the wisest Greek or Roman.

Questions and Exercises

REVIEW OF CHAPTER

1. What are some of the reasons why peoples have moved from one location to another? Do you recall any of the earlier migrations? any modern ones? Describe how the German tribes lived and the way they fought. How did they get a foothold in the Roman Empire?

2. Trace the history of the West Goths. Where did they finally settle? Contrast the fate of the eastern and western portions of the Empire. What happened to the Roman province of Britain?

3. How did the invasion of the Franks differ from that of other German peoples? What did Clovis accomplish and what was the extent of the Frankish kingdom under his successors?

4. On what terms do the Germans seem to have lived with the people of the Roman Empire? In what ways could a party in a German lawsuit prove his case? Why have the Middle Ages been called the "Dark Ages"?

USEFUL TERMS

See how much meaning you can give to the following: *Teutonic, Ostrogoths, Visigoths, code, Merovingian, medieval, migration, barbarian, ordeal.*

DIRECTIVE QUESTIONS

1. What modern languages are derived from Latin and what from the Germanic tongues?

2. Were any of the barbarian kingdoms permanent? What modern states have finally developed from the Germanic invasions?

3. Why did Christians destroy the libraries and temples in the Empire?

DISCUSSION TOPICS

1. The Justinian Code is a part of the Roman law.

2. Anglo-Saxon is an early form of the English language.

3. The barbarians did not permanently ruin European civilization.

4. The Middle Ages were not entirely given over to fighting and disorder.

5. The United States has a large population of peaceful invaders.

ADDITIONAL ADVENTURES IN LEARNING

1. Studies in Source Materials. ROBINSON, *Readings in European History*, Vol. I, chap. ii, sect. iv, Comparison of the Romans and barbarians. Chap. iii, sect. i, (*a*) A description of the Huns, (*b*) The Goths in the Roman Empire; ii, The sack of Rome; iii, A description of the court of Attila; iv, How Pope Leo saved Rome; v, The conversion of Clovis to Christianity.

2. Supplementary. Look up in a large dictionary the uses of the words *Vandal, Goth*, and especially *Gothic*. On a map of France block in the sections added to the Frankish kingdom by the successors of Clovis. Make your own map of the migrations of the German tribes in the fifth century. Write a description of the early Germans, their life and customs. Tacitus, *Germania*, sects. 1–29.

CHAPTER XX · HOW CHRISTIANITY
BECAME THE RELIGION OF EUROPE

GROWTH OF THE CHRISTIAN CHURCH · HOW THE POPE BECAME THE HEAD OF THE
CHURCH · THE MONKS AT HOME · THE MONKS BECOME MISSIONARIES · CHRISTIANITY
IN CONFLICT WITH MOHAMMEDANISM

WE NOW turn from the story of the conflicts and confusion which overcame the Roman Empire to see how Christianity became the religion of Western civilization and one of the great religions of the world. There are, as we know, several other "world" religions, each with its millions of faithful followers, — for example, the Buddhists and Confucianists in the Far East, the Hindus and Mohammedans in India, Asia, and Africa, and the Jews scattered in all parts of the earth. Each of these religions has a long past.

We may well ask how the religion of Jesus, with its humble beginnings among the fishermen on the shores of the Lake of Galilee, grew into a mighty power which affected the lives of all the peoples of the Western world. While the Roman Empire was falling into the hands of marauding chieftains, the Christian Church was rapidly growing in strength and importance. It replaced in many ways the great unifying power of the Roman Empire and dominated the civilization of Europe for many centuries.

We may recall that the emperors, after having persecuted the early Christians for years, finally adopted Christianity themselves and made it the religion of their realms. It was the emperors, therefore, who laid the foundations of the worldly power of the Church and strengthened it with their might. In the Theodosian Code, a collection of the laws of the Empire made under Theodosius (A.D. 438), we find the edicts which had been issued in regard to Christianity up to that time. It is plain from these that the government would permit no other form of religion than the one it had approved. The code goes so far as to call all who do not believe in the Trinity "mad and demented" and to threaten them with the punishment of the state as well as the wrath of Almighty God. Heretics are liable to be sent into exile or put to death and their books burned. The clergy are set apart as a privileged class, freed from taxation and all public burdens, lest these interfere with the performance of their sacred duties. Subjects are encouraged to bequeath their lands and wealth to the church.

In these provisions we can see the framework of what was to become the most important institution in medieval Europe. Although it was granted its first privileges by the emperors, it finally became powerful enough to defy kings and emperors when they opposed its will. For the present it will be

392

enough to understand that the Church had much to offer to the people of a disordered world. Christianity brought comfort and guidance in daily life, it held up standards of righteousness and peace in an age of bloodshed and cruelty, and it offered salvation and happiness in a life to come. The Church preserved what learning and culture survived the wreckage of the Roman Empire. Let us see how it built up an organization which was able to carry on its important work.

---

1. Growth of the Christian Church

How Christianity Spread. Jesus had said to his Apostles, "Go ye into all the world and preach my Gospel to every living creature." So faithfully had his disciples and their fellow missionaries carried out this commandment that Christian communities multiplied rapidly. By the third century people began to speak of an all-embracing, or "catholic," church. The early Church, in the midst of other religions and troubled by differences of opinion among Christians, asserted that its beliefs were the one "true" religion and that no other faiths were genuine. The emperors had set a standard of intolerance by making it an offense to differ from the orthodox, or "right-teaching," church. But Christianity was much affected by other religions already existing within the Empire and by such philosophies as that of the Stoics. Its teachings were thus easily understood by people who had lived in the Empire and had been familiar with such ideas as the fatherhood of God and the brotherhood of man.

We cannot overestimate the influence which the Church came to have over people in both private and public life. As the Roman Empire fell to pieces and the kingdoms of the German chieftains sprang up and were conquered by some mightier leader, the Church remained permanent, teaching the Gospel of peace, comforting the sick, aiding the poor, praying for those about to die. As the Church grew in strength Rome won back its place of leadership in the eyes of Europe. Its old glory as the capital of a *political* empire had vanished; but men now turned toward Rome as the capital of a *religious* empire, the *center* of Christendom, the *seat* of the Holy Roman Apostolic Church.

The Church as the Means of Salvation. Religion to the devout pagan was, as we have seen, mainly an affair of this life: the gods were worshiped with a view to securing happiness and success in this world and not in a life to come. To the Greeks and Romans, existence after death, when it was thought of at all, seemed but a shadowy dream in which men were neither sad nor glad. Christianity, on the other hand, held a widely different view. It taught that man's brief stay on this earth was but a preparation for the far more important life to come. Those who were good Christians here below would enter into never-ending bliss, while the wicked would suffer everlasting punishment for their sins. Moreover, it declared, the fate of mankind in the next world depended largely upon the Church. Only those whom the Church had baptized could hope to reach heaven; but even baptism washed away only past sins and did not prevent new ones. These sins which man committed every day, if they were grievous and were not removed through the help of the Church, would surely drag the soul down to hell.

The Monks. The anxiety about the future became so great that thousands gave up their ordinary occupations altogether and devoted their entire attention to preparation for the world to come. They shut themselves in lonely cells, and, not satisfied with giving up most of their natural pleasures, they inflicted bodily suffering upon themselves by undergoing hunger, cold, and other discomforts. They trusted that in this way they might avoid some of the sins into which they were apt to fall, and that, by self-inflicted punishment in this world, they might perchance escape some of that reserved for them in the next. Those who left their homes and joined religious brotherhoods living apart under a special rule became *monks* (from a word meaning "solitary").

Miracles. The divine power of the Church was, furthermore, established in the eyes of the people by the wonderful works which Christian saints were constantly performing. They healed the sick, and made the blind to see and the lame to walk. They called down God's wrath upon those who opposed the Church, and inflicted terrible punishments upon those who treated her holy sacraments with contempt. To the reader of today the frequency of the miracles narrated by medieval writers seems astonishing. The lives of the medieval saints, of which hundreds and hundreds have been preserved, contain little else than accounts of them, and no one appears to have doubted their everyday occurrence.

The Church Frees itself from Government Control. The chief interest of the Church for the student of medieval history does not lie, however, in its religious duties, important as they were, but rather in its remarkable relations to the government. As long as the Roman Empire remained strong and active, there was no chance for the clergy to free themselves from the control of the emperor, even if they had wished to do so. He made such laws for the Church as he saw fit, and the clergy did not complain. The government was, indeed, very useful to them. It undertook to root out paganism by destroying the heathen temples and preventing heathen sacrifices, and it punished severely those who refused to accept the teachings of the Church.

But as the great Empire began to fall apart, the churchmen in the West began to dislike the interference of the new rulers, whom they did not respect. Consequently they managed gradually to free themselves in large part from the control of the government.

The Church performs the Duties of a State. The authority of the various barbarian kings was seldom sufficient to keep their realms in order. There were always many powerful land-holders scattered throughout the kingdom who did pretty much what they pleased and who settled their grudges against their fellows by neighborhood wars. Fighting was the main business as well as the chief amusement of this class. The king was unable to maintain peace and protect the oppressed, however anxious he may have been to do so.

Under these circumstances it naturally fell to the Church to keep order, when it could, by either threats or persuasion, and to see that contracts were kept, the wills of the dead

FIG. 84. *Santa Maria Maggiore*

This beautiful church at Rome was built shortly after the emperor Constantine's reign. Above its stately columns are fine mosaics, which can still be seen. The ceiling is of the sixteenth century

carried out, and marriage obligations observed. It took the defenseless widow and orphan under its protection and gave help to the poor; it promoted education at a time when few besides the clergy were able even to read. These conditions serve to explain why the Church was finally able so greatly to extend the powers which it had enjoyed under the Roman Empire, and why it undertook duties which seem to us today to belong to the state rather than to a religious body.

The Early Churches. The Romans were accustomed to build near their market places a kind of public hall, in which townspeople could meet one another to carry on business and in which judges could hear cases and public officials attend to their duties. These buildings, as we have seen, were called *basilicas*. There were several magnificent ones in Rome itself, and there was doubtless at least one to be found in every large town. The roofs of these spacious halls were usually supported by long rows of columns; sometimes there were two rows on each side. forming aisles. When, after Constantine had given his approval to Christianity, large, fine churches began to be built, they were constructed much like these familiar public halls and, like them, were called basilicas.

Almost all the early churches have disappeared; but the beautiful church of Santa Maria Maggiore, still standing in Rome, gives us an excellent notion of a Christian basilica, with its fine rows of columns and its handsome decorations. In general, the churches were plain and unattractive on the outside. A later chapter will describe how the basilica grew into the Gothic cathedral, which was beautiful outside as well as in the interior (Chapter XXVI).

2. HOW THE POPE BECAME THE HEAD OF THE CHURCH

Origin of the Pope's Power. We must now turn to a consideration of the origin and growth of the authority of the Popes, who, by raising themselves to the head of the Western Church, became in many respects more powerful than any of the kings and princes with whom they frequently found themselves in bitter conflict.

The bishop of Rome and his congregation had almost from the first enjoyed a leading place among the Christian communities. The Christian group which had early developed in Rome was the only one in the *West* which claimed the distinction of having been founded by the immediate followers of Christ — the "two most glorious Apostles, Peter and Paul."

Belief that Peter was the First Bishop of Rome. The New Testament speaks repeatedly of Paul's presence in Rome. As for Peter, there had always been an unquestioned belief, accepted throughout the Christian Church, that he was the first bishop of Rome. Peter enjoyed a prominent place among the Apostles, and was singled out by Christ upon several occasions. In a passage of the New Testament (Matthew xvi, 18–19), which has affected history more profoundly than the decrees of the most powerful monarch, Christ says:

And I say also unto thee, That thou art Peter, and upon this rock I will build my church; and the gates of hell shall not prevail against it. And I will give unto thee the keys of the kingdom of heaven: and whatsoever thou shalt bind on earth shall be bound in heaven; and whatsoever thou shalt loose on earth shall be loosed in heaven.

This the Popes have always quoted as their particular claim to the powers which they believe to be theirs.

How the Roman Church came to be regarded as the Mother Church. Thus it was natural that the Roman Church should early have been looked upon as the "mother church" in the West. Its doctrines were considered the purest, since they were believed to have been handed down from its founders, the Apostles Peter and Paul. When there was a difference of opinion in regard to a particular teaching, it was customary to turn to the bishop of Rome for his view. Moreover, the majesty of Rome helped to raise its bishop above his fellows. It was long, however, before all the other bishops, especially those in the large cities, were ready to accept the supreme authority of the bishop of Rome, although they acknowledged his leading position.

We know but little of the bishops of Rome during the first three or four centuries of the Church's existence. It is only with the accession of Leo the Great (440–461) that our knowledge of the history of the papacy may, in one sense, be said to begin.

Title of Pope. The name "pope" (meaning "father") was originally given to all bishops, and even to priests. It began to be especially applied to the bishops of Rome, perhaps as early as the sixth century, but apparently was not confined to them until two or three hundred years later. Gregory VII (d. 1085) was the first to declare plainly that the title should be used only for the bishop of Rome.

Not long after the death of Leo the Great, Odoacer put an end to the Western line of emperors (p. 378). Then, as we know, Theodoric and his East Goths settled in Italy, only to be followed by still less desirable invaders, the Lombards. During this disorderly period the people of Rome, and even of all Italy, came to regard the Pope as their protector and leader. The Eastern emperor was far away, and his officers, who managed to hold a portion of Italy around Rome and Ravenna, were glad to accept the aid and advice of the Pope.

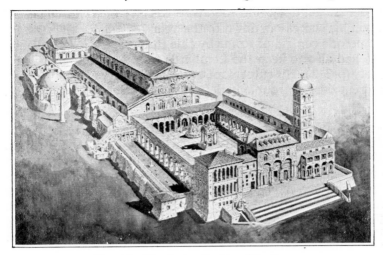

FIG. 85. *The Ancient Basilica of St. Peter*

Of the churches built by Constantine in Rome, that in honor of St. Peter was, next to the Lateran, the most important. It was constructed on the site of Nero's circus, where Saint Peter was believed to have been crucified. It retained its original appearance, as here represented, for twelve hundred years; and then the Popes (who had given up the Lateran as their residence and come to live in the Vatican Palace close to St. Peter's) determined to build the new and grander church one sees today. Constantine and the Popes used in their buildings great numbers of columns and stones from older Roman buildings, which in this way came to be torn down

Pope Gregory the Great (590–604). Gregory the Great was one of the most distinguished heads that the Church has ever had. When he was chosen Pope (in 590) and most sorrowfully left his monastery, ancient Rome, the former capital of the Empire, was already changing into medieval Rome, the capital of Christendom. The temples of the gods had furnished building materials for many Christian churches. The tombs of the Apostles Peter and Paul were soon to become the center of religious interest and to be visited by many earnest Christians from every part of western Europe.

Gregory's letters show clearly what the power of the Pope was coming to mean for Europe when it was in the hands of a really great man. While he assumed the humble title of "Servant of the Servants of God," which the Popes still use, Gregory was a statesman whose influence extended far and wide. It fell upon him to govern the city of Rome (as it did upon his successors down to the year 1870); for the Eastern emperor's control of Rome by this time existed in name only. He had also to keep the Lombards from overrunning central Italy (p. 382). His successors, as we shall see, continued to have a great deal of trouble in defending the region around Rome.

Gregory sends the Monks as Missionaries. Beyond the borders of Italy, Gregory was in constant correspondence with the emperor and the Frankish and Burgundian rulers. Everywhere he used his influence to have good clergymen chosen as bishops, and everywhere he watched over the interests of the monasteries. But his chief work was sending missionaries to the lands which we now know as England, France, and Germany. In this way a large part of western Europe was Christianized and brought under the rule of the Roman Catholic Church.

As Gregory had himself been a devoted monk, it was natural that he should rely chiefly upon the monks in his important work of converting the heathen. Consequently, before considering his missionary achievements, we must glance at the origin and character of the monks, who are so important throughout the Middle Ages.

3. THE MONKS AT HOME

What it Meant to become a Monk. Monasticism was not created by Christianity. Before the Christian Era there were, in India and Asia, followers of other religions who retired from the world to lead a pious life and devote their time to fasting and the study of their faith. In these religions, as well as in Christianity, such religious persons sometimes formed little groups and sometimes preferred to live entirely alone. Those who followed a solitary life were called *hermits*. Those who lived in communities, or orders, were the *monks*. There were also groups of pious women who preferred the monastic life. These were called *nuns* and lived in *nunneries*, or *convents*.

Monks and nuns had to give up all idea of expressing their own personality, for they became merely members of their order. They had strictly to obey the rules of the house and do whatever was commanded by its head. They also gave up all earthly possessions and, penniless, offered themselves to the service of the Lord.

Why People Became Monks. There were many different reasons why a person might wish to enter a monastery. The monastic life was safe and peaceful, as well as holy. The monastery was the natural refuge not only of those who were religious but of those who were studious and thoughtful and wished to lead a quiet and protected life. Even the most heartless warriors hesitated to attack a monastery and disturb the life of those who were believed to enjoy God's special favor. The monastery furnished, too, a refuge for the friendless, an asylum for the disgraced, and even food and shelter for the idle, who would otherwise have had to earn their living. Kings and nobles, for the good of their souls, readily gave land upon which to found colonies of monks, and there were plenty of far-off spots in the mountains and forests which seemed inviting to those who wished to escape from the world and its temptations, its dangers, or its cares.

Rule of Saint Benedict (A.D. 526). Christian monks first appeared on a large scale in Egypt in the fourth century. The idea, however, was quickly taken up in Europe. In the sixth century monasteries multiplied so rapidly in western Europe that it became necessary to establish definite rules which had to do with the life of the monks and the regulation of the monasteries. Accordingly Saint Benedict drew up, about the year 526, a sort of constitution for the monastery of Monte Cassino, in southern Italy, of which he was the head. He called his monastery "a school for the service of the Lord." His plan worked so well that it was rapidly accepted by other monasteries and gradually became the "rule" according to which a great many of the Western monks lived.[1]

---

[1] Those who lived under a "rule" (*regulum*) came to be called *regular* clergy, in contrast to those who lived out in the world (*saeculum*) and were referred to as *secular* clergy.

The Rule of Saint Benedict provided that, since not everyone was fitted for the monk's life, one wishing to enter the monastery should pass through a period of trial, or testing, called the *novitiate,* before he was permitted to take the solemn final vows. The brethren were to elect the head of the monastery — the abbot, as he was called. Along with frequent prayer and meditation, the monks were to do the necessary cooking and washing for the monastery and raise the necessary vegetables and grain. They were also to read and teach. Those who were not strong enough for outdoor work were given lighter tasks, such as copying books.

The Monastic Vows, or Pledges. The monk had to take the three vows of obedience, poverty, and purity. He was to obey the abbot without question in all matters. He agreed to a life of absolute poverty in which everything he used was the property of the monastery. He was not permitted to own anything whatsoever — not even a book or a pen. Along with the vows of obedience and poverty, he was also required to pledge himself never to marry; for not only was the single life considered more holy than the married but the monastic organization would have been impossible unless the monks remained single.

The influence of the Benedictine monks upon Europe was very great. From their numbers no less than twenty-four Popes and forty-six hundred bishops and archbishops have been chosen. They boast almost sixteen thousand writers, some of great distinction. During the Middle Ages their monasteries furnished retreats where the scholar might study and write in spite of the confusion and disorder of the times. In a later chapter we shall describe the two great religious orders of Franciscans and Dominicans that developed in the thirteenth century (Chapter XXIX).

How the Monks contributed to Civilization. The copying of books, as has been said, was a constant occupation of the monks. Doubtless their work was often done carelessly, with little heart and less understanding. But with the serious loss of manuscripts due to the destruction of libraries and the

FIG. 86. *A Monk at Work Copying a Manuscript*
From a mural painting by Willy Pogany in the Jonas Bronck School, New York

general lack of interest in books, it was necessary that new copies should be made. Even poor and incorrect ones were better than none. Almost all the books written by the Romans disappeared altogether during the Middle Ages, but from time to time a monk would copy the poems of Virgil, Horace, or Ovid, or the speeches of Cicero. In this way some of the chief works of the Latin writers have continued to exist down to the present day.

The monks regarded good hard work as a great aid to salvation. They set the example of careful cultivation of the lands about their monasteries and in this way introduced better farming methods into the regions where they settled. They entertained travelers at a time when there were few or no inns and so increased communication between the various parts of Europe.

Arrangement of a Monastery. The monastery, or abbey, of the monks was arranged to meet their particular needs and was usually at some distance from any town, in order to secure solitude and quiet.[1] It was modeled upon the general plan of the Roman country house. The buildings were arranged around an uncovered yard, or court. On all four sides of this was a covered walk, called the *cloister*, which made it possible to reach all the buildings without going outdoors in the rain or the hot sun. Not only the Benedictines but all the orders which grew up later arranged their homes in much the same way.

On the north side of the court was the *church*, which always faced west.[2] As time went on and certain groups of monks were given a great deal of property, they erected very beautiful churches for their monasteries. Westminster Abbey was originally the church of a monastery lying outside the city of London, and there may be seen today in Great Britain many picturesque remains of former abbey churches.

On the west side of the court were storerooms for provisions; on the south side, opposite the church, was the "refectory," or dining-room, and a sitting-room that could be warmed in cold weather. In the cloister, near the dining-room, was a wash room where the monk could wash his hands before meals. To the east of the court was the "dormitory," where the monks slept. This always adjoined the church, for the Rule required that the monks should hold services seven times a day. One of these services, called vigils, came well before daybreak; and it was convenient when one was called in the darkness out of his warm bed to be able to go down a short passage that led from the dormitory into the choir of the church, where the service was held.

The Benedictine Rule provided that the monks should, so far as possible, derive everything for their support from their own land. So outside the main group of buildings

---

[1] Later monasteries were sometimes built in towns or just outside the walls.
[2] The high altar was at the eastern end of the church, so that the priest when he stood before it to celebrate the Mass could face east, as was the custom.

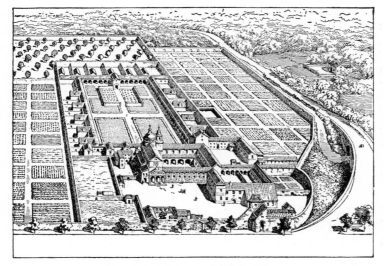

Fig. 87. *Monastery of Val di Cristo*

This monastery in southern Spain has two courts, the main one lying to the left.
The buildings were surrounded by vegetable gardens and an orchard, which supplied the monks with food. We know that we are viewing the monastery from the
west, for the church faces us

would be found the garden, the orchard, the mill, a fishpond,
and fields for raising grain. There were also a hospital for the
sick and a guest house for pilgrims or poor people who happened to come along. In the chief monasteries there were
also quarters where a king or nobleman might spend a few
nights in such comfort as was possible in those days.

4. The Monks become Missionaries

The Monks as Missionaries. The monks were a great help
in spreading the Christian faith. Their first notable undertaking was the conversion of those German peoples who had
not yet been won over to Christianity. These the monks
made not merely Christians but also faithful subjects of the
Pope. In this way the strength of the Roman Catholic
Church was substantially increased. The first people to attract the attention of the monks were the heathen German
tribes who had conquered the once Christian Britain.

Conversion of Britain. Pope Gregory the Great, while still a simple monk, had been struck with the beauty of some Angles whom he saw one day in the slave market at Rome. When he learned that they had been brought there from the heathen island of Britain, he was grieved that such handsome beings should still belong to the kingdom of the Prince of Darkness. He wished to go as a missionary to their people, but permission was refused him. So when he became Pope he sent forty monks to Britain, under the leadership of a prior named Augustine (who must not be confused with the Church Father of that name). The heathen king of Kent, in whose territory Augustine and his monks landed with fear and trembling (A.D. 597), had a Christian wife, the daughter of a Frankish king. Through her influence the monks were kindly received and were given an ancient church at Canterbury, dating from the Roman occupation (before the German invasions). Here they established a monastery, and from this center the conversion, first of Kent and then of the whole island, was gradually accomplished. Canterbury has always maintained its leadership among the English churches and may be considered the religious capital of England. The Archbishop of Canterbury holds the highest office in the English Church and is called "the Primate of all England."

England thus became a part of the ever-growing territory embraced in the Roman Catholic Church and remained for nearly a thousand years as faithful to the Pope as any other Catholic country. The most distinguished writer of the seventh and early eighth centuries in Europe was the English monk Bæda, often called "the Venerable Bede" (A.D. 673–735), from whose admirable history of the Church in England most of our information about the period is derived.

Saint Boniface, the Apostle to the Germans. In the year 718 Saint Boniface, an English monk, was sent by the Pope as a missionary to the Germans. Boniface succeeded in converting many of the more remote German tribes who still clung to their old pagan beliefs. His energetic methods are illustrated by the story of how he cut down the sacred oak of the old German god Odin, at Fritzlar, in Hesse, and used the wood to build a chapel, around which a monastery soon grew up.

5. CHRISTIANITY IN CONFLICT WITH MOHAMMEDANISM

Mohammed founds a New Religion. Just about the time that Gregory the Great was doing so much to strengthen the power and influence of the Popes in Rome, a young Arab camel-driver in far-away Mecca was dreaming of a religion which was one day to spread with astonishing rapidity into Asia, Africa, and Europe and to become a dangerous rival of Christianity. Today the millions who believe in Mohammed as God's true prophet are probably equal in number to those who are faithful to the Pope.

Before the time of Mohammed the Arabs (a branch of the Semitic people) had not played any notable part in the world's history. The scattered tribes were constantly at war with one another, and each tribe worshiped its own gods, when it worshiped at all. Mecca was considered a sacred spot, however, and the fighting was stopped four months each year so that all could peaceably visit the *Kaaba*, a sort of temple, full of idols and containing, in particular, a black stone, about as long as a man's hand, which was regarded as specially worthy of reverence.

As Mohammed traveled back and forth across the desert with his trains of camels heavily laden with goods he had plenty of time to think, and he became convinced that God was sending him messages which it was his duty to reveal to mankind. He met many Jews and Christians, of whom there were large numbers in Arabia, and from them he got some ideas of the Old and New Testaments. But when he tried to convince people that he was God's prophet, and that the Angel Gabriel had appeared to him in his dreams and told him of a new religion, he was treated with scorn.

Finally he discovered that his enemies in Mecca were planning to kill him, and he fled to the neighboring town of Medina, where he had friends. His flight, which took place in the year 622, the Arabs call the *Hegira*. It was taken by his followers as the beginning of a new era — the Year One, as the Mohammedans reckon time.

FIG. 88. *Pilgrims Visiting the Kaaba at Mecca*

Long before the time of Mohammed, Mecca was a holy place on account of its
ancient square temple called the Kaaba, which contained a sacred black stone.
Pilgrims had long come to Mecca to pay homage at the temple, and Mohammed
did not interfere with the custom. After his death the Moslems built a large
court around the Kaaba. Moslem believers still come to this shrine every year
in great numbers; those from Egypt bring annually the richly brocaded curtains
with which the sides of the Kaaba are hung

Mohammed calls his Religion Islam. There were many
wars between the Meccans and those who had joined Mohammed in and about Medina. In eight years, however,
Mohammed had a following strong enough to enable him to
enter Mecca as a victor. He destroyed the idols in the city,
but spared the sacred black stone of the Kaaba. Before his
death (in 632) he had gained the support of many Arab
chiefs, and the new religion was spreading rapidly throughout
the whole Arabian peninsula. Mohammed called his religion
Islam, by which he meant "reconciliation," or submission to
the will of Allah, the sole God. His followers are called
Moslems (*Muslims*), or *Mohammedans.* From the first, Mohammedanism was a religion of conquest, which its members
justified as righteous since their enemies were "unbelievers."

The Mohammedan Bible, the Koran. Mohammed could probably neither write nor read well; but when, from time to time, he fell into trances, he would repeat to his eager listeners the words which he heard from heaven, and they, in turn, wrote them down. These sayings, which were collected into a volume shortly after his death, form the *Koran*, the Mohammedan Bible. This contains the chief beliefs of the new religion, as well as the laws under which all good Mohammedans were to live.

The Koran announces a day of judgment when the heavens shall be opened and the mountains be powdered and become like flying dust. Then all men shall receive their reward. Those who have refused to accept Islam shall be banished to hell, there to be burned and tormented forever. "They shall not taste therein coolness or drink, save scalding water," and the scalding water they shall drink like thirsty camels.

Those, on the other hand, who have obeyed the Koran, especially those who die fighting for Islam, shall find themselves in a garden of delight. They shall recline in rich brocades upon soft cushions and rugs and be served by surpassingly beautiful maidens,

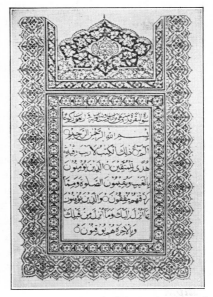

Fig. 89. *A Page of a Manuscript Copy of the Koran, the Bible of the Moslems*

This writing has descended from the ancient alphabet used by the Phœnicians (p. 127), and, like the Phœnician writing, it is still written and read from right to left. The Arab writers love to give their letters decorative flourishes, producing a handsome page. The rich ornamental border is a good example of Moslem art. The whole page was done by hand. In such handwritten books as these the educated Moslems wrote out translations of the books of the great Greek philosophers and scientists, like Aristotle. At the same time the Moslems wrote their own treatises on algebra, astronomy, grammar, and other sciences in similar books. These books later came to the knowledge of Christian scholars, who learned much from them

with eyes like hidden pearls. Wine may be drunk there, but
"their heads shall not ache with it, neither shall they be confused." They shall be content with their past life and shall
hear no foolish words; and there shall be no sin but only the
greeting, "Peace, peace."

The Mosque Unlike the Christian Church. The religion of
Mohammed was much simpler than that of the medieval
Christian Church; it did not have priests or any great number of ceremonies. The Mohammedan mosque, or temple, is
a house of prayer and a place for reading the Koran; no
altars or images or pictures of any kind are permitted in it.
Mosques are often extremely beautiful buildings, especially
in great Mohammedan cities such as Jerusalem, Damascus,
Cairo, and Constantinople. They have spacious courts surrounded by covered colonnades and are adorned with beautiful marbles and mosaics. The delightful windows are made
of bright stained glass. The walls are adorned with passages
from the Koran, and the floors are covered with rich rugs.
The mosques have one or more minarets, or towers, from
which the call to prayer is heard five times a day.

Rise of the Oriental Empire of the Moslems. The Moslem
leaders who succeeded to Mohammed's power were called
caliphs. As rulers they proved to be men of the greatest
ability. The caliphs organized the untamed desert nomads,
who now added a burning religious zeal to the wild courage of barbarian Arabs. This combination made the Arab
armies of the caliphs hard to defeat. Within a few years
after the death of Mohammed they took Egypt and Syria,
including Jerusalem and the Holy Land, from the feeble
successors of Justinian at Constantinople. They thus reduced the Eastern Empire to Asia Minor and a portion
of southeastern Europe (map, p. 411). The Arabs then
crushed the empire of the New Persians (p. 357) and brought
the Sassanian line of kings to an end (A.D. 640), after it had
lasted a little over four hundred years. Thus the Moslems
built up a great Oriental empire, with its center at the east
end of the Fertile Crescent.

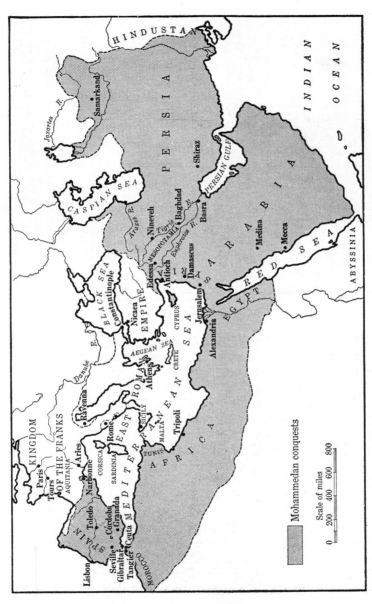

The Mohammedan Conquests at their Greatest Extent, about the Year 750

Fig. 90. *Interior of the Mosque at Cordova*

The Moslem Tribes learn to live in Cities. Just as the people of Sargon and Hammurapi adopted the higher civilization of the conquered Sumerians and learned to live in cities, so now the wandering Moslem Arabs of the desert took over the civilization of the New Persians. Indeed, the Arabs had a genius for adapting and preserving the civilizations with which they came in contact, much as the Romans had done. They had admired the beautiful buildings which they had seen in Egypt, Babylon, Assyria, and Persia. They now determined to have for themselves buildings which would rival these. With the ruins of Babylon looking down upon them, the Moslems established a splendid capital at Bagdad, beside the New Persian royal palace of Ctesiphon. The Mohammedans learned to read and write and so to put their sacred Koran in a form that all could read.

They learned the business of government and became experienced rulers. Thus alongside the shapeless mounds of the older capitals — Akkad, Babylon, and Ctesiphon — the

Fig. 91. *The Hall of Justice in the Alhambra, at Granada*

power and civilization of the Orient rose into new life for the last time. Bagdad became the finest city of the East. The caliphs extended their power eastward to the frontiers of India.

The Moslems invade Europe: the Battle of Tours. Westward the Moslems pushed along the African coast of the Mediterranean, as the Phœnicians, who were of the same race, had done so many centuries before (p. 127). Only two generations after the death of Mohammed the Arabs crossed over from Africa into Spain (A.D. 711). Here they overthrew the feeble kingdom of the West Goths (p. 378); then they moved on into France and threatened to surround the entire Mediterranean. At the battle of Tours (A.D. 732), however, they were checked by the army of the Franks (under Charles the Hammer). Unable to push farther westward, they withdrew permanently from France into Spain, where they established a western Moslem, or Moorish, kingdom.[1]

[1] The Mohammedans of northern Africa and those who crossed into Spain are commonly called Moors. The name "Morocco" still recalls this.

The Moslems develop a Higher Civilization. **The** Moorish kingdom developed a civilization far higher than that of the Franks, and, indeed, the highest in Europe of that age. While Europe was sinking into the ignorance of the Middle Ages, the Moslems were the leading students of such subjects as mathematics, astronomy, and grammar. There was soon much greater knowledge of these matters among the Moslems than in Christian Europe. Such common words as "algebra," "alcohol," "almanac," "coffee," "cotton," "mattress," "muslin," "sherbet," "sirup," and "sofa," and our figures, 1, 2, 3, 4, 5, 6, 7, 8, 9, 0, which we received from the Arabs, suggest to us how much we owe to them.

© Publishers' Photo Service

Fig. 92. *Part of the Mosque and Tower or Minaret at Seville*

This tower was built not long before 1200 out of the ruins of Roman and West Gothic buildings found here by the Moors. Blocks bearing Latin inscriptions are to be seen in a number of places in its walls. After alterations at the top by Christian architects it was converted into the bell tower of a Christian church

Some of the buildings which they erected soon after their arrival in Spain still stand. Among these is the mosque at Cordova, with its countless columns and arches.[1] They erected also a

[1] The huge mosque which the Mohammedan rulers built at Cordova (Fig. 90) was second in size only to the mosque at Mecca. The beautiful holy of holies is richly adorned with magnificent mosaics. The whole mosque is about the size of St. Peter's in Rome.

lofty tower at Seville (Fig. 92). The Mohammedans built beautiful palaces and laid out charming gardens. One of these palaces, the Alhambra (Fig. 91), built at Granada some centuries after they settled in Spain, is a marvel of loveliness. They founded also a famous university at Cordova, to which Christians from the North sometimes went to study.

Historians commonly regard it as exceedingly fortunate that Charles the Hammer and his barbarous soldiers succeeded in defeating and driving back the Mohammedans at Tours. But had the Moslems been permitted to settle in southern France, they might have developed science and art far more rapidly than did the Franks. It is difficult to say whether it was a good thing or a bad thing that the Moors, as the Mohammedans in Spain were called, did not get control of a portion of Gaul.

Questions and Exercises

REVIEW OF CHAPTER

1. What privileges did the Roman emperors grant the Christian clergy? How did the Church unite European peoples in a period of disorder? How would the Church have justified its intolerance of any religious beliefs other than its own? How did the Church come to play the part of a government? What were its chief duties?

2. Why was the Pope called the successor of Saint Peter? How was the Pope able to become the head of the Church? Tell something of Gregory the Great.

3. To what different kinds of people did the life of a monk appeal? Describe a monastery. How did the monks spend their time?

4. Describe the missionary work of the monks on the Continent. How was Britain reconverted to Christianity?

5. Compare the Mohammedan religion with Christianity. What countries did the Mohammedans conquer after Mohammed's death? Compare the Mohammedan conquests with those of the Romans.

USEFUL TERMS

See how much meaning you can give to the following: *orthodox, Catholic, heretic, monasticism, papacy, vigils, basilica, Islam, Koran, Moslem, Hegira. cloister.*

DIRECTIVE QUESTIONS

1. What is meant by "the See of Peter"? (Look this up.)

2. Why is the Pope called the Supreme Pontiff?

3. Why did the monks have to copy out books by hand?

4. Why has Rome been called the Eternal City?

5. England has two archbishops. One is the Archbishop of Canterbury. Can you find out the title of the other?

DISCUSSION TOPICS

1. Christianity was and is a missionary religion.

2. Churches are exempted from taxation. When did this practice start? Do you approve?

3. Is education controlled by the Church in America?

4. Does our government have an official religion?

5. Is religious freedom necessary?

6. Is religious freedom more than the right to your own religion? If religion were official, what should you be compelled to do that is not required now?

7. "America is the home of religious liberty." What does this mean?

ADDITIONAL ADVENTURES IN LEARNING

1. Studies in Source Materials. ROBINSON, *Readings*, Vol. I, chap. ii, sect. iii, "The Church and the Roman Emperors"; chap. iv, sect. i, "The Rise of the Papacy"; chap. v, sect. i, "The Monks"; chap. vi, sect. i, "Passages from the Koran."

2. Supplementary. Make a map of the Mohammedan conquests. What is a hermit? Read the account of Saint Anthony in an encyclopedia. For the experiences of the hermit Martin, see *Readings*, chap. v, sect. ii, 37.

3. Look up in an encyclopedia: Venerable Bede; Benedictines; Mohammedan art, especially buildings and mosaics. Can you find the pictures of any famous monasteries?

4. Write a short account of Mohammed and his religion. For further reference helps, see bibliography for Chapter XX.

CHAPTER XXI · HOW FEUDALISM DEVELOPED IN AN AGE OF DISORDER

A BISHOP who lived during the Age of Disorder described the people of Europe as divided into three classes: the nobility, who did the fighting; the clergy, who did the praying; and the others, who did the work. This little summary shows us that as early as Charlemagne's time people had already begun to fall into large social groups based on the way they spent their time.

The clergy was described in the previous chapter. The present chapter tells how the other two classes, the *nobility* and the *serfs*, developed. The disorder and danger of the early Middle Ages, and the inability of the kings to keep peace within their realms or protect them from enemies without, led to the growth of a class of persons whose main occupation was to fight. They fought invaders, they protected their followers, and too often they fought each other. These fighters, because of their high station, were called nobles (from *nobilitas*). They did no manual work but lived on the income from their estates. Charlemagne and other kings were wont to pay their officials with grants of land and other privileges rather than with money. In this way land became the most important form of wealth. The feudal system was a system in which great landowners obtained the help of other men by granting them part of their land and so making *them also* independent and free to fight. In this way there grew up a large landowning class which, because of its independence and wealth, formed the upper, or privileged, class and is called the *nobility*.

The rest of the people, other than the clergy, were peasants, who were farmers on the estates of the rich and did many other kinds of work to provide for all the needs of their masters and themselves. These workers, or *serfs*, labored long and hard and got little in return.

1. DIFFICULTIES OF CHARLEMAGNE IN FOUNDING AN EMPIRE

Pepin becomes King of the Franks. We have seen how the kings of the Franks, Clovis and his successors, conquered a large territory including what is today western Germany and France. For two centuries or more this land was fought over and parceled out among rival heirs. It is a long story of bloodshed and cruelty into which we need not go. As time went on, the Frankish kings were too weak, dissipated, or lazy to take proper care of their realms themselves, and the real business of governing fell to the chief official of the royal household. This was the *Major Domus*, or Mayor of the Palace. This chief steward not only had charge of the royal estates and handled the taxes but led the army to war. He was thus in a fortunate position to increase his own wealth and power and, moreover, was looked upon by those who fought under him as the real leader of the state. Finally, in the seventh century, one of the ambitious Frankish "mayors" succeeded in getting this office made hereditary in his family. It was now only a step to take over the kingship itself and get rid of a useless and "do-nothing" line of rulers. This is just what was done by Pepin, the son of that Charles the Hammer who, as Mayor of the Palace, had checked the Mohammedans at Tours (p. 413).

Before taking this bold and dangerous step, however, Pepin wisely decided to make sure that he had the support of the Church. He therefore consulted the Pope, who replied that the one who had the real power was the one who should be king. Upon the approval of Rome the Frankish dukes and counts rallied to Pepin's cause and raised him upon their shields to signify that they accepted his leadership. Pepin was thereupon anointed and crowned king of the Franks. The Pope gave his blessing to the new ruler as "God's anointed." The old line of kings which was displaced by Pepin is known as the Merovingian line, named for an early Frankish king. Pepin and his successors are called the Carolingian line, from Charlemagne, the most famous member of the dynasty.

It was not long before Pepin was able to repay the Pope handsomely for his assistance. The Lombards, who had for years been a danger to Rome, were again attacking the city. When the Pope appealed to the Frankish king for help, Pepin set out for Italy, drove out the Lombards, and presented the Pope with a wide strip of land extending from Ravenna, on the Adriatic, across Italy to a point south of Rome. This territory, over which the Popes thereafter ruled like other sovereigns, was known as the Papal States.

FIG. 93. *At the Battle of Tours* (A.D. 732)

Charlemagne builds up an Empire. It was the dream of Pepin's famous son, Charlemagne, however, to bring all the German peoples together into one great Christian empire.[1] The ideal of a vast Roman Empire uniting all Europe had never died out, and Charlemagne spent most of his long reign of nearly fifty years (A.D. 768–814) in trying to make this dream come true. Charlemagne's first military expedition was into Italy. Summoned by the Pope to protect him from his old enemies the Lombards, Charlemagne invaded Lombardy (773), took possession of the capital at Pavia, sent the Lombard king to a monastery, and the next year had himself acknowledged by all the Italian counts and dukes as king of the Lombards.

Charlemagne turned his attention a few years later to Spain, where certain dissatisfied Mohammedans sought his aid against the Emir of Cordova.[2] Charles, hoping to Christianize this pagan region, crossed the Pyrenees in 778. After some years of hard fighting he succeeded in conquering a wide district north of the Ebro, later known as the Spanish *March* (meaning border, or boundary). Charlemagne's achievement marked the beginning of a long and gradual expulsion of the Mohammedans from the Spanish peninsula.

The Conquest of the Saxons. To the east Charlemagne conquered the Bavarians and added their possessions to his realms. After several years he was able to push his boundaries still further eastward by overcoming the Avars. But the most difficult of all his military undertakings was that of subduing the Saxons, who occupied the region lying east of Cologne and extending to the Elbe. These people were still pagans and appear to have lived much the same way they did when the Roman historian Tacitus described them seven centuries earlier. They had no towns or roads and were thus very difficult to conquer, as they could retreat with their few

[1] "Charlemagne" is the French form for the Latin name *Carolus Magnus* (Charles the Great). We must never forget, however, that Charlemagne was not French: he spoke a German language, namely, Frankish; and his favorite palaces — at Aix-la-Chapelle (Aachen), Ingelheim, and Nimwegen — were located in German regions.

[2] The caliphate broke up in the eighth century, and the ruler of Spain first assumed the title of "Emir" (about 756) and later (929) that of "Caliph."

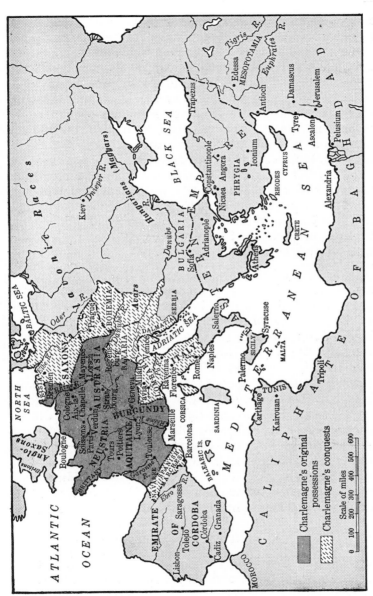

Europe in the Time of Charlemagne

possessions into the forests or swamps as soon as they found
themselves unable to meet an invader in the open field. Yet
as long as they remained unsubdued they constantly threatened the borders of the Frankish realms. Besides, their country was needed to round out the Frankish boundaries.

Charles believed it was his duty to Christianize these pagans by any means, however harsh. Although he defeated the
Saxons from time to time in battle, he had to return again
and again as rebellion broke out or the Saxons were guilty of
massacre. Before the Frankish conquest the Saxons had had
no towns; but after Charlemagne was able finally to bring
them under his control (about 803) settlements began to form
around the church of a bishop or about a monastery, and
cities finally grew up. A century after they had submitted to
Charlemagne's rule, the Saxons became the leading Germanic
people in Europe.

Charlemagne crowned Emperor by the Pope. By the year 800
Charlemagne had managed to bring most of western Europe
under his control. No ruler had governed such a vast territory since the days of the Empire. Indeed, it included all the
Western Empire except England, Mohammedan Spain, and
southern Italy. In the year 800 Charlemagne was called to
Rome to help Pope Leo III, who was heartily disliked at
Rome, to settle his disputes with his enemies. To celebrate
the satisfactory outcome of the trouble, the Pope held a
solemn service in St. Peter's on Christmas Day. As Charlemagne was kneeling before the altar, the Pope, without warning, approached him and placed a crown upon his head,
saluting him, amid the acclamation of those present, as "Emperor of the Romans." This extraordinary act had important
consequences; for, as we shall see, the Popes from this time
on claimed the right of making and unmaking emperors.

2. Renewal of Disorder

Break-up of Charlemagne's Empire. It would have taxed
the powers of the gifted and untiring Charlemagne to govern
successfully these vast dominions, but it was quite impossible
for any of the rulers who followed him to do so. Charle-

Map of Treaty of Verdun

This map shows the division of Charlemagne's empire made in 843 by his grandsons in the Treaty of Verdun

magne's empire passed on intact to his son, Louis the Pious. On his death his sons fought over its partition. By the Treaty of Verdun (843) they divided the empire into three kingdoms. Charles took the West Frankish kingdom, Louis the East Frankish kingdom, and Lothair received a middle kingdom which included central and northern Italy and a wedge of territory separating the other two kingdoms. By the Treaty of Mersen (870) this wedge, separated only a few years before from Italy, was split between the East and West Frankish kingdoms.

The significance of the Treaty of Verdun is that its divisions happened to "stick." It outlined the future map of western Europe. The territory of the middle kingdom was to be fought over for centuries and to cause trouble down to modern times. Out of the West Frankish realm France was to develop. The speech of its people was derived from the *spoken* Latin. This Latinized speech finally developed into French as we know it today. The East Frankish kingdom was the beginning of Germany. Never having been Romanized, it was German in language and customs. In Italy the spoken Latin of the people finally developed into Italian.

Many Causes for Disorder. Although each main division of the empire was finally to grow into one of the great states of modern Europe, hundreds of years were to elapse before the kings of these realms got sufficient power to control their subjects and establish orderly and unified governments.

In the first place, the king found it very hard to get quickly from one part of his realms to another. No new roads had been built during the long period of fighting, and the fine roads which the Romans had so carefully made were now mostly in ruins. Many of the bridges had been washed away by floods. So the king had to go by foot or on horseback, for he had no trains or automobiles to carry him. His army had to make its way over rough and difficult country before it could put down a rebellion in a distant part of his lands.

There was another and more serious difficulty, one that had important consequences for the king: he had very little money. There were not many gold or silver mines in western Europe, and there was no supply of precious metals coming from other countries, for business had largely died out since the days of the Roman Empire. How, then, could the king pay his officials to carry on the government and keep order, and how could he support an army if he had no treasury to draw on? All he had to give the important counts and dukes who brought their own followers to fight for him was *land*. The kings had to give away so much land for the assistance they received that the nobles often became richer and more powerful than the kings themselves.

Origin of Titles of Nobility. The officials upon whom the Frankish kings were forced to rely chiefly were the counts, who were supposed to be the "hand and voice of the king" wherever he could not be in person. They were expected to maintain order, see that the laws were kept in their district, and raise troops when the king needed them. On the frontier

FIG. 94. *The Amphitheater at Arles in the Middle Ages*

The great Roman amphitheater at Arles (built probably in the first or second century) is about fifteen hundred feet in circumference. During the eighth century, when the Mohammedans were invading southern France, it was converted into a fortress. Many of the inhabitants lived inside its walls, and towers were constructed which still stand. This picture shows it before the buildings were removed in 1830

were the counts of the "march," or margraves (marquises). These titles, together with that of "duke," still exist as titles of nobility in Europe. Those who hold them, however, have no longer any governmental duties except in cases where they have the right to membership in the upper house of Parliament.

New Invasions. Another source of trouble for the kings was the frequent invasion from every direction, which kept the three parts of Charlemagne's empire, and England as well, in a constant state of terror and disaster. These new invasions were almost as serious as those which had occurred before Charlemagne's time. They prevented western Europe from becoming peaceful and prosperous, and serve to explain the unsettled period of two hundred years which followed the break-up of Charlemagne's empire.

In the first place the Mohammedans who had conquered Spain got control of the island of Sicily shortly after Charlemagne's death and continued to terrorize Italy and southern France. Even Rome itself suffered from them. Fig. 94 shows how the people of Arles, in the southern part of France, built their houses inside the old Roman amphitheater in order to protect themselves from these Mohammedan invaders.

On the east the German rulers had constantly to fight the Slavs. Charlemagne, as we have seen, had defeated them in his time; but they continued to make much trouble for at least two centuries more. Then there were also the Hungarians, a savage race from Asia, who overran Germany and northern Italy and whose wild horsemen penetrated even into the West Frankish kingdom. Finally they were driven back eastward and settled in the country now named after them — Hungary.

The Northmen. Lastly there came the Northmen, bold and adventurous pirates from the shores of Denmark, Sweden, and Norway. These skillful and daring seamen not only attacked the towns on the coast of the West Frankish kingdom but made their way up the rivers, plundering and burning the villages and towns as far inland as Paris.[1]

So there was danger always and everywhere. If rival nobles were not fighting one another, there were foreign invaders of some kind laying waste the country and robbing, maltreating, and enslaving the people whom they found in the towns and villages and monasteries. No wonder that strong castles had to be built and the towns surrounded by walls! Even the monasteries were in some cases protected by fortifications.

3. How Feudalism afforded Some Protection

Feudalism a System of Defense. It is hard for us who live in a well-governed land to imagine how helpless one would feel in the midst of such confusion, danger, and insecurity as we have just described. There was, of course, neither a police

[1] These Scandinavian pirates are often called *vikings*, from their habit of leaving their long boats in the *vik*, which meant in their language "bay," or "inlet."

Fig. 95. *Coucy-le-Château*

This castle of Coucy-le-Château was built by a subject of the king of France in the thirteenth century. It was at the end of a hill and protected on all sides but one by steep cliffs. One can see the moat (*A*) and the double drawbridge and towers which protected the portal. The round donjon (*B*) was probably the largest in the world, one hundred feet in diameter and two hundred and ten feet high. At the base its walls were thirty-four feet thick. At the end of the inner court (*C*) was the residence of the lord (*D*). To the left of the court was a great hall, and to the right were the quarters of the garrison. This ancient building was destroyed during the World War

system such as we have to keep order in the kingdom nor a strong army to guard the boundaries against invaders. Since the king was not able to protect them, men had to find some way of standing together to defend themselves. So it came about that an individual would attach himself to some stronger man in his community and promise to fight for him; or a noble who had only a few followers would put himself at the service of a more powerful noble, in return for his protection. In this way the relation of *lord* and *vassal* grew up, and this system of leaders and followers is called the *feudal system*. Its name means a system based not on feuds, or fighting, but on the *fief* (Latin *feodum*, *feudum*), or grant of land.

The Feudal System based on Land. We have seen how kings who had little money were sometimes forced to give the nobles part of the royal lands as payment for their services. In the same way, landholders with large estates who were in need of strong men to fight for them found it to their advantage to grant the use of part of their property on certain conditions. The one who received the land (the vassal) must swear to be loyal to the giver, fight for him when he was in need, and lend him aid when other difficulties arose. The lord, or *suzerain*, on his part, not only gave the vassal the use of his land but also agreed to protect him when necessary. Land granted on these terms was called a *fief*.

One who held a fief larger than he needed might himself become a lord by granting a portion to a vassal upon terms similar to those upon which he held his own lands of his lord. The vassal of a vassal was called a *subvassal*.

The feudal system was not established by any decree of a king nor because of any general agreement among landholders. It grew up gradually because it seemed the most satisfactory way of meeting the difficulties and dangers of the times. It rested not on written laws but on promises, custom, and the principle of honor.

The Ceremony of Homage. Upon becoming a vassal there was a picturesque ceremony in which the vassal knelt before the lord and rendered him *homage*[1] by placing his hands

---

[1] "Homage" is derived from the Latin word *homo*, meaning "man."

between those of the lord and declaring himself the lord's "man" for such and such a fief. Thereupon the lord gave his vassal the kiss of peace and raised him from his kneeling posture. Then the vassal swore an oath of fidelity upon the Bible or some holy object, solemnly binding himself to fulfill all his duties toward his lord. This act of rendering homage by placing the hands in those of the lord and taking the oath of fidelity was the first and most important duty of the vassal (p. 368). For a vassal to refuse to do homage for his fief when he received it amounted to a declaration of revolt and independence.

Duties of a Vassal. Several forms of service were expected by a lord of his vassal. In the first place, he must join him when he went to war. It was understood, however, that the vassal need not serve at his own expense for more than forty days. In the second place, the vassal had to attend the lord's court, where he and his fellow vassals had to hear cases and assist their lord in administering justice.

Under certain conditions vassals had to make money payments to their lord; for instance, when the lord was required to meet the expenses involved in knighting his eldest son or in providing a marriage dowry for his daughter, or when he was captured by an enemy and was held for ransom. Lastly, a vassal might be obliged to entertain his lord should he be passing the vassal's castle. There are amusing accounts in some of the feudal agreements of exactly how often the lord might visit his vassal, how many followers he might bring, and what he should have to eat during his stay.

Complications of the Feudal System. There were fiefs of all sizes and of all grades of importance, from that of a duke or count, who had received his fief from the king himself and who had the powers of a practically independent prince, down to the fief of the simple knight, whose bit of land, cultivated by peasants or serfs, was barely sufficient to enable him to support himself and provide the horse upon which he rode to perform his military service for his lord.

It was perfectly possible for a man to hold fiefs of several lords and, in turn, to grant his lands to as many vassals as could be obtained for the amount of land he himself had to offer. This subdivision of fiefs proved very confusing. Moreover, it is easy to see that where a vassal had promised allegiance to several lords it might on occasion be a difficult matter to choose which one to be faithful to, especially if the lords happened to be fighting against one another.

How Land became Hereditary. It is important to observe that the fief was not granted for a fixed number of years, or simply for the life of the vassal, to go back at his death to the owner. On the contrary, it became *hereditary* in the family of the vassal and passed down to the eldest son from one generation to another. So long as the vassal and his heirs remained faithful to the lord and performed the services they had agreed upon, *neither the lord nor his heirs could rightfully regain possession of the land.*

The result was that little was left to the original owner of the fief except the services and dues to which the vassal had agreed in receiving it. In short, the fief came really to belong to the vassal, and the lord was owner in name only. Nowadays the owner of land either makes some use of it himself or leases it for a definite period at a fixed money rent. But in the Middle Ages most of the land was held by vassals who neither really owned it outright nor paid a regular rent for it, and yet who could not be deprived of it by the real owner or his successors so long as they performed the services they had agreed upon.

The Nobility become more Powerful than the King. The great vassals who held their land directly from the king became almost independent of him as soon as their fiefs were granted to them and their descendants. Their vassals, since they had not done homage to the king himself, often paid little attention to his commands. From the ninth to the thirteenth century the king of France or the king of Germany did not rule over a great realm occupied by subjects who owed him obedience as their lawful sovereign, paid him taxes, and were bound to fight under his banner as the head of the state. As a feudal landlord himself, the king had a right to demand fidelity and certain services only from those who were his vassals. But the great mass of the people over whom he ruled in name, whether they belonged to the nobility or not, owed little to the king directly, because they lived upon the lands of other feudal lords more or less independent of him.

The Kings finally get the Better of the Feudal Lords. Yet we must not think that the state ceased to exist altogether during the centuries of confusion that followed the break-up of Charlemagne's empire, or that it fell entirely apart into little local governments independent of each other. In the first place, a king always retained some of his ancient majesty. He might be weak and without the means to enforce his rights and to compel his more powerful subjects to perform their duties toward him. Yet he was, after all, the *king*, solemnly anointed by the Church as God's representative on earth. He was always something more than a feudal lord. Before many centuries the kings were to get the upper hand in England, France, and Spain, and finally in Italy and Germany, and to destroy the castles behind whose walls their haughty nobles had long defied the royal power.

Neighborhood Warfare. One has only to read an account of the time to discover that brute force governed almost everything outside of the Church. The feudal obligations were not fulfilled except when the lord was sufficiently powerful to enforce them. The oath of fidelity was constantly broken by both vassal and lord, who paid little attention to their solemn promises.

We may say that war, in all its forms, was the law of the feudal world. War formed the chief occupation of the restless nobles who held the land and were supposed to govern it. An ambitious vassal was likely to make war, first, upon each of the lords to whom he had done homage; secondly, upon the bishops and abbots with whom he was brought into contact, and whose control he particularly disliked; thirdly, upon his fellow vassals; and lastly, upon his own vassals. The feudal bonds, instead of offering a guarantee of peace and concord, appear to have been a constant cause of violent ill-feeling and conflict. Everyone seemed bent upon profiting to the full by the permanent or temporary weakness of his neighbor.

In theory, the lord could force his vassals to settle their disputes in an orderly manner before his court; but often he was neither able nor inclined to bring about a peaceful agreement, and he would frequently have found it hard to carry out the decisions of his own court if he had wished to do so. So the vassals were left to fight out their quarrels among themselves, and they found their chief interest in life in so doing.

Justs and Tourneys. Justs and tourneys were military exercises — play wars — to fill out the tiresome periods which occasionally occurred between real wars. They were, in fact, small battles in which whole troops of hostile nobles sometimes took part. These rough plays were condemned by the Popes and even by the kings. The latter, however, were much too fond of the sport not to take part themselves.

The Truce of God. The horrors of this constant fighting led the Church to try to check it. About the year 1000 several church councils in southern France declared that the fighters were not to attack churches or monasteries, churchmen, pilgrims, merchants, and women, and that they must leave the peasant and his cattle and plow alone. Then church councils began to decree what was known as the "Truce of God," which provided that all warfare was to stop during Lent and various other holy days, as well as on Thursday, Friday, Saturday, and Sunday of every week. During the truce no one was to attack anyone else. Those besieging castles were to cease from any assaults during the period of peace, and people were to be allowed to go quietly to and fro on their business without being disturbed by soldiers.

If anyone failed to observe the truce, he was to be *excommunicated*, that is, cast out of the Church. If he fell sick no Christian should dare to visit him, and on his deathbed he was not to receive the comfort of a priest, and his soul was condemned to hell if he had refused to repent and mend his ways. It is hard to say how much good the Truce of God accomplished. Some of the bishops and even the heads of great monasteries liked fighting pretty well themselves. It is certain that many disorderly lords paid little attention to the truce and found three days a week altogether too short a time for plaguing their neighbors.

4. Life in the Feudal Age

Nobles and Serfs. The incessant warfare and constant necessity for protection produced a class of persons whose only business was fighting. These nobles, both lords and vassals, did no work, but relied upon their farms to supply enough for their own needs, and often had enough land to turn over part to others who used it for the same purpose. At the top of feudal society therefore developed this large landowning class, who believed it beneath them to work. When not fighting they lived on their estates, which the rest of the people (peasants) farmed for them. These peasants had to do all the work, which included many other things beside farming, and got along themselves as best they could. They were called *serfs*.

How the Nobles Lived; the Castle. As one travels through England, France, or Germany today he often comes upon the picturesque ruins of a medieval castle perched upon some rocky cliff and overlooking the surrounding country for miles. As he looks at the thick walls and great towers he may well wonder why so many of these forts were built and why people lived in them. But when he recalls the danger and disorder which overtook Europe in the Middle Ages after the various invasions, he can see that it was necessary for persons not only to be ready to fight on occasion but also to have some fortified place in which to live in case of attack.

The Romans had been accustomed to build walls around their camps, which were called *castra*; in the names of such places as Rochester, Winchester, Gloucester, Worcester, we have reminders of the fact that these towns were once fortresses. These camps, however, were all *government* fortifications, and did not belong to private individuals.

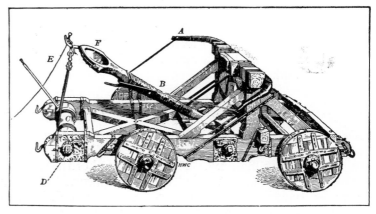

Fig. 96. *Machine for Hurling Stones*

This machine was a medieval device for throwing stones and bolts of iron, which were often heated red-hot before they were fired. It consisted of a great bow (*A*) and the beam (*B*), which was drawn back by the windlass (*C*), turned by a crank applied at the point *D*. Then a stone was put in the pocket (*F*), and the trigger pulled by means of the string (*E*). This let the beam fly up with a bang against the bumper, and the stone went sailing against the wall or else over it among the defenders of the castle

But as the Roman Empire grew weaker, and the disorder caused by the incoming barbarians became greater, the various counts and dukes and even other landowners commenced to build forts for themselves. At first these were only wooden buildings on top of a great mound of earth encircled by a deep ditch and by a wall constructed of stakes interwoven with twigs.

But as the method of warfare changed it was found that wooden castles were not strong enough to withstand attack, and stone towers were put up instead. The Romans had used machines to hurl great stones and stakes when besieging a walled town. The barbarian invaders had not used these machines; but about the year 1100 the stone-throwers were introduced again into European warfare from the Eastern Empire, and it was found that only stone would withstand their assault. Square towers were built until it was realized that round towers were harder to batter down; and so these became common as time went on.

Arrangement of a Castle. When the castle was not on a steep, rocky hill, which made it very hard to approach, a deep ditch, called the *moat,* was constructed outside the walls. This was filled with water and crossed by a bridge, which could be drawn up when the castle was attacked, leaving no way of getting across. The doorway was further protected by a grating of heavy wood or iron bars, called the *portcullis,* which could be quickly dropped down to close the entrance or to crush an enemy as he tried to enter the castle. Inside the castle walls was the great *donjon,*

Fig. 97. A Fortified Gate of a Medieval Castle

Here one can see the way in which the entrance to a castle was carefully protected : the moat (*A*); the drawbridge (*B*) ; the portcullis (*C*)

or chief tower, which had several stories. There was sometimes also a fine hall, as at Coucy, and handsome rooms for the use of the lord and his family ; but sometimes they lived in the donjon. There were buildings for storing supplies and arms, and usually a chapel.

The Vill, or Manor. The owner of a castle had, of course, to obtain supplies to support his family and servants and the armed men who stayed on the estate. The medieval estates were called *vills* or *manors* and closely resembled the Roman "villas" that had existed in former centuries. The peasants who tilled the soil were called *villeins,* a word derived from "vill." A portion of the estate was reserved for the lord's use, while the rest of the land was divided among the peasants for their own farming.

Fig. 98. *Serfs Treading Grapes in September*

From Queen Mary's Psalter, early fourteenth century. (Courtesy of the British Museum)

How the Serfs Lived. The peasants were generally serfs (from Latin *servus*, meaning "servant" or "slave"), who did not own their fields, but could not, on the other hand, be deprived of them so long as they worked for the lord and paid him certain dues. They were not free, but were regarded as belonging with the land and so passed from one master to another when the land changed hands. The serfs were required to till those fields which the lord reserved for himself and to gather in his crops. They might not marry without their lord's permission. Their wives and daughters helped with the indoor work of the manor house. In the women's buildings the women serfs engaged in spinning, weaving, sewing, baking, and brewing, thus producing clothes, food, and drink for the whole community.

We get our clearest ideas of the position of the serfs from the ancient descriptions of manors, which give an exact account of what each member of a particular community owed to the lord. For example, we find that the abbot of Peterborough held a manor upon which Hugh Miller and seventeen other serfs, mentioned by name, were required to work for him three days in each week during the whole year, except one week at Christmas, one at Easter, and one at Whitsuntide. Each serf was to give the lord abbot one bushel of wheat and eighteen sheaves of oats, three hens, and one

FIG. 99. *The Castle of Pierrefonds*

This great feudal castle, not very far from Paris, was built by the brother of the
king of France about 1400. It has been very carefully restored in modern times
and gives one a good idea of the way in which the feudal lords lived. Pierrefonds
was one of the strongest and handsomest of the castles of that period. Its eight
massive towers, one hundred and twelve feet in height, have walls from fifteen
to twenty feet thick. Within the walls of the castle are a handsome central
courtyard and magnificent apartments

cock yearly, and five eggs at Easter. If he sold his horse
for more than ten shillings, he was to give the said abbot
fourpence.

One of the most striking characteristics of the manor was
its independence of the rest of the world. It produced nearly
everything that its members needed, and might have continued to exist almost indefinitely without communication
with those who lived beyond its bounds. Little or no money
was necessary, for the peasants paid what was due to the
lord in the form of labor and farm products. They also
helped one another and found little occasion for buying and
selling.

But there was almost no opportunity to better one's condition, and life must have gone on, generation after generation,
in a weary routine. The life was not merely monotonous, —

it was wretched. The food was coarse, and there was little variety, as the peasants did not even take pains to raise many kinds of fruit and vegetables. The houses usually had but one room, which was ill-lighted by a single little window and had no chimney.

How the Increased Use of Money Destroyed Serfdom. When, in the twelfth and thirteenth centuries, towns began to grow up, and goods were made and bought and sold, money began to be used once more as it had been in Greek and Roman times. The increased use of money tended to break up the manor. The old habit of trading one thing for another without the use of money began to disappear. As time went on, neither the lord nor the serf was satisfied with the old system, which had answered well enough in the time of Charlemagne. The serfs, on the one hand, began to get money from the sale of their products in the markets of neighboring towns. They soon found it more profitable to pay the lord a certain sum instead of working for him, for they then had time to attend to their own farms.

The landlords, on the other hand, found it to their advantage to accept money in place of the services of their tenants. With this money the landlord could hire laborers to cultivate his fields and could buy the luxuries which were brought to his notice as manufacturing and business increased. So it came about that the lords gradually gave up their control over the peasants, and there was no longer very much difference between the serf and the freeman who paid a regular rent for his land. A serf might also gain his liberty by running away from his manor to a town. If he remained undiscovered, or was unclaimed by his lord for a year and a day, he became a freeman.

It took a long time, however, to get rid of the medieval feudal system. Nobles continued to be disorderly and oppressive, and serfdom lingered on in some countries into the nineteenth century. Reformers had constantly to fight for the abolition of various evils which had their origin in the Middle Ages, and this explains why the word "medieval" has a bad sound to many people.

Questions and Exercises

REVIEW OF CHAPTER

1. Tell how Pepin became king of the Franks. What special importance had his coronation? How did Charlemagne build up an empire? What were the difficulties of a ruler in the early Middle Ages?

2. Give some results of the lack of money in the early Middle Ages. How was land used to pay government officials? What were the causes of a renewal of disorder? Who were the new invaders? How did the titles of nobility originate?

3. Describe the origin of feudalism. What was the position of the serfs? How did feudalism weaken the power of the kings? What did the Church do about neighborhood warfare? What was the Truce of God?

4. Describe the life of a noble, of a serf. Tell about medieval castles. What effect had the increased use of money on serfdom?

USEFUL TERMS

See how much meaning you can give to the following terms: *suzerain, feudalism, fief, homage, vassal, subvassal, Major Domus, hereditary, manor, excommunicate.*

DIRECTIVE QUESTIONS

1. How do countries protect their citizens today against invasion?

2. Who furnishes the armies today?

3. Give an account of the nobles in Egypt and in Greece. (Look up earlier chapters in this book.)

4. Was money used in Greek and Roman times? Why not in the Middle Ages?

DISCUSSION TOPICS

1. Money is a better means of exchange than land.

2. Vassals belonged to a different class of society from serfs; yet both were granted the use of land by feudal lords.

3. Though they did not go to war, the serfs had a harder life than the vassals.

4. The custom of anointing a king was an old one. (See the Bible and an encyclopedia.)

5. The vikings were pirates.

6. Charlemagne could not write. What about other kings in the Middle Ages?

ADDITIONAL ADVENTURES IN LEARNING

1. Studies in Source Materials. ROBINSON, *Readings*, Vol. I, chap. vii, sect. i, "Charlemagne's personal appearance and habits"; sect. iii, "How Charlemagne was made Emperor"; sect. vi, "Charlemagne's Ideals of Government"; sect. vii, Charlemagne's interest in education.

Prepare a short account of Charlemagne, choosing your facts from source materials only. See also *The Early Lives of Charlemagne by Eginhard and the Monk of St. Gall,* translated by A. J. Grant.

Write a paragraph on the value of annals as a historical source (*Readings*, p. 147).

Chap. ix, sect. i, The origins of feudalism; sects. ii–v, Feudal customs and ceremonies.

2. Supplementary. Make a list of the titles of nobility you can discover, and try to find their origin. Are such titles used today?

Look up in an encyclopedia money and its uses; also castles, noting especially the pictures of fortified castles from the Middle Ages.

3. Topical Studies. How the nobles lived: DAVIS, *Life on a Medieval Barony*; TAPPAN, *In Feudal Times.* Armor and weapons in the Middle Ages: E. L. CUTTS, *Scenes and Characters of the Middle Ages,* Part II. The Vikings: encyclopedia; A. MAWER, *The Vikings.* How the peasants lived: SALZMANN, *English Life in the Middle Ages,* chap. ii; TAPPAN, *In Feudal Times,* chap. vi.

CHAPTER XXII · THE RIVALRY
OF POPES AND EMPERORS

ORIGIN OF THE HOLY ROMAN EMPIRE · HOW THE CHURCHMEN BECAME FEUDAL LORDS ·
THE STRUGGLE OVER INVESTITURE · EFFECTS OF THE STRUGGLE BETWEEN POPES AND
EMPERORS ON GERMANY AND ITALY

IN THE previous chapter we saw how the kings of the Franks and the Popes at Rome established friendly relations. We saw how a Frankish noble sought the blessing of the Pope before proclaiming himself king; how the Pope asked the help of the new king against his enemies and was given the lands which the Frankish king conquered in Italy; how a Pope crowned a king "Emperor of the Romans" and hailed him as "Augustus" and "Caesar."

These seemingly innocent arrangements had far-reaching results. In the first place, the Pope, by virtue of his new possessions, became a sovereign prince like any other ruler in Europe. In the second place, the king, in receiving the Pope's blessing, was from this time on looked upon as "God's anointed." There soon grew up the idea that there was a sacred character to kingship and that a sovereign ruled his people as God's representative. On the other hand, the Pope, in assuming the power to crown an emperor, raised himself to a position above all earthly monarchs. As long as the Popes and emperors were friends, all went well. The kings went to Rome to be crowned by the head of the Church. The Popes did not hesitate to call upon earthly rulers to keep them out of their troubles. The kings and feudal lords gave lands freely to the Church, but expected in return the support of the Church and the privilege of taking part in the appointment of its officials

It is the object of this chapter to show how the emperors, who were at the head of the government, came into bitter conflict with the head of the Church. The emperors demanded the right to have a hand in selecting the important churchmen, even the Pope himself. The Pope denied this right, and declared religion was far more important than government. In this way there arose the question of the relation of Church and State, which has been a troublesome problem down to the present day. In most countries the matter has now been adjusted by their separation. The Church is to take care of the religious interests of the people; the state is to keep the peace, defend its citizens, and make laws for them.

1. ORIGIN OF THE HOLY ROMAN EMPIRE

German Kings seek the Support of the Church. In spite of the invasions and disorder which distracted Europe, the ideal of a great Roman Empire uniting all peoples never wholly died out. Ambitious rulers who were successful in conquering their neighbors and increasing their realms naturally began to dream of reviving the Western Empire and placing themselves at its head. Rome, though no longer the capital of an empire, was still the most famous city of the West. There dwelt the Pope, the head of the Universal Church. For a king to secure the Pope's approval of an undertaking amounted to having the blessing of Heaven in the eyes of his Christian followers. When, therefore, Pepin decided to proclaim himself king of the Franks and do away with the reigning line of kings, he first made sure that he had the support of the Pope. In acknowledging the new king as "God's anointed," the Pope asserted the power of the Church to determine who was the rightful ruler of a people. But when, later, the Pope actually crowned Charlemagne as "Emperor of the Romans," he assumed the power to appoint the emperor himself.

The coronation of Charlemagne had two important consequences which we must now consider. One had to do with the affairs of government only, the revival of the Empire in the West; the other, with the relation of the Church to the state. For from the time of Charlemagne the Popes assumed the right to deprive an emperor of his realms as well as to allow him to take office. We shall see how this high claim resulted in a bitter conflict between the emperors and Popes in the attempt of each to establish his superiority over the other.

Otto I builds up a Strong Kingdom in Germany. Charlemagne's empire soon fell apart after his death, as we have seen. His successors in the German part of his empire found it quite as hard as did the kings of his western, or French, realms to keep control of their vassals. Germany, like France, was divided into big and little fiefs, and the dukes and counts who held them were continually waging war upon each other and upon their kings.

EUROPE

ABOUT A. D. 1000

0   100   200   300

Scale of Miles.

Longitude   West   5   from Greenwich

M.-N. ENG., BUFFALO.

LITHUANIANS

55

OF DENMARK

Roskilde   Lund

leswig   Bornholm

Rugen

Minsk

BILLINGS MARK

Kolberg   Danzig

PRUSSIANS

Stettin

POMERANIA (To Poland)

Pinsk   Pripet

Tchernigov

NORTH MARK

avelburg   Brandenburg

deburg

Vistula   Plock

Gnesen

R   S   S   I   A

Kiev (Kiew)

50

in   Halberstadt

EAST MARK

erseburg (Lusatia)

URINGIA   Meissen

Erfurt

Posen

DUCHY

Oder

OF

POLAND

Krakow

Belsk

Haliac

Dniester

 MARK OF MEISSEN

DUCHY OF

Prague   Olmütz

BOHEMIA

Brünn

MARK OF MORAVIA

CROATIA

Erlau

MARK OF urzburg NORDGAU

ichstadt   Regensburg

Danube

MARK OF VERONA

Pressburg

Gran

Pruth

rance   Freising

Augsburg D Y OF AUSTRIA

Salzburg

StuBlweissenburg

H   U   N   G   A   R   Y

TRANSYLVANIA

45

BAVARIA

Brixen

D Y OF CARINTHIA

Villach

Belluno

Maros

Danube

PETCHENEGS (PATZINAKS)

Trent

MARK OF VERONA

antua

Aquileia

Drave

Fünfkirchen

Venice

K. OF

Save

Sirmium

Belgrade

Varna

Canossa

ologna

ROMAGNA

Ravenna

VENETIAN POSSESSIONS

Zara

CROATIA

Vidin

Nicopolis   Periathlava

Tirnovo

lorence

TUSCANY

SPOLETO

Ancona

Spalato

SERBIA

Nissa

Triaditza (Sofia)

THEME OF

Siena

STATE

OF THE

Ragusa

Diocica

Scodra

Skopia

STRYMON

Philippopli

THEME OF

EMONT

THEME OF

Adrianople

THEME OF

Sutri

Rome

CHURCH

THEME OF LOMBARDY

Benevento

Dioclea

Durazzo

Dyrrhachium

Okhrida

THEME OF MACEDONIA

Constantinople

THRACE

BENEVENTO

Bari

Salonika

THEME OF

40

Naples

Salerno

Brindisi

Kastoria

THESSALONICA

Adramyttium

SALERNO

Greeks

THEME

OF

CALABRIA

THEME

OF

EASTERN

THEME OF HELLAS

Larissa

THEME OF THE

AEGEAN

ONS

Messina

Reggio

CEPHALENIA

THEME OF NICOPOLIS

Athens

ISLANDS

Palermo

SICILY

Catania

Corinth

Argos

THEME

OF

PELOPONNESUS

CRETE

erta

When Otto I came to the throne in 936, he determined to get as many of the great fiefs under his control as possible and build up a strong kingdom for himself. He succeeded in over-coming a number of the troublesome vassals who defied the royal power and in placing their lands in the hands of his rela-tives. Other large fiefs Otto granted to churchmen, who then became his vassals and furnished him with fighting men as did any other great lord. Otto's idea in appointing so many churchmen to his fiefs was that these lands would always re-main in his direct control. For as bishops and abbots could not marry, they would have no descendants to whom the land would pass at their death. It would then naturally fall back into the hands of the king.

Otto also strengthened his kingdom by fighting off the Slavs and by defeating the Hungarians, who had long been a source of danger to Germany.

Otto the Great becomes King of Italy and Emperor (962). It would seem as if Otto had quite enough trouble at home, but he thought that it would make his reign more glorious if he added northern Italy to his realms. So when, in 951, he was urged to come to the assistance of one of the warring factions in Italy, he crossed the Alps, won a victory over one of the rivals, and was generally acknowledged as king of Italy. Ten years later he was called to Rome by the Pope, who was seeking protection from the attacks of his enemies. Otto accepted the invitation, restored order, and the grateful Pope in return crowned him emperor (962).

The coronation of Otto was a very important event in German history; for, from this time on, the German kings, instead of giving all their attention to maintaining order in their own kingdom, were constantly in trouble trying to keep hold of their Italian kingdom, which lay on the other side of a great range of mountains.

The German emperors who succeeded Otto had usually to make several costly and troublesome journeys to Rome, — a first one to be crowned, and then others either to remove an unfriendly Pope or to protect a friendly one from the attacks of neighboring lords. These expeditions were very inconvenient, especially to a ruler who left behind him in Germany a rebellious nobility that always took advantage of his absence to revolt.

The Holy Roman Empire. With the crowning of Otto the Western Roman Empire was revived a second time. But the "Holy Roman Empire" (as it came to be called later), which was to last, in name at least, for more than eight centuries, was even less like that of the ancient Romans than was Charlemagne's. As *kings* of Germany and Italy the German rulers had almost all the powers that they enjoyed as *emperors*. The title of "Emperor" was of course a proud one, but it gave the German kings no additional power except the right that they eagerly claimed of taking part in the election of the Pope. We shall find that, instead of making themselves feared at home and building up a great state, the German emperors wasted their strength in a long struggle with the Popes, who proved in the end far stronger and finally reduced the Empire to a mere shadow.

2. How the Churchmen became Feudal Lords

How the Church acquired Vast Territories. In order to understand the long struggle between the emperors and Popes, we must stop a moment to see how the Church as owner of a vast amount of land was drawn into the feudal system. During the Middle Ages it was the custom for rulers and rich landowners to give lands for "the good of their souls" to bishops and monasteries. In this way a very considerable portion of western Europe had come into the hands of the Church.

A king, or landed proprietor, might also grant fiefs to churchmen as well as to laymen. The bishops became the vassals of the king or of other feudal lords by doing homage for a fief and swearing fidelity, just as any other vassal would do. An abbot would sometimes secure for the monastery of which he was the head the protection of a neighboring lord by giving up his land and receiving it back again as a fief.

FIG. 100. *Saint Peter gives the Pallium to Pope Leo III, and the Standard to Charlemagne*

From an eighth-century mosaic at Rome

Church Lands not Hereditary. One great difference, however, existed between the church fiefs and the ordinary fiefs. As we have said, according to the law of the Church the bishops and abbots could not marry and so could have no heirs to whom they might hand down their property. Consequently, when a landholding churchman died, someone had to be chosen in his place to take over his property and perform his duties. The law of the Church had always been that the *clergy* of the bishopric should choose the bishop, their choice being approved by the people. The abbots were, according to the Rule of Saint Benedict, to be chosen by the members of the monastery of which they were in charge.

Meaning of "Investiture." But the rules of the Church had come to be disregarded. As many of the church lands were held as fiefs, the bishops and abbots were selected by the various kings and lords who granted the land. It is true that the outward forms of a regular election were usually permitted; but the feudal lord made it clear whom he wished chosen, and if the wrong person was elected he simply refused to hand over to him the lands attached to the bishopric or monastery.

When a bishop or abbot had been regularly chosen, the feudal lord proceeded to the *investiture,* or ceremony of giving him (*investing* him with) the symbols of his new office and lands. The new bishop or abbot became the "man" of the lord by doing him homage (p. 428), and then the lord transferred to him the lands and rights attached to the office. No careful distinction appears to have been made between the property and the religious powers. The lord often conferred both by presenting the bishop a ring and a crosier (the bishop's pastoral staff), the signs of religious authority. It seemed shocking enough that the king or feudal lord, who was often a rough soldier, should control the selection of the bishops; but it was still more shocking that he should dare to confer religious powers with religious emblems.

In Germany the king, who was especially eager to have the support of the Church, had, from about the beginning of the eleventh century, often conferred upon the bishops the authority of a count in the districts around them. In this way they might have the right to collect tolls, coin money, and perform other important governmental duties. To forbid the king to take part in the investiture was therefore to rob him of his authority over many of his own government officials. Hence he found it necessary to take care who got possession of the important church offices.

Not only the appointment of bishops and abbots but even that of the Popes had come into the hands of secular rulers. In the tenth century, the papacy having become the victim of warring factions in Italy, unsuitable persons, sometimes even boys, were placed in this high office. The German king Otto I thereupon determined that henceforth only his own candidates should occupy the papal throne. Otto issued a decree declaring that no Pope should be consecrated until he had sworn his allegiance to the emperor.

The Marriage of the Clergy. Still another danger threatened the power of the Church. During the tenth and eleventh centuries the rule of the Church prohibiting the clergy from marrying appears to have been widely disregarded in Italy, Germany, France, and England. To the stricter people of the time this appeared very shocking, for they believed that the clergy should be unhampered by family cares and affections and should devote themselves wholly to the service of God. The question, too, had another side. It was clear that the property of the Church would soon be divided if the clergy were allowed to marry, since they would wish to provide for their children. Just as the feudal lands were handed down from father to son (p. 430), so the church lands would pass into the families of the clergy and be lost to the Church unless the clergy were forced to remain unmarried.

Simony, or the Buying and Selling of Church Offices. Another evil effect of the feudal system on the Church was the temptation it offered to buy and sell church offices. The income from a great church estate and the high rank that went with the office led many to seek church positions merely for their worldly interests. The feudal lord who had the right of investiture was also influenced in granting the benefice by the amount a vassal would be willing to pay.

The sin of buying or selling church offices was recognized as a most serious one. It was called *simony*, a name derived from Simon the Magician, who, according to the account in the New Testament (Acts viii, 9–24), offered money to the Apostle Peter if he would give him the power of imparting the Holy Spirit to those upon whom he should lay hands.

It must be remembered, however, that when a king or lord accepted a gift from one for whom he had secured a *benefice*, that is, a church office endowed with lands or income, he did not regard himself as *selling* the office; he merely shared its advantages. No transaction took place in the Middle Ages without accompanying gifts and fees of various kinds.

The evil of simony (or "graft," as we should call it today) spread downward and affected the whole body of the clergy. A bishop who had spent a large sum in securing his office naturally expected something from the priests whom he appointed. Then the priest, in turn, was tempted to ask too much for baptizing and marrying his parishioners and for burying the dead.

The introduction of worldly gain into religious offices had a very sad effect on the morals of the clergy. It also made the Church the victim of many scheming adventurers who became clergymen only because the Church offered prospects of wealth and position and an easy life.

Beginning of a Reform Movement. The growth of these evils in the Church seriously threatened its power and religious influence. A reform movement finally developed which had as its first object the freeing of the papacy from the control of princes. This movement was largely the work of the monks at the abbey of Cluny, in eastern France. This abbey was unique in being entirely free from any regulation save that of the Pope. The monks of Cluny were noted for their piety and learning and for their high ideals. The reform movement gradually spread until it reached Rome, where it was championed by the celebrated Hildebrand, who later became Pope Gregory VII.

Many difficulties had to be overcome in the gigantic task of ridding the Church of the evils that had grown up and making it a strong and independent institution.

Nicholas II reforms the Election of Popes. The first great step toward the freeing of the Church from the control of the kings and feudal lords was taken by Pope Nicholas II. In

1059 he issued a famous decree which took the election of the head of the Church once for all out of the hands of both the emperor and the people of Rome and placed it definitely and forever in the hands of the *cardinals*, who represented the Roman clergy.[1]

The reform party, headed by Hildebrand, which directed the policy of the Popes, now proposed to free the Church as a whole from worldly things: first, by strictly forbidding the clergy to marry; secondly, by depriving the kings and feudal lords of their influence over the choice of the bishops and abbots; thirdly, by abolishing simony. The character of the task which the Popes had undertaken first became clear when Hildebrand ascended the papal throne, in 1073, as Gregory VII.

Gregory VII's View of the Papacy. Among the writings of Gregory VII there is a very brief statement, called the *Dictatus*, of the powers which he believed the Popes to possess. Its chief claims are the following: The Pope enjoys a unique title; he is the only *universal* bishop and may remove and reinstate other bishops or transfer them from place to place. No council of the Church may be regarded as speaking for Christendom (the Christian world) without his consent. The Roman Church has never erred, nor will it err to all eternity. No one may be considered a Catholic Christian who does not agree with the Roman Church. No book has full authority unless it has received the Pope's approval.

Gregory does not stop with asserting the Pope's complete supremacy over the Church. He says that "the Pope is the only person whose feet are kissed by all princes"; that he may depose emperors and "free subjects from allegiance to an unjust ruler." No one shall dare to condemn one who appeals to the Pope. No one may annul (abolish) a decree of the Pope,

---

[1] The cardinals (Latin *cardinalis*, "principal") are the highest dignitaries in the Roman Catholic Church next to the Pope. They form a kind of council to the Pope in the government of church affairs. Originally the cardinals were clergy connected with churches in the Roman district, but later they came to be chosen from parishes outside Rome. Officially each cardinal today, even those in the United States, has a post in one of the Roman churches. In 1586 the number of cardinals was fixed at seventy. When a Pope dies the Sacred College of Cardinals meets in Rome and elects his successor, usually one of their own number.

though the Pope may declare of no effect the decrees of all other earthly powers; and no one may pass judgment upon his acts.

Gregory VII puts his Theories into Practice. Immediately upon his election as Pope, Gregory began to put into practice his high ideas of the rôle that the religious head of Christendom should play. He explained, kindly but firmly, to the king of England that the papal and kingly powers are both established by God as the greatest among the authorities of the world, just as the sun and moon are the greatest of the heavenly bodies. But the papal power is clearly superior to the kingly, for it is responsible for the deeds of princes. At the Last Day, Gregory urged, he would have to render an account of the king as one of the flock intrusted to his care. The king of France was warned to give up his practice of simony, lest he be excommunicated and his subjects freed from their oath of allegiance. All these acts of Gregory appear to have been dictated not by worldly ambition but by an earnest belief in their righteousness and in his heavy responsibility to God and toward all men.

3. The Struggle over Investiture

Struggle over Investiture between Henry IV and Gregory VII. The Popes who came just before Gregory had more than once forbidden the churchmen to receive investiture from laymen. Gregory reissued this prohibition in 1075. In forbidding a newly chosen church official to accept his lands and rights from the hands of a king or feudal lord Gregory attempted nothing less than a revolution. He attacked the power of kings and landholders all over Europe and, especially, that of the emperor, whose power rested largely in his control over the bishops and churchmen. The bishops and abbots were often officers of government, exercising in Germany and Italy powers in all ways like those of the counts. Not only did the German king rely upon them for advice and assistance in carrying on his government, but they were among his chief allies in his constant struggles with his vassals.

Fig. 101. Pope Gregory VII and Henry IV at Canossa

This act of Gregory's led to a long and bitter struggle between the Popes and German rulers, lasting for two hundred years. Gregory's legates, or ambassadors, so irritated the young German king, Henry IV, that he had the Pope deposed as a wicked man (1076).

Gregory's reply to Henry and the German bishops who had deposed him was speedy and to the point. "Incline thine ear to us, O Peter, chief of the Apostles. As thy representative and by thy favor has the power been granted especially to me by God of binding and loosing in heaven and earth. . . . I withdraw, through thy power and authority, from Henry the King, who has risen against thy Church with unheard-of insolence, the rule over the whole kingdom of the Germans and over Italy. I absolve all Christians from the bonds of the oath which they have sworn, or may swear, to him; and I forbid anyone to serve him as king."

For a time after the Pope had deposed him, everything went against Henry. Instead of resenting the Pope's interference, the discontented Saxons, and many other of Henry's vassals, believed that there was now an excellent opportunity to get rid of Henry and choose a more agreeable ruler.

Henry Submits to the Pope at Canossa (1077). Henry was so discouraged that he hastened across the Alps in midwinter and appeared as a humble suppliant before the castle of Canossa,[1] whither the Pope had come on his way to Germany. For three days the German king stood before the closed door, barefoot in the snow, clad in the coarse garments of a pilgrim and a penitent, before the Pope consented to receive him.

The sight of this mighty prince of distinguished appearance, in tears before the little man who humbly styled himself the "servant of the servants of God," has always been regarded as a most striking illustration of the power of the Church in the Middle Ages and the fear of her curses hurled against even the most exalted of the earth.

The famous scene at Canossa settled nothing, however, and the struggle went on. The Pope took sides with Henry's

[1] The castle of Canossa belonged to Gregory VII's ally and admirer, the Countess of Tuscany.

enemies in Germany, but the German king was later able to march down into Italy, drive Gregory from Rome, and set up a new Pope in his place.

Settlement of Investiture Controversy. After a long succession of troubles between the Popes and emperors who followed Gregory VII and Henry, an agreement was reached in the Concordat of Worms (1122), which put an end to the troubles over investitures in Germany. The emperor promised to permit the Church freely to elect the bishops and abbots and gave up his old claim to invest with the religious emblems of the ring and the crosier. But the elections were to be held in the presence of the king, and he was permitted, in a separate ceremony, to *invest* the new bishop or abbot with his fiefs and his governmental powers by a touch of the scepter. In this way the religious powers of the bishops were conferred by the churchmen who elected them; and although the king might still interfere with an election by refusing to hand over the lands, nevertheless the actual appointment of the bishops and abbots was taken out of his hands.

4. EFFECTS OF THE STRUGGLE BETWEEN POPES AND EMPERORS ON GERMANY AND ITALY

Struggle between Popes and Emperors Goes On. In the long conflict between the Popes and emperors the Popes had gained much, even if they did not win the complete triumph which Gregory VII would have wished. The Church had shown its great power and was well on its way to becoming the most important institution in medieval Europe.

Although the Popes and emperors had agreed to a compromise on the question of investiture, their quarrel did not come to an end with the Concordat of Worms. The continued attempts of the emperors to manage Italy, and their many invasions of that country, were a constant irritation to the Popes, who saw what a danger a strong empire would be to their own possessions in the Italian peninsula.

Frederick I of Hohenstaufen. The most famous of German emperors after Charlemagne was Frederick I, commonly known as Barbarossa (from his red beard). He belonged to the family of Hohenstaufen, so called from their castle in southern Germany. When Barbarossa came to the throne in 1152, he wished, like Charlemagne and Otto, to restore the Roman Empire in its old extent and glory. He believed that his office was quite as truly established by God himself as that of the papacy. This attitude naturally kept alive the antagonism of the Popes, who never forgot the claims of Gregory VII that the Popes had the right to control the emperors as well as other rulers. Throughout his reign Barbarossa constantly engaged in fighting, trying to maintain his empire. He had always his rebellious nobles at home to deal with, and he wasted much time and energy in a hopeless attempt to keep control of Italy.

Italian Towns Oppose the Emperor. Barbarossa's task in keeping hold of his Italian possessions was even more difficult than had been that of Otto the Great ; for in the two hundred years that had passed since Otto's day the towns of northern Italy had grown rich and prosperous and had formed their own governments. Milan, Cremona, Verona, and other cities were now practically independent states which resented the interference of a German king in their affairs. But they were also keen rivals of each other and for this reason were slow in combining against him.

Barbarossa was forced to make many trips across the Alps, hoping to conquer these rich Italian towns which at times would seem to be subdued only to rise anew against him. Finally, with doubtless some urging on the part of the Pope, the cities united to form the Lombard League and defeated the emperor decisively (1176) at Legnano. After all the years of fighting and hopeless ambition, Barbarossa was compelled to let the towns go their own way and to content himself with their vague acknowledgment of his overlordship.

Frederick II lives in Southern Italy. After some forty years of fighting, in Germany and Italy, Barbarossa decided to undertake a Crusade to the Holy Land and lost his life on the journey (p. 526). His grandson, Frederick II, continued the

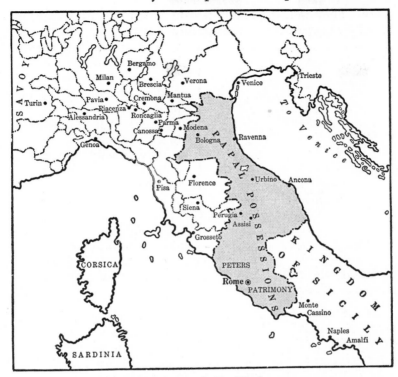

Italian Towns in the Twelfth Century

wearisome struggle between the emperors and Popes. There were five Popes during his reign with whom to make terms. Frederick, while still a mere child, inherited from his mother the kingdoms of Naples and Sicily. As he was brought up in the south, he preferred to live in this part of his realms rather than in Germany.

Frederick II was unable to bring any order into German affairs or those of northern Italy, but in his southern kingdom he built up a strong, well-regulated state — the first strong modern monarchy in Europe.

We cannot relate here his long struggle with the Popes, — how he was excommunicated from time to time and even deposed, and how the Popes tried to set up other rulers in his

place. They were especially fearful, when they saw a strong
kingdom developing to the south of them, that if Frederick

Kingdom of the Two Sicilies

were successful in controlling the Lombard cities,
the Papal States would be
wedged in, and held as if
in a vise. Consequently
they did all in their power
to oppose him.

After Frederick's death
(1250) his sons maintained
themselves for a few years
in the Sicilian kingdom,
but finally gave way before
a French army. This was
led by the brother of Saint
Louis, Charles of Anjou,
to whom the Pope, hoping to rid himself of the Hohenstaufens, presented their southern realms.

The Empire becomes a Mere Shadow. With Frederick's
death the medieval Empire may be said to have come to an
end. It is true that the German kings continued to call themselves emperors, and the "Holy Roman Empire" existed in
name down to 1806. But few of the emperors took the trouble
to go to Rome to be crowned. No serious effort was ever
made to reconquer the Italian territory for which Otto the
Great, Frederick Barbarossa, and his grandson had made
such serious sacrifices. Germany was hopelessly divided, and
its king was no real king. He had no capital city and no well-
organized government. Such power as existed was mainly in
the hands of the king's powerful vassals.

Condition of Germany and Italy. By the middle of the
thirteenth century it becomes clear that neither Germany nor
Italy was ready to develop into a strong single kingdom like
England and France. The map of Germany shows a confused
group of duchies, counties, archbishoprics, bishoprics, abba-
cies, and free towns, each one of which asserted its practical
independence of the weak king who called himself an emperor

In northern Italy each town, including a certain district about its walls, had become an independent state, dealing with its neighbors as with independent powers. The Italian towns, during the fourteenth and fifteenth centuries, were to become the birthplace of our modern learning. Venice and Florence, in spite of their small size, came to be reckoned among the most important states of Europe. In the central part of the peninsula the Pope maintained more or less control over his possessions, but he often failed to subdue the towns within his realms. To the south the kingdom of Naples, which the Hohenstaufens had lost, remained for some time under the French dynasty which the Pope had called in, and the island of Sicily drifted into Spanish hands (p. 631, n.).

Questions and Exercises

REVIEW OF CHAPTER

1. How did the Holy Roman Empire originate? What was the basis of the claims of the German kings on Italy? How did Otto strengthen the German kingdom? How did he weaken it? What was the importance of the Treaty of Mersen?

2. How did the Church come to be rich in land? How were the churchmen drawn into the feudal system? Why was it important for the clergy to remain unmarried? What was simony, and what is it now called in politics? Why was the ceremony of investiture so important? How was the election of the Pope arranged by Nicholas II? What were the claims of Gregory VII?

3. What was the great issue between Popes and emperors? Tell about the conflict between Henry IV and Gregory VII. Was the Holy Roman Empire any of the things its name implies? What was the Concordat of Worms?

4. Who were the chief characters in the struggle of Popes and emperors after Henry IV? What was the effect on Italy and Germany of the policy of the emperors? Do you know when Germany and Italy were finally unified?

USEFUL TERMS

See how much meaning you can give to the following: *secular, benefice, investiture, compromise, laymen, simony, anointed, suppliant, cardinals, concordat, crosier.*

DIRECTIVE QUESTIONS

1. Why were men sometimes more loyal to the Pope than to their own king?

2. Contrast the old Roman Empire with the Holy Roman Empire in extent, government, institutions, and interests.

3. What became of the emperor's privilege of naming the Popes?

4. How are the Popes elected today? What is the Sacred College of Cardinals?

5. How many cardinals are there? Where do they live?

6. What advantage was it to a lord to grant land to a churchman instead of to a layman?

DISCUSSION TOPICS

1. The Popes were more powerful than the emperors.

2. It was an unwise thing to give lands to the Church.

3. The Roman Empire could not be revived.

4. The title of "Emperor" in the Middle Ages was an empty one.

5. Should the government appoint church officials?

6. The State and Church are today entirely separate institutions in most countries.

ADDITIONAL ADVENTURES IN LEARNING

1. Studies in Source Materials. ROBINSON, *Readings*, Vol. I, chap. xii, sect. i, 103, The election of Otto I; chap. xiii, sect. iii, Gregory VII's ideas of the papacy; sects. ii and v, 113, Difficulties between Gregory and Henry IV; sect. v, 114, Gregory's account of Canossa; sect. vi, Gregory defends papal supremacy; sect. vii, 117, The settlement of the question of investiture by the Concordat of Worms; chap. xiv, sect. ii, The Italian cities and the emperor.

2. Supplementary. Look up in the Old Testament the anointing of an early king (1 *Samuel* x, 1–24). Can you find other instances? Write a short account of the career of Hildebrand (or Gregory VII) (THORNDIKE, *History of Medieval Europe*, chap. xv, pp. 286 ff.).

Part Six

HOW OUR FOREFATHERS BEGAN
TO RESTORE ORDER AND BUSINESS,
RECOVERED WHAT THE GREEKS
AND ROMANS HAD KNOWN,
AND COMMENCED TO FIND OUT
NEW AND IMPORTANT THINGS
FOR THEMSELVES

The Kings of England and France succeeded in Establishing Modern Nations ; Towns grew up, with Active Business and Fine Buildings. The Books of the Greeks and Romans were Rediscovered, and a New Way of Reproducing them Cheaply by Printing was invented. Writers began to use the Modern Languages as well as Latin. The Invention of Gunpowder Revolutionized the Ways of Fighting, and the Compass encouraged Bold Navigators to learn more about the Earth than the Ancients had known

Louis IX at the Abbey of Royaumont, Studying Mathematics under the Direction of Vincent de Beauvais (1223)

From a painting by Chartran, in the Sorbonne

CHAPTER XXIII · FROM FEUDALISM
TO MONARCHY IN FRANCE

HOW THE FRENCH KINGS LOST THEIR POWER FOR A TIME · HOW THE KINGS RE-
COVERED THEIR REALMS · THE HUNDRED YEARS' WAR · STRENGTHENING OF FRANCE
AFTER THE HUNDRED YEARS' WAR

AFTER the break-up of Charlemagne's empire France was for centuries hopelessly divided among innumerable nobles who were ever scheming to see how much of one another's land they could get to add to their own holdings. France was in a state of *feudal anarchy*.

The poor French kings had almost nothing left of their former realms, and a tremendous task was ahead of them if France was ever to be a strong nation. Moreover, they now had a new difficulty to deal with: a large part of France had actually fallen into the hands of a *foreign* ruler.

In 1066 Duke William of Normandy had become king of England. His descendants inherited his Norman lands and had by marriage come to possess a large amount of territory in central and southern France. Later one of the English kings even laid claim to the throne of France.

For many years the French were at war with the English, trying to rid their land of them. Finally this was accomplished. The French kings not only regained the French possessions of the English kings but recovered most of the territory which had been held by their French vassals. They brought their unruly subjects to terms, improved the central government, increased their income, and built up the powerful French nation, which has played a very important part in the development of modern civilization.

1. How the French Kings lost their Power for a Time

The Nobles get Possession of the Land. By the Treaty of Verdun (843), it will be recalled, Charlemagne's empire was divided into an eastern and a western Frankish kingdom and a middle kingdom (p. 423). The western portion, which we shall hereafter call France, soon fell into the hands of many dukes, counts, and other nobles, who built strong castles, maintained armies of fighting men, and came to possess most of the privileges formerly enjoyed by the king. The king himself had little left besides his crown.

Charlemagne's income had been largely derived from the revenues of his vast estates and from the rewards of his conquests. He had granted to his officials, the dukes and counts who helped him to manage his realms, large tracts of land in payment for their services. One of their duties was to levy and support armies for his warlike enterprises. The trouble started here. For whereas Charlemagne was a strong and a shrewd monarch who kept sufficient power in his own hands to *rule* as well as *reign*, his feeble successors soon became less powerful than their most important vassals. As the kings had little money, they were forced to give away more and more of their land in return for assistance against the attacks of rebellious vassals or of outside invaders who were constantly threatening the kingdom. With their land went their income, and with their income went their power. They had no armies under their direct control and were unable to force their vassals into obedience. They could no longer collect fines that had formerly been paid to the royal courts, and were too weak to force tribute from their subjects. The tolls from roads and bridges were now taken by the feudal lords who actually held the lands. Moreover, the kings could no longer count on the plunder from war. Their vassals, who owed them military service, would fight for them only when it suited their own interests. So for several hundred years France was controlled by nobles and landholders who paid little respect to their overlord, the king. Feudalism was at its height. If ever royal power was to be reëstablished and the country united under one government, the kings would have to find some way to regain their lands and, with them, the power to enforce their will upon their rebellious subjects.

Great Fiefs practically Independent States. By the eleventh century most of the country was consolidated in the hands of a few great landholders who held large fiefs. These were the dukes of Normandy, Brittany, Burgundy, and Aquitaine, and the counts of Flanders, Champagne, Anjou, and Aquitaine. These nobles had increased their lands through conquest or purchase or through marriage with members of families who also held large estates. They made sure of their control over their vassals by promptly destroying the castles of those who did **not** fulfill their obligations.

FIG. 102. *L'Abbaye-aux-Dames, Caen*

William the Conqueror married a lady, Matilda, who was remotely related to him. This was against the rules of the Church, and he took pains to get the Pope's sanction to his marriage. But he and his queen were afraid that they might have committed a sin in marrying; so William built a monastery for men, and Matilda a nunnery for women, as a penance. The churches of these monasteries still stand in the Norman city of Caen. William was buried in his church. The picture represents the interior of Matilda's church and is a good example of the so-called Norman style of architecture. (See Fig. 106)

The Duke of Normandy conquers England. Of these little nations none was more important or interesting than Normandy. The Northmen had for many years been the terror of those who lived near the North Sea. Finally one of their leaders, Rollo, made terms with the French king and received a district on the north coast where he and his followers might settle down. He was also permitted to take possession of Brittany if he would cease making raids on the French realms.

Rollo took the title of "Duke of the Normans" and introduced the Christian religion among his people. For some time the newcomers kept up their Scandinavian habits and language. Gradually, however, they learned to appreciate and imitate the ways of their more advanced neighbors. By the twelfth century their capital, Rouen, was one of the finest cities of Europe. Normandy became a source of endless trouble to the French kings when, in 1066, Duke William laid claim to the English crown, invaded and conquered that country, and became its king.

This event had important consequences for both the English and the French nation. When we turn to the study of England, we shall describe the influence of the Norman Conquest on English civilization. We shall speak here only of the effect of the Norman Conquest on France, though the affairs of England and France were entangled for centuries as a result of the adventures of this bold and able Norman duke.

French Possessions of the Plantagenets. By the time of Henry II (1154–1189), the great-grandson of William the Conqueror, the French possessions of the English king were about six times the size of those ruled over by the French king himself. For Henry inherited the duchy of Normandy and the overlordship of Brittany as a descendant of King William : and as his mother had married the Count of Anjou and Maine, these fiefs also came to him. Lastly, he married Eleanor of Aquitaine, thereby doubling the extent of his French lands. Henry II and his successors are known as the "Plantagenets," owing, it is supposed, to the habit of his father (the Count of Anjou) of wearing a sprig of broom (Latin, *planta genista*) in his helmet.

Plantagenet Lands

So it came about that the French kings, already deserted by their vassals at home, faced a new danger arising within their borders; for the lands of the English royal family included more than half the territory which they themselves should rightfully rule. The holder of these lands really owed the French king homage, according to feudal law, so there was a new kind of *international* feudalism added to the complicated situation already existing. But the English kings were no more ready to acknowledge the power of their French overlord than were the French nobles themselves.

2. How the Kings Recovered their Realms

Philip Augustus Strengthens the French Monarchy. A few years before Henry died, an ambitious and able monarch, Philip Augustus (1180–1223), ascended the French throne and made it the chief business of his life to get control of his feudal vassals, — above all, the *Plantagenets.*

Henry II of England divided his French possessions among his three sons, Richard, Geoffrey, and John; but father and sons were engaged in constant disputes with one another, since none of them were easy people to get along with. These quarrels were most fortunate for the French king. If the Plantagenets had only held together, they might have crowded out the royal house of France, for their possessions hemmed in the narrow dominions of the French monarch on the west and south.

Philip gains the Plantagenet Lands. So long as Henry II lived, there was little hope of driving the Plantagenets out of France; but when his sons came to rule, the prospects of the French king brightened wonderfully. Philip was kept busy trying first to outwit Richard and afterwards John, Richard's younger brother.

John, who has the reputation of being the most contemptible of English kings, soon gave Philip an excuse for seizing a great part of his French lands. John was suspected of secretly consenting to the brutal murder of his nephew Arthur (the son of Geoffrey [1]). He was also guilty of the less serious offense of carrying off and marrying a lady engaged to one of his own vassals. Philip Augustus, as John's suzerain, or over-lord, summoned him to appear at the French court to answer the latter charge. Upon John's refusal to appear or to do homage for his possessions in France, Philip caused his court to issue a decree taking possession of almost all the Plantage-net lands, leaving to the English king only the southwest corner of France.

Philip found little difficulty in winning over Normandy itself, which showed no hesitation in accepting him in place of the Plantagenets. Six years after John became king the English rulers had lost almost all their French fiefs. It should be noted that Philip, unlike his ancestors, was no longer merely suzerain of the new conquests but was himself duke of Normandy, count of Anjou, of Maine, etc. The bound-aries of his domain — that is, the land which he himself con-trolled directly as feudal lord — now extended to the sea.[2]

Philip Augustus improves the National Government. Philip Augustus not only regained most of the important lands of the Plantagenets, but exercised his rights as feudal overlord to interfere in the affairs of his French vassals, and by skillful maneuvering sometimes managed to get their fiefs back into his own hands. By the end of his reign he had, in one way and another, brought a large part of France under royal control.

Along with the recovery of territory, Philip made the power of the king felt by improving and strengthening the central government. He appointed a large number of officials to administer his lands, but he was careful not to place his affairs in the hands of undependable nobles. Instead he called upon members of the clergy, — who were the educated class

---

[1] Geoffrey, John's next-older brother, who would naturally have succeeded Richard, had died in 1186. (See genealogical table, p. 488.)

[2] Saint Louis, Philip's successor, arranged with Henry III (John's successor, in 1258 that the English king should do him homage for Guienne and Gascony, and should give up every claim to all the rest of the former possessions of the Plantagenets. So it came about that the English kings, in spite of their losses, continued to hold a portion of France for several hundred years.

of that day, — students of the Roman law (which was being revived at Bologna (p. 593)), and officials of the towns to assist him. He encouraged trade, and strengthened the growing towns by including their representatives in his assemblies along with the clergy and nobility. The towns furnished aid for his conquests, either militia or a payment of money. Philip was also successful in his relations with the clergy and nobility. He protected their interests and property, but he also saw to it that they made substantial contributions to the government from time to time.

Philip the Fair introduces Taxation. Philip's policy of strengthening the national government was carried on by his successors, especially Louis IX, called Saint Louis (1226–1270), and Philip the Fair (1285–1314). As the kings got more power they were better able to bring the unruly vassals to terms and to prevent further rebellion against the monarchy. They established the superiority of the royal courts, or *parlements*, in place of the old feudal courts of the nobles, by receiving appeals from the feudal courts. This, of course, brought revenue in the form of fees and fines into the royal treasury. Philip the Fair found various ways of increasing his income by securing gifts and loans, which he did not always repay, and by levying taxes on property, on income, and even on trade. He demanded the military service that was due him as feudal lord, but often accepted money in place of actual service.

The Estates-General. In Philip's reign a French national assembly was also established, called the *Estates-General* (1302). This was composed of representatives from the three *estates*, or classes, of people in the nation, — the nobility, the clergy, and the merchants, or townsmen. It was called *general* to indicate that it represented the people of the *whole* realm rather than some *local* community.

The history of the Estates-General forms a striking contrast to that of the English Parliament, which was laying the foundation of its later power during this very period. While the French king occasionally summoned the Estates when he needed money, he did so only in order that their approval of new taxes might make it easier for him to collect them. But he never admitted that he had not the right to levy taxes if he wished to without consulting his subjects.

In England, on the other hand, the kings, ever since the time of Edward I, had repeatedly agreed that no *new* taxes should be imposed without the consent of Parliament. Edward I, as we shall see, had gone farther and accepted the representatives of the people as his advisers in all important matters touching the welfare of the realm (p. 500). While the Estates-General was never so important or powerful as the English Parliament, it was appealed to in later years, and one of its meetings was the first step toward bringing about the great French Revolution of 1789.

3. The Hundred Years' War

Edward III claims the French Crown. By the early fourteenth century the king of France had got the better of the feudal lords, and a parliament had been established in which the townspeople, as well as the clergy and nobility, were represented. This progress toward a strong national state was interrupted, however, by a long series of conflicts with England known as the Hundred Years' War, which began in 1337.

As a matter of fact, the trouble between England and France lasted more nearly four hundred years, for it had started with the conquest of England by Duke William of Normandy. The Hundred Years' War was only one part of the contest. On the other hand, actual war was not going on continuously for one hundred years between the two countries. There were long stretches of time within the century when there was no fighting, the two enemies observing a truce. Two treaties were made during the period in the hope of ending the conflict ; but these were later disregarded and the fighting was renewed.

King John of England had lost almost all the French possessions of the Plantagenets. For what remained to him he had to do homage to the king of France and become his vassal. This arrangement lasted for many years; but in the time of Edward III the old line of French kings died out (1328), as none of the sons of Philip the Fair had a male heir to the throne. Edward thereupon declared that he himself was the rightful ruler of France because his mother, Isabella, was a daughter of Philip the Fair and sister of the last French king.[1]

Edward III invades France. The French lawyers, however, decided that the crown could not pass to a woman or her descendants. A nephew of Philip the Fair was chosen, therefore, who took the title Philip VI. Edward nevertheless insisted that he was rightfully the king of France, and he added the French emblem of the lilies (fleur-de-lis) to the lions on the English coat of arms. In 1346 he landed in Normandy with an English army, laid waste the country, and marched up the Seine toward Paris. He met the troops of Philip at Crécy, where a celebrated battle was fought in which the English,

[1] The French kings during the fourteenth and fifteenth centuries:

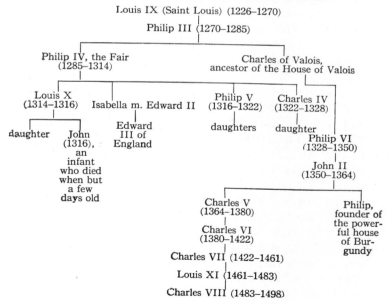

with their long bows and well-directed arrows, put to rout the French knights. Ten years later the English made another attack on France and again defeated the French cavalry (Poitiers, 1356). The French king, John II, was captured and carried off to London. A treaty of peace was soon signed at Brétigny (1360) which temporarily halted the fighting.

The Estates-General Summoned. While the French king was living in captivity in England and his young son, the *Dauphin*, was ruling in his place, the French nobles seized this opportunity to try to overthrow the royal power. When the Dauphin called the Estates-General together to vote taxes

FIG. 103. *Royal Arms of Edward III*

On the upper left-hand and the lower right-hand quarter are the lilies of France

to carry on the struggle, he was unable to get any aid. The Estates-General, however, presented a list of reforms providing, among other things, that they should meet regularly even when the king failed to summon them, and that the collection and spending of the government's money should no longer be entirely under the control of the king but should be supervised by themselves as representatives of the people. The agitation for reform caused such disorder in Paris that the attempts to change the old system were finally given up, and the plans of the Estates-General came to nothing.

Edward III fails to Conquer France. When the Dauphin became king, as Charles V, in 1364, he reasserted the power of the monarchy. He determined not to be ruled by an Estates-General that had failed him. Shortly after his accession the war with England was renewed.

Edward III had found it impossible to conquer France; for, although the English won many victories, they could

not occupy the whole of French territory at once, and the
French would not tolerate the idea of giving up the fight
and acknowledging a foreigner as their king. Under Charles V
success was with the French, and by the end of Edward III's
reign (1377) the English had lost almost all their possessions
in France. Then war ceased for another forty years.

Last Stages of the War. During this long truce civil war
was raging in France, for the French now had a king who
was most of the time insane. Again the nobles attempted
to divide up the realms among themselves. A French party
known as the Burgundians allied themselves with the English against the French monarch, and Henry V, the English
king, was encouraged to attack the French again in 1415.
He won another great victory at Agincourt, similar to that
won at Crécy. Once more the English bowmen slaughtered
great numbers of French knights. Fifteen years later the
English, with the aid of the Burgundians, had succeeded in
occupying a great part of France north of the river Loire.
Though a considerable region to the south was still in the
possession of the feeble heir to the French throne, Charles VII,
he was doing nothing to check the English victories. The
English were engaged in besieging the great town of Orléans
when help and encouragement came to the French from a
most unexpected quarter. A peasant girl put on a soldier's
armor, mounted a horse, and led the faint-hearted French
troops to victory.

Joan of Arc. To her family and her companions Joan of
Arc seemed only "a good girl, simple and pleasant in her
ways"; but she brooded much over the disasters that had
overtaken her country, and a "great pity on the fair realm
of France" filled her heart. She saw visions and heard
voices that bade her go forth to the help of her poor king
and lead him to Reims to be crowned.

It was with the greatest difficulty that she got anybody to
believe in her mission or to help her to get an audience with
the king. But her own firm faith in her divine guidance triumphed over all doubts and obstacles. She was at last

The Treaty of Brétigny (1360)

In 1360 Edward III gave up the claims of the English kings to the French crown and to the northern lands that had once belonged to the Plantagenets. In return he was granted outright Poitou, Guienne, Gascony, and the town of Calais. Before Edward died the French king managed to get most of these lands back. When the Hundred Years' War was renewed, over half a century later, the English for a time occupied all the old Plantagenet lands, but, as we shall see, soon lost them for good

accepted as a God-sent champion and placed at the head of some troops sent to the relief of Orléans. This city, which was the gateway to southern France, had been besieged by the English for some months and was on the point of surrender. Joan, who rode at the head of her troops, clothed in armor like a man, had now become the idol of the soldiers and of the people. Under the guidance and inspiration of her courage, sound sense, and burning enthusiasm, Orléans was relieved and the English completely overcome. The Maid of Orléans, as she was henceforth called, was now free to conduct the king to Reims, where he was crowned in the cathedral (July 17, 1429).

The Maid now felt that she had done her part and begged permission to return to her home and her brothers and sisters. To this the king would not consent, and she continued to lead his battles with success. But the other commanders were jealous of her, and even her friends, the soldiers, were ashamed of being led by a woman. During the defense of Compiègne in May, 1430, she was allowed to fall into the hands of the Duke of Burgundy, who sold her to the English. The English were not satisfied with holding as a prisoner the strange maiden who had so outwitted them; they wished to belittle everything that she had done, and so declared, and undoubtedly believed, that she was a witch who had been helped by the devil. She was tried by a court of clergymen, found guilty, and burned at Rouen in 1431. Her bravery and patriotism touched even her executioners, and an English soldier who had come to triumph over her death was heard to exclaim, "We are lost — we have burned a saint!" The English cause in France was indeed lost, for her spirit and example had given new courage and vigor to the French armies.

England Loses her French Possessions. The English Parliament became more and more unwilling to grant money when there were no more victories gained. From this time on, the English lost ground steadily. They were expelled from Normandy in 1450. Three years later the last remnant of their possessions in southern France passed into the hands of the French king. The Hundred Years' War was over, and, although England still retained Calais, the great question whether she should extend her control on the mainland of Europe was finally settled.

Fig. 104. *Joan of Arc at the Court of Chinon, Appealing to the Dauphin to Accept her Aid*
From a painting by Boutet de Monvel. (Courtesy of the Art Institute of Chicago)

4. STRENGTHENING OF FRANCE AFTER THE HUNDRED YEARS' WAR

Effects of the War on the Country. France had suffered a great deal more than England from the war, for the fighting had all been done on her soil. Her lands were devastated and her crops ruined for years. Besides, the country had been plagued by soldiers who, when they found themselves without occupation, wandered about in bands plundering and maltreating the defenseless country folk.

The King gets a Standing Army (1439). On the other hand, the experiences of the long struggle with England brought about a number of changes which tended to strengthen permanently the monarchy of France. In the first place, the king had come to have a well-organized standing army, that is, an army paid by the government and always prepared to fight. The feudal armies had long since disappeared. Even before the opening of the Hundred Years' War the nobles had begun to be paid for their military services and no longer furnished troops as a condition of holding fiefs. But the soldiers had found their work and their pay very uncertain, and so plundered their countrymen as well as the enemy to get a living.

The Estates-General agreed in 1439 to an annual direct tax, called the *taille*, to support a regular army. The king now had a permanent fighting force that he could depend on, and money to maintain it. He no longer had to appeal to his vassals for assistance or hire bands of soldiers in times of trouble. He alone had the power to maintain troops — an arrangement which was likely to do away with the constant neighborhood warfare that had so long disturbed the general peace. The French king was thus independent of the approval of his subjects; for he had the right to collect the *taille* and was not, like the English ruler, forced to beg from a Parliament grants of money which often lasted only a short period.

The King subdues the Nobles. But before the king of France could hope to establish a strong, unified state, he had to conquer his ambitious vassals, some of whom were almost as powerful as the monarch himself. It will be remembered that in the thir-teenth century Philip Augus-tus and his successors had greatly increased the royal power by recovering the ter-ritory of some of the feudal nobles. But since that time the kings had made the same mistake as their predecessors: they granted large districts to the younger members of the royal family, who often still further increased their do-mains by marrying into other important landowning fami-lies. Most of the large fiefs were therefore again held by

FIG. 105. *Louis XI of France*

relatives of the king, who did not hesitate to plot against him and prevent the unification of the country under one ruling monarch.

Success of Louis XI. The task of uniting France remained for the son of Charles VII, the shrewd and cunning Louis XI (1461–1483). The most powerful and dangerous of Louis XI's vassals were the dukes of Burgundy, who had long given the monarchy a great deal of trouble and had even allied themselves with the English against their own king. Louis had arranged that he should fall heir to a number of prov-inces in central and southern France, — Anjou, Maine, Pro-vence, etc., — which by the death of their rulers now came under the king's immediate control (1481). He took revenge in various ways on the vassals who in his early days had combined in a league against him. At his death, except for Artois, Brittany, and the county of Burgundy, Louis had won possession of nearly all the territory today included in France. In 1491 Louis's son, Charles VIII, added Brittany to the crown lands by marrying the heiress to that province.

The government had been much strengthened by the measures which had been taken to bring all power into the hands of the king. The nobles were now forbidden to coin money, to keep armies of their own, or to tax their subjects. Moreover, the authority of the king's judges was supreme throughout the realm. Business and industry had increased the people's wealth, and this not only gave the government a larger income to meet its expenses but raised up a strong middle class who were loyal to the king, since they realized that only under a peaceful, unified government could business and trade flourish. In short, France was on the way to becoming a strong modern state.

Questions and Exercises

REVIEW OF CHAPTER

1. Why were the French kings powerless in the Middle Ages? What was the result of the Norman conquest of England for France? How did Henry II of England come to have so much French territory?

2. How did Philip Augustus strengthen his power? How did he recover the Plantagenet possessions? What classes were represented in the Estates-General? What did Philip the Fair do about taxation?

3. What claim did the English king have on the French throne? What advantages and what disadvantages did the English have in carrying on the Hundred Years' War?

4. What did Louis XI accomplish for France? Compare his position with that of the kings who followed Charlemagne. What are the advantages of a standing army?

USEFUL TERMS

See how much meaning you can give to the following terms: *feudal anarchy, centralized government, civil war, Plantagenets, Estates-General, Dauphin, taille.*

DIRECTIVE QUESTIONS

1. In what does a strong central government consist? Has your own government these features? Contrast this condition with that of France in the Feudal Age.

2. Why did the towns prefer a monarchy to feudalism?

3. Why could the English not conquer France though they won many victories? How does one nation conquer another?

4. Explain how French and English affairs were entangled for centuries because a Frenchman became king of England and an English king tried to become king of France.

DISCUSSION TOPICS

1. Peace is more likely under monarchy than under feudalism.

2. The English had no right to the possession of French territory.

3. Foreigners have no right under any circumstances to invade a country and try to rule the people living there

4. Was Joan of Arc a heretic, as the Church ruled, a witch as the English believed, a saint as the Church afterwards said, or a simple peasant girl?

ADDITIONAL ADVENTURES IN LEARNING

1. Studies in Source Materials. ROBINSON, *Readings*, Vol. I, chap. x, sect. i, How Hugh Capet became king of France; sects. ii–iii, Feudal anarchy in France; sect. iii, pp. 202 f., Position and duties of a medieval French king; sect. iv, How Philip Augustus restored order and built up his kingdom; sect. vi, Saint Louis, the ideal ruler. CHEYNEY, *Readings in English History*, chap. x, The Hundred Years' War; chap. xi, sect. iii, Description of Joan of Arc by a contemporary chronicler.

2. Supplementary. Draw a map of the great French fiefs in the eleventh century. Indicate on a map the Plantagenet lands in the time of Henry II.

3. Look up in an encyclopedia the fleur-de-lis, the symbol of the French kings. Can you draw one from memory? What is the Ile de France, from which France derives its name? Why are the names "Britain" and "Brittany" alike? Is there any connection?

4. Topical Studies. Write a short account of Joan of Arc. See reference above; also GREEN, *Short History of the English People*, chap. vi, sect. 1.

How the French people lived in the Middle Ages: JOAN EVANS, *Life in Medieval France*.

Why was Louis IX called Saint Louis?

CHAPTER XXIV · FOUNDATIONS
OF A FREE GOVERNMENT LAID IN ENGLAND

HOW THE NORMAN KINGS DEVELOPED GOVERNMENT IN ENGLAND · FOUNDATION OF
ENGLISH LIBERTIES: THE GREAT CHARTER AND PARLIAMENT · EFFORTS TO BRING
GREAT BRITAIN UNDER ONE GOVERNMENT · A PERIOD OF ABSOLUTE MONARCHY
IN ENGLAND

ENGLAND, like other parts of the Roman Empire, was a prey to invaders who plundered her shores and sought to get control of the
island. German tribes settled down in England as they did in the rest
of Europe, and established a kingdom of their own. In the eleventh century, however, England was conquered by a more highly civilized people
from across the Channel, the Normans. This was the last invasion of
Britain, for the Norman kings established a strong and permanent monarchy. They had a gift for governing, and soon succeeded in subduing the
nobles and unifying their realms under royal control.

One of the features of a well-organized state is a *central government*
strong enough to protect the country against foreign invaders and also to
keep order within the realm. This requires an *army* which is ready to
fight when needed, and *officers* to see that the peace is kept through the land.
It requires *money* to pay the soldiers and to support the many officials needed
to carry on the business of the state. To get this money the government
must have a system of *taxation* by which those who can afford to do so pay
for the services which the government provides for all the people. The
state must also see that the subjects deal fairly with one another and are
responsible to the government. This requires the making of *laws* and the
establishing of *courts* where disputes and complaints can be heard and
settled.

It was the foundations of these elements of good government that the
Norman kings laid in England. It took many centuries to perfect a national
state; for the kings were sometimes unwise and demanded too much power.
But the English people learned how to protect themselves against a tyrannical sovereign and to win rights for themselves which could not be taken
away. They developed a great council of their own representatives, called
a *Parliament*, which met to work out with the king the problem of governing
the country.

In the meantime business, manufacturing, and trade increased, and England was the first country to emerge as a strong, unified, and independent
modern state.

1. How the Norman Kings developed Government in England

Importance of English History. So far we have had little occasion to speak of England. In telling the story of Europe after the break-up of the Roman Empire we have been concerned first with the conditions that developed in the various kingdoms which grew up on the Continent. England was the most remote province of the Empire, and after it was abandoned by the emperor its affairs remained for centuries largely unrelated to those of the rest of Europe. After the Duke of Normandy conquered the island in 1066, however, England was brought into closer connection with the Continent; for the Norman kings of England held possession of a large part of France, and the affairs of England and France were for centuries greatly entangled. In later days, when business and trade developed and colonies were founded in new lands, the little island of Britain became the most important country in the world. The real greatness of England is bound up with the story of her ships, to be told later.

English history is of special interest to English-speaking peoples throughout the world; for it is from England that they have inherited not only their language but their ways of thinking, many of their laws and principles of government, and in many cases even their country.

Early Invasions of England. The conquest of the island of Britain by the Angles and Saxons has already been spoken of, as well as the conversion of these pagans to Christianity by Augustine and his monks (p. 406). The various kingdoms founded by the invaders were brought under the overlordship of the southern kingdom of Wessex by Egbert (830), who lived during the time of Charlemagne.

The Danes and Alfred the Great (871–901). But no sooner had the long-continued invasions of the Angles and Saxons come to an end, and the country acknowledged the overlordship of one ruler, than the Northmen (or Danes, as the English called them), who were overrunning France, began

Early German Kingdoms in England

England in the Time of Alfred the Great

to cross over to England. Before long they had conquered a large district north of the Thames and were making permanent settlements. They were defeated, however, in a series of attacks by Alfred the Great, the first English king about whom we know very much. He forced them back beyond the old Roman road, called Watling Street, and made the Danish king and his principal followers accept Christianity, as a sign that they would cease plundering their neighbors.

England from Alfred to the Norman Conquest (901–1066). But more Danes kept coming, and the Danish invasions continued for more than a century after Alfred's death (901). Sometimes they were bought off by a money payment called the *Danegeld*, which was levied on the people of England like any other tax. But finally a Danish king (Cnut) succeeded in making himself king of England in 1017. The Danes ruled, however, for only a few years. Then a last timid but well-meaning Saxon king, Edward the Confessor, reigned for twenty-four years. Edward had been brought up in Normandy. His father, having fled there to escape the Danes, had married the daughter of the Norman duke. When Edward was called to England as its king, therefore, he was accompanied by Norman relatives, nobles, and followers. During his reign he was much influenced by his Norman associates, but the government was for the most part carried on by an able and powerful noble named Godwin, whose son Harold of Wessex later claimed the English crown as his right.

Upon the death of Edward one of the greatest events in all English history occurred. The most powerful of the vassals of the king of France crossed the English Channel, conquered England, and made himself king. This was William, duke of Normandy.

A Norman claims the English Crown. William of Normandy claimed that he was entitled to the English crown, but we are somewhat in the dark as to the basis of his claim. There is a story that he had visited the court of Edward the Confessor, who was his cousin, and had become his vassal on condition that, should Edward die childless, he

FIG. 106. *L'Abbaye-aux-Hommes at Caen, Founded by*
William the Conqueror (1066)
See legend, Fig. 102

was to declare William his successor. However this may be, Harold of Wessex, the most powerful noble in England, and son of Edward's chief adviser, was elected king upon Edward's death and paid no attention to William's demand that Harold should hand over his crown to him.

William thereupon appealed to Rome, promising that if he came into possession of England he would see that the English clergy submitted to the authority of the Pope. Thereupon the Pope, Alexander II, condemned Harold and blessed in advance any expedition that William might undertake to secure the throne. The conquest of England thus took on the character of a holy war; and as the expedition was widely heralded and was approved by the Church.

many adventurers hastened to join William. During the spring and summer of the year 1066, ships were being built in most of the Norman harbors for the purpose of carrying William's army across the Channel.

Battle of Hastings (October, 1066). The English took their stand on the hill of Senlac, west of Hastings, and awaited the coming of the enemy. They had few horses and fought on foot with their battle-axes. The Normans had horses, which they had brought across in their ships, and the troops were supplied with bows and arrows. The English made a brave fight, repulsing the Normans as they tried to press up the hillside. But the English army was at last thrown into confusion, and Harold was killed by a Norman arrow which pierced his eye.

William in this way destroyed the English army in the famous battle of Hastings, and the legitimate English king was dead. But the Norman duke was not satisfied to take possession of England as a conqueror merely. In a very few weeks he managed to persuade a number of powerful nobles and several bishops to agree to accept him as king, and London opened its gates to him. On Christmas Day, 1066, he was *chosen* king by an assembly in Westminster Abbey and duly crowned. Thus he made it seem as if the English had desired him for their ruler.

William establishes a Strong Monarchy (1066–1087). William's authority was far greater than that of an ordinary ruler. He was the elected, anointed king of England, the military conqueror of the land, and he was the feudal overlord of his most important subjects. He declared that as successor of the Anglo-Saxon kings he did not intend to change the English customs but to carry on the government as it had been in the time of Edward the Confessor. As a matter of fact, William combined certain features of the old government with Norman customs in such a way as to secure the advantages of both and create a strong and impressive monarchy. He retained the council of bishops and nobles (the *Witenagemot*) whose advice the Saxon kings had sought in important matters, and held meetings regularly

Fig. 107. *Scenes from the Bayeux Tapestry*

This tapestry, made shortly after 1066, is a band of linen (two hundred and thirty-one feet long) on which are embroidered in colored wools scenes from the Norman Conquest. In this panel, to the left a group of men are pointing to a strange star which they regard as an evil omen. We now know that this was Halley's comet, which appeared in 1066. To the right King Harold listens to a messenger who brings him news, probably of the ships in the border below. (Bayeux Museum)

and with great ceremony. But he was careful to keep control, nevertheless, in his own hands. He continued to collect the *Danegeld* (p. 484), a tax which, though no longer needed to buy off the Danes, was useful in increasing his own income. He issued a code of laws, based on earlier ones, and retained the county and local courts.[1]

William, however, introduced feudalism into England; for he gave to Norman knights and barons the lands taken from the English who had refused to support him. Fortunately, these lands were so scattered that no feudal lord was able rapidly to collect an army against him. Toward the end of his reign he made all the landholders in the kingdom take an oath of fidelity to him so that he *directly* controlled all the vassals and subvassals in the land. William had his officials make a survey of the whole kingdom by showing the number of tenants, the size and value of their

---

[1] An interesting custom brought into England by William was the curfew law. This required that all fires be covered at nightfall (*couvre-feu*), to avoid danger of a fire during the night.

holdings, and the payments they owed the crown. This information we now call a *census*. It was written down in two
volumes known as the *Domesday Book*.

In these and many other ways William the Conqueror laid
the basis of a strong and unified national government.

King Henry I Further develops the Government (1100–1135).
The principles of monarchy were still further developed
by William's son Henry I, who made the royal power felt
throughout the land through the work of his able officials.
These ministers met together to attend jointly to government affairs in what was called the *curia regis*, or king's
council. All lawsuits involving land and other matters of
concern to the king were brought before this council, or
court, and gradually most of the important cases throughout
the realm came to the king's court. Justices representing the
king's council were sent from time to time through the country to settle cases, so that the royal authority was exercised
in the local communities.

Civil War weakens the Government. At the death of Henry
the country went through a long period of civil war; for
some of the nobility supported the claim of the Conqueror's
grandson, Stephen, to the crown, and some that of Henry's
daughter, Matilda.[1] After the death of Stephen, who reigned

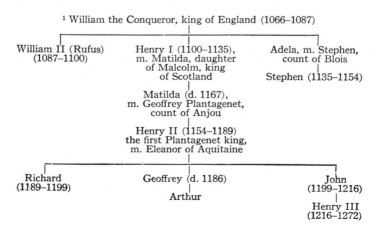

[1] William the Conqueror, king of England (1066–1087)

William II (Rufus) (1087–1100)	Henry I (1100–1135), m. Matilda, daughter of Malcolm, king of Scotland	Adela, m. Stephen, count of Blois
		Stephen (1135–1154)
	Matilda (d. 1167), m. Geoffrey Plantagenet, count of Anjou	
	Henry II (1154–1189) the first Plantagenet king, m. Eleanor of Aquitaine	

| Richard (1189–1199) | Geoffrey (d. 1186) | John (1199–1216) |
| | Arthur | Henry III (1216–1272) |

England and Normandy under William the Conqueror

for some nineteen years, Matilda's son came to the throne as Henry II. He found the kingdom in a confused and unruly state. The nobles had taken advantage of the general disorder and the lax rule of Stephen to build castles without permission and to reëstablish themselves as almost independent rulers. Many of the gains made by the earlier Norman kings had been lost, and the respect for royal authority had lapsed.

The Task of Henry II (1154–1189). Henry's first task was to establish order and reorganize the central government. Councils were held, the king's courts were revived, able officials were appointed to administer state business, and foreign soldiers who had been hired were sent out of the country. The fortified castles of the barons were confiscated, and lands which had been taken from their owners by force were returned. The nobles who resisted these changes were subdued, and royal control was restored.

Henry, with the help of his ministers, made several lasting contributions to the development of English government. In the first place, he laid the foundations of fair and equal treatment of all citizens in his organization of the courts, in establishing trial by jury, and in the recognition of the old laws of England, called the *common law*.

The king's courts, which had been disregarded for a score of years, were reëstablished and their importance was soon increased. They extended to every freeman the privilege of having any case concerning land tried by the king's justices. In order to avoid private warfare over difficulties which arose among his subjects, Henry arranged that his judges should make regular rounds throughout the country so that they might try cases on the spot at least once a year. As the decisions of the king's judges were respected more than those of a local court, the importance of the government's courts grew while that of the feudal courts declined.

The Jury System. Henry also established the beginning of what is now known as trial by jury. It will be recalled that the medieval trials were decided by ordeal, compurgation, and wager of battle (p. 389). Henry's judges introduced a better type of decision, called "recognition," which later grew into trial by jury. The judges ordered a number of men — usually twelve — to investigate the facts of a case, to attend court, and to give a sworn "verdict," or statement, as to which party had the better claim. These men were called *jurors* (from the Latin *jurare*, "to swear") because they had to swear to tell the truth. We know that at a trial today there are witnesses selected to tell what they know of the facts of a case, and a *petty*, or small, jury of men who hear these facts and decide which side shall win the case. While not all the features of a modern trial were worked out until later, it was in Henry's reign that the old methods were gradually discarded for what seemed a fairer method of determining the truth.

Another feature, familiar to us today, which was introduced by Henry was the so-called *grand* jury. This was a body of men, selected in each neighborhood, whose business it was to give information concerning any crimes or misdemeanors that were committed and, by accusing wrongdoers, bring them to justice. Without this method criminals could go undiscovered and unpunished; for it was nobody's concern to protect the people at large against burglary, murders, and other evil deeds. These ways of dealing with court cases constituted what is called the jury system. It differs from the Roman trial, where the judges made the decision, and the medieval system, which attempted to get the decision of God.

The Common Law. The king's council in earlier times had kept records of the decisions of the king's justices, who were learned men and had, in general, based their opinions on principles of reason and fairness. Henry's judges, when traveling through the country, formed their decisions according to the principles of these earlier jurists, and this body of opinion and custom was the foundation of the *common law*. The common law is unwritten. Together with the written statutes of the realm, it forms the body of law by which the English peoples are governed.

Creation of a National Army. Henry spent much of his time fighting. When on the Continent he hired soldiers, called *mercenaries,* whose trade was fighting. Finding that the military service of his vassals in England was insufficient, Henry made a law requiring every freeman to be prepared and ready to fight when called to the king's service. The knights must have full armor and a horse; those of lower rank were not required to furnish such complete equipment. So the king had at his command not only his hired soldiers and his vassals but a national militia composed of the people at large.

Relations between the Church and Government. In attempting to unify his realms Henry had still another problem to deal with besides the feudal barons. This was the Church. In England, as on the Continent, the same questions regarding the powers of earthly rulers and of the head of the Church had arisen. The peace of the realm was thus threatened by the claims of an outside monarch who divided the loyalty of English subjects. After the Norman Conquest, William, although he had been encouraged by the Pope to undertake the invasion of England and was himself a good Catholic, nevertheless refused to take an oath of submission to Gregory VII when the Pope demanded it. The high claims which Gregory made for the papal power seemed to William to endanger his own supremacy within his kingdom. William went farther and forbade his subjects to recognize any Pope, receive any papal demands, or attend any councils without first having his consent. His successors were also careful to safeguard the powers of the English throne against the influence of Rome. The question of investiture was fought out in England as on the Continent, but was finally arranged in a peaceable manner between Henry I and his archbishop.

By Henry II's time the Church possessed a large amount of property and had its own laws and its own courts, in which great sums were collected as fees and penalties. The church courts got an increasing number of cases into their hands besides those affecting the clergy or religious matters:

for there were cases involving church property, marriages, wills, and inheritances. There was always the question as to how far this separate organization within the realm should be regulated and whether the officers of the Church should be under the control of the king or of the Pope.

Thomas Becket and Henry II. Henry's reign was rendered very unhappy by the famous struggle with Thomas Becket, which illustrates admirably the peculiar dependence of the monarchs of his day upon the churchmen. Becket was born in London and became an ecclesiastic; but he grew up in the king's service and was able to aid Henry in

© British Museum

Fig. 108. *The Murder of Thomas Becket in Canterbury Cathedral (December, 1170)*

From a thirteenth-century manuscript

gaining the throne. It appeared to Henry that there could be no better head for the English clergy than this loyal Becket; he therefore determined to make him Archbishop of Canterbury.

In securing the election of Becket as Archbishop of Canterbury, Henry intended to establish his own complete control of the Church in England. He proposed to punish like other offenders all churchmen who committed crimes, to make the bishops fulfill their feudal obligations, and to abolish appeals from his own authority to that of the Pope. Becket, however, immediately gave up the gay life he had previously led, and opposed every effort of the king to reduce the independence of the Church by bringing it under the control of the king rather than of the Pope. After a final refusal to come to terms with Henry, Thomas Becket fled from the wrathful and disappointed monarch to France and sought the protection of the Pope. Henry confiscated the estates of Thomas and of all his adherents, friends, and relatives and banished four hundred of his sympathizers from England.

After six years Becket was permitted to return to England and take up his neglected duties. He thereupon proceeded to excommunicate some of the great English prelates (that is, higher clergy), who had taken the king's side in their quarrel, and, as Henry believed, was planning to rob his son of the crown. In a fit of anger Henry exclaimed among his followers, "Is there no one to avenge me of this miserable churchman?" Unfortunately, certain of Henry's knights took the hasty expression seriously, and Becket was murdered in his own cathedral of Canterbury, whither he had returned. The king really had not meant that he wished Becket to be killed, and his sorrow and distress when he learned of the dreadful deed, and his terror at the results, were most genuine. The Pope proposed to excommunicate him. Henry, however, finally made peace with the papal legates (or ambassadors) who had been sent to England, by solemnly declaring that he had never wished the death of Thomas and by promising to return to Canterbury all the property which he had taken possession of for his own uses. He promised also to send money to aid in the capture of the Holy Sepulcher at Jerusalem, which had fallen into the hands of the Mohammedans, and even to undertake to lead an expedition to the Holy Land himself.

The French Possessions of the Plantagenets. Although Henry II was one of the most important kings in English history, he spent a great part of his time across the Channel in his French possessions. We have already seen in the previous chapter that rather more than half of his realms lay to the south of the English Channel. The trouble that these possessions made for the English kings has already been described.

John becomes a Vassal of the Pope. It will be recalled
that it was John, the son of Henry II, who lost Normandy
and other territories that had belonged to the earlier Norman kings. The relation of England to the Church of Rome
is well illustrated by John's conflict with the Pope, in which
he actually agreed to become the Pope's vassal, receive
England as a fief from the papacy, and pay tribute to Rome.
This strange affair came about in this way. When the
Archbishop of Canterbury died, in 1205, the clergy, without
consulting the king, had dared to select one of their own
number as the new archbishop and send him to Rome for
the approval of the Pope. This so angered John that he
compelled the clergy to hold another election and make one
of his ministers archbishop. The Pope at that time was no
less a person than Innocent III, one of the greatest of medieval rulers. Innocent rejected both the men who had been
elected, sent for representatives from Canterbury, and bade
them choose Stephen Langton, a man of great ability. As
John refused to accept the Pope's appointee or give up his
own, Innocent after three years placed England under the
interdict; that is to say, he ordered the clergy to close all
the churches and stop holding public services — a very terrible thing to the people of the time. John was excommunicated, and the Pope threatened that unless the king submitted
to his wishes he would depose him and give his crown to
Philip Augustus of France. As Philip made haste to collect an
army for the conquest of England, John humbly submitted to
the Pope in 1213. He went so far as to hand England over to
Innocent III and receive it back as a fief, thus becoming the
vassal of the Pope. He agreed also to send a sum of money
every year to Rome.

2. FOUNDATION OF ENGLISH LIBERTIES: THE GREAT CHARTER AND PARLIAMENT

The Granting of the Great Charter (1215). We must now
turn to another very important event in John's reign — the
drawing up of the Great Charter of English liberties.

When, in 1213, John proposed to lead his English vassals
across the water in order to attempt to reconquer his lost

possessions in France, they refused to accompany him on the ground that their feudal obligations did not bind them to fight outside of their country. Moreover, they showed a lively discontent with John's tyranny and his neglect of those limits of the kingly power which several of the earlier Norman kings had solemnly recognized. In 1214 a number of the barons met and took a solemn oath that they would compel the king, by arms if necessary, to sign a charter (an agreement in writing) containing the things which, according to English traditions, a king could *not* do. As John would not agree to do this, it became necessary to get together an army and march against him. The determined nobles met him at Runnymede, not far from London. Here, on the fifteenth of June, 1215, they forced him to swear to observe what they believed to be the rights of his subjects, which they had carefully written out.

The Importance of the Charter. The Great Charter is perhaps the most famous document in the history of government. For the first time the king was forced to acknowledge that his subjects had certain rights — that the government does not exist for the ruler alone but also for the people. In electing a king the people enter into a kind of feudal contract in which, in return for their obedience and support, they are promised good government. If the king fails in his obligations the people have the right to take him to task. This view of the monarchy had been entirely neglected by King John.

The Charter was also important in showing not only that the people had the *right* but also the *power* to compel a king to rule as they wished. For without their aid and support he was helpless. If the people turned against him, he could be deposed. A later king, Charles I, was actually beheaded for continuing to defy his people and finally going to war against them (p. 740).

Provisions of the Charter. While the provisions of the Charter may seem limited to us today, they were a great achievement for the people to have made at that time. It

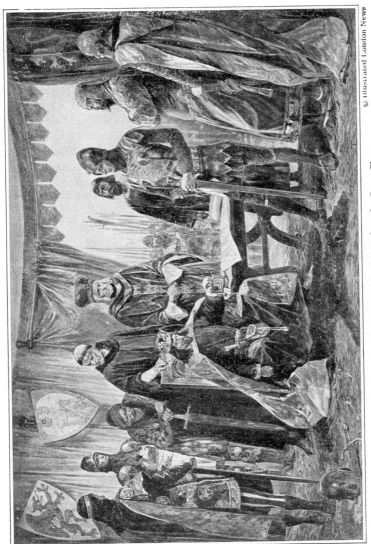

FIG. 109. *King John Putting his Seal on the Great Charter*

was definitely stated that the king was to impose no tax besides the three feudal dues,[1] except with the consent of the Great Council of the nation. The Council was to include the prelates and the greater barons and all the king's vassals. The Charter also promised that "to no one will we sell, to no one will we deny or delay, right or justice."

There is no more notable clause in the Charter than that which provides that no *freeman* is to be arrested, or imprisoned, or deprived of his property unless he be immediately sent before a court of his peers (that is, equals) for trial. In France, on the other hand, down to 1789 — nearly six hundred years later — the king exercised such unlimited powers that he could order the arrest of anyone he pleased and could imprison him for any length of time without bringing him to trial or even letting him know what wrong he was supposed to have done.

The Great Charter provided a further measure of liberty and protection to the king's subjects by stating that merchants should be safe to come and go throughout the land and to leave and return to England without being oppressed by "evil tolls." The privileges which the towns had secured were not to be interfered with. Another very important provision was the restrictions put upon the king's officials. No constable or bailiff was to take away goods or implements "or anyone's grain or other chattels without immediately paying for them in money," nor the horses and wagons of a freeman for carrying purposes without the owner's permission, nor the wood of another man for castles. All fines levied were to be in proportion to the importance of the offense and the position of the offender, and the fines should be imposed only by the "oaths of honest men of the neighborhood."

It must be remembered, however, that the barons, who forced the Charter on the king, had their own interests especially in mind. The nobles, churchmen, merchants, and other freemen made up only about a sixth of the population,

[1] These three regular feudal dues were payments made when the lord knighted his eldest son, gave his eldest daughter in marriage, or had been captured and was waiting to be ransomed.

and the Charter had little or nothing to say of serfs, or villeins, who formed the great mass of the English people at that time. They could still be illtreated as before by their masters, the lords of the manor. Nevertheless, in later centuries, when the serfs had become free, the Charter could be appealed to in support of the common people against attempts of the ruler to oppress them.

Lasting Value of the Charter. In spite of his solemn agreement, John, with his usual treachery, made an unsuccessful effort to break his promises in the Charter; but neither he nor his successors ever succeeded in getting rid of the document. Later there were times when the English kings disregarded its provisions and tried to rule as absolute monarchs. But the people sooner or later always remembered their Charter, which thus continued to afford protection against any permanent oppression in England.

The Beginnings of Parliament. The Great Charter was a statement of the rights of the people to which the ruler was forced to consent. There now developed in England, through the course of the thirteenth century, an institution which was, if possible, even more important than the Charter; for it gave the people an actual part in the everyday government of the realm. This was the *Parliament.*

The Great Council of the Norman kings, like the older Witenagemot of Saxon days, was a meeting of nobles, bishops, and abbots which the king summoned from time to time to give him advice and aid and to approve important undertakings (p. 486). During the reigns of Henry I and II the kings' ministers had taken an increasingly active part in the conduct of the business of state and the administration of justice.

Owing to the difficulties which arose during the reign of John, and that of his son Henry III, the council met very often, and the name *parliament* was gradually adopted for it (from *parler*, a French word meaning "to speak" or "discuss"). Parliament began to be much more outspoken in its disapproval of Henry III's bad management of the government, and when he refused to adopt the reforms it demanded, part of its members went to war with their sovereign.

England becomes English. With the accession of Edward I (1272–1307) the nation came under the leadership of a wise and farseeing king, such as some of the earlier Norman kings had been, and the unifying of the country made great progress. For the first time England came to be more truly English. The earlier Norman kings, while wise rulers, had really been French in spirit, as well as birth, and had spent much time away from their kingdom. Some, like Richard the Lion-Hearted, had looked upon the country only as a source of income. But Edward I loved England, and from his time the island began to assume an independent national character. One of the most decisive features in the development of unity and strength in the kingdom was the growth of the importance of Parliament. Government began to be a joint enterprise of the ruler and the governed. The king found it wise to have the approval and support of his people, and the people held it as their right to take part in the government and, above all, to say how their money should be spent.

The "Model Parliament" of Edward I. The most far-reaching advance was the admission of a new class of members to Parliament — the middle classes, or commons. It will be recalled that only the nobles and great churchmen had formerly attended the councils, and that even in the Charter it was chiefly their interests that were guarded.

In 1295, however, a Parliament was summoned which, because it formed the standard for all future meetings, is called the "Model Parliament." To this gathering the king not only summoned the nobles and higher clergy but, in addition, arranged that two knights representing each county, and two townsmen representing each city and borough, should be present. There was a very good reason for including these new members in the government councils. The nobles and higher clergy were no longer the only powerful classes in the country from the standpoint of wealth.

With the increase of business and trade there had grown up a large group of freemen — landholders, merchants, and townspeople — who, although below the rank of nobility, were yet rich, active, and intelligent. Since the king could no longer tax the people without their consent, one of the main reasons for calling a Parliament was to obtain grants of money. The kings soon saw that they could not afford to overlook such an important source of wealth and neglect a group who often had more money than those who possessed only land.

In calling the "Model Parliament," therefore, Edward introduced a principle which is today the very cornerstone of modern representative government. Ever since the Model Parliament of 1295, the commons, or representatives of the "freemen," have always been included along with the nobility and clergy when the national assembly of England has been summoned, and no Parliament has ever met without them.

Growth of the Powers of Parliament. The Parliament early took the stand that the king must agree to the "redress of grievances" before it would grant him any money. This meant that the king had to promise to remedy any acts, of himself or his officials, of which Parliament complained before it would agree to let him raise the taxes. Moreover, instead of following the king about and meeting wherever he might happen to be, the Parliament, from the time of Edward I, began to hold its sessions in the city of Westminster, now a part of London, where it still continues to meet. In 1327 Parliament showed its power by deposing an incompetent king, Edward II, and declaring his son, Edward III, the rightful ruler of England.

Parliament becomes a Lawmaking Body. Under Edward III (1327–1377) Parliament was able greatly to extend its powers. The king was carrying on an expensive war with France (the Hundred Years' War, pp. 469 ff.), in which the people took little interest. There seemed to be nothing to be gained by it, and as the fighting was far from home they were not much concerned with the king's enterprise. The armies which fought in France were composed largely of hired soldiers; so the king was in constant need of money. He therefore summoned Parliament nearly every year to persuade it to grant additional funds. This gave Parliament its opportunity; for when the king made his demands he had to listen to Parliament's grievances and take its advice. In return for each appropriation Parliament saw to it that the king's consent was given to some new law or reform. In bargaining in this fashion Parliament not only succeeded in improving the government but established itself as a law-making body. No new law was passed without expressly stating that it was with the consent of the great men and the *commons* of the realm. This custom continued to be observed, and an acknowledgment of the consent of the "lords spiritual and temporal" and "commons" has been included in every statute of the realm.

House of Lords and House of Commons. During the reign of Edward III, Parliament separated into two sections, or *Houses.* The small landholders and the representatives of shires and towns had much in common and came to act together as one body. The difference in their rank from that of the nobility and clergy finally led them to prefer to hold their meeting in one room while the "lords spiritual and temporal" met in another. In this way Parliament became divided into the House of Commons and the House of Lords.

As time went on, the House of Commons grew more and more important, and finally came to have more power than the Upper House. Today no money can be spent by the government without the approval of the Commons, regardless of the wishes of the House of Lords, nor can any law be passed without their consent. The House of Commons can, moreover, pass a law over the veto of the Lords. The Parliament of Great Britain is now so powerful a body that we should understand something of its humble beginnings, way back in the fourteenth century.

3. Efforts to bring Great Britain under One Government

Extent of the King of England's Realms before Edward 1 (1272–1307). The Norman kings not only strengthened the government of England but sought to bring the whole island of Great Britain under their control. The English kings, however, who preceded Edward I had ruled over only a portion of the island. To the west of their kingdom lay the mountainous district of Wales, inhabited by that remnant of the original Britons which the Angles and Saxons had been unable to conquer. To the north of England was the kingdom of Scotland, which was quite independent, except when occasionally a Scotch king acknowledged an English king as his feudal lord. Edward I, however, succeeded in conquering Wales permanently and Scotland for a short time.

Edward I conquers Wales. For centuries a border warfare had been carried on between the English and the Welsh. When Edward I came to the throne he demanded that Llewellyn, prince of Wales (as the head of the Welsh clans was called), should do him homage. Llewellyn, who was a man of energy and independence, refused the king's summons, and Edward marched into Wales. Two campaigns were necessary before the Welsh were finally defeated. Llewellyn was killed (1282), and with him the independence of the Welsh people passed away. Edward divided the country into shires, or counties, and introduced English laws and customs, but his method of winning the confidence of his new subjects was so successful that there was but a single uprising in the country for a whole century. Later, at a public ceremony, he presented his son to the Welsh as their prince, and from that time down to the present the title of "Prince of Wales" has usually been given to the heir to the English throne.

Edward interferes in Scotch Affairs. The conquest of Scotland proved a far more difficult matter than that of Wales. When the Angles and Saxons conquered Britain some of them wandered north as far as the Firth of Forth and occupied the so-called Lowlands of Scotland. The mountainous region to the north, known as the Highlands, continued to be held by wild tribes, related to the Welsh and Irish, who spoke a language similar to theirs, namely, Gaelic. There was constant warfare between the older inhabitants themselves and between them and the Anglo-Saxon invaders; but the Highlands and the Lowlands were finally united under a line of Scotch kings, who moved their residence down to Edinburgh, which, with its fortress, became their chief town. It was natural that the language of the Scotch Lowlands should be English, but in the mountains the Highlanders to this day continue to use the ancient Gaelic spoken by their forefathers.

It was not until the time of Edward I that the long series of troubles between England and Scotland began. When the old line of Scotch kings came to an end, there appeared a number of claimants to the crown in 1290. In order to avoid civil war Edward was asked to decide who should be king. He agreed to make the decision on condition that the one whom he selected should hold Scotland as a *fief* from the English king. This arrangement was adopted, and the crown was given to John Baliol. But Edward unwisely made demands upon the Scotch which aroused their anger, and their king renounced his homage to the king of England. The Scotch, moreover, formed an alliance with Edward's enemy, Philip the Fair of France; thenceforth, in all the difficulties between England and France, the English kings had always to reckon with the hostile Scotch, who were glad to aid the French against England.

Edward attempts to Conquer Scotland. Edward marched in person against the Scotch (1296) and speedily put down what he regarded as a rebellion. He declared that Baliol had forfeited his fief through treason, and that consequently the English king had become the real ruler of Scotland. He emphasized his claim by carrying off the famous Stone of Scone (now in Westminster Abbey), upon which the kings of Scotland had been crowned for centuries. As the Scotch

W. F. Taylor

FIG. 110. *Conway Castle*

Edward built this fine castle in 1284 on the north coast of Wales, to keep the Welsh in check. Its walls are twelve to fifteen feet in thickness. There were buildings inside, including a great banqueting hall one hundred and thirty feet in length

continued to resist him, Edward attempted to make their country a part of England in the same way that he had treated Wales. But a heroic leader, Robert Bruce, had arisen to defend the Scotch against the English king, and Edward was unable to conquer them.

Edward I died, old and worn out, in 1307, when on his way north to put down a rising under Bruce, and left the task of dealing with the Scotch to his incompetent son, Edward II. The Scotch acknowledged Bruce as their king and completely defeated Edward II in the great battle of Bannockburn (1314), the most famous conflict in Scottish history. But still the English refused to acknowledge the independence of Scotland. For nearly three hundred years England and Scotland were from time to time at war with one another. The bitter opposition of the Scotch came to an end only when a Scotch king, James VI, succeeded to the throne of England in 1603, as James I (p. 725).

The Scotch Nation Differs from the English. In the course of their struggles with England the Scotch people of the Lowlands had become more closely bound together. The long independence of Scotland, although it caused much bloodshed, served to develop certain permanent differences between the little Scotch nation and the rest of the English race. No Scotchman to the present day likes to be mistaken for an Englishman. The peculiarities of the language and habits of the people north of the Tweed have been made familiar to all readers of good literature by the novels of Sir Walter Scott and Robert Louis Stevenson and by the poems of Robert Burns.

4. A Period of Absolute Monarchy in England

The Power of Parliament Declines. It was during the Hundred Years' War, waged by King Edward III and his successor against France, that Parliament made its extraordinary gains in power. It achieved the right not only to decide on the levying of taxes but to make laws and, on occasion, to express frankly its disapproval of the king's policy.

This development of parliamentary power, however, did not continue. Although, in the seventeenth century, Parliament finally established itself permanently as the great power in English government, there was a period of some two hundred years when it let itself be managed by the king and when England was under absolute monarchs who used Parliament merely to carry out their wishes. This was the period of the Tudors and early Stuarts. The decline of Parliament came about as a result of general conditions in England.

The Wars of the Roses (1455–1485). When the war with France was brought to an end, England did not enter a period of peace, for there followed thirty years of civil war within the kingdom itself. This was carried on by groups of powerful nobles and their retainers. The parties were led by members of rival branches of the royal family, the House of Lancaster and the House of York.[1] The emblem of the House of York was a white rose; so the House of Lancaster adopted a red rose as its badge, and the long struggle came to be called the *Wars of the Roses*. This conflict, which had no other reason behind it than jealousy and greed, is a disgraceful record of treachery, murder, and the execution of defeated rivals. Most of the great nobles of England were killed and their estates confiscated. Finally the last victor of the Lancastrian line, Henry Tudor, came to the throne as Henry VII.

Absolutism under the Tudors. With the accession of the House of Tudor the period of absolute monarchy begins. In the first place, nearly all the nobles who could have made trouble for the new king had perished on the battlefield or had been executed. The king had come into possession of vast estates which had been confiscated, and his wealth made him far more independent than most of his predecessors had been. Moreover, by avoiding foreign wars, he was not forced to ask Parliament for money and so made himself independent of its approval. He could circumvent Parliament, even if he could not do away with it entirely.

[1] Descent of the rival Houses of Lancaster and York, and the beginning of the Tudor line of kings:

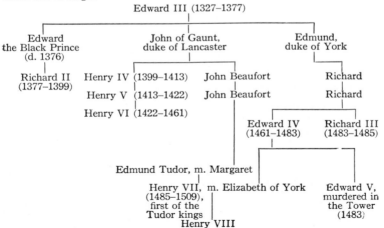

Fig. 111. *Origin of the Symbols of the Parties of Lancaster and York*

The wrangling nobles are walking in the Temple Gardens. Richard Plantagenet, the great Duke of York (left foreground), challenges those who would support him in his quarrel with the Duke of Somerset (right) "to pluck a white rose from the brier with me." Those at the left pluck "a pale and maiden blossom" (the white rose of York), while Somerset's sole follower picks a red rose (the badge of the Lancaster party). (From a painting by Henry A. Payne in the British House of Lords. Reproduced by permission of the Fine Arts Publishing Company)

It should be said, however, that though the Tudors were despotic they knew how to get along with their Parliaments by appearing to seek their advice. Moreover, during the long period of fighting, new business and interests had developed in England. The nobles who were always seeking more power were gone, and the middle classes were absorbed in other matters than that of government.

Growth of Towns in the Fifteenth Century. This was a period of prosperity for the middle classes. English towns

were developing. Better buildings were being constructed, streets were being paved and houses improved, and wharves and markets were multiply-
ing. Townspeople were se-
curing charters for the towns, and laws that protected their business and trade. The development of towns resulted from increased manufactur-
ing carried on in England, and from trade not only within the country but with foreign countries as well. Ships brought products of European countries and the East and carried away English wool and manufactured articles. Foreign workmen came to England, and the English learned from them many ways of improving their manufacturing and many new

FIG. 112. *Henry VII of England*

From a bust by Torrigiano in the Vic-
toria and Albert Museum

arts and crafts. The business class was strongly against war, for only in time of peace could business and trade flourish.

Effects of the Normans on English Civilization. A well-
known historian has said that the Norman Conquest was "the most important single event" in English history. In leaving this topic we may do well, therefore, to remember some of the ways in which England was permanently affected by this memorable invasion.

In the first place, the coming of William meant not merely a change of kings but the introduction of a new people into the English nation. The Conqueror and his companions were French. For centuries Frenchmen ruled England; the nobility, bishops, abbots, and government officials were mainly French. Besides these, the architects who built the castles, fortresses, cathedrals, and abbeys came from Normandy, and one may see throughout England today ex-

Fig. 113. *Ely Cathedral. The Prior's Door, Showing Late-Norman Decoration*

amples of the Norman architecture of this period. Merchants from Rouen and Caen followed the Conqueror, and weavers from Flanders settled in England. The influence of all these foreigners on business, manufacturing, government, religion, and art is beyond measure. New occupations, trades, interests, and ideas were added to English civilization, to say nothing of a new language; for French was the language of the court and of the nobility, while Anglo-Saxon remained the speech of the peasants. Latin was used by the Church, and later in the law. This combination finally resulted in making English a far richer language than it would otherwise have been; for many words and expressions derived from Latin and French became a part of modern English.

The Norman kings laid the foundations of the future government of their country. They unified the people under a strong monarchy; they developed the means of administering justice to all in the courts by introducing the jury system; they replaced feudal courts by the king's courts and created a respect for the "common law." Educated in the principles of justice, the people finally forced from a tyrannical ruler the great charter of liberties which has ever since been the pride of the English people. Representative government was developed by including the "commons" in the national council, and the success of this method of government has given to England the name "Mother of Parliaments."

Questions and Exercises

REVIEW OF CHAPTER

1. What is the importance of English history for English-speaking peoples? What were William's claims to the English throne? What measures did he take to strengthen his power? What permanent contributions were made by Henry II to the English system of government? Explain the jury system.

2. Give the chief provisions of the Great Charter. How did the English Parliament originate? Describe its hold over the kings. Who were included in the House of Lords? in the House of Commons?

3. How did the English kings get control of Wales and Scotland?

4. How did the Tudor line of monarchs originate? What was the policy of Henry VII? Summarize some of the effects of the Norman Conquest on later England.

USEFUL TERMS

See how much meaning you can give to the following: *Danegeld, Witenagemot, Domesday Book, curia regis, justice* (two meanings), *confiscate, jury, verdict, indictment, precedent, common law, charter, prelate, excommunicate, fees, fines and penalties, lords spiritual, lords temporal, commons, arts and crafts.*

DIRECTIVE QUESTIONS

1. What is a census? Do governments have censuses today? Did William the Conqueror have one?

2. Name some of the features of a strong, unified government which began to develop in England between the time of William the Conqueror and that of Henry VII.

3. How did the medieval trials compare, in their fairness, with trial by jury? How are citizens of the United States tried today?

4. What is representative government? Compare the state of the government in England, from this point of view, in the time of William the Conqueror, Edward I, Henry VII, and, if you can, today.

5. What is an archbishop? How many archbishops are there in England? How far back in history does this arrangement go?

6. What is the origin of the title " Prince of Wales," and to whom does this title belong?

DISCUSSION TOPICS

1. English-speaking peoples have inherited much from England.

2. One invasion proved to be a benefit to the conquered.

3. The knowledge of Latin aids one in understanding and using English. (A few examples are such words as "verdict," "jury," "excommunicate," "justice." Support your position with additional words.)

4. The opinion of a jury of twelve is likely to be fairer than the opinion of one. Is this true if the twelve are uneducated and the one is a highly trained judge?

ADDITIONAL ADVENTURES IN LEARNING

1. **Studies in Source Materials.** ROBINSON, *Readings*, Vol. I, chap. xi, sect. i, How Alfred the Great tried to improve learning; sect. ii, The battle of Hastings; p. 227, The condition of England before the Norman Conquest; sect. iii, The Doomsday Book; sects. iv–v, The Great Charter and its provisions; sect. vi, How the bishops, barons, and commoners were summoned to the "Model Parliament." CHEYNEY, *Readings in English History*, chap. vii, sect. i, Result of the coming of William the Conqueror to England; chap. viii, sect. i, The reforms of Henry II; chap. x, sect. ii, Edward III establishes the Order of the Garter.

2. **Supplementary.** Make a list of the important rights gained by the English in the Great Charter. Are these laws still in force?

3. **Topical Studies.** The effects of the Norman Conquest on English civilization, in language, laws, manufacture, etc.: CHEYNEY, *Short History of England*; QUENNELL, *The Making of Everyday Things in England*. How the English people lived: SALZMANN, *Life in Medieval England*; BOISSONADE, *Life and Work in Medieval Europe*. How Parliament developed in England: CHEYNEY, *Short History of England*; C. P. ILBERT, *Parliament*.

4. Look up, in an encyclopedia, Robert the Bruce. GREEN, *Short History of the English People*, chap. iv, sect. vi.

CHAPTER XXV · THE WEST LEARNS FROM THE EAST: THE CRUSADES

TROUBLES OF THE EASTERN ROMAN EMPIRE · A HUNDRED AND FIFTY YEARS OF CRU-
SADING · CHIEF RESULTS OF THE CRUSADES

WE HAVE had little reason to refer to the eastern portion of the old Roman Empire, of which Constantinople was the capital. This region had also been repeatedly invaded by barbarous peoples, but it retained more of the old civilization of the Greeks and Romans than did the West. When an Eastern emperor called on the Pope to send him aid against new enemies, and great numbers of western Europeans trooped eastward to Constantinople and the Near East, they discovered many things of which they had never heard in their villages and little Western towns. This makes it important to bring into our story the expeditions called the Crusades.

The new enemies who threatened the Eastern Empire were the Seljuk Turks, who, coming from the interior of Asia, had overrun the Holy Land and treated Christian pilgrims with great cruelty. The emperor, in desperation, appealed to the Pope and to all Christians to aid him in driving back these fierce infidels. The astonishing response of Western Christians was a widespread enthusiasm for setting out to recapture the Holy Land from the hands of the unbelievers. Tens of thousands of persons, of all ages and conditions of life, started out on the long pilgrimage to Jerusalem. Their sufferings were terrible; many never lived to return home, and some never even reached their goal.

One of the most striking features of this movement was the fact that Christians all over Europe combined for the first time in a common undertaking. Warring nobles gave up their quarrels with one another, and rich and poor, lords and simple folk, were ready to devote themselves to the great cause of saving Christendom from unholy hands. Europe had united in the defense of Christianity, which was permanently to be the leading religion of our civilization.

Another important result of the Crusades was the new and lasting relations established between western Europe and the East. Thousands of Europeans were brought into contact with civilizations, including that of the Arabs, which were higher than their own. They saw new lands and unfamiliar customs, and became acquainted with luxuries of which they had never dreamed. All these ideas and experiences were an education which stimulated the people of the West to seek ways to obtain for themselves the refinements and knowledge they had found in the East.

1. TROUBLES OF THE EASTERN ROMAN EMPIRE

The Empire attacked on All Sides. Although the Empire in the East was able to maintain itself for a thousand years longer than the western portion of the Roman Empire, it had many dangerous experiences and lost many of its provinces. Outside peoples threatened and invaded its territory as they had that of the West. Sometimes they settled down within its boundaries, but sometimes they conquered the armies sent against them and took the land away from the empire altogether. Constantinople itself was besieged more than once, but its strong natural defenses helped it always to hold off its enemies. While many emperors, good and bad, came and went, and the government was often weakened by dissensions, conspiracies, and murders, yet the ancient capital continued the tradition of the old Roman Empire.

We cannot take the space here to tell the story of the barbarian tribes which were a constant danger to the northern boundaries. Among these were the Avars, a tribe from southern Russia who were long a serious menace and raided the Empire from time to time. Then there were the Slavs, who, driven by the Avars, invaded the Empire and pushed down into the Balkan Peninsula, where they established themselves permanently. The Eastern Empire was even more directly exposed to the wandering tribes from Asia than was the West, and we find Bulgars, Russians, and Magyars, or Hungarians, among those who plundered its lands and settled where they wished.

While the Empire was still suffering from the effects of long wars with Persia, its eastern portions fell victim to the Mohammedans, of whom we have spoken earlier (p. 412) In a few years the Persian kingdom was in the hands of the Moslems, who within a century had taken possession of Syria, the Holy Land, Egypt, northern Africa, and Spain. They attempted to take Constantinople, but were unable to capture the capital city. The struggle between the Christians and Moslems continued for two hundred years, until by the year 1000 the emperors had freed Asia Minor and extended their rule as far as Antioch.

The New Danger from the Turks. Before long a new and powerful foe threatened the lands of the Empire. This was a rude people from Turkestan called the *Seljuks* (named from their leader). After conquering the Persian kingdoms and adopting the religion of Islam, they began a new period of Mohammedan conquest. When, in the seventh century, the city of Jerusalem had fallen into the hands of the Arabs, Christians had been allowed to visit, untroubled by Mohammedans, the places associated with the life of Christ. But with the arrival of the Seljuk Turks the pilgrims began to bring home news of great hardships and cruel treatment. Moreover, the Eastern emperor was defeated by the Turks in 1071 and lost Asia Minor. The Turks, who had taken possession of the fortress of Nicæa, just across from Constantinople, were now a serious danger to the Eastern Empire. Finding himself unable to drive them away, Emperor Alexius appealed to the Pope, Urban II, for aid.

The Western (Latin) Church and the Eastern (Greek) Church. The Eastern and Western churches had drifted apart. The Eastern Church had refused to acknowledge the leadership of the Pope and was under the direct control of the emperor. The "patriarch," as the head of the Greek church was called, was a mere deputy of the crown and enjoyed no such power and influence as did the Popes at Rome. Moreover, the churches of East and West had seriously disagreed in regard to certain doctrines and in 1054 had broken completely with each other. The Roman Catholic Church looked upon the Greek Church as a body of *schismatics*, who had refused to join their fellow Christians in the West.

Under these circumstances it might seem surprising that Pope Urban responded so promptly to the appeal of the emperor. But, aside from the desire to protect his fellow Christians, there were doubtless other practical considerations which influenced him. In the first place, the struggle over investiture was still dragging on, and the opportunity which was thus presented to Urban to place himself at the head of a movement uniting all Christians might greatly increase the importance of the papacy. The Pope may also have hoped that sponsoring the Crusade would bring the Greek Church once more under his control. It would certainly bring the Holy Land and the East under the influence of the Latin Church. Then, too, there was the fear that the Turks, if not halted, might overcome the Eastern Empire and then invade Europe. So there were many good reasons, besides those which the Pope emphasized in his address, which gave his appeal power to move greatly those who listened to him at Clermont.

2. A Hundred and Fifty Years of Crusading

Urban II issues Call to First Crusade (1095). Urban responded to the emperor's cry for help at the church council held at Clermont, in France (1095). In an address which produced more remarkable immediate results than any other which history records, the Pope exhorted knights and soldiers of all ranks to give up their usual wicked business of destroying their Christian brethren in private warfare (see pages 431 ff.) and to turn, instead, to the assistance of their fellow Christians in the East. He warned them that the Turks would, if unchecked, extend their sway still more widely over the faithful servants of the Lord. Urban urged, besides, that France was too poor to support all its people, while the Holy Land flowed with milk and honey. "Enter upon the road to the Holy Sepulcher; wrest the land from the wicked race and subject it to yourselves."

When the Pope had finished, all who were present exclaimed, with one accord, "It is the will of God." This, the Pope declared, should be the rallying cry of the Crusaders, who were to wear a cross upon their bosoms as they went forth, and upon their backs as they returned, as a holy sign of their sacred mission. It was this symbol of the cross (Latin, *crux*) that led these expeditions to be called "Crusades."

Many Reasons for Joining the Crusades. The Crusades are a striking illustration of the simple faith and religious enthusiasm which existed in the Middle Ages. Thousands of earnest Christians started on the dangerous journey to

Jerusalem with the sole object of helping to free the Holy Sepulcher from the hands of unbelievers. But there were also thousands who joined the Crusades for less noble reasons. In a movement attracting such vast crowds there were bound to be many kinds of people, all with their own interests in mind. There were the merely adventurous, who liked to go on a far journey and were caught by the wide-prevailing excitement of the enterprise. There was many a noble who dreamed of securing a piece of territory for himself over which he might rule; there was the merchant who saw the opportunity for new business; and there were the discontented and restless who wished to get away from home and its responsibilities, and even criminals who saw in the Church's promises a way to escape from the results of their past offenses.

In his famous address Urban had appealed to those who had been "contending against their brethren and relatives" and to those "who have hitherto been robbers now to become soldiers of Christ." The behavior of the

Fig. 114. *A Crusader in Armor*

From a model in the Musée de l'Armée, Paris

Crusaders when they reached strange lands seems to show that many of those who had been warlike and even criminal had taken the Pope at his word.

The Pope held out inducements which were very tempting to the ordinary man. The faithful Crusader was to be free of all punishment for his past sins; he was promised immediate entrance into heaven if he died repentant. Later the

Church went so far as to interfere in business contracts; for those who entered upon the journey "with a pure heart" it dared to free from the payment of interest on their debts. It also permitted them to carry on business transactions against the wishes of their feudal lords, thus freeing them from their solemn obligations as vassals.

Crowds of Simple People Start Ahead of the Crusade. The Council of Clermont met in November. After this meeting Urban preached the Crusades elsewhere in southern France, and others followed his example. The most famous was Peter the Hermit, who rode from place to place on a mule preaching and exhorting the people. His feet were bare, he ate very little, and he was a strange-looking figure as he journeyed about urging repentance upon his fellows. Soon he came to be regarded as a saint sent from God and drew thousands of simple folk after him. By the spring of 1096 a great army of common folk — peasants, workmen, vagabonds, and even women and children — were impatient to start off, blindly intent on rescuing the Holy Sepulcher, several thousand miles away. They were sure that the Lord would sustain them during the weary miles of the journey and that when they reached the Holy Land he would grant them a prompt victory over the unbelievers. Although the Pope had set August as the time for the departure of the First Crusade, the excited crowds of simple folk were unwilling to wait and so started off ahead in several different divisions, under the leadership of Peter the Hermit, Walter the Penniless, and other simple knights utterly unfit to manage successfully such an undisciplined crowd of people. Many of these "Crusaders" were slaughtered by the Hungarians, who rose to protect themselves from the plunderings of this motley horde in its passage through their country. Part of them got as far as Nicæa, only to be massacred by the Turks. This is but an example of what was going on for a century or so after this first great catastrophe. Individual pilgrims and adventurers, and sometimes groups of Crusaders, fell a prey to starvation, slavery, disease, and death in their persistent endeavors to reach the far-away Holy Land.

FIG. 115. *Departure of a Group of Knights for a Crusade*

From a fourteenth-century miniature

The First Crusade (1096). The most striking figures of the
long period of the Crusades are not, however, to be found
among the lowly followers of Peter the Hermit but are the
knights, in their long coats of flexible armor. It was nearly
a year after the summons issued at Clermont before the great
armies of fighting men which had been collected in the West
under distinguished leaders were ready to start out. The
Pope speaks of three hundred thousand soldiers. Of the various divisions which were to meet in Constantinople, the
following were the most important: the volunteers from
southern France, under the papal legate and Count Raymond
of Toulouse; inhabitants of Germany, particularly of Lorraine, under Godfrey of Bouillon and his brother Baldwin,
both of whom later became rulers of Jerusalem; and, lastly,
an army of French and of the Normans of southern Italy
under Bohemond and Tancred.[1]

---

[1] For the routes taken by the different crusading armies, see the map on
pages 524–525

Upon the arrival of the Crusaders at Constantinople it soon became clear that they had not much more in common with the "Greeks"[1] than with the Turks. Emperor Alexius ordered his soldiers to attack Godfrey's army, encamped in the suburbs of his capital, because their chief at first refused to take the oath of feudal homage to him. The emperor's daughter Anna, in her history of the times, gives a sad picture of the outrageous conduct of the Crusaders on their way to the Holy Land. They, on the other hand, denounced the Greeks as traitors, cowards, and liars.

The Eastern emperor had hoped to use his Western allies to reconquer Asia Minor and force back the Turks. The leading knights, on the contrary, had little interest in the emperor's plans but dreamed of carving out realms for themselves in the former dominions of the emperor and of controlling them by right of conquest. Later we find both Greeks and Western Christians shamelessly allying themselves with the Mohammedans against each other.

Crusaders take Jerusalem. The first real allies that the Crusaders met with were the Armenians, who were Christians, and who gave them aid after their terrible march through Asia Minor. With their help Baldwin got possession of Edessa, of which he made himself prince. The chiefs induced the great body of the Crusaders to postpone the march on Jerusalem, and a year passed during which they were engaged in taking the rich and important city of Antioch. Then Raymond of Toulouse set to work and conquered a principality for himself on the coast about Tripoli.

In the spring of 1099 about twenty thousand warriors were at last able to move upon Jerusalem. They found the city well walled, in the midst of a desolate region where neither food nor water nor the materials to construct the siege machinery necessary for the capture of the Holy City were to be had. However, the fortunate arrival at Jaffa of galleys sent from Genoa furnished the besiegers with supplies, and, in spite of all the difficulties, the place was taken in a couple of

---

[1] The people of the Eastern Empire were called Greeks because the Greek language continued to be used in Constantinople.

FIG. 116.   *Crac-des-Chevaliers*

This is an example of the strong castles that the Crusaders built in Syria. It was completed, in the form here represented, about the year 1200 and lies halfway between Antioch and Damascus.   It will be noticed that there was a fortress within a fortress. View taken from the air

months. The Crusaders showed no mercy to the people of the city, but with shocking barbarity massacred the inhabitants. Godfrey of Bouillon was chosen ruler of Jerusalem and took the modest title of "Defender of the Holy Sepulcher." He soon died, and was succeeded by his brother Baldwin, who left Edessa in 1100 in order to take up the task of extending the bounds of the kingdom of Jerusalem.

Founding of Kingdoms in Syria by the Franks. It will be observed that the "Franks," as the Mohammedans called all the Western folk, had established the centers of four principalities. These were Edessa, Antioch, the region about Tripoli conquered by Raymond, and the kingdom of Jerusalem. The last was further increased by Baldwin, who, with the help of the mariners from Venice and Genoa, succeeded in getting possession of Acre, Sidon, and a number of smaller coast towns.

The Crusaders' States in Syria

The news of these Christian victories quickly reached the West, and in 1101 tens of thousands of new Crusaders started eastward. Most of them were lost in passing through Asia Minor, and few reached their destination. The original conquerors were consequently left to hold the land against the Mohammedans and to organize their conquests as best they could. This was a very difficult task—too difficult to accomplish under the circumstances.

The permanent hold of the Franks upon the eastern borders of the Mediterranean depended upon the strength of the colonies which their various princes were able to establish. It is impossible to learn how many pilgrims from the West made their permanent homes in the new principalities. Certainly the greater part of those who visited Palestine returned home after fulfilling the vow they had made — to kneel at the Holy Sepulcher.

Still, the princes could rely upon a certain number of soldiers who would be willing to stay and fight the Mohammedans. The Turks, moreover, were so busy fighting one another that they showed less energy than might have been expected in attempting to drive the Franks from the narrow strip of territory (some five hundred miles long and fifty wide) which they had conquered.

The Second and Third Crusades. Fifty years after the preaching of the First Crusade, the fall of Edessa (1144), an important outpost of the Christians in the East, led to a second great expedition. This was forwarded by the famous preacher Saint Bernard, who went about persuading volunteers to take the Crusader's cross. In a fierce hymn of battle he cried to the Knights Templars: "The Christian who slays the unbeliever in the Holy War is sure of his reward, the more sure if he himself be slain. The Christian glories in the death of the infidel, because Christ is glorified." The king of France readily consented to take the cross, but the emperor, Conrad III, yielded only after Saint Bernard had preached before him and given a vivid picture of the terrors of the Judgment Day.

In regard to the majority of the Crusaders, a historian of the time tells us that so many thieves and robbers hastened to take the cross that everyone felt that such enthusiasm could only be the work of God himself. Saint Bernard, however, the chief promoter of the expedition, afterward gave a most unflattering description of the "soldiers of Christ." "In that countless multitude you will find few except the utterly wicked and impious, the sacrilegious, homicides, and perjurers, whose departure is a double gain. Europe rejoices to lose them and Palestine to gain them; they are useful in both ways, in their absence from here and their presence there." It is unnecessary to describe the movements and

Metz

Vézelay

Ratisbon

Frederick Barbarossa

Godfrey of Bouillon

Louis VII

HUNGARY

Lyon

Philip Augustus

Venice

Rhône R.

Marseille

Richard

Genoa

Raymond of Toulouse →

D A L M A T I A

A D R I A T I C   S E A

CORSICA

Rome

North French

Thessalonica

SARDINIA

Naples

Richard

Bari

Durazzo

Normans

Brindisi

Otranto

Philip Augustus →

SICILY

Reggio

Richard 1191

M E D I T E R R A N E A N

MALTA

Routes

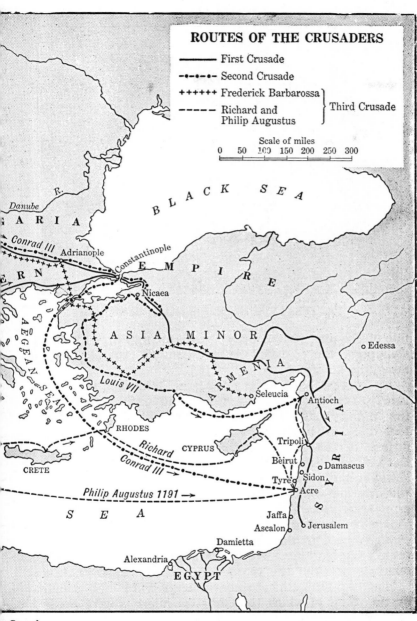

ROUTES OF THE CRUSADERS

——— First Crusade
-·-·-·- Second Crusade
++++++ Frederick Barbarossa ⎱ Third Crusade
------ Richard and ⎰
Philip Augustus

Scale of miles
0   50   100   150   200   250   300

BLACK   SEA

R.
Danube

ARIA

Conrad III   Adrianople   Constantinople

RN

EMPIRE

Nicaea

AEGEAN SEA

ASIA   MINOR

ARMENIA

Edessa

Louis VII

Seleucia

Antioch

RHODES

CYPRUS

Tripoli

SYRIA

Richard

Beirut

Damascus

Conrad III

CRETE

Tyre   Sidon

Philip Augustus 1191 →

Acre

SEA

Jaffa

Ascalon

Jerusalem

Damietta

Alexandria

EGYPT

Crusaders

Fig. 117. *Church of the Holy Sepulcher in Jerusalem*

fate of this unorganized body of Crusaders. From a military standpoint the so-called Second Crusade was certainly a miserable failure.

In the year 1187, forty years later, Jerusalem was recaptured by Saladin, the most heroic and distinguished of all the Mohammedan rulers of that period. The loss of the Holy City led to the most famous of all the military expeditions to the Holy Land, in which Emperor Frederick Barbarossa, Richard the Lion-Hearted of England, and his rival, Philip Augustus of France, all took part. Frederick was drowned while crossing a stream in Asia Minor, and his army scattered. The accounts of this Third Crusade show that while the Christian leaders hated one another heartily enough, the Christians and Mohammedans were coming to respect one another. We find examples of the most polite relations between the representatives of the opposing religions. In 1192 Richard concluded a truce with Saladin, by the terms of which the Christian pilgrims were allowed to visit the holy places in safety and comfort.

Later Crusades. In the thirteenth century the Crusaders began to direct their expeditions toward Egypt as the center of the Mohammedan power. The first of these undertakings was diverted in an extraordinary manner. The Venetians, who had arranged to furnish ships and provisions for the enterprise, persuaded the Crusaders with their help to attack Constantinople instead. The city was captured, its works of art were destroyed, and its treasure was divided among the invaders. But the Latin empire established as a result of this disgraceful expedition lasted but a short time.

The further expeditions of Emperor Frederick II and Saint Louis, king of France, need not be described. Jerusalem was permanently lost in 1244; and, although the hope of recovering the city was not given up, the Crusades may be said to have come to a close before the end of the thirteenth century.

3. Chief Results of the Crusades

Military Religious Orders. A noteworthy outcome of the crusading movement was the foundation of several orders, or societies, of which the Hospitalers and the Templars were the most important. These orders combined the two great interests of the time, those of the monk and of the soldier. They permitted a man to be both at once: the knight might wear the habit of a monk over his coat of armor.

The Hospitalers grew out of a monastic association that was formed before the First Crusade for the aid of the poor and sick among the pilgrims. Later the society admitted noble knights to its membership and became a military order, at the same time continuing its care for the sick. This charitable association, like the earlier monasteries, received generous gifts of land in western Europe and built and controlled many fortified monasteries in the Holy Land itself. After the Christians left Syria in the thirteenth century, the Hospitalers moved their headquarters to the island of Rhodes, and later to Malta. The order still exists, and it is considered a distinction to this day to have the privilege of wearing its emblem, the cross of Malta.

The Templars. Before the Hospitalers were transformed into a military order, a little group of French knights banded together in 1119 to defend pilgrims, on their way to Jerusalem, from the attacks of enemies. These knights were given quarters in the king's palace at Jerusalem, on the site of the former Temple of Solomon; hence the name "Templars," which was to become famous. The "poor soldiers of the Temple" were enthusiastically approved by the Church. They wore a white cloak adorned with a red cross, and were under a very strict monastic rule which bound them by the vows of obedience, poverty, and celibacy. The fame of the order spread throughout Europe, and persons belonging to the highest rank, even dukes and princes, were ready to renounce the world and to serve Christ under the black and white banner of this distinguished order.

From the first the order was aristocratic, and it soon became very rich and independent. It had its collectors in all parts of Europe, who forwarded the "alms" they received to the Grand Master at Jerusalem. Towns, churches, and estates were given to the order, as well as vast sums of money. The Pope showered privileges upon the Templars. They were excused from tithes and taxes and were brought under his immediate protection; they were released from feudal obligations, and bishops were forbidden to excommunicate them.

No wonder they grew insolent and aroused the jealousy and hate of princes and clergy alike! Early in the fourteenth century, through the combined efforts of the Pope and Philip the Fair of France, the order was brought to a terrible end. Its members were accused of the most abominable practices, such as the worship of idols and the systematic insulting of Christ and his religion. Many distinguished Templars were burned as heretics; others perished in dungeons. The once powerful order was abolished and its property taken away.

Settlements of the Italian Merchants. For one class, at least, the Holy Land had great and permanent charms, namely, the Italian merchants, especially those from Genoa, Venice, and Pisa. It was through their early interest and by means of supplies from their ships that the conquest of the

Fig. 118. *Crusaders Viewing the Wares of the Merchants at Constantinople*

Holy Land had been made possible. The merchants always made sure that they were well paid for their services. When they aided in the successful siege of a town, they arranged that a definite quarter should be assigned to them in the captured place where they might have their market, docks, church, and all that was necessary for a permanent center for their business. This district belonged to the town from which the merchants came. Venice even sent governors to live in the quarters assigned to its citizens in the kingdom of Jerusalem. Marseille also had independent quarters in Jerusalem, and Genoa had its share in the county of Tripoli.

Oriental Luxury introduced into Europe. This new trade with the Orient had a most important influence in bringing the West into permanent relations with the East. Eastern products from India and elsewhere — silks, spices, camphor, musk, pearls, ivory, and the like — were brought by the Mohammedans from the East to the commercial towns of Palestine and Syria; then, through the Italian merchants, they found their way into France and Germany, bringing with them ideas of luxury hitherto scarcely dreamed of by the still half-barbarous Franks.

Effects of the Crusades on Warfare. Moreover, the Crusades had a great effect upon the methods of warfare; for the soldiers from the West learned from the Greeks the old Roman methods of using machines for attacking castles and walled towns. This led, as has been pointed out in a previous chapter (pp. 434–435), to the building in western Europe of stone castles, first with square towers and later on with round ones, whose remains can still be seen in France, Germany, England, and other countries. In addition, the Crusades produced heraldry, or the use of "coats of arms." These were the badges that single knights or groups of knights adopted in order to distinguish themselves from other people.

Other Results of the Crusades. Some of the effects of the Crusades upon western Europe may readily be seen, even from this very brief account. Thousands and thousands of Frenchmen, Germans, and Englishmen had traveled to the Orient by land and by sea. Most of them, whether they came from simple dwellings or from castles, could never have learned much of the great world beyond the limits of their native village or province. They suddenly found themselves in great cities and in the midst of unfamiliar peoples and customs. This could not fail to make them think and give them new ideas to carry home. The Crusade was an education. The Crusaders came into contact with those who knew more than they (above all, the Arabs), and brought back with them new notions of comfort and ways of living other than their own.

Yet in attempting to discover what were the direct effects of the Crusades on the West, it should be remembered that many of the new things may well have come from Constantinople, or through the Mohammedans of Sicily and Spain, quite independently of the armed expeditions into Syria. The western Europeans derived many important ideas from the Mohammedans in Spain, such as *Arabic* numerals, alchemy, algebra, and the use of paper. Moreover, during the twelfth and thirteen centuries towns were rapidly growing up in Europe, trade and manufactures were developing, and the universities were being founded. It would be absurd to suppose that without the Crusades this progress would not have taken place. So we may conclude that the distant expeditions and the contact with strange and more highly civilized peoples, if they did no more, at least hastened the improvement which was already beginning before Urban made his ever-memorable address at Clermont.

Questions and Exercises

REVIEW OF CHAPTER

1. From what invaders did the Eastern Empire suffer? How had the Eastern and Western Christian churches become separated? How nearly had the Turks reached Constantinople before the Crusades?

2. What reasons did Urban II urge for joining in a crusade? What other reasons did men have for going to the Holy Land? What were the results of the First Crusade? What reasons were given for the Second Crusade? What highly important rulers joined the Third Crusade?

3. Tell something about the military religious orders. What cities used the Crusades to increase their business? What were some of the effects on our civilization of bringing Western people into contact with the East?

USEFUL TERMS

See how much meaning you can give to the following terms: *patriarch, provinces, pilgrimages, council, sepulcher, flexible armor, principalities, alms, homicide, perjurer.*

DIRECTIVE QUESTIONS

1. Was the pilgrimage a new idea at the time of the Crusades?

2. How far, roughly, did a Crusader have to journey if he came from Lorraine? from Toulouse? from northern Germany?

3. How did the Eastern Empire serve as a protection to the West during the Middle Ages?

4. Can you name any of the elements of Eastern and Saracen civilization which would have seemed new to a western European at the time of the Crusades?

DISCUSSION TOPICS

1. The Crusades were not entirely a religious enterprise.

2. The Eastern Empire helped to preserve Roman civilization.

3. European civilization was affected by the Crusades.

4. The civilizations of the East were higher than that of the West in the eleventh century.

ADDITIONAL ADVENTURES IN LEARNING

1. **Studies in Source Materials.** ROBINSON, *Readings*, Vol. I, chap. xv, sect. i, A report of Pope Urban's address at Clermont; sect. ii, An account of the First Crusade by a historian of the twelfth century; 125, "A Greek princess describes the bad manners of a crusading prince"; sect. iii, Letters from the Crusaders; sect. iv, Saint Bernard promotes the Second Crusade; sect. v, The pilgrimage of Udalrich; sect. vi, Privileges granted by the Popes to the Crusaders; sect. vii, An account of the luxury at the court of Constantinople (949).

2. **Supplementary.** Make a map showing the routes of the First and Second Crusades. Look up in an encyclopedia the word "cross." Draw pictures showing the difference between the Latin cross, the Maltese cross, the cross patée, and the swastika, or hooked cross.

Do you know any of Scott's novels which deal with this period? Who were the royal knights that took part in the Third Crusade?

3. **Topical Studies.** Pilgrims in the Middle Ages: CUTTS, *Scenes and Characters of the Middle Ages*, Part III; SALZMANN, *English Life in the Middle Ages*, pp. 274 ff.; J. J. JUSSERAND, *English Wayfaring Life*, Part III, "Religious Wayfarers." The civilization of the Arabs: MUNRO and SONTAG, *The Middle Ages*, chap. xix. Anecdotes of the Crusades: *Memoirs of the Crusades*, by Villehardouin and Joinville (Everyman Edition).

CHAPTER XXVI · HOW THE GROWTH
OF TOWN LIFE ADVANCED CIVILIZATION

REAPPEARANCE OF TOWNS · DEVELOPMENT OF BUSINESS · OVERCOMING BUSINESS
DIFFICULTIES · THE ITALIAN CITIES AND THE RENAISSANCE · HOW BUSINESS ENTER-
PRISE LED TO THE DISCOVERY OF NEW LANDS · HOW THE TOWNS BUILT THE
GOTHIC CHURCHES

D URING the Feudal Age almost all the people of Europe from whom
we are descended were serfs on the estates of the nobility. The
number of families on a manor might differ greatly; but they all raised their
own food, and supplied their other needs without having much to do with
the outside world. They did the same things and thought the same thoughts
as had their ancestors. Life brought little change, and there was no chance
of progress.

After about the year 1000, towns began to grow up. People had begun
to turn from farm life to manufacturing and trade. They began once more
to use money instead of paying for things with labor or with farm produce.
If a serf could get money for his work, he could buy things he had never had
before or he might even run away from the farm altogether.

The growth of towns and, later, of large cities is one of the most important developments in the story of civilization. When great numbers of people live close together, they can combine and so secure advantages that no
village could possibly afford. Commerce developed and extended. Business
carried merchants or their agents from place to place and greatly broadened
the knowledge of the townspeople. The Italian cities took the lead in trade
and richness of life; but the northern towns soon followed their example.
Business enterprise led to bold attempts to cross the ocean and to the discovery of lands unknown to the Greeks and Romans. Had not the towns
grown rich, they could never have built the marvelous churches, called
cathedrals, which are among the most beautiful structures men ever combined to create.

1. REAPPEARANCE OF TOWNS

Progress Impossible in an Age of Disorder. During the
turmoil and disorder of the early Middle Ages there was no
chance for progress in civilization, and, as we have seen,
much that man had earlier gained was forgotten or lost.
When, however, kings got control of their rebellious and

warring vassals and were able to maintain a fair amount of order in their realms, conditions were established under which improvements could be made along many lines and new arts could be encouraged.

In England the Norman kings secured order and were able to lay the foundations of a strong, unified state, and afterwards the principles of representative government were gradually developed. In France, until much later, the kings were so occupied in trying to get complete possession of their royal territories that there was little time for anything else.

Reappearance of Towns a Sign of Progress. One of the first evidences of progress after the Age of Disorder was the reappearance and growth of towns. From the break-up of the Roman Empire to the time of William the Conqueror there were no large, flourishing towns in Europe. Towns or cities are necessarily the chief centers of progress and enlightenment for the simple reason that people must live near each other in large numbers before they can join together in any enterprise, whether it be improving the conditions of living, establishing schools and colleges, building hospitals and museums, developing business on a large scale, or organizing trade with a far-off country. Until our own time the country people have been too scattered and too poor to have the conveniences which were possible in the cities.

Disappearance of the Roman Cities. The Roman towns were already decreasing in population before the German invasions. The changes and confusion which followed the migrations hastened the decline, and a great number of them disappeared altogether. Those which managed to survive were of little importance during the early Middle Ages. For over six centuries by far the greater part of the people of England, Germany, and northern and central France were living in the country, on the great estates of the feudal lords, abbots, and bishops.

How the Towns Grew Up. Most of the medieval towns, of which we begin to have some scanty records about the year 1000, started on the manors of feudal lords or around a castle or monastery. The French name for "town," *ville,* comes from the Latin word *villa,* which means an estate or manor (compare *vill* and *villein,* p. 435). We can now understand why the names of towns — such as Abbeyville, Harrisville, and Jacksonville — often have the ending "ville."

The little towns were by no means safe from the attacks of neighboring feudal lords, so that a wall was often built around them to protect the inhabitants as well as the country people who might seek shelter in time of danger. Crowded within its wall, the medieval town had to be built up very closely. The streets were often mere alleys, above which the overhanging upper stories of the higher buildings nearly met, shutting out the sunlight. Aside from the

Fig. 119. *A Street in Vitré, France, a Medieval Town on the River Vilaine*

The narrow, crooked streets are very picturesque. The second stories of some of the old houses project over the pavements below

market place there were few open spaces, and there were no amphitheaters or public baths such as the Roman towns had had. Moreover, the high, thick wall prevented the town from growing easily, as our towns are able to do today.

How the Medieval Towns developed Trade. All towns outside of Italy (p. 454) were small in the eleventh and twelfth centuries and, like the manors on which they had grown up, had little business, as yet, with the outside world. They produced almost all that their inhabitants needed except the farm products which came in from the neighboring country. Gradually the townspeople learned to make things for a wider market, especially if they were situated where they could get raw materials or if they were skillful in any one line. When new and attractive goods began to be brought to them from the South or from the East, the townsmen became interested in making articles which they could send to a neighboring fair and sell, in order to purchase the products from the distant regions. In this way manufacturing and trade developed.

The Towns find it Necessary to get Charters. The towns, especially those which were successful in business, soon found it necessary to secure some form of agreement with the lord of the manor which permitted them more freedom in regulating their own affairs. As long as the town remained under the absolute control of the lord or the monastery on whose ground it was situated, there was little prospect of growth or development. The townspeople were scarcely better off than serfs, in spite of the fact that they lived in a protected community and were workmen and traders and not farmers. They still had dues to pay, like the country serfs.

Moreover, when the townspeople began to engage in manufacturing and trade with the outside world, they found that their landlords could tax them heavily in order to share in the profits. Consequently, during the twelfth century there were many insurrections of the towns against their lords, and there was a general demand that the lords should grant the townsmen *charters*, in which the rights of both lord and people should be clearly stated.

These charters were written contracts, between the lord and the town government, containing the rules by which the town was to be governed. The old dues and services which the townspeople owed as serfs (pp. 436 f.) were either abolished or changed into money payments.

The free towns often had a belfry, a high building with a watchtower, where a guard was kept day and night who

Ewing Galloway

FIG. 120. *Nuremberg*

On the left is a watchtower of masonry, with four corner turrets, built by the people of Nuremberg in 1377. Immediately adjoining is the Granary, with its tall roof with many dormers, built in 1494–1495. This building was used as a stable during the visits of the emperor and so acquired the name *Kaiserstallung* (Imperial Stables). The tower at the right, known even in the Middle Ages as "Old Nuremberg," is considered the oldest structure in the town; it is possibly of Roman origin. The upper part fell in the Middle Ages and was replaced with brick work. In the foreground is a portion of the city wall and moat, which is filled with trees and bushes

could ring the bell to warn the people in case of approaching danger. The building contained an assembly hall, where those who governed the town held their meetings, and a prison. In the fourteenth century stately town halls began to be erected which, with the exception of the cathedrals and other churches, are usually the most interesting buildings that the traveler sees today in the old commercial cities of Europe.

2. DEVELOPMENT OF BUSINESS

Decline of Business during the Age of Disorder. The chief reason for the growth of the towns and their increasing prosperity was a great development of trade throughout western Europe. Commerce — that is, extensive trading — had pretty much disappeared with the decline of the Roman roads and the general disorder produced by the barbarian invasions. In the early Middle Ages there was no one to mend the ancient Roman roads. The great network of highways which spread from Persia to Britain fell apart when independent nobles or poor local communities took the place of a world empire. All business declined; for there was little demand for those articles of luxury which the Roman settlements in the north had been accustomed to get from the south, and there was but little money to buy what we should consider the comforts of life, — even the nobility lived uncomfortably enough in their rudely furnished castles.

Italian Cities trade with the Orient. In Italy, however, trade does not seem to have altogether ceased. Venice, Genoa, Amalfi, and other towns appear to have developed a considerable Mediterranean commerce even before the Crusades (map, p. 524). Their merchants, as we have seen, supplied the destitute Crusaders with the material necessary for the conquest of Jerusalem (p. 520). The enthusiasm for pilgrimages encouraged the Italian merchants to make journeys to the Orient; for they transported the pilgrims to the Holy Land and, returning, brought back the products of the East. The Italian cities set up trading stations in the East and carried on a direct business with the caravans which brought as far as the shores of the Mediterranean the products of Arabia, Persia, India, and the Spice Islands. The southern French towns and Barcelona entered into trading relations with the Mohammedans in northern Africa.

The Luxuries of the East introduced into Europe. The stories of the twelfth century show that the West was astonished and delighted by the luxuries of the East — the silks and other rich fabrics, rugs, precious stones, perfumes, drugs, and porcelains from China, spices from India, and cotton from Egypt. Venice introduced from the East the silk industry and the manufacture of those glass articles which the traveler may still buy in the Venetian shops. The people of the West learned how to make silk and velvet as well as light and gauzy cotton and linen fabrics. The Eastern dyes were introduced, and Paris was soon imitating the tapestries of the Orient. In exchange for those luxuries which they were unable to produce, the Flemish towns sent their woolen cloths and Italy its wines to the East.

Business Centers in Northern Countries. The northern merchants dealt mainly with Venice and brought their purchases across the Brenner Pass and down the Rhine, or sent them by sea to be exchanged in Flanders (map, p. 540). By the thirteenth century important centers of trade had come into being, some of which are still ranked among the world's foremost commercial cities. Bremen, Lübeck, and Hamburg carried on active trade with the countries on the Baltic and with England. Augsburg and Nuremberg, in southern Germany, attained great importance on account of their situation on the line of trade between Italy and the north. Bruges and Ghent sent their manufactures everywhere. English commerce was relatively unimportant, as yet, compared with that of the great ports of the Mediterranean.

Business Difficulties. Medieval business was hampered by many obstacles which do not exist today. Modern business is recognized, encouraged, and protected by the government, as essential to the welfare and prosperity of the nation. In the Middle Ages, however, business was pretty much a private affair, and business men had to look after their own interests if they wished to succeed at all. We can better understand the difficulties that the early townsmen had to face if we compare their situation with that of today.

Scarcity of Money. In the first place, as has been said earlier, there was little money, and business could not develop so long as people merely exchanged, or *bartered*, one thing for another. Money is necessary to buying and selling on a large scale. There were few gold and silver mines in western Europe, and the kings and feudal lords could not obtain much metal for coins. Such coins as were issued were rudely made, and the edges were so rough and irregular that many

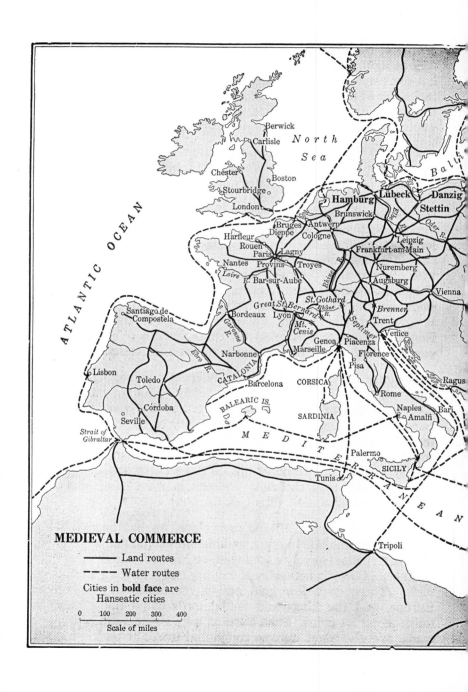

MEDIEVAL COMMERCE

——— Land routes

- - - - Water routes

Cities in **bold face** are
Hanseatic cities

0   100   200   300   400
Scale of miles

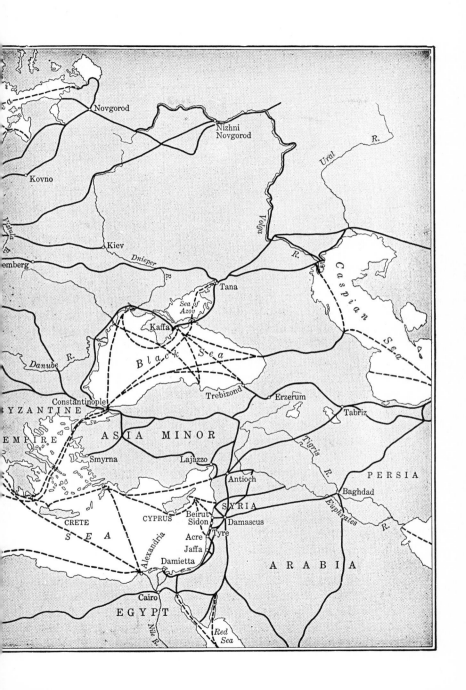

people were tempted to pare off a little of the precious metal before they passed the money on. "Clipping," as this was called, was harshly punished; but that did not stop the practice. Modern coins are perfectly round, with milled edges, specially finished so that no one can grind off bits of them without its being very easily detected.

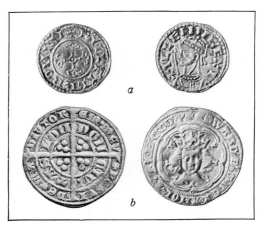

Fig. 121. *Medieval Coins*

a, face and back of a silver penny of William the Conqueror's reign; *b*, a silver groat of Edward III's reign. (Courtesy of American Numismatic Society)

In modern times there is plenty of money to carry on business, and also there is a system of *credit*, by which people can obtain things without paying *cash* at the moment if they have the reputation of being honest and reliable and agree to settle their bills later. Not only do individuals make use of credit, but business men buy their goods or finance their undertakings in this way because of its convenience. A great deal of business is carried on every day without the use of any cash. Yet the banks have money stored away which can be called for at any moment.

The Just Price versus the Profit System. In the second place, the whole question of profits — that is, what a business man should make out of his venture — was entirely different from what it is today. It was universally believed that everything had a "just" price, which was merely enough to cover the cost of the materials used in its manufacture and to repay the maker for the work involved. It was considered outrageous to ask more than the just price, no matter how eager the purchaser might be to buy the article.

It would be very difficult today to determine the just price of any article, since business methods are so different from what they were in the Middle Ages. Many people ordinarily take part in a business transaction besides the person who makes the goods and the one who buys them, and the amounts these people receive for handling, marketing, and advertising have all to be added to the final cost. Business men ordinarily go into enterprises for as large profits as possible, and would think the medieval idea of a "just price" extremely little reward for their pains and risk.

No Wholesale Business Allowed. Every manufacturer was required to keep a shop in which he offered at retail all that he made. Those who lived near a town were permitted to sell their products in the market place within the walls on condition that they sold directly to the consumers. They were not permitted to dispose of their whole stock to one dealer, for fear that if he had all there was of a commodity he might raise the price above the just one. These ideas made all wholesale trade very difficult.

Today it would seem impossible to get along without wholesale business, since everything is made on such a large scale, usually by the use of machinery. Great numbers of people have now to be supplied with many things which were undreamed-of in the little medieval towns. Great stocks of goods and of raw materials have to be brought together and distributed to retail dealers and manufacturers. Any attempt to keep within the limits once imposed upon wholesale trade would destroy the whole modern business system.

Payment of Interest on Money Forbidden. Akin to these prejudices against wholesale business was that against charging *interest* for lending money. Money was believed to be a dead and barren thing, and no one, it was thought, had a right to demand any return for lending it. If this view were held today, there would be no banks or trust companies, and a large part of all the business and financial transactions which contribute to our modern civilization would at once disappear. The convenience of borrowing money is now regarded as so great as to be worth a recompense to the person or institution that accommodates the borrower. But in the Middle Ages interest was considered wicked, since it was often exacted by those who took advantage of the needs and embarrassments of others. This, of course, is still true, though to a less degree, perhaps, than in medieval times. The changed view as to charging interest is due to an entirely different business system, which is greatly aided by a regulated practice of lending and a reasonable charge for the use of money.

"Usury," as the taking of even a moderate and reasonable rate of interest was then called, was strictly forbidden by the laws of the Church. So money-lending, which is necessary to all great business undertakings, was left to the Jews, who were not required to obey the rules established by the Christian Church for its own members.

The Jews as Money-lenders. This unfortunate people played a most important part in the business development of Europe; but they were terribly illtreated by the Christians, who held them guilty of the supreme crime of putting Christ to death. The active persecution of the Jews did not, however, become common before the thirteenth century, when they first began to be required to wear a peculiar cap, or badge, which made them easily recognized. Later they were sometimes shut up in a particular quarter of the city, called the Jewry, or ghetto. As they were kept out of the guilds, they not unnaturally turned to the business of money-lending, which no Christian might practice. Undoubtedly this occupation had much to do with causing their unpopularity. The kings permitted them to make loans, often at a most extravagant rate; Philip Augustus allowed them to charge 46 per cent, but he reserved the right to extort their gains from them when the royal treasury was empty. In England the usual rate was a penny a pound for each week.

In the thirteenth century the Italians began to go into a sort of banking business which helped merchants to pay their debts more conveniently. In England these Italian bankers were called Lombards, and there is a Lombard Street in London today where several banks have their buildings.

Tolls and Other Annoyances. Another serious disadvantage the medieval merchant had to face was the payment of an endless number of tolls and dues, which were demanded by the lords through whose property his route passed. Not only were charges made for using the highways and bridges and crossing fords, but those barons who were so fortunate as to have castles on a river blocked the stream in such a way that a merchant could not bring his vessel through without paying for the privilege.

The charges were usually small, but the way in which they were collected and the repeated delays must have been a serious source of irritation and loss to the merchants. For example, a certain monastery lying between Paris and the sea required that those hastening to town with fresh fish should stop and let the monks pick out what they thought worth threepence, with little regard to the condition in which they left the goods. When a boat laden with wine passed up the Seine to Paris, the agent of the lord of Poissy could have three casks opened, and, after trying them all, he could take a measure from the one he liked best. At the markets all sorts of dues had to be paid, such, for example, as fees for using the lord's scales or his measuring rod. Besides this, the great variety of coinage which existed in feudal Europe caused infinite perplexity and delay.

It must have seemed to the business man as though everything were arranged to interfere with his operations and that everyone wished to get something from him before he had a chance to make any profit for himself. The older classes of society —"the men of prayer, men of war, and men of work," as Alfred the Great had called them — were jealous of the new business class. There is a sermon dating from the thirteen hundreds in which the preacher says, "God made the clergy, knights, and laborers, but the Devil made the burghers and usurers."

The modern business man has many taxes to pay, some of which may seem to him unreasonable ; but they are fixed by law, and all citizens pay the same in the same situation. On the other hand, governments sometimes establish *tariffs* (taxes on goods coming from other countries), with a view to aiding their own manufacturers. They also grant *sub-sidies* (money assistance) to certain businesses — especially shipping — which they wish to encourage for the public benefit.

Pirates. Commerce by sea had its own particular trials, by no means confined to the dangers of wind and wave, rock and shoal. Pirates were numerous in the North Sea. They were often organized and sometimes led by men of high rank, who appear to have regarded the business as no disgrace. The coasts were dangerous, and lighthouses and beacons were few. Moreover, natural dangers were increased by false signals which were used to lure ships to shore by those who wished to plunder them.

3. Overcoming Business Difficulties

Medieval Business Men discover the Benefits of Organization. Medieval townsmen, workmen, and merchants early discovered what modern workers and employers know very well, that in union there is strength; that in order to promote their own special interests, or to secure any reform, it is necessary for those wishing the change to organize and unite. The townsmen of the Middle Ages, when they found themselves oppressed by their feudal lords, organized into *communes* for the purpose of forcing their lords to make some definite agreement in which their rights and liberties should be stated.

The Craft Guilds. Another form of organization for protection was the *guild*. The tradesmen within the town were divided into groups according to their particular trade. These groups were called guilds. There were, for example, the bakers, the butchers, the weavers, the sword-makers, and the hatters. These organizations were formed to protect the interests of each special trade, and no one was allowed to carry on a business until he was a member of the proper guild. The oldest statutes, or rules, of a guild in Paris are those of the candle-makers, which go back to the year 1061.

FIG. 122. *Glassmaking in the Fifteenth Century*

The rules strictly regulated the manufacture and sale of the goods of each particular guild. They arranged the hours of labor, the quality of materials, the kind of workmanship, and the prices to be charged for the wares. In this way the guilds not only maintained the standard of their manufactures but, by making all details public, prevented any craftsman in the guild from taking advantage of another in his work or materials or in the prices charged. The number of trades differed greatly in different towns, but the guilds were organized with one object — that of preventing anyone from practicing a trade who had not been admitted to the guild.

A young man had to spend several years in learning his trade. During this time he lived in the house of a "master workman" as an "apprentice," or "learner," but received no pay. He then became a "journeyman" and could earn wages, although he was still allowed to work only for master workmen and not directly for the public. A simple trade might be learned in three years, but to become a goldsmith one had to be an apprentice for ten years. The number of apprentices that a master workman might employ was strictly limited, in order that the journeymen might not become too numerous.

Comparison between the Guilds and Trade Unions. The strict regulations of the guilds later interfered with progress; but in the beginning they protected their members from the oppression of their lords. The guilds were, moreover, a sort of benefit society. Dues were paid into the treasury and might be used in times of sickness or other misfortune to help out the unfortunate.

It might seem at first sight that the guilds were a good deal like our modern trade unions, but they were really quite different. The whole business situation has greatly changed since the introduction of machinery on a large scale. Those who formed the guilds were workers who owned their shops and materials. Even the apprentices and journeymen looked forward to becoming master workmen and owners. When machines came to be used, great factories were built by individual capitalists or companies. These owned the buildings, machinery, materials, and products, and took the profits or faced the loss, as the case might be. The employees, or workmen, nowadays usually have to rely entirely upon their wages and have no rights as owners. They form themselves into unions in order to prevent what they believe to be "unfair" treatment by their employers and to be able to bargain collectively in regard to wages, hours of labor, and working conditions.

Ewing Galloway

FIG. 123. *The Famous Cloth Hall at Ypres, Belgium*
Begun in 1201. Destroyed in the World War, 1916

The Merchant Guilds. There had been traveling merchants,
or traders, even before the towns developed. As these merchants increased in numbers they too combined and formed
guilds to protect their special interests. Competition was
strictly regulated; for the interests of the group were considered more important than those of any individual member.
The guilds prohibited forestalling (that is, buying up goods
before they got to market), selling short weight, or asking
more than the established price. They purchased goods to
sell in other towns, supplied raw materials to the craft
guilds, and fixed the prices of incoming goods. They established offices and warehouses, policed trade routes, improved
harbors, built ships and docks, and insured member merchants against loss.

The groups had their own meeting place, or guild hall,
where the sessions were held. As the members were usually
the most influential persons in the communities, the governments soon saw that the organizations were favored.

The Hanseatic League. With a view to overcoming the difficulties of trade, the towns early began to form unions for mutual, or joint, defense. The most famous of these was that of the German cities, called the Hanseatic League. Lübeck was always the leader, but among the seventy towns which at one time or another were included in the League we find Cologne, Brunswick, Danzig, and other centers of great importance. The union purchased and controlled settlements in London — the so-called Steelyard, near London Bridge — and at Wisby, Bergen, and the far-off Novgorod (in Russia). They managed to get control of nearly the whole trade on the Baltic and the North Sea, either through treaties or through the influence that they were able to bring to bear.

The League made war on the pirates and did much to reduce the dangers of traffic. Instead of sending out separate and defenseless merchantmen,[1] it had its ships sail in fleets under the protection of a man-of-war. On one occasion the League undertook a successful war against the king of Denmark. At another time it declared war on England and brought her to terms. For two hundred years before the discovery of America the League played a great part in the commercial affairs of western Europe; but it had begun to decline even before the discovery of new routes to the East and West Indies revolutionized trade.

Trade carried on by Towns, not by Nations. It should be observed that during the thirteenth, fourteenth, and fifteenth centuries trade was not carried on between *nations* but between various *towns*, like Venice, Lübeck, Ghent, Bruges, and Cologne. A merchant did not act or trade as an independent individual but as a member of a particular merchant guild, and he enjoyed the protection of his town and of the treaties it arranged. If a merchant from a certain town failed to pay a debt, a fellow townsman might be seized if found in the town where the debt was due. An inhabitant of London was considered as much of a foreigner in Bristol as was the merchant from Cologne or Antwerp. Only gradually did the towns merge into the nations to which their people belonged.

[1] The ships of the Hanseatic League were very small (Fig. 185).

Rise of a New Class in Society. The increasing wealth of the merchants could not fail to raise them to a position of importance which earlier tradesmen had not enjoyed. They began to build fine houses and to buy the various comforts and luxuries which were finding their way into western Europe. They wished their sons to be educated, and so it came about that other people besides clergymen began to learn how to read and write. As early as the fourteenth century many of the books appear to have been written with a view to meeting the tastes and needs of the business class.

Representatives of the towns were summoned to the councils of the kings — to the English Parliament and the French Estates-General (about the year 1300); for the monarch was obliged to ask their advice when he demanded their money to carry on his government and his wars. The rise of the business class alongside the older orders of the clergy and nobility is one of the most important changes of the thirteenth century.

4. The Italian Cities and the Renaissance

The Renaissance. We have been speaking so far of the town life in northern Europe in the twelfth and thirteenth centuries. We must now see how the Italian towns in the following two centuries reached a degree of prosperity and refinement undreamed-of north of the Alps. Within their walls learning and art made such extraordinary progress that a special name is often given to the period when they flourished — the *Renaissance*,[1] or "new birth." The Italian towns, like those of ancient Greece, were little states, each with its own individual life and government. Some of them, like Rome, Milan, and Pisa, had been important in Roman times; others, like Venice, Florence, and Genoa, did not become of importance until about the time of the Crusades.

The map of Italy at the beginning of the fourteenth century was still divided into three zones, as it had been in the time of the Hohenstaufens.[2] To the south lay the kingdom

---

[1] This word, although originally French, has come into such common use that it is quite permissible to pronounce it as if it were English, — *rĕ-nā'sạns.*

[2] See map, p. 455.

Fig. 124. *A Street Scene in Venice*

Boats, called gondolas, are used instead of carriages in Venice; one can reach any point in the city by some one of the numerous canals, which take the place of streets. There are also narrow lanes along the canals, crossing them here and there by bridges, so that one can wander about the town on foot

of the Two Sicilies (or Naples). Then came the States of the Church, extending diagonally across the peninsula. To the north and west lay the group of city-states to which we now turn our attention.

Venice and its Trade with the East. Of these city-states none was more celebrated than Venice, which in the history of Europe ranks in importance with Paris and London. Venice was built upon a group of sandy islets lying in the Adriatic Sea, about two miles from the mainland.[1] It was protected from the waves by a long, narrow sand bar similar to those which fringe the Atlantic coast from New Jersey southward. Such a location would not ordinarily have been chosen as the site of a great city; but it was a good place for fishermen, and its very desolation and remoteness

[1] It is the only surviving successor to the pile villages of the lake-dwellers who wandered down the valley of the Po.

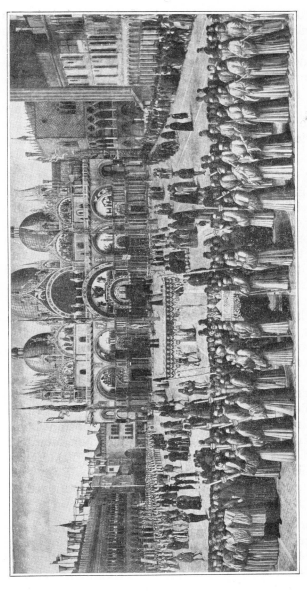

FIG. 125. *A Procession in the Piazza di San Marco*

The church of St. Mark's, modeled after one in Constantinople, was planned before the First Crusade. It is adorned with numerous colored marble columns and slabs brought from the East. The interior is covered with mosaics, some of which go back to the twelfth and thirteenth centuries. The façade is also adorned with brilliant mosaics. St. Mark's "is unique among the buildings of the world in respect to its unparalleled richness of material and decoration." (From a painting by G. Bellini in the Royal Academy, Venice)

recommended it to those settlers who fled from their homes on the mainland during the barbarian invasions. As time went on, the location proved to have its advantages commercially, and even before the Crusades Venice had begun to engage in foreign trade. Its business carried it eastward, and it early gained territory across the Adriatic and in the Orient. The influence of this trade with the East is plainly shown in the celebrated church of St. Mark's, whose domes and decorations suggest Constantinople rather than Italy (Fig. 125).

Venice extends its Control on the Mainland. It was not until early in the fifteenth century that the rulers of Venice began to extend their control upon the Italian mainland. It doubtless seemed dangerous to permit Venice's rival, Milan, to get possession of the Alpine passes through which Venetian goods found their way north. It may be, too, that it seemed safer to get its food supplies from the neighborhood instead of transporting them across the Adriatic from its Eastern possessions. Moreover, all the other Italian cities already controlled a larger or smaller area of country around them.

About this time Venice reached the height of its prosperity. It had a population of two hundred thousand, which was very large for those days. It had three hundred seagoing vessels which went to and fro in the Mediterranean, carrying wares between the East and the West. It had a war fleet of forty-five galleys, manned by eleven thousand marines ready to fight the battles of the republic. But when Constantinople fell into the hands of the Turks (1453), and when, later, the route to India by sea was discovered (pp. 562 ff.), Venice could not maintain control of the trade with the East, and, while it remained an important city, it no longer enjoyed its former influence and power.

Government of Venice. Although Venice was called a republic, it was really governed by a very small group of persons. In 1311, after a rebellion, the famous Council of Ten was created, as a sort of committee of public safety. The government was placed under its guidance and that of the senate and the *doge* (duke), who acted as the head of the

FIG. 126. *The Senate Chamber in the Doge's Palace*

The Doge's Palace contained the government offices and the magnificent halls in which the senate and the Council of Ten held their meetings. The palace was begun about 1350 and shows the influence of the Gothic style of architecture. The walls of the palace were decorated by celebrated painters in the sixteenth century, when Venice became famous for its artists

republic. The government, thus intrusted to a very few, was carried on with great secrecy, so that public discussion, such as prevailed in Florence and led to so many revolutions there, was unheard-of in Venice. The Venetian merchant was such a busy person that he was quite willing that the state should carry on its duties without his interference.

Venice often came to blows with other rival cities, especially Genoa; but while its soldiers fought its enemies, its citizens lived quietly at home under the government of its senate, the Council of Ten, and the doge. Not only were the other Italian towns fighting one another much of the time, but their government was frequently in the hands of *despots*, somewhat like the old Greek tyrants.

Position of the Italian Despots. There are numerous stories of the unbelievable ferocity exhibited by the Italian despots.

FIG. 127. *Cathedral and Bell Tower at Florence*

The church was begun in 1298 and completed in 1436. The great dome built by the architect Brunelleschi has made his name famous. It is three hundred feet high. The façade is modern, but after an old design. The bell tower, or campanile, was begun by the celebrated painter Giotto about 1335 and completed about fifty years later. It is richly adorned with sculpture and colored marbles and is considered the finest structure of the kind in the world

It must be remembered that they were very rarely rightful rulers but usurpers, who could hope to retain their power only so long as they could manage to keep their subjects under control and, besides, defend themselves against other equally unlawful usurpers in the neighboring cities. This situation developed a high degree of shrewdness, and many of the despots found it to their interest to govern well, and even to give dignity to their rule by favoring artists and literary men. But the despot usually made many bitter enemies and was almost necessarily suspicious of treason on the part of those about him.

The Condottieri. The Italian towns carried on their wars among themselves largely by means of hired troops. When a military expedition was proposed, a bargain was made with one of the professional leaders (*condottieri*), who provided the necessary helpers. As the soldiers had no more interest in the conflict than did those whom they opposed, who were likewise hired for the occasion, the fight was not usually very bloody; for the object of each side was to capture the other without unnecessarily rough treatment.

Florence. The history of Florence, perhaps the most important of the Italian cities, differs in many ways from that of Venice and that of the despotisms of which Milan was an example. Florence was a republic, so that all classes claimed the right to interest themselves in the government. This led to constant changes in the constitution and to frequent struggles between the different parties to obtain control of the government.

Fig. 128. *The Palace of the Medici in Florence*

This palace was erected about 1435 by Cosimo de' Medici, and in it Lorenzo the Magnificent conducted the government of Florence and entertained the men of letters and artists with whom he liked best to associate. It illustrates the fortress-like lower portions of a Florentine palace, which were designed to protect the owner from attack

When one party got the upper hand, it generally expelled its chief opponents from the city. Exile was a terrible punishment to one who loved his native town.

The Medici; Lorenzo the Magnificent. By the middle of the fifteenth century Florence had come under the control of the great family of the Medici, whose members played the rôle of very enlightened political bosses. By quietly watching the elections and secretly controlling the selection of city officials, they governed without letting it be suspected that

Fig. 129. *A Bedroom in the Fourteenth-Century Davanzati Palace, Florence*

the people had lost their power. The most distinguished member of the house of Medici was Lorenzo the Magnificent (d. 1492). Under his rule Florence not only prospered in industry and commerce but also reached the height of its glory in the production of art and literature, for Lorenzo was a sincere admirer and generous patron of men of genius.

As one wanders about Florence today he is impressed with the contradictions of the Renaissance period. The streets are lined with the palaces of the noble families to whose rivalries much of the continual disturbance was due. The lower stories of these buildings are constructed of great stones, like fortresses, and their windows are barred like those of a prison (Fig. 128); yet within they were often furnished with the greatest taste and luxury. For in spite of the disorder, against which the rich sought protection by building their houses like strongholds, the beautiful churches and noble public edifices, and the many works of art which now fill the museums, show that mankind has never, perhaps, reached a higher degree of perfection in the arts of peace than amid the turmoil and agitation of this restless town.

Fig. 130. *St. Peter's and the Vatican Palace*

St. Peter's, the largest church in the world, is about seven hundred feet long and four hundred and forty-eight feet high. The reconstruction was begun as early as 1450. Several great architects — Bramante, Raphael, Michelangelo, and others — were intrusted with the work. The new church was finally in condition to consecrate in 1626. It is estimated that it cost over $50,000,000. The vast palace of the Popes, to the right of the church, was constructed during the same period. Some of its rooms are celebrated for frescoes by Raphael, Michelangelo, and others of Italy's greatest artists

Rome again the Capital of the Papacy. During the same period in which Venice and Florence were becoming leaders in wealth and refinement, Rome, the capital of the Popes, was likewise undergoing a great change. After the Popes returned from seventy years' residence in France and Avignon (pp. 652 f.), they found Rome in a dilapidated state. For years they were able to do little to restore it, as the papacy was weakened by the existence of a rival line of popes who continued to live at Avignon and to assert that they were the true Popes. But when the "Great Schism" (division) was over, and all the European nations had once more acknowledged the Pope at Rome to be the true head of the Church (1417), it became possible to improve the city and revive some of its ancient glory. Architects, painters, and literary men were handsomely paid by the Popes to erect and adorn magnificent buildings and to collect a great library in the Vatican Palace.

St. Peter's and the Vatican. The ancient basilica of St. Peter (Fig. 85) no longer satisfied the ambitions of the Popes. It was gradually torn down, and after many changes of plan the present famous church, with its vast dome and impressive approach (Fig. 130), took its place. The old Lateran Palace, where the government of the Popes had been carried on for a thousand years, had been deserted after the return from Avignon, and the new palace of the Vatican was built to the right of St. Peter's and added to by successive Popes. It has thousands of rooms, some of them adorned by the most distinguished Italian painters. Besides it has numerous halls, courts, and gardens. Its art treasures include magnificent examples of the work of Raphael, Michelangelo, Botticelli, and others. Its museum has the choicest collection of Greek and Greco-Roman sculpture in existence; while the vast Vatican library contains not only thousands of volumes but many priceless manuscripts.

As one visits Venice, Florence, and Rome today he may still see, almost perfectly preserved, many of the finest of the buildings, paintings, and monuments which belong to the period we have been discussing.

5. How Business Enterprise led to the Discovery of New Lands

Medieval Commerce on a Small Scale. The business and commerce of the medieval towns was on what would seem to us, after all, a rather small scale. There were no great factories, such as have grown up in recent times with the use of steam and machinery, and the ships which sailed the Mediterranean and the North Sea were small and held only a very light cargo as compared with modern merchant vessels. The gradual growth of a *world* commerce began with the sea voyages of the fifteenth century, which led to the exploration by Europeans of the whole globe, most of which was entirely unknown to the Venetian merchants and those who carried on the trade of the Hanseatic League. The Greeks and Romans knew little about the world beyond southern Europe, northern Africa, and western Asia, and much that they knew was forgotten during the Middle Ages. The Crusades took many Europeans as far East as Egypt and Syria.

Marco Polo. About 1260 two Venetian merchants, the Polo brothers, visited China and were kindly received at Peking by the emperor of the Mongols. On a second journey they were accompanied by Marco Polo, the son of one of them. When they got back to Venice in 1295, after a journey of twenty years, Marco gave an account of his experiences which filled his readers with wonder. Nothing excited the interest of the West more than his marvelous description of the abundance of gold in Zipangu (Japan) and of the spice markets of the Moluccas and Ceylon.

The Discoveries of the Portuguese. About the year 1318 Venice and Genoa opened up direct communication by sea with the towns of the Netherlands. Their fleets, which touched at the port of Lisbon, aroused the business ambition of the Portuguese, who soon began to undertake larger maritime expeditions. By the middle of the fourteenth century Portuguese mariners had discovered the Canary Islands, Madeira. and the Azores. Before this time no one had ven-

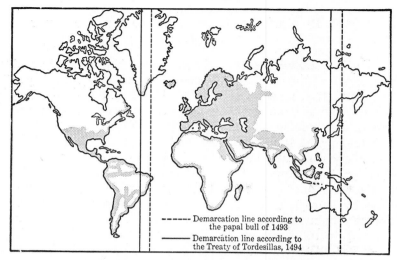

- - - - - Demarcation line according to
the papal bull of 1493
————— Demarcation line according to
the Treaty of Tordesillas, 1494

The World as the Europeans knew it in 1550

tured along the coast of Africa beyond the desert region of Sahara. In 1445, however, some adventurous sailors came within sight of a headland beyond the desert, and, struck by its luxuriant growth of tropical trees, they called it Cape Verde (the "green cape"). Its discovery put an end once for all to the idea that there were only parched deserts to the south.

For a generation the Portuguese ventured farther and farther along the coast, in the hope of finding it coming to an end, so that they might make their way by sea to India. At last, in 1487, Dias rounded the Cape of Good Hope. Eleven years later (1498) Vasco da Gama, spurred on by Columbus's great discovery, sailed around the Cape of Good Hope. He proceeded northward to a point beyond Zanzibar, and thence, aided by an Arab pilot, steered eastward straight across the Indian Ocean and reached Calicut, in Hindustan, by sea.

The Spice Trade. Vasco da Gama and his fellow adventurers were looked upon with natural suspicion by the Mohammedan spice merchants, who knew very well that

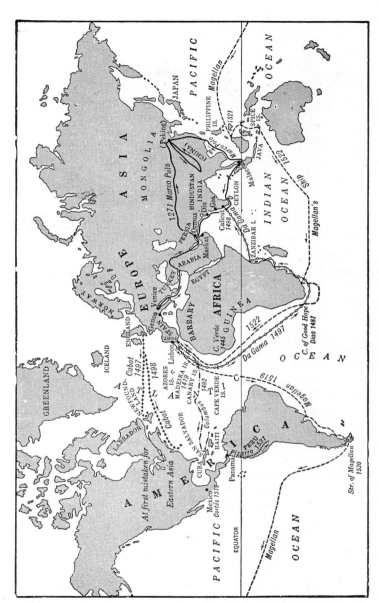

The Voyages of Discovery

The Malay Archipelago
The area of Portuguese exploration at the opening of the sixteenth century

their object was to establish *direct* trade between the Spice Islands (Moluccas) and western Europe. Hitherto the Mohammedans had had the entire control of the spice trade between the Moluccas and the eastern ports of the Mediterranean, where the products were handed over to Italian merchants. The Mohammedans were unable, however, to prevent the Portuguese from making treaties with the Indian princes and establishing trading stations at Goa and elsewhere. In 1512 a successor of Vasco da Gama reached Java and the Moluccas, where the Portuguese speedily built a fortress. By 1515 Portugal had become the greatest among sea powers; and spices reached Lisbon regularly without the assistance of the Mohammedan merchants or of the Italian towns, especially Venice, whose business was fatally hurt by the change (p. 554).

There is no doubt that the desire to obtain spices was at this time the main reason for the exploration of the globe. This motive led European navigators to try in succession every possible way to reach the East: by going around Africa; by sailing west in the hope of reaching the Indies (before they knew of the existence of America); then, after

A Map of the Globe in the Time of Columbus

In 1492 a German mariner, Behaim, made a globe which is still preserved in Nuremberg. He did not know of the existence of the American continents or of the vast Pacific Ocean. It will be noticed that he places Japan (Cipango) where Mexico lies. In the reproduction many names are omitted, and the outlines of North and South America are sketched in so as to make clear the misconceptions of Columbus's time

America was discovered, by sailing around it to the north or south, and even sailing around Europe to the north.

It is hard for us to understand this enthusiasm for spices, for which we care much less nowadays. One former use of spices was to preserve food, which could not then, as now, be carried rapidly, while still fresh, from place to place; nor did our conveniences then exist for keeping it by the use of ice. Moreover, spice served to make even spoiled food more palatable than it would otherwise have been.

Idea of Reaching the Spice Islands by Sailing Westward. It finally occurred to thoughtful men that the East Indies could be reached by sailing *westward.* Many intelligent people knew, all through the Middle Ages, that the earth was a globe. The chief authority upon the form and size of the earth continued to be the ancient astronomer Ptolemy, who lived about A.D. 150. He had reckoned the earth to be about one sixth smaller than it is; and as Marco Polo had given an exaggerated idea of the distance which he and his companions had traveled eastward, and as no one suspected the existence of the American continents, it was supposed that it could not be a very long journey from Europe across the Atlantic to Japan.[1]

Columbus discovers America (1492). In 1492, as we all know, a Genoese navigator, Columbus (b. 1451), who had had much experience on the sea, got together three little ships and undertook the journey westward to Zipangu, — the land of gold, — which he hoped to reach in five weeks. After thirty-two days from the time he left the Canary Islands he came upon land, the island of San Salvador, and believed himself to be in the East Indies. Going on from there he discovered the island of Cuba, which he believed to be the mainland of Asia, and then Haiti, which he mistook for the longed-for Zipangu. Although he made three later expeditions and sailed down the coast of South America as far as the Orinoco, he died without realizing that he had not been exploring the coast of Asia.

Magellan's Expedition around the World. After the bold voyages of Vasco da Gama and Columbus, an expedition headed by the Portuguese Magellan succeeded in sailing around the globe (1519–1522). There was now no reason why the new lands should not become more and more familiar to the European nations. The coast of North America was

[1] See reproduction of Behaim's globe on page 565.

explored principally by English seamen, who for over a century pressed northward, still in the vain hope of finding a northwest passage to the Spice Islands.

The Spanish Conquests in America. Cortes began the Spanish conquests in the western world by undertaking the subjugation of the Aztec empire, in Mexico, in 1519. A few years later Pizarro established the Spanish power in Peru. Spain now superseded Portugal as a sea power, and her importance in the sixteenth century is to be explained largely by the wealth which came to her from her possessions in the New World.

By the end of the century the Spanish Main — that is, the northern coast of South America — was much frequented by adventurous seamen, who combined in about equal parts the occupations of merchant, slaver, and pirate. Many of these came from English ports, and it is to them that England owes the beginning of her commercial greatness.

It is hardly necessary to say that Europeans showed an utter disregard for the rights of the people with whom they came in contact and often treated them with heartless cruelty. The exploration of the globe and the conquest by European nations of peoples beyond the sea led finally to the vast colonization of modern times, which has caused many wars but has served to spread European ideas throughout the world.

6. How the Towns built the Gothic Churches

Churches, the most Important Medieval Buildings. As the business and commerce of the medieval towns increased and brought more wealth into the communities they began to improve their buildings and to vie with each other in giving an air of prosperity to their towns. The most important and imposing building erected in each town or city was, of course, its main church; for in the church the real life of the group centered. Not only was the Catholic Church as an institution possessed of great wealth, but in each community the local church could count on the regular contribution of the members to its treasury. The church buildings were therefore the measure of the wealth and taste of each community.

Most of the buildings of the medieval towns, except the churches, have long since disappeared. Constructed of wood, they have either fallen to pieces or been torn down. As a town grew in importance the walls, no longer needed for protection, were removed, and new streets and avenues carried its houses far beyond its former narrow limits. The old buildings were cleared away in order to straighten and widen the streets and to make room for more modern dwellings. So few walled towns remain today that these are of great interest to the student of the past.

Stone Churches and Cathedrals still Remain. Most of the churches, however, were built of stone and still stand to fill the beholder with wonder and admiration. No modern churches equal them in beauty and grandeur. It seems impossible that the cities of the twelfth and thirteenth centuries, which were neither very large nor very rich as compared with ours today, could possibly have found money enough to pay for them. It has been estimated that the Cathedral of Notre Dame at Paris would cost more than five million dollars to reproduce, and there are a number of other cathedrals in France, England, Italy, Spain, and Germany which must have been almost as costly. They are the most striking memorial of the religious spirit and town pride of the Middle Ages.

How Cathedrals were Built. Of course, it was only in the larger towns, where a bishop resided, that a bishop's church, or cathedral, was erected, and the cathedrals are the most elaborate and expensive of the medieval churches. The construction of a cathedral sometimes extended over two or three hundred years. The work went on slowly, for the money must have been collected penny by penny. Since everybody belonged to the one great Catholic Church, the building of a church was a matter of interest to the whole community — to people of every rank, from the bishop him-

Fig. 131. *The Cathedral of Amiens*

self to the workman and the peasant. The cathedrals, then, represent the interest and devotion of many hearts and the labor of many hands, as well as the savings of the poor and the gifts of the wealthy; for guilds of skilled craftsmen in stone and glass put something more than their daily labor into the construction of these magnificent buildings.

Fig. 132. *The Romanesque Church of Châtel-Montagne, in the Department of Allier, France*

A pure Romanesque building, with no alterations in a later style. Heavy as are its walls, they are reënforced by buttresses along the sides. All the arches are round

Romanesque the Style of the Early Middle Ages. Up to about the twelfth century, churches were built in what is called the *Romanesque,* or Roman-like, style because they resembled the solid old basilicas referred to in an earlier chapter (see pages 396–397). These Romanesque churches had stone ceilings, and it was necessary to make the walls very thick and solid so as to support them (Figs. 84, 132). There was a main aisle in the center, called the *nave,* and a narrower aisle on either side, separated from the nave by massive stone pillars, which helped to hold up the heavy ceiling. These pillars were connected by round arches of stone above them. The tops of the smallish windows were round, and the ceiling was constructed of round arches, or *vaults,* somewhat like a stone bridge; so the use of the *round* arch represents a striking feature of the Romanesque style which distinguishes it from the later Gothic style. The windows had to be small so that the walls should not be weakened.

The Gothic Style. The architects of France were not satisfied, however, with this method of building, and in the twelfth century they invented a new and wonderful way of constructing churches and other buildings that made it possible to do away with the heavy walls and to put high, wide, graceful windows in their place. This style of architecture is known as the *Gothic*. Its underlying principles can readily be understood by studying the accompanying diagram, which shows how a Gothic cathedral is supported not by heavy walls but by *buttresses*.

The architects discovered, first, that the concave stone ceiling, known as the *vaulting* (*A*), could be supported by means of *ribs* (*B*). These ribs could be brought together and supported on top of pillars which rested upon the floor of the church. So far so good! But the builders well knew that the pillars and the ribs would be pushed over by the weight and outward "thrust" of the stone vaulting unless firmly supported from the outside. Instead of erecting heavy walls to give

Fig. 133. *Cross Section of Amiens Cathedral*

It will be noticed that there is a row of rather low windows opening under the roof of the aisle. These constitute the so-called *triforium* (*E*). Above them is the *clerestory* (*F*), the windows of which open between the flying buttresses. So it came about that the walls of a Gothic church were, in fact, mainly windows. These were made of stained glass and gave a beautiful light. The Egyptians were the first to invent the clerestory (Fig. 15)

Fig. 134. *Flying Buttresses*

this support they invented *buttresses* (*D*), built quite outside
the walls of the church and connected by means of "flying"
buttresses (*C*) with the points where the pillars and ribs had
the most tendency to push outward. *Thus a vaulted stone ceiling could be supported without a massive wall.* This clever use
of buttresses instead of walls is the fundamental principle
of Gothic architecture. It was discovered by the architects
in the medieval towns and was probably quite unknown to
earlier builders.

The wall, no longer needed to support the ceiling, was used
only to inclose the building, and windows could be made as
high and wide as pleased the architect. By the use of *pointed*
instead of *round* arches it was possible to give great variety
to the windows and vaulting. So pointed arches came into
general use; and the Gothic is often called the "pointed"
style on this account, although the use of the ribs and buttresses is its chief peculiarity.[1]

---

[1] The misleading name "Gothic" was given to the beautiful churches of the
north by Italian architects of the sixteenth century, who did not like them and
preferred to build in the style of the ancient Romans. The Italians, with their
"classical" tastes, assumed that only German barbarians — whom they carelessly
and ignorantly called Goths — could admire a Gothic cathedral.

Fig. 135. *Interior of the Sainte-Chapelle, Paris*

Colored-Glass Windows. The light from the huge windows (those at Beauvais are fifty to fifty-five feet high) would have been too intense had it not been softened by the stained glass, set in exquisite stone tracery, with which they were filled. The stained glass of the medieval cathedrals, espe-

FIG. 136. *Grotesque Heads, Reims Cathedral*

Here and there about a Gothic cathedral the stone-carvers were accustomed to place grotesque and comical figures and faces. During the process of restoring the cathedral at Reims a number of these heads were brought together, and the photograph was taken upon which the illustration is based

cially in France, where the glass workers brought their art to the greatest perfection, was one of their chief glories. By far the greater part of this old glass has, of course, been destroyed; but it is still so highly prized that every bit of it is now carefully preserved, for it has never since been equaled. A window set with odd bits of it pieced together like crazy patchwork is more beautiful, in its rich and jewel-like coloring, than the finest modern work.

Gothic Sculpture. As the skill of the architects increased they became bolder and bolder and erected churches that were marvels of lightness and delicacy of ornament, without sacrificing dignity or beauty of proportion. The façade, or front, of the cathedral at Amiens, finished in the fourteenth century (Fig. 131), has three beautiful entrances, and a rose window thirty-eight feet across. The Sainte-Chapelle, in Paris, was built in the time of Saint Louis. Its walls are almost completely replaced by windows (Fig. 135).

One of the charms of a Gothic building is the profusion of carving — statues of saints and rulers and scenes from the Bible, cut in stone. The same kind of stone was used both for constructing the building and for making the statues; so they harmonize perfectly. Here and there the Gothic stone-carvers would introduce amusing faces or comical animals (Figs. 136, 137).

In the fourteenth and fifteenth centuries Gothic buildings other than churches were built. The most striking and important of these were the guild halls, erected by the rich corporations of merchant and craft groups, and the town halls of the important cities. But the Gothic style has always appeared specially suitable for churches. Its lofty aisles and open floor spaces, its soaring arches leading the eye toward heaven, and its glowing windows suggesting the glories of paradise (to

Ewing Galloway

Fig. 137. *Figures on Notre Dame, Paris*

Such grotesque figures as these are very common adornments of Gothic buildings. They are often used for spouts to carry off the rain and are called gargoyles, that is, "throats" (compare our words "gargle" and "gurgle"). The two here represented are perched on a parapet of one of the church towers

which men had been taught from childhood they should go when death claimed them if they had lived a godly life) strengthened the faith of the medieval Christian.

Questions and Exercises

REVIEW OF CHAPTER

1. Why did towns disappear in the early Middle Ages? How did the towns grow up? Compare the life of townsmen with that of the serfs. Why were towns necessary to the advance of civilization?

2. What effect did the incoming of Oriental luxuries have on medieval business? Enumerate and discuss the obstacles business formerly faced as compared with our present conditions.

3. Describe the organization of the craft guilds. What were the aims of the merchant guilds? Compare the guilds with modern trade unions. What services were rendered by the Hansa? How did the rise of a business class affect medieval government?

4. Why did the Italian cities excel the northern towns in wealth and the beauty of their buildings? Describe Venice. Tell something about Florence under the Medici. How was Rome developed under the Popes of the time?

5. Why did the search for trade lead to the exploration of the earth? Describe the chief discoveries before Columbus; those after Columbus.

6. What were the characteristics of the Romanesque churches? What was the great discovery made before Gothic buildings could be erected?

Useful Terms

See how much meaning you can give to the following terms: *villa, ville, villein; amphitheater, belfry, tapestries, subsidies, usury, interest on money, credit, guild, apprentice, journeyman, "just price," doge, Renaissance, tariffs, charter, commerce, commune, community.*

Directive Questions

1. What is meant by "the profit system"?

2. How does modern business justify the taking of interest on money?

3. How does wholesale selling promote large business? Why was it prohibited in the Middle Ages?

4. What enterprises can you think of which could take place only in a town or city?

5. What trade routes existed in Roman times?

6. How did business serve as a means of promoting civilization in other than material comforts?

Discussion Topics

1. The "just price" is fairer than the profit system.

2. The discovery of America was an accident.

3. Arts and letters flourish under a tyrannical form of government.

4. The secret of success in any enterprise is organization. Examples in the Middle Ages.

5. Money is necessary for the conduct of business.

Additional Adventures in Learning

1. Studies in Source Materials. ROBINSON, *Readings*, Vol. I, chap. xviii, sect. i, 157, Description of a manor and the services required of the serfs; 158, Description of an English manor house; 160, How a serf was legally made free; sect. ii, Examples of the rules of craft guilds; sect. iii, How the merchants gained protection; sect. iv, 169, The story of a knight of the thirteenth century; 170, "A picture of German life in the thirteenth century"; sect. v, How the Jews were treated.

2. Supplementary. Can you find examples of the influence of the Romanesque or Gothic styles in the architecture you know? Look up in an encyclopedia "Pirates" and "Piracy." Select any article of clothing or furniture and try to find out how many steps intervened between the raw material and the finished product.

3. Topical Studies. Life in a medieval town: SALZMANN, chap. iii; ABRAM, *English Life and Manners in the Later Middle Ages*, chap. iii; TICKNER, *Social and Industrial History of England*, chaps. iv–vi; COULTON, *The Medieval Village*. Life in the country: SALZMANN, chap. ii; LIPSON, *Economic Introduction to the History of England*, chap. iii; TICKNER, chaps. ii–iii. Medieval markets and fairs: LIPSON, chap. vi; THOMPSON, *Social and Economic History*, chap. xxiii. Medieval people at work: HARTLEY and ELLIOTT, *Life and Work of the People of England in the Fifteenth Century*; *Life and Work of the People of England in the Sixteenth Century*; QUENNELL, *A History of Everyday Things in England, 1066–1499*. Early travelers and discoverers: SYNGE, *A Book of Discovery*, chap. xvii (Marco Polo), chap. xx (Prince Henry of Portugal), chap. xxiii (A Great New World); *The Travels of Marco Polo* (Everyman Edition); OLIVERA. *The Golden Age of Prince Henry the Navigator.*

CHAPTER XXVII · HOW OUR FOREFATHERS REGAINED LOST KNOWLEDGE AND MADE NEW DISCOVERIES

HOW OUR MODERN LANGUAGES GREW UP · WHY MEDIEVAL SCIENCE IS NOW A CURIOSITY · ORIGIN OF OUR COLLEGES AND UNIVERSITIES · THE RENAISSANCE · BEGINNINGS OF MODERN INVENTIONS · PROFOUND EFFECTS OF PRINTING · THE ART OF THE RENAISSANCE · THE BEGINNINGS OF OUR SCIENTIFIC AGE

IN THE last chapter we saw that when people began to live in towns again they were able to carry on business on a much larger scale than previously. They erected beautiful buildings, extended their trade into distant regions, and discovered lands of which the Greeks and Romans had known nothing. In this chapter we shall see how some of the most important books of Greek and Roman writers were sought out, copied, and carefully studied, so that men caught up once more with what had been discovered in ancient times. Our modern languages were developing—such as English, French, Italian, and German — in which new books could be written and into which the old Greek and Latin works could be translated. Scholars gathered in universities to study the old writers, especially Aristotle, who they believed knew more than any of the others.

Some thoughtful men were not satisfied with merely learning what had been handed down from former times ; so they began to make investigations for themselves and find out things that nobody had known before. Thus modern science and invention began, which was to change men's ways of living as nothing before had done. Among the earliest inventions were lenses, which were later used for microscopes and telescopes, enabling scientists to learn vastly more than would have been possible without them. With the compass long voyages could be safely made out of sight of land; printing spread knowledge by means of cheap books. Gunpowder greatly altered the old ways of fighting. Artists began to paint more beautiful pictures than any that had been produced in ancient times. Sculptors and architects used old models to make new and original statues and buildings So we may say that from about the year 1100 onward our forefathers not only were recovering all that their predecessors had known but were making wonderful advances of their own.

1. How our Modern Languages grew up

Languages, Living and Dead. Today we use the same language in talking and writing, and we think nothing of it. It seems to us a matter of course. But very commonly the spoken language has been used just for *talking*, and there has been another and older language in which books were written and which the learned used when conversing with one another. This is still the case in China. The daily speech of the Jews in the time of Christ was no longer Hebrew, but the Bible and the ancient laws were in that old language. The spoken language is constantly changing; new words come in and old words are dropped. The language of books tends to remain the same for long periods. If a college professor writes a Latin oration, he will try to imitate the way Cicero wrote two thousand years ago. In former days the speech of the people was called the "mother" tongue or the "vernacular" (from the Latin word *verna*, "household slave"). It was the way the ignorant talked, and was regarded by educated persons as very low and inferior compared with the noble Latin. A few scholars still regard Latin and Greek as far superior to any modern language. But there are now many wonderful books in English, French, German, Italian, Spanish, and Russian. The living languages may be said finally to have gained the victory over the dead ones. Those who have taken the trouble to learn Latin and Greek are usually glad they did so; but there are many fine old books in English, and interesting new ones are constantly appearing.

Use of Latin in the Middle Ages. Latin, of course, was the language used throughout the Roman Empire. After the Empire fell apart, the Church kept on using Latin in its services and its official communications. The standard version of the Bible was in Latin. All books that made any claim to learning were in Latin and continued to be for centuries. Not until about 1700 were there more books published in Germany in the mother tongue than in Latin. In England famous men like Lord Bacon, Milton, and Newton were still writing some of their books in Latin when the early settlements were being made in America. All these authors could, however, write beautiful English and were not ashamed to do so. We still retain many Latin terms in law and medicine, and scientists make up new terms from Latin and Greek words. The Roman Catholic Church still uses Latin in its services. The ability of every educated person to make use of Latin, as well as of his native tongue, was a great advantage at a time when there were many obstacles to communication among the various nations. It helps to explain, for example, the remarkable way in which the Pope kept in touch with all the clergymen of western Christendom, and the ease with which students, monks, and merchants could get along with the people when they wandered from one country to another. There is no more interesting or important revolution than that by which the languages of the people in the various European countries gradually pushed aside the ancient tongue and took its place, so that even scholars scarcely ever think now of writing books in Latin.

The Germanic Languages. It was in the twelfth and thirteenth centuries that the vernacular tongues began to be written and came into rivalry with Latin. These spoken languages belonged to two different groups, with different origins. Those German peoples who had continued to live *outside* the Roman Empire naturally kept the language they had always used, namely, the particular Germanic dialect, or local form of German, which their forefathers had spoken for untold generations. From the various languages used by the German barbarians, modern English, German, Dutch, Swedish, Norwegian, Danish, and Icelandic are largely derived.

The Romance Languages. The second group of languages developed *within* the territory which had formed a part of the Roman Empire, and includes modern French, Italian, Spanish, and Portuguese. These *Romance* languages were derived from the *spoken* Latin, employed by the soldiers, merchants, and people at large. This differed considerably from the elaborate and elegant *written* Latin which was used, for example, by Cicero and Cæsar. It was much simpler in its grammar and varied a good deal in different regions; a Gaul, for instance, could not pronounce the words like a Roman. Moreover, in conversation people did not always use the same words as those employed in books. For example, a horse was commonly spoken of as *caballus*, whereas a writer would use the word *equus*; it is from *caballus* that the words for "horse" in Spanish, Italian, and French are derived (*caballo, cavallo, cheval*).

As time went on, the *spoken* language differed more and more from the *written*. Latin is a troublesome speech, on account of its complicated grammar, and can be mastered only after a great deal of study. The people of the more remote Roman provinces and the incoming barbarians naturally paid very little attention to the niceties of grammar and found easy ways of saying what they wished.[1]

Yet it was several centuries after the German invasions before there was anything written in this conversational language. So long as the uneducated could understand the correct Latin of the books when they heard it read or spoken, there was no necessity of writing anything in their familiar daily speech. But by the time Charlemagne came to the throne the gulf between the spoken and the written language had become so great that he advised that sermons be given thereafter in the language of the people, who could no longer follow the Latin. While little was written in any German tongue before Charlemagne's time, the Germans no doubt possessed an unwritten literature, passed down by word of mouth for several centuries before any of it was written out.

Old English, or Anglo-Saxon. The oldest form of English is commonly called Anglo-Saxon. It is so different from the language which we use that, in order to be read, it must be learned like a foreign language. We hear of an English poet as early as Bede's time (p. 406), a century before Charlemagne.

---

[1] Even the monks and others who wrote Latin in the Middle Ages often did not know enough to follow strictly the rules of the language. Moreover, they introduced many new words to meet the new conditions and the needs of the time, such as *imprisonare*, "to imprison"; *utlagare*, "to outlaw"; *baptizare*, "to baptize"; *foresta*, "forest"; *feudum*, "fief"; etc.

A manuscript of an Anglo-Saxon epic, called *Beowulf*, has been preserved which belongs perhaps to the close of the eighth century. King Alfred displayed great interest in the English language. He actually translated several old Latin works and encouraged the writing of a history of England, the *Anglo-Saxon Chronicle*. This old form of our language prevailed until after the Norman Conquest; the *Anglo-Saxon Chronicle*, which was continued down to 1154, is written in pure Anglo-Saxon. Here is an example:

"Here on thissum geare Willelm cyng geaf Rodberde eorle thone eorldom on Northymbraland. Da komon tha landes menn togeanes him & hine ofslogen, & ix hund manna mid him."[1] In modern English this reads: "In this year King William gave the earl Robert the earldom of Northumberland. Then came the men of the country against him and slew him, and nine hundred men with him."

By the middle of the thirteenth century, two hundred years after the Norman Conquest, English begins to look somewhat familiar, as may be seen in the example which follows:

> And Aaron held up his hond
> To the water and the more lond;
> Tho cam thor up schwilc froschkes here
> The dede al folc Egipte dere;
> Summe woren wilde, and summe tame,
> And tho hem deden the moste schame;
> In huse, in drinc, in metes, in bed,
> It cropen and maden hem for-dred.

In modern English this reads:

> And Aaron held up his hand
> To the water and the greater land;
> Then came there up such host of frogs
> That did all Egypt's folk harm;
> Some were wild, and some were tame,
> And those caused them the most shame;
> In house, in drink, in meats, in bed,
> They crept and made them in great dread.

---

[1] In writing Anglo-Saxon two old letters are used for *th*, one (þ) for the sound in "thin," and the other (ð) for that in "father." The use of these old letters serves to make the language look more unlike that of today than it is.

© British Museum

FIG. 138. *Canterbury Pilgrims, Described by Chaucer in One of his Poems*

Chaucer (about 1340–1400) was the first great English writer whose works are now read with pleasure, though one is sometimes puzzled by his spelling and by certain words which are no longer used. This is the way one of his tales opens:

> A poure wydow somdel stope in age,
> Was whilom dwellyng in a narwe cotage,
> Bisyde a grove, stondyng in a dale.
> This wydwe of wichh I telle yow my tale,
> Syn thilke day that sche was last a wif,
> In pacience ladde a ful symple lyf.

French and Provençal. In the later Middle Ages, however, French, not English, was the most important of the national languages of western Europe. In France the vast literature produced in the language of the people had a great influence on the books written in Italy, Spain, Germany, and England.

Two quite different languages had grown up in France, both derived from the spoken Latin of the old Roman Empire. To the north, an early form of modern French was spoken. This was called the *langue d'oïl*, that is, the speech in which the word for "yes" was *oïl* (modern *oui*). In the south, where Provençal was used, the word for "yes" was *oc*, and the language was accordingly known as *langue d'oc*.

Earliest French Poems. Very little in the ancient French language written before the year 1100 has been preserved. The West Franks undoubtedly began much earlier to sing of their heroes, — of the great deeds of Clovis and Charles the Hammer. These famous rulers were, however, completely overshadowed later by Charlemagne, who became the unrivaled hero of medieval poetry and story. It was believed that he had reigned for a hundred and twenty-five years, and the most marvelous deeds were attributed to him and his knights. He was supposed, for instance, to have led a crusade to Jerusalem. Such themes as these — more legend than history — were woven into long epics, or poems concerning heroes, and were the first written literature of the Frankish people. The most famous of all these long hero songs was the story of Roland (one of Charlemagne's generals) and his marvelous deeds. These poems, combined with the stories of adventure, developed a spirit of patriotic enthusiasm among the French which made them regard "fair France" as the especial care of Providence.

Besides the long and elaborate epics, like the *Song of Roland*, and the romances in verse and prose, there were numberless short stories in verse (the *fabliaux*), which usually dealt with the incidents of everyday life, especially with the comical ones.

Origin of Knighthood. For students following the story of our civilization the chief interest of these early works in the modern languages is the knowledge they give us of the ideals of conduct and character which had developed under feudalism. These are usually summed up under the terms *chivalry* and *knighthood*, which still mean in our own day fine and

FIG. 139. *Medieval Knights Jousting*

The joust was a mock combat between two knights on horseback who charged at each other with blunted weapons to display their skill at arms. To reduce the danger of injury, strict regulations were enacted as to the kind of weapons used and the rules to be followed in the sport. One of these rules was that the paths of the opponents should be separated by a barrier (at first of cloth, later of wood), across which the knights should tilt at each other. The *tournament*, in which a number of contestants on each side took part, was a favorite form of entertainment in the Middle Ages

noble actions. The knights were the heroes of the medieval romances of which we have been speaking, and many modern stories and moving pictures owe their popularity to new kinds of knights who perform wondrous deeds to save ladies from villains and disaster. So we ought to see how the idea of chivalry and knightly deeds grew up hundreds of years ago.

The custom of creating knights had no founder but seems to have developed in western Europe to meet the ideas of the time. When a young man of "good" family had been carefully trained to ride his horse, use his sword, and hunt with skill, he might be made a *knight*. The Church blessed him, and urged him to be true and faithful in his new and honorable position. The actual knighthood was, however, conferred by some older knight by tapping the kneeling young man on the back with the flat of a sword.

Ideals of Chivalrous Conduct. The knight was a Christian soldier, and he and his fellows were supposed to form, in a way, a separate order, with high ideals of the conduct befitting their class. Knighthood was not, however, membership in an association with officers and a definite constitution. It was an ideal, half-imaginary society — a society to which even those who enjoyed the title of king or duke were proud to belong. One was not born a knight, as he might be born a duke or count, and could become one only through the ceremony mentioned above. Although most knights belonged to the nobility, one might be a noble and still not belong to the knightly order, and, on the other hand, one who was baseborn might be raised to knighthood on account of some deed of bravery.

The knight must, in the first place, be a Christian and must obey and defend the Church on all occasions. He must respect all forms of physical weakness and defend the helpless wherever he might find them. He must fight the infidel Mohammedans ceaselessly, pitilessly, and never give way before the enemy. He must perform all his feudal duties, be faithful in all things to his lord, never lie or break his promised word. He must be generous and give freely and ungrudgingly to the needy. He must be faithful to his lady and be ready to defend her and her honor at all costs. Everywhere he must be the champion of the right against injustice and oppression. Chivalry was the ideal and rule according to which the Christian soldier and gentleman should live.

The Troubadours. Turning now to southern France, the beautiful songs of the *troubadours*, which were the glory of the Provençal tongue, reveal a gay and polished society at the courts of the numerous feudal princes. The rulers not only protected and encouraged the poets — they desired to be poets and to enter the ranks of the troubadours themselves. These songs were always sung to an accompaniment of some instrument, usually the lute. The troubadours often traveled from court to court, not only in France but north into Ger-

FIG. 140.   A *Troubadour at a Medieval Castle*

many and south into Italy, carrying with them the southern French poetry and customs. We have few examples of Provençal before the year 1100; but from that time on, for two centuries, countless songs were written, and many of the troubadours enjoyed a very wide reputation.

Romances of King Arthur and the Knights of the Round Table. The famous *Song of Roland* was written before the First Crusade. In the latter part of the twelfth century the romances of King Arthur and his Knights of the Round Table were developed. These enjoyed great popularity in all western Europe for centuries, and they are by no means forgotten yet. Arthur, of whose historical existence no one can be quite sure, was supposed to have been king of Britain shortly after the Saxons gained a foothold in the island.

Sir Thomas Malory, an Englishman who was fighting in France toward the end of the Hundred Years' War, found in what he calls a "Frensshe Booke" the stories about King Arthur and his knights — Tristan and Lancelot, and the magician Merlin and the lady Guenevere — and wrote them out in charming English. He called his book *Morte d'Arthur* ("The Death of Arthur"). Much the easiest way to get some idea of the early notions of knighthood is to hunt up a copy of Malory's famous work, which is not hard to find.

The German Minnesingers. The Germans also made their contribution to the literature of chivalry. The German poets of the twelfth and thirteenth centuries are called *minnesingers*. Like the troubadours, whom they greatly admired, they usually sang of love; hence their name (from the German *Minne*, which is the poetic name for love). The most famous of the Minnesingers was Walther von der Vogelweide (d. about 1228), whose songs are full of charm and of enthusiasm for his German fatherland.

Survival of Medieval Stories. It is wonderful how long-lived these medieval stories have been. Tennyson, in the nineteenth century, revived a number of the tales of Arthur's knights, and an American poet, Edwin Arlington Robinson, has written on the same theme. Some of Wagner's most famous operas revive the old tales that so delighted those who listened to the troubadours and minnesingers seven hundred years ago.

How Italian began to be Written. We have seen how French and Provençal were first used in writing long poems about famous heroes. Another Romance language, Italian, had a different start. It more nearly resembled Latin than the languages outside of Italy and was not written so early. It happened that a very celebrated poet, Dante (1265–1321), although quite able to write in Latin, decided to use his mother tongue, Italian, when he came to compose his immortal work, *The Divine Comedy.* In it he represents himself as led through hell, purgatory, and up into the heavens; he sees and talks with the great men of the past. He also wrote the first treatise on the modern languages. Petrarch (1304–1374), who had a great enthusiasm for the old books (p. 597), wrote mostly in Latin, but composed many charming verses in Italian. His friend Boccaccio wrote in Italian as well as

Latin, and it was under the auspices of these three renowned authors that Italian started on its career.

As the national states of our own time developed they encouraged the use of their particular speech. The sense of union which comes from the speaking of the same language has done much to strengthen nationalism. Nowhere do the peoples of our civilization any longer regard ancient Greek or Latin as superior to their own modern speech.

2. Why Medieval Science is now a Curiosity

Comparison of Modern and Medieval Science. One of the most important studies in our schools and colleges today is *science.* "Science" is a broad term, which really means knowledge (Latin, *scientia*, from *scire*, "to know"); but it has become customary to apply it to certain branches of study concerned with nature and the world about us, — for example, our knowledge of the stars (astronomy), of the earth (geology), of plants (botany), of animals (zoölogy), of the elements of which matter is composed (chemistry). It is within the last hundred years that most of the reliable information that we have about these and many other subjects, such as light, electricity, and atoms and molecules, has been patiently collected. The fact that our civilization today is built on this information, or is profoundly affected by it, has led to calling our era the *Scientific* Age.

Most that passed for knowledge in the Middle Ages is now only a curiosity. Instead of being based on facts that had been observed, tested, and tried, it rested largely on hearsay, folklore, old wives' tales, superstitions, and collections of misinformation reported by well-intentioned but ignorant persons. Popular beliefs were a mixture of fear, superstition, and belief in magic, miracles, and the devil's power. In such an atmosphere learning could make little advance.

General Ignorance of the Past. So long as books had to be copied by hand, they were of course very scarce, and difficult to obtain. Even the things that men had found out in the past and written down were not known except by a very few edu-

FIG. 141.　*A Deep-Sea Monster*

As late as the middle of the sixteenth century it was generally believed that the
Atlantic Ocean was inhabited by weird monsters and swept by fierce winds. Yet
men and women dared to attempt to cross the unknown waters in tiny boats, to
make their homes in a wilderness. (From Olaus Magnus, *Historia de Gentibus
Septentrionalibus*, Rome, 1555)

cated people. Most of what people knew they *heard*. There
were no translations of the great Greek and Roman writers,
— of Homer, Plato, Cicero, or Livy; so only those familiar
with Latin or Greek could learn much about the past.

Wherever the wandering troubadour or minnesinger appeared, he was sure of a delighted audience for his songs and
stories, both serious and light; for all that ordinary folk
could learn of the past they derived from these fantastic
romances which had for their theme the quite impossible
deeds ascribed to Alexander the Great, Æneas, and Cæsar.
As for their own past, the epics relating to the history of
events in France and the rest of Europe were hopelessly
confused. For example, the writers attributed to Charlemagne a great part of the acts of the Frankish kings from
Clovis to Pepin.

We shall see that for the sake of progress in scientific
knowledge many things were needed that the Middle Ages
did not have. In the first place, an entirely different attitude
toward knowledge was necessary. Some effort had to be

made to distinguish between what might be false and what was true. It was necessary for men to observe for themselves the things around them, to compare, to measure, and to use their own intelligence. But some of these required apparatus which they did not yet have. We shall refer to this again when we come to Roger Bacon and the story of inventions (pp. 598 f.).

Medieval Popular Science. Of what we should call scientific books there were practically none. It is true that there was a kind of encyclopedia in verse which gave a great deal of misinformation about things in general. Everyone continued to believe, as the Greeks and Romans had done, in strange animals like the unicorn, the dragon, and the phœnix, and in still stranger habits of real animals. A single example will suffice to show what passed for zoölogy in the thirteenth century.

"There is a little beast made like a lizard, and such is its nature that it will extinguish fire should it fall into it. The beast is so cold and of such a quality that fire is not able to burn it, nor will trouble happen in the place where it shall be." This beast signifies the holy man who lives by faith, who "will never have hurt from fire nor will hell burn him. . . . This beast we name also by another name, salamander. It is accustomed to mount into apple trees, poisons the apples, and in a well where it falls it poisons the water."

It will be noticed that the habits of the animals were supposed to have some moral or religious meaning and carry with them a lesson for mankind. It may be added that this and similar stories were centuries old and are found in the encyclopedias of the Romans. The most improbable things were repeated from generation to generation without its occurring to anyone to inquire if there was any truth in them.

From the Roman and early Christian writers the Middle Ages got the idea of strange races of men and manlike creatures of various kinds. We find the following in an encyclopedia of the thirteenth century:

Satyrs be somewhat like men, and have crooked noses, and horns in the forehead, and are like to goats in their feet. . . . Those be wonderful creatures that have heads as hounds, and seem beasts rather than men; and some be called Cyclops, and have that name because each of them hath but one eye, and that in the middle of the forehead; and some be all headless and noseless and their eyes be in the shoulders; and some have plain faces without nostrils, and the lower lips of them stretch so that they veil therewith their faces when they be in the heat of the sun. Also in Scythia be some with so great and large ears that they spread their ears and cover all their bodies with them, and these be called Panchios.

Astrology. Two ancient subjects of study were revived and received great attention in Europe from the thirteenth century onwards until recent times. These were *astrology* and *alchemy.* Astrology was based on the belief that the stars influence the make-up of men and consequently their fate. The theory of the Greek philosophers, especially Aristotle, that all things were compounded of the "four elements"— earth, air, fire, and water — was also accepted. Each person was a particular mixture of these four elements, and the position of the planets at the time of his birth was supposed to influence his mixture, or "temperament,"— that is to say, his character.

For example, if one were born under the influence of Venus, — that is, when Venus was ascendant in the heavens, — he should be on his guard against violent love and should choose for a trade something connected with dress or adornment; if he were born under Mars he might make armor or horseshoes or become a soldier. Many common words are really astrological terms, such as "ill-starred," "disastrous," and "jovial," "saturnine," "mercurial" (derived from the names of the planets). Astrology was taught in the universities, because it was supposed to be necessary for physicians to choose times when the stars were favorable for particular kinds of medical treatment.

Alchemy. Alchemy consisted in experimenting with various chemicals with the hope of discovering a substance that would turn the baser metals, like lead and copper, into gold and silver. It was believed that this same substance, or *elixir,* would restore youth and prolong life indefinitely. The alchemists, even if they did not succeed in their chief aim, learned a great deal incidentally in their laboratories, and finally our modern chemistry developed from alchemy. Like astrology, which later grew into astronomy, alchemy goes back to ancient times. The people of the thirteenth century got most of their ideas from the Mohammedans, who had, in turn, got theirs from the Greek books on the subjects.

3. Origin of our Colleges and Universities

Origin of the Universities. All the countries in which our civilization now prevails have excellent schools, colleges, and universities. These had their beginning in the later Middle Ages. With the incoming of the barbarian Germans and the break-up of the Roman Empire, education largely disappeared, and for hundreds of years there was nothing in western Europe, outside of Italy and Spain, corresponding to our universities and colleges. Whatever learning remained was in the hands of the clergy.

But by the end of the twelfth century the teachers had become so numerous in Paris that they formed a union, or guild, to protect and promote their own interests. This union of professors was called by the usual name for corporations in the Middle Ages, *universitas*; hence our word "university." The king and the Pope both favored the university and granted the teachers and students many of the privileges of the clergy, — a class to which they were regarded as belonging because learning had for so many centuries been confined to the clergy.

About the time that we find the beginnings of a university, or guild of professors, at Paris, another great institution of learning was growing up at Bologna. Here the chief attention was given not to theology, — that is, the study of religion, — as at Paris, but to the study of the law, both Roman and church (canon) law. Students streamed to Bologna in greater and greater numbers. In order to protect themselves in a town where they were regarded as strangers, they also organized themselves into such powerful unions that they were able to force the professors to obey the rules which they laid down.

The University of Oxford was founded in the time of Henry II, probably by English students and masters who had become discontented at Paris. The University of Cambridge, as well as numerous universities in France, Italy, and Spain, was founded in the thirteenth century. The German universities were established much later, most of them in the latter half of the fourteenth century and in the fifteenth. The northern institutions generally took the great mother university at Paris as their model, while those in southern Europe ordinarily adopted the methods of Bologna.

The University Degrees. When, after some years of study, a student was examined by the professors, he was, if successful, admitted to the guild, or corporation, of teachers and became a *master* himself. What we call a *degree* today was originally, in the medieval universities, nothing more than the right to teach; but in the thirteenth century many who did not care to become professors in our sense of the word began to desire the honorable title of *master* or *doctor* ("master," "doctor," "professor," meant about the same thing in the thirteenth century).[1]

Simple Methods of Instruction. The students in the medieval universities were of all ages, from thirteen to forty, and even older. There were no university buildings, and in Paris the lectures were given in the Latin Quarter, in Straw Street (so called from the straw strewn on the floors of the hired rooms where the lecturer explained the textbook, with the students squatting on the floor before him).[2] There were no laboratories, for there was no experimentation. All that was required was a copy of the textbook. This the lecturer explained sentence by sentence, and the students listened and sometimes took notes.

[1] The origin of the bachelor's degree, which comes at the end of our college course nowadays, may be explained as follows: The bachelor in the thirteenth century was a student who had passed part of his examination in the course in "arts," as the college course was then called, and was permitted to teach certain elementary subjects before he became a full-fledged master. So the A. B. (Bachelor of Arts) was inferior to the A. M. (Master of Arts) then as now.

[2] The Latin Quarter, located on the left bank of the Seine, is the section of Paris where the university and other educational institutions grew up and where the students still live.

FIG. 142. *Lecturer Presiding over his Class in a Medieval University*
From a fourteenth-century miniature

Aristotle the Supreme Authority. The most striking peculiarity of the instruction in the medieval university was the
unquestioning confidence in Aristotle (p. 250). Most of the
courses of lectures were devoted to the explanation of some
one of his numerous works. The Latin translations were bad
and difficult, and the lecturer had enough to do to give some
meaning to them and to bring them into harmony with the
teachings of Christianity.

The teachers of the thirteenth century were so fascinated
by his logic (that is, method of reasoning) and astonished
at his learning that the great religious writers of the time,
Albertus Magnus (d. 1280) and Thomas Aquinas (d. 1274),
prepared elaborate commentaries, or books of explanations
and comments, upon all his works. He was called "The
Philosopher"; and so fully were scholars convinced that it
had pleased God to permit Aristotle to say the last word
upon each and every branch of knowledge that they rev-

erently accepted him as an unquestioned authority, along with the Bible, the Church Fathers, and the canon and Roman law.

Course of Study. No attention was given in the medieval universities to the great subject of history, nor was Greek taught. Latin had to be learned in order to carry on the teaching at all; but little time was given to the study of Roman classics, that is, to the best works of the Roman writers. The new modern languages were considered entirely unworthy of the learned. It must, of course, be remembered that none of the books which we consider the great classics in English, French, Italian, or Spanish had as yet been written.

Scholasticism. The name "scholasticism" is commonly given to the beliefs and ways of reasoning and teaching adopted by the medieval professors of whom we have been speaking. They discussed God's nature, man's soul, the essence of things, the mysteries of the Christian religion, and other deep matters in ponderous treatises full of elaborate distinctions and long arguments. The scholastic movement was at its height in the thirteenth century, which has been called the Golden Age of Scholasticism.

During the period of its greatest vigor it numbered among its prominent teachers Anselm, Abelard, Peter Lombard, Alexander of Hales, Albertus Magnus, John Duns Scotus, and William of Occam. To those interested in scientific experiments the scholastics seemed to discuss questions which they could not possibly answer. Those who admired Greek and Roman literature accused the scholastics of giving too much attention to Aristotle, and of engaging in too extensive disputations on philosophical and religious propositions that they maintained were of little value. Scholasticism is still taught in Roman Catholic colleges and universities throughout the world. It is no longer in use in Protestant universities.

4. THE RENAISSANCE

Petrarch tries to learn Greek. Although the medieval professors paid the greatest respect to the Greek philosopher Aristotle and made Latin translations of his works the basis of the college course, very few of them could read any Greek, and none of them knew much about Homer or Plato or the Greek writers of plays and histories. In the fourteenth century Petrarch, an Italian poet (1304–1374), set the example in Italy of carefully collecting all the writings of the Romans, which he greatly admired. He made an unsuccessful effort to learn Greek; for he found that Cicero and other Roman writers were constantly referring with enthusiasm to the Greek books to which they owed so much. Petrarch had a great influence in starting the new movement called the Renaissance or Revival of Learning, to which we shall come in a moment.

Chrysoloras begins to teach Greek in Florence (1396). Petrarch had neither the patience nor the opportunity to master Greek; but twenty years after his death a learned Greek prelate from Constantinople, named Chrysoloras, came to Florence and found pupils eager to learn his language so that they could read the Greek books. Soon Italian scholars were going to Constantinople to carry on their studies, just as the Romans in Cicero's time had gone to Athens. They brought back copies of all the ancient writers that they could find, and by 1430, after a thousand years of neglect, Greek books were once more known in the West.

The Humanists. In this way western Europe caught up with ancient times : scholars could once more know virtually all that the Greeks and Romans had known, and could read in the original Greek the works of Homer, Sophocles, Plato, Aristotle, Demosthenes, and other philosophers, historians, and writers of plays. Those who devoted their lives to a study of the literature of Greece and Rome were called *Humanists*. The name is derived from the Latin word *humanitas*, which means "culture." In time the colleges gave up the exclusive study of Aristotle and substituted a wider study of the Greek and Latin literature, and in this way what is known as our "classical" course of study originated.

Exaggerated Importance of the Renaissance. The revival of interest in Latin and Greek is sometimes called the Revival of Learning. In the latter half of the nineteenth century the word *Renaissance,* or "rebirth," began to be used by historians who believed that Europe awoke from a winter sleep of ignorance when Petrarch began to collect Latin and Greek books. The term "Renaissance" was extended to include all the advance made in painting, architecture, and sculpture. One cannot read much history without coming upon this term. It covers the period between the late Middle Ages and modern times — from 1325 to 1525. Certainly a great many important advances were made during these two centuries, but it is a mistake to suppose that the renewed interest in Latin and Greek literature was responsible for all of them. The enthusiasm for the works of the ancients did not encourage new discoveries. These were made in spite of Aristotle and the old authorities. The defenders of dead languages forgot that the Greeks whom they worshiped had no dead language to sharpen their wits on; nor had the Romans. In the time of Cicero, Virgil, and Horace, Greek was a modern and living language, which the Romans found it most important to learn on account of the books written in it, just as we often learn French or German in order to profit by the literature and scientific works written in those tongues.

5. BEGINNINGS OF MODERN INVENTIONS

Roger Bacon Criticizes Reliance on Old Books. So long as intellectual men confined themselves to studying the old books of Greece and Rome, they could not advance beyond what the Greeks and Romans had known. In order to explain modern discoveries and inventions it is necessary to take account of those who began to suspect that Aristotle might be ignorant and mistaken upon many important matters. and who set to work and urged others to examine things around them with the hope of finding out more than anyone had ever known about the world before.

Even in the thirteenth century there were a few scholars who criticized the habit of relying upon Aristotle for all knowledge. The most distinguished faultfinder was Roger Bacon, an English Franciscan monk (d. about 1290), who declared that even if Aristotle was very wise he had only planted the tree of knowledge and that this had "not as yet put forth all its branches nor produced all its fruits."

If we could continue to live for endless centuries, we mortals could never hope to reach full and complete knowledge of all the things which are to be known. No one knows enough of nature completely to describe the peculiarities of a single fly and give the reason for its color and why it has just so many feet, no more and no less.

Progress certainly could not be made, Bacon pointed out, either in ideas or inventions, so long as man looked continually backwards. He pointed out clearly the reasons why men persisted in their old and false beliefs:

There are four principal stumblingblocks . . . to comprehending truth, which hinder well-nigh every scholar; to wit, the example of weak and unworthy authority, long-established custom, the sense of the ignorant crowd, . . . and the hiding of one's own ignorance under the show of wisdom. . . . For in every act of life, or business or study, these three worst arguments are used for the same conclusion : namely, this is the way of our ancestors, this is the custom, this is the common view ; therefore it should be held. But the opposite of this conclusion follows much better from the premises, as I will prove through authority, experience, and reason.

Roger Bacon foresees Great Inventions. Bacon declared that if men would only study the common, everyday things round about them, instead of reading the books of the ancients, science would outdo the wonders which people of his day thought could be produced by magic. He said that in time men would be able to fly, would have carriages which needed no horses to draw them, and ships which would move swiftly without oars, and that bridges could be built without piers to support them.

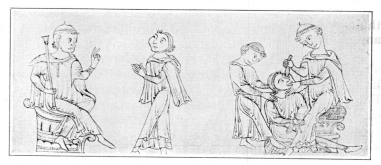

Fig. 143. *Left, Medieval Doctor Giving Advice ; Right, Doctor Operating for Cataract*

From an early-fifteenth-century manuscript in Trinity College Library, Cambridge

All this and much more has come true, but inventors and modern scientists owe but little to the books of the Greeks and the Romans, which the scholastic philosophers and the Humanists relied upon. Although the Greek philosophers devoted considerable attention to *natural science* (study of nature), they were not much inclined to make long and careful experiments or to invent anything like the microscope or telescope to help them. Aristotle thought that the sun and all the stars revolved about the earth and that the heavenly bodies were perfect and unchangeable. He believed that heavy bodies fell faster than light ones and that all earthly things were made of the four elements — earth, air, water, and fire. The Greeks and Romans knew nothing of the compass or gunpowder or the printing press or the uses to which steam can be put. Indeed, they had scarcely anything that we should call a machine.

Our Debt to the Mohammedans. From the thirteenth century onward our forefathers in western Europe began their great advance in knowledge and invention which has made Western peoples the leaders in the revolution that scientific discovery has made in men's lives. They were aided by the Mohammedans with whom they came in contact in Spain and during the Crusades. The Mohammedans also owed a good deal to other peoples, and handed on to Europeans things that they had learned from India and China. A good example of this is found in the figures we use every day. Though these are called "Arabic" numerals, they seem really to have been discovered in India and are sometimes called "Hindu" numerals. Their convenience, as compared with the old Roman method of using letters for numbers, is marvelous. How could anyone divide cxliv by viii? But we all can divide 144 by 8. Before the introduction of the Arabic figures people had to use the strings of beads on an abacus or calculating machine in order to do sums. This method is still common in Japan and China. "Algebra" is an Arabic word, and the branch of mathematics which bears this name, as well as other improvements in that department, appears to have come from the Moslems.

Assisting Men's Eyes. Mirrors and lenses began to come into use in the thirteenth century. We hear for the first time of spectacles, as an aid to failing sight. As time went on, lenses were to be used to make telescopes and microscopes, spectroscopes, and cameras. Men were able to discover billions of stars previously invisible; to study minute animals and plants often very important in our lives but too small to be detected with the naked eye. But telescopes and microscopes did not come before the seventeenth century, and many of our most ingenious optical instruments were devised in the nineteenth century. Without the lenses very little that we now know could have been discovered.

Finding One's Way at Sea. The peoples of Europe have proved to be the greatest wanderers in history and have now visited every part of the habitable globe, carrying their civilization with them and teaching it to others. The Chinese seem to have known about the compass, but the fact that a magnetized needle, when free to move, will turn to the north may have been discovered by western Europeans. In any case, the compass began to be used by them in the thirteenth and fourteenth centuries, and encouraged much bolder ventures at sea than ever before because mariners could tell the *direction* in which they were going even in darkest night, when all the stars were hidden. By the use of the astrolabe (the ancestor of the modern sextant), which was not wholly new,

Fig. 144. *Effects of Cannon on a Medieval Castle*

sailors could tell the *position* of their ship, its latitude and longitude, by observing the sun or stars. So men came to feel at home hundreds of miles from land, since they could direct their course and calculate their position.

Effects of Gunpowder. Quite a different type of novelty, with its terrible effects, was the introduction of gunpowder into warfare. This explosive (a compound of sulphur, saltpeter, and charcoal) was slowly introduced. Although there is a record of the making of cannon and balls in Florence in 1326, and a little later of gunpowder works in a few towns in France and Germany, it was some hundred and fifty years before the old method of fighting with bows and arrows and axes and lances was given up for this new form of attack. When the destructive power of gunpowder was realized, all the old methods of defense had to be abandoned. It was seen that iron armor was of no use against the force of the new bullets, and so it was discarded. As feudal stone castles were not proof against cannon balls, they were no longer built. Kings and nobility now lived in unprotected palaces. Even the old ways of fortifying towns were useless, and new means of protection had to be discovered. Since the introduction of gunpowder great national armies have been built up, and the destruction caused by war has been vastly increased. As compared with some modern explosives, gunpowder is rather feeble. With the ever-improving means of destruction it may be that men will decide some day to give up war entirely, as too terrible and dangerous to civilization, and invent a new method of solving their difficulties.

6. Profound Effects of Printing

How Printing spread Learning Far and Wide. The invention which proved to be of widest benefit to mankind was printing with movable type; for printing served well every other invention and discovery by making it known all over the world. After printing was invented and books were made in quantity, more people learned to read, thus raising the level of general intelligence of mankind. An *illiterate* person is one who is unable to read, and reading is now recognized as one of the most fundamental parts of education.

After the invention of printing people no longer had to get their information by listening to the songs of wandering minstrels or to stories repeated by any chance person; they could read more accurate accounts of what had been done or thought. As many people began to read the same things there grew up a body of common knowledge in many fields which gave men a foundation on which they could base further information. As years went by, this fund of information increased enormously until there were great libraries with hundreds of thousands of books on every imaginable subject. This knowledge is the very basis of civilization; for it is the written record of what is known about the past from the most remote period down to yesterday.

All study and progress are made possible because books give us information on what has been found out and tried and tested in any subject. The student of history or mathematics or medicine or law tries to find the best books on those subjects, for in them he may read what the most learned students of those subjects already know. With this background the new inquirer can go on by his own observation, experimenting, or reasoning, and add to what has already been found out.

Printing, then, has put into the hands of countless millions of people the knowledge of the past and present that they would never otherwise have had. It now furnishes information, aid, and amusement to young and old, in books, pictures, magazines, and newspapers.

How Books were made before the Invention of Printing. Before printing was invented, everything that was to be set down as a record had to be written or lettered by hand. If you will think how long it would take you to make a copy by hand of today's newspaper, you will easily see how slow and painful the writing out of a book would be. You can readily guess that many mistakes would creep in when various persons made copies of the same article, and how many mistakes the same person would make at different times. No two copies would be *exactly* alike. When you consider how much this slow labor would cost nowadays, you can see how machines which are quick, accurate, automatic, and can run off thousands of copies in a short time have revolutionized the learning of mankind.

Beautiful Work of Medieval Copyists. While it was impossible for scribes not to make mistakes when they copied, and a careless one would make a great many, the books of the best copyists are works of art. The professional copyists were incredibly skillful with their quills, as may be seen in Fig. 145, a page from a Bible of the thirteenth century which is given in its original size. The letters are as clear, as small, and almost as regular as if they had been printed. The whole volume, containing the Old and New Testaments, is about the size of this book. After the scribe had finished his work, the volume was often turned over to the *illumi-*

---

* Fig. 145 is a reproduction, exactly the size of the original, of a page in a thirteenth-century manuscript Bible (in Latin) belonging to the library of Columbia University. The page represented is taken from 1 Maccabees i, 56–ii, ŏ5 (a portion of the Scriptures not usually included in the Protestant Bibles). It begins, "...ditis fugitivorum locis. Die quintadecima mensis Chalen, quinto quadragesimo et centesimo anno edificavit rex Antiochus abhominandum ydolum desolationis super altare Dei; per universas civitates Jude in circuitum edificaverunt aras et ante januas domorum, et in plateis incendebantur thura, et sacrificabant et libros Dei legis combusserunt." The scribes used many abbreviations, as was the custom, and what is transcribed here fills a little over five lines of the manuscript.

FIG. 145. Page from a Copy of the Bible Made in the Thirteenth Century, Showing
Perfection of the Best Work *

nator, who would put in gay illuminated initials and sometimes page borders, delightful in both design and color. The word "miniature," which is often applied to them, is derived from *minium,* the Latin name for one of the favorite colors, vermilion. Later the word came to be applied to anything small. Books designed to be used in the church services were adorned with pictures, as well as with ornamented initials and decorative borders.

The written books were often both compact and beautiful, but they were never cheap or easily produced in great numbers. When Cosimo, the father of Lorenzo the Magnificent, wished to form a library, just before the invention of printing, he applied to a contractor, who engaged forty-five copyists. By working hard for nearly two years they were able to produce only two hundred volumes for the new library.

Paper introduced into Western Europe. After the supply of papyrus — the paper of the Egyptians, Greeks, and Romans — was cut off from Europe by the conquest of Egypt by the Mohammedans, the people of the Middle Ages used *parchment,* made from the skin of lambs and goats. This was so expensive that printing would have been of but little use, even if it had been thought of, before paper was introduced into Europe by the Mohammedans. The Arabs seem to have derived their knowledge of paper-making from the Chinese. Paper began to become common in the thirteenth and fourteenth centuries and was already replacing the expensive parchment before the invention of printing.

The Earliest Printed Books. We have seen how the interest in books was increasing. The Humanists were seeking everywhere for ancient Greek and Latin works, which they carefully copied and corrected with their quills; new books were also being written in the modern languages, which were being used more and more. It was therefore a favorable time for certain ingenious mechanics, who had been experimenting in Dutch and German cities, to introduce a new invention by which pages of a book could be set up in lead types, inked, and printed on paper in a press, instead of being painfully

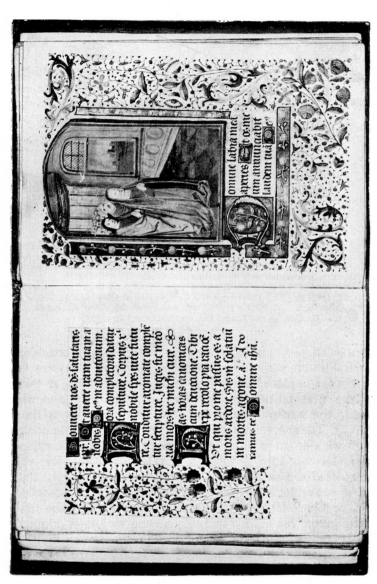

FIG. 146. *From Horae Beatae Mariae Virgini cum Calendaria, a Fifteenth-Century Manuscript on Vellum*

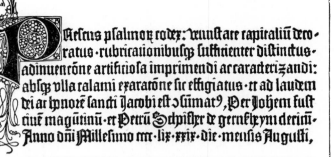

Fɪɢ. 147.   Closing Lines of the Psalter of 1459

The closing lines (the so-called *colophon*) of the second edition of the Psalter, which are shown here much reduced, are essentially the same as those of the first edition. They may be translated thus: "The present volume of the Psalms, which is adorned with handsome capitals and is clearly divided by means of rubrics, was produced not by writing with a pen but by an ingenious invention of printed characters; and was completed to the glory of God and the honor of Saint James by John Fust, a citizen of Mainz, and Peter Schöffer of Gernsheim, in the year of our Lord 1459, on the 29th of August"

written with pen and ink. The first book of any considerable size to be printed was the Bible, which appears to have been completed at Mainz in the year 1456. A year later the first edition of the famous Mainz Psalter was finished, the earliest book we have which bears a date (Fig. 147). There are, however, earlier examples of little books printed with engraved blocks and even with movable types. In the German towns, where the art spread rapidly, the printers used the same style of letters which the scribe had found it convenient to make with his quill — the so-called *Gothic*, or black letter. In Italy, however, where the first printing press was set up in 1466, a type was soon adopted which resembled the letters used in ancient Roman inscriptions. This was quite similar to the style of letter commonly used today; for example, in this book. The Italians invented also the compressed slanting *italic* type, which enabled them to get a great many words on a page and so economize paper. Whole volumes are no longer printed in italics, and this type is now used when one would emphasize a word or heading, as in the present volume. It is also employed for book titles.

The early printers did their work very conscientiously, and used excellent ink and beautiful paper; so some of the very earliest books, made before Columbus set sail, have lasted down to the present, looking fresher than much more recent ones.

By the year 1500, after printing had been in use for less than half a century, there appear to have been at least forty printing presses in operation in various towns of Germany, France, Italy, the Netherlands, and England. These presses had, it is estimated, already printed eight millions of volumes. So there was no longer any danger of the old books' being lost again, and the encourage-

Fig. 148. *An Old-fashioned Printing Office*

Until the nineteenth century, printing was carried on with very little machinery. The type was inked by hand; then the paper was laid on, and the form was slipped under a wooden press operated by hand by means of a lever

ment to write and publish new books was greatly increased. From that date our sources for history become far greater in number than those which exist for the previous history of the world.

7. THE ART OF THE RENAISSANCE

Development of Art in Italy. We have already described briefly the work of the medieval architects and referred to the beautiful carvings that adorned the Gothic cathedrals and to the pictures of saints and angels in stained glass which filled the great church windows. But in the fourteenth and fifteenth centuries art developed in a most astonishing manner in Italy and set new standards for all of western Europe.

FIG. 149.   *Ghiberti's Doors at Florence*

Opposite the cathedral at Florence (Fig. 127) stands the ancient baptistery. Its northern bronze doors, with ten scenes from the Bible, surrounded by a very lovely border of foliage, birds, and animals, were completed by Lorenzo Ghiberti in 1452. Michelangelo declared them worthy to be the gates of heaven

Florence was the great center of artistic activity during the fifteenth century. The foremost sculptors and nearly all the most famous painters and architects of the time either were natives of Florence or did their best work there. During the first half of the century sculpture once more took the lead. The bronze doors of the baptistery at Florence, by Ghiberti, completed in 1452, are among the finest products of Renaissance art (Fig. 149).

Florence reached the height of its glory as an art center during the reign of Lorenzo the Magnificent, a devoted admirer of art, who assisted and encouraged artists. With his death (1492) Rome, which was fast becoming again one of the great capitals of Europe, became also the leader in art. Pope Julius II as well as Pope Leo X took pains to secure the services of the most distinguished painters, sculptors, and

FIG. 150. *Michelangelo's Statue of Giuliano de' Medici, Son of Lorenzo the Magnificent and Brother of Pope Leo X (see page 662)*

He is here represented in Roman costume. The statue is much more celebrated than the man

architects of the time, including Raphael and Michelangelo, in the building and adornment of St. Peter's (the papal church) and the Vatican Palace, the home of the Popes (see page 559). The ceiling paintings of the Sistine Chapel, in the Vatican, are among the best of Michelangelo's work.

Fig. 151. *Interior of a Dutch House*

From a painting by Pieter de Hooch (1632–1681). This is one of the artist's many charming pictures of Dutch home life

Height of Renaissance Art —Da Vinci, Michelangelo, Raphael. During the sixteenth century the art of the Renaissance attained its highest development. Among all the eminent artists of this period three stand out prominently: Leonardo da Vinci, Michelangelo, and Raphael. The first two were masters in the three arts of architecture, sculpture, and painting, and Leonardo was an engineer and inventor as well. It is impossible to give in a few lines any idea of the quality and beauty of the work of these great geniuses. Both Raphael and Michelangelo left behind them so many and such magnificent frescoes and paintings, and Michelangelo so many statues as well, that it is very easy to appreciate their importance. Leonardo, on the other hand, left but little completed work. His influence on the art of his time, which was probably greater than that of either of the others, came

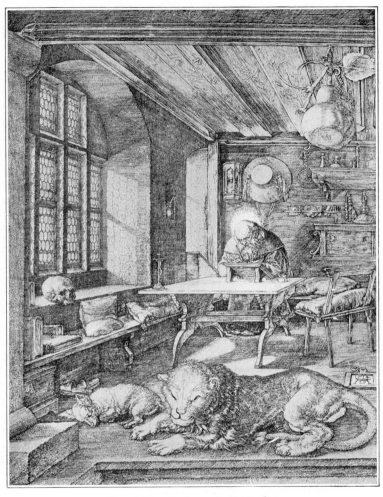

FIG. 152. *St. Jerome in his Study*
From an engraving by Albrecht Dürer (1471–1528)

from his many-sidedness, his originality, and his unflagging interest in the discovery and application of new methods. He has contributed to the world of art almost as much through his experiments as through his finished paintings.

FIG. 153. *The Young Spanish Prince Don Balthazar Carlos on Horseback*

From a painting by Velásquez

Although Florence could no longer boast of being the art center of Italy, it still produced celebrated artists, among whom Andrea del Sarto may be particularly mentioned. But the most important center of artistic activity in the sixteenth century, outside of Rome, was Venice. The distinguishing characteristic of the Venetian pictures is their glowing color. This is strikingly illustrated in the paintings of Titian, the most famous of all the Venetian painters (Fig. 155).

Painting in Northern Europe. It was natural that artists living in the northern countries should be attracted to Italy by the fame of its great masters and, after learning all that Italy could teach them, should return home to practice their art in their own particular fashion. About a century after painting began to develop in Italy, two Flemish brothers, Van Eyck by name, not only showed that they were able to paint quite as excellent pictures as the Italians of their day but also discovered a new way of mixing their colors superior to that employed in Italy. Later, when painting had reached its height in Italy, Albrecht Dürer and Hans Holbein the Younger in Germany vied with even Raphael and Michelangelo in the mastery of their art. Dürer, though a painter, is especially celebrated for his wonderful woodcuts and copper-plate engravings, in which field he has perhaps never been excelled. Holbein, like Dürer, made many drawings, but is chiefly known for his marvelous portrait painting (Figs. 163, 168).

When, in the seventeenth century, painting had declined south of the Alps, Dutch and Flemish masters — above all, Rubens and Rembrandt — developed a new and admirable school of painting. To Van Dyck, another Flemish master, we owe many notable portraits of historically important persons (Figs. 173 and 179). Spain gave to the world in the seventeenth century a painter whom some would rank higher than even the greatest artists of Italy, namely, Velásquez (1599–1660). His genius, like that of Van Dyck, is especially conspicuous in his portraits (Fig. 153).

8. The Beginnings of our Scientific Age

A New Era in Science. Our modern science may be said to have begun about the seventeenth century. Its beginnings were due not to those who slavishly followed the words of Aristotle and spent their time trying to combine the conclusions of the Greek philosopher with the theology of the medieval Church (pp. 595 ff.), but rather to the men who patiently observed the world of nature around them. It is to them that we owe the first contributions to a new science and a new attitude toward knowledge.

A New Way of Learning. Medieval science, so called, was a mixture of some truth and much superstition and folklore. There was nothing about man or the world too absurd to be accepted in the Middle Ages. Even the educated class believed many things which had no foundation in fact. Roger Bacon (pp. 598 f.) had deplored the excessive veneration for the works of ancient writers; for although these were used as textbooks in the universities, they were full of statements which could not be proved to be true. Bacon declared that instead of relying on what previous generations had thought, men should examine the world about them and observe its ways in order to determine its laws and to discover new and important truths. This could be accomplished not by reading old books but by observing, examining, measuring, questioning the reason of things, analyzing results, and experimenting — or trying things in new conditions and relations — to see what would happen. Bacon believed that if men would go about their studies in these ways, astonishing discoveries would be made. Bacon was right; for these are the methods which scientists have used to learn more and more about the universe.

The Discovery of Copernicus. The Polish astronomer Copernicus published a work in 1543 in which he rejected the old idea that the sun and the stars revolved around the earth as a center, as was then taught in all the universities. He showed that, on the contrary, the sun was the center about which the earth and the rest of the planets revolved, and that the reason the stars seem to go around the earth each day is that our globe revolves on its axis. Although Copernicus had been encouraged to write his book by a cardinal and had dedicated it to the Pope, the Catholic as well as the Protestant theologians declared that the new theory contradicted the teachings of the Bible, and they therefore condemned it as a bad book. But we know now that Copernicus was right and that the theologians and universities were wrong.

Later scientists supported the theory of Copernicus and, by the development and use of mathematics, made great contributions to the knowledge of astronomy. Among these was Johannes Kepler (1571–1630), a German, who formulated several important laws describing the motion of the heavenly bodies. Kepler showed that the planets follow an elliptical and not a circular orbit around the sun and that there is a fixed relationship between their distance from the sun and their revolution.

Galileo and his Telescope. Bacon had recognized that, in order to carry on the kind of investigation that he recommended, special apparatus would be necessary. As early as the thirteenth century it had been discovered that lenses could be made that would magnify the size of objects. This knowledge was used to develop the microscope to enlarge small objects close at hand, and the telescope to see bodies at a great distance. The Italian scientist Galileo (1564–1642), by the use of a telescope that he had perfected, was able to behold many heavenly bodies never before seen; he was able to discover the mountains and the valleys of the moon, and to observe the moons revolving around Jupiter. In 1611 he discovered the spots on the sun. As he watched these spots on the revolving sphere he knew that the sun was not, as Aristotle had declared, a perfect, unchanging body but, as Copernicus had said, revolved on its axis.

Fig. 154.   *Galileo, One of the World's Greatest Scientists*

From a painting in the Pitti Gallery, Florence

Galileo made careful experiments by dropping objects from the leaning tower of Pisa. He proved that Aristotle was wrong in saying that a body weighing a hundred pounds fell a hundred times as fast as a body weighing but one. He wrote in Italian as well as in Latin. His opponents might have forgiven him had he confined his discussions to the learned, that is, to those who could read Latin; but they thought it very dangerous to have the new ideas set forth in such a way that the people at large might come to doubt what the theologians and universities were teaching. Galileo was finally summoned before the Inquisition; some of his theories were condemned, and he was imprisoned by the church authorities.

Newton and the Law of Gravitation.   The year that Galileo died the famous English mathematician Isaac Newton was born (1642–1727). Newton carried on the work of the earlier astronomers, using his great knowledge of mathematics to aid him. His name has become famous through his description of the universal law of *gravitation*, which means the force, or attraction, that causes bodies to fall and the planets to remain in their orbits. He found that the attraction between two heavenly bodies varies inversely as the square of the distance between them.

Harvey discovers the Circulation of the Blood. Another Englishman, William Harvey, a court physician, had published in 1628 a book in which he announced the discovery of the circulation of the blood. Harvey began his work with an apology for contradicting the older authorities on this subject, but described his own experiments and offered many proofs for his daring theories.

What the Microscope Revealed. While the telescope aided the astronomer, the microscope opened up a great world of minute things never before seen by man. Rude and simple microscopes were used as early as the seventeenth century. Leeuwenhoek, a Dutch merchant, improved his lenses so that he discovered (1665) the corpuscles in the blood and the "animalcula" or tiny organisms of various kinds, found in pond water and elsewhere. This was but the beginning of a marvelous story of what the microscope has revealed to man.

Scientific Societies Founded. The earliest societies to promote scientific study grew up in Italy. Later the English Royal Society and the French Institute were founded, as well as similar associations in Germany. They were the first societies of the kind in the history of the world, except perhaps the ancient Museum at Alexandria (p. 246). Their object was not, like that of the old Greek schools of philosophy and the medieval universities, mainly to hand down and explain the knowledge derived from the past, but to find out what had never been known before.

Questions and Exercises

REVIEW OF CHAPTER

1. Explain why Latin was the language of the educated classes in the Middle Ages. Explain why there are two groups of modern languages in western Europe. Give the main examples of each. What are the earliest examples of written modern languages? Give an account of chivalry. Under what circumstances was Italian first written? When did English become easily readable to us?

2. What was the character of popular medieval science? Give examples. Compare the medieval ideas of science with our own. Tell something about astrology. What was medieval chemistry called, and what were its aims?

3. How did the medieval universities grow up? How did the students carry on their work? Why was the study of Aristotle so important? What is the meaning of "scholasticism"?

4. What does the word "Renaissance" mean? Who were the Humanists, and what was their great interest? Has the importance of the Renaissance been exaggerated?

5. What objections did Roger Bacon urge against scholasticism? Discuss the chief early inventions and explain how they altered men's lives and ambitions.

6. Describe the older ways of making books. What is printing? What effects did the invention of printing have on knowledge?

7. Why did modern art develop in Italy? Name some of the most famous Italian artists and some in northern lands.

USEFUL TERMS

See how much meaning you can give to the following terms: *prelate, chivalry, epic, fables, astrology, alchemy, compass, quill, miniature, parchment, classics, humanism, liberal arts, natural science, scholasticism, minnesinger, abacus, astrolabe.*

DIRECTIVE QUESTIONS

1. How do inventions revolutionize life?

2. What advantages have modern universities over the medieval ones?

3. What makes language change from generation to generation?

4. Why did knowledge fail to make progress in the early Middle Ages?

5. In what professions does a knowledge of Latin still prove of help?

6. Why do people disbelieve fantastic tales about animals today?

DISCUSSION TOPICS

1. The classical question.

2. Language is a living, growing thing. (How many everyday words can you list that were unknown in the time of George Washington?)

3. Printing revolutionized learning. (Try to imagine what it would be like if newspapers and books had to be written out by hand instead of printed.)

4. Investigation is a sounder basis for gaining knowledge than is authority.

ADDITIONAL ADVENTURES IN LEARNING

1. Studies in Source Materials. ROBINSON, *Readings*, Vol. I, chap xix, sect. i, "Development of the Modern Languages"; 176–179, The troubadours and their songs; sect. ii, Examples of medieval scientific ideas; sect. iv, Abelard, a great medieval teacher; 191–192, Student life at the University of Paris; sect. v, Reverence for Aristotle in the Middle Ages; sect. vi, "Roger Bacon and the Beginning of Modern Experimental Science"; chap. xxii, sect. i, " The Italian Despots"; sect. ii, Humanism — Dante and Petrarch; sect. iii, "Artists of the Renaissance."

2. Topical Studies. The troubadours: CUTTS, Part V; JUSSERAND, *English Wayfaring Life.* Chivalry: TAPPAN, *In Feudal Times*; CUTTS, Part VI, chap. ix. Tournaments: CUTTS, *ibid.*, and ABRAM, pp. 232 ff. Medieval universities: HASKINS, *Rise of the Universities.* Heraldry: H. W. C. DAVIS (ed.), *Medieval England*, chap. vi; TICKNER, chaps. iii–iv; see also an encyclopedia. The making of printed books: TICKNER, chap. xiv, and the article "Printing" in an encyclopedia. Examples of medieval poetry: CHAUCER, *The Canterbury Tales*; *The Song of Roland*; *The Nibelungenlied.* What great composer has used medieval literature as the theme for his operas? Look up in an encyclopedia the Holy Grail.

CHAPTER XXVIII · THE GROWTH
OF OUR MODERN NATIONS

A GOOD deal has been said in this book about nations and their governments. They are among the most striking results of civilization
and are of great importance to all of us. One of the main problems of
civilized mankind, which the Greeks began to discuss, is how peoples are
to be ruled in such a way as to bring them happiness, security, and prosperity. The Greeks and Romans made a number of experiments in government, as described earlier in this volume. In the Age of Disorder the Church,
and to some extent feudalism, supplied a certain degree of safety and
authority. When the towns appeared, they discovered methods of governing themselves in a way to protect their citizens and extend their trade.
France and England had developed out of feudalism into monarchies with
extensive territories and able kings.

In this chapter we shall tell the story of the progress in the formation of
national states about four hundred years ago. We must see how the map
of Europe looked shortly after the year 1500—who were the rivals in the
struggle carried on by governments for lands, business, and power. We
shall notice that the lands that were to become Germany and Italy enjoyed
little of the importance in world affairs that they gained in the latter part
of the nineteenth century. Another reason for learning about the European
states in the sixteenth century is to be able to follow the great revolt
against the Roman Catholic Church, called the Protestant Reformation,
and to become acquainted with the kings and other rulers who played such
an important part in the long, bitter struggle.

1. BEGINNINGS OF MODERN NATIONS

Our Debt to the Middle Ages. The progress in modern
times is based, as we have seen, on the advances made during the previous centuries. The languages we speak, the
studies we pursue, the universities we attend, the literature,
architecture, and art that we enjoy today — all these elements of our civilization, and many more, had begun to
develop in the late Middle Ages. Some of our most important
inventions, such as printing, gunpowder, and the compass,

were made by the men of this period, while the beginnings of world trade and colonization were the result of the marvelous discoveries of the fifteenth century.

Besides these things we find those experiments in the business of government which gave men experience in political life. There was the constant question whether those who were powerful and rich should be free of control, and indifferent to the welfare of the rest of the population, who might fare as best they could, or whether one ruler should control all the people in a given territory, rich and poor, and combine them into a great "national" family, governed by the same laws and contributing to the treasury of one central government. Very slowly, as we have seen, in some countries of Europe the feudal system gave way to monarchy, and the ideal of a strong national state grew up.

Reasons for Studying the History of Governments. The study of European governments in the sixteenth century may seem, at first thought, unnecessary and distasteful. But it is important, nevertheless; for an understanding of the development of the countries of Europe has a direct bearing on the problems of our civilization today. For example, Germany and Italy, as national states, are much younger than France and England or even the Netherlands, Spain, and Portugal. They were unified only in the last half of the nineteenth century. During the age of exploration and colonization, expeditions were sent out only by countries which had central governments to back them. It was these countries — above all, England and France — that gained vast colonial possessions. Most of the inhabitable land was taken up before Germany and Italy became great powers, and during their short existence these nations have been able to add but little to their over-sea territory.

Italy's war with Ethiopia, begun in 1935, was a move for expansion and was justified by her on the ground that she too had a right to colonies. Germany, deprived of her colonial possessions after the World War, did not give up hope of recovering them and became a constant threat to the peace of Europe. It is the rivalry between powers, based on their long history, that keeps the world in ferment. And it is this history which, in some part at least, we should understand.

England and France establish Strong National Governments. At the opening of the sixteenth century England was a strong monarchy in the hands of Henry VII. The Wars of the Roses had so reduced the number of nobles that the king's power was undisputed (see page 507). France, after years of conflict, had finally grown into a united country, and its boundaries were approaching those which it has today. Louis XI had triumphed over most of his great vassals and added their fiefs to the crown, while his son Charles VIII had married the heiress of Brittany (p. 477).

The central government in both England and France was becoming stronger; business and trade increased the wealth of the people and supplied the monarch with sufficient income to support a standing army, so that he was no longer dependent on the assistance of faithful vassals.

Arab Civilization in Spain. The Mohammedan conquest served to make the history of Spain very different from that of the other states of Europe. The presence in the peninsula of a large population of alien race and religion made the task of unifying Spain doubly difficult; for it had also the same problem of curbing the ambitious nobles as France and England. During the tenth century, which was so backward a period in the rest of Europe, the Arab civilization in Spain reached its highest development. Cordova, with its half-million inhabitants, its stately palaces, its university, its three thousand mosques, and its three hundred public baths, was perhaps unrivaled at that period in the whole world.

The Rise of New Christian Kingdoms in Spain. But the Christians were finally able to reconquer the peninsula. As early as the year 1000[1] several small Christian kingdoms — Castile, Aragon, and Navarre — had come into existence in northern Spain. Castile, in particular, began to push back the Mohammedans and, in 1085, reconquered Toledo. By

[1] Map, p. 625.

1250 the long war of the Christians against the Mohammedans, which fills the medieval records of Spain, had been so successfully carried on that Castile extended to the southern coast and included the great towns of Cordova and Seville.

The Moors, as the Spanish Mohammedans were called, held out for two centuries more in the mountainous kingdom of Granada, in the southern part of the peninsula. Not until 1492, after a long siege, was the city of Granada captured by the Christians and the last remnant of Mohammedan rule disappeared.

Spain becomes a European Power. The first Spanish monarch whose name need be mentioned here was Queen Isabella of Castile, who, in 1469, married Ferdinand, the heir of the crown of Aragon. It is with this union of Castile and Aragon that the great importance of Spain in European history begins. For the next hundred years Spain was to enjoy more military power than any other European state.

The year 1492 was a momentous one in Spanish history; for it saw not only the completion of the conquest of the peninsula but the discoveries made by Columbus, under the auspices of Queen Isabella, which opened up sources of undreamed-of wealth beyond the seas. The greatness of Spain in the sixteenth century was largely due to the riches derived from her American possessions. The shameless and cruel looting of the Mexican and Peruvian cities by Cortes and Pizarro (pp. 831 f.), and the silver mines of the New World, enabled Spain for a time to hold a position in Europe which her ordinary resources would never have permitted.

Unfortunately, the most industrious, skillful, and thrifty among the inhabitants of Spain — that is, the Moors and the Jews, who well-nigh supported the whole kingdom by their toil — were bitterly persecuted by the Christians. So anxious was Isabella to rid her kingdom of the infidels that she revived the court of the Inquisition (p. 645). For several decades its courts arrested and condemned innumerable persons who were suspected of heresy, and thousands were burned at the stake during this period.

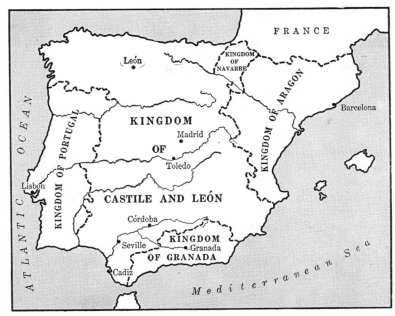

Spain, 1250–1492

Portugal as a Sea Power. The Christian kingdom of Portugal was already as large as that country is today. Although small in size as compared with her neighbors, she became an important state owing to her marvelous explorations and discoveries (p. 561). In the sixteenth century Portugal developed a flourishing trade and was for a time the leading sea power in Europe.

The Netherlands. The Netherlands, or Low Countries, included seventeen provinces stretching for a hundred miles or so along the North Sea, where we now find the kingdoms of Holland and Belgium. By the fourteenth century there had grown up in this region important towns which were centers of manufacture and trade: in the north, Haarlem, Leiden, Amsterdam, and Rotterdam; to the south, Ghent, Bruges, Brussels, and Antwerp. The business of these practically independent provinces had brought great wealth to the Low Countries (map. p. 705).

In 1384 the county of Flanders, in the Netherlands, had come into the possession of the Duke of Burgundy through marriage, and one by one the provinces were added to the Burgundian possessions. At the death of Charles the Bold this region was inherited by his daughter Mary, who was married to Emperor Maximilian. In this way the Netherlands passed into the hands of the Austrian house of Hapsburg. (See page 628.)

The Turks put an End to the Eastern Empire (1453.) The Crusades, as we have seen, ended in failure, and the Mohammedans again gained possession of Palestine and the eastern Mediterranean. The last of the Christians were driven out of Syria in 1291. The Eastern Empire, weakened by the conflicts with the Crusaders, would have fallen an easy prey to the infidels had not the Seljuk Turks themselves been threatened by a new and terrible enemy, the Mongols, from the region northwest of China. The Mongols were related to the Huns and the Turks. Having conquered northern China, the Mongols pushed westward through Asia and Russia into Europe. The Poles, however, drove them back into Russia, where they remained for three centuries. These Asiatic invaders overran the Turkish realms in Asia Minor and prevented the Turks from seizing Constantinople.

In the fifteenth century, however, a band of Turks, led by Othman and therefore called the Ottoman Turks, crossed the Dardanelles and conquered the Balkan regions. The territory of the Empire was reduced to the land surrounding its capital, and in 1453, unable longer to resist the siege of the Turks, the capital finally surrendered. So Constantine's city, after more than a thousand years, fell into the hands of Asiatic invaders, and the Eastern Empire, the last vestige of the old Roman Empire, disappeared. But the Turks were not satisfied with their conquests, and continued to plague and threaten eastern and southern Europe for centuries.

2. GERMANY BEHIND THE PROCESSION

Why the German Kings were Unable to establish a Strong State. The German kings had failed to create a strong kingdom such as those over which Louis XI of France and Henry VII of England ruled. Their fine title of "Emperor," as we have seen (pp. 443–444), had made them a great deal of trouble and done them no good. Their attempts to keep Italy as well as Germany under their rule, and the alliance of the mighty bishop of Rome with their enemies, had well-nigh ruined them. Their position was further weakened by the fact that their office was not strictly hereditary, that is, did not pass down from father to son without question. Although the emperors were often succeeded by their sons, each new emperor had to be *elected*, and those great vassals who controlled the election naturally took care to bind the candidate by solemn promises not to interfere with their privileges and independence. The result was that, after the downfall of the Hohenstaufens, Germany fell apart into a great number of practically independent states, of which none were very large and some were extremely small.

The "Germanies." These two or three hundred states, which the French called the "Germanies," differed greatly from one another in size and character. This one had a duke, that a count, at its head, while others were ruled over by archbishops, bishops, or abbots. There were many cities, like Nuremberg, Frankfurt, and Cologne, just as independent as the great duchies of Bavaria, Württemberg, and Saxony. On the other hand, there were the knights, whose possessions might consist of a single strong castle with a wretched village lying at its foot.

As for the emperor, he no longer had any power to control his vassals. He had neither money nor soldiers. At the time of Luther's birth (see page 660) the poverty-stricken Frederick III (Maximilian's father) might have been seen picking up a free meal at a monastery or riding behind a slow but economical ox team. The real power in Germany lay in the hands of the more important vassals, seven of whom were called the *electors* because, since the thirteenth century, they had enjoyed the right to elect the emperor.

The towns, which had grown up since the revival of business and the use of money in the thirteenth century, were centers of culture in the north of Europe, just as those of Italy were in the south. Some of the towns were direct vassals of the emperor and were consequently independent of the particular prince within whose territory they were situated. These were called *free*, or *imperial*, cities and must be reckoned among the states of Germany.

The knights, who ruled over the smallest of the German territories, had earlier formed a very important class; but the introduction of gunpowder and new methods of fighting put them at a disadvantage, for they clung to their medieval habits. Their tiny realms were often too small to support them, and they frequently turned to robbery for a living and proved a great nuisance to the merchants and townspeople whom they were accustomed to plunder from time to time.

Neighborhood War. It is clear that these states, little and big, all tangled up with one another, would be sure to have frequent disputes among themselves. The emperor was not powerful enough to keep order, and each ruler had to defend himself if attacked. Neighborhood war was permitted by law, if only some polite rules were followed. For instance, a prince or town was required to give warning three days in advance before attacking another member of the Empire.

Germany had a national assembly, called the *diet*, which met at irregular intervals, now in one town and now in another; for Germany had no capital city. The towns were not permitted to send delegates until 1487, long after the townspeople were represented in France and England. The restless knights and other minor nobles were not represented at all and consequently did not always consider the decisions of the diet binding upon them.

The Imperial Title becomes Hereditary in the House of Austria. Among those who had enjoyed the title of Emperor there was, toward the end of the thirteenth century, one Rudolph of Hapsburg. The original seat of the Hapsburgs, who were destined to play such a great part in European affairs, was in northern Switzerland, where the ruins of their original castle may still be seen. Rudolph was the first prominent member of the family; he established its position and influence by seizing the duchies of Austria and Styria, which became, under his successors, the center of the extensive Austrian possessions.

About a century and a half after the death of Rudolph the German princes began regularly to choose as their emperor the ruler of the Austrian possessions, so that the title of emperor became, to all intents and purposes, hereditary in the Hapsburg line. The Hapsburgs were, however, far more interested in adding to their family domains than in advancing the interests of the German Empire as a whole.

Maximilian I lays the Foundation of Hapsburg Power. It is an old saying that some families fight their way, others intrigue their way, to power; the Hapsburgs *married* their way. It was the young Maximilian I (1493–1519) who laid the foundations of the Hapsburg power by arranging an unusual number of profitable marriages. As a young man he himself had married Mary of Burgundy, thereby gaining the Burgundian possessions. He arranged that his son Philip should wed the daughter and heiress of Ferdinand and Isabella of Spain, thus adding a still greater territory to the large holdings of the family.

The Vast Possessions of Charles V. When Philip died, in 1506, his son Charles, the next Hapsburg successor, could look forward to an unheard-of accumulation of glorious titles as soon as his grandfathers, Maximilian of Austria and Ferdinand of Aragon, should pass away.[1] He was soon to be

[1] AUSTRIA	BURGUNDY	CASTILE (AMERICA)	ARAGON, NAPLES, ETC.
Maximilian I, m. Mary (d. 1482), (d. 1519)	dau. of Charles the Bold (d. 1477)	Isabella, m. Ferdinand (d. 1516) (d. 1504)	
	Philip (d. 1506), m.	Joanna the Insane (d. 1555)	
Charles V (d. 1558), Emperor. 1519–1556		Ferdinand (d. 1564), m. Anna, heiress to kingdoms Emperor, 1556–1564 of Bohemia and Hungary	

duke of Brabant, margrave of Antwerp, count of Holland,
archduke of Austria, count of Tyrol, and king of Castile,

Aragon, Naples,[1] and
of the vast Spanish
possessions in Amer-
ica — to mention a
few of his more im-
portant titles.

Ferdinand died in
1516, and Charles,
now a lad of sixteen,
who had been born
and brought up in
the Netherlands, was
not a little bewil-
dered when he first
set foot in his Span-
ish dominions. The
Burgundian advisers
whom Charles had
brought with him
were distasteful to
the Spaniards, who,
of course, regarded
them as foreigners.
Opposition and sus-
picion awaited him
in each of his several
Spanish realms, for

FIG. 155. *Charles V at the Age of Forty-eight*
From a painting by Titian at Munich

he found by no means a united Spain. Each kingdom
claimed special recognition of its rights and proposed important reforms before it would acknowledge Charles as king.

The Election of Charles as Emperor (1519). It seemed as
if the boy would have his hands full in asserting his authority
as the first "king of Spain"; nevertheless, a still more imposing title and still more perplexing responsibilities were to fall

[1] Naples and Sicily were in the hands of the king of Aragon at this time (see
note, p. 631)

upon his shoulders before he was twenty years old. It had long been Maximilian's ambition that his grandson should succeed him upon the imperial throne. He died in 1519, and the electors finally chose Charles as emperor — the fifth of that name — instead of the rival candidate, Francis I of France. By this election the king of Spain, who had not yet been in Germany and who never learned its language, became the ruler of the confused German territories at the time when the teachings of Luther were adding a new kind of trouble to the old disorders (see Chapter XXX).

3. ITALY BECOMES THE BATTLEGROUND OF FOREIGN POWERS

Charles VIII of France invades Italy. In order to understand the Europe of Charles V and the constant wars which occupied him all his life, we must turn back and review the questions which had been engaging the attention of his fellow kings before he came to the throne. It is particularly necessary to see clearly how Italy had suddenly become the center of commotion — the battlefield for Spain, France, and Germany.

Charles VIII of France (1483–1498) possessed little of the shrewdness of his father, Louis XI (p. 477). He dreamed of a mighty expedition against the Turks and of the conquest of Constantinople. As the first step he determined to lead an army into Italy and assert his claim, inherited from his father, to the kingdom of Naples, which was in the hands of the House of Aragon.[1] While Italy had everything to lose by permitting a powerful foreign monarch to get a foothold in the south, there was no probability that the various Italian states would lay aside their quarrels and combine against the invader. On the contrary, Charles VIII was urged by some of the Italians themselves to come.

[1] It will be remembered that the Popes, in their struggle with Frederick II and the Hohenstaufens, finally called in Charles of Anjou, the brother of Saint Louis, and gave to him both Naples and Sicily (p. 456). Sicily revolted in 1282 and was united with the kingdom of Aragon, which still held it when Charles V came to the Spanish throne. Naples also was conquered by the king of Aragon, and was in his family when Charles VIII undertook his Italian expedition. Louis XI, although he claimed the right of the French to rule in Naples, had prudently refused to attempt to oust the Aragonese usurpers, as he had quite enough to do at home.

The success of the French king seemed marvelous; he marched down the Italian peninsula without opposition. As he approached Florence the people, roused by the preaching of a famous Dominican friar, Savonarola, revolted against the rule of the Medici and established a republic. But the insignificant and ugly figure of the French king sadly disappointed them. So he soon deemed it wise to continue his way southward. Naples speedily fell into his hands. But he and his troops were demoralized by the wines and other pleasures of the south, and his enemies at last began to form a combination against him. Ferdinand of Aragon was fearful lest he might lose Sicily, and Emperor Maximilian objected to having the French control Italy. Charles's situation became so dangerous that he may well have thought himself fortunate, at the close of 1495, to escape, after losing only a single battle, from the country he had hoped to conquer.

Results of Charles's Expedition. The results of the expedition of Charles VIII appear at first sight trivial; in reality they were momentous. In the first place, it was now clear to Europe that the Italians had no real national feeling, however much they might despise the "barbarians" who lived north of the Alps. From this time down to the latter half of the nineteenth century Italy was dominated by foreign nations, especially Spain and Austria. In the second place, the French learned to admire the art and culture of Italy (pp. 551 ff.). The nobles began to change their feudal castles, which since the invention of gunpowder were useless as fortresses, into luxurious palaces and country houses. The new scholarship of Italy also became known and flourished not only in France but in England and Germany as well, and Greek began to be studied outside of Italy. Consequently, just as Italy was becoming the victim of foreign invaders, it was also losing, never to regain, that leadership in learning which it had enjoyed since the revival of interest in Latin and Greek literature.

Francis I and his Attempt to conquer Northern Italy. It would be wearisome and unprofitable to follow the attempts of the French to get a foothold in northern Italy. Suffice it to say that Charles VIII soon died and that his successor, Louis XII, laid claim to the duchy of Milan in the north as well as to Naples in the south. But he concluded to sell his claim to Naples to Ferdinand of Aragon and centered his attention on holding Milan. He did not succeed in his purpose, however, largely owing to the Pope, who managed to drive the French out of Italy in 1512.

FIG. 156. *Francis I*

From a painting by Clouet in the Louvre

Francis I, who came to the French throne in 1515, at the age of twenty, is one of the most famous of the French kings. He was gracious and chivalrous in his ideas of conduct, and his proudest title was "the Gentleman King." Like his contemporaries, Pope Leo X, son of Lorenzo de' Medici, and Henry VIII of England, he helped artists and men of letters, and was interested in fine buildings, of which a striking example is shown on page 634.

Francis opened his reign by a very astonishing victory. He led his troops into Italy, over a mountain pass which had hitherto been believed to be too steep for cavalry, and defeated the Swiss — who were in the Pope's pay — at Marignano. He then occupied Milan and communicated with Leo X, who was glad to make terms with the victorious young king. The Pope agreed that Francis should retain Milan, and Francis on his part approved Leo's plan for turning over Florence once more to the Medici, the family to which the Pope himself belonged. This was done, and some years later this wonderful republic became the grand duchy of Tuscany, governed by a line of petty princes under whom its former glories were never renewed.

Fig. 157. *Court of the Palace at Blois*

The expedition of Charles VIII to Italy called the attention of French architects to the beautiful Renaissance style used there. As cannon had by this time begun to render the old kind of castles with thick walls and towers useless as a means of defense, the French kings began to construct beautiful palaces, of which several still exist. Charles VIII's successor, Louis XII, began a handsome structure at Blois, on the river Loire, and Francis I added a wing, the inner side of which is here reproduced. Its magnificent open staircase and wide, high windows have little in common with the old donjons of feudal times

Sources of Trouble between France and the Hapsburgs. Friendly relations existed at first between the two young sovereigns Francis I and Charles V, but there were several circumstances which led later to an almost incessant series of wars between them. France was clamped in between the northern and southern possessions of Charles and had at that time no natural boundaries, such as a river or range of mountains. Charles also believed that, through his grandfather Maximilian, he was entitled to Milan, which the French kings had set their hearts upon retaining. For a generation the rivals fought over these and other matters, and the wars between Charles and Francis were but the beginning of a conflict lasting over two centuries between France and the overgrown power of the House of Hapsburg.

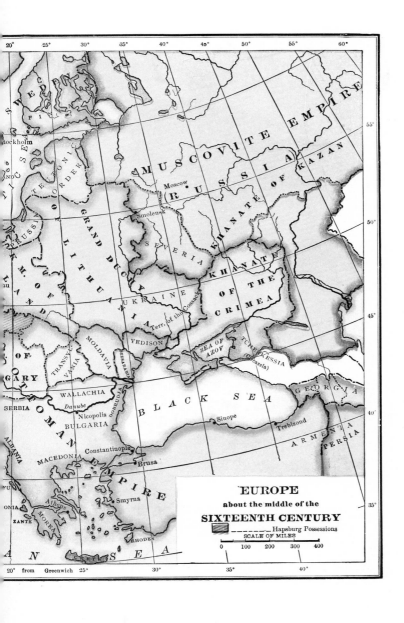

EUROPE

about the middle of the

SIXTEENTH CENTURY

Hapsburg Possessions

SCALE OF MILES

0   100   200   300   400

Charles V goes to Germany. In 1520 Charles V started for Germany to receive his crown as emperor at Aix-la-Chapelle. On his way he landed in England with the purpose of persuading Henry VIII not to form an alliance with Francis. He then set sail for the Netherlands, where he was duly crowned King of the Romans. From there he proceeded, for the first time, to Germany, where he summoned his first national assembly, or *diet*, at Worms. The most important business of this assembly proved to be the consideration of the case of a university professor, Martin Luther, who was accused of writing heretical books, and who had begun what proved to be the first successful revolt against the powerful medieval Church.

Questions and Exercises

REVIEW OF CHAPTER

1. Recall some important contributions to our civilization made in the late Middle Ages. How did England and France develop strong monarchies in the sixteenth century? What difficulties did Spain have in developing a unified state?

2. Why did Germany remain divided up between feudal lords? What were the foundations of the Hapsburg power? Why was the Holy Roman Empire a failure? How were the emperors elected?

3. How was Italy divided in the sixteenth century? Why was it difficult to unify Italy? What were the troubles between the French kings and the Hapsburgs?

USEFUL TERMS

See how much meaning you can give to the following terms: *electors, knights, diet, mosque, Inquisition.* Distinguish between *feudalism, monarchy,* and *democracy*; between *Seljuk* and *Ottoman Turks.*

DIRECTIVE QUESTIONS

1. What is meant by saying that the Holy Roman Empire was a dream rather than a reality?

2. Contrast a national state and an empire. Did the people of an empire all speak the same language?

3. What earlier rulers aspired to rule a world empire?

4. Compare the empire of Charlemagne with that of Charles V.

1. Progress is more likely under a monarchy than under feudalism.

2. The study of medieval government is important in understanding present-day Europe.

3. "The Holy Roman Empire was neither holy, Roman, nor an empire." — VOLTAIRE

4. The year 1492 was momentous in the history of Spain.

ADDITIONAL ADVENTURES IN LEARNING

1. Studies in Source Materials. ROBINSON, *Readings*, Vol. II, chap. xxiii, sect. i, "The Expedition of Charles VIII into Italy"; 231a, "Florence and the Medici"; sect. ii, The troubles of Italy in the sixteenth century described by Machiavelli; sect. iii, The story of the good Chevalier Bayard; 233a, How Francis I succeeded Louis XII; 233b, The battle of Marignano and the bravery of Francis I; p. 21, Adventures of the Good Chevalier and his horse Carman; pp. 22–23, note, How Francis I was knighted; sect. iv, 234, "Spain at the Opening of the Sixteenth Century"; chap. xxiv, "Germany in the time of Maximilian I."

2. Topical Studies. Europe at the opening of the sixteenth century: HAYES, *Political and Cultural History of Europe*, Vol. I, chap. i. The later years of Charles V: WELLS, *The Outline of History*, Vol. II, pp. 207 ff. The Mohammedans in Spain: THOMPSON, *The Middle Ages*, chap. xxiii.

Part Seven

HOW SOME OF THE RULERS OF EUROPE REVOLTED FROM THE CHURCH OF THEIR ANCESTORS, AND PROTESTANTS CAME INTO EXISTENCE; THE VARIOUS IMPORTANT CHANGES THAT TOOK PLACE DURING THE SO-CALLED "WARS OF RELIGION"

Religion has always been a very Important Part of Civilization, and the Differences of Opinion on this Subject have caused Many Bitter Struggles. Luther and Calvin Broke Away from the Church as it had Previously Existed, as an International Institution under the Headship of the Pope. Henry VIII of England Also declared his Independence of the Pope. A Powerful Protestant Party developed in France. The Catholic Ruler of Spain tried to Subdue the Protestants in England and the Netherlands. All these Things led to the Wars of Religion and Important Changes in the Christian Church as it had existed Earlier

Martin Luther Preaching at the Wartburg
From a painting by Hugo Vogel

CHAPTER XXIX · THE CHURCH
BEFORE THE PROTESTANT REVOLT

WE HAVE already seen that the Christian Church in the Middle Ages was very different in many ways from the churches with which we are familiar in English-speaking countries today. In the next chapter we shall come to the revolt against this church under which western Europe had lived since the break-up of the Roman Empire. Some countries broke away from the rule of the Pope and adopted Protestantism; others remained faithful to the Pope and defended the church of their ancestors. Before taking up this revolt, which is called by Protestants the "Reformation," we ought to see how strong was the Holy Roman Catholic Church, which still has far more people faithful to it in the United States, a Protestant country, than has any single Protestant sect.

In order to understand the Wars of Religion we have first to consider the *one* Church which existed before the Reformation, to realize that everyone in western Europe was forced to belong to it and to contribute to its support. We shall see that many of the churchmen were very wealthy and powerful, and that the Church was much more like a state than a present-day church. It performed many of the duties that our governments do now. We must realize the reasons why reformers complained of the teachings and actions of the Church and were able finally to induce a number of rulers to throw off their allegiance to the Pope and establish churches of their own. From these some of our modern Protestant sects are descended. When once the power of the Catholic Church to force people to belong to it was lost, religious leaders arose and established a great number of sects, each claiming to represent the true Christian faith.

1. RESEMBLANCE BETWEEN THE CHURCH AND A STATE

The Importance of the Medieval Church. The Catholic Church was by far the most powerful and important institution all through the Middle Ages. Its Popes, bishops, and abbots were the soul of nearly every great undertaking. Although we have already spoken of its early development, we cannot properly understand the history of Western civilization without appreciating what a dominant position it occupied in the life of medieval Europe.

Comparison with Modern Churches. In the first place, the medieval Church influenced men's lives in far more ways than do our numerous churches today. Everyone was required to belong to it, as we must all now belong to some nation. Everyone was baptized into it while a mere infant. All western Europe formed a single religious association, from which it was a crime to revolt. To refuse loyalty to the Church or to question its authority or teaching was *heresy*, or treason against God, and was punishable by death.

Secondly, modern churches, especially Protestant organizations, are supported by voluntary contributions, that is, by what their members are willing to give. The medieval Church, however, not only had its revenue from its vast lands and a great variety of fees for its services but collected a regular tax, the *tithe* (or tenth), from everyone who had any income.

Thirdly, the medieval Church was not merely a religious body. Besides its duties in the saving of men's souls, it performed many services which today are carried on by other institutions. There were then no government forms of relief or charity, nor were there any public educational institutions. The Church looked after the poor, the sick, the forlorn; saw that justice was provided for the helpless; and performed much useful work which is now divided between government and other non-religious organizations.

Finally, the Church, unlike Protestant churches, had one official head — the Pope — to whom all ministers and religious associations were responsible. Whether in Italy, Germany, France, Spain, or England, every church office was really controlled by the Supreme Pontiff at Rome. Moreover, the Church had one official language, Latin, known by the members of the clergy; and in this tongue all its communications were written and its religious services conducted.

The Medieval Church an International Monarchy. The medieval Church was, in short, an international monarchy —

a state to which the rulers of the countries of Europe as Christians owed their allegiance. Besides its official language and its organization under one head, it had its own system of law — the canon law — and its own courts, in which it tried many cases which are nowadays settled in our government courts.[1] One may get some idea of the business of the church courts from the fact that the Church claimed the right to try all cases in which a clergyman was concerned or anyone connected with the Church or under its special protection, such as monks, students, crusaders, widows, orphans, and the helpless. Then all cases which had to do with the business of the Church or with offenses against its teachings usually came before the church courts, as, for example, those concerning marriages, wills, sworn contracts, blasphemy, and heresy. The Church even had its prisons, to which it might sentence offenders for life.

Organization of the Church: the Pope. At the head of this international monarchy was an all-powerful and absolute ruler, the Pope. He was the supreme lawgiver. He might set aside or repeal any law of the Church, no matter how ancient, so long as he did not believe it to be commanded by the Scriptures or by Nature. He might, for good reasons, make exceptions to all merely human laws; as, for instance, permit cousins to marry, or free a monk from his vows. Such exceptions were known as *dispensations.*

The Pope was not merely the supreme lawgiver but also the supreme judge. Anyone, whether clergyman or layman, in any part of Europe could appeal to him at any stage in the trial of a large number of cases. Of course, this system had serious drawbacks. Grave injustice might be done by carrying to Rome a case which ought to have been settled in Edinburgh or Cologne, where the facts were best known. The rich, moreover, always had the advantage, as only they could afford the time and expense of bringing a suit before so distant a court.

---

[1] The law of the Church was known as the *canon law*. It was taught in most of the universities and was practiced by a great number of lawyers. It was based upon the acts of the various church councils. from that of Nicæa (A.D. 325) down, and, above all, upon the decrees and decisions of the Popes.

The Pope's control over the entire Christian Church was exercised by his *legates*, whom he sent, when occasion required, as his special messengers or representatives to all parts of the Christian world. These papal ambassadors were intrusted with great powers. Their haughty manner sometimes offended the prelates and rulers to whom they brought home the authority of the Pope, — as, for instance, when the legate Pandulf grandly freed all the subjects of King John of England, before his very face, from their oath of loyalty to him.

The task assumed by the Pope of governing the whole Western world naturally made it necessary to create a large body of officials at Rome in order to transact all the varied business and prepare and send out the innumerable legal documents.[1] The cardinals and the Pope's officials constituted what was called the papal *curia*, or court.

Sources of the Pope's Income. To carry on his government and to meet the expenses of his palace and officials, the Pope had need of a vast income. This he secured from various sources. Heavy fees were required from those who brought cases to his court for decision. The archbishops, bishops, and abbots were expected to make generous contributions when the Pope approved their election. In the thirteenth century the Pope himself began to fill many benefices throughout Europe, and he customarily received half the first year's revenues from those whom he appointed. For several centuries before the Protestants finally threw off their allegiance to the Popes, there was widespread complaint on the part of both clergy and laymen that the fees and taxes levied by the Roman curia were too large.

The Archbishops and Bishops. Next in order below the head of the Church were the archbishops and bishops. An archbishop was a bishop whose power extended beyond the boundaries of his own *diocese*, or district, and who exercised a certain control over all the bishops within his province. There is perhaps no class of persons in medieval times whose position it is so necessary to understand as that of the

---

[1] Many of the edicts, decisions, and orders of the Popes were called *bulls*, from the seal (Latin, *bulla*) attached to them.

bishops. They were regarded as the successors of the Apostles, whose powers were held to be divinely handed down to them.

They represented the Church Universal in their respective dioceses, under the supreme headship of their "elder brother," the Pope, the bishop of Rome, the successor of the chief of the Apostles. Their symbols of office, the miter and crosier, are familiar to everyone (see Fig. 158). Each bishop had his especial church, called a cathedral, which ordinarily surpassed the other churches of the diocese in size and beauty.

Fig. 158. *An English Bishop Ordaining a Priest*

The picture is taken from a manuscript of Henry II's time. The bishop is wearing his miter, or cap, and holds his pastoral staff, the *crosier*, in his left hand while he raises his right, in blessing, over the priest's head

The bishop had to look after his diocese and the lands and other possessions which belonged to the bishopric. Lastly, the bishop was usually a feudal lord. He might have vassals and subvassals, and often was himself a vassal, not only of the king but also of some neighboring lord.

The Parish Priest and his Duties. The smallest division of the Church was the parish. At the head of the parish was the parish priest, who conducted services in the parish church and absolved, baptized, married, and buried his parishioners. The priests were supposed to be supported by the lands belonging to the parish church and by the tithes. But both these sources of income were often in the hands of laymen or of a neighboring monastery. The poor priest who performed all these services often received scarcely enough to keep soul and body together.

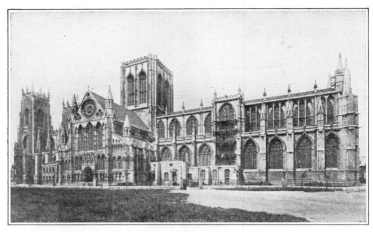

Fig. 159. *The Cathedral at York, England*

The bishop's church was called a cathedral, because in it stood the bishop's chair, or throne (Latin, *cathedra*). It was ordinarily much more imposing than the parish churches, although sometimes the abbey churches belonging to rich monasteries vied with the bishop's church in beauty

The Clergy a Peculiar and Powerful Class. The *clergy* were a class set quite apart from the members of the churches, or *laymen*, as they were called. Their dress was different from that of the ordinary citizen. They were not supposed to fight, though the great bishops and abbots, who were feudal lords, had vassals who fought for them. They were not supposed to marry. On taking orders the clergy were said to have "indelible characters," or marks of spiritual grace and power, granted them at their consecration, which were not possessed by the layman. They had the power to act as mediators between God and man, and to officiate at the miracle of the Mass, to dispense the Sacraments, or means of grace, and to absolve men from their sins.

Benefit of Clergy. They owed their first allegiance not to the ruler of their country but to the Pope. They were excused from paying taxes. They had the right, if accused of crimes or unlawful acts, to be tried in the church courts. This privilege was called the "benefit of clergy."

The influence of the clergy was greatly increased by the

fact that they alone were educated. For six or seven centuries after the break-up of the Roman Empire very few outside of the clergy ever dreamed of studying, or even of learning to read and write. Even in the thirteenth century a wrongdoer who wished to prove that he belonged to the clergy, so that he might be tried by a church court, had only to show that he could read a single line; for it was supposed by the judges that no one unconnected with the Church could read at all.

2. How the Church dealt with Traitors

The Crime of Heresy. In spite of the power and wonderful organization of the Church, there were, almost from the first, those who differed in belief from its teachings. As time went on and the Church became more powerful, the number of those who objected to its teaching and practices increased. The rebels were of two kinds: some merely rejected certain practices and teachings of the Church while they remained Christians. Others denied the truth of the Christian religion itself. In the eyes of the Church both classes were guilty of the supreme crime of *heresy*; and heresy was a sin against God and a crime, according to the laws of Christian countries, punishable by death. Against these offenders, therefore, the Church took the sternest measures. Those who openly denounced the Church or the truths of Christianity could be met with armed force. It was more difficult, however, to discover secret objectors, who were nevertheless also regarded as traitors and worthy of punishment.

The Albigensian Crusade. In the thirteenth century there was a group of Albigensians (named from their town of Albi in southern France) who taught that the Christian religion was false in its teaching. Against these unfortunate people Pope Innocent III preached a crusade in 1208. An army from the northern part of France marched into the doomed region and after a bloody war put down the heresy by wholesale slaughter.

The Inquisition. To search out and bring to trial secret offenders against the Church, the Pope established a special system of courts. These courts, which devoted their whole attention to the discovery and conviction of heretics, were called the *Holy Inquisition*. This system gradually grew up after the Albigensian Crusade. The unfairness of the trials and the cruel treatment of those suspected of heresy — long imprisonment, or torture inflicted with the hope of forcing them to confess their crime or to accuse others — have made the name "Inquisition" infamous. Without by any means attempting to defend the methods employed, it may be remarked that the inquisitors were often earnest and upright men, and the methods of the Inquisition were not more cruel than those used in the government courts of the period.

The statement of the suspected person that he was not a heretic did not receive any attention; for it was assumed that he would naturally deny his guilt, as would any other criminal. A person's belief had, therefore, to be judged by outward acts. Consequently one might fall into the hands of the Inquisition by mere accidental conversation with a heretic, by some unintentional neglect to show proper respect toward the church services, or by the malicious accusation of one's neighbors.

If the suspected person confessed his sin and renounced his heresy, he was forgiven and received back into the Church; but he still had to suffer imprisonment for life as the only means of wiping away the unspeakable sin of which he had been guilty. If he persisted in his heresy he was "relaxed to the secular arm"; that is to say, the Church, whose law forbade it to shed blood, handed over the convicted person to the government, which burned him alive.

3. Reformers Within the Church: Franciscans and Dominicans

The Wealth of the Church a Temptation. The wealth and power of the Church constituted in themselves a great danger. Its vast lands, its rich livings, its enormous treasury, the high position and privileges enjoyed by its important officials, all made the Church a prey to worldly and scheming persons who sought to secure church appointments for themselves, their families, or their friends. Kings and nobles were ever watchful to see how they might profit by some connection with so powerful an institution or influence its policy for their own advantage. Within the organization itself there was many a temptation for weak and worldly churchmen to make use of its resources for their own personal benefit.

Founding of Mendicant Orders. There were, however, many pious persons within the Church who saw that it was in need of reform. They held that the clergy should lead simpler lives and devote themselves entirely to good works. It was this conviction, that the negligence and failure of the clergy to perform their duties was essentially to blame for the evils of the time, which led to the formation of two organizations within the Church, the Franciscans and Dominicans. Saint Francis and Saint Dominic, the founders of the two orders, strove to meet the needs of their day by inventing a new kind of clergyman, the begging brother, or "mendicant

Fig. 160. *Saint Francis of Assisi Preaching to the Birds*

There is a legend that Saint Francis once preached to the birds, who listened attentively. This is a fifteenth-century artist's conception. (From a fresco by Benozzo Gozzoli in the Church of St. Francis at Montefalco, Italy)

friar" (from the Latin *frater*, "brother"), as he was called because he depended for his support on charity. He was to do just what the bishops and parish priests often failed to do, — namely, lead a life of self-sacrifice, defend the Church's beliefs against the attacks of heretics, and awaken the people to a new religious life. The founding of the mendicant orders is one of the most interesting events of the Middle Ages.

Saint Francis of Assisi (1182?–1226) *and his Order.* There is no more lovely or more fascinating figure in history than Saint Francis. He was born (probably in 1182) at Assisi, a little town in central Italy. He was the son of a well-to-do merchant, and during his early youth lived a very gay life and had everything that money could buy. But he was of a sensitive and chivalrous nature, and the contrast between his own life of luxury and the sad state of the poor early troubled him. When he was about twenty, after a long and serious illness which made a break in his gay life and gave him time to think, he suddenly lost his love for the old pleasures and began to visit the poor and forsaken, — above all, the lepers. His father objected to his son's strange ideas. Finally the young man decided to give up all his inheritance, and, casting aside his rich apparel, he put on the worn-out garment of a gardener and became a homeless wanderer living on charity. He soon began to preach in a simple way, and before long a rich fellow townsman resolved to follow his example — to sell his all and give to the poor. Others soon joined them, and these joyous converts, free of worldly burdens, went barefoot and penniless about central Italy preaching the Gospel.

Missionary Work of the Franciscans. The Pope, with some hesitation, gave his approval to the work of the Franciscan brothers (1210). Seven years later, when the followers of Francis had greatly increased in numbers, missionary work was begun on a large scale, and brethren were sent to Germany, Hungary, France, Spain, and even Syria. It was not long before an English writer was telling with wonder of the arrival in his country of these barefoot men, in their

Fig. 161. *Church of St. Francis at Assisi*

Assisi is situated on a high hill, and the monastery of the Franciscans is built out on a promontory. The monastery has *two* churches, one above the other. The lower church, in which are the remains of Saint Francis, was begun in 1228 and contains pictures of the life and miracles of the saint. To reach the upper church (completed 1253) one can go up by the stairs, seen on the right of the entrance to the lower church, to the higher level upon which the upper church faces

patched gowns and with ropes about their waists, who, with Christian faith, took no thought for the morrow, believing that their Heavenly Father knew what things they had need of.

The Franciscans become a Powerful Order. When the Pope saw the success of their missionary work, he bestowed many privileges on the Franciscans. But Francis did not wish his band of companions to become great and powerful lest they cease to follow the simple life of Christ. After the death of Saint Francis many of the members wished to continue the life of poverty, but the new head of the order believed that much good might be done with the wealth which people were anxious to give them. A stately church was immediately built at Assisi to receive the remains of the humble founder of the order, and a great chest was set up in the church to receive the offerings of those who desired to give to the work of the Franciscans. Many beautiful churches and monasteries were constructed.

The Founding of the Dominican Order. Saint Dominic (b. 1170), the Spanish founder of the other great mendicant order, was not a simple layman like Francis. He was a churchman and took a course of religious study for ten years in a Spanish university. He then (1208) accompanied his bishop to southern France on the eve of the Albigensian Crusade and was deeply shocked to see how many people were heretics. His host at Toulouse, where he stayed, happened to be an Albigensian, and Dominic spent the night in converting him. He then and there determined to devote his life to fighting heresy.

By 1214 a few sympathetic followers from various parts of Europe had joined Dominic, and they asked Pope Innocent III to approve their new order. The Pope again hesitated, but is said to have dreamed a dream in which he saw the great Roman Church of the Lateran tottering and ready to fall had not Dominic supported it on his shoulders. He interpreted this as meaning that the new organization might sometime become a great aid to the papacy, and gave it his blessing. As soon as possible Dominic sent forth his followers, of whom there were but sixteen, to preach, just as the Franciscans were undertaking their first missionary journeys. By 1221 the Dominican order was thoroughly organized and had sixty monasteries scattered over western Europe.

Work of the Begging Friars. "Wandering on foot over the face of Europe, under burning suns or chilling blasts, rejecting alms in money but receiving thankfully whatever coarse food might be set before the wayfarer, enduring hunger patiently, taking no thought for the morrow, but busied eternally in the work of snatching souls from Satan and lifting men up from the sordid cares of daily life" — in this way did the early Franciscans and Dominicans win the love and honor of the people.

The Dominicans were called the "Preaching Friars" or Black Friars and were carefully trained in religious debate in order the better to answer the arguments of the heretics. The Pope intrusted to them especially the task of conducting the Inquisition. They early began to extend their influence over the universities, and the two most distinguished religious teachers of the thirteenth century, Albertus Magnus and Thomas Aquinas, were Dominicans.

4. Sources of Conflict between Church and State

Difficulties between Church and State. It was inevitable that the power and wealth of the Church not only should be a source of temptation and danger within the Church itself but should bring it into conflict with the interests of the growing national states.

1. Within their realms the rulers of the new monarchies beheld a large body of churchmen who, although they were their subjects, nevertheless owed their first loyalty to the Pope and who looked to Rome, rather than to the national government, for aid in all matters concerning their lives and advancement. The kings also saw vast tracts of land within their boundaries which were outside of their control since they belonged to the Church. They could hope for no revenue from these, for they could not tax church lands. The clergymen, too, were freed from taxation, although the Church permitted them to make gifts of their own free will to the king when there was great necessity. These gifts were, however, a very uncertain source of income. Was this vast amount of wealth to go on increasing and the Church bear no part of the expense of the government? The churchmen usually argued that they needed all their money to carry on the church services, keep up the churches and monasteries,

take care of the schools, and aid the poor ; for the state left them to bear all these necessary burdens.

2. Another cause of conflict was the question of appointments. Should the king or the Pope have the advantage of selecting the bishops and the abbots of rich monasteries? Naturally both were anxious to place their friends and supporters in these important positions. Moreover, the Pope, like the king, could claim a considerable contribution from those whom he appointed, and the king naturally grudged him the money.

3. Then there was the trouble about the number of cases which could be tried in the church courts. The fees which might have been collected by the king's court found their way into the treasury of the Church ; for not only did the cases concerning clergymen go to the church courts, but, as we have seen, a wide variety of matters concerning wills and inheritances could be taken there for settlement.

4. Lastly, there was the question of how far the Pope, as head of the Christian Church, had a right to interfere with the government of a particular state when he did not approve of the way in which a king was acting. The powers of the Pope were very great ; but even the most devout Catholics differed somewhat as to just how great they were.

The "Babylonian Captivity." Philip the Fair determined to demand a tax of one hundredth, later one fiftieth, of the possessions of the clergy and laity alike. This led to a bitter conflict between the French king and Pope Boniface VIII about the year 1300. The Pope at first forbade all such payments, but in the end was forced to permit the clergy to pay their feudal dues and make loans to the king.

After the death of Boniface (1303) King Philip proposed to have no more troubles with the Popes. He had a French archbishop chosen as head of the Church, with the understanding that he should move the papacy from Rome to France. The new Pope was crowned Clement V, and remained in France during his whole Pontificate (or term of office). Clement V's successors built a gorgeous palace at Avignon, just outside the French frontier of those days, and lived there in great splendor for sixty years. The long exile of the Popes from Rome is called the "Babylonian Captivity." Although the Popes of this period were for the most part good and earnest men, they were all Frenchmen; and the nearness of their court to France led to the suspicion that they were controlled by the French kings. This tended to weaken the influence of the papacy in other countries.

How the Popes increased their Income. Another element which brought criticism on the Popes was their method of securing money to support their splendid papal court. Living at Avignon they were naturally deprived of some of the income they had enjoyed from their Italian possessions when they were located at Rome. To make up this shortage in revenue they demanded larger fees for the trial of lawsuits in church courts, and larger contributions for dispensations and for appointments to important church offices. They began to get the control of as many rich benefices (church offices) into their hands as possible, by promising their supporters appointments ahead of time, to take effect as soon as the office should fall vacant. Men appointed in this way were very unpopular; for they were often foreigners and were suspected of receiving their nomination only on account of the revenue that they had promised to give the Pope.

The "Great Schism" in the Church (1378–1415). A further misfortune befell the Church when, after the Popes had moved back to Rome, a new Pope was to be chosen. The Roman populace clamored for the appointment of an Italian; and when the new Pope attempted to introduce a number of reforms, the cardinals, claiming that they had been forced to choose Urban VI, met and elected a second pope, Clement VII, who reëstablished the papacy at Avignon. For forty years thereafter there were two popes, each claiming the right to the office. There were two colleges of cardinals, and all Catholic Europe was divided in its loyalty to the one it deemed to be the true head of the Church. Italy supported Urban, while France obeyed Clement; and England, hostile to France, accepted the Pope at Rome. We cannot tell of all the difficulties of this unusual situation. Peace was finally restored when, at the Council of Constance, in 1415, a new Pope, Martin V, was elected, and the long schism in the Church was finally healed.

5. Reformers Before the Reformation

The Statute of Provisors: John Wycliffe. There were many loyal Catholics who felt that certain evils in the Church should be remedied and so advocated some steps toward reform. One of the most famous of the early reformers was a professor at Oxford, John Wycliffe (*c.* 1320–1384), who rose to the defense of the government against what he regarded as the unjust claims of the Popes. The papal taxes met with the greatest opposition in England because the Popes were thought to favor France, with which country the English were at war. A law was passed by Parliament, in 1351, ordering that all who procured appointment to a church office in England from the Pope should be outlawed, since they were enemies of the king and his realm. This Statute of Provisors,[1] as it was called, failed, however, to prevent the Pope from filling English benefices. The English king was unable to keep the money of his realm from flowing to Avignon, and at a meeting of the English Parliament held in 1376 a report was made to the effect that taxes levied by the Pope in England were five times those raised by the king.

When Pope Urban V demanded that England should pay the tribute promised by King John at the time he became the Pope's vassal (p. 495), Parliament declared that John had had no right to bind the people without their consent. Wycliffe began his career of opposition to the papacy by trying to prove that John's agreement was void. About ten years later we find the Pope issuing bulls against the teachings of Wycliffe, who had begun to assert that the state might take possession of the property of the Church if it was misused, and that the Pope had no authority except as he acted according to the teachings of the Gospel. Soon

---

[1] "Provisor" meant one who had an order from the Pope appointing him to a church office when it should become vacant.

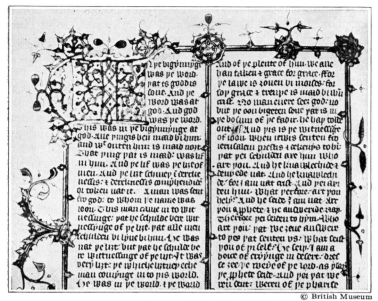

FIG. 162. *A Page from Wycliffe's Translation of the Bible*

This is the first page of the Gospel according to John and contains verses 1–30. The lettering was done with a quill, and the scribe of the time made *y* and *th* in somewhat the same way. The page begins "In the bigynnyge was the word that is goddis love. And the word was at god. And god was the word. This was in the bigynnynge at god. Alle thingis ben maad bi him and wtouten him is maad noght. That thing that is maad was lif in him. And the lif was the light of men." While the spelling is somewhat different from ours, it is clear that the language used by Wycliffe closely resembles that used in the familiar Authorized Version of the New Testament, made two centuries and a half later

Wycliffe went further and boldly attacked the papacy itself, as well as many of the church practices.

Wycliffe's anxiety to teach the people led him to have the Bible translated into English. In addition, he prepared a great number of sermons and pamphlets in English. He is known as the father of English prose; for we have little in English before his time except poetry.

Wycliffe's Influence: John Huss. Wycliffe's followers, the Lollards, as they were called, carried on his teachings, but in a more extreme form, and they were soon put down by persecution. Wycliffe's doctrines, however, were spread abroad in Bohemia by another ardent reformer, John Huss, who went so far as to claim that, as many of the clergy were themselves sinful, men should not be forced to obey them. The Church naturally viewed this theory as dangerous to all order and authority. Huss was tried as a heretic at the Council of Constance, in 1415, and condemned. He was turned over to the secular government and was burned at the stake.

FIG. 163. *Erasmus*

This wonderful picture by Hans Holbein the Younger (1497–1543) hangs in the gallery of the Louvre at Paris. We have every reason to suppose that it is an excellent portrait, for Holbein lived in Basel a considerable part of his life and knew Erasmus well. The artist was, moreover, celebrated for his skill in catching the likeness when depicting the human face. He later painted several well-known Englishmen, including Henry VIII and his little son, Edward VI

Erasmus (1466?–1536). Among the critics of the Church in the early days of Charles V's reign the most famous and influential was Erasmus. He was a Dutchman by birth, but spent his life in various other countries — France, Italy, England, and Germany. He was constantly writing to literary men in different parts of Europe, and from his letters we can get an excellent idea of the feeling of the times. He was greatly interested in the Greek and Latin authors; but his main purpose in life was to better the Church, which he believed was stifled by unnecessary beliefs and practices.

The Councils fail to Reform the Church. Proposals for reform had been brought before the church council at Pisa, in 1409, and later at the Council of Constance. The latter council had succeeded in healing the Great Schism, had burned one whom they deemed an enemy of the Church, and undertook to remedy some of the evils that had grown up in the institution. But after three years of discussion its members lost hope. They did, however, provide for the regular summoning of church councils every ten years. In this way it was hoped that the absolute power of the Pope would be controlled, since he would share some of the responsibility of deciding on important matters with the councils.

A century after the Council of Constance, demands for reforms had become so general that when a revolt started in Germany there were many who took part in the discussion. Before long the "universal" Church was divided, separating Christendom into Roman Catholics, who remained loyal to the older organization, and Protestants, who refused longer to regard the Pope as the head of the Church and rejected many of the beliefs of their ancestors. Instead of a single powerful Church, many sects developed under different leaders, all claiming to represent the true faith as they believed they discovered it in the Bible.

Questions and Exercises

REVIEW OF CHAPTER

1. How did the medieval Church differ from our modern churches? What were the features of its organization which resembled those of a state? In what ways was it really an *international* monarchy? How did the Church support itself? Why were the clergy a powerful class? Explain the meaning of "benefit of clergy."

2. How did the Church deal with heretics? What was the object of the Inquisition? What were the views of the Albigensians?

3. How did its wealth prove to be a danger to the Church? Give a short account of the life of Saint Francis. Did the Franciscan order continue to follow the wishes of its founders? Do you recall the story connected with the founding of the Dominican order?

4. What were the chief subjects of disagreement between the Church and the State? What events led up to the "Babylonian Captivity"? How did the Great Schism come about?

5. What reforms did John Wycliffe demand in the Church?

USEFUL TERMS

See how much meaning you can give to the following terms: *tithe, heresy, heretic, dispensations, legates, benefices, parish, ecclesiastical, spiritual and temporal, canon law, mendicant friar, schism, absolve.*

DIRECTIVE QUESTIONS

1. What public services that were performed by the Church are now taken care of by public organizations?

2. How did the life of the begging friars work for reform in the ideals of the Church?

3. Contrast the life of the Franciscans with that of the secular clergy.

4. Why was the sojourn of the Popes in France called the "Babylonian Captivity"?

DISCUSSION TOPICS

1. It is better for churches not to possess great wealth.

2. The government rather than the Church should be required to look after the needy.

3. Church property should not be taxed. (What other property is free from taxation?)

4. People should be permitted their own religious beliefs without interference of the government.

ADDITIONAL ADVENTURES IN LEARNING

1. Studies in Source Materials. ROBINSON, *Readings*, Vol. I, chap. xvi, sect. i, "The preëminence of the Church"; sect. iv, "The Privileges of Benefit of Clergy"; sect. v, "How the Church and Monasteries were Supported"; chap. xvi, sect. vi, and chap. xvii, sect. v, The attitude toward heretics; chap. xvii, sect. vi, "Life and Character of St. Francis"; chap. xxi, sect. i, The question of taxing church property; sect. iii, John Wycliffe and his teachings; sect. iv, The Popes at Avignon.

2. Topical Studies. Religious orders of the Middle Ages: CUTTS, *Scenes and Characters of the Middle Ages*, Part I, chap. ii (The Benedictine Orders), chap. iv (Military Orders), chap. v (The Orders of Friars); JESSOPP, *The Coming of the Friars*; HEATH, *Pilgrim Life in the Middle Ages*. Write a short account of Saint Francis: *The Little Flowers of St. Francis of Assisi* (translated by Alger); *The Writings of St. Francis* (translated by P. Robinson). Saint Dominic and the founding of the Dominican Order. The work of Erasmus: P. SMITH, *Erasmus*. The story of John Huss.

3. Make a list of the ways in which the medieval Church resembled a great political state.

CHAPTER XXX · THE BREAK-UP
OF THE MEDIEVAL CHURCH

THE medieval Church was rich and powerful, and had been able to defend itself for centuries against the attacks of its enemies before the first successful revolt against the Pope. So long as the rulers were willing to put to death those whom the Church held to be treasonable, no rebellion could succeed. Early in the sixteenth century, however, when Charles V was still a youth, a certain Professor Luther, in the University of Wittenberg, Germany, ventured to denounce some of the beliefs and practices of the Church which he declared to be unchristian. This protest would have endangered his life had not certain of the German rulers decided to support him against the Church. It was in this way that the first successful revolt against the Holy Roman Apostolic Church began.

Other reformers arose in Switzerland, France, and Scandinavia. The English king determined to throw off the authority of the Pope and make himself religious head of his kingdom. All these " protestants," as they were called, accepted, however, most of the beliefs of the older Church, although they rejected some of them and agreed in refusing longer to regard the Pope at Rome as the head of their Church.

Today, in many European countries, especially in England, and in the English-speaking countries (like the United States and Canada), Catholics, Protestants, and Jews get along together without any fear that the government will interfere with their particular way of worshiping God. Quarrels over religious matters seem shocking to us nowadays. We shall see, however, how peoples fought one another for over a hundred years after Luther's time and much blood was shed before the religious freedom which we now enjoy was established.

1. MARTIN LUTHER STARTS THE REVOLT IN GERMANY

The Church divided into Catholics and Protestants. By far the most important event in the sixteenth century was the withdrawal of a large portion of western Europe from the Mother Church. In various European countries *Protestant* groups arose who declared themselves entirely independent of the Pope and who rejected a number of religious beliefs which the older Church held sacred. With the exception of England, all those countries that lay within the ancient bounds of the Roman Empire — Italy, France, Spain, Portugal, as well as southern Germany and Austria — continued to be faithful to the Pope and the Roman Catholic Church. On the other hand, the rulers of the northern German states, England, Holland, Denmark, Norway, and Sweden, sooner or later became Protestants. In this way Europe was divided into two great religious parties, and the enmity between them led to terrible wars and cruel persecutions which fill the history of the sixteenth and seventeenth centuries.

The Germans find Fault with the Papacy. The revolt began in Germany. The Germans, while good Catholics, were suspicious of the Popes, whom they regarded as foreigners, bent upon getting as much money as possible out of the simple people north of the Alps. The revenue flowing to the Popes from Germany was very large. The great German prelates, such as the archbishops of Mainz, Treves, and Cologne, were expected to contribute no less than ten thousand gold guldens to the papal treasury upon having their election approved by the church authorities at Rome. The Pope enjoyed the right to fill many important church offices in Germany and frequently appointed Italians, who collected the income without going to Germany or performing the duties attached to the office. One person often held several church offices.

At first, however, no one thought of withdrawing from the Church or of attempting to destroy the power of the Pope. All that the Germans wished was that the money which flowed toward Rome should be kept at home, and that the clergy should be upright, earnest men who faithfully performed their religious duties.

Early Years of Luther. Martin Luther was born in 1483. He was the son of a poor miner, and he often spoke in later life of the poverty and superstition in which his boyhood was spent. His father, however, was determined that his son should be a lawyer, and so Martin was sent to the University of Erfurt. After he finished his college course and was about to take up the study of the law, he became very religious, however, and decided to become a monk. In the monastery he devoted himself to the study of the Bible and of the writings of the Church Fathers. He proved himself a good scholar and was chosen as a professor by the new University of Wittenberg. Here he had a large following of students who flocked to listen to the young professor lecture on theology. For Luther early had ideas of a simpler form of Christianity than that taught by the Church, and he aroused interest on account of his criticisms of the old system.

When he was thirty years old he suddenly came into great prominence; for he found himself engaged in a controversy with the leaders of the Catholic Church in which the government soon took a hand. It came about in this way.

Luther objects to the Grant of Indulgences. In Luther's younger days the Popes had undertaken the rebuilding of St. Peter's, the huge central church of Christendom, at Rome (p. 560). The cost of this enterprise was enormous. In order to secure money for the purpose, Pope Leo X arranged that those who made contributions might in return receive special *indulgences*, or "pardons," as the people called them.

The Church taught that when men died they were, on account of their sinful nature, not yet ready to enter heaven. They must first pass a long period in *purgatory* (a place between the earth and heaven), where they could be purified from sin by suffering some form of punishment.

An indulgence was a pardon, issued usually by the Pope, which freed the person to whom it was granted *from a part or all of his suffering in purgatory.* It did not forgive his sins or in any way take the place of true repentance and confession; it only reduced the punishment which a truly repentant sinner would otherwise have had to endure, either in this world or in purgatory, before he could be admitted to heaven.[1]

---

[1] It is a common mistake of Protestants to suppose that the indulgence was forgiveness granted beforehand for sins to be committed in the future. There is absolutely no foundation for this idea. A person proposing to sin could not possibly be sorry in the eyes of the Church, and even if he had secured an indulgence it would, according to the Church, have been quite worthless.

The contribution to the Church which was made in return for indulgences varied greatly : the rich were required to give large sums, while the very poor were to receive these pardons without payment. The representatives of the Pope were naturally anxious to collect all the money possible, and did their best to induce everyone to secure an indulgence, either for himself or for his deceased friends in purgatory. In their eagerness they made many claims for the value of the indulgences to which no thoughtful churchman or even layman could listen without doubting their truth.

Fig. 164. *Pope Leo X*

Leo, a son of Lorenzo de' Medici, was Pope from 1513 to 1521. Leo was greatly interested in the artists of his time and in the rebuilding of St. Peter's. (From a painting by Raphael)

Luther's Theses on Indulgences. Tetzel, a Dominican monk, in October, 1517, began preaching about indulgences in the neighborhood of Wittenberg and making claims for them which appeared to Luther wholly against the teachings of Christianity. Therefore, in accordance with the custom of the time, he wrote out a series of ninety-five statements in regard to indulgences. These *theses,* as they were called, he fastened on the church door and invited anyone interested in the matter to enter into a debate with him on the subject, which he believed was very little understood. In posting these theses Luther did not intend to attack the Church and had no expectation of creating a sensation. The theses were in Latin and addressed, therefore, only to learned men. It turned out, however, that everyone, high and low, learned and ignorant, was ready to talk about indulgences.

The theses were promptly translated into German, printed, and scattered abroad throughout the land. In these *Ninety-*

five Theses Luther declared that the indulgence was very un-important and that the poor man would better spend his money for the needs of his household. The truly repent-ant, he argued, do not seek to escape punishment, but bear it willingly in sign of their sorrow. Faith in God, not the securing of pardons, brings forgiveness, and every Christian who feels true sor-row for his sins will receive full relief from the punish-ment as well as from the guilt. Could the Pope know, said Luther, how his agents misled the people, he would rather have St. Peter's burn to ashes than build it up with money gained under false pretenses. Then, Luther adds, there is danger that

Fig. 165.   *Martin Luther*

From a painting by Lucas Cranach the Elder. Courtesy of the John G. John-son Art Collection, Philadelphia

men will ask awkward questions. For example, "If the Pope releases souls from purgatory for money, why not for charity's sake?" or, "Since the Pope is rich as Crœsus, why does he not build St. Peter's with his own money, instead of taking that of the poor man?"

Luther Widens his Attack. There were many who were loyal to the papacy in Germany; but, on the other hand, many had become irritated with the state of affairs in the Church and were in sympathy with Luther's ideas. A con-troversy now began in which Luther became more and more outspoken. He soon attacked the papacy in harsh terms, and even suggested that the German rulers punish churchmen in their lands who refused to reform their ways.

In his *Address to the German Nobility* (1520), his most noted work, he denied that there was anything especially sacred about a clergyman except the duties which he had been appointed to perform. If he did not attend to his work, it should be possible to deprive him of his office at any moment, just as one would turn off a poor tailor or farmer, and in that case he should become a simple layman again. Luther claimed, moreover, that it was the right and duty of the rulers to punish a churchman who did wrong, just as if he were the humblest layman.

The *Address to the German Nobility* closed with a long list of evils which must be done away with before Germany could become prosperous. Luther saw that his view of religion, if adopted, would introduce many changes. He recommended reducing the monasteries to a tenth of their number and permitting those monks who were disappointed in the good they got from living in them to leave. He pointed out the evils of pilgrimages and of the numerous church holidays, which interfered with daily work. The clergy, he urged, should be permitted to marry and have families like other citizens. The universities should be reformed, and "the accursed heathen, Aristotle," should be cast out from them.

Luther Excommunicated; burns the Papal Bull. In 1520 the Pope finally excommunicated Luther, issuing a bull against him which provided that any place sheltering him was to be placed under the *interdict*. As a heretic he should be delivered at once to the government authorities. But no one thought of arresting him. On the contrary, the bull irritated the German princes, who resented having the Pope issue commands to them. Luther, instead of taking back his statements, summoned his students to witness what he called a "pious religious spectacle" and publicly burned the bull, together with a copy of the laws of the Church and a textbook of scholastic theology which he specially disliked.

Luther before the Diet at Worms (1521). Among the enemies of Luther none was more important than the young emperor. It was toward the end of the year 1520 that Charles came to Germany for the first time (p. 635). After being crowned King of the Romans at Aix-la-Chapelle he took, with the Pope's consent, the title of "Emperor-Elect," as his grandfather Maximilian had done. He then moved on to the town of Worms, where he was to hold his first diet and face the German situation. He realized the need of reforming the Church, but he had no sympathy whatever with any change of religious belief. He proposed to live and die a devout Catholic, such as his ancestors had been. Luther was ordered to appear before the diet and answer the serious charges brought against him. Here, in the presence of the emperor, the nobility, and the clergy, he acknowledged his writings and declared that he could not conscientiously deny that what he had written was true.

The Edict of Worms (1521). There was now nothing for the emperor to do but to outlaw Luther, who had denied the binding character of the commands of the Church. He thereupon issued an edict which declared Luther an outlaw on the following grounds: that he scorned and defamed the Pope, despised the priesthood and stirred up the laity to dip their hands in the blood of the clergy, denied free will, taught loose living, despised authority, advocated a brutish existence, and was a danger to Church and State alike. Everyone was forbidden to give the heretic food, drink, or shelter, and was required to seize him and deliver him to the emperor.

Moreover, the decree provided that "no one shall dare to buy, sell, read, preserve, copy, print, or cause to be copied or printed, any books of the aforesaid Martin Luther, condemned by our holy father the Pope, as aforesaid, or any other writings in German or Latin hitherto composed by him, since they are foul, noxious, suspected, and published by a notorious and stiff-necked heretic."

So general was the disapproval of the edict by the people that few were willing to pay any attention to it. Charles V immediately left Germany and for nearly ten years was occupied outside it with the government of Spain and a succession of wars.

Luther begins a New Translation of the Bible. As Luther was on his way home from Worms he was kidnaped by his friends and carried to the Wartburg, a castle belonging to the elector of Saxony. Here he was hidden until any danger from the action of the emperor or diet should pass. His chief occupation during his months of hiding was to begin a new translation of the Bible into German. He had finished the New Testament before he left the Wartburg in March, 1522. Up to this time German translations of the Scriptures, while not uncommon, had been poor and difficult to understand. Luther's task was a hard one. He was anxious above all that the Bible should be put into language that would seem perfectly clear and natural to the common folk. So he went about asking the mothers and children and the laborers questions, hoping that their answers might suggest to him an expression that would be useful in his work. Luther's translation of the Bible came to be regarded as a German classic, just as the translation into English (the King James Version), made about ninety years later, became one of the foremost English classics.

2. GERMANY DIVIDED INTO CATHOLIC AND PROTESTANT COUNTRIES

Spread of Lutheran Ideas. Within the next few years Luther's teachings spread throughout Germany. They appealed to many classes: to the pious who desired a simpler religion than that of the Catholic Church; to the German rulers who wished to lay their hands on the possessions of the Church; to patriotic Germans who were irritated by the interference of Rome; and to those who were shocked by the abuses that had grown up in the Church. The peasants saw in Luther's ideas some hope of escaping from their own sad lot. They were taxed beyond their powers by the upper classes and the higher clergy. Insurrections had taken place from time to time. The peasants were only too glad, therefore, to hear Luther denounce the clergy and urge the princes to seize the church lands. They thought that this might in some way right the wrongs which they suffered under the feudal system.

The Revolt Begins. While Luther was quietly living in the Wartburg, translating the Bible, people began to put his teachings into practice. The monks and nuns left their

GERMANY

ABOUT 1550

- Boundary of Empire
- Hapsburg Territories
- Hohenzollern Territories
- Ecclesiastical Territories
- Imperial Cities

0 10 20 30 40 50   100

Scale of Miles.

M.-N. ENG., BUFFALO.

monasteries in his own town of Wittenberg. Some of them married, in spite of their solemn promises to remain single, and this seemed a very wicked thing to all who held to the old beliefs. The students and citizens tore down the images of the saints in the churches and even went so far as to oppose the celebration of the Mass, the chief Catholic ceremony.

Luther was greatly troubled by news of this disorderly attempt at reform. He did not approve of sudden and violent changes and left his hiding place to protest. He preached a series of sermons in Wittenberg in which he urged that all changes in religious services and practices should be introduced by the *government* and not by the *people* themselves. But his advice was not heeded.

The Peasant War (1525). In 1525 the serfs rose, in the name of "God's justice," to avenge their wrongs. Luther was not responsible for the civil war which followed, but he had certainly helped to stir up discontent; for he had asserted that the German feudal lords were hangmen, who knew only how to swindle the poor man. "Such fellows were formerly called rascals, but now must we call them 'Christian and revered princes.'" Yet in spite of his harsh talk about the princes, Luther really relied upon them to forward his movement, and he justly claimed that he had greatly increased their power by attacking the authority of the Pope and subjecting the clergy in all things to the government.

The peasants stated their demands, many of which were perfectly reasonable, in various petitions to their masters. The most famous of these statements was the dignified "Twelve Articles." In these they claimed that the Bible did not mention any of the dues which the lords demanded of them, and that, since they were Christians like their lords, they should no longer be held as serfs. They were willing to pay all the old and well-established dues, but they asked to be properly paid for extra services demanded by the lord. They thought, too, that each community should have the right to choose its own pastor and to dismiss him if he neglected his duties.

There were, however, leaders who were more violent and who proposed to kill the "godless" priests and nobles. Hundreds of castles and monasteries were destroyed by the frantic peasantry, and some of the nobility were murdered with shocking cruelty. Luther tried to induce the peasants — with whom, as the son of a peasant, he was at first inclined to sympathize — to remain quiet; but when his warnings proved vain and the revolt spread over central and southern Germany, he turned against them. He declared that the peasants were guilty of the most fearful crimes, and urged the government to put down the uprising without pity.

The Peasant Revolt put down with Great Cruelty. Luther's advice was followed in a terrible manner by the German rulers, and the nobility took fearful revenge on the peasants. In the summer of 1525 their chief leader was defeated and killed, and it is estimated that ten thousand peasants were put to death, many with the utmost cruelty. Few of the rulers or landlords introduced any reforms, and the despair due to the destruction of property and to the misfortunes of the peasants cannot be imagined. The people concluded that the new gospel was not for them, and talked of Luther as "Dr. Lügner," that is, liar. The old demands of the lords of the manors were in no way lightened, and the situation of the serfs for centuries following the great revolt was worse rather than better.

Religious Division of North and South Germany. It became clear not long after the Peasant War that some of the German rulers were going to follow Luther's ideas and take over the property and affairs of the churchmen in their domains without regard to the Pope's wishes. Other princes and towns agreed that they would remain faithful to the Pope if certain reforms were introduced, especially if the papal taxation were reduced. Southern Germany decided for the Pope, and it remains Catholic down to the present day. Many of the northern rulers, on the other hand, adopted the new teachings, and finally all of them fell away from the papacy and became Protestant. Since there was no one powerful enough to de-

POLAND

Wittenberg

Erfurt

Aix-la-Chapelle *Wartburg*

Worms

Speyer

Augsburg

Basel

Zürich

Bern

Trent

HUNGARY

PAPAL
STATES

Rome

Elbe R.

Rhine R.

Danube R.

F R A N C E

- - - Boundary of the
Holy Roman Empire
at the time of Luther

The Holy Roman Empire and Papal States in the Time of Luther

cide the great question for the whole of Germany, the diet
which met at Speyer in 1526 determined that until a church
council should be summoned each ruler should "so live,
reign, and conduct himself that he would be willing to answer
to God and His Imperial Majesty." For the moment, then,
the various German governments were left to determine the
religion of their subjects.

Origin of the Term "Protestants." The emperor, finding himself free for a time to attend to German affairs, commanded the diet, which again met at Speyer in 1529, to order the enforcement of the Edict of Worms against the heretics. The Lutheran princes and towns drew up a *protest*, in which they claimed that the majority had no right to do away with the edict of the former diet of Speyer, which had been passed unanimously, and which all had solemnly pledged themselves to observe. Those who signed this appeal were called from their action *Protestants*. Thus originated the name which came to be generally applied to those Christians who do not accept the rule and teachings of the Roman Catholic Church.

The Augsburg Confession. At the Diet of Augsburg, held the following year (1530), a statement of the Lutheran beliefs drawn up by Melanchthon, Luther's great friend, was presented to the emperor. The Augsburg Confession, as it later came to be called, is the most important manifesto of the Protestant position of this period and, in general, is the official creed of the Lutheran churches today. Melanchthon was a learned man and possessed a mild and reasonable temper. The Confession states, in a scholarly and moderate manner, the main beliefs of the reformers, the grounds on which they agreed with the Catholic Church, and the points in which they differed. It is a historical document of great importance for the student of the Protestant Revolt.

The Peace of Augsburg (1555). For ten years after the emperor left Augsburg he was kept busy in southern Europe by new wars; and in order to secure the support of the Protestants he was forced to let their religion alone. Meanwhile the number of rulers who accepted Luther's teachings gradually increased. Finally there was a brief war between Charles and the Protestant princes. The emperor even brought his Spanish soldiers into Germany and captured both John Frederick of Saxony and his ally Philip of Hesse, the chief leaders of the Lutheran cause, whom he kept prisoners for several years. Luther himself died in 1546.

In 1555 the religious Peace of Augsburg was signed. Its provisions are noteworthy. Each German prince and each town and knight directly under the emperor was to be at liberty to make a choice between the beliefs of the venerable Catholic Church and those contained in the Augsburg Confession. If, however, an archbishop, bishop, or abbot declared himself a Protestant, he must surrender his possessions to the Church. Every German was either to conform to the religious practices of his particular state or to leave it. Everyone was supposed to be either a Catholic or a Lutheran, and no provision was made for any other belief.

This settlement in no way established religious freedom except for the rulers. Their power, it must be noted, was greatly increased, inasmuch as they were given the control of religious as well as of government matters. An arrangement which permitted the ruler to determine the religion of his realm was more natural in those days than it would be in ours, since the Church and government had been so closely associated with one another for centuries. No one as yet dreamed that every individual might safely be left quite free to believe what he would and to practice any religious rites which afforded him help and comfort.

3. Zwingli and Calvin in Switzerland

Beginnings of Switzerland. For at least a century after Luther's death the great struggle between Catholics and Protestants fills the history of all the countries with which we have to do, except Italy and Spain, where Protestantism never took permanent root. In Switzerland, England, France, and Holland the revolt against the medieval Church produced discord, wars, and profound changes, which must be understood in order to follow the later development of these countries.

During the Middle Ages the region which was later to become Switzerland was a part of the Holy Roman Empire and was hardly to be distinguished from the rest of southern Germany. As early as the thirteenth century the three districts — or *cantons,* as the little Swiss states are called — on the shores of the winding Lake of Lucerne formed a union to protect themselves against the advances of their neighbors, the Hapsburgs (pp. 628 f.). It was about this tiny center that Switzerland gradually grew up. Lucerne and the free towns of Zurich and Bern soon joined the Swiss league. By brave fighting the Swiss were able to defeat the various efforts of the Hapsburgs to control them. Several districts in the neighborhood joined the Swiss union, and even the region lying on the Italian slopes of the Alps was brought into the group. Gradually the bonds between the members of the Swiss union and the Empire were broken. Finally, in 1499, they were freed from the control of the emperor, and Switzerland became a practically independent country. Although the original union had been made up of German-speaking people, a number of districts had been annexed in which Italian or French was spoken.[1] The Swiss did not, therefore, form a unified nation speaking one language, and consequently for some centuries their little country was loosely held together and the government was poorly organized.

Zwingli leads the Revolt against the Old Church. In Switzerland the first leader of the revolt against the Church was a young priest named Zwingli, who was a year younger than Luther. He lived in the well-known monastery at Einsiedeln, near the Lake of Zurich, which was the center of pilgrimages on account of a wonder-working image. "Here," he says, "I began to preach the Gospel of Christ in the year 1516, before anyone in my locality had so much as heard the name of Luther." Three years later he was called to a prominent position as preacher in the cathedral of Zurich, and there his great work really commenced. He then began to denounce the evils in the Church, as well as the shameless hiring out of soldiers, which he had long regarded as a blot upon his country's honor.[2]

[1] This condition has not changed; all Swiss laws are still issued in three languages.

[2] Switzerland had made a business, ever since the time when Charles VIII of France invaded Italy, of supplying troops of soldiers — mercenaries, as they are called — to fight for other countries, especially for France and the Pope. It was the Swiss mercenaries that Francis I defeated at Marignano (p. 633), and Swiss guards may still be seen in the Pope's palace, the Vatican.

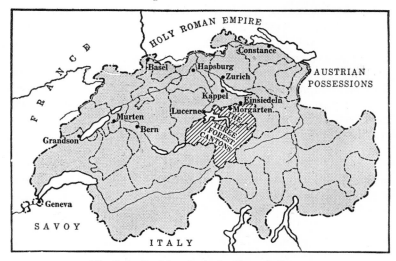

The Swiss Confederation in the Sixteenth Century

But the original cantons around the Lake of Lucerne, which feared that they might lose the great influence that, in spite of their small size, they had hitherto enjoyed, were ready to fight for the old faith. The first armed outbreak between the Swiss Protestants and Catholics took place at Kappel in 1531, and Zwingli fell in the battle. The various cantons and towns never came to an agreement in religious matters, and Switzerland is still part Catholic and part Protestant.

Calvin (1509–1564) *and the Presbyterian Church.* Far more important than Zwingli's teachings, especially for England and America, was the work of Calvin, which was carried on in the ancient city of Geneva, on the very outskirts of the Swiss union. It was Calvin who organized the *Presbyterian Church* and wrote out a statement of its beliefs. He was born in northern France in 1509, and was early influenced by the Lutheran teachings, which had found their way into France. A persecution of the Protestants under Francis I drove him out of the country, and he settled for a time in Basel. Here he issued the first edition of his great work, *The Insti-*

tute of the Christian Religion (c. 1536), which has been more widely discussed than any other Protestant treatise on religion. It was the first complete and well-ordered statement of the principles of Christianity from a Protestant standpoint and became a convenient book for study and discussion. The *Institute* holds that the Bible should be the chief guide and authority in religion, rather than the Church; for the Bible can be entirely relied on as God's word, while it is possible for the Pope and the Church to be mistaken.

Calvin's Work at Geneva. When Calvin was about twenty-seven years old, he was prevailed upon by the Protestant leaders in Geneva to join them in their work of reform. Calvin finally agreed to live in Geneva; but he found himself faced with a difficult task, for the people of Geneva had adopted Protestantism more to be rid of their Catholic duke of Savoy than because they understood very well the religious meaning of the movement. Calvin got into many controversies with other religious leaders in Switzerland on account of his particular views and his strict ideas of what the Christian life should be. He was a preacher at the cathedral and drew up a catechism for the instruction of the people. For many years he not only led the reformation movement at Geneva but took an active part in government affairs. He was consulted on matters of law, police, trade, and manufactures as well as on religious questions. Calvin believed that every member of the state was under the discipline of the Church, and that the government should therefore look to the Church for guidance. He was also the founder of the University of Geneva.

Calvin's name has become most famous perhaps through his ideas of church government. He believed that according to the New Testament the Church should be managed not by bishops but by ministers and elders, or *presbyters*. He is therefore looked upon as the founder of the Presbyterian Church, which still flourishes in our own times. The Protestantism which found its way into France, Scotland, and to a great extent England and the United States was not that of Luther but of John Calvin.

4. ENGLAND DESERTS THE PAPACY

Division of Opinion as to the Papacy. Five years after the Lutheran princes had drawn up their protest at Speyer (p. 670), Parliament, in the Act of Supremacy (passed 1534), declared the English king to be the supreme head on earth of the Church in England, and by this and other statutes separated the nation from all connection with the papacy. The special circumstances which led to England's final break with the Catholic Church were the result of Henry VIII's determination to have his own way in spite of the disapproval of the Pope. There were, however, many people in England eager to see the realm independent of Rome, and willing to support the king in his decision.

There had been much dissatisfaction in earlier times with the interference of the Popes in England's affairs and with the amount of wealth which was sent out of the kingdom to Rome. The people, also, had not forgotten the humiliating occasion when King John had been forced to hand over the realm to Innocent III, nor the claims which the Popes thereafter made as a result of this episode. Since the time of William the Conqueror the government had found it necessary from time to time to pass laws guarding the realm from the interference and demands of Rome. In 1351, as we have seen, a Statute of Provisors had been passed, to do away with appointments by the Pope to English church positions. Reformers, like Wycliffe, had pointed out the evils which had grown up in the Church. Humanists, like Erasmus, had awakened a critical attitude toward the Church by emphasizing the importance of relying on the Bible rather than merely accepting the orders of the Pope. The writings of Luther had found their way from the Continent into England and were taken seriously at the University of Oxford. When, therefore, the king and the Pope became engaged in their famous quarrel, opinion was divided. Many remained loyal to the Catholic Church, while others, though they may have disapproved the king's actions privately, nevertheless supported him, seeing in this occasion a chance to free England from the control of a foreign potentate.

Henry VIII's Divorce Case. The cause of controversy between Henry and the Pope was this. Henry VIII had come to the throne when he was but eighteen years old. He had married Catherine of Aragon, the aunt of Charles V (p. 629). Only one of their children, Mary, lived to grow up. As time went on, Henry was very anxious to have a son and heir; for he was fearful lest a woman might not be permitted to succeed to the throne. Moreover, he had tired of Catherine, who was a good deal older than he.

Catherine had first married Henry's older brother, who had died almost immediately after the marriage. Since the Church forbade a man to marry his deceased brother's wife, Henry professed to fear that he was committing a sin by retaining Catherine as his wife and demanded to be divorced from her on the ground that his marriage had never been lawful. His anxiety to rid himself of Catherine was greatly increased by the appearance at court of a black-eyed girl of sixteen, named Anne Boleyn, with whom the king fell in love.

Unfortunately for his case, his marriage with Catherine had been permitted by a *dispensation* (a special act of the Pope exempting one from the law of the Church in a particular case) by a previous Pope; so Pope Clement VII, to whom the king appealed to annul the marriage, could not have granted Henry's request, even if he had been willing to run the risk of angering the queen's nephew, Charles V. Henry induced Parliament to cut off some of the Pope's revenue from England; but, as this did not bring Clement VII to terms, Henry lost patience and secretly married Anne Boleyn, relying on getting a divorce from Catherine later. He then summoned an English church court, which declared his marriage with Catherine null and void. He had persuaded Parliament to make a law providing that all lawsuits should be definitely decided within the realm, and in this way cut off the possibility of the queen's appealing to the Pope.

Parliament, which did whatever Henry VIII asked, also declared Henry's marriage with Catherine unlawful and that with Anne Boleyn lawful. Consequently it was decreed that Anne's daughter, Elizabeth, born in 1533, was to succeed her father instead of Mary, the daughter of Catherine.

How Henry VIII threw off the Papal Authority. By a series of laws (1530–1535) Parliament effected a complete separation of England from the papacy and established a national (Anglican) Church. The king was given the right to appoint all the prelates and to enjoy the income that had formerly gone to Rome. In the Act of Supremacy, Parliament pronounced the king to be "the only supreme head in earth of the Church of England," and declared that he should enjoy all the powers which the title naturally carried with it. Two years later every officer in the kingdom

Fig. 166. *Henry VIII*

The portrait shows Henry as a young man. (From a painting by Hans Holbein the Elder in the Royal Palace, Naples)

was required to swear to renounce the authority of the bishop of Rome. Refusal to take this oath was to be declared high treason. Many English people were unwilling to deny the Pope's headship merely because king and Parliament renounced it; and this law led to a persecution, in the name of treason against the king, even more horrible than that which had been carried on in the name of religion.

Henry VIII not a Protestant. Although Henry VIII broke every bond between England and Rome and had Parliament declare him to be the head of the English national Church, he was *not* a Protestant. He continued to believe most of the doctrines of the old Church and never accepted the teachings of Luther, Zwingli, or Calvin. Moreover, Henry had no

Fig. 167. *Henry VIII*

A symbolic picture showing the king with his new Bible in his hand and with his feet upon the Pope. (From John Foxe's *Ecclesiastical History*, 1576)

desire to arouse the hostility of the Catholic monarchs on the Continent, nor even of his faithful Catholic subjects. While he was determined to have his own way in personal matters, he was at the same time eager to prove himself a stanch Catholic. Especially after he had seized the property of the monasteries, and the gold and jewels which adorned the cases in which the relics of the saints were kept, he believed it wise to show that he was not a looting Protestant, without reverence for the sacred traditions of the Mother Church. He presided personally at the trial of one of Zwingli's followers, and took part in the argument by quoting Scripture to show that Zwingli's teachings were wrong. The prisoner was condemned and burned as a heretic.

On the other hand, to please his Protestant subjects, who placed their faith in the Scriptures rather than in the Church, Henry ordered a new translation of the Bible into English. A fine edition of this was printed (1539), and every parish was ordered to place a copy in the church where all the people could readily make use of it. Henry may have wished it to be known that Popes were not mentioned in the Bible.

FIG. 168. *Sir Thomas More*

From a painting by Holbein in the Uffizi Gallery

Despotic Character of Henry VIII. Henry VIII, in spite of any religious views he may have held, was heartless and despotic. With a barbarity not uncommon in those days, he had his old friend and adviser Sir Thomas More beheaded for refusing to take the Oath of Supremacy. More was a learned and pious man, and Henry well knew that he was loyal to the crown, but that, as a good Catholic, he believed it a sin against God to acknowledge that Parliament could make the king, who was only a layman, the head of the Holy Church. Other equally innocent persons Henry permitted to be beheaded for opposing him. He did not hesitate to leave those whom he disliked to die of starvation and disease in the filthy prisons of the time.

How Henry plundered the Monasteries. The king wanted money. Some of the English abbeys were rich, and the monks were quite unable to defend themselves against the charges which were brought against them. Henry sent commissioners about, to inquire into the state of the monasteries. A large number of scandalous tales were easily collected, some of which were undoubtedly true. Some of the monks were doubtless often lazy and sometimes wicked. Nevertheless, they were kind landlords, hospitable to the stranger, and good to the poor. The royal commissioners took possession of the monasteries and sold every article upon which they could lay hands, including the bells and even the lead on the roofs. The picturesque remains of some of the great abbey churches are still among the chief objects of interest to the sight-seer in England. The monastery lands were, of course, taken possession of by the king. They were sold for the benefit of the government or given to nobles whose favor the king wished to secure.

Destruction of Shrines and Images. Along with the destruction of the monasteries went an attack upon the shrines and images in the churches, which were adorned with gold and jewels The shrine of Saint Thomas of Canterbury (p. 493) was destroyed, and the bones of the saint were burned. These acts resembled the Protestant attacks on images which occurred in Germany, Switzerland, and the Netherlands. The main object of the king and his party was probably to get the treasure; the reason urged for the destruction of the relics and images, however, was the superstitious veneration in which they were held by the people, who were still pious Catholics.

Henry's Third Marriage and the Birth of Edward VI. Henry's family troubles by no means came to an end with his marriage to Anne Boleyn. Of her too he soon tired, and three years after their marriage he had her executed on a series of outrageous charges. Ten days later he married his third wife, Jane Seymour, who was the mother of his son and successor, Edward VI. Jane died a few days after her son's birth, and later Henry married in succession three other women, who are historically unimportant since they left no children as claimants for the crown. Henry took care that his three children, — Mary, Elizabeth, and Edward, — all of whom were one day to reign, should be given their

due place in the line of inheritance by act of Parliament.[1]
His death, in 1547, left the great problem of Protestantism
and Catholicism to be settled
by his son and daughters.

*England becomes Protestant
under Edward VI.* While the
revolt of England against the
papacy was carried through
at a time when the greater
part of the nation was still
Catholic, the number of eager
and enthusiastic Protestants
continued to increase during
Henry VIII's reign. By the
time that Henry's son, Edward, came to the throne, in
1547, there was a sufficient
Protestant party to change
the character of the religious
doctrines and services of the
Church without serious opposition. During the six years

© H. M. the King of England

Fig. 169. *Edward VI*

This interesting sketch by Holbein was
made before Edward became king; he
could have been scarcely six years old,
as Holbein died in 1543. (From a
drawing at Windsor Castle)

of the boy Edward's reign (he died in 1553, at the age of
sixteen) those who had charge of the government favored the
Protestants and did what they could to strengthen them by
bringing over a number of reformers from the Continent as
teachers in the universities.

It was decided that the king should appoint bishops without troubling to follow the old forms of election (p. 453), and
Protestants began to be put into the high offices of the Church.
Parliament took possession of funds which had been left for
the purpose of having Masses chanted for the dead, and
handed them over to the king. It was decreed that the

---

[1] Henry VIII, m. (1) Catherine   (2) Anne Boleyn   (3) Jane Seymour

Mary (1553–1558)   Elizabeth (1558–1603)   Edward VI (1547–1553)

It was arranged that the son was to succeed to the throne. In case he died
without heirs, Mary and then Elizabeth were to follow.

clergy should thereafter be permitted to marry. The feeling against Catholicism grew so strong that a general destruction of all sacred images was ordered; even the beautiful stained-glass windows, the glory of the cathedrals, were broken by fanatical Protestants because they often represented saints and angels.

Church Services become Protestant. The old Catholic services, which had been conducted in Latin, were done away with, and a prayer book written in English was substituted, not unlike the one in use today. Forty-two articles of faith were drawn up, and approved by Parliament as representing the official beliefs of the national Church.[1]

The changes in the Church must have been very shocking to those who were still faithfully attached to the older beliefs and services. Earnest Catholics who disliked those who conducted Edward's government must have felt that the Protestants were using their new faith chiefly as an excuse for plundering the Church. The great zeal of unbalanced enthusiasts resulted in much disorder. We learn that Edward was forced to forbid "quarreling and shooting in churches" and "the bringing of horses and mules through the same, making God's house like a stable or common inn." Although many were heartily in favor of the recent changes, it is no wonder that after Edward's death there was a tendency to return to the old religion.

Queen Mary (1553–1558) *restores Catholicism.* Edward VI was succeeded in 1553 by his half sister Mary, the daughter of Catherine, who had been brought up in the Catholic faith and held firmly to it. Her earnest hope of bringing her kingdom back once more to her religion did not seem altogether ill-founded; for the majority of the people were still Catholics at heart, and many who were not Catholics disapproved of the policy of Edward's ministers, who had removed abuses "in the devil's own way, by breaking in pieces."

The Catholic cause appeared, moreover, to be strengthened by Mary's marriage with the Spanish prince Philip, son of

---

[1] These, reduced to Thirty-nine Articles in Elizabeth's reign, remain the official statement of the beliefs of the Church of England.

the Roman Catholic Charles V. But although Philip, when he became king of Spain, distinguished himself, as we shall see, by the merciless way in which he strove to put down heresy within his realms, he never gained any great influence in England. By his marriage with Mary he acquired the title of "King," but the English took care that he should have no hand in the government nor by any means be permitted to ascend the English throne.

Mary succeeded in bringing about peace between England and the Roman Church. A special ambassador was sent to ask forgiveness of the Pope. In 1554 a papal legate came to England to restore to the communion of the Catho-

FIG. 170. *Queen Mary*

This lifelike portrait, in the Madrid collection, is by Antonio Moro, a favorite painter of Philip II, Mary's husband (see Fig. 173). It was painted about 1554, and one gets the same impressions of Mary's character from the portrait that one does from reading about her. Moro had Holbein's skill in painting faces

lic Church the "Kneeling" Parliament, which represented the whole nation. During the last four years of Mary's reign a serious religious persecution occurred. No less than two hundred and seventy-seven earnest Protestants were put to death for refusing to renounce their faith; hundreds more lay suffering in the miserable prisons of the time. The majority of the victims were humble workmen. The three most notable sufferers were Archbishop Cranmer and Bishops Latimer and Ridley, officials of the Anglican Church, who refused to accept Catholicism and were burned in Oxford.

Elizabeth establishes a Protestant Church of England. When, on the death of Mary, Anne Boleyn's daughter, Elizabeth,

Fig. 171. *Queen Elizabeth*
Courtesy of the British Museum

came to the throne, the official Church of England once more became Protestant. Queen Elizabeth (1558–1603) was not a very pious person and was willing to adopt a form of religion which would be agreeable to the largest number of her subjects. The result was that the English (Anglican) Church, as it was finally established by Parliament, followed a middle way between the Catholic Church and that of the Protestant reformers. It was hoped that through a moderate policy the national Church would gain the affection and loyalty of all English people. In outward form the Anglican Church remained like the old Church. It was managed by archbishops and bishops, and its services and ceremonies resembled in many ways those of the older organization. In doctrines and belief, however, the Anglican Church was Protestant. It did not follow Luther, but was much influenced by Calvin and the Swiss reformers. Edward VI's prayer book, with the English service, was improved and became the official guide for church services, while his articles of faith, now thirty-nine in number, gave a clear statement of the position of the national Church. All English subjects were required to accept the official religion of the government.

The Roman Catholic churchmen who had held positions under Queen Mary were naturally dismissed, and replaced by those who would obey Elizabeth and use her book of prayer. Her first Parliament gave the sovereign the *powers* of supreme head of the Church of England, although the *title*, which her father, Henry VIII, had taken, was not revived.

Presbyterian Church established in Scotland. While the English adopted a middle course in matters of religion, the Scotch became Presbyterians, and this fact occasioned Elizabeth no little trouble. The ancient Catholic Church in Scotland was abolished, for the nobles wished to get the lands of the bishops into their own hands and enjoy the revenue from them. John Knox, a second Calvin in his stern energy, secured the introduction of the Presbyterian form of faith and church government which still prevails in Scotland.

5. TROUBLES OF THE ENGLISH CHURCH

The Religious Settlement fails to bring Peace. Unfortunately, the settlement of religion which the queen and Parliament believed would recommend itself to all people did not bring the peace and harmony that was hoped for. In the first place, the Catholics, of whom there were still many, were eager to have England return to the leadership of Rome. In the second place, the Protestants themselves soon began to differ and make trouble for the official Church. Some supported the Anglican Church, but others felt that it resembled too closely the old Catholic organization and that the reformation had not gone far enough. They wished to abolish the vestments worn by the clergy, and the elaborate ceremonial which was still retained. Later they urged that the Church should no longer be managed by archbishops and bishops but by ministers and *presbyters*, thus following Calvin's ideas of church government. These objectors came to be known as *Puritans*, because they advocated great simplicity in the Church, as well as strict conduct in daily life. Later many other sects grew up which differed from the Church and one another in their ideas of how the Bible should be interpreted and religious life conducted.

Mary Stuart, the Hope of the Catholics. While the constant complaints of the Puritans were very irritating to the government, the hostility of the Catholics was a danger not only to the English Church but to the throne as well. In 1561 the Scottish queen Mary Stuart, whose French husband, Francis II,[1] had just died, landed at Leith. She was but nineteen years old, of great beauty and charm, and, by reason of her Catholic faith and French training, almost a foreigner to her subjects. Her grandmother was a sister of Henry VIII, and Mary claimed to be the rightful heiress to the English throne should Elizabeth die childless. Consequently the beautiful Queen of Scots became the hope of all those who wished to bring back England and Scotland to the Roman Catholic faith. Chief among these were Philip II of Spain and Mary's relatives the Guises (p. 710) in France.

Mary quickly disgraced herself with both Protestants and Catholics by her conduct. After marrying her second cousin, Lord Darnley, she discovered that he was a worthless fellow and came to despise him. She then formed an attachment for a reckless nobleman named Bothwell. The house near Edinburgh in which Darnley was lying ill was blown up one night with gunpowder, and he was killed. The public suspected that both Bothwell and the queen had some knowledge at least of the murder. How far Mary was responsible for her husband's death no one can be sure. It is certain that she later married Bothwell and that her indignant subjects thereupon deposed her as a murderess. After unsuccessful attempts to regain her power she abdicated in favor of her infant son, James VI, and then fled to England to appeal to Elizabeth. While the cautious Elizabeth denied the right of the Scotch to depose their queen, she was afraid of her rival's claims and took good care to keep her practically a prisoner.

The Rising in the North (1569), *and Catholic Plans for Deposing Elizabeth.* As time went on, it became more and more difficult for Elizabeth to keep to her policy of moderation in the treatment of the Catholics. A rising in the north of England (1569) showed that there were many who would

---

[1] Son of Henry II. See table, p. 709.

gladly reëstablish the Catholic faith by freeing Mary and placing her on the English throne. This revolt was followed by the excommunication of Elizabeth by the Pope, who at the same time absolved her subjects from their allegiance to their "heretical" ruler. Happily for Elizabeth, the rebels could expect no help either from Philip II or from the French king. The Spaniards had their hands full, for the war in the Netherlands had just begun; and Charles IX of France was at that moment in hearty accord with the Protestants. The rising in the north was suppressed, but the English Catholics continued to look to Philip for help. They opened correspondence with the Spanish Duke of Alva (p. 702) and invited him to come with six thousand Spanish troops to dethrone Elizabeth and make Mary Stuart queen of England in her stead. Alva hesitated; for he thought that it would be better to kill Elizabeth, or at least capture her. Meanwhile the plot was discovered and came to naught.

English Mariners capture Spanish Ships. Although Philip found himself unable to harm England, the English mariners caused great loss to Spain. In spite of the fact that Spain and England were not openly at war, Elizabeth's seamen extended their operations as far as the West Indies and seized Spanish treasure ships, with the firm conviction that in robbing Philip they were serving God. The daring Sir Francis Drake even ventured into the Pacific, where only the Spaniards had gone heretofore. Though he lost all his ships except one, he was able to carry off much booty in his tiny vessel.

Relations between England and Catholic Ireland. One hope of the Catholics has not yet been mentioned, namely, Ireland, whose relations with England from very early times down until recently form one of the most cheerless pages in the history of Europe. The population was divided into numerous clans, and their chieftains fought constantly with one another as well as with the English, who were vainly endeavoring to gain control of the island. Several attempts were made by Catholic leaders to land troops in Ireland with the purpose of making the island a base for an attack on England. Elizabeth's officers were able to frustrate these enterprises, but the resulting disturbances greatly increased the misery of the Irish. In 1582 no less than thirty thousand people are said to have perished, chiefly from starvation.

Persecution of the English Catholics. As Philip's troops began to get the better of the opposition in the southern Netherlands, the prospect of sending a Spanish army to England grew brighter. Two Jesuits were sent to England in 1580 to encourage the Catholics and to urge them to assist the foreign forces against their queen when the Spaniards should come. Parliament now grew more intolerant and ordered fines and imprisonment to be inflicted on those who said or heard Mass or who refused to attend the English services. One of the Jesuit priests was cruelly tortured and executed for treason; the other escaped to the Continent.

In the spring of 1582 the first attempt by the Catholics to assassinate the heretical queen was made at Philip's suggestion. It was proposed that when Elizabeth was out of the way an army should be sent to England to assist the Catholics.

Execution of Mary Queen of Scots (1587). Mary Queen of Scots did not live to witness Philip's attack. She became involved in another plot for the assassination of Elizabeth. Parliament now realized that as long as Mary lived Elizabeth's life was in constant danger; whereas, if Mary were out of the way, Philip II would have no interest in the death of Elizabeth, since Mary's son, James VI of Scotland, who would succeed Elizabeth on the English throne, was a Protestant. Elizabeth was therefore finally persuaded by her advisers, in 1587, to sign a warrant for Mary's execution.

Destruction of the Spanish Armada (1588). Philip II, however, by no means gave up his project of reclaiming Protestant England. In 1588 he brought together a great fleet, including his best and largest warships, which was proudly called by the Spaniards the "Invincible Armada" (or fleet). This was to sail through the English Channel to the Netherlands and bring over the Spanish commander there and his

FIG. 172. *The Spanish Armada*

This picture shows a large Spanish ship which has run aground at night as it was trying to escape a small English fire ship in the Bay of Calais

experienced soldiers, who, it was expected, would soon make an end of Elizabeth's raw militia. The English ships were inferior to those of Spain in size, although not in number; but they had trained commanders, such as Francis Drake and Hawkins.

These famous captains had long "sailed the Spanish Main" and knew how to use their cannon without getting near enough to the Spaniards to suffer from their short-range weapons. When the Armada approached, it was permitted by the English fleet to pass up the Channel before a strong wind, which later became a storm. The English ships then followed, and both fleets were driven past the coast of Flanders. Of one hundred and twenty Spanish ships, only fifty-four returned home; the rest had been destroyed by English guns or by the gale, to which Elizabeth herself ascribed the victory. With the destruction of the Armada the danger from Spain came to an end, and England remained permanently a Protestant country.

Questions and Exercises

REVIEW OF CHAPTER

1. What were the sources of discontent with the Church in Germany? What objections did Luther have to the sale of indulgences? Give some of Luther's views as stated in the Ninety-five Theses. What were the main points of his *Address to the German Nobility?*

2. Explain, if you can, why Luther's views spread so rapidly and became influential. What is the origin of the term "Protestant"? How did Luther's teachings encourage the uprising of the peasants? Describe the Peace of Augsburg.

3. How was the Swiss union formed? What reforms did Zwingli preach? What organization of the Church did Calvin recommend? Describe Calvin's work at Geneva. In what countries was Calvin's teaching more important than Luther's?

4. Under what circumstances did England break her relations with the papacy? What earlier instances of dissatisfaction with the papacy were there in England? By what legal steps did Henry VIII establish the Church of England? What changes, if any, were made by Henry in the Church? When did the Anglican Church become Protestant in doctrine? Review briefly the changes in the nature of the Church until it was finally established by Elizabeth. What was the character of the Elizabethan Church? What features of the Catholic faith did it retain? What features of the Protestant faith? Why was Elizabeth's settlement not satisfactory to all her subjects? What were the main grievances of the Puritans?

5. What plans did the Catholics develop for restoring the Church of Rome? What was Mary Stuart's claim to the throne of England? Why was the dissatisfaction of the Catholics more dangerous than that of the Puritans?

USEFUL TERMS

See how much meaning you can give to the following terms: *theses, indulgence, purgatory, prelate, Gulden, excommunicate, to outlaw, papal bull, edict, cantons, Presbyterian, dispensation, relics, papal legate, mariners, armada.*

DIRECTIVE QUESTIONS

1. Do you think that the ideas of the Wittenberg professor would have been so influential if the German princes had not supported Luther? Why was Charles V so eager to suppress Luther?

2. Do you think the peasants were justified in their complaints? Were they justified in their abuse of Luther?

3. Why did not the English people rebel against Henry's treatment of the Pope? Give illustrations of the power of the Tudor monarchs over Parliament.

4. In what respects was the Anglican Church, as finally constituted, a moderate church?

DISCUSSION TOPICS

1. The Protestant Revolt was not wholly a religious movement.

2. Religious unity is not necessary to national happiness.

3. Religious toleration is founded on reason.

4. Compare Luther and Calvin as reformers.

ADDITIONAL ADVENTURES IN LEARNING

1. **Studies in Source Materials.** ROBINSON, *Readings*, Vol. II, chap. xxv, "Martin Luther and his Revolt against the Church"; chap. xxvii, "The Protestant Revolt in Switzerland and England." CHEYNEY, *Readings in English History*, chap. xii, "The Early Tudor Period."

2. Topical Studies. How the German princes were led to revolt against the papacy : ROBINSON, *Readings*, Vol. II, chap. xxv, sect. vi, 245; sect. vii; PRESERVED SMITH, *The Age of the Reformation*; McGIFFERT, *Martin Luther*. Personal characteristics of Queen Elizabeth: ROBINSON, *Readings*, Vol. II, chap. xxviii, sect. vii, 288; sect. viii, 291; CHEYNEY, *Readings*, chap. xiii, sects. i, v–vi. Drake's expedition around the world, 1577–1580: CHEYNEY, *Readings*, chap. xiii, sect. iii, 229; *Short History of England*, pp. 358–359; PAYNE, *Voyages of Elizabethan Seamen*, Vol. I, pp. 196–230. Life in Elizabethan England : CHEYNEY, *Short History of England*, pp. 369–381; TRAILL, *Social England*, pp. 383–390; HARRISON, *Elizabethan England*, chap. ix; SAINTSBURY, *Elizabethan Literature*; DAVIS, *Life in Elizabethan Days*; QUENNELL, *The Making of Everyday Things in England*.

CHAPTER XXXI · HOW MEN FOUGHT OVER RELIGION AS THEY DID OVER LAND

THE CATHOLIC REFORMATION: THE JESUITS · PHILIP II AND THE REVOLT OF THE NETHERLANDS · THE FATE OF THE PROTESTANTS IN FRANCE · THE THIRTY YEARS' WAR IN GERMANY

THIS chapter is not a cheerful one. It tells of the long and disastrous wars, lasting a century and more, which men fought in the name of religion. The desire to rule men's daily lives (absolutism) and to control their religious beliefs (religious intolerance) led kings to war on their own subjects. Not only this, but Christian princes fought each other, sacrificing the lives of their people and drenching the land in blood.

The very horror of these dark years finally taught men the necessity of establishing liberty and peace. The events recorded in this chapter show us very vividly what a terrific price has been paid for " religious and civil liberty," those blessings of modern civilization which we accept with little thought of how deeply men had to suffer before they learned the mad folly of their ways.

The world is a better place to live in than it was in the days of Philip II or when Henry II was king of France. Protestants and Catholics dwell peacefully together in many countries, and every attempt is now made to keep religious interests separate from those of the state.

1. THE CATHOLIC REFORMATION: THE JESUITS

The Catholic Church determines to Reform itself. While northern Germany, England, and portions of Switzerland withdrew from the Catholic Church, a great part of western Europe remained faithful to the Pope and to the old beliefs which had been accepted for centuries. Complaints of the evils which had grown up in the Church had not been confined, as we have seen, to those who wished to break away from its control. There were many good Catholics who criticized the bad practices which existed in the organization, but who desired to reform the Church and maintain its unity, rather than depart from it. The Catholic Church therefore set itself the task of a great reform which proved so effective in its methods as to preserve loyalty to the papal monarchy throughout southern Europe and establish the influence of the Roman Catholic Church beyond the seas.

The program called not only for a reform of the papal government, and the character and practices of the clergy, but for the summoning of a great church council to restate the Catholic doctrines and to rebuke those who by their evil ways brought criticism on the Church. A religious order also was shortly formed which not only defended the papacy but taught the young the true faith and carried on missionary work in foreign fields. In all these ways the Church set to work to strengthen itself and meet the attacks of its enemies.

Reform started by the Popes. With the accession of Paul III (1534–1549) a line of able and upright rulers came to the head of the Church who saw the importance of appointing only men of piety and learning to high offices. They also reduced the scandal which had arisen over the scramble for position and wealth in the priestly offices. In time the influence of this reform worked a wonderful transformation in the character of the clergy from the Pope down to the humblest parish priest.

The Council of Trent (1545–1563). In order to try to reconcile differences in religious beliefs and refute the enemies of the Church, the Pope in 1545 summoned a great council to meet at Trent, on the frontier of Germany and Italy. After a few sessions the Council of Trent was interrupted, and it did not complete its task for nearly twenty years. The work of the council was of two kinds: (1) it stated what it held to be the true teachings of the Roman Catholic Church and condemned those beliefs of the Protestants which it regarded as heretical or erroneous; (2) it passed on many decrees designed to do away with the evils of long standing and insure the choice of high-minded and religious men for office in the Church. In order to refute the errors which it saw in the Protestant teachings and to defend the Church against its critics, the council restated the dogmas of the Catholic Church. It reaffirmed the familiar doctrine that "tradition" and the decisions of Popes and councils, as well as the Bible, formed the basis of the Christian religion, and asserted that the interpretation of the Scriptures belonged not to individuals but to the Church. It reaffirmed the Catholic belief in the doctrines which had been rejected by the Protestants, including the Mass, the invocation of saints, the veneration of images and relics, purgatory, and the merit of indulgences, and reasserted the spiritual superiority of the Pope. The Protestant beliefs which differed from those of the Catholic Church it then denounced as "anathema."

To effect specific reforms in the Church, the council issued a volume of disciplinary rules. These prohibited the sale of church offices and the charging of fees for administering the Sacraments; they compelled the bishops and prelates to reside in the place where they held their positions; and they warned the clergy against trying to make money out of their sacred office. They ordered sermons to be preached from time to time in the language of the people, so that the unlearned might understand. Seminaries were to be established for the instruction of the young. A new catechism was to be prepared for the benefit of the laymen, and a new edition of the Catholic Bible, the Vulgate, was printed.

By these and other measures a permanent reform was made in the Catholic organization; but the Inquisition was also revived, bringing horrible suffering to those who fell under its suspicion.

The Index of Prohibited Books. The council suggested that the Pope's officials should make a list of dangerous books which faithful Catholics should not read for fear that their faith in the Church would be disturbed. Accordingly, after the council broke up, the Pope issued the first "Index," or list of books which were no longer to be printed or circulated on account of the false religious teachings they contained. Other lists have since been printed from time to time. The establishment of this "Index of Prohibited Books" was one of the most famous of the council's acts. It was hoped that in this way the spread of heretical doctrines and of immoral ideas could be checked.

Ignatius Loyola (1491–1556), *the Founder of the Jesuits.*
Among those who, during the final sessions of the council, steadfastly opposed every attempt to reduce in any
way the exalted power of the Pope, were members of a new
religious society which was becoming the most powerful
Catholic organization in Europe. The Jesuit order, or the
Society of Jesus, was founded by a Spaniard, Ignatius
Loyola. He had been a soldier in his younger days, and
while bravely fighting for his king, Charles V, had been
wounded by a cannon ball (1521). Obliged to lie inactive
for weeks, he occupied his time in reading the lives of the
saints and became filled with a burning desire to equal their
deeds. Upon recovering he dedicated himself to the service
of the Church, put on a beggar's gown, and started on a
pilgrimage to Jerusalem.

Later he went to Paris and sought to influence his fellow students at the university; and finally, in 1534, seven
of his companions agreed to follow him to Italy and devote themselves to the service of the Pope. When asked
to what order they belonged, they replied, "To the Society
of Jesus."

Strict Discipline of the Jesuit Order. In 1538 Loyola summoned his followers to Rome, and there they worked out
the rules of their order. When this had been done, the Pope
gave his blessing to the new society. Loyola had been a
soldier, and he laid great stress upon absolute and unquestioning obedience. Not only were all the members of the
new association to obey the Pope as Christ's representative
on earth and to undertake without hesitation any journey,
no matter how distant or dangerous, which he might command, but each member was to obey his superiors in the
order as if he were receiving directions from Christ in person. He must have no will or preference of his own, but
must be as the staff which supports and aids its bearer in
any way in which he sees fit to use it. This admirable organization and the long and strict training which the order
required of its members were the great secret of the later
success and influence of the Jesuits.

The Jesuits as Teachers. The object of the society was to promote piety and the love of God, especially through the example of its members. The Jesuits were to pledge themselves to lead a pure life of poverty and devotion. A great number of the members were priests, who went about preaching, hearing confession, and holding devotional exercises. But the Jesuits were teachers as well as preachers and confessors. They clearly saw the advantage of bringing young people under their influence; they opened schools and seminaries and soon became the schoolmasters of Catholic Europe. So successful were their methods of instruction that even Protestants sometimes sent their children to them.

Missionary Work of the Jesuits. Before the death of Loyola over a thousand persons had joined the society. Under his successor there were three times that number, and the order went on increasing in size for two centuries. The founder of the society, as we have seen, had been attracted to missionary work from the first, and the Jesuits rapidly spread not only over Europe but throughout the whole world. Francis Xavier, one of Loyola's original little band, went to Hindustan, the Moluccas, and Japan. Brazil, Florida, Mexico, and Peru were soon fields of active missionary work at a time when Protestants as yet scarcely dreamed of carrying Christianity to the heathen. We owe to the Jesuits' reports much of our knowledge of the condition of America when white men first began to explore Canada and the Mississippi Valley; for the followers of Loyola boldly penetrated into regions unknown to Europeans and settled among the natives with the purpose of bringing the Gospel to them.

The Jesuits early directed their energies against Protestantism. They sent their members into Germany and the Netherlands and even made serious efforts to reclaim England. Their success was most apparent in southern Germany and Austria, where they became the confessors and trusted advisers of the rulers. They not only succeeded in checking the progress of Protestantism but were able to reconquer for the Catholic Church some districts in which the old faith had been given up.

2. Philip II and the Revolt of the Netherlands

Religion an Added Cause for War. Neither the winning of their independence of the papacy by the Protestants nor the thoroughgoing reforms of the Catholic Church put an end to the religious troubles in Europe. On the contrary, there followed another century in which religious differences only lent greater animosity to the old struggles of the princes for land and power. The age was one in which men readily resorted to cruelty, murder, and war to gain their ends, and they were encouraged in their undertakings when they could give a religious reason to justify their deeds.

Religion, then, in the sixteenth century did not seem to promote peace but ill will. Protestants quarreled bitterly with one another over the slightest difference in belief, while Catholics and Protestants were at open enmity with one another.

Division of the Hapsburg Possessions. Charles V, crippled with the gout and old before his time, laid down the cares of government in 1555–1556. To his brother, Ferdinand, who had acquired by marriage the kingdoms of Bohemia and Hungary, Charles had earlier transferred the *German* possessions of the Hapsburgs. To his son, Philip II (1556–1598), he gave Spain with its great American colonies, Milan, the kingdom of the Two Sicilies, and the Netherlands.[1]

---

[1] Division of the Hapsburg possessions between the Spanish and German branches:

Maximilian I (d. 1519), m. Mary of Burgundy (d. 1482)
|
Philip (d. 1506), m. Joanna the Insane (d. 1555)
|

Charles V (d. 1558), Emperor, 1519–1556	Ferdinand (d. 1564), m. Anna, heiress to kingdoms Emperor, 1556–1564 of Bohemia and Hungary
Philip II (d. 1598) inherits Spain, the Netherlands, and the Italian possessions of the Hapsburgs	Maximilian II (d. 1576), Emperor, and inherits Bohemia, Hungary, and the Austrian possessions of the Hapsburgs

The map of Europe in the sixteenth century (see page 634) indicates the vast extent of the combined possessions of the Spanish and German Hapsburgs.

From this time on we find two branches of the Hapsburg family: the Austrian, in which line the title of "Emperor" descended, and the Spanish, consisting of the descendants of Philip II. Over Ferdinand and the story of the Austrian realms we need not linger at this point. We must turn our attention to Philip II, for he was responsible for several of the most important events in the Europe of the sixteenth century.

Fig. 173. *Philip II*

From a painting by Van Dyck in the
Rosso Palace, Genoa

Philip fails to make Spain a Great Power. Philip was an upright and loyal man; but he was an autocratic ruler, and ruthless in carrying out his designs. He believed in the absolute right of a monarch to rule as he saw fit. He determined to unify the Spanish peninsula and make Spain the greatest country in Europe. The Church had no more faithful ally in its fight against Protestantism in the sixteenth century than Philip. His loyalty to the Catholic cause he carried to the point of fanaticism, and he set himself to be the champion of the Church against its Protestant enemies and to make the Church everywhere victorious. In both these cherished schemes, however, Philip failed; for his methods were cruel and merciless, and he stirred up forces which were too strong for him to overcome. When he died he had lost one of his most promising realms, — the Netherlands, — and the wealth and importance of Spain had greatly declined.

Philip's Policy in Spain. In attempting to get control of the Spanish peninsula and make a strong kingdom for himself he did many unwise things. He abolished local government, ignored the wishes and advice of his nobles, disregarded the parliament, and imposed on the people crushing taxes which brought the country to the verge of ruin. He subdued the rebellious kingdom of Aragon and put down a revolt of the Moors in southern Spain with the greatest cruelty. He revived the Inquisition, to stamp out heresy from the realm, and terrified his subjects with his despotism.

Philip's Treatment of the Netherlands. Philip's greatest failure was a result of his policy in dealing with the Netherlands. This region, which he had inherited from his father, Charles V, had, through the patience and industry of its inhabitants, become rich and flourishing. Large tracts of lowlands which had formerly been under water had been reclaimed by building dikes or embankments to keep out the sea. The land was fertile and excellent for farming. The towns had developed manufactures, especially the spinning and weaving of linens and woolens, which they sent to all parts of Europe. The people of the northern provinces were Dutch, a Teutonic folk akin to the Germans and the English. The population of the southern provinces was mainly Gallic in origin. Between the two sections (in Flanders) were the Flemish, who spoke a Dutch dialect.

Philip Disliked by the People of the Netherlands. Philip's haughty manner made a disagreeable impression upon the people at Brussels when his father first introduced him to them as their future ruler. They regarded him as a Spaniard and a foreigner, and he ruled them as such after he returned to Spain. Instead of attempting to win them by meeting their reasonable demands, he did everything to antagonize all classes in his Burgundian realm and to increase their hatred and suspicion of the Spaniards. The heavy taxes which had been imposed by Charles V were increased by Philip. Commerce was interfered with in the interests of Spanish traders. Spaniards were sent to the Netherlands,

FIG. 174. *View of a Dike along the Shores of the Zuider Zee, the Netherlands*

and placed at the head of government offices which had been held by the native nobles and members of the old Dutch families. The people were forced to house Spanish soldiers, whose insolence drove them nearly to desperation.

What was still worse, Philip proposed that the Inquisition should carry on its work far more actively than hitherto and put an end to the heresy which appeared to him to spoil his fair realms. The Inquisition was no new thing to the provinces. Charles V had made the most cruel laws against the followers of Luther, Zwingli, and Calvin. According to a law of 1550, heretics who persistently refused to recant were to be burned alive. Even those who confessed their errors and gave up their heresy were, if men, to lose their heads; if women, to be buried alive. In either case their property was to be forfeited. The lowest estimate of those who were executed in the Netherlands during Charles's reign is fifty thousand. Although these terrible laws had not checked the growth of Protestantism, all of Charles's decrees were solemnly put into force again by Philip in the first month of his reign. For ten years the people suffered Philip's rule; nevertheless their king, instead of listening to the protests of their leaders, who were quite as earnest Catholics as himself, appeared to be bent on the destruction of the land. So in 1566 some five hundred of the nobles ventured to protest against Philip's government.

Alva's Cruelty (1567–1573). Thereupon Philip took a step which led finally to the revolt of the Netherlands. He decided to send to the Low Countries the heartless Duke of Alva, whose conduct has made his name associated with blind and unmeasured cruelty. The report that Alva was coming caused the flight of many of those who especially feared his approach. William of Orange, who was to be the leader in the war against Spain, went to Germany. Thousands of Flemish weavers fled across the North Sea to England.

Alva brought with him a fine army of Spanish soldiers, ten thousand in number and superbly equipped. He appeared to think that the wisest and quickest way of quieting the discontented provinces was to kill all those who dared to criticize "the best of kings," of whom he had the honor to be the faithful servant. He accordingly established a special court for the speedy trial and conviction of all those whose loyalty to Philip was suspected. This was known as the Council of Blood, for its aim was not justice but butchery. As long as Alva remained in the Netherlands (1567–1573), there was bloodshed and terror.

William of Orange, called the Silent (1533–1584). The Netherlands found a leader in William, prince of Orange and count of Nassau. He is a national hero whose career bears a striking resemblance to that of Washington. Like the American patriot, he undertook the seemingly hopeless task of freeing his people from the oppressive rule of a distant king. To the Spaniards he appeared to be only a poor nobleman at the head of a handful of armed peasants and fishermen, who dared to oppose the sovereign of the richest realm in the world.

William had been a faithful subject of Charles V and would gladly have continued to serve his son Philip after him had

the oppression and injustice of the Spanish ruler not become intolerable. But Alva's policy convinced him that it was useless to send any more complaints to Philip. He accordingly collected a little army in 1568 and opened the long struggle with Spain. William found his main support in the northern provinces, of which Holland was the chief. The Dutch, who had in large part become Protestants, were purely German in blood, while the people of the southern provinces, who

Fig. 175. William the Silent

From a painting by Mierevelt

adhered (as they still continue to do) to the Roman Catholic faith, were more akin to the people of northern France.

The Spanish soldiers found little trouble in defeating the troops which William collected. Like Washington, again, he seemed to lose almost every battle and yet was never conquered. The first successes of the Dutch were gained by the seamen whom William hired to attack enemy ships. These "sea beggars," as they were called, were able to capture many Spanish ships and sold them in Protestant England. Encouraged by this, many of the towns in the northern provinces of Holland and Zeeland ventured to choose William as their governor, although they did not throw off their allegiance to Philip. In this way these two provinces became the heart of the United Netherlands.

Both the Northern and Southern Provinces combine against Spain (1576). Alva recaptured a number of the towns which had revolted, and he treated their inhabitants with his usual cruelty; even women and children were slaughtered in cold blood. But instead of putting an end to the rebellion he aroused the Catholic southern provinces to revolt.

After six years of this tyrannical and mistaken policy, Alva was recalled to Spain. His successor soon died and left matters worse than ever. The leaderless soldiers, following Alva's example, indulged in wild orgies of robbery and murder; they plundered and partially reduced to ashes the rich city of Antwerp. The "Spanish fury," as this outbreak was called, together with the hated taxes, created such bitter feelings that representatives from all of Philip's Burgundian provinces met at Ghent in 1576 with the purpose of combining to put an end to the Spanish tyranny.

This union lasted only a short while. Philip sent to the Netherlands wiser and more reasonable governors, who soon succeeded in winning back the southern, or Catholic, provinces. So the northern provinces went their own way. Guided by William the Silent, they refused to consider the idea of again recognizing Philip as their king. In 1579 seven provinces, all lying north of the mouths of the Rhine and the Scheldt, formed the new and firmer Union of Utrecht. The articles of this union served as a constitution for the United Provinces, — later called Holland, — which at last declared themselves independent of Spain (1581).[1]

Assassination of William the Silent. Philip realized that William was the soul of the revolt and believed that without him it might be put down. He therefore offered to give a title of nobility and a large sum of money to anyone who should make way with the Dutch patriot. After several unsuccessful attempts upon his life, William, who had been chosen hereditary governor of the United Provinces, was shot in his house at Delft (1584). He died praying the Lord to have pity upon his soul and "on this poor people."

[1] The southern provinces (now called Belgium) remained in the possession of the Hapsburgs for over two centuries longer. They were called the "Spanish Netherlands" and later the "Austrian Netherlands."

The Netherlands in 1581

Independence of the United Provinces. The Dutch had long hoped for aid from Queen Elizabeth or from the French, but up to this time had been disappointed. Finally the English queen decided to send troops to their assistance. While the English gave but little actual help, Elizabeth's action so enraged Philip that he at last decided to attempt the conquest of England. The destruction of the Armada, the great fleet which he sent against England (p. 688), interfered with further attempts to conquer the United Provinces.

Philip's Policy hastens the Decline of Spain. Moreover, the resources of Spain were being rapidly exhausted, and the state was on the verge of bankruptcy in spite of the wealth which it had been drawing from across the sea. But even though Spain had to surrender the hope of winning back the lost provinces, which now became a small but important European power, she refused formally to acknowledge their independence until 1648 (Peace of Westphalia, p. 720). Spain itself had suffered most of all from Philip's reign. His policy at home and his expensive wars had sadly weakened the country. The income from across the sea was bound to decrease as the mines were exhausted. After Philip II's death Spain sank to the rank of a secondary European power.

3. The Fate of the Protestants in France

How the French Kings got along with the Popes. In France the spread of Protestant ideas did not lead to the development of a national reformed religion as it did in England, Switzerland, the Netherlands, portions of Germany, and Scandinavia. The majority of the people in France remained loyal Catholics, and the French rulers (except for Henry IV) were consistent defenders of the older faith. Religiously and politically France remained on the conservative side in the struggles of the sixteenth century.

There were several reasons why Protestant ideas did not get such a hold on the French people as they did on those of some other countries. In the first place, the language, traditions, and culture of Catholic Italy were more congenial to the French than to the people of the northern countries, and the Italians were not so hated as foreigners. Moreover, the French rulers, the court, and the nobility were all strongly Catholic in sympathy. All this determined the character of the official religion of the state. The kings of France had established a much more satisfactory relation to the papacy than had the emperor or the king of England. Ever since the time of Philip the Fair the French monarchs had maintained their independence of papal control. During the long period when the Popes lived at Avignon, they were in no position to defy the French rulers. In 1438, in the Pragmatic Sanction of Bourges, the French monarch (Charles VII) had definitely restricted the power of the Popes in France. The liberties of the Gallican Church were explicitly stated in this document; the Pope was not to interfere in church elections nor to levy taxes in France. It was further declared that a church council was superior in power to the Pope. In 1516 a new arrangement gave the sovereign the nomination of bishops and abbots and the power to dispose of benefices. Francis I (1515–1547), who virtually controlled the management of the wealth of the Church in France, had therefore no grievance against the papacy.

Origin of the Reform Movement in France. The reform movement in France came from a force quite outside the Church. As in England, the humanistic movement led to a study of the Scriptures in the original tongue. Lefèvre, the most noted of the French Humanists, began his translation of the New Testament in 1512. In his commentary he practically asserted the Lutheran doctrine that there is no merit in human works without the grace of God (that is, the Protestant theory of justification by faith). He also held the Lutheran view of the Communion before he had ever heard of the German reformer. When, later (1519), Luther's writings were spread abroad in France, an enthusiastic movement began, and a group of Protestants in the south of France preached the new doctrines. By 1521 the Sorbonne (the theological school of the University of Paris), aroused by the danger of these heretical ideas, condemned the works of Luther, and the French reformers began to be sought out and persecuted. When the Protestants openly showed disrespect for the Catholic faith, Francis I, though he had no interest in religious matters, forbade the circulation of Protestant books and took measures to suppress the reformers. However, as he was eager to form an alliance with the German princes, Francis wavered in his policy, at times tolerating the Protestants and at other times encouraging persecution of the men of the new faith by reviving the Inquisition. As a result, many Protestants were burned, while hundreds were driven into exile. Calvin was forced to flee to Basel, where he prepared a defense of his beliefs which he published as a sort of preface to his famous *Institute of the Christian Religion.*

Before his death Francis became so intolerant that he ordered the massacre of three thousand defenseless peasants who dwelt on the slopes of the Alps, and whose only offense was that they followed the simple teaching of the Waldensians. This sect had been founded by Peter Waldo, of Lyon, about 1170. His followers believed that they could get along without priests and churches, and they denounced the evil ways of the clergy. The Church regarded them as heretics, and they had long been persecuted by the Inquisition. But the policy of repression, while it drove the reformers to practice their faith secretly, only increased their fervor, and Protestantism spread throughout France and even into the universities, where professors of theology dared to teach the new doctrines.

Francis I's son Henry II (1547–1559) swore to wipe out the Protestants, and hundreds of them were burned. At his death the kingdom fell into the hands of his three weak sons, the last heirs of the House of Valois, who succeeded in turn to the throne. During their reigns France suffered from a terrible period of civil and religious wars; for Protestantism became involved with political rivalries and added another issue to the conflict.

During the reign of Henry II and his sons the chief champion of Catholicism was the powerful family of Guise. The Duke of Guise and the Cardinal of Lorraine, the wealthiest

Relations of the Guises, Mary Stuart, the Valois, and the Bourbons

Francis I (d. 1547)

Henry II (d. 1559), m. Catherine de' Medici

Claude, duke of Guise (d. 1550)

Francis, duke of Guise (killed 1563)

Charles, cardinal of Lorraine

Mary, m. James V of Scotland, son of Henry VIII's sister

Henry, duke of Guise (murdered 1588)

Mary Stuart; m. Francis II (d. 1560 without heirs) Queen of Scots

Francis II (d. 1560 without heirs)

Charles IX (d. 1574 without heirs)

Henry III (d. 1589 without heirs)

Margaret, m. Henry IV (d. 1610), king of Navarre, a descendant through the younger, *Bourbon*, line from Saint Louis

Elizabeth, m. Philip II of Spain

James VI of Scotland, I of England, by Mary's second marriage, with Lord Darnley

Louis XIII (d. 1643), by Henry's second marriage, with Mary de' Medici

Louis XIV (d. 1715)

Louis XV (d. 1774), great-grandson of Louis XIV

churchman in France, not only were ardent defenders of the faith but believed in the violent suppression of heresy. With the accession of Francis II (1559–1560) the government virtually passed into their hands. For although but a boy of fifteen, Francis was married to the niece of the Guises, Mary Queen of Scots. Francis, however, reigned only one year and was succeeded by his brother Charles IX (1560–1574). As Charles was but ten years old, his mother, Catherine de' Medici, of the famous Florentine family, claimed the right to conduct the government until her son should become of age. There now followed a terrific struggle between the supporters of the Catholic cause, headed by the Guises, and the Protestants.

The Huguenots and their Ambitions. By this time the Protestants in France had become a powerful party. They were known as *Huguenots* (the origin of the name is uncertain) and accepted the religious teachings of their fellow countryman Calvin. Many of them, including their great leader Coligny, belonged to the nobility. They had a strong support in the king of the little realm of Navarre, on the southern boundary of France. He belonged to a side line of the French royal house known as the Bourbons, who were later to occupy the French throne (see the genealogical table, p. 709). It was natural that the Huguenots should try to get control of the government, and they consequently formed a *political* as well as a *religious* party and were often fighting for worldly ends.

Catherine tried at first to make friends with both Catholics and Huguenots, and granted a Decree of Toleration (1562), which withdrew the former edicts against the Protestants and permitted them to assemble for worship during the daytime and outside of the towns. Even this limited toleration of the Protestants appeared unbearable to the more fanatical Catholics, and a savage act of the Duke of Guise brought on civil war.

The Massacre of Vassy. As the duke was passing through the town of Vassy on a Sunday he found a thousand Huguenots assembled in a barn for worship. The duke's followers rudely interrupted the service, and a tumult arose in which the troops killed a considerable number of the defenseless multitude. The news of this massacre aroused the Huguenots and was the beginning of a war which continued, broken only by short truces, for over thirty years, until the last weak descendant of the House of Valois ceased to reign. As in the other religious wars of the time, both sides showed inhuman cruelty. France was filled for a generation with burnings, pillage, and barbarity. The leaders of both the Catholic and the Protestant party, as well as two of the French kings, fell by the hands of assassins.

FIG. 176. *Armor of Admiral de Coligny*

From a model in the Musée de l'Armée, Paris

Coligny's Influence. In 1570 a brief peace was made. The Huguenots were to be tolerated, and certain towns were given them, where they might live and defend themselves in case of renewed attacks from the Catholics. For a time both Charles IX and his mother, Catherine de' Medici, were on the friendliest terms with the Huguenot leader Coligny, who became a sort of prime minister. He was anxious that Catholics and Protestants should join in a great national war against France's old enemy, Spain.

Massacre of St. Bartholomew (1572). The strict Catholic party of the Guises upset this plan by a most fearful scheme. They easily induced Catherine de' Medici to believe that she was being deceived by Coligny, and an assassin was engaged to put him out of the way; but the scoundrel missed his aim and only wounded his victim. Fearful lest the young king, who was faithful to Coligny, should discover her part in the attempted murder, Catherine invented a story of a great Huguenot conspiracy. The innocent king was deceived, and the Catholic leaders at Paris arranged that not only Coligny but all the Huguenots, gathered in the city in great numbers to witness the marriage of the king's sister to the Protestant Henry of Navarre, should be massacred on the eve of St. Bartholomew's Day (August 23, 1572).

Fig. 177. *Henry IV of France*

From a painting by Pourbus in the Louvre

When the signal was given, no less than two thousand persons were cruelly murdered in Paris before the end of the next day. The news of this attack spread into the provinces, and it is probable that, at the very least, ten thousand more Protestants were put to death outside the capital.

Henry IV (1589–1610) *accepts the Catholic Faith.* Civil war again broke out, and at the same time there was a struggle between three claimants for the throne of France. As a result the Huguenot Henry of Navarre ascended the throne in 1589 as Henry IV. The new king had many enemies, and his kingdom was ruined by years of war. He soon saw that he must accept the religion of the majority of his people if he wished to reign over them. He accordingly asked to be readmitted to the Catholic Church (1593), excusing himself for his change of religion on the ground that "Paris was worth a Mass." He did not forget his old friends, however, and in 1598 he issued the Edict of Nantes.

The Edict of Nantes (1598). By this edict of toleration the Calvinists were permitted to hold services in all the towns and villages where they had previously held them, but in Paris and a number of other cities all Protestant services were prohibited. The Protestants were permitted to enjoy the

Fig. 178. *Cardinal Richelieu*
From a painting by Philippe de Champagne

same rights under the government as Catholics and could also hold government offices. A number of fortified towns were to remain in the hands of the Huguenots, particularly La Rochelle, Montauban, and Nîmes. Henry's only mistake lay in granting the Huguenots the right to control these fortified towns.

Ministry of Sully. Henry IV chose Sully, an upright and able Calvinist, for his chief minister. Sully at once set to work to strengthen the king's power, which had suffered greatly under the last three brothers of the House of Valois.

He undertook to lighten the tremendous burden of debt which weighed upon the country. He laid out new roads and canals and encouraged farming and commerce; he dismissed the useless noblemen and officers whom the government was supporting without any advantage to itself. Had his administration not been early interrupted, it might have brought France such power and prosperity as she had never enjoyed before; but religious fanaticism put an end to his reforms.

In 1610 Henry IV, like William the Silent, was assassinated just in the midst of his greatest usefulness to his country. Sully could not agree with the regent, who was Henry's widow, and so gave up his position and retired to private life.

Cardinal Richelieu protects the Monarchy against the Huguenots. Before many years Cardinal Richelieu, perhaps the greatest minister France has ever had, rose to power, and from 1624 to his death in 1642 he governed France for Henry IV's son Louis XIII (1610–1643). Richelieu's ambition was to build up the absolute power of the monarch. He soon determined to suppress the Huguenots, not so much on religious grounds as on account of their independent position, which suggested too strongly that of the former feudal nobles. He therefore deprived them, by force of arms, of all their fortified towns and removed all danger of armed opposition from the Protestant party in France.

4. The Thirty Years' War in Germany

The Thirty Years' War really a Series of Wars. The last great conflict caused by the religious and political differences between the Catholics and Protestants was fought out in Germany during the first half of the seventeenth century. Though it is generally known as the Thirty Years' War (1618–1648), there was in reality a series of wars; and although the fighting was done upon German territory, Sweden, France, and Spain played quite as important a part in the struggle as the various German states.

Just before the abdication of Charles V the Lutheran princes had forced the emperor to acknowledge their right to their own religion and to the church property which they had seized. The religious Peace of Augsburg (p. 671) had, however, as we have seen, two great weaknesses. In the first place, only those Protestants who held the Lutheran faith were to be tolerated. The Calvinists, who were growing in numbers, were not included in the peace. In the second place, the peace did not put a stop to the seizure of church property by the Protestant princes.

Protestantism, however, made rapid progress and spread into the Austrian possessions and, above all, Bohemia. So it looked for a time as if even the Catholic Hapsburgs were to see large portions of their territory falling away from the old Church. But the Catholics had in the Jesuits a band of active and able missionaries. They not only preached and founded schools but also succeeded in gaining the confidence of some of the German princes, whose chief advisers they became. Conditions were very favorable at the opening of the seventeenth century, the Catholics believed, for regaining part of their lost property.

Opening of the Thirty Years' War (1618). The long war began in Bohemia in 1618. This portion of the Austrian possessions was strongly Protestant and decided that the best policy was to declare its independence of the Hapsburgs and set up a king of its own. It chose Frederick, the elector of the Palatinate, a Calvinist who would, it was hoped, enjoy the support of his father-in-law, King James I of England. So Frederick and his English wife moved from Heidelberg to Prague. But their stay there was brief; for the Hapsburg emperor (Ferdinand II), with the aid of the ruler of Bavaria and the Catholic League, which had been formed a few years before, put to flight the poor "Winter King," as Frederick was called on account of his reign of a single season. The Hapsburg power was reëstablished in Bohemia, and the Protestant religion forbidden. The king of Bavaria was given the Palatinate, while poor Frederick, with neither lands nor money, was now driven into exile.

The Protestants became so alarmed at this victory of the Catholics that the Protestant king of Denmark, Christian IV, decided to take a hand. Not only did the Danish king wish to defend his fellow Protestants but, as duke of Holstein, he was a member of the Holy Roman Empire and was eager to throw off the Hapsburg domination. Moreover, he desired to extend his influence over the ports along the North Sea. With these various motives, Christian IV entered the war, supported by the German princes, only to find himself confronted by a vast army made up of many nationalities which had been gathered together by an adventurous but able soldier, Wallenstein. Wallenstein, having enriched himself by plundering defeated Bohemia, had offered the emperor the services of an army which was to be rewarded only by the spoils of war. The Danes were terribly defeated by this motley horde, under its brilliant leader, and retired from the war in 1629.

The Edict of Restitution (1629). The emperor was encouraged by the successes of the Catholic armies in defeating the Bohemian and Danish Protestant armies to issue that same year an Edict of Restitution (that is, restoration). In this he ordered the Protestants throughout Germany to give back all the church possessions which they had seized since the religious Peace of Augsburg (1555). Moreover, he decreed that only the Lutherans might hold religious meetings; all other "sects," including the Calvinists, were to be broken up. As a result the Catholics recovered a number of bishoprics, some thirty towns, and a hundred or more monasteries.

Dismissal of Wallenstein; Gustavus Adolphus of Sweden (1594–1632). The Catholic League, which had by this time become alarmed at Wallenstein's power, joined in the complaints, which came from every side, of the terrible extortions and robbery and unbelievable cruelty of Wallenstein's troops. The emperor consented, therefore, to dismiss this most inhuman though competent commander. Just as the Catholics were thus weakened, a new enemy arrived upon the scene who proved far more dangerous than any they had yet had to face, namely, Gustavus Adolphus, king of Sweden.

The Kingdom of Sweden. We have had no occasion hitherto to speak of the Scandinavian kingdoms of Norway, Sweden, and Denmark, which the northern Germanic peoples had established about Charlemagne's time; but they now begin to take part in the affairs of central Europe (map, p. 634). The Union of Calmar (1397) had brought these three kingdoms, previously separate, under a single ruler. About the time that the Protestant revolt began in Germany, the union was broken by the withdrawal of Sweden, which became an independent kingdom. Gustavus Vasa, a Swedish noble, led the movement and was later chosen king of Sweden (1523). In the same year Protestantism was introduced. Vasa took possession of the church lands, got the better of the aristocracy, — which had formerly made the kings much trouble, — and started Sweden on its way toward national greatness.

Motives of Gustavus Adolphus. Gustavus Adolphus, the grandson of Gustavus Vasa, was a sincere and enthusiastic Protestant and by far the most generous and attractive figure of his time. He was induced to invade Germany for two reasons. In the first place he was genuinely grieved by the misfortunes of his Protestant brethren and anxious to help them. Secondly, he undoubtedly hoped by his invasion not only to free his fellow Protestants from the oppression of the emperor and of the Catholic League but also to gain a strip of German territory for Sweden.

Fate of Gustavus and Wallenstein. Gustavus was not received very warmly at first by the Protestant princes of the north, but they were brought to their senses after the awful destruction of Magdeburg by the troops of the Catholic League under General Tilly. Magdeburg was the most important town of northern Germany. When it finally yielded, after an obstinate and difficult siege, twenty thousand of its inhabitants were killed and the town burned to the ground. Although Tilly's reputation for cruelty is quite equal to that of Wallenstein, he was probably not responsible for the fire. After Gustavus Adolphus had met Tilly near Leipzig and routed the army of the League, the Protestant princes began to look with more favor on the foreigner.

The next spring Gustavus entered Bavaria and once more defeated Tilly (who was fatally wounded in the battle) and

FIG. 179. *Gustavus Adolphus*
From a painting by Van Dyck

forced Munich to surrender. There seemed now to be no reason why he should not continue his progress to Vienna. The emperor, however, decided to recall Wallenstein, who collected a new army of which he was put in absolute command. After some delay Gustavus met Wallenstein on the field of Lützen, in November, 1632, where, after a fierce struggle, the Swedes gained the victory. But they lost their leader and Protestantism its hero; for the Swedish king ventured too far into the lines of the enemy and was surrounded and killed. The Swedes did not, however, retire from Germany, but continued to take part in the war, which now became only a series of raids by leaders whose soldiers ruined the land and mercilessly slaughtered the people. Wallenstein, who had long been detested even by the Catholics, was deserted by his soldiers and murdered (in 1634), to the great relief of everyone.

Richelieu renews the Struggle of France against the Hapsburgs. Just at this moment Richelieu, who was guiding the policy of France for Louis XIII (p. 714), decided that it would be an advantage to renew the old struggle with the Hapsburgs. France was still shut in, as she had been since the time of Charles V, by the Hapsburg lands, Austrian and Spanish. Except on the side toward the ocean her boundaries were in the main artificial ones and not those established by great rivers and mountains. She therefore determined to weaken her enemy and strengthen herself by winning Roussillon on the south and so make the crest of the Pyrenees the border line between France and Spain. She dreamed, too, of extending her control toward the Rhine by adding the county of Burgundy (that is, Franche-Comté, as it was often called), and a number of fortified towns which would afford protection against the Spanish Netherlands.

Richelieu had already arranged an alliance with the chief enemies of the house of Austria and had furnished money and support to the Protestant princes. He declared war against Spain in May, 1635. At first the French met serious defeats; but they went on increasing their armies and sending them in every direction, — to the Netherlands, Alsace, Franche-Comté, and Roussillon. French troops joined Swedish, Spanish, and German soldiers, who continued to despoil an already exhausted country for a decade longer. The scarcity of provisions was so great that the armies had to move quickly from place to place in order to avoid starvation. After suffering a serious defeat by the Swedes the emperor (Ferdinand III, 1637–1657) sent a Dominican monk to protest to Cardinal Richelieu for his crime in aiding the German and Swedish heretics against Catholic Austria.

France succeeds Spain in Military Supremacy. The cardinal had, however, just died (December, 1642), doubtless well content with the results of his diplomacy. The French were in possession of Roussillon and of Lorraine and Alsace.

Under the direction of Cardinal Mazarin, who continued the foreign policy of Richelieu, the war went on with brilliant leadership. The military achievements of the French generals, especially Turenne and Condé, during the opening years of the reign of Louis XIV (1643–1715), showed that a new period had begun in which the military and political supremacy of Spain was to give way to that of France (see Chapter XXXIII).

Close of the Thirty Years' War (1648). The countries in the war were now so numerous and their objects so various and conflicting that it is not strange that it required some years to arrange the conditions of peace, even after everyone was ready for it. It was agreed (1644) that France and the Empire should confer at Münster, and the emperor and the Swedes at Osnabrück — both of which towns lie in Westphalia. For four years the representatives of the several powers worked upon the difficult problem of satisfying everyone, but at last the treaties of Westphalia were signed late in 1648.

Provisions of the Treaties of Westphalia. (1) The religious troubles in Germany were settled by extending the toleration of the Peace of Augsburg so as to include the Calvinists as well as the Lutherans. (2) The Protestant princes were to keep the lands which they had in their possession in the year 1624, regardless of the Edict of Restitution, and each ruler was still to have the right to determine the religion of his state. (3) The break-up of the Holy Roman Empire was practically acknowledged by permitting the individual states to make treaties among themselves and with foreign powers; this amounted to recognizing the virtual independence which they had, as a matter of fact, already long enjoyed. (4) While portions of northern Germany were given to Sweden, this territory did not cease to form a part of the Empire, for Sweden was thereafter to have three votes in the German diet. (5) The emperor also gave to France three important towns — Metz, Verdun, and Toul — and all his rights in Alsace, although the city of Strassburg was to remain with the Empire. (6) Lastly, the independence both of the United Netherlands and of Switzerland was acknowledged.

Disastrous Results of the War in Germany. The accounts of the misery of Germany caused by the Thirty Years' War can hardly be believed. Thousands of villages were wiped out altogether; in some regions the population was reduced by one half, in others to a third, or even less, of what it had been at the opening of the conflict. The flourishing city of Augsburg was left with but sixteen thousand souls instead of eighty thousand. The people were fearfully demoralized by privation and suffering and by the atrocities of the soldiers of all the various nations. Until the end of the eighteenth century Germany remained too poor to make any considerable contribution to the culture of Europe.

Questions and Exercises

REVIEW OF CHAPTER

1. What program of reform did the Church adopt? What was accomplished by the Council of Trent? Describe the rules and purposes of the Jesuit order. For what activities is the Jesuit order chiefly noted? What was the purpose of the Index of Prohibited Books?

2. What were the chief aims of Philip II? Describe Philip's policy in the Netherlands. How did it happen that the Netherlands belonged to Spain? Why did Philip's projects fail?

3. Why did France remain a Catholic country? What were the relations of the French kings to the papacy? Describe the rise of the Huguenot party. Why were the Huguenots looked upon as dangerous to the government? How did the Guise family promote civil war in France? Describe Richelieu's attitude toward the Huguenots.

4. What were the weaknesses in the Peace of Augsburg? What led Gustavus Adolphus to enter the Thirty Years' War? Describe Richelieu's interest and activity in the conflict. What were the provisions of the treaties of Westphalia?

USEFUL TERMS

See how much meaning you can give to the following: *tradition, Sacraments, fanaticism, pillage, alliance, toleration, dogmatic, seminary, Index, Huguenots, restitution, fortified towns, Palatinate.*

DIRECTIVE QUESTIONS

1. What did the Catholic reformation accomplish?

2. Is an Index of Prohibited Books still in existence? If so, are additions made to it?

3. What do you consider the most important provisions of the treaties of Westphalia as regards later times?

4. Was the Edict of Restitution a just measure?

DISCUSSION TOPICS

1. Religious wars are never justifiable.

2. Philip II was shortsighted in fighting the Dutch.

3. Should reading be censored by church authorities?

4. Religious wars have taught men the necessity of religious liberty.

ADDITIONAL ADVENTURES IN LEARNING

1. **Studies in Source Materials.** ROBINSON, *Readings*, Vol. II, chap. xxviii, sect. i, The Council of Trent; sect. iv, Philip II; sect. vi, "The Wars of Religion in France"; chap. xxix, sect. i, The Thirty Years' War; sect. iii, "The Treaty of Westphalia."

2. **Topical Studies.** The Order of the Jesuits: *Readings*, chap. xxviii, sect. ii; SMITH, *The Age of the Reformation*; HAYES, *Political and Cultural History of Modern Europe*, Vol. I, pp. 188 ff. The revolt of the Netherlands, and William the Silent: *Readings*, chap. xxviii, sect. v; HAYES, Vol. I, p. 245; PUTNAM, *William the Silent*; GRIFFIS, *Brave Little Holland*. Gustavus Adolphus: *Readings*, chap. xxix, sect. ii; C. R. L. FLETCHER, *Gustavus Adolphus*; HAAREN and POLAND, *Famous Men of Modern Times*, chap. xiii; HAYES, Vol. I, pp. 268 ff. The Huguenots: ADAMS, *The Growth of the French Nation*; WAKEMAN, *The Ascendancy of France*.

Part Eight

HOW OUR ANCESTORS IN EUROPE WERE GETTING READY FOR OUR OWN AGE

In Part Eight we shall see Monarchy brought to its Height. We shall find that it accomplished much in Establishing Strong National States; but we shall see also how the Abuse of Kingly Power worked to bring about its Own Undoing. For it was Oppressive Autocracy which woke the Common People to a Realization of their Own Rights and led to an Ever-Increasing Demand on their Part for Fairer Treatment and a Share in the Government. Part Eight also shows us how European Ideas were carried across the Seas and how our Own Country was founded — a Free Nation in the New World, the Heir of that Western Civilization whose Story we have followed in this Volume

Peter the Great at the French Court

Saint-Simon, in his *Memoirs*, tells how Peter astonished the court by lifting
the youthful Louis XV in his arms

CHAPTER XXXII · THE MAKING OF MODERN ENGLAND

THE seventeenth century was an important period in the history of England, for it was during that time that the forms and principles of government were adopted which have ever since been followed in Great Britain. Much had already been accomplished in the development of Parliament, the establishment of the jury system, the courts, and the unification of the island under a strong monarchy. A struggle between two rival theories of government was, however, fought out in England in the seventeenth century. Should England be ruled by monarchs who claimed to hold the throne by *divine right*, and were therefore responsible for their actions to God alone, or should England be governed by monarchs who were responsible to the people as well, and who shared the sovereign power with the representatives of the subjects elected to Parliament? In the triumph of this second principle of "constitutional monarchy" England achieved an enlightened form of rule under which she became the foremost power in Europe and the first modern state.

During this century England also settled her religious problem, and her national Church was permanently established. The Revolution of 1688 not only defined the *civil* rights of the people but guaranteed some measure of *religious* liberty. For though England kept her State Church, those who "dissented" were recognized as having the legal right to believe what they liked and to conduct their own favorite church service.

The seventeenth century marks also the beginning of England's supremacy on the seas and the founding of her vast colonial empire (Chap. XXXV).

1. The Struggle between King and Parliament

The Stuarts ascend the Throne of England. At the death of Elizabeth, in 1603, James VI of Scotland became king of England as James I. He was the son of Mary Stuart, Queen of Scots, and Lord Darnley. With James's accession a new family came to the throne of England, the House of Stuart, and Scotland and England were brought under the same ruler. The Stuart family ruled England, with two short

725

interruptions, for over one hundred years. The first four Stuarts were autocratic and attempted to reign as absolute monarchs. They were engaged in a continual and losing struggle with Parliament for control of the government. The great question was, Should the Stuart *kings*, who claimed to be God's representatives on earth, rule as they saw fit or should *Parliament* have the right to control them and the government of the country?

How the Tudors managed Parliament. From the days of Edward I, when Parliament was established, the rulers of England had been forced to consider the wishes of Parliament, for it was that body which granted the money of which the kings were generally in need. Before making the grants, Parliament had an opportunity to compel the ruler to agree to some needed reform in exchange. Parliament had also asserted its powers in other ways, on occasion even going so far as to depose the king (p. 501).

The Tudors, however, had been able to develop an absolute form of monarchy in which Parliament on the whole was favorably disposed toward the wishes of the crown. Henry VII, the first of the Tudor rulers, had been able, by shrewd management of various sources of income and by restricting expenses, to make himself financially independent of Parliament and had summoned it only a few times throughout his reign. When it did meet, it was very ready to follow the wishes of the ruler. Henry VIII, while tyrannical and cruel, had for a long time been extremely popular and had had the ability to get along even in trying situations. Elizabeth, also autocratic and headstrong, had a shrewd and cunning wit and the wisdom to keep on good terms with her Parliament. Her confidence in herself, her general popularity, and her broad interest in the nation were all in her favor. The Tudors were clever enough not to *talk* about their rights as monarchs and were content to *exercise* them.

The Tactlessness of James I. The Stuarts, on the other hand, especially James I, had a very irritating way of asserting their claims to be the sole and divinely appointed rulers of England. "It is atheism and blasphemy," James declared, "to dispute what God can do; ... so it is presumption and high contempt in a subject to dispute what a king can do, or say that a king cannot do this or that." James was a learned man and was fond of writing books. Among them was a work on monarchs, in which he claimed that the king could make any law he pleased without consulting Parliament; that he was the master of every one of his subjects, high and low, and might put to death whom he pleased. A good king would act according to law, he said, but was not bound to do so and had the power to change the law at any time to suit himself.

The "Divine Right of Kings." These ideas seem strange and very unreasonable to us; but James was only defending the powers which the Tudor monarchs had actually exercised, and which the kings of France

Fig. 180. *James I*

From a painting by Marcus Geerarts in Dulwich College Picture Gallery

enjoyed down to the French Revolution of 1789. According to the idea of the "divine right of kings" it had pleased God to appoint the monarch as the father of his people, who must obey him as they would God and ask no questions. The king was responsible to God alone, to whom he owed his powers, — not to Parliament or the nation. These notions were supposed to be based on the teachings of the Bible.

James Antagonizes the Parliament. It is unnecessary to follow the troubles between James I and Parliament; for they were but slight as compared with those of his son Charles I. Nevertheless, it was James who laid the foundation of the fatal quarrel between the Stuarts and their government. James talked of the kingly powers in a lofty way, but his appearance and manners were by no means such as would command the respect or fear of his people. Awkward and shambling in his gait, with indistinct speech, a Scotch accent, and an unpleasant voice, peevish and irritable in manner, he exasperated the members of Parliament when he scolded them as if they were children and insolently asserted that they had no right to meddle in "deep matters of state." James got into endless disputes, lost his temper, and would angrily declare a Parliament dissolved.

Parliament Hits Back. From the first he was at odds with his people as well as Parliament. He was hostile to the Puritans and treated their representatives in a disagreeable and unfair manner, though the Puritans were growing in number and power, were gaining seats in Parliament, and were becoming hostile and outspoken in their criticism of the government. James had great difficulty with Parliament over money, which he spent extravagantly or wasted on his favorites. His arguments over money came to a climax in 1621, when Parliament replied to his demands with a list of reforms to be made in the government. It recommended aiding the Protestants on the Continent at the opening of the Thirty Years' War, and enforcing the laws against the Roman Catholics. It urged the marriage of the heir to the throne to a Protestant princess instead of to a Catholic, and the curbing of expenses. James was exceedingly angry; he forbade the mention of such matters in Parliament and threatened its members with punishment. This led to the Great Protestation, in which Parliament entered on the record its rights, privileges, and jurisdictions. But James sent for the journal, tore out the page, and dismissed Parliament. He had prepared the way for very serious trouble, which cost his son his head

Fig. 181. *An Early Session of Parliament*
Courtesy of the British Museum

Great Writers of James's Reign. The writers of James's reign constituted its chief glory. They outshone those of any other European country. William Shakespeare is generally admitted to be the greatest dramatist that the world has produced. While he wrote many of his plays before the death of Elizabeth, some of his finest — *Othello, King Lear,* and *The Tempest,* for example — belong to the time of James I.

During the same period Francis Bacon was writing his *Advancement of Learning,* which he dedicated to James I in 1605 and in which he urged that men should cease to rely upon the old textbooks, like Aristotle, and turn to a careful examination of animals, plants, and chemicals, with a view to learning about them and using the knowledge thus gained to improve the condition of mankind. Bacon's ability to write English is equal to that of Shakespeare, but he chose to write prose, not verse. It was in James's reign that the authorized English translation of the Bible was made, which is still used in all countries where English is spoken. It is known as the King James Version. This was based on earlier translations made by Wycliffe and in the time of Henry VIII.

Charles I (1625–1649) *quarrels with Parliament.* Charles I, who succeeded James, was a handsome man and more dignified and kingly in appearance than his father; but he was equally obstinate and intent on having his own way. He had the same high ideas of his authority and believed that a king might rule as he wished, regardless of the desires of his people. Accordingly he did nothing to improve the disagreeable impressions of his father's reign and immediately began to quarrel with Parliament.

The Duke of Buckingham, who had been James's favorite, was a close friend of Charles and was retained in power. He and the new king soon had the country at war with the Netherlands, France, and Spain, and all these adventures were not only expensive but turned out to be miserable failures. Hence when Charles applied to Parliament for funds, he was urged first to dismiss Buckingham from office. But Charles became very angry at the suggestion, and twice dissolved Parliament rather than see its wishes carried out. Finding that he could not secure money from the government, he attempted to raise it in a number of irregular ways.

Despotic Measures of Charles. The law prohibited the king from asking for *gifts* from the people; but it did not forbid asking them to *lend* him money, even though there was no prospect that he would repay it. Loans were therefore practically forced from the people by Charles's officials on pain of the king's displeasure. When several prominent men refused to make such loans, they were arrested by order of the king and thrown into prison. Another grievance of the people was that great numbers of soldiers from the wars were lodged with families who had to support them and have them in their homes, however distasteful this might be.

The Petition of Right (1628). Charles's attacks on the liberties and rights of the people — his defiance of the laws of the land — aroused Parliament. In 1628 that body drew up the celebrated *Petition of Right,* which is one of the most important documents in the history of the English constitution. In it Parliament called the king's attention to his unlawful ways of forcing money from his subjects and to the acts of his agents who had in various ways molested and disquieted the people of the realm. Parliament therefore "humbly prayed" the king that no man need thereafter "make or yield any gift, loan, benevolence, tax, or such like charge" without consent of Parliament; that no free man should be imprisoned or suffer any punishment except according to the laws and statutes of the realm as presented in the Great Charter; and that the people should not be forced to lodge soldiers in their houses on any excuse whatever.

Very unwillingly Charles consented to sign a document which clearly stated the limits to which an English king might go; for Charles firmly believed that his power was, and ought to be, absolute within the realm. The Petition of Right and the Great Charter, both forced from arbitrary rulers, guaranteed certain fundamental rights to the English people. They clearly showed that the nation did not intend to yield to an unreasonable monarch but was destined to be a great and free commonwealth in which the king, like his people, should be responsible to the laws of the realm.

The Religious Question makes More Trouble. The Petition of Right, however, by no means settled Charles's troubles. The disagreement between king and Parliament was made much more serious by their opposition to each other on religious matters. The king had married a French Catholic princess and was known to be sympathetic to the Catholic cause. Just at this time the Catholics seemed to be gaining in the religious wars on the Continent. The king of Denmark had just been defeated by Wallenstein (p. 716), and Richelieu had succeeded in depriving the Huguenots of their fortified cities (p. 714). Both James I and Charles had shown their readiness to enter into agreements with France and Spain to protect Catholics in England. Parliament, which was growing strongly Puritan in its membership, began to fear that the king might be planning to go still farther in support of the Roman Catholics; for there had been a growing tendency in England to restore some of the older ceremonies of the Church, a fact which irritated and alarmed the stricter Protestant members of the House of Commons. Since the king was squarely behind the Anglican Church in its Catholic tendencies, the breach between the king and many of his subjects was growing ever wider.

Charles continues to Defy Parliament and the Law. When Charles found that Parliament would not grant him funds unless he followed their advice in matters of government, he began to seek other ways to increase his income. There was an ancient source of revenue, which former kings had always enjoyed, called "tonnage and poundage." This was an import and export duty on wine, wool, and other articles which entered or left the country. When Charles came to the throne, Parliament, fearing the extravagance of Buckingham, had been willing to grant this revenue to the king only for a year at a time. This greatly angered the king, who asserted that Parliament was attempting to take away his rights. Parliament now replied that no taxes were legal without its approval according to the Petition of Right.

Charles claimed that tonnage and poundage was not a *tax* but a *customs duty*, and he continued to have it collected. Realizing that Charles would be independent if he continued to get hold of this large sum, Parliament summoned to trial certain customs officials who had seized the goods of persons refusing to pay this tax. Charles, however, forbade his customs officers to appear before Parliament. After several stormy sessions the king dissolved Parliament and determined to rule without its help.

Fig. 182. *Charles I*

From a painting by Van Dyck in the Louvre

How Charles got along without Parliament. Charles's determination to rule with the aid of his ministers alone marks the beginning of a long and bitter contest between king and Parliament. Would the king be able to conduct the government and prove that his power was supreme, or would he finally be forced to call Parliament to his aid and acknowledge that its powers were superior to those of the crown?

For eleven years Charles ruled England without Parliament, and at first his government seemed likely to be a success. His ministers were able men. By wise management, expenses were reduced and income was increased. The country was at peace, and there was no drain on the treasury for troops to fight in foreign lands. A number of schemes for raising money were tried, but they made the king and his advisers very unpopular. Old feudal dues were revived, so that some of those who held property found that they were suddenly forced to pay special taxes, and fines were collected for breaking ancient laws that had long been neglected. There was a very irritating tax called "ship money." This had been a levy on seaport towns to help to keep up the navy. It was now extended to all towns, and, when the people protested, it was said that it was not a tax but a payment which the subjects owed for the defense of the country. As a matter of fact, the money did not go into building ships but was used for other purposes, according to the pleasure of the king. Monopolies were also granted to corporations, which were given the sole right to carry on a certain business on the payment of handsome sums for the privilege.

How Charles dealt with the Religious Situation. In the meantime the religious situation was growing worse. William Laud, archbishop of Canterbury, was the king's adviser in all matters connected with the Church. He was an able and conscientious man, but autocratic and severe. Eager to uphold the dignity and authority of the Established Church, Laud made every effort to enforce conformity throughout the realm. The Puritans, however, had greatly increased in number, and their hatred of the High Church party was growing more widespread. The Puritans came to think of their cause as united to that of liberty and the rights and powers of Parliament, while the king, the bishops, and the government ministers were strong in support of the High Church party.

In order to find out for himself whether clergymen and laymen were conforming to the services ordered by the State Church, Laud began a series of *visitations* to the parishes throughout his province. Every clergyman who refused to use the prayer book, or opposed placing the communion table at the east end of the church, or objected to any other forms of the Anglican service, even though it was for conscience' sake, was referred to the archbishop for discipline. If he persisted he was tried, and if convicted lost his parish. Extreme cases were brought before the Court of High Commission, a court composed of the bishops and other officers of the Church. This court was so arbitrary that a victim was practically condemned before his case was tried. The Star Chamber — a court composed of the king and his ministers — and the Court of High Commission were notorious for the severity of their sentences and became the symbol of oppression to the people. The punishments inflicted by these courts, from our modern standpoint, seem very shocking. They included such penalties as flogging, the pillory, cutting off the ears, heavy fines, or imprisonment with no chance of a trial. Many of the victims died from the foul conditions in the prisons.

Growth of Protestant Sects. Many of the violent and outspoken Puritans were arrested and brought to trial for their writings and speeches. But the sufferings they endured seemed to increase rather than diminish the enthusiasm for their cause. The Protestants were at this time divided into a number of separate sects. Besides Presbyterians, there were Quakers and Baptists and many less well-known groups. There were also a growing number of Independents, or Separatists. These did not wish to join either the Church of England or the Presbyterians, and believed that each religious community should govern itself independently. They felt that the Church and the State should be entirely separate. So the government found itself face to face with an ever-growing body of devout, conscientious men who felt that they had the right to worship in their way, and yet were interfered with by the bishops and the defenders of the Church of England.

Rebellion in Scotland. Charles's personal government, although tyrannical and unpopular with a large part of the people in England, was brought to an end by trouble which originated in Scotland. There the Presbyterian form of religion had been established by John Knox in Elizabeth's time. Neither James nor Charles had been satisfied to leave the Scotch Church alone, but had gradually secured the appointment of bishops and restored to them some of their former

powers. Charles, who desired to have the Scotch Church
like the English organization, had tried to introduce a new
prayer book much like the one used in the Established
Church of England. When, however, an attempt was made
to compel the Scotch Church to use the new book, a riot
broke out. Opposition spread rapidly, and within a year
(1638) many of the Scotch signed a National Covenant,
pledging themselves to restore the purity and liberty of the
Gospel. This, to most of the *Covenanters*, meant Presbyterianism. A Scotch assembly claimed the right to regulate
all religious matters for the country, defied the commissioners
sent by the king, and reëstablished their own form of worship.

Charles forced to call Parliament once more. This action
amounted to rebellion. Charles determined to crush it immediately by going to Scotland with an army. He was now
forced to summon Parliament, for he could not carry on a
war in Scotland without money. He first tried to raise funds
independently, by buying on credit a large cargo of pepper
which had just arrived in the ships of the East India Company, and selling it for cash. The soldiers whom he hired did
not wish, however, to fight the Scotch, with whom they sym-
pathized in religious matters. After several unsuccessful
attempts Charles found himself unable to handle the situation
and in the embarrassing position of having to summon Parliament. But the return of Parliament did not mean support
for the king. It was, rather, the opening act of a great
tragedy which ended in the overthrow of the Anglican
Church and the execution of the king.

The Long Parliament (1640–1653). The Long Parliament,
so called because it lasted for thirteen years, began by calling to account those who had oppressed the people. They
were now accused by Parliament of high treason. Some
of the ministers escaped, but Charles's chief financial adviser
and Archbishop Laud were sent to the Tower of London.
Both were tried and executed, in spite of all Charles could do
to save them. Parliament now passed a bill providing that
it could not be dissolved without its own consent, and an-

other, the Triennial Act, requiring Parliament to meet every three years even if the king failed to summon it. It abolished the Star Chamber and the Court of High Commission, declared "ship money" illegal, and prohibited the collection of tonnage and poundage and other taxes which the people had been forced to pay. By these and other measures Parliament abolished entirely the despotic government of Charles's personal rule and substituted permanent constitutional reforms. Moreover, it proved its power superior to that of the crown in protecting the liberties and rights of the English people.

The Grand Remonstrance. Fearing lest the king might somehow get control of an army and forcibly dissolve Parliament, a "Grand Remonstrance" was drawn up in which all of Charles's wrongdoings and offenses were boldly and fully stated and a number of reforms proposed. This document was printed and sent throughout the country with the idea of gaining the sympathy of the people for the action of Parliament. Angry at the conduct of the Commons, Charles attempted to frighten the group that opposed him by undertaking to arrest five of its most active leaders, whom he declared to be traitors. But when he entered the House of Commons and looked around for his enemies, he found that they had taken shelter in London, whose citizens later brought them back in triumph to Westminster, where Parliament held its meetings.

The Beginning of Civil War (1642); *Cavaliers and Round-heads.* Both Charles and Parliament now began to gather troops for the unavoidable conflict, and England was plunged into civil war. Those who supported Charles were called *Cavaliers.* They included not only most of the aristocracy and the Catholic party but also a number of members of the House of Commons who were fearful lest Presbyterianism should succeed in doing away with the English Church. The parliamentary party were popularly known as the *Roundheads,* since some of them cropped their hair close because of their dislike for the long locks of their more aristocratic and worldly enemies. The Cavaliers, in turn, scorned the Roundheads as a set of hypocrites, on account of their solemn ways and for liking to go to meeting and singing psalms instead of trying to have a good time.

Overthrow of the Anglican Church. By this time Parliament was sharply divided on the great religious question. Some of the moderate members wished merely to limit the power of the bishops and leave the Church under the control of the government. The more ardent Presbyterians, however, succeeded in getting an assembly of Puritan clergymen appointed to draw up a plan for the organization, doctrines, and services of a new national Church. The report of this Westminster Assembly, as it was called, was accepted by Parliament, and a bill was passed by both houses making the English Church *Presbyterian.* The Anglican organization as it had existed since Elizabeth's time was overthrown, there were no longer any bishops, and the authority of the Church was now in the hands of a General Assembly. The use of the prayer book was forbidden, and a simple service was substituted for the older form. All the furniture and decorations of the Anglican Church were removed. Yet religious toleration was not achieved by this change. One party of Protestants had succeeded in replacing another, but religious opinion was as divided as before.

Oliver Cromwell; the Defeat of Charles's Armies at Marston Moor and Naseby. The Roundheads soon found a distinguished leader in Oliver Cromwell (b. 1599), a country gentleman and member of Parliament, who was later to become the most powerful ruler of his time. Cromwell organized an army of God-fearing men, who were not permitted to indulge in profane words or light talk, as was the habit of soldiers, but advanced upon their enemies singing psalms. The king had the support of northern England and also looked for help from Ireland, where the royal and Catholic causes were popular.

The war continued for several years, and a number of battles were fought which, after the first year, went in general

Fig. 183. *Children of Charles I*

This very interesting picture, by the Flemish artist Van Dyck, was painted in 1637. The boy with his hand on the dog's head was destined to become Charles II of England. Next on the left is the prince who was later James II. The girl to the extreme left, the Princess Mary, married the governor of the United Netherlands, and her son became William III of England in 1688 (see page 750). The two princesses on the right died in childhood

against the Cavaliers. The most important of these were the battle of Marston Moor in 1644 and that of Naseby the next year, in which the king was completely defeated. The enemy came into possession of his letters, which showed how their king had been endeavoring to bring armies from France and Ireland into England. This encouraged Parliament to carry on the war with more energy than ever. The king, defeated on every hand, put himself in the hands of the Scotch army which had come to the aid of Parliament (1646), and the Scotch soon turned him over to Parliament. During the next two years Charles was kept in prison.

Pride's Purge. There were, however, many in the House of Commons who still sided with the king, and in December, 1648, that body attempted to make peace with the monarch, whom they had safely imprisoned on the Isle of Wight. The next day Colonel Pride, representing the army, — which was now a party in itself and was opposed to all negotiations between the king and the Commons, — stood at the door of the House with a body of soldiers and kept out all the members who were known to take the side of the king. This outrageous act is known in history as "Pride's Purge."

Execution of Charles (1649). In this way the House of Commons was brought completely under the control of those most bitterly hostile to the king, whom they immediately proposed to bring to trial. They declared that the House of Commons, since it was chosen by the people, was supreme in England and the source of all just power, and that consequently neither king nor House of Lords was necessary. This remnant of the lawful House of Commons appointed a special High Court of Justice made up of Charles's sternest enemies, who alone would consent to sit in judgment on him. They passed sentence upon him, and on January 30, 1649, Charles was beheaded in front of his palace of Whitehall, London. It must be clear from the foregoing account that it was not the nation at large which demanded Charles's death, but a very small group of extremists who claimed to be the representatives of the nation.

2. ENGLAND TRIES A REPUBLIC

England becomes a Commonwealth, or Republic. On May 19, 1649, the "Rump Parliament," as the remnant of the House of Commons was contemptuously called, proclaimed England to be thereafter a "commonwealth," that is, a republic, without a king or House of Lords. The authority was in the hands of Parliament, but Cromwell, who soon became the head of the army, was nevertheless the real ruler of England. He was mainly supported by the Independents; and it is very surprising that he was able to maintain himself so long, considering what a small portion of the English people were in sympathy with the religious ideas of that sect and with the abolition of kingship. Even the Presbyterians were on the side of Charles I's son, Charles II, the lawful heir to the throne. Cromwell was a vigorous and skillful statesman, however, and had a well-organized army of fifty thousand men at his command; otherwise the republic could scarcely have lasted more than a few months.

Ireland and Scotland Subdued. Cromwell found himself faced by every kind of difficulty. The three kingdoms had fallen apart. The nobles and Catholics in Ireland proclaimed Charles II as king, and raised an army of Irish Catholics and English royalist Protestants with a view to overthrowing the Commonwealth. Cromwell accordingly set out for Ire-

Fig. 184. *Oliver Cromwell*

land, where, after taking Drogheda, he mercilessly slaughtered two thousand of the "barbarous wretches," as he called them. Town after town surrendered to Cromwell's army, and in 1652, after much cruelty, the island was once more conquered. A large part of it was taken possession of by the English, and the Catholic landowners were driven into the mountains. In the meantime (1650) Charles II, who had taken refuge in France, had landed in Scotland, and upon his agreeing to be a Presbyterian king the whole Scotch nation was ready to support him. But Scotland was subdued by Cromwell even more promptly than Ireland had been. So completely was the Scottish army destroyed that Cromwell found no need to draw the sword again in the British Isles.

The Navigation Act (1651). Although it would seem that Cromwell had enough to keep him busy at home, he engaged in a war against the Dutch. England and Holland had both been increasing their trade in Europe and overseas, but enterprise, skill, and government support made the Dutch dangerous competitors. The ships which went out from

FIG. 185. *Ship such as was used by the Hanseatic League*

This is taken from a picture painted in 1409. Like other pictures of the time, it makes it clear that the Hanseatic ships were tiny as compared with those used two hundred and fifty years later, when Cromwell fought the Dutch

Amsterdam and Rotterdam were the best merchant vessels in the world and had got control of the carrying trade between Europe and the colonies. In order to put an end to this, the English Parliament passed the Navigation Act (1651), which permitted only English vessels to bring goods to England, unless the goods came in vessels belonging to the country that had produced them. This crowded out the Dutch vessels and left them only the trade in the products of their own country.

The Dutch protested, and finally war broke out between Holland and England. A series of battles followed between the English and Dutch fleets, and in a few years the Dutch recognized the Navigation Act. This war is a good example of the struggles over business and trade which were thereafter to take the place of the religious conflicts of the preceding period.

Cromwell dissolves the Long Parliament (1653) *and is made Lord Protector.* Cromwell failed to get along with Parliament any better than Charles I had done. The "Rump Parliament" had become very unpopular; for its members, in spite of their boasted piety, accepted bribes and eagerly sought the promotion of their relatives to government offices. The members had been holding office for thirteen years with-

FIG. 186. *Dutch War Vessel in Cromwell's Time*

This vessel should be compared with the ship in Fig. 185 in order to realize the progress that had taken place in navigation since the prosperous days of the Hanseatic League (p. 550)

out new elections, and the head of the army now felt that new men should be sent to Parliament as representatives of the people. When he found that they proposed to pass a bill prolonging their own power, Cromwell became angry and scolded them for their selfishness. On being interrupted by a member, he cried out: "Come, come, we have had enough of this. I'll put an end to this. It's not fit that you should sit here any longer"; and, calling in his soldiers, he turned the members out of the House and sent them home. Having thus made an end of the Long Parliament (April, 1653), he summoned a Parliament of his own, made up of "God-fearing" men whom he and the officers of his army

FIG. 187. *Great Seal of England under the Commonwealth* (1651)

This seal is reduced considerably in the illustration. It gives us an idea of the appearance of a session of the House of Commons when England was for a short period a republic. It is still the custom today for members to sit with their hats on, except when making a speech

chose. This extraordinary body is known as Barebone's Parliament, because of the Puritan name of one of its members, Praisegod Barebone. Many of these godly men were unbusinesslike and hard to deal with. A small number of the more sensible ones got up early one winter morning (December, 1653) and, before their opponents had a chance to protest, declared Parliament dissolved and placed the supreme authority in the hands of Cromwell.

The Protector's Foreign Policy. For nearly five years Cromwell, as Lord Protector, — a title similar to that of " Regent," — was practically king of England, though he refused actually to accept the royal emblems of office. Cromwell had a council to aid him, but he was really a dictator with an army behind him. England had been through a long period of conflict, and the leadership of one man — provided he was upright and able like Cromwell — seemed for the time the only possible form of government. While he did not succeed in permanently establishing the government at home, he had remarkable success in his dealings with foreign nations. He promptly formed an alliance with France, and English troops assisted the French in winning a great victory over Spain. England gained thereby Dunkirk and the West Indian island of Jamaica. The French king, young Louis XIV, at first hesitated to address Cromwell, in the usual courteous way of monarchs, as "my cousin," but soon admitted that he should have to call Cromwell even "father" should the English ruler wish it. The Protector was undoubtedly the most powerful person in Europe. Indeed, Cromwell found himself forced to play the part of a monarch, and it seemed to many persons that he was quite as despotic as James I and Charles I.

Cromwell's Death (1658). In 1658 Cromwell died; and as a great storm passed over England at that time, the Cavaliers asserted that the devil had come to fetch home the soul of the usurper. Cromwell was dying, it is true, but he was no instrument of the devil. He closed a life of honest effort for his fellow beings with a last touching prayer to God, whom he had faithfully sought to serve:

> Thou hast made me, though very unworthy, a mean instrument to do Thy people some good and Thee service: and many of them have set too high a value upon me, though others wish and would be glad of my death. Pardon such as desire to trample upon the dust of a poor worm, for they are Thy people too; and pardon the folly of this short prayer, even for Jesus Christ's sake, and give us a good night, if it be Thy pleasure. Amen.

3. THE ENGLISH RECALL THEIR KING

Charles II called to the Throne (1660–1685). It was soon evident in the confusion that followed the death of Cromwell that the people were tired of a military rule and would be glad to have a king once more. The new Parliament which assembled in 1660 received a message from the exiled Prince Charles in which he offered to pardon all those who had taken part in the rebellion, to permit royalist property which had been confiscated to remain in the hands of its present owners, and to consent to any bill which Parliament might propose granting religious toleration. Upon receipt of this declaration Parliament solemnly resolved that "according to the ancient and fundamental laws of this kingdom, the government is, and ought to be, by king, lords, and commons."

A few weeks later Charles was welcomed in England with great manifestations of joy on the part of the people. The period of Puritan revolution was over, the republic and dictatorship were things of the past, and England once more took to its heart the family of Stuart.

The Powers of Parliament Recognized. In ascending the throne Charles II swore to uphold the Great Charter, the Petition of Right, and other important statutes safeguarding the liberties of the people. In all the promises made by the new king it was evident that the lessons of the recent bitter experiences had been learned, and that there was no longer in the king's mind, nor in that of the people, any question of absolutism. The full powers of Parliament, if not its supremacy, in the government were recognized.

Charles II was quite as fond of having his own way as his father, but he took things less seriously and had more foresight. Besides, he had a sad reminder to warn him how far he could go. Although he was indolent and pleasure-loving, and might try to outwit Parliament, he was never stubborn and defiant. He knew when to give in; for he did not intend, as he himself said, to let anything send him on his travels again. The king now realized that he held his throne not by *divine right* but at the *pleasure of the people.*

Reaction against Puritanism. The nation for the most part was genuinely glad to have a king once more. They were tired not only of the strict army rule but of the severity and drabness of the Puritan influence. They longed for life to be more gay and free. During the Puritan régime the theaters had been closed, and popular games like bear-baiting, cockfighting, and bowling forbidden. Sports and games on Sunday had been prohibited, and the Puritan Sabbath substituted for a day of rest and outdoor pleasures. The churches had been stripped of their works of art and stained-glass windows and were bare and ugly places. A natural reaction to such austere repression had taken place, and this accounts for the reckless extravagance and lavish expenditures for which the Restoration period is noted.

The Anglican Church Reëstablished and Conformity Required. With the return of the king came the reëstablishment of the national Anglican Church. A number of intolerant acts designed to curb Puritanism and insure conformity to the State Church were passed, and an effort was made to keep Presbyterians and Independents out of town offices. In 1662 the Act of Uniformity required every clergyman and schoolmaster to give his full approval to everything contained in the prayer book. About two thousand ministers resigned their positions rather than agree to this requirement against their conscience. The Conventicle Act (1664) forbade any religious meetings not in conformity with the law. The Five-Mile Act (1665) prohibited ministers who had been turned out of their parishes from going within five miles of their former churches unless they took an oath renouncing the Solemn League and Covenant and declaring that it was unlawful to bear arms against the king. The Corporation Act (1661) had required all those who held town or city offices to take the same oath. All city offices were therefore held by members of the Church of England. These acts established the Anglican Church once more in its former position of power and threw all Protestants who differed from its rules — Presbyterians, Baptists, Quakers, Independents, and other sects — into one legal class called *Dissenters.* They were very numerous, and since they had been connected with the former rebellion they were feared as revolutionary and dangerous unless strictly regulated by law.

Toleration favored by the King. The king endeavored several times to issue declarations stating that the laws against worship other than that of the Established Church would not be enforced, and later did issue one suspending the enforcement of laws against the Roman Catholics. The king was secretly a convert to Catholicism and was eager to help his fellow Catholics. When Parliament protested, however, against the declarations, Charles withdrew them. Parliament then passed the intolerant Test Act (1672), which kept everyone from holding public office who did not accept the views of the English Church and take the Communion according to its usage. This law excluding all but members of the English Church from office remained in force down into the nineteenth century.[1]

War with Holland Renewed. The old war with the Dutch, begun by Cromwell, broke out again as a result of rivalries over trade and colonies in the East and West Indies and in North America. Both countries were prospering, and each was exceedingly jealous of the good fortune of the other. Neither could gain a decisive victory; but the English seized some West Indian islands from the Dutch and in 1664 captured the Dutch settlement of New Amsterdam, which they renamed New York in honor of the king's brother, the Duke of York. Peace was made in 1667, the English retaining their conquests and ceding to Holland the Spice Islands.

4. ENGLAND ESTABLISHES A CONSTITUTIONAL MONARCHY

Charles II and his Parliament. We shall now see how the policy of Charles II and his successor led to the establishment in England of a constitutional monarchy. It must not be assumed that Charles was always at one with Parliament in its actions. His whole attitude toward the religious question was different. For many years he was secretly in the pay of Louis XIV, who supplied him with large sums of money to support the French policy. But Charles did not openly oppose Parliament. He had many able ministers, but when they became unpopular with Parliament he did not hesitate to dismiss them.

[1] It was in view of such acts that the United States constitution declares that no religious test shall ever be required as a qualification to any public office.

The King refuses to exclude his Brother from the Succession.
In only one matter did he stand firm, and that was in maintaining the right of his brother James to succeed him. James
was an ardent Catholic, and there was a general fear that
when he became king he would attack the Protestant religion. While Charles was willing to restrict the powers of a
Catholic successor (and directed that James's two daughters,
Mary and Anne,[1] should be brought up in the Protestant
faith), he was unwilling to let Parliament pass a bill preventing James from inheriting the crown. Three times he
dissolved Parliament rather than permit the bill to come to
a final vote. So firmly did he take his stand on this matter
that it looked at one time as if civil war might result. But
the people were more afraid of war than of Catholics, and
finally a reaction set in in favor of the king. When a plot
to seize Charles was discovered, sympathy turned to the
king, and James was assured of his accession.

James II becomes King (1685–1688). At the death of
Charles II his brother came to the throne as James II. James
made no attempt to conceal his sympathy with the Catholics.
He had none of the quick wit, ease of manner, or adaptabil-
ity which served his brother in difficult situations. On the
contrary, from the first he did everything to alienate his
subjects by his tactless and stubborn manner. The severity
with which he punished his enemies, and his reckless violation of the laws of the land in order to force through his own
ideas, aroused general dislike. Most of his troubles came from
his determination to champion the Catholic cause. He made
use of the so-called "dispensing" power to appoint Catholics
to government and university offices in spite of the Test Act,
and dissolved Parliament when it opposed him, as his father,
Charles I, had done. He finally issued a Declaration of Indulgence suspending all laws against Catholics and Dissenters
and ordered it read from the pulpits. Those ministers who
refused were brought to trial as rebels.

Matters came to a climax when a son was born to James
and his Catholic wife, Mary of Modena. The English had

[1] See table, p. 753.

tolerated James II, in spite of his religious views, as long as they expected that he would be succeeded by his Protestant daughter Mary, who had married her cousin the Protestant prince William of Orange. The birth of a Catholic heir to the throne entirely changed the situation. James was already very unpopular, and there now seemed no reason for putting up with him any longer. Representatives of Parliament were therefore dispatched to Holland to invite William and Mary to come to England as king and queen (1688).

The "Glorious Revolution" of 1688. William landed in November, 1688, and marched to London, where he received general support from all the English Protestants regardless of party. James II started to oppose William, but his army refused to fight and his courtiers deserted him. William was glad to forward James's flight to France, as he would hardly have known what to do with him had James insisted on remaining in the country. A new Parliament declared the throne vacant, on the ground that King James II, "having violated the fundamental laws and withdrawn himself out of the kingdom, had abdicated the government."

The Bill of Rights (1689). A Bill of Rights was then drawn up, condemning James's breaking of the constitution, and appointing William and Mary joint sovereigns. The Bill of Rights, which is an important monument in English constitutional history, once more stated the fundamental rights of the English nation and the limitations which the Petition of Right and the Great Charter of King John had placed upon the king. By this peaceful revolution of 1688 (the "Glorious Revolution," as they are fond of calling it) the English rid themselves of the Stuarts and their claims to rule by divine right; the rights of Parliament were once more established; and the Catholic question was practically settled by the dethroning of a king who openly favored the rule of the Pope.

The *Toleration Act* was passed by Parliament, which freed Dissenters from all penalties for failing to attend services in Anglican churches and allowed them to have their own meetings. Even Catholics, while not included in the act of toleration, were permitted to hold services undisturbed.

5. England after the Revolution of 1688

What the "Glorious Revolution" Accomplished. A well-known historian has said that the Revolution of 1688 is called the "Glorious Revolution" not because of any feat of arms or heroic sacrifices but because it took place without bloodshed. There was no fighting in this revolution, but a peaceful settlement, by consent, of two troublesome questions which had long divided the country into angry and hostile camps — the questions of religion and of the best form of government. The adjustment of these differences made in 1688 has, moreover, stood the test of time. Further, the settlement which has proved so successful was not made by means of a *written* constitution. There were, of course, the Bill of Rights, defining the limits of the royal power, and the Toleration Act, permitting a limited degree of religious liberty; but the machinery of the new constitutional government was worked out later, as circumstances called for it, and it became law. The revolution laid the foundation principles on which a system of government congenial to British taste and traditions, and suited to British needs, could be gradually reared.

England to remain a Protestant Country. The Bill of Rights declared, once for all, that England was to remain permanently a Protestant country. It was expressly stated that no Catholic, or one who should "marry a papist," should ever "inherit, possess or enjoy the crown and government of the realm." William and Mary were both Protestants, and William was looked upon as the leader of the reformed princes of Europe. Some years later the Protestant character of the government was reaffirmed in the Act of Settlement (1701), which provided for a Protestant succession to the throne. As there were no Protestant heirs in the reigning family, Parliament arranged that after the death of Anne the crown should go to the nearest Protestant relative, who happened to be a German princess of the House of Hanover (p. 753).

Religious toleration was extended, if not completely achieved, by the Toleration Act of 1689. The Dissenters had shown their loyalty to the principles of the revolution

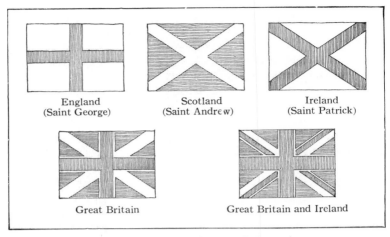

FIG. 188. *The Union Jack*

The flag of Great Britain, combining the crosses of Saint George and Saint Andrew, was called the Union Jack from *Jacques*, the French form of "James" (referring to James I, the first king of Great Britain). The cross of Ireland was added upon its union with Great Britain in 1801. Upright lines indicate red; horizontal lines, blue

by joining with the Anglicans in supporting it. The Dissenters were therefore legally recognized and were permitted to have their own churches and carry on their own form of worship unmolested. They were, however, not allowed to hold public office; this was reserved for Church of England men. Catholics and Unitarians were not granted toleration by the government. They held religious services privately, however, and were no longer persecuted. Although many harsh laws still stood, these were in general neglected.

Constitutional Monarchy Established. The other great question settled by the revolution was the relative power of the king and Parliament in the government of the country. An end was put once and for all to the old rivalry between king and Parliament, and a constitutional monarchy was established in which the powers of the crown and those of the people's representatives in Parliament were carefully distinguished. This will be discussed later.

The Union of Scotland and England (1707). William out-lived Mary by some eight years, and during this time he ruled alone. At his death, in 1702, Mary's younger sister, Anne, came to the throne. It was during Anne's reign that the final union of England and Scotland took place. The two countries, it is true, had been under the same ruler since the accession of James I, but each had maintained its own independent parliament and system of government. Finally, in 1707, both nations agreed to unite their governments into one. Forty-five members of the British House of Commons were to be chosen thereafter in Scotland, and sixteen Scotch lords were to be added to the English House of Lords. In this way the whole island of Great Britain was placed under a single government, and the danger of trouble was thereby greatly reduced. The Union Jack was adopted as the flag of the United Kingdom of Great Britain (Fig. 188).

Accession of George I (1714–1727) *of Hanover.* Since none of Anne's children survived her, she was succeeded, accord-ing to the arrangement made before her accession, by the nearest Protestant heir. This was the son of James I's grand-daughter Sophia, who had married the Elector of Hanover;[1]

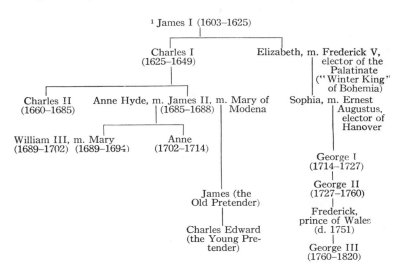

[1] James I (1603–1625)

Charles I
(1625–1649)

Elizabeth, m. Frederick V,
elector of the
Palatinate
("Winter King"
of Bohemia)

Charles II   Anne Hyde, m. James II, m. Mary of   Sophia, m. Ernest
(1660–1685)   (1685–1688)   Modena   Augustus,
                                                              elector of
                                                              Hanover

William III, m. Mary   Anne
(1689–1702) (1689–1694)   (1702–1714)

George I
(1714–1727)

George II
(1727–1760)

James (the
Old Pretender)

Frederick,
prince of Wales
(d. 1751)

Charles Edward
(the Young Pre-
tender)

George III
(1760–1820)

consequently the new king of England, George I, was also elector of Hanover and a member of the Holy Roman Empire.[1]

English Foreign Policy after the Revolution. The coming of William of Orange to the throne in 1689 had an important effect on the foreign policy of England in the eighteenth century. The old commercial rivalry between the Dutch and English died out, and the two countries established friendly relations; for they had much in common. Not only was a Dutch prince the English king but England and Holland were leaders in religious toleration and in permitting the liberty of the press. Both countries were hostile to Louis XIV and, as we shall see, were always on the side of the enemies of France. As Prince of Orange, William had delivered his country from the attempts of Louis to take possession of Holland (p. 777). Louis maintained the exiled James II in royal fashion and threatened to reinstate him on the throne of England; for Louis preferred to see a Catholic ruler in England.

During the eighteenth century England took part in the wars on the Continent, not for the purpose of gaining territory but to equalize the strength between the various nations and so maintain a "balance of power." The wars which she waged for her own advantage were fought in distant lands. In these France was her chief rival; and this, added to their other differences, kept England and France enemies for over a century.

What Limited Monarchy in England Meant. The most important part of the settlement made by the Revolution of 1688 was the determination of the permanent form which the English government was to take. The theory of an absolute monarch governing by divine right was given up once and for all. The long-standing question as to the power of the king and the power of Parliament was settled. Henceforth the king owed his crown not to any hereditary right

---

[1] Originally there had been seven electors (p. 628); but the duke of Bavaria had been made an elector during the Thirty Years' War, and in 1692 the father of George I had been permitted to assume the title of "Elector of Hanover."

of a divine nature but to the Parliament. The king and Parliament were to rule together, but Parliament was supreme. On the other hand, the fact that the monarchy had not been abolished, as in the time of the Commonwealth, meant that Parliament preferred to have a constitutional monarchy, that is, one in which the king rules not according to his own ideas but according to the constitution. His power is therefore strictly limited.

The British Constitution. One may well ask what the British constitution really is, since there is no written document that goes by that name as does the constitution of the United States. The Great Charter of 1215 (p. 495), the Petition of Right (p. 731) of 1628, and the Bill of Rights of 1689 (p. 750) are the three most important documents of the British constitution; but they are not all, for the British constitution is not written. It is the name given to the accepted form of English government. This form has grown up gradually on the basis of these charters of liberty, of other laws and statutes, and of many customs. The written documents are important because they plainly define the right of the people to govern themselves through Parliament and place definite limits on the power of their king.

Further Restrictions on the Monarchy. Several other matters which affected the division of power between Parliament and king were settled shortly after the revolution. A large part of the taxes which had formerly been granted to the king for life were now awarded for but a year at a time. This insured the annual meeting of Parliament; for otherwise no taxes could be legally voted or revenue collected to carry on the government. The Mutiny Act of 1689 provided for the upkeep of the army for a year at a time, also making necessary the annual summoning of Parliament. These measures prevented the king from getting control of the army or handling any large amount of funds, and made the crown dependent on Parliament both for its revenue and for the maintenance of troops. Thus the old evils which darkened the Stuart period were to be made forever impossible.

Political Parties: Whigs and Tories. In an *absolute* monarchy there are no political parties such as we are familiar with today; there can be none. Political parties arise only where the people have a share in the government, — where the people or their representatives, assembled in a congress or parliament, are free to express their views on matters of state. In an absolute monarchy, only the king's wishes are important, and there is no discussion of the ideas of the people. If the people have opinions contrary to those of the crown, they do well to keep them to themselves.

In a *constitutional* monarchy or a *democracy*, however, where the representatives of the people run the government and where the people themselves are free to express their preferences, many ideas are expressed as to how the state should be managed; and these ideas naturally differ. There arise groups, or factions, which agree on certain principles and programs of action. These factions organize into political parties, which by the vote try to place in power those who represent their views.

England had political parties before the other national states of Europe because, in the struggle between Parliament and king during the reign of the Stuarts, Parliament got sufficient power to make its ideas felt in spite of the opposition of the king. The members of Charles I's Parliament disagreed about both religion and government, and, as we recall, there were the parties of the Cavaliers and Roundheads (p. 737). In the time of Charles II the same questions divided the people, and we find political parties again active. The *Tories*, the successors of the Cavaliers, upheld the divine right of kings and the supremacy of the Anglican Church; the *Whigs*, who succeeded the Roundheads, believed in the power of Parliament and favored religious toleration of Dissenters. The contest between the Whigs and Tories was very serious during the reign of Charles II; for the Whigs wished to have the Exclusion Bill passed which would prevent the king's brother James, an avowed Catholic, from inheriting the crown. The Tories, on the other hand, while loyal to the Anglican Church, believed so strongly in the divine character of hereditary kingship that they were ready to accept James as king.

After the revolution both parties continued to hold distinct views as to the best policy to be followed in domestic and foreign affairs. We cannot relate their history here. In general, the Tories were the party of the landholders and the Anglicans, while the Whigs represented the merchants, business men, the Dissenters, and a small section of the aristocracy. In the nineteenth century the Tories became the Conservative party; the Whigs, the Liberal party.

The Cabinet System and the Prime Minister. The cabinet system, which has become such an important part of the machinery of British government, grew up gradually. There was no provision for a cabinet at the time of the revolution, but later this system developed as the most efficient means of carrying on the government. The name "cabinet" came from the habit of the king and his chief ministers of meeting together privately in a room, or cabinet. William at first chose his ministers from either party, but their differences of opinion hindered the smooth carrying on of state affairs. Finally it was found best to choose the ministers from the party which had a majority in the House of Commons.

The cabinet, then, was the small group of the king's chief ministers, who were chosen from the party which had the majority in the House of Commons. It was, and is today, responsible for the government of the country. Headed by the prime, or chief, minister as its spokesman, the cabinet proposes the policies to be followed by the government. These proposals are submitted to Parliament, to be debated upon and finally voted on. If they are approved by Parliament, they are carried out as the will of the people, whose representatives have had a chance to accept or reject them. If, however, they are rejected by vote of Parliament, the cabinet usually resigns in a body. The king then chooses a cabinet made up of members of the opposition party. When any law is passed it is taken to the king for his signature. This is a matter of form, or courtesy, since the king has no power to veto an act of Parliament.

William was his own first minister, and, during the reign of Anne, the Duke of Marlborough took charge of military affairs in time of war. It was Robert Walpole who, as the leading minister in the cabinet of George I, became England's first prime minister, though he did not assume the title.

Walpole, England's First Prime Minister. At the death of Anne, many of the Tories, disregarding the Act of Settlement, were ready to assist the son of James II (popularly called the "Old Pretender") to secure the throne. This gave the Whigs the opportunity of making their rivals very unpopular by denouncing them as Jacobites and traitors. They made the new Hanoverian king, George I, believe that he owed everything to the Whigs, and for a period of nearly fifty years, under George I (1714–1727) and George II (1727–1760), they were able to control Parliament.

As George I could speak no English, he soon ceased to attend the meetings of the cabinet and left the management of the government in its hands. When someone was needed to straighten out a difficult financial situation, Robert Walpole, who was noted for his ability with figures, was appointed First Lord of the Treasury and Chancellor of the Exchequer. Walpole, owing to his skill in handling the situation and to his general wisdom and reasonableness, soon rose to prominence and became the recognized leader of the cabinet.

George II also seldom met with his cabinet, trusting the management of affairs to Walpole, so that for twenty-one years, as spokesman of the group, Walpole was really prime minister. Walpole was affable, judicious, and cautious. His policy was to avoid war and to prevent party differences at home from causing trouble. In maintaining peace he was enabling the country to build up its business and trade and to grow in prosperity.

Corruption in Parliament. The Whig cabinet could remain in power so long as it could keep the Whig party in the majority in Parliament. In order to do this, Walpole did not hesitate to resort to a regular system of bribery to secure the votes necessary to carry through his measures and insure party control. It must be said that while Walpole shamelessly corrupted the members of Parliament by open bribery and influence, he was never known to accept a bribe himself.

George III attempts to rule Independently. George III, who
came to the throne in 1760, attempted to recover some of the
power enjoyed by former kings, — to rule as well as reign. He
did not like the cabinet system, and he succeeded in creating
a party of his own, known as the "King's Friends." He
adopted the Whig methods of using bribery and various forms
of graft to obtain the support of a little group which would
assist him in running the government as he wished. His
mother, a German princess, had taught him that he should
be a king like those on the Continent; and, in spite of the restrictions imposed by Parliament, he managed to rule in a
high-handed and headstrong way. It was during his reign
that the American colonies declared their independence of
the mother country, and there is no doubt that his tactless
manner in handling the situation was partly the cause of the
American Revolution (p. 845). During the war George III
was practically his own prime minister.

Parliament not really Representative of the People. England,
it is true, had made great progress toward representative government, but she had a great deal farther to go to reach what
is considered *representative* government today. While her Parliament, in the eighteenth century, was a famous body, it represented only a small portion of the English people. The
scheme of voting was very old-fashioned and unfair. There
were two representatives from every county and every
moderate-sized town. But as the list had not been revised
since the sixteenth century, many changes had taken place
which made the representation very unequal. Many towns,
for various reasons, had declined in size or disappeared altogether; yet the owners of the land were still able to send two
members to Parliament even if they represented only a few
houses or a stretch of fields or parkland where the town had
been. On the other hand, owing to the increase of manufacturing and business, new and flourishing centers had grown
up which had no representatives other than those for the
whole county in which the towns were located. The control of
Parliament was in the hands of a very few persons who had
great influence and who could dispose of government offices

as they desired. Moreover, only those who owned a certain amount of land had the privilege of voting. This, it will be seen, excluded the larger part of the middle class and all of the poorer people. Only a small portion of the English people therefore were fairly represented.

Seats in Parliament were bought and sold, and votes on measures could easily be influenced by money. Not only the government but the Church had yielded to the general practice; for church offices were often reserved for the nobility. The army and navy were also full of opportunities for graft.

Growing Demand for Reform. In spite of the progress that had been made, the English system was still an aristocracy, which did not represent the English nation as a whole. There was much discontent with the influence which the lords of great estates and the rich merchants enjoyed in Parliament. There was an increasing number of writers who pointed out to the people the defects in the English system. They urged that every man ought to have the right to share in the government by casting his vote and that the unwritten constitution of England should be written down and so made clear and unmistakable. Political clubs were founded, which entered into correspondence with political societies in France; newspapers and pamphlets poured from the press in enormous quantities, and reform found champions in the House of Commons.

The Younger Pitt. This demand for reform finally induced the younger Pitt (son of the Earl of Chatham), who was prime minister from 1783 to 1801, to introduce bills into the House of Commons for remedying some of the inequality in representation. But the violence of the French Revolution, which began in 1789, involved England in a long and tedious war. The disorder in France discouraged Englishmen who had formerly favored change, to say nothing of the Tories, who regarded with horror any proposal to give the people more power.

England had a Modern Free Government, but was not a Democracy. It is clear that England had a free government as compared with that of other European countries; for her king was master of neither the persons nor the purses of his subjects, nor could he issue arbitrary laws. Public affairs were discussed in newspapers and pamphlets, so that weighty matters of government could not be decided secretly in the king's palace, without the knowledge of the people. Nevertheless, it would be far from correct to regard the English system as democratic. A hereditary House of Lords could block any measure introduced in the House of Commons, and the House of Commons itself represented not the nation but a small minority of landowners and rich business men. Government offices were monopolized by members of the Established Church, and the poor were oppressed by cruel laws. Workingmen were prohibited from forming associations to promote their interests. It was more than a century after the accession of George III before the English farmer could go to the ballot box and vote for members of Parliament.

Yet England had already established a system which could be gradually improved as the vote was extended to one class after another. No revolution such as France suffered was necessary to create a modern democracy in England.

Questions and Exercises

Review of Chapter

1. Why did James I quarrel with Parliament? What were the two main difficulties between Charles I and Parliament? What other charter of liberties did the English have besides the Petition of Right? Describe the religious problems which became so acute in Charles I's reign. Why did the Puritans ally themselves with Parliament? What was the attitude of the English Church in the struggle between Parliament and king? What were the Star Chamber and the Court of High Commission? What circumstances led to the execution of the king?

2. What form of church government was substituted for the Anglican? Describe the government of the Commonwealth. Describe the personality and methods of Cromwell.

3. What promises did Charles II make before he was invited to become king? Describe Charles's relations with Parliament. What acts were passed to protect the Anglican Church? How did New York get its present name?

4. Why was James II unpopular? What led to the loss of his throne? How did William and Mary propose to remedy the situation? What are some of the provisions of the Bill of Rights?

5. What national questions were settled by the Revolution of 1688? Why did the government treat Dissenters more leniently than Catholics after the revolution? Give some reasons why England and France were on opposite sides in the European wars of the eighteenth century. How were England and Scotland finally united?

USEFUL TERMS

See how much meaning you can give to the following: *jurisdiction, fundamental, visitations, triennial, elaborate ceremonies, pillory, flogging, commonwealth, navigation, trade war, Dissenters, uniformity, nonconformity, Unitarian.*

DIRECTIVE QUESTIONS

1. Can you show the relationship on both sides of the family of the Stuarts to Henry VII? What relation was James I to Elizabeth?

2. What are some of the characteristics of a military rule?

3. What qualities of an absolute monarchy are always offensive to the English? Give earlier examples.

4. Why were the religious acts of Charles II's reign so intolerant?

5. Was England more tolerant in religious matters after the revolution than other European countries, such as Holland? What is the nature of the British constitution? What important documents does it include?

DISCUSSION TOPICS

1. The seventeenth century was an important period in the history of English government.

2. The Puritan régime was a very drab period.

3. The Lord Protector was really a dictator.

4. The English followed a very selfishly national policy in their shipping laws and competition with the Dutch.

5. The Bill of Rights affects the powers of the English sovereign today.

6. "A man should stick to his party, right or wrong."

ADDITIONAL ADVENTURES IN LEARNING

1. Studies in Source Materials. ROBINSON, *Readings*, Vol. II, chap. xxx, sect. i, 302, James's dislike of the Puritans; sect. ii.

"The Petition of Right"; sect. iii, "The Personal Government of Charles I; Religious Parties"; sect. iv, "The Early Acts of the Long Parliament"; sect. v, "The Civil War"; sect. vi, "The Execution of Charles I"; sect. vii, "The Commonwealth and Cromwell"; sect. viii, "The Restoration of the Stuarts: Charles II"; sect. ix, "Religious Questions under Charles II"; sect. x, "James II and the Revolution of 1688." CHEYNEY, *Readings in English History*, chap. xiv, "The Personal Monarchy of the Stuarts"; chap. xv, "The Great Rebellion and the Commonwealth"; chap. xvi, "Restoration and Revolution."

2. Supplementary. Find out what important countries have the cabinet system of government today. If a British cabinet's proposals are rejected by Parliament, the cabinet resigns. What happens in the United States under similar circumstances? What is the Union Jack? Can you draw one from memory?

3. Topical Studies. The theory of the "divine right of kings": ROBINSON, *Readings*, chap. xxx, sect. i, 303. The attitude of the government toward the Puritan Sunday: CHEYNEY, chap. xiv, 246; ROBINSON, *Readings*, chap. xxx, 308–309. What are "blue laws"? Oliver Cromwell: CHEYNEY, *A Short History of England*, chap. xv; FIRTH, *Oliver Cromwell*; JOHN BUCHAN, *Oliver Cromwell*.

CHAPTER XXXIII · THE ABSOLUTE MONARCHY OF LOUIS XIV

LOUIS XIV is the most perfect example of a monarch "by the grace of God." The Stuart kings of England had tried to make the English people believe in their "divine right" to rule as they saw fit. But after a long and tragic struggle they were forced to accept a crown whose powers were definitely limited by Parliament.

In France, however, two great cardinals of the Church had built up the royal power until the king was absolute master of his realm. Moreover, a famous bishop taught the people that this idea of government was drawn from the Scriptures themselves. He even asserted that anyone who criticized the king was finding fault with God himself; for the king is the very "image of God."

The wonder, then, is not that Louis believed himself to be a sort of God but that the French people accepted these ideas and so long paid for the extravagance and suffered the tyranny of their rulers. Eighty years after Louis's death, however, the French monarchy came to an awful end in a revolution which established in France the "rights of man."

We who live in a democracy can hardly realize what it meant to live under such oppression; but by the measure of our own liberty we can mark the advance of civilization since the time when men's lives and fortunes could be disposed of by an arbitrary ruler in the name of God.

1. THE KINGDOM THAT LOUIS XIV INHERITED

Louis XIV brings Absolute Monarchy to its Height. Under Louis XIV absolute monarchy reached its height. Never had it attained so perfect and full an expression. The kings of the Middle Ages, as we have seen, were usually little more than feudal lords and hardly more important than their great vassals, on whom they had to depend for their armies. For many centuries the kings struggled to get the better of their unruly nobles, and were successful only when they got hold of enough money to have a large standing army of their own. With this support they could build up a national state and manage its affairs from their palace.

Henry VII and Henry VIII of England were absolute monarchs, to be sure; for there were no nobles strong enough to dispute their power. But there was always Parliament in the background to consider. While that body was the obedient and loyal servant of the Tudor monarchs, it nevertheless remained a possible check and had often to be consulted. Moreover, a people who had once risen to demand its rights in a great charter had shown that it could, and if necessary would, oppose the actions of a too despotic sovereign.

What a Personal Monarchy meant. The government of Louis XIV, on the other hand, was a *personal* monarchy, that is, a government in which the king not only is the sole authority but also can dispose of the lives of his subjects, their money, and the welfare of the country without interference. Louis had no Parliament which could dispute his ideas or to which he must apply for funds. He carried on the business of state with the assistance of ministers whom he himself appointed to carry out his will without criticism or complaint. Everything centered in the king; his ideas, his desires, his projects, however foolish or dangerous, were the law of the land. So great an impression did such power and privilege make on the people of his times that a great French writer called a history of his reign "The Age of Louis XIV." In order to see how unlimited monarchy worked, let us first recall what kind of kingdom Louis inherited, then how he thought a monarch should live and govern, and, lastly, what things he desired which led him to make war on his neighbors.

How Two Great Cardinals had strengthened the French Monarchy. After the disastrous civil wars of the sixteenth century (Chap. XXXI), Henry IV and his able minister, Sully, had done much to restore the authority of the king and the prosperity of France. They had put down the ambitious nobles who had threatened the king; they had managed the finances of the realm wisely, encouraging manufactures, farming, and commerce.

It was Cardinal Richelieu, however, who, in the days of Louis XIII, laid the foundations of that policy which made the king supreme in France. With great shrewdness, audacity, and determination Richelieu gradually got the entire control of the government into the hands of the monarch. Richelieu refused to summon or consult the Estates-General, which had been dismissed in 1614. He encouraged the idea that their meetings were a hindrance rather than a help to the government, which, he claimed, could be conducted better by the appointees of the king than by a group of old-fashioned representatives of the classes in the realm. The king and his associates therefore controlled the entire administration of the state. The local assemblies that continued were largely useful in collecting taxes, and were managed by the king's great minister. Without a parliament, the king now had the power to levy taxes and to spend money without giving an account of what he did. A large standing army, paid and directed by the king, served to secure independence. The two sources of danger to the crown — the Huguenots and the nobles — Richelieu speedily dealt with. The Huguenots, who had developed into a political power of some importance, the cardinal left free as to their religious views, but deprived of their fortified towns and prohibited from holding assemblies. The nobles, who in some cases had been governors of provinces and had been able to have armies at their disposal and to collect taxes, were removed, and replaced by governors (*intendants*) appointed directly by the crown. All fortified castles of the nobility which were not needed for the protection of the country were destroyed. By a system of spies Richelieu was able to learn of any conspiracies against the royal power, and the conspirators were immediately put to death.

Richelieu's successor, Cardinal Mazarin, who was in charge of the government during Louis XIV's boyhood, carried forward the policy of his predecessor, and put down a last uprising of the discontented nobility. Therefore, when Louis came to the throne as actual ruler, the stage was already set for him to play the "grand monarch." This he did with such perfection and amid such grandeur that he became the envy and despair of every prince in Europe.

Louis believed in the Divine Right of Kings. Louis not only played the grand monarch with perfect mastery but believed he was divinely ordained to do so. He had the same idea of kingship that James I had tried in vain to make the English people accept. God had given kings to men, it was argued. It was His will that monarchs should be regarded as His representatives, and that all the king's subjects should be absolutely obedient without asking any questions or making any complaints; for in submitting to their prince they were really submitting to God himself. If the king was good and wise, his subjects should thank the Lord; if he proved foolish or cruel, they must nevertheless accept their evil ruler as a well-deserved punishment which God had sent them for their sins. But in no case might they limit his power or rise up against him.

English and French differed as to Absolute Monarchy. This theory of absolute monarchy had not been very well received in England. James had written it all out very carefully in his book *On the True Law of Monarchies*; but neither he nor his son and grandsons found that it would work successfully with Parliament.

Louis XIV had several advantages over James I. In the first place, the tradition of Parliament, the courts, and the various declarations of the people's rights in England made it impossible for the Stuarts to establish any claim to be absolute rulers. In France, however, the Estates-General had not met for forty-seven years when Louis began to rule, and a century and a quarter were still to pass before another call to the representatives of the nation was issued, in 1789. There was no strong feeling against the excessive authority of kingship, nor had the people ever voiced their grievances so effectively as had the English. There were no state documents showing what the people were entitled to enjoy in the way of rights or powers.

The French people depended more on their king than did the English. France was not protected by sea as England was. On every side France had neighbors who could take advantage of any disagreement between her king and Estates-

General to invade the country. So the French felt it best to leave all important questions to the king, even if the nation suffered at times from his tyranny.

Fig. 189. *Louis XIV*

From a painting by Rigaud at Versailles

Louis Looked and Acted like a King. Louis had another advantage over James I in making people believe that he was born to be a great king: as the saying is, he "looked the part." The memoirs of several persons who frequented his court give a very vivid description of the king. He was a handsome man, of "proportions such as a sculptor would choose to model." He had "the very figure of a hero," with a natural and impressive majesty in his slightest gestures; even when playing billiards he is said to have retained the air of a mighty monarch. Yet with all his dignity he had a grace which gave all his actions a singular charm. "He was," says the writer Saint-Simon, "as dignified and majestic in his dressing gown as when clad in robes of state or on horseback at the head of his troops." While James was awkward, and slouching in his gait, and talked in a stilted and tiresome way, Louis had "a perfect countenance and the grandest air and mien ever granted to men." He loved the out-of-doors and spent hours daily in exercise, braving every extreme of weather. There is small wonder that his belief in his own unusual powers and importance was shared by those who looked upon his commanding figure. Moreover, although not brilliant, Louis had a quick understanding. He said neither too much nor too little. He was industrious for a king and kept regular hours for work, attending personally to many of the details of government.

How Louis governed his Realms. The fact that Louis wished to keep personal control of all departments of state made it necessary for him to give far more energy and attention to the business of government than would have been necessary had he left affairs in the hands of his officials. Louis had able ministers; but he never permitted them to get too much power, nor did he like them to have too many independent ideas of their own. He would never have consented to be dominated by an adviser as his father had been by Richelieu.

Louis's vanity would hardly have permitted him to realize how much of the glory of his reign and the standing of France was due to the work of the gifted experts who surrounded him. Louvois, his war minister, is one of the most famous of military organizers. He recruited and maintained for France the largest and finest standing army in Europe. Vauban, a master engineer, built the great row of fortifications across the northern and eastern boundaries of the state. In Prince Condé and Turenne, Louis also had great generals to command his troops.

The Reforms of Colbert. Of all Louis's ministers, however, it was Colbert, the great finance minister, who did most for France. During Louis's reign Colbert held many important government offices, and in all of them he did brilliant work. He put an end to the wasting and stealing of large sums of government money by officials. He introduced a new system of bookkeeping which was more up to date, and he tried to appoint honest agents. He found that he could do little to correct the old system of taxation, which freed the nobility from payment yet permitted officials to extract every penny they could from the poor, defenseless peasants. But he introduced a system of customs duties in which the burden would fall more nearly alike on all classes. He promoted farming and protected the peasant against the loss of his implements when he got into debt. He improved roads and canals; he encouraged manufactures and inaugurated a strict government supervision over the quantity and quality of goods that were made. He introduced new industries and protected the rights of inventors. He established tariffs to keep out foreign goods that would compete with those made at home. He granted government money payments, or subsidies, to build up merchant shipping. He also sought to increase the navy and to secure colonies as a market for French manufactures.

2. MONARCHY AT ITS HEIGHT

Impression which Louis's Reign made. One of the chief reasons why Louis XIV's reign was so celebrated was that it was conducted amid such splendor as to give it the character of a pageant. Louis set the fashion for absolute monarchy on a scale which his fellow rulers could not hope to achieve. The importance which court life attained under Louis was something new. Other monarchs, such as the Tudors and Stuarts, had lived in luxury, but never had the court been so sumptuous nor the courtiers seemed so privileged as they now did, dwelling in a gay world of their own, far removed from the rest of the people and from the ordinary duties and responsibilities of life. The lavish display of the king's court at Versailles made a deep impression on other princes and their luxury-loving nobles. But the wasteful extravagance which it represented finally helped to destroy the power of the French kings.

The King's Palace at Versailles. Louis XIV was careful that his surroundings should suit the grandeur of his office. His court was magnificent beyond anything that had been dreamed of in the West. He had an enormous palace constructed at Versailles, about ten miles from Paris, with endless halls, reception rooms, and bedrooms, and a vast park stretching away behind it. About this a town was laid out where those lived who were privileged to be near His Majesty or to supply the wants of the royal court. This palace and its outlying buildings, including two or three less gorgeous residences

EUROPE

WHEN LOUIS XIV BEGAN

HIS PERSONAL GOVERNMENT

1661

Spanish Possessions
Austrian Possessions
Boundary of the Holy Roman Empire

0   100   200   300

Scale of Miles

Fig. 190. *The Palace at Versailles*

for the king when he occasionally tired of the pomp and ceremony of Versailles, probably cost the nation about a hundred million dollars, in spite of the fact that thousands of peasants and soldiers were forced to turn to and work without pay. The furnishings and decorations were as rich and costly as the palace was splendid, and still fill the visitor with wonder. For over a century this magnificent "château" at Versailles continued to be the home of the French kings and the seat of their government.

Life at Louis XIV's Court. This splendor and luxury helped to attract the nobility, who no longer lived on their estates in well-fortified castles, prepared to fight the king's troops. They now rejoiced in being the king's companions and waiting on him. They saw him to bed at night, and in stately procession they greeted him in the morning. It was thought a high honor to hand him his shirt as he was being dressed or, at dinner, to provide him with a fresh napkin. Only by living close to the king could the courtiers hope to gain favors, pensions, and well-paying offices for themselves and their friends, and, perhaps, occasionally to influence a little the policy of the government. For they were now entirely dependent upon the good will of their monarch.

Louis's Court vividly pictured by H. G. Wells. H. G. Wells, in his *Outline of History*, has given in a short space a very striking picture of the brilliance of the court at Versailles, and the luxuries which had to be manufactured in order to supply Louis's family and courtiers.

His great palace at Versailles, with its salons, its corridors, its mirrors, its terraces and fountains and parks and prospects, was the envy and admiration of the world. He provoked a universal imitation. Every king and princelet in Europe was building his own Versailles, as much beyond his means as his subjects and credits would permit. Everywhere the nobility rebuilt or extended their châteaux to the new pattern. A great industry of beautiful and elaborate fabrics and furnishings developed. The luxurious arts flourished everywhere: sculpture in alabaster, faïence, gilt woodwork, metal work, stamped leather, much music, magnificent painting, beautiful printing and bindings, fine cookery, fine vintages. Amidst the mirrors and fine

Fig. 191. *One of the Great Halls at Versailles*

furniture went a strange race of "gentlemen" in vast powdered wigs, silks and laces, poised upon high red heels, supported by amazing canes; and still more wonderful "ladies" under towers of powdered hair and wearing vast expansions of silk and satin sustained on wire. Through it all postured the great Louis, the sun of his world, unaware of the meager and sulky and bitter faces that watched him from those lower darknesses to which his sunshine did not penetrate.[1]

Louis XIV as a Patron of Art and Literature. Louis was wise enough to know that it was part of the business of a grand monarch to be the gracious patron of art, literature, and learning and to make his court the center of the great talents of the day. Molière, who was at once a writer of plays and an actor, delighted the court with comedies in which he gently poked fun at people's vanity and foolish ways. Corneille, who had gained renown by the celebrated tragedy of *The Cid* in Richelieu's time, found a worthy successor in Racine, the most distinguished, perhaps, of French tragic

---

[1] H. G. Wells, *The Outline of History*, Vol. II, p. 238. The Macmillan Company, 1920.

poets. The charming letters of Madame de Sévigné are beautifully written and serve at the same time to give us a glimpse of life at court. In the famous memoirs of Saint-Simon the weaknesses of the king, as well as the numberless intrigues of the courtiers, are freely exposed with rare skill and wit.

Men of letters were generously aided by the king with pensions. Colbert encouraged the French Academy, which had been created by Richelieu. This body gave special attention to making the French tongue more eloquent and expressive by selecting what words should be used. It is now the greatest honor that a Frenchman can obtain to be made one of the forty members of this association. A magazine which still exists, the *Journal des Savants*, was founded at this time for the promotion of science. Colbert had an astronomical observatory built at Paris; and the Royal Library, which possessed only about sixteen thousand volumes, began to grow into that vast collection of about four million volumes — one of the largest in existence — which today attracts scholars to Paris from all parts of the world. In short, Louis XIV and his ministers believed one of the chief objects of any government was to aid and encourage artists, writers, and men of science.

3. Why Louis made War on his Neighbors

The Dark Side of the Picture. There was a darker side to this bright picture which Louis, dazzled by his surroundings, could not see. The same writer, Saint-Simon, who describes the king's fine appearance also gives an account of his unlimited vanity. He tells how the king relished the silly flattery of his courtiers, how he enjoyed the verses and pictures which represented him in some heroic pose, and how he believed his own judgment to be superior to that of any of his ministers. All this explains why he made such fatal mistakes.

Besides, the king was very ambitious, and his ambitions were by no means always peaceful. Instead of being content with his own fair realms and devoting his energy to increasing their strength and prosperity, he did quite the reverse. Not only did he waste on himself and his nobility the vast sums which his ministers collected but he turned to war as a means of still further increasing his glory. He coveted the lands of his neighbors, much of which belonged to the rival family of Hapsburg. He began to invent all sorts of claims to adjoining territory, and finally, in the latter part of his reign, dragged France through many years of war and almost into bankruptcy.

Louis desires Natural Boundaries for France. Louis was very proud of his fine army and his great generals. He began to think he might be able to realize the dream of his ancestors to extend the kingdom to the ancient boundaries of Gaul in the time of Cæsar. The "natural limits" of France appeared to be the river Rhine on the north and east, the Jura Mountains and the Alps on the southeast, and to the south the Mediterranean Sea and the snow-capped Pyrenees. Richelieu had believed that it was the chief task of his ministry to restore to France the boundaries established for it by nature. Mazarin had tried hard to win Savoy and Nice and to reach the Rhine on the north. Before his death France at least gained Alsace and reached the Pyrenees (map, p. 776).

The Invasion of the Spanish Netherlands (1667). Louis XIV first turned his attention to the conquest of the Spanish Netherlands. He claimed that the region rightly belonged to his wife, the elder sister of the Spanish king, Charles II (1665–1700). He easily took a number of towns on the border of the Netherlands and then turned south and completely conquered Franche-Comté. This was an outlying province of Spain, isolated from her other lands, and a tempting morsel for the hungry king of France. These conquests alarmed Europe, especially Holland, which could not afford to have the barrier between itself and France removed; for Louis XIV would be an uncomfortable neighbor. A Triple Alliance, composed of Holland, England, and Sweden, was accordingly organized to stop Louis's advance and force him to make peace with Spain. Louis satisfied himself for the moment with the dozen border towns which he had taken and which Spain ceded to him on condition that he would return Franche-Comté.

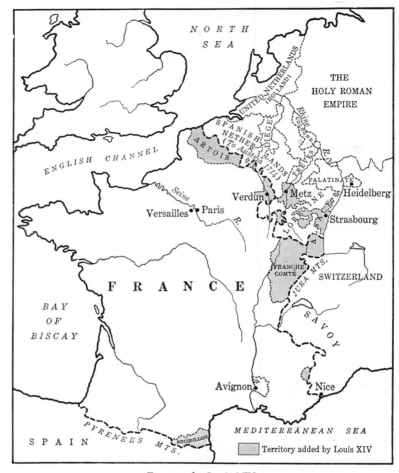

France under Louis XIV

Louis XIV breaks up the Triple Alliance. The success with which Holland had managed, by calling in England and Sweden, to bring the proud king of France to a halt produced much joy in that tiny country. This was very irritating to Louis XIV. He was thoroughly vexed that he should have been blocked by so trifling an obstacle as the Dutch. He consequently conceived a strong dislike for Holland, which was increased by the protection that it afforded to writers who annoyed him with their attacks. Moreover, Louis looked with envy on the successful trade and colonial ventures of the Dutch. He broke up the Triple Alliance by bribing Charles II of England to sign a secret treaty which pledged England to help France in a new war against the Dutch (p. 748).

Louis XIV's Invasion of Holland (1672). Louis XIV then startled Europe again by seizing the duchy of Lorraine, which brought him to the border of Holland. At the head of a hundred thousand men he crossed the Rhine (1672) and easily conquered southern Holland. For the moment the Dutch cause appeared to be lost. But William of Orange showed the spirit of his great ancestor William the Silent: the sluices in the dikes were opened and the country flooded, so that the French army was checked before it could take Amsterdam and advance into the north. The emperor sent an army against Louis, and the English Parliament compelled Charles II to break off the French alliance and make peace with Holland.

When a general peace was concluded (1678), at the end of six years, the chief provisions were that Holland should be left as it was and that France should this time retain Franche-Comté, which had been conquered by Louis XIV in person. This bit of the Spanish possessions thus became at last a part of France, after France and Spain had quarreled over it for a century and a half. For the ten years following there was no open war, but Louis seized the important free city of Strassburg and made many other less striking but equally unjustifiable additions to his territory.

He had pushed his frontier nearer the Rhine, but at heavy cost. The treasury was empty, and Colbert was nearly distracted in trying to raise money by taxes and foreign loans. Louis, however, was untroubled by such difficulties as long as his armies could remain the talk and terror of Europe.

How Louis treated his Protestant Subjects. Louis XIV revealed as woeful a want of statesmanship in the treatment of his Protestant subjects as in the waging of disastrous wars.

The Huguenots had turned to manufacture, trade, and banking; "as rich as a Huguenot" had become a common saying in France. There were perhaps a million of them among fifteen million Frenchmen, and they undoubtedly formed the most thrifty and enterprising part of the nation. The Catholic clergy, however, did not cease to urge the complete suppression of the Protestants.

Revocation of the Edict of Nantes, and its Results. Louis XIV had scarcely taken the reins of government into his own hands before the perpetual nagging and injustice to which the Protestants had been subjected at all times took a more serious form. Upon one pretense or another their churches were demolished. Rough troopers were sent to live in the houses of the Huguenots, with the hope that the insulting behavior of the soldiers might frighten the Protestant "heretics" into accepting the religion of the king.

At last Louis XIV was led by his officials to believe that practically all the Huguenots had been converted by these harsh measures. In 1685, therefore, he revoked and annulled the Edict of Nantes, granted the Huguenots for their protection in 1598 by their friend Henry IV (p. 713). The Protestants thereby became outlaws and their ministers subject to the death penalty. Thousands of the Huguenots succeeded in escaping from the country and fled, some to England, some to Prussia, some to America, carrying with them their skill and industry to strengthen France's rivals. This was the last great and terrible example in western Europe of that fierce religious intolerance which had produced the Spanish Inquisition and the Massacre of St. Bartholomew.

Louis attacks the Palatinate. Louis XIV now set his heart upon conquering the Palatinate, a Protestant land on the Rhine, to which he easily invented a claim. The rumor of his plan, and the indignation aroused in Protestant countries by the revocation of the Edict of Nantes, resulted in an alliance against the French king headed by William of Orange. Louis speedily justified the suspicions of Europe by a frightful devastation of the Palatinate, burning whole towns and destroying many castles, including the beautiful one of the elector at Heidelberg. Ten years later, however, Louis agreed to a peace which put things back as they had been before the struggle began. He was preparing for the final and most ambitious undertaking of his life, which precipitated the longest and bloodiest war of all his warlike reign.

4. How Louis Secured a Crown and Lost an Empire

The Question of the Spanish Succession. The fourth and last of Louis's wars is the most important because of its effects on later history. In his eagerness to secure a crown for his grandson Louis involved France in a war which put an end to the possibility of her building an empire in the New World. It was her rival, England, who emerged victorious from the conquest and began to command the seas and to found a vast colonial empire in America and India.

The king of Spain, Charles II, had neither children nor brothers, and Europe had long been discussing what would become of his vast realms when his sickly life should come to an end. For while Spain no longer had the wealth that she possessed when Philip II came to the throne, the last feeble representative of the Spanish Hapsburgs had some twenty-two crowns to dispose of (p. 630).

Louis XIV had married the elder sister of Charles II; the emperor Leopold, a younger sister. These two rulers had both been considering for some time how they might divide the Spanish possessions of Charles between them. The matter was also one of keen interest not only to those who hoped to profit by the poor king's death but to all Europe. For it was easily seen that if France gained the Spanish crown a great Bourbon monarchy would be established in western Europe, whereas if Leopold inherited his cousin's dominions he would have an empire as vast as that of Charles V. Nor was this all. The over-sea colonies of Spain joined to those of France would create a real empire in the New World, and the monopoly of trade which would be established would strike a fatal blow at the commercial and colonial ambitions of the English and Dutch. It was therefore to the interest of these nations, especially England, to see that the balance of power was maintained; that is, that no country on the continent became dangerously powerful.

Louis XIV had great skill in diplomacy. Although Spain had been the victim of Louis's earlier wars, he was able to make himself so agreeable to the Spanish monarch that when Charles died it was found he had made Philip, the grandson of Louis XIV, heir to the Spanish throne, on condition that France and Spain should never be united.

Philip of Anjou becomes King of Spain. There now arose a momentous decision for Louis to make. Should he permit his grandson to accept the coveted crown which would place the Bourbon family in control of western Europe from Holland to Sicily, as well as give them a great part of North and South America? Or should he refuse to take the chances? Louis knew that the emperor and the ever-watchful William of Orange, now king of England (p. 750), would never permit this extension of French influence. They had already shown themselves ready to make great sacrifices in order to check far less serious aggressions on the part of the French king. Nevertheless, family pride led Louis criminally to risk the welfare of his country. He accepted the will and informed the Spanish ambassador at the French court that he might salute Philip V as his new king. The leading French newspaper of the time boldly proclaimed that the Pyrenees were no more.

The War of the Spanish Succession. King William of England soon succeeded in forming a new Grand Alliance (1701), in which Louis's old enemies, England, Holland, and the emperor, were the most important members. William himself died just as fighting began, but Queen Anne (1702–1714) carried on vigorously the long War of the Spanish Succession. The great English general, the Duke of Marlborough, and the Austrian commander, Eugene of Savoy, drove the French out of the Netherlands, the Holy Roman Empire, and Italy; even in America there was fighting between French and

English colonists, which is known in American histories as Queen Anne's War. All the more important battles went against the French; and after ten years of war, which was rapidly ruining France by the destruction of its people and its wealth, Louis XIV was willing to consider some compromise. After long discussion a peace was arranged in 1713.

The Treaty of Utrecht (1713). The Treaty of Utrecht changed the map of Europe as no previous treaty had done, — not even that of Westphalia. Each of the chief combatants got his share of the Spanish booty over which they had been fighting. The Bourbon Philip V was permitted to retain Spain and its colonies on condition that the Spanish and French crowns should never be united.

To Austria fell the Spanish Netherlands, hereafter called the Austrian Netherlands, which continued to serve as a barrier between Holland and France. Austria also received the Spanish possessions in Italy (Naples and Milan), which established a hold on Italy lasting down to 1866.

Holland won back certain barrier fortresses protecting her against France.

The elector of Brandenburg was recognized as "King in Prussia." This provision will be of special interest when we follow, in the next chapter, the way in which the Hohenzollern family built up Prussia and finally became the rulers of a new German Empire.

England gained most from the war. From Spain she received the island of Minorca and Gibraltar, which has permitted her from that time to the present to command the narrow entrance to the Mediterranean Sea. Her principal gains were not in Europe, however, but in the New World, where she obtained Newfoundland, Nova Scotia, and the Hudson Bay region and so began to push the French out of North America.

France at the End of Louis XIV's Reign. Although France lost no territory, she was practically ruined at the end of the war. Its cost had emptied the treasury and brought the people to the depths of poverty. There followed a marked increase in taxes. the currency was debased, and the king-

EUROPE

AFTER THE TREATIES OF
UTRECHT AND RASTADT
1713 - 1714

Austria and its possessions

Prussia and its possessions

Boundary of the Empire

Scale of miles
0   100   200   300

Europe after the Treatie

KINGDOM OF
DENMARK
AND
NORWAY

Copenhagen

KINGDOM OF
SWEDEN

BALTIC SEA

Stralsund

SWEDISH POMERANIA

Königsberg

PRUSSIA

Bremen
Verden

PRUSSIA

Berlin

Vistula

P O L A N D

Hannover

Osnabrück

SAXONY

SILESIA

BOHEMIA

Prague

R.

THE EMPIRE

ELECTORATE
OF
BAVARIA

Rastadt
Blenheim

Strasbourg

Munich

MORAVIA
ARCH. DUCHY
OF
AUSTRIA

Vienna

Buda Pest

KINGDOM OF HUNGARY

TRANSYLVANIA

Baden

ERLAND

TYROL

Temesvar

DUCHY OF MILAN
(To Austria)

REPUBLIC OF
VENICE

Venice

Danube

R.

Piacenza

MONT.

D. OF
PARMA

REP. OF GENOA

Genoa

D. OF
MODENA

STATES OF THE CHURCH

Lucca
Florence

GR. D.
OF
TUSCANY

Ragusa

Cattaro

OTTOMAN

DOMINIONS

CORSICA

Rome

N A P L E S
(To Austria)

Naples

SARDINIA
(To Austria)
(later, 1720, to Savoy)

MOREA

Palermo

Messina

R

R

A

SICILY
(To Savoy)
(later, 1720, to Austria)

CANDIA

N

E

A

N

S E A

C A

of Utrecht and Rastadt

dom was bankrupt. Such was the condition of France when the magnificent Louis, after a reign of seventy-two years, handed on his country to his great-grandson Louis XV. This is what *absolute monarchy* had done to the prosperous and influential country which Cardinal Mazarin had turned over to his young king in 1661. Thus closed the record of the most glorious of all monarchs "by the grace of God."

Questions and Exercises

REVIEW OF CHAPTER

1. What is meant by absolute monarchy? Contrast the position of Louis XIV and the Stuarts in regard to their power. What had become of the Estates-General in France? How did Louis get the money to support his palace and court? Where did the nobles obtain money?

2. Describe the court at Versailles. What did Louis do to encourage art and literature?

3. What were the reasons lying behind the warlike enterprises of Louis? Why did Louis wage war upon the Dutch? What was one of the results of Louis's treatment of the Huguenots?

4. Make a list of the four great wars of Louis XIV and set down what he achieved from each and what he lost. What was the most disastrous effect of the War of the Spanish Succession? Contrast the position of France at Louis's accession and at his death.

USEFUL TERMS

See how much meaning you can give to the following: *autocracy, democracy, absolute monarchy, revocation, patron, mien, château, Triple Alliance, succession, monopoly.*

DIRECTIVE QUESTIONS

1. Why did France and England differ in the history of their theories of government?

2. What is the difference between an absolute monarch and a constitutional monarch? What form of monarchy has Great Britain today? What form of government has France?

3. What disadvantages might there be to such an interference in business by the government as Colbert instituted?

4. What earlier instances can you give of the sacred character of kingship?

1. Constitutional monarchy is an advance over absolute monarchy.

2. The persecution of the Huguenots was an injury to the welfare of France.

3. All countries should have "natural boundaries."

4. Louis XIV helped to prepare the way for a great revolt against monarchy.

1. Studies in Source Materials. ROBINSON, *Readings*, Vol. II, chap. xxxi, sect. i, How Richelieu strengthened the French monarchy; sect. ii, The theory of "divine right" as set forth by Bishop Bossuet; sect. iii, "Colbert and his Work"; sect. iv, An Englishman's description of France in the first part of Louis XIV's reign; sect. v, How the Prince of Condé entertained Louis; 340, "Saint-Simon's portrait of Louis XIV"; sect. vi, How Louis treated the Huguenots; sect. vii, "How the War of the Spanish Succession came about"; 344, Louis proclaims Philip of Anjou king of Spain.

2. Topical Studies. Richelieu and Mazarin: ROBINSON (reference above); HAYES, *Modern Europe*, Vol. I, chap. vi; PERKINS, *Richelieu* and *France under Mazarin*. The work of Colbert: ROBINSON (reference above); HAYES, *Modern Europe*, Vol. I, chap. vi. The Huguenots: ROBINSON (reference above); WAKEMAN, *The Ascendancy of France*, chap. xi; HASSALL, *Louis XIV*, chap. ix.

CHAPTER XXXIV · HOW RUSSIA, AUSTRIA, AND PRUSSIA BECAME GREAT POWERS

YOU have doubtless often seen in the newspapers references to "European powers," "great powers," or "small powers," meaning European states, great or small. The word *power* for "government" or "state" would not have been appropriate in feudal times; for there was then no central government strong enough to represent an entire kingdom. But with the development of our modern national states "power" has become a familiar term. It signifies that the state is unified so that its government acts for it and negotiates with other states. Moreover, because the powers can act and express their will as if they were individuals, we sometimes speak of them as if they were persons. So we see such expressions as "America thinks" or "France feels" or "Great Britain will not tolerate" an act. This is a careless way of speaking; for no body of persons can actually all be of one mind. The meaning is that the government of these countries has taken a definite stand, or that majority public opinion is this or that, according as it is expressed in the newspapers or perhaps by the votes of the people.

We have already seen how France and England developed into strong national states. The eighteenth century saw the rise of three other important powers in central and eastern Europe — Russia, Austria, and Prussia. These powers still belong to the great family of European nations.

In order to understand the serious problems in Europe today we must learn something of how these powers grew up and of how they dealt with one another; for international policy is greatly influenced by long-standing habits of friendship or enmity between nations. In seeing how old is the tradition of settling quarrels by war we may understand why it is so difficult to achieve the security of permanent peace in Europe.

1. THE DEVELOPMENT OF RIVAL POWERS IN EUROPE

How Feudal Kingdoms grew into National States. In feudal times, as we know, the kings were kept busy fighting their warring nobles and trying to regain possession of the land which had formerly been their own. When, in the later Middle Ages, they had conquered their rebellious vassals and had made their power supreme in their kingdoms, they established standing armies, paid by the crown, which could be relied upon to fight their battles.

Having achieved unity in their disorderly kingdoms, they were then free to look about them to see how they might enlarge their territories and increase the importance of their realms. We have already seen how England built up a strong national government, and how France, under the guidance of her shrewd ministers of state, had by the time of Louis XIV come to occupy the leading place in European affairs. Louis, however, was not content with the fair kingdom he inherited but was ever looking around to see how he might extend its boundaries and thus gain more "glory" for France. Louis set a pattern which became the ambition of every less fortunate prince in Europe.

Europe permanently Divided: Nationalism. It was the fate of Europe not to remain one great empire bound together by allegiance to an emperor at Rome. On the contrary, its lands were to be fought over for centuries and to pass back and forth through countless hands. By the eighteenth century the old ideal of a universal Empire and a universal Church had been given up. It was evident that Europe was to be permanently divided into national states with an ever-increasing feeling of separateness, or *nationalism*, between them, — a feeling which encouraged and promoted a growing attitude of rivalry toward one another. Indeed, so great was the fear of empire that various alliances had already been formed, during times of war, to maintain the "balance of power," that is, to prevent any one state from creating too large and dangerous a realm.

With the development of strong national states in the eighteenth century, the map of Europe began to look much more as it does today. In central and eastern Europe three powers emerged which have remained important states down to our own time. Under Frederick the Great the kingdom of Prussia became the most important power in northern

Europe; this was to become the center of modern Germany. The possessions of the Hapsburgs in central Europe were growing into the Austro-Hungarian Empire, which lasted till the World War. Under Peter the Great, Russia began to push westward and to transform itself from an Oriental into a European power.

How the Monarchs Viewed themselves. There were in the eighteenth century certain "political theories," or ideas of government, which were shared by all monarchs alike. We should know what some of these were; for many persisted for a long time before they were given up, while others have continued to our own day.

The eighteenth-century rulers believed rather generally that they held their office with divine approval and that they were therefore responsible to God rather than to their subjects for their actions. They believed in *autocracy*, that is, the supreme right of the ruler to do as he pleased, with no check put upon him. They believed they should do what was best for their subjects, but that they themselves must decide what this was, regardless of what their people thought or wished. Moreover, they should have the power of life and death over those whom they ruled. They looked upon their kingdoms almost as a personal possession, and this possession was to be handed down as a hereditary gift in their own family. As long as these ideas prevailed, it is easy to see that the fortunes of a state depended on the wisdom or foolishness of its ruler. And it was the ambition of most rulers to have their realms grow in size and importance at whatever cost.

How Monarchs Dealt with One Another. There were various ways by which the monarchs set about to achieve these ends. One was through the marriage of the members of their family with other reigning families so that their realms might be consolidated. Another was through bargaining, — making treaties and forming alliances, — in which they employed a good deal of intrigue, trying to outwit one another. These negotiations between governments are generally called *diplomacy*. Then they readily resorted to war on the slightest pretext, as the easiest way to settle difficulties, and they believed thoroughly in the rights of the conqueror, that "might is right."

Naturally they came into frequent conflict. So the eighteenth century, like those before it, is a story of wars. We cannot hope to remember all that were fought or what they were about. We shall speak of only a few of the more important ones, — ones that had a lasting effect on the future of Europe. These will be enough to show the nature of what is called the "great game of politics," — a game which is very old and still goes on. As one looks back it seems as if these monarchs, as well as many others, had used Europe as a gaming board around which they sat ever watchful. Each power played its hand, using its army, its navy, its money, or its diplomacy to gain an advantage over its opponents. The stakes of the game were more land, more power, more glory. Let us see how these great powers, Austria, Russia, and Prussia, entered the game and how they played their hands.

2. RUSSIA BECOMES A WESTERN STATE

The Slavic Peoples. We have had little occasion so far to speak of the Slavic peoples, to whom the Russians, Poles, and many other nations of eastern Europe belong. Yet together they form the most numerous race in Europe, and those who use the Slavic languages number about one hundred and fifty million people. We must turn now to a study of the greatest of these Slavic countries, Russia; for, from this time on, Russia plays an ever more important part in world affairs.

The Slavs, whose language is one of the Indo-European group to which Greek, Latin, Celtic, and German also belong, were settled along the Dnieper, Don, and Vistula rivers, in what is now southwestern Russia, as early as the beginning of the Christian Era. After the East Goths pushed their way into the Roman Empire (p. 379), the Slavs followed their example and invaded and conquered a great part of southeastern Europe. When the Lombards moved south into Italy, the Slavs pressed behind them into the eastern Alps, where they still live to the north of the Adriatic Sea. There are three main branches of Slavs: (1) the **Russians**; (2) the group lying between Russia and Germany, which includes Poles, Bohemians (Czechs), Moravians, and Slovaks; (3) the Balkan Slavs, now to be found in Yugoslavia and Bulgaria.

The "Slavic Peril." By that shifting of peoples which we found to be so characteristic of the human race when we studied the "barbarian invasions" (pp. 369–371), the Slavs moved from their earlier settlements westward into Russia and Europe, spreading in all directions and increasing in number. Today they occupy a large part of eastern Europe. The map (p. 791) shows the territory already occupied by Slavs. Since to the east there is the vast Slavic population of Russia, Europeans have feared lest the Slavs advance in overwhelming numbers. Hence there has been much talk in recent years of the "Slavic peril."

Beginnings of Russia. The greatest of all Slavic empires, Russia, began by the gradual expansion to the north and east of the tribes living on the eastern slopes of the Carpathian Mountains. These tribes pushed their way through the forests of central Russia, made clearings, and founded settlements that became villages and later grew into towns.

We cannot follow the history of these Slavic tribes through the centuries nor tell of their many wars with other nomadic tribes who overran the country from time to time. As early as the ninth century, however, we know that bands of Northmen — those bold adventurers of whose exploits we read on page 426 — invaded the districts east of the Baltic Sea. These enterprising Northmen — Swedes in this case — followed the great waterways of western Russia and found their way south to the Black Sea. They founded trading stations and settlements, and in the later tenth century we find that they hired themselves to the emperor at Constantinople as soldiers of his bodyguard. The Swedish invaders had great influence in the development of Russia; for the early Russian rulers mentioned in the chronicles of the time have Swedish rather than Slavic names. It is from *Rous* or *Rus*, the name of one of their tribes, that Russia is supposed to derive its name.

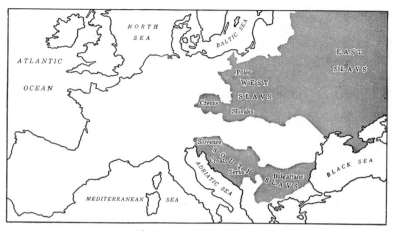

Slav Penetration into Europe

Greek Church established in Russia. The first Russian ruler whom we need mention is Vladimir the Great (980–1015). Vladimir married the sister of the emperor at Constantinople and accepted Christianity. In this way Russia was brought under the Eastern, or Greek, Church. For two centuries the officials of the Russian Church were Greeks, and the Patriarch of Constantinople rather than the Pope at Rome was the head of the Church. The contact now so fully established between the rulers of Russia and Constantinople might have led to a rapid advance in Russian civilization had it not been for a great disaster which put Russia back for centuries.

The Mongol Invasions. Russia is geographically nothing more than an extension of the vast plain of northern Asia, which the Russians were destined finally to conquer. It was therefore exposed to the great invasion of the Mongols, who swept in from the east in the thirteenth century. The powerful Mongol ruler, Genghis Khan (1162–1227), conquered northern China and central Asia, and the bands of fierce horsemen sent by his successors crossed into Europe and overran Russia, which had fallen apart into numerous principalities. The Russian princes became the dependents of the Great Khan and had frequently to visit his far-distant court, some three thousand miles away, where he might, as he chose, give them crowns or cut off their heads. The Mongols required tribute of the Russians, but left them undisturbed in their laws and religion.

Influence of the Mongol Occupation on Russia. Of the Russian princes who went to prostrate themselves at the foot of the Great Khan's throne, none made a more favorable impression upon him than the prince of Moscow, in whose favor the Khan was wont to decide all disputes between the prince and his rivals. When the Mongol power had begun to decline in strength and the princes of Moscow had grown more powerful, they ventured to refuse to pay tribute any longer and thus freed themselves from the Mongol yoke. The Mongol occupation had left its mark, however; for the princes of Moscow imitated the khans and the emperors at Constantinople rather than the rulers of western Europe, of whom, in fact, they knew nothing. The costumes and etiquette of the court seem to have come from Constantinople. The Russian armor suggested that of the Chinese, and their headdress was a turban.

Russia becomes a Free Monarchy. Under Ivan the Great (1462–1505) and his successors Russia began to take the form of a united monarchy. The yoke of the Mongols was thrown off (1480), the country greatly extended in size, and its vast territories brought under the direct control of the duke at Moscow. Moreover, the Russian Church achieved its independence from Constantinople. The Byzantine Church had yielded in 1439 to the influence of the Pope at Rome, and in 1453 the capital itself had fallen into the hands of the Turks (p. 626). Moscow now claimed, therefore, to be the "third Rome" and its patriarch the head of the true church of Orthodox Greek Christians. Ivan the Terrible (1533–1584) had himself crowned Tsar, which was the equivalent of king or emperor.[1] He deprived the nobles of much of their power

---

[1] The word "Tsar," or "Czar," is derived from *Caesar* (German, *Kaiser*), but was used in Slavic books for the title of the kings of antiquity as well as for the Roman emperors. Peter the Great called himself *Imperator*; that is, "Emperor." The Tsar was also known as "Autocrat of all the Russias."

by taking from them their *hereditary* lands and giving them other estates in their place. He made their service to the crown compulsory. He introduced many reforms in the administration of the government and in the collection of taxes, all with a view to making his own power absolute. He enforced his authority with such cruelty and bloodshed that his reign was a nightmare of terror.

FIG. 192. *Peter the Great*
After a painting by Kneller

The Romanovs (1613–1917). After the reign of Ivan the Terrible the country passed through a period of civil war and anarchy which was finally ended by the election of a new Tsar, Michael, a member of the family of Romanov. The choice of Michael was important; for it brought to the throne the Romanov family, which ruled Russia for three hundred years, down to the great revolution in 1917. The most noted of the Romanovs was Peter I, the grandson of Michael, who ascended the throne in 1682. It was Peter who determined to change Russia from an Oriental to a Western country and bring it into the family of European nations.

Peter I becomes Tsar of Russia. Peter I (reigned 1682–1725) was a very giant, seven feet tall, strong, and active. He combined shrewd, practical good sense with some idealism and a good deal of the coarsest brutality. Although he himself had little education, he had great respect for learning. As a boy, he was much interested in mechanics and especially in everything that had to do with ships. He learned how to build boats with his own hands. Never idle a moment, he worked hard at government, yet spent hours at drinking bouts in the lowest company.

Peter makes Russia a European Power. At the time of Peter's accession, Russia was still a backward country and was looked upon by Europeans as a semibarbarous state. Although much had been done by his predecessors in laying the foundation of a central government, Russian manners and customs were still Oriental, and the country remained almost entirely unaffected by the progress in government, military affairs, manufacture, learning, science, and art which had been made in Europe. Moreover, Russia still had no outlet to the sea. Peter realized that his kingdom was very much behind the countries of western Europe and his government much like that of a Mongol prince. He had no objection to the despotic power that fell to him, but he knew that his crudely equipped soldiers could never cope with the well-armed and well-disciplined troops of Western states. Without a seaport and ships Russia could not gain trade nor take part in world affairs. Peter therefore determined to introduce Western institutions and habits into his barbarous realms and to "make a window," as he expressed it, through which Russia might look abroad.

Peter's Travels in Europe. In 1697–1698 Peter, under a disguise, joined a commission which was visiting Europe in the hope of securing help for Russia against the Turks. While the commission had no success, Peter himself had an opportunity to visit Germany, Holland, and England and to learn about every art and science in which he was interested, as well as about the newer methods of manufacture, from the making of a man-of-war to the etching of an engraving. Nothing escaped the keen eyes of this rough, half-savage northern giant. For a week he put on the wide breeches of a Dutch laborer and worked in the shipyard at Zaandam, near Amsterdam. In England, Holland, and Germany he engaged workmen, scientific men, architects, ship captains, and experts in artillery and in the training of troops, all of whom he took back with him to aid in the reform and development of Russia.

Peter was called home by a revolt of Russian nobles, the *Streltzi*, or royal bodyguard. He took a fearful revenge upon the rebels and is said to have himself cut off the heads of many of them. Like the barbarian that he was, he left their bodies lying about all winter, unburied, in order to make the terrible results of revolt against his power quite plain to all.

Peter makes the Power of the Tsar Absolute in Russia. Peter now determined to make his power absolute throughout his realms. He therefore began by abolishing the *Streltzi* and creating a strong military machine upon which he could depend. He recruited a large standing army directly under his control. He had his troops trained and disciplined by foreign officers responsible to him alone. He reorganized the country into provinces, each under the management of a military officer whose business it was to see that sufficient taxes were collected in his district to support a certain number of regiments. He abolished all local self-government and brought the country under the oversight of the Tsar's own appointed officials. The old assembly of nobles, the duma, was replaced by an advisory council of nobles appointed by Peter himself.

In making himself absolute "autocrat" of Russia, Peter determined to have no trouble with the Church. He therefore made it virtually a department of state. The patriarch of Moscow was removed as head of the Church, and a "Holy Synod" was created, to whose care was intrusted the oversight of all religious activities in Russia. This body was appointed by Peter, and its members were directly responsible to the Tsar.

The Condition of the Serfs. The peasant farmers in Russia had formerly been free to move about from one place to another, especially if they had settled all their debts to their landlords. As time went on, however, their condition had changed ; for many of them were unable to keep up their rents and so fell into the control of the landowners. Sometimes, when they could not pay the heavy taxes, the farmers handed over their little property to the Church or to a noble and became tenants. In the early seventeenth century a number of decrees were passed which deprived the peasants of their former freedom to go where they wished and which set a strict watch on the payments of their debts. So it was that the serfs became merely a part of the lord's estate, to be sold or exchanged along with the land itself. This reduced them to virtual slavery.

The laws of Peter the Great served to fasten this state of affairs on the people and to cause an ever-widening gap between the rights and privileges of the upper classes and the miserable lot of the serfs. The latter had no way of protecting themselves and were often illtreated by their masters, having to submit to flogging and other bodily punishment, and even torture.

Peter Westernizes his Realms. Peter determined to give a European appearance as well as organization to Russia. He made his people give up their cherished Oriental beards and long, flowing garments and wear costumes like those of the Europeans. He forced the women of the richer classes, who had been kept in Oriental seclusion, to come out and meet the men in social assemblies, such as were common in the West. He invited foreigners to settle in Russia and sent young Russians abroad to study.

Peter gains an Outlet to the Sea. Peter realized that, above all, he must gain for Russia some land bordering on the sea. He looked with longing eyes toward the Black Sea. But in this direction he was confronted by the Ottoman Turks. While he was not destined to have much success against this formidable power, he was able to gain a much desired shore line on the Baltic. The provinces which Peter desired lay between the Russian boundary and the Baltic Sea. These belonged to Sweden, which happened to have at that time a very warlike and energetic young monarch, Charles XII. This spirited young ruler filled Europe with astonishment for a time by engaging in war with Denmark, Poland, and Russia and gaining many surprising victories. But his attempt to penetrate into Russia was unsuccessful, for his army was defeated. Charles managed to escape into Turkish territory but was unable to get sufficient aid from the Sultan

Russia, Showing Territory added by Peter and Catherine the Great

to gain a victory over the Tsar's forces. Peter's plans to reach the Baltic were delayed by the young Swedish ruler; but three years after Charles's death (1718) Peter forced Sweden to cede to him Livonia, Estonia, and other Swedish territory which had previously cut Russia off from the sea.

Peter founds a New Capital at St. Petersburg. Finding that the capital, Moscow, clung persistently to its ancient habits, Peter built a fine new capital for his new Russia, on part of the land which he had conquered from Sweden. He drained the marshy land on the Neva and at enormous expense created

Russia's first real port. He had handsome buildings con-- structed on European models for his new city and transferred the seat of government from Moscow to the new capital, St. Petersburg, which bore his name.[1]

Catherine II, Tsarina of Russia (1762–1796). Peter was followed by a number of unimportant rulers; but in 1762 a German princess of remarkable ability came to the throne and took the title of Catherine II. Catherine was the daughter of one of Frederick the Great's officers (p. 809), and had been selected by him, at the request of the Tsarina Elizabeth, Peter's daughter, as a suitable wife for her nephew, the heir to the throne.

At the age of fourteen this inexperienced girl found herself in the midst of the intrigues of the court at St. Petersburg. She joined the Greek Church, exchanged her name of Sophie for that of Catherine, and by the study of books and men prepared to make her new name famous. Her husband, who ruled for six months as Peter III, proved to be a worthless fellow, who early began to maltreat her. Catherine won over the imperial guard and had herself proclaimed empress. Peter was forced to abdicate and was carried off by some of Catherine's supporters, who put him to death, probably with her silent consent.

Catherine makes Russia a Great Power. It has been said that Peter the Great made Russia a *European* power, but that Catherine II made it a *great* power. Catherine was ambitious, thoroughly unscrupulous, and hypocritical, but she was shrewd in the choice and management of her ministers and played the game of politics like a man. All her measures were intended to increase the royal authority; for, like her fellow monarchs of the eighteenth century, Catherine was a thorough despot.

As a result of a successful war against the Ottoman Turks (p. 626), Catherine gained the possession of Azov and the surrounding territory north of the Black Sea. Moreover,

---

[1] Changed during the World War to *Petrograd*, and in 1924 to *Leningrad*, in honor of the chief leader of the communists, who had overthrown the Tsarist government.

Russian ships were now granted the right to pass through the Dardanelles and the Bosporus and thus to reach the Mediterranean Sea. As we shall learn later (pp. 815 f.), Catherine was also able to push the boundary of her realms still further westward into Europe. A glance at the map will show how much greater in extent was the territory added to Russia by Catherine II than that acquired by Peter the Great.

Fig. 193. *Catherine the Great*
After a portrait by Rosselin

Why Know about Russia? Russia, as we have seen, not only grew into a major European power but has become one of the greatest problems in our world affairs today. When you hear people talking about the *Soviet Republic* and *communism*, they are speaking of that country about which you have been learning in this chapter. For these are the names of the present government of Russia and its economic system.

Some two hundred and fifty years have passed since the time of Peter the Great. Russia is today a world power, whose inhabitants no longer live under the rule of a Tsar but under a government of the working class. For most of that long period since Peter's day — until about twenty years ago — the mass of the people remained serfs, ignorant, hard-working, poor, often almost starving. The nobility, on the other hand, which constituted only a small part of the population, owned the land and wealth of the country and kept in subjection the millions who toiled for them. The despotic Tsars and their officials did nothing to change the lot of the masses. This is, of course, only a part of the dreadful story of slavery, hardship, torture, and exile to Siberia which the people suffered under the Tsars.

The Russian Revolution of 1917. In 1917 a great revolution took place. The Tsar and his family were murdered (July, 1918), all the nobility who did not manage to escape to other countries were killed, and all their lands and wealth were confiscated. The private property of those who lived on their income was taken away. The control of the country was seized by representatives of the working classes, who took over not only the government but mines, banks, railroads, the management of all industries, and the control of daily life. No one was permitted to own anything without the consent of the government. This system is called *communism*.

Why Russia is a Problem Today. The rule of the workers still continues in Russia ; and because it is such an unheard-of situation in the history of government, and has not yet convinced the world that it can permanently maintain itself, it is referred to as the "Russian experiment." The Soviet Republic and its communistic doctrines have caused great alarm throughout the world and have made many enemies. Many people were shocked by the brutal character of the revolution and the ruthless, oppressive measures of the Soviet government. While there was widespread sympathy for the masses of Russia in their sufferings under the Tsarist régime, many people do not believe that the workers are capable of directing the affairs of a great country. They disapprove of the Russian economic and social doctrines, especially of the attack on private property.

Above all, they fear the effects of Russian propaganda. They believe that the communists have no right to try to influence the people of other countries to create disorder and to encourage others to follow the revolutionary ideas and methods which they have chosen for themselves.

3. The Hapsburgs build an Austrian "Empire" in Central Europe

Weakness of the Holy Roman Empire. The Thirty Years' War left the Holy Roman Empire in a sad plight. During the long and bloody battles which were fought upon its soil, villages were plundered or wiped out altogether, and the population was reduced to half its former size. By the treaties that ended the war the Empire lost territory to Sweden and France, while Switzerland and the Dutch Netherlands gained their complete independence. Moreover, the German princes achieved the right to keep the lands they had taken from the Church, as well as the power to act as independent sovereigns over their districts, without the interference of the emperor. Contrary to the general movement toward unification in other states of Europe, there was in the Empire no such tendency. Each prince was too intent on increasing the importance of his own principality and in imitating the ways of Louis XIV to yield his rights to a higher power. Nor was there any economic or patriotic motive strong enough to weld the parts of the Empire into one strong national state. It remained, therefore, a voluntary alliance of duchies, counties, archbishoprics, and free cities which since medieval times had constituted the "Germanies."

The Austrian Hapsburgs and their Realms. Although the Hapsburg emperor of this shadowy realm had no real power to back up his fine title of "Emperor," as archduke of Austria he was ruler over a vast territory of his own. A distinction must therefore be made between the position of the Hapsburg monarchs as overlords of the Holy Roman Empire and their position as rulers of their family possessions which centered in Austria. Although Austria itself lay within the Empire, its archduke (who was also emperor) had other vast realms which lay entirely outside its boundaries. As the sovereign of these family dominions he could raise armies and exercise powers which he could not enjoy as nominal emperor of the miscellaneous "Germanies."

How the Austrian Empire Grew Up. By the eighteenth century the Hapsburgs had built up a large empire of their own in central Europe, consisting of many different lands and many different peoples, owing allegiance to their rule. It will be remembered that in dividing his vast realms Charles V gave to his brother Ferdinand, who had already acquired the kingdoms of Bohemia and Hungary by marriage, the

Turkish Possessions in Europe about 1660

German possessions of the Hapsburg family (p. 698). These included Austria, with its districts of Carinthia, Carniola, Styria, and the Tyrol. Since that time the Hapsburgs had, by marriage, inheritance, and conquest, greatly added to their dominions.

Struggle of the Hapsburgs with the Turks. The control of Hungary was the cause of serious trouble to the Hapsburgs; for it involved a continual struggle with the Turks, who almost completely conquered it. After the Ottoman Turks captured Constantinople, in 1453 (p. 626), they began to invade southeastern Europe and steadily to press further north. It fell to the lot of the republic of Venice and to the Hapsburgs to try to hold the Mohammedans in check. But the Turks were nevertheless able to press forward and occupy nearly all of Hungary. In 1683, with a large force, they invaded Austria and besieged Vienna. The Austrian capital

Austrian possessions, 1730

- - - - Boundary of
    Holy Roman Empire

POLAND

AUSTRIAN
NETHERLANDS
THE   EMPIRE
SILESIA
BOHEMIA
AUSTRIA
Vienna
STYRIA
KINGDOM OF
HUNGARY
MOLDAVIA
FRANCE
SWITZERLAND
TYROL
CARINTHIA
CARNIOLA
Milan
PARMA
BOSNIA
SERVIA   BULGARIA
OTTOMAN
EMPIRE
TUSCANY
ADRIATIC SEA
NAPLES
MEDITERRANEAN   SEA

Austrian Possessions in 1730

might very well have fallen into their hands had it not been
for the timely assistance of the king of Poland, who defeated
the Turks and freed the city. After this the Christian powers
of Europe became alarmed at the Mohammedan invasion and
furnished money and men to aid the emperor in driving the
Turks back. After a struggle of some sixteen years the invaders were forced back, and the Hapsburgs regained all of
Hungary and Transylvania (to the east). In 1699 the Sultan
acknowledged the right of the Hapsburgs to these lands.

Various Peoples in the Hapsburg Realms. After the close
of the War of the Spanish Succession the Hapsburgs saw the
Spanish portions of Charles V's empire pass into the hands
of their enemies the Bourbons (p. 781); yet to them fell the

Spanish Netherlands, the duchy of Milan, and the kingdom of the Two Sicilies. Austria thus got a firm foothold in Italy, as well as possession of a region on the North Sea.

FIG. 194. *Maria Theresa*

From a painting by Von Listard

But the problem of unifying and governing such a miscellaneous group of peoples, each with its own language, customs, and institutions, taxed to the full the power and ingenuity of the Hapsburgs. In Austria there were mainly Germans; in Bohemia and Moravia there were Germans and a Slavic people called Czechs; there were Poles in Galicia (after the partitions of Poland, p. 815); Hungarians, or Magyars, along with Rumanians and smaller groups of peoples, in Hungary and Transylvania; Croats and Slovenes, both Slavs, in the south; Italians in Milan; and Flemish and Walloons in the Netherlands.

Although the Hapsburgs had no real power in Germany and were faced with a constant problem of keeping their own miscellaneous peoples under their control, they were nevertheless one of the chief reigning families in Europe down to the World War. They were related by marriage to most of the other ruling families; they were stanch champions of Catholicism; they shared the absolutist ideas of their fellow monarchs; and they were able, with the large armies which they could gather together in their wide realms, to make their ideas law within their own dominions and to play their hand in the great game of international rivalry.

Maria Theresa comes to the Throne (1740). When, in 1700, the last direct male heir of the Spanish Hapsburgs died, a European war resulted, to determine who should gain control of his great kingdom (p. 779). A similar disaster overtook the

German Hapsburgs a generation later; for in 1740 Emperor Charles VI died, leaving only a daughter, Maria Theresa, to inherit and rule over his vast realms. Charles, knowing what had happened in Spain, had taken great pains to secure from the other European powers a promise to accept his will, by which he left his dominions to Maria Theresa. But no sooner had she started her reign than her greedy neighbors disregarded the "Pragmatic Sanction," as their agreement was called, and began to plan to seize her lands. Her foremost enemy was the newly crowned king of Prussia, Frederick II. We must now see how this rival to the north had become strong enough to prove a serious danger to the ancient Hapsburg power.

4. Frederick the Great makes Prussia a Powerful Kingdom

Brandenburg sold to the Hohenzollerns. The electorate of Brandenburg had been part of Germany for centuries, and there was no particular reason to suppose that it was ever to become of great importance. Early in the fifteenth century the old line of electors of Brandenburg had died out, and the emperor had sold Brandenburg to a hitherto unimportant family of landowners, the Hohenzollerns. Beginning with a strip of territory extending some ninety or a hundred miles to the east and to the west of the little town of Berlin, the Hohenzollerns gradually extended their boundaries until, in the nineteenth century, the kingdom of Prussia occupied nearly two thirds of Germany. Of the earlier little annexations nothing need be said. While it has always been the pride of the Hohenzollern family that almost every one of its reigning members has added something to what his ancestors handed down to him, no great extension took place until just before the Thirty Years' War. About that time the electors of Brandenburg inherited Cleves and Mark and thus got their first hold on the Rhine district.

Prussia acquired by the Elector of Brandenburg. What was quite as important, a few years later the electors of Brandenburg won, far to the east, the duchy of Prussia, which was separated from Brandenburg by Polish territory. "East Prussia" was originally the name of a region on the Baltic inhabited by heathen Slavs. These had been conquered in the thirteenth century by one of the orders of crusading knights (the Teutonic order), who, when the conquest of the Holy Land was abandoned, in the thirteenth century, looked about for other occupation.

After the German knights had conquered Prussia, it began to fill up with German colonists. In Luther's day (1525) the knights were converted to Protestantism and broke up their order. They then formed their lands into the duchy of Prussia, and their Grand Master, who was a relative of the elector of Brandenburg, became their first duke. About a hundred years later (1618) this branch of the Hohenzollerns died out, and the duchy then fell to the elector of Brandenburg.

The Territories of the Great Elector (1640–1688). Notwithstanding this gain in territory, there was little promise that the hitherto obscure electorate would ever become a formidable power when, in 1640, Frederick William, known as the Great Elector, came to the throne of Brandenburg. His territories were scattered from the Rhine to the Vistula and beyond, his army was of small account, and his authority was opposed by powerful nobles. The center of his domain was Brandenburg. Far to the west was Mark, bordering on the Rhine valley, and Cleves, lying on both banks of that river. Far to the east, across the Vistula, was the duchy of Prussia (map, p. 807).

The Great Elector was, however, well fitted for the task of welding these domains into a powerful state. He was coarse by nature, heartless in destroying opponents, treacherous in dealing with other rulers, and entirely lacking in the refinement of his contemporary, Louis XIV. He resolutely set to work to increase his territories and his power.

By shrewd tactics during the closing days of the Thirty Years' War he managed to secure, by the Treaties of Westphalia (p. 720), the bishoprics of Minden and Halberstadt and the duchy of Farther Pomerania, which gave him a good shore line on the Baltic.

Territories of the Great Elector of Brandenburg

Reforms of the Great Elector. Knowing that the interests of his house depended on military strength, he organized, in spite of the protests of the taxpayers, an army out of all proportion to the size and wealth of his dominions. He succeeded in creating an absolute monarchy on the model furnished by Louis XIV. He joined with England and Holland in their alliances against Louis, and the army of Brandenburg began to be known and feared. Though a good Protestant, he permitted religious freedom to a remarkable degree. He admitted Catholics to public offices and, on the other hand, welcomed the persecuted Huguenots of France (p. 778), even offering them special inducements to settle in his realms.

Brandenburg becomes the Kingdom of Prussia (1701). It was accordingly a splendid legacy which the Great Elector left in 1688 to his son, Frederick I; and although the career of the latter was by no means so brilliant as that of his father, he induced the emperor to permit him to change his title from "elector" to "king" and so to transform his *electorate* into a *kingdom.*[1] The title "King in Prussia"[2] seemed better than

[1] As king in Prussia his title was Frederick I.
[2] He was not king of all of Prussia. Frederick the Great changed his title to "King of Prussia."

Prussia at the Death of Frederick the Great

the more natural "King of Brandenburg," because Prussia lay wholly without the bounds of the Empire, and consequently its ruler was not in any sense subject to the emperor but was entirely independent.

Frederick William I builds up a Strong Army (1713–1740). The second ruler of the new kingdom, Frederick William I, the father of Frederick the Great, was a rough and boorish king who devoted himself entirely to governing his realm, collecting tall soldiers, drilling his battalions, hunting wild game, and smoking strong tobacco. He was passionately fond of military life from his childhood. He took special pride in stalwart soldiers and secured them at great expense from all parts of Europe. He raised the Prussian army, which numbered twenty-seven thousand in the days of the Great Elector, to eighty-four thousand, making it almost equal to that maintained by France or Austria. He was constantly drilling his men, whom he addressed as "my blue children."

Moreover, by constant saving and entire indifference to luxury, Frederick William amassed a huge sum of money. He discharged a large number of court servants, sold at auction many of the royal jewels, and had a great part of the family table silver coined into money. Consequently he was able to leave to his son, Frederick II, not only an admirable army but an ample supply of gold. Indeed, it was his toil and economy that made possible the achievements of his far more distinguished son.

Fig. 195. *Frederick the Great*
From a painting by Antoine Pesne

Frederick II, called "the Great" (1740–1786). In his early years Frederick II grieved and disgusted his boorish old father by his dislike for military life and his interest in books and music. He was a particular admirer of the French and preferred their language to his own. No sooner had he become king, however, than he suddenly showed such marvelous energy and skill in warlike enterprises that he gained the title of "the Great." Fortune favored his designs.

Frederick takes Silesia from Austria. The young Maria Theresa had just succeeded her father, Charles VI, as ruler of the Hapsburg realms. Frederick determined to seize the opportunity of occupying Silesia, a strip of Hapsburg territory, southeast of Brandenburg (map, p. 808), populated by Germans. Since Prussia contained a large Slavic element, Frederick eagerly desired to get possession of Silesia, not only because it was a rich and fertile province but because it would add a large number of Germans to his subjects. He accordingly marched his army into the coveted district and occupied the important city of Breslau, without declaring war or offering any excuse except a vague and ancient claim to a portion of the land.[1]

---

[1] As no woman had ever been elected empress, the duke of Bavaria managed to secure the headship of the Holy Roman Empire, as Emperor Charles VII. Upon his death, however, in 1745, Maria Theresa's husband, Francis, duke of Lorraine, was chosen emperor. Their son, Joseph II, succeeded his father in 1765 and upon his death, in 1790, his brother Leopold II was elected.

The War of the Austrian Succession. France, following Frederick's example, joined with Bavaria in the attack upon Maria Theresa. It seemed for a time as if her struggle to keep her realms would be vain, but the loyalty of all the various peoples under her scepter was roused by her extraordinary courage and energy. The French were driven back, but Maria Theresa was forced to grant Silesia to Frederick in order to induce him to retire from the war. Finally, England and Holland joined in an alliance for maintaining the balance of power, for they had no desire to see France annex the Austrian Netherlands. A few years later (1748) all the powers, tired of the war, — which is known as the War of the Austrian Succession, — laid down their arms and agreed to what is called in diplomacy the *status quo ante bellum*, which simply means that things were to be restored to the condition in which they had been before the opening of hostilities.

Frederick II strengthens Prussia. Frederick was, however, permitted to keep Silesia, which increased his dominions by about one third of their former extent. He now turned some of his attention to making his kingdom richer by draining the swamps, encouraging manufacturing, and drawing up a new code of laws. He found time, also, to associate with distinguished writers and invited Voltaire, the famous French author, to make his home at Berlin. It will not seem strange to anyone who knows anything of the character of these two men that they quarreled after two or three years and that Voltaire left the court of the Prussian king.

The Powers try to Defeat Frederick in a Seven Years' War. Maria Theresa was by no means reconciled to the loss of Silesia, and began to lay her plans for expelling the treacherous Frederick and regaining hold of her lost territory. This led to one of the most important wars in modern history, in which not only almost every European power joined but the whole world was involved, from the Indian rajahs of Hindustan to the colonists of Virginia and New England. This Seven Years' War (1756–1763) will be considered in its broader aspects in the next chapter. We shall mention here only the part played in it by the king of Prussia.

Maria Theresa's ambassador at Paris was so skillful in his dealings with the French court that in 1756 he induced it, in spite of its two hundred years of hostility to the House of Hapsburg, to enter into an alliance with Austria against Prussia. Russia, Sweden, and Saxony also agreed to join in an attack on Prussia. Their armies, coming as they did from every point of the compass, threatened the complete destruction of Maria Theresa's enemy. It seemed as if Frederick's armies might be wiped out and the new kingdom of Prussia might disappear altogether from the map of Europe.

Frederick's Victorious Defense. It was in this war, however, that Frederick earned his title of "the Great" and showed himself the equal of the ablest generals the world has seen, from Alexander the Great to Napoleon. Undaunted by the overwhelming numbers of his enemies and by the loss of several battles, Frederick defeated the French and his German enemies in 1757 at Rossbach, in perhaps the most famous of all his battles. A month later he put to flight the Austrians at Leuthen, not far from Breslau. Thereupon the Swedes and the Russians retired from the field and left Frederick for the moment master of the situation.

At this point England occupied the attention of the French and left Frederick at liberty to deal with his other enemies. Money paid him by the English government helped him to keep his army active, though for a time it looked as if he might, after all, be vanquished. The accession of a new Tsar, however, who was an ardent admirer of Frederick, led Russia to conclude peace with Prussia, whereupon Maria Theresa reluctantly agreed to give up once more her struggle with her old enemy. Shortly afterwards England and France came to terms, and a general settlement was made at Paris in 1763 (p. 842).

5. How "Enlightened" Monarchs divided Poland
among them

The "Benevolent" Despots. The monarchs whose wars we have been following — Frederick the Great, Catherine the Great and Maria Theresa — and also Maria Theresa's son

Joseph II are often called "enlightened" or "benevolent" despots. In one sense they were more "enlightened" than the older kings: they read books, interested themselves in reforms, and associated with the learned men of their day. But they were no more benevolent than Charlemagne, Alfred the Great, Saint Louis, or many other monarchs of earlier times who believed it their duty to do all they could for the welfare of their people. On the other hand, the monarchs of the eighteenth century were despots in the full sense of the word. They took very seriously the business of ruling; for they had no idea of permitting their subjects any share in the government. They believed that all the powers of the state belonged to them, and they intended to exercise them. Moreover, they waged war upon one another as freely as any earlier kings had done, and had no hesitation in robbing one another of their territories on the slightest pretext.

Frederick the Great a Hard Worker. When Frederick the Great became king, he devoted himself less to music and philosophy and more to the practical problems of state. He rose early and was busy all day. He was his own prime minister and the active head of all branches of the government, inspecting the army and leading it to battle, attending to foreign affairs, guarding his treasury, overseeing the law courts, and journeying up and down the kingdom watching the conduct of his officials. While not a religious man himself, he was tolerant toward others and believed that his subjects should be allowed to worship God in any way they pleased. He welcomed Huguenots and Jesuits with equal cordiality, and admitted Catholics as well as Protestants to his service.

Maria Theresa and Catherine the Great. Maria Theresa showed a passionate devotion to her country and, as we have seen, met reverses with dignity and courage. She endeavored to unify the various peoples in her scattered realms and favored educational and legal reforms and also a greater degree of religious toleration, — all, however, only so far as they did not weaken the absolute authority of the crown.

Catherine the Great, like Frederick, was a hard worker. She rose at six o'clock daily and prepared her own breakfast, after which she turned to the dull business of examining the reports laid before her relating to the army, the navy, finances, and foreign affairs. Like Frederick, Catherine was also interested in philosophy and liked to correspond with distinguished and learned persons. She talked much of reform; but she made the lot of the serfs harder than it had been before, for she forbade them even to complain of the treatment they received at the hands of their masters.

Joseph II and his Unsuccessful Reforms. Maria Theresa's son Joseph II, who came to the throne at her death in 1780, was honestly interested in making a thoroughgoing improvement in his realms. With a view to making his kingdom a unified and well-organized state, he redivided the territory into new provinces and replaced the older officials by specially chosen representatives who were to carry on his new system of government. German was to be the official language of the realm. He reduced the power of the Church by abolishing hundreds of monasteries and used the property for charitable purposes and schools. He appointed his own bishops and forbade money to be sent to Rome. He favored religious toleration. He taxed the nobles and clergy, who had formerly been exempt. In part of his dominions he freed the serfs and in other parts reduced the services due from the peasants to their lords. But Joseph's startling reforms were not received as he had expected. Those who had lost their old privileges regarded him as an oppressor, and on all hands he met with a storm of protest. While his intentions were good, his autocratic methods in introducing changes defeated his own good purpose. He died a defeated and discouraged man.

Poland a Prey to her Neighbors. The "enlightened" monarchs were ambitious as well as autocratic. Most of them had no scruples about adding to their kingdoms land that did not belong to them. Let us see how they took advantage of one of their weak neighbors and so completely divided up its territory that the kingdom of Poland entirely disappeared.

With the exception of Russia, Poland was the largest kingdom in Europe. It covered an immense plain and had no natural boundaries. Its population was mixed, consisting of Poles, Germans, Russians, and Jews. Its government was the worst imaginable. Instead of developing into a strong monarchy which could defend itself, Poland had remained in a condition of feudal anarchy. The kingship was not hereditary, but each new ruler was elected by the diet of nobles. The elections were disorderly, and the European powers regularly interfered to secure the selection of a candidate who might favor their interests. The king was given no power : he could not declare war, make peace, impose taxes, or institute a law without the consent of the diet. Yet the diet itself amounted to little ; for no measure could be passed if any one of the nobles vetoed it. Since they rarely agreed on any measure, most of their meetings broke up without accomplishing anything.

The Polish Nobles and Peasants. The nobles in Poland were very numerous. There were perhaps a million and a half of them, mostly very poor, owning only a trifling bit of land. There was a saying that the poor noble's dog, even if he sat in the middle of his master's estate, was sure to have his tail upon a neighbor's land. There was no business class except in the few German towns. The peasants were miserable indeed. They had sunk from serfs to slaves, whom their masters had even the right to put to death under certain circumstances. It is easy to see that Poland was in danger of falling a victim to the greedy and powerful neighbors — Prussia, Russia, and Austria — who hemmed in the unfortunate kingdom on all sides.

Frederick desires West Prussia. Frederick's success in seizing and holding one of Austria's finest provinces did not satisfy him. The central portions of his kingdom — Brandenburg, Silesia, and Pomerania — were completely cut off from East Prussia by a large tract known as West Prussia. This belonged to the kingdom of Poland. The map on page 807 will show how great must have been Frederick's temptation

Fig. 196. *A Cartoon of the Partition of Poland*

Catherine II, Emperor Joseph II, and Frederick II are pointing out the part of the map of Poland they each propose to take. The king of Poland is trying to hold his crown from falling off his head. What is left of Poland on the map is out at sea

to fill this gap in his kingdom, especially as he well knew that Poland was in no condition to defend its territory.

Catherine the Great, who was ruling in Russia, was at one with Frederick in wishing to prevent any improvement in Poland's affairs and in desiring to keep up the disorder so that Russia might profit from the general confusion.

The Partitions of Poland (1772, 1793, 1795). In 1772 Prussia, Russia, and Austria agreed, therefore, to take each a slice of the unhappy kingdom. Austria was assigned a strip inhabited by three million Poles and Russians. She thus added two new kinds of peoples and two more languages to her already varied collection of races and tongues. Prussia was given a smaller piece; but it was the coveted West Prussia, with its German population. Russia's portion on the east was inhabited entirely by Russians. The Polish diet was forced by the advance of Russian troops to approve the partition.

Partition of Poland

Russia and Prussia continued their policy of keeping Poland in disorder and then treacherously declared that they could no longer put up with such a dangerous neighbor. In 1793 they proceeded to make a second partition. In this division Austria was put off with a promise that the others would try to aid her to secure Bavaria in exchange for the Austrian Netherlands.

In 1795 a third and final partition was made in which the remnants of the dismembered country were divided, after much bitter contention, between the three — Russia, Prussia, and Austria. The Polish king was compelled to abdicate, and Poland was blotted from the map.

Questions and Exercises

REVIEW OF CHAPTER

1. What problems were created by the permanent division of Europe into separate states? What means did the monarchs employ to increase the power of their states? Can you name three reigning families of the period and tell what modern states they built up?

2. Why did the Russians adopt the Greek form of Christianity rather than become part of the Roman Catholic Church? What effect did the Mongol invasion have on the habits and institutions of Russia? How did Peter the Great Westernize his realms? What measures did he take to make the Tsar's power absolute?

3. Why did the emperor of the Holy Roman Empire have no power? Distinguish between the importance of the Hapsburg ruler as emperor and his importance as archduke of Austria. How did the Hapsburgs get possession of such vast realms?

4. How did Brandenburg grow into the kingdom of Prussia? What permanent effect did Frederick William I's policy have on the history of Prussia? How did Frederick II win the title of "the Great"?

5. Why were some of the eighteenth-century monarchs called "enlightened"? What conditions in Poland made her an easy victim for powerful neighbors? What happened to Poland?

USEFUL TERMS

See how much meaning you can give to the following: *nationalism, personification, political theories, autocratic, diplomacy, Muscovy, soviet, communist, Pragmatic Sanction, natural boundaries.*

DIRECTIVE QUESTIONS

1. What distinguishes a great power from a small one? Name some of the great powers today; some small ones. Do you see any objections to hereditary rulers as compared with elected ones?

2. What countries are Slavic today? Louis XIV and Peter the Great were reigning at the same time; compare the civilization of the two countries at that time.

3. How did the population of the Hapsburg realms differ from that of England or France? What problems did this create which the other countries did not have?

4. What did Frederick the Great accomplish for Prussia?

5. Is there a country called Poland at the present time? When was it restored?

DISCUSSION TOPICS

1. The nationalistic spirit encourages war.

2. The present government of Russia is largely due to the oppression of the people under the Tsars.

3. Hapsburg rulers controlled at one time or another nearly every part of Europe.

4. Frederick William and his son started Prussia as a military state; Frederick the Great carried on their work.

5. The enlightened monarchs of the eighteenth century were not truly enlightened. The powers that divided Poland claimed that she was better off under their rule.

ADDITIONAL ADVENTURES IN LEARNING

1. Studies in Source Materials. ROBINSON, *Readings*, Vol. II, chap. xxxii, sect. ii, 347, 350, Impressions of Peter the Great; 348, How Peter dealt with rebellion; 351, Peter founds St. Petersburg; 352, How Peter Westernized his realms; sect. iii, "How the Turks were defeated before Vienna"; sect. iv, The Great Elector welcomes the Huguenot refugees; sect. v, 358, The education of Frederick the Great as directed by his father; 359 and 359a, The relation of Frederick the Great and his father as shown in two letters; sect. vii, Frederick's estimate of German literature, — a German who did not praise the German writers; sect. viii, How Maria Theresa viewed her part in the partition of Poland.

2. Supplementary. The habit of personifying nations is an old one; find examples in the Old Testament. What instances do you find in the current newspapers? Make a map of Russia showing what territory was added by Peter and what by Catherine the Great. Make a table showing the line-up of allies in Frederick the Great's two important wars. Give the reasons why these countries chose the sides they did.

3. Topical Studies. Genghis Khan (see encyclopedia). The influence of the French on Frederick the Great: CARLYLE, *History of Frederick the Great.*

CHAPTER XXXV · EUROPEAN CIVILIZA- TION CARRIED OVERSEAS

EUROPEAN EXPANSION MARKS A NEW ERA OF CIVILIZATION · EARLY EXPEDITIONS TO THE EAST · THE CONTEST OF FRANCE AND ENGLAND FOR CONTROL IN INDIA · EARLY DISCOVERERS OF THE WESTERN WORLD · THE ENGLISH AND FRENCH IN NORTH AMERICA · THE STRUGGLE OF FRANCE AND ENGLAND FOR NORTH AMERICA · ENGLAND LOSES HER THIRTEEN AMERICAN COLONIES

EUROPE occupies scarcely one twelfth of the land upon the globe, and yet over three fifths of the world is today inhabited by the descendants of Europeans or ruled by European states. The possessions of France in Asia and Africa, for example, cover a larger territory than that of the whole of Europe. The island of Great Britain is but a hundredth part of the area of the British Empire, which includes one fifth of the world's dry land. Europeans and their descendants have peopled the United States of America.

The way in which Europeans began to cross the oceans and claim a large part of the world as their own constitutes one of the most important chapters in the story of man. It means that European civilization was carried to all parts of the earth, molding the life of distant countries, and being influenced by the ideas and conditions which it found, until it merged into a *world* civilization which is today the common heritage of mankind.

1. EUROPEAN EXPANSION MARKS A NEW ERA OF CIVILIZATION

Europeans go forth to Discover the World. In this, our last chapter, the curtain rises on a great drama — the drama of our modern world. In it we learn how Europeans sailed west and found America, a new continent that was unexplored and undeveloped; how they sailed east and came upon India, a continent where there already existed an ancient civilization; how they found other lands and islands in both East and West. A whole new world to explore and to exploit rewarded the early adventurers across the seas.

The story of how Europeans established relations with distant parts of the globe is the opening act in the great drama which is still being played by the nations of the world. For when the tiny ships of European mariners first ventured forth timidly across the waters, it took months and months for them to reach their distant goal. Today great steamers sail on regular weekly schedules east and west, in an endless procession, and in a minimum of time can reach a foreign port. Regular "lanes" of travel are charted across the waves, like broad avenues, and are carefully followed by ocean-going vessels. Airplanes can encircle the earth, and telegraph cables and wireless keep all parts of our world in instantaneous communication. News from all over the globe is being flashed every moment back and forth across its surface.

Interchange of Products and of Knowledge. Not only this, but the products of the East are carried to the West, and those of the West are sent to the East. By this constant interchange every nation can now enjoy the food, clothing, and articles of household use, as well as the luxuries and art, of other countries. So life is everywhere enriched by the variety of material things available and by the knowledge and scientific discoveries of far-distant peoples.

Another striking feature of this world-wide drama which opened in Europe with the Age of Discovery is the fact that *European* civilization was carried to all parts of the world. It was the West that went to the East and left its imprint there. European civilization was carried not only to the East but to the West as well — to the continent of America, where we now live and inherit its traditions. While the first voyages were made in the pursuit of trade, Europeans later went forth with the idea of settling down in the New World and forming colonies belonging to their mother country.

America the Child of Europe. In America the settlers took possession of the land and developed a great continent whose population is today largely composed of the descendants of these pioneers. The roots of America lie therefore in Europe — in the Europe about which we have learned in this book. So this volume has been dealing all the time with our own ancestors, starting a long, long time ago and gradually moving nearer to our own day.

Influence of the East on the West. We have not had occasion so far to say much about the Far East. A very old civilization existed, however, in India and China. Until the eighteenth century, Oriental ideas influenced but little the daily life of our ancestors; but when the West became acquainted with the East, Eastern civilization began to affect the people of Europe. This subject will be taken up in the following volume, where it will be shown how much the West is indebted to the learning and philosophy of the East. It was Western civilization, however, which was to prevail in a large part of the modern world, owing to its genius for improving and developing the material things of life and to its progress in science. For example, only when Japan adopted Western civilization, in the nineteenth century, did it rapidly develop into one of the great world powers.

Expansion of Europe Overseas. Only the outlines of the great drama of Europeans in the far parts of the world can be given. A detailed account of the rôles played by the various powers would take more space than we have left in the concluding chapter of our book. Yet if we recall some of the facts which we have learned about the powers of Europe, we shall see why some of them played only a small part or none at all, while others, better fitted to compete, eagerly entered the contest for control in distant lands. In the great adventure of Europe overseas we again see the powers at their old international game, using the same methods of outwitting their rivals that they had so long employed in their struggles on the continent of Europe.

Why Some Powers did not Join the Race. There were good reasons why some of the powers did not take part in the new venture, gained no trade, and founded no colonies. Italy, Russia, the Holy Roman Empire, Austria, Prussia, and many less important states had little or nothing to do with the rivalry for supremacy across the seas.

The early expeditions for discovery and trade were in general undertaken either by a government or with its approval and support. Italy was still divided into the Papal States, petty kingdoms, and the independent cities of the north. There was no central government strong or rich enough to forward a foreign project for either gain or glory. Although the Italian city-states had been the first to establish a lively trade in the luxuries of the East through the near-by ports (p. 554), they were in no position to fit out expeditions to cross the oceans and guard settlements in distant lands. Russia had a vast undeveloped territory in the East, while her "window" in the West looked out upon the Baltic. The ambition of the Tsars was limited to the conquest of the lands in these regions and those of the Black Sea to the south, as well as to what might be gained in the continual struggles in Europe. The "Germanies," still a collection of kingdoms, electorates, city-states, and bishoprics, under the nominal overlordship of the emperor, had no central policy, no navy, and no common patriotism. The Austrian Hapsburgs had all they could do to consolidate and control their scattered dominions and alien peoples. Prussia, which by the eighteenth century had grown into a strong military power, was looking in all directions for territory that would strengthen its position and power on the Continent. The eyes of these nations could see no farther than the realms of their neighbors; so they recklessly wasted their money and strength in an endless scramble for European land. There was neither money nor energy left for expeditions to foreign shores.

The Powers who saw Opportunity Abroad. There were other states, however, whose eyes had been opened and whose imaginations had been kindled by the tales of the riches of the East and who, in searching for this treasure, had come upon a new world in the West and begun to discover its resources as well. The Portuguese and Spanish, as we know, had been the pioneers in exploration and foreign trade (pp. 561 ff.). Holland, after escaping from the yoke of Spain, had built up a sea power that had been the cause of much irritation to England (pp. 741 f.). France, during the reign of Louis XIV, had greatly increased her fleet, owing to the efforts of her minister Colbert (p. 770). England had for a long time been adding to her ships and, while other European powers were exhausting themselves in fruitless wars on the Continent, had been slowly establishing her supremacy on the seas.

Let us see how, one after another, these countries held the lead, then fell behind, until finally England emerged victorious in the race for power overseas, with a vast territory under her control. For England not only saw the advantage of foreign trade but soon realized the importance of building up on foreign shores an enlarged Britain destined one day to make her tiny isle the center of a powerful world empire.

2. EARLY EXPEDITIONS TO THE EAST

Portugal establishes Trade with the East. The voyages that had brought America and India to the knowledge of Europe during the fifteenth and early sixteenth centuries were undertaken, as we know, mainly by the Portuguese and the Spaniards (pp. 561 ff.). Portugal was the first to realize the advantages of establishing direct trade with the East; and after Vasco da Gama returned home in 1498 with his precious cargo, the Portuguese regarded the East Indies as their own.

In 1493 Pope Alexander VI undertook to divide the uncivilized world between these two pioneers, who claimed it by right of discovery. The map on page 562 will show the line of "papal demarcation" by which eastern Brazil, Africa, and the East were allotted to Portugal and the unknown lands of the West to Spain. The Portuguese established trading stations at Ormuz, at Diu and Goa in India, and on the islands of Ceylon, Java, and Sumatra. They even reached the long-sought Spice Islands, two thousand miles farther away. For a large part of the sixteenth century Portugal monopolized the rich trade between the Orient and Europe. This had formerly been in the hands of the Mohammedans, who brought the products of the East to the Mediterranean ports, where they were turned over to Italian traders.

As the prosperity of the Italian cities declined, Lisbon grew in wealth and importance; for the merchants of other nations eagerly flocked to her port to obtain the luxuries which her ships brought. But Portugal was too small and too powerless to keep other countries, who enviously watched her success, from sharing in this new and profitable enterprise. The Portuguese trading stations were scattered thousands of miles apart, with no proper protection, and the mother country lacked a population large enough to send out settlers to the new lands to defend them. In 1580 Philip II of Spain annexed Portugal, and the port of Lisbon was closed to France, England, and Holland, with whom Spain was at war. This gave the Dutch an opportunity to seize the trade of Portugal and establish themselves in Java, Sumatra, and other Portuguese possessions.

Spain enjoys a Brief Supremacy. While Portugal was busy in the East Indies, the interest of Spain was centered in her vast empire in America. The untold wealth of the gold and silver mines in Mexico and Peru and her enormous territory in the New World had raised her to a place of supreme importance in Europe (see page 567). Moreover, when Philip II annexed Portugal he gained control for a time of the Portuguese possessions and trade in the East. But the Spanish nobles soon wasted the treasure that came to them from the West; and high taxes imposed by the government destroyed the trade with her colonies. The inhuman treatment of the Netherlands by Philip II led to the revolt of his richest European provinces, and in 1588 Spain lost her "Invincible Armada." By the end of the century, her resources having been exhausted by extravagance and mismanagement, Spain sank to the rank of a secondary power.

The Dutch supplant the Portuguese in India; the Dutch East India Company. After the Dutch gained their freedom from Spain, they turned their attention to the sea and built up a strong fleet to increase the already flourishing trade of their rich cities. They had little to fear when, in 1595, they sent out their first expedition to India by way of the Cape of Good Hope; for the Spanish were too busily occupied policing the sea over which the wealth from America was carried to guard the trade routes of their dependency Portugal. The success of the first expedition aroused great enthusiasm among the Dutch, and by 1602 from sixty to seventy vessels had sailed to India and the Malay Archipelago. In the same year the Dutch East India Company was formed, to regulate and protect the growing Dutch trade. This company rapidly established trading houses and seized one by one the most favorable stations belonging to the Portuguese, until by the close of the seventeenth century only Goa and a few minor posts remained of the vast commercial empire which the Portuguese had built up.

The English become Rivals of the Dutch; the English East India Company. Meanwhile the energetic Dutch discovered that the English were not inclined to sit idly by and have their neighbors reap an enormous profit from the goods they brought to England to sell. As early as 1591 some English traders had sent out an expedition from Plymouth. Although their venture was not successful, London merchants had in 1600 organized the East India Company and been granted a charter by the government which gave them the monopoly of the English trade with India, with the power to govern themselves and defend themselves against rivals. The English succeeded in establishing a number of agencies in India, including one near Calcutta, and built a fort at Madras (1640).

But the Dutch owned half the merchant ships of Europe and controlled a large part of the carrying trade between the East and Europe. Hoping to reduce the Dutch trade and to increase English shipping, Parliament in 1651 passed the Navigation Act, providing that only English vessels should be permitted to bring to England goods from Asia, Africa, and America. This led, as we know, to a short war between the Dutch and English, fought at sea (pp. 741 f.).

A few years later King Charles II granted the East India Company a new charter which gave it the right to coin money, administer justice, punish independent English merchants who sailed ships into Eastern waters on their own account, and, finally, to wage war and make peace with non-Christian states. The Navigation Act of 1651 was strengthened by requiring that vessels bringing commodities to England from across the seas should hereafter be *built* in England, and English agents were ordered to prevent the Dutch from getting

any of the English trade. War broke out again between the
two rivals. In 1664 the English got possession of some of the
West Indies belonging to the Dutch, as well as of the island
of Manhattan. On the other hand, the Dutch succeeded in
driving the English out of the Spice Islands. When William
of Orange became king of England, in 1689, the Dutch no
longer opposed the English in India.

The Dutch during the Eighteenth Century. While no longer
dominating the seas, the Dutch continued to enjoy a profitable trade during the eighteenth century and to hold important possessions. These included the Cape of Good Hope
as a halfway post to India, the island of Ceylon, several important settlements in India, and dominion or predominance
in the Moluccas, or Spice Islands, Java, Sumatra, Borneo,
Celebes, the Malaccan peninsula, and Siam. They monopolized the trade with Japan and the greater part of the spice
business. Nevertheless, their progress was checked, and it
was not they but the French who were now to fight with
England for the control of India and North America.[1]

*The French get a Start in India; the French East India
Company.* French merchants had for some fifty years been
going to India; but it was not until 1664 that Louis XIV
chartered the French East India Company, granting it a monopoly of trade for fifty years, and the right to cast cannons,
raise troops, and garrison posts, and to declare war and make
peace in the name of their sovereign. The king also assisted
the company with grants from the royal treasury in overcoming the difficulties which the enterprise necessarily
involved.

In 1669 the first French expedition under the new company
arrived at Surat, where they established an agency beside
those of the English and Portuguese. From here they sent
out their agents in every direction. Three years later the
French became the rivals of the English in Bengal by fortifying themselves at Chandernagor, just north of Calcutta.

---

[1] The Dutch, in spite of losses in later wars, still hold Java, Sumatra, Celebes,
the Moluccas, portions of Borneo, and other islands, comprising an area of over
700,000 square miles, with a population of some 60,000,000.

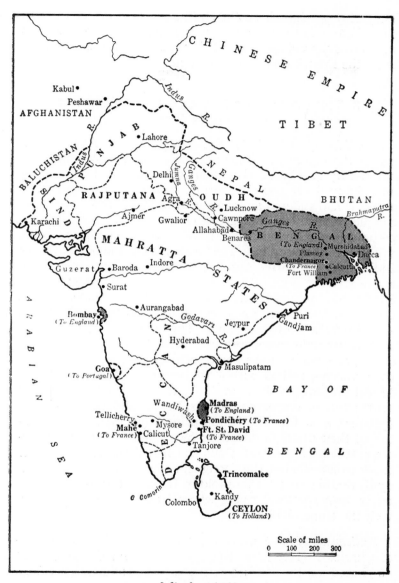

India about 1763

They also purchased, on the southeastern shores of India, a plot of ground of about one hundred and thirteen acres, upon which was the village of Pondichéry, destined to be the capital of the French dominions in India.

3. The Contest of France and England for Control in India

Condition of India in the Eighteenth Century. At the opening of the eighteenth century India was a vast empire inhabited by two hundred millions of people, with an ancient and highly developed civilization. Some two hundred years earlier it had suffered an invasion of Mohammedans, who had conquered the northern part of the peninsula. A line of emperors called "Moguls" had established a magnificent court at Delhi as their capital. The larger part of the population of India were the native Hindus, who had an ancient religion and a strict system of "castes," or classes of society. The Hindus had never felt any loyalty to the alien emperors, and they cherished a strong hostility — a feeling they still possess — toward the Mohammedans. The emperors, at their best, were never able to secure strict control over the vast peninsula, and many of the native princes continued to manage their various realms within the empire. When the Great Mogul Aurangzeb died, in 1707, the empire began to fall apart; for the emperor's officials, the subahdars and nawabs (nabobs), as well as the Hindu princes (rajahs), got the control of their districts into their own hands. Though an emperor still held court at Delhi, he had little power. Under these circumstances the foreigners who began in the eighteenth century to get a foothold in India had to deal more directly with the local rulers whose lands they coveted than with the emperor himself.

Settlements of the English and French in India. In the time of Charles I (1639) the English East India Company had purchased, on the southeastern coast of Hindustan, a village which grew into the important station of Madras. About the same time, posts were established in the district of Bengal,

L. Green; from Gendreau

FIG. 197. *Jain Temple, Calcutta, India*

The Jains are a small, but wealthy and important, sect in India
who are dissenters from Hinduism

and later Calcutta was fortified. Bombay was already an
English station. The Mogul, or emperor, at first scarcely
deigned to notice the presence of a few foreigners on the
fringe of his extensive realms; but before the end of the
seventeenth century, hostilities began between the English
East India Company and the native rulers, making it plain
that the foreigners would have to fight to maintain their hold.

The center of the French dominion was Pondichéry. It
had a population of sixty thousand, of which only two hundred were Europeans. Dupleix, governor of Pondichéry, was
a soldier of great ambition and energy who proposed to take
advantage of the quarrels between native rulers to make himself leader in India and drive out the English. He made alliances with natives of importance and fortified Pondichéry.
Dupleix had very few French soldiers; but he began the
enlistment of natives, a custom which was quickly adopted
by the English. These native soldiers, whom the English
called *sepoys*, were trained to fight in the European manner.

Struggle between Dupleix and Robert Clive. But the English colonists, in spite of the fact that they were mainly traders, discovered among the clerks in Madras a leader equal in military skill and energy to Dupleix himself. This was Robert Clive, who was but twenty-five years old at the time. He organized a large force of sepoys and gained a remarkable influence over them by his astonishing bravery. Just at the time that the Seven Years' War was beginning in Europe (1756), word reached Clive that the nawab of Bengal had seized the property of some English merchants and imprisoned one hundred and forty-six Englishmen in a little cell — the "Black Hole" of Calcutta — where most of them died of suffocation before morning. Clive hastened to Bengal and forced the nawab to hand over Calcutta to the English. Later, with a small army of Europeans and sepoys, he won a brilliant victory over a much larger force of the nawab at Plassey (1757). He then placed a nawab of his own choice in power in Bengal. As France and England were already at war, he took possession of the French settlement at Chandernagor. Before the Seven Years' War was over, the English had won Masulipatam and Wandiwash, captured Pondichéry, and so deprived the French of their former power in the region of Madras and established themselves as masters in India.

Although France received back the towns which the English had taken from her, she had permanently lost her influence over the native rulers, while Clive had made Britain's name greatly feared among them. The forces of the English East India Company not only had put an end to the danger of French control in India but had begun the conquest of Bengal, which became the center from which, in the nineteenth century, British power spread throughout India.

4. EARLY DISCOVERERS OF THE WESTERN WORLD

The Spanish and Portuguese in America. While the Portuguese, Dutch, English, and French were struggling to gain control of the trade with the East, a vast new world lay in the West awaiting development. The early expeditions westward were undertaken not for the sake of this prize but in search of a shorter route to the fabled riches of the East. As the explorers sailed west, however, they came upon an immense continent in their path. Little did they dream what they had found. Columbus, although he could not find the treasures of Cathay, after four expeditions to America died believing he had been exploring the coast of Asia. It was the Spanish queen, Isabella, who had furnished Columbus with the money for his undertaking, and consequently the new-found islands and the adjacent mainland were claimed by Spain.

While Columbus and others were exploring the Caribbean Sea in the interests of Spain, Cabral, a Portuguese commander on his way around Africa to India, sailed so far to the west that he came upon Brazil. Thereupon the coast southward was rapidly explored by the Portuguese, who in this way came into possession of a vast region in the New World.

The Spanish sailed across the Gulf of Mexico, skirted the coast of Central and South America, and in 1513 Balboa crossed the Isthmus of Panama and from the mountain heights beheld the broad waters of the Pacific. Magellan's voyage had carried him along the barren coast of Patagonia to the strait which bears his name and thence into the Pacific.

The Spanish find Treasure in Mexico and Peru. In Mexico the Spaniards finally came upon the treasure that they had so long and eagerly sought. In 1519, Cortes, the boldest of their explorers, sailed westward from Cuba with a small company and landed at Vera Cruz. Hearing of the wealth of the inland kingdom, Cortes made his way some two hundred miles to the high plateau on which was situated the rich capital of the Aztec Indians. Here he seized the emperor Montezuma, captured the City of Mexico, and began the conquest of New Spain, as he called the region, a tract eight hundred miles in length, extending from the Gulf of Mexico to the Pacific Ocean. Cortes plundered the city of its vast store of silver, gold, jewels, and ornaments of exquisite Aztec workmanship which the natives had been accumulating for centuries. Spanish ships returned home laden with treasure which amazed and excited all Europe.

Before long, rumors reached the Spaniards that there was even greater wealth to be found among the Incas of Peru. Ten years after Cortes had won Mexico, Pizarro invaded Peru and cruelly subjugated its people. The country was plundered, and the silver and gold from Peruvian mines was carried across the Andes to the Isthmus of Panama, whence it was shipped twice a year to Spain. Spanish treasure from the New World was trebled by the conquest of Peru. It is no wonder that the English, French, and other mariners found excuses for attacking Spanish galleons and capturing a share of the wealth which Spain was seizing in the New World.

The Spaniards lose Interest in North America. After reaping such a rich harvest in Peru, the Spaniards sent expeditions to North America to search for further stores of silver and gold. But when they had tramped through forests and swamps without finding anything more than an occasional Indian village, they lost interest in North America and left it, with the exception of Florida and Mexico, to be fought over by other European powers, especially France and England.[1]

How Spain Ruled and Converted the Natives. It was the policy of Spain to keep a firm hold on her possessions in the New World, and for three centuries she ruled the conquered natives by means of viceroys. As the conversion of the heathen was always regarded as important by the Spaniards, friars followed the explorers, establishing missions from Chile to California, and in 1600 there were four hundred monasteries in New Spain alone.[2] The Spaniards did not emigrate in great numbers; but by the close of the eighteenth century there were, in all the colonies, probably some three or four millions of them whose blood was unmixed with that of the native races, besides many half-breeds.

Spain occupies the Philippines (1565). Spain, however, pressed on westward where Magellan had shown the way. Forty-four years after he had laid claim in her name to the

---

[1] Spain, however, founded, to the north of her main possessions, St. Augustine (Florida) in 1565, and Santa Fe (New Mexico) in 1598.

[2] The old missions in California have in some cases been kept in repair and may be seen today.

archipelago which he had discovered far to the south of Japan, an expedition of soldiers and friars was sent out from New Spain (Mexico) to occupy the islands. These they discovered to be "large and rich, well provided with inhabitants, food, and gold." The group had earlier been named the Philippine Islands, after Philip II, who was then heir to the Spanish throne. In 1571 the town of Manila was established on the island of Luzon and made the seat of the Spanish government in the islands.

The archipelago consists of seventeen or eighteen hundred islands, inhabited by three distinct races which are divided into many tribes differing in language and civilization. The Spaniards were early defeated by the sultan of Sulu and never gained complete control over the more savage tribes, especially the Moros, who still cling to Mohammedanism. The friars and Jesuits, however, Christianized a great part of the islands. Under their care the natural products, such as hemp, tobacco, coffee, sugar, and rice, were developed.

5. The English and French in North America

England's Claim to North America Based on Cabot's Discovery. Although England was later to exert a great influence in the New World, she allowed a hundred years or more to elapse after its discovery before her mariners did much more than hunt in vain for a western passage to India and plunder such Spanish ships as they might encounter. In 1497 John Cabot, an Italian by birth, sailed from Bristol westward with the hope of reaching "the island of Zipango and the lands from which Oriental caravans brought their goods to Alexandria." He discovered, however, only the barren coast of Labrador, which he believed to be a part of Asia. For at least a century and a half thereafter so little was known concerning North America that mariners continued to search for a passage westward to the Pacific Ocean and the Spice Islands.

Verrazano (1524) *and Cartier* (1534) *lay Claim to North America for France.* Verrazano, an Italian commander in the French service, had captured two of the treasure ships dispatched by Cortes to Spain in 1522 and turned them over to the French king. Francis I was so impressed by the riches which were flowing into Spain that he commissioned Verrazano to explore the shore from Florida to Newfoundland and to search for a northwest passage to the East Indies. Upon this exploration France based her claim to North America, which she named New France. Ten years later Jacques Cartier made his way up the St. Lawrence River and took possession of the land in the name of his sovereign.

French Settlements in Nova Scotia and Canada. A French company succeeded in 1604 in establishing a permanent settlement at Port Royal in Acadia, as Nova Scotia was then called; four years later Champlain founded a colony at Quebec, from which, as a base, French explorers, traders, and missionaries worked their way westward and southward. In 1642 Montreal was permanently founded. The French companies offered every inducement to Frenchmen who would agree to settle in Canada, but the severe climate and hard life kept back all except the most adventurous. French explorers and missionaries pressed westward in the hope of finding the Pacific; instead they discovered the Great Lakes and laid claim to all the surrounding lands.

Exploration of the Mississippi. In 1673 Father Marquette, a Jesuit missionary, and Joliet, a veteran explorer and trader, undertook to explore the Mississippi. Untroubled by the warnings of the Indians that the river was full of monsters that would devour them, the brave adventurers found their way down the river nearly to the Gulf of Mexico. La Salle completed their work some years later by setting out with his companions from Lake Michigan in January, 1682, and reaching the mouth of the Mississippi in April. La Salle then solemnly claimed for France all the region watered by the great river and named it Louisiana after his king, Louis XIV.

England's Seaboard Colonies. The most promising of the English possessions in North America were the colonies which were to develop into the United States. While the French were roaming about the Great Lakes and the Mississippi

Ewing Galloway

Fig. 198. *Ruins of the Old Church Built at Jamestown, Virginia, in 1639*
The tower is part of the original building. The church proper is of a later date ᾿

Valley, the English were slowly occupying and settling the Atlantic coast from New England to Florida. A year before Champlain founded Quebec, Englishmen had established their first successful colony, which they named Jamestown after their king, James I. After a period of great hardship, help came from the mother country, and the colonists, becoming more prosperous, began to find their way inland and take possession of the fertile valley of Virginia. The New England colonists differed essentially from those of Virginia. The Virginia colony had been promoted by a London company as a business enterprise; the New England colony had an entirely different origin. In 1620 the *Mayflower* had landed at Plymouth, bringing stern, religious Englishmen who could not endure the ceremonies of the English Church and who had fled to the New World to found permanent homes where they might worship as they pleased. Nine years later the Massachusetts Bay Company began to attract thousands of well-to-do Puritans, whose worldly prosperity contributed not a little to the success of the colony. A group from Massachu-

FIG. 199. *Henry Hudson's Little Boat, the "Half-Moon," in which he sailed up the River that bears his Name*

From a painting by H. A. Ogden

setts established themselves as a colony in Connecticut, being attracted by the rich farming land in the valley of the Connecticut River. Another group, headed by Roger Williams, founded the colony of Rhode Island, seeking for themselves more religious freedom than was possible under the rule of the

Puritans in Massachusetts. Maryland, granted to Lord Baltimore in 1632, became a refuge for Roman Catholics who were persecuted in the mother country. North and South Carolina were founded by English courtiers to whom Charles II had granted a large tract south of Virginia. Pennsylvania, granted to William Penn by Charles II in 1681, developed into a thriving colony of Quakers, whose religious convictions and opposition to war made them hated in England. New Hampshire became a separate colony in 1679, Georgia was founded in 1733, and Delaware, though it had its own assembly earlier, remained under the management of the Pennsylvania governors down to the Revolution.

England wins New Amsterdam from the Dutch. An important settlement was taken from the Dutch in one of the commercial wars. Henry Hudson, an English mariner sailing under the Dutch flag, had discovered (1609) the river which bears his name, and the island of Manhattan at its mouth. On this island the Dutch West India Company established its colony of New Amsterdam, and the Dutch occupied the valley of the Hudson and what is now New Jersey, calling it New Netherland. But the short history of the Dutch in North America came to an end in 1664, when their possessions were conquered by the English.

England gains Nova Scotia, Newfoundland, and the Hudson Bay Region. The wars in Europe, moreover, were usually accompanied by little wars among the colonists of the various nations involved. During the War of the Spanish Succession (called Queen Anne's War by the colonists) the New England settlers had captured the French stronghold of Port Royal[1] in Nova Scotia (then Acadia). By the Peace of Utrecht (1713) at the end of the war, France ceded Nova Scotia to England and acknowledged her right to Newfoundland and the region about Hudson Bay which had been in dispute between the two countries.[2]

---

[1] Now Annapolis.

[2] The English had organized a Hudson's Bay Company in 1670 and laid claim to the vast region north of New France.

Map of the New World in 1750. The map of the New World in 1750 indicates that it was divided up as follows among the various European countries which had participated in its exploration and colonization during the two centuries and a half that they had known of its existence. Besides New France (Canada), the French held Louisiana, extending from the Alleghenies to the Rocky Mountains and from the Great Lakes to the Gulf of Mexico. This was defended by scattered forts, extending from New Orleans (founded by the French Mississippi Company in 1718) to Montreal. France held also a portion of the island of Haiti and of Guiana (Cayenne), on the northeastern coast of South America. The English Hudson's Bay Company claimed the vast ill-explored region, frequented by adventurous trappers, which lay to the north of New France. English colonies occupied all the Atlantic coast from Newfoundland to a point south of Savannah. England had settlements, besides, in the Bahamas, Jamaica, and Belize (British Honduras). Like France she had colonized also a portion of Guiana, on the coast of South America; but this she ceded to the Dutch, in 1667, in exchange for New Amsterdam and their other North American possessions. In general, however, the entire region to the south of Santa Fe and St. Augustine, including Mexico, Florida, Central America, the West Indies, and all of South America, except Brazil (which was Portuguese) and Guiana, belonged to the Spanish crown. All the outlying regions, such as the northwestern parts of North America, the interior of Brazil, and the southern part of South America, were little known or entirely unexplored.

6. The Struggle of France and England for North America

Comparison of French and English Colonies. In the contest between France and England for possession of North America the French were at a distinct disadvantage. Their territory was so immense that it could not be easily protected. The exhausting wars of Louis XIV had checked emigration to America and prevented the sending of proper financial support to the colonies. The Huguenots, who might have sought

The New World in 1750

refuge in the New World after the revocation of the Edict of Nantes (p. 778), were forbidden entrance on the ground that they were heretics. The French king kept strict control of the colonies and permitted them no self-government or freedom in the management of their affairs. Moreover, the French who came to America were mainly traders, explorers, and missionaries who were not interested in forming permanent settlements like the English. As a result the scattered population of the French colonies numbered less than a hundred thousand when war broke out with England in 1754.

The situation in the English colonies from Massachusetts to Georgia was quite different. They varied greatly in size, population, religion, trade, and industry; but they had a common bond of loyalty to England and, moreover, were so situated that they could combine in any enterprise far more readily than the French. Again, four fifths of the English lived within a short distance of the seacoast, and hence were in ready communication with the mother country as compared with a Frenchman in Kaskaskia or Detroit. Each of the colonies had its own government and its representative assembly, which voted taxes and passed laws subject to the approval of the king. The English settlers were, for the most part, seeking permanent homes; there were few traders, trappers, missionaries, and wandering adventurers. Colonial industry and commerce were prospering, and the population was increasing rapidly. Although at the close of the War of the Spanish Succession there were less than half a million English settlers, by 1750 the number had trebled.

The French and Indian War (1754). As the English colonies grew they gradually pressed inland and so came into conflict with the French, who claimed all the region south of the Great Lakes. In 1754 the French captured an English fort (which they named Duquesne) on the spot where Pittsburgh now stands. During the two years following, the war went badly for the English. The British were unaccustomed to fighting in the forests and were terrified by the Indians. Moreover, the British generals were too proud to take advice from the colonial officers.

In 1757, however, the situation changed. William Pitt, the great British statesman, came to the head of the government. He immediately sent reënforcements to the hard-pressed colonies and also recognized the ability of colonial officers to command their own forces. The colonists on their part responded with money and troops. They took Louisburg, on Cape Breton Island, captured Fort Duquesne, which they renamed Pittsburgh, and drove the French from western New York.

© National Portrait Gallery

FIG. 200. *The Elder Pitt*

William Pitt, earl of Chatham, more than any other one man, was responsible for the victories of England in the Seven Years' War. A great orator, as well as a shrewd statesman, he inspired his country with his own lofty ideals. He boldly upheld in Parliament the cause of the American colonists, but died in 1778 before he could check the policy of the king. (From a painting by Richard Brompton)

The English capture Canada. The following year the English were able to begin the conquest of Canada. They took Ticonderoga and Crown Point, on Lake Champlain, and Fort Niagara. Then, from Louisburg, the English under General Wolfe made their way up the St. Lawrence to attack Quebec, the key to the French power in Canada. After trying for three months to secure a landing place for his troops, Wolfe, with his followers, one dark night scaled the heights of the citadel upon which the town stands. The next morning the French general, Montcalm, was amazed to see his army confronted by the English. In a short battle the British were victorious, but both Wolfe and Montcalm were killed. From this time on, the conquest of Canada progressed rapidly. The French forts surrendered in quick succession, and when Montreal was captured (1760) the French gave up the unequal contest and recalled their troops to France.

England gains Control of North America. In the Peace of Paris (1763), which brought the Seven Years' War to a close, France gave up all her territory in North America. Canada and the region east of the Mississippi, with the exception of New Orleans, she ceded to England; that to the west of the river, together with New Orleans, she gave to her ally, Spain.[1] Spain on her part ceded Florida to England, on condition that England would return Havana and Manila, both of which the English had captured. In this way England got possession of practically all that part of North America which had been explored and developed, with the exception of Mexico. While Spain's territory was greatly enlarged by Louisiana, she was not in a position to colonize this vast region west of the Mississippi. Forty years later it was purchased by the United States.

7. ENGLAND LOSES HER THIRTEEN AMERICAN COLONIES

British Trade and Navigation Laws. England had no sooner gained Canada and driven the French from the broad region that lay between her dominions and the Mississippi than she lost her thirteen American colonies, which refused to submit longer to her interference with their freedom.

While the English settlements enjoyed more liberty than those of Spain and France, England, like other European countries, looked upon her colonies as a legitimate source of profit. Like the other colonizing countries she had therefore enacted a number of trade and navigation laws by which she sought to control the business and commerce of the colonies

---

[1] The only traces of the French occupation of North America today are the French-speaking Creoles of New Orleans and the French Canadians in and about Montreal and Quebec. We still retain the name "prairie," which the French explorers gave to the grassy plains of Illinois; and names like "Detroit," "Vincennes," "Terre Haute," "Des Moines," and "Baton Rouge" remind us of the nationality of the first explorers and missionaries. Joliet, La Salle, and Marquette each have a town dedicated to their memory.

in her own interest. The laws were not enacted to injure a part of her empire but to protect British commerce against that of her rivals. But to the colonists these measures seemed to deprive them of their rights as British subjects and to interfere with the free development of their new homes. They objected to having their business and trade regulated by ministers living three thousand miles away. Moreover, their rapidly increasing wealth and population gave them confidence in themselves and in their future and made Parliamentary interference intolerable to them.

How the Home Government Interfered in the New Land. One of the offensive trade laws (1660) specified that certain articles. including sugar, tobacco, cotton, and indigo, could be sold only to England or to English colonies.[1] Other articles the colonists were forbidden to export at all, or even to produce. For instance, though they had the finest furs in abundance, they could not sell any caps or hats to any foreign country or even to England. They had built up a profitable lumber and provision market with the French Indies, from which they bought in return large quantities of sugar and molasses. But British merchants objected to this competition with their own business, and the colonies were forbidden to import these commodities.

Furthermore, there was another act (1663) which forbade the importation into the colonies of goods from European countries unless they were first sent to England, where a duty was collected, and, besides, they were required to be carried in British ships. So if a merchant of Philadelphia wished to get French wines or Dutch watches, he would have to buy them through English merchants. If a colonist wished to sell his goods to foreigners, he was forced to send them in English ships and by way of England.

The Colonists Ignore the Trade Laws. The colonists naturally disobeyed these laws. They carried on a flourishing trade and built up their industries in spite of the restrictions imposed by the home government. The navigation and trade

---

[1] This law renewed an earlier Navigation Act against the Dutch (pp. 741 f.).

laws were not strictly enforced, and business men engaged in a good deal of "smuggling." Besides, the home country was occupied with its own wars in Europe. After the Peace of Utrecht, Walpole, the prime minister, refused for twenty years to interfere with the independence of the colonies.

Change in English Policy after 1763. With the close of the Seven Years' War and the conquest of Canada and the Ohio valley, the attitude of the English government changed. In the first place, it would require a large army to protect this vast new territory against the Indians. The cost of the war had been great, — the British debt was doubled and home taxes had soared, — and the government believed that the colonies should pay their part of the expense. It therefore devised for the colonies a new policy. Customs offices and courts for the trial of cases of smuggling were to be reorganized, to see that the trade laws were now strictly enforced. Duties were levied on silk, wine, coffee, and other articles imported into the colonies from foreign countries. The colonies were forbidden to issue paper money when they had no gold or silver. Finally, Parliament decided to secure a fixed revenue by means of taxation.

The Stamp Act Arouses the Colonists. In March, 1765, Parliament passed an act requiring stamps costing from a few pence to several shillings to be placed on all legal and business papers, such as leases, wills, mortgages, and bills of sale, as well as newspapers, pamphlets, etc. This act angered the colonists as no previous measure had done. Everywhere there were protests and denunciations of the new bill, on the ground that it was "taxation without representation." Colonial assemblies denounced the measure, and a petition was sent to the king in protest. So great was the excitement that the stamp tax was repealed. Parliament then decided to raise a revenue by duties on glass, paper, and tea, but again the protests of the colonists were so violent that all duties were removed except that on tea. This was retained because of the active lobbying of the East India Company.

FIG. 201. *The Doak House, Marblehead, Massachusetts*

The "Boston Tea Party" (1773). The effort, however, to make the colonists pay a very moderate duty on tea and to force upon the Boston markets the East India Company's tea at a very low price produced trouble in 1773. Those who had supplies of "smuggled" tea to dispose of and who were likely to be undersold even after the small duty was paid raised a new cry of unjust taxation. A band of young men boarded a tea ship in Boston harbor and threw the cargo into the water.

A considerable number of the members of Parliament were opposed to forcing the colonists to obey. Edmund Burke, perhaps the most able member of the House of Commons, urged the ministry to leave the Americans to tax themselves; but George III, and the Tory party in Parliament, could not forgive the colonists for their opposition. Believing that the trouble was largely confined to New England, they closed the port of Boston to trade, forbade the assembling of town meetings without permission of the governor, and quartered troops in the colony. This severe punishment stirred the people of all the colonies to resistance.

The Continental Congress declares War. Instead of bringing Massachusetts to terms, these measures so roused the fears of the rest of the colonies that a congress of representatives from all the colonies was held at Philadelphia in 1774 to see what could be done. This was the first united action of the colonies in defense of their liberties. The Congress published a Declaration of Rights and Grievances asking for the repeal of acts passed since 1763; but most important of all, it declared that trade with Great Britain should cease until the complaints of the colonists had been attended to. The following year the Americans encountered the British troops at Lexington, in Massachusetts, and made a brave stand against them at Bunker Hill. The second Congress (1775) decided to prepare for war and raised an army which was placed under the command of George Washington. On July 6 it finally declared war against Great Britain.

The Declaration of Independence (July 4, 1776). Up to this time few colonists had openly urged the separation of the colonies from the mother country; the war was begun to recover the rights which, as British subjects, they believed had been taken from them. But the king charged his colonists with being rebels and increased the number of British troops in America. Events moved rapidly, and in July, 1776, Congress declared that "these united colonies ought to be free and independent; that they are absolved from all allegiance to the British crown."

The party which favored an attempt to gain independence was a minority of the population. The so-called "Tories," who opposed separation from England, were perhaps as numerous as the "patriots" who advocated the war. About a third of the colonists appear to have been indifferent.

France Aids the Colonists. The colonists immediately sought the aid of France in their fight against her old enemy. But King Louis's ministers were uncertain whether the colonies could maintain their resistance against the overwhelming strength of the mother country. After the Americans had defeated Burgoyne at Saratoga in 1777, however, France

Fig. 202. *The Inauguration of Washington*
From a miniature group by Dwight Franklin in the Museum of the City of New York

concluded a treaty of alliance with the United States in which the independence of the new republic was recognized. This was equivalent to declaring war upon England. The French government aided the colonists with loans, and enthusiasm for the American cause was so great in France that a number of the younger nobles, including the Marquis of Lafayette, crossed the Atlantic to fight as volunteers in the American army.

Success of the Revolution. There was so much difference of opinion in England in regard to the advisability of the war and so much sympathy in Parliament for the colonists that the military operations were not carried on with much vigor. Nevertheless, the Americans found it no easy task to win the war. In spite of the skill and heroic self-sacrifice of Washington and the bravery of the troops, they lost more battles than they gained. The aid of the French fleet was of great importance in bringing the war to a successful close by forcing the English general Cornwallis to surrender at Yorktown (1781). The chief result of the war was the recognition by England of the independence of the United States, whose territory was to extend to the Mississippi River. To the west of the Mississippi the vast territory of Louisiana still remained in the hands of Spain, as well as Florida, which England had held since 1763 but now gave back.

Spain and Portugal were able to hold their American possessions a generation longer than the English, but in the end practically all the Western Hemisphere, with the exception of Canada, freed itself from European rule. Cuba, one of the very last remnants of Spanish control in the West, gained its independence with the aid of the United States in 1898.

Epilogue

With the events of the late eighteenth century, five thousand years of history, written and unwritten, has been studied. Many events of great significance have transpired: great wars have been fought; new lands have been discovered; new nations have been established. Yet when modern man

rises in the morning and clothes his body in *textile garments*, when he sits down to the breakfast table spread with spotless *linen*, set with vessels of *glazed pottery* and with drinking goblets of *glass*, when he puts forth his hand to any implement of *metal* on that table except aluminum, when he eats his morning *roll* or *cereal* and drinks his glass of *milk*, or perhaps eats his morning chop cut from the flesh of a *domesticated animal*, when he rolls downtown, on a vehicle supported on *wheels*, when he enters his office building through a porticus supported on *columns*, when he sits down at his desk and spreads out a sheet of *paper*, grasps his *pen*, dips it in *ink*, puts a *date* at the head of a sheet, writes a *check*, or a *promissory note*, or dictates a *lease* or a *contract* to his secretary, when he looks at his watch with the *sixty-fold division* of the circle on its face, in all these and in an infinite number of ways other commonplaces of life—things without which modern life could not go on for a single hour, the average man of to-day is using items of an inheritance which began to pass across the eastern Mediterranean from the Orient when Europe was discovered by civilization five thousand years ago.[1]

[1]Breasted, James H., "The New Past," *University of Chicago Record*, 1920, Volume VI, p. 245.

Since the material well-being of man was not greatly changed in five thousand years, it might be well to consider what mankind had achieved in that long, long period of time. The first, and perhaps most important, fact of all is the establishment of civilization. How many thousands of years human beings had existed without achieving civilized status is almost conjectural. At the very best, only rough estimates of time may be made. But however long men lived in a sub-civilized state, the fact was that at least by 2500 B.C. a civilization, with almost all the material comforts known to the eighteenth century, was established.

A second significant development was spiritual rather than material. Dwelling in ignorance men were enslaved by their own fears and superstitions. Slowly, however, man evolved a philosophy which enabled him to place himself in the great universe of material things, many of which he understood not at all, others only dimly. As men came to have an understanding of their place in the universe, the great religions were born, offering to men a new way of life and a new theory of man's relationship to man.

Third, many great inventions were made. One, however, is of incomparable significance, and that is the invention of the printing press, which made possible not only the rapid duplication of information, but extensive dissemination. The printing press paved the way for the great advancement of the human mind that opened up an age of learning unequaled in all preceding history.

Still another great achievement of this long period of time was a new concept of government. The notion that kings ruled by divine right or that rulers were especially endowed with a strength that gave them royal prerogatives was challenged by a new social philosophy called Democracy. This theory held that men could live in a form of social organization in which the decisions affecting the general welfare were determined by the voice of the people themselves. The establishment of the government of the United States was an experiment of world-wide importance, engaging the attention of people everywhere. It was a fitting climax to five thousand years of class struggle; the ultimate realization of the highest form of organized human freedom the world had ever seen.

The events that were to transpire in modern history were all tempered by these great epochal movements. The new age would see great material progress accelerated by the ever westward movement of people from the Old World into a New. The great achievements were to be accompanied by issues and problems just as significant as those that faced the people in the five thousand years of human history just completed. The great quest for the full meaning of human living courses onward through all human history. In the new age, men were to have at their command vastly better facilities for aiding and understanding their fellow beings. Human knowledge was to increase; human ignorance decline. Yet as we stand in the midst of the twentieth century, by far the greatest fear we feel is the fear of other men. Perhaps the lessons of five thousand years have not been well learned, or perhaps having been well learned they are only now about to be applied to usher in a new age of human fellowship and understanding.

Questions and Exercises

REVIEW OF CHAPTER

1. Contrast the means of communication possible between Europe, America, and India in the eighteenth century and today. What motives led Europeans to go forth to seek foreign lands? What powers took no part in the exploration or colonizing of distant lands? Why were they uninterested? Do you think greater gain was to be had from wars for European land or for distant territory?

2. What country first established trade with the East? How did Portugal lose her important position in India? Why was Spain unsuccessful as a colonizing country?

3. How did the English first get a foothold in India? Where did the French make their settlements? Describe the way in which Clive established the supremacy of the British in India.

4. Describe the conquests of the Spanish in Mexico and Peru. Why did the Spanish lose interest in North America?

5. Describe the explorations of the French in Canada. Give an account of the English settlements in North America. What regions did the English gain by the Treaty of Utrecht?

6. Describe the difficulties which the French colonies faced. Why were the English colonies more successful? What territory did England gain at the end of the Seven Years' War?

7. Describe England's navigation and trade laws. Give the chief events leading to the revolt of the American colonies. Give the chief results of the Revolution.

USEFUL TERMS

See how much meaning you can give to the following: *chartered companies, monopoly, Mogul, sepoys, castes, subahdar, nawab (nabob), Cathay, Zipangu, Aztecs.*

DIRECTIVE QUESTIONS

1. What led men to prefer a hard life in a new country to life in their homeland? What classes of articles are exchanged between countries today?

2. Why did the West seek the East rather than the East the West?

3. What is Great Britain's relation to India today?

4. On a map show the extent of Spanish, French, and English territory in North America about 1750.

5. Why was England the most successful colonizing country in the world?

6. What traces of French occupation remain today in the United States and Canada?

7. Why were the French in sympathy with the American colonies?

DISCUSSION TOPICS

1. Compare the migration of Europeans to America with the barbarian invasions as to the civilization of the invaders, the objects of the migration, and the results.

2. What is meant by the phrase "one hundred per cent American"? Is there such a person, as regards either birth or culture?

3. Canada and the United States are neighbors, yet they erect no border defenses. Why is this?

4. Discuss the debt of America to European civilization.

5. To what extent have the nations changed their ideas since the eighteenth century in regard to conquest and the annexation of foreign territory? Some Europeans objected to the policy of Japan and Italy.

6. The contribution of America to world civilization.

ADDITIONAL ADVENTURES IN LEARNING

1. Studies in Source Materials. ROBINSON, *Readings*, Vol. II, chap. xxxiii, sect. ii, "Letter of the Great Mogul to James I"; sect. iii, "Condition of India before the English Conquest"; sect. iv, "How England established her Control over India"; sect. vi, "The Settlements in New England and Pennsylvania."

2. Supplementary. Arrange a debate between an Englishman and an American at the time of the Revolution. The Englishman defends the colonies; the American, the mother country. Suggested aids: *Readings*, Vol. II, chap. xxxiii, sect. vi; MUZZEY, *A History of Our Country*, chap. v; BEARD, *The Rise of American Civilization*, chap. v; BURKE, *Essay on Conciliation*. Make a table comparing the area and population of the colonizing countries with their present colonies. Add Italy and Germany to the list. When did Germany lose her colonies? Read Marquette's description of his discovery of the Mississippi River: *Readings*, Vol. II, chap. xxxiii, sect. v. Write a short account of chartered companies: CHEYNEY, *The European Background of American History*, chap. vii.

Bibliography

The following bibliography supplements the references given at the end of each chapter. It is intended primarily for the teacher. While it necessarily contains many works too advanced for high-school students, it includes also books well within the grasp of young people. From these the teacher will be able to select assignments according to the abilities of her pupils.

CHAPTER I

BREASTED, J. H., *Ancient Times* (2d ed., Boston, 1935). BURKITT, M. C., *Old Stone Age* (New York and Cambridge University Press, 1933); *Our Early Ancestors* (New York and Cambridge University Press, 1929); *Our Forerunners* (London, 1924). BUXTON, L. H. D., *Primitive Labour* (London, 1924). CHILDE. V. G., *The Most Ancient East* (New York, 1929). COLE, F. C., *The Long Road from Savagery to Civilization* (Baltimore, 1933). GARDNER, H., *Art through the Ages* (New York, 1926), chap. i. HIBBEN, T., *The Carpenter's Tool Chest* (Philadelphia, 1933). KUMMER, F. A., *First Days of Knowledge* (New York, 1923). MACALISTER, R. A. S., *A Text-book of European Archæology* (Cambridge, 1921), Vol. I. MARETT, R. R., *Anthropology* (New York, 1912). OSBORN, H. F., *Man Rises to Parnassus* (2d ed., Princeton University Press, 1928); *Men of the Old Stone Age* (3d ed., New York, 1919). QUENNELL, M. and C. H. B., *Everyday Life in Prehistoric Times* (2d ed., London, 1931). WILDER, H. H., *Man's Prehistoric Past* (rev. ed., New York, 1923).

CHAPTER II

A. Histories. BREASTED, J. H., *History of the Ancient Egyptians* (New York, 1913); *History of Egypt* (2d ed., New York, 1924). HALL, H. R. H., *The Ancient History of the Near East* (7th ed., London, 1927). QUIBELL, A. A., *Egyptian History and Art* (New York, 1923).

B. Art and Archæology. AMERICAN COUNCIL OF EDUCATION, COMMITTEE ON MATERIALS OF INSTRUCTION, Achievements of Civilization Series (5835 Kimbark Avenue, Chicago, Illinois). BELL, E., *The Architecture of Ancient Egypt* (London, 1915). BOSTON MUSEUM OF FINE ARTS, *Bulletin*, 1903–   . BRITISH MUSEUM, *A General Introductory Guide to the Egyptian Collections* (new ed., rev. and enlarged, London, 1930). CROSS, L. (Ed.), *Pre-Greek Art* (Student Series M of The University Prints, Cambridge, Massachusetts, 1925). GARDNER, H., *Art through the Ages*, chaps. ii–iii. MASPERO, SIR G., *Art in Egypt* (Ars Una: Species Mille. General History of Art series, New York, 1930). METROPOLITAN MUSEUM OF ART (New York), *Bulletin*, 1905–   . PETRIE, SIR W. M. F., *The Arts and Crafts of Ancient Egypt* (Edinburgh and London, 1923).

C. Mythology and Religion. BREASTED, J. H., *The Dawn of Conscience* (New York, 1934); *Development of Religion and Thought in Ancient Egypt* (New York, 1912). GARDINER, A. H., article "Egypt: Ancient Religion" in *Encyclopædia Britannica* (11th ed.). SHORTER, A. W., *An Introduction to Egyptian Religion* (London, 1931).

D. Social Life. ERMAN, A., *Life in Ancient Egypt* (New York, 1894) (new edition in German by Ranke, Tübingen, 1923). GLANVILLE, S. R. K., *Daily Life in Ancient Egypt* (London, 1930); *The Egyptians* (London, 1933). GULICK, C. B., *Modern Traits in Old Greek Life* (New York, 1927). SHORTER, A. W., *Everyday Life in Ancient Egypt* (London, 1932).

E. Excavations and Discovery. CARTER, H., and MACE, A. C., *The Tomb of Tut-ankh-Amen* (3 vols.; New York, 1923–1933).

F. Original Sources in English. BREASTED, J. H., *Ancient Records of Egypt* (5 vols.; University of Chicago Press, 1906–1907). ERMAN, A., *The Literature of the Ancient Egyptians* (London, 1927). PEET, T. E., *A Comparative Study of the Literatures of Egypt, Palestine, and Mesopotamia* (Oxford University Press, 1931).

G. The Monuments as they are Today. BAIKIE, J., *Egyptian Antiquities in the Nile Valley* (London, 1932). BREASTED, J. H., *Egypt through the Stereoscope; a Journey through the Land of the Pharaohs* (Keystone View Co., Meadville, Pennsylvania, 1908; 100 views, with guidebook and maps). MURRAY, M. A., *Egyptian Temples* (London, 1931).

853

CHAPTER III

A. Histories. BAILEY, A. E., and KENT, C. F., *History of the Hebrew Commonwealth* (New York, 1920). DELAPORTE, L. J., *Mesopotamia* (New York, 1925). GADD, C. J., *History and Monuments of Ur* (New York, 1929). GOODSPEED, E. J., *The Story of the Old Testament* (University of Chicago Press, 1934). HALL, H. R. H., *Ancient History of the Near East*. KENT, C. F., *History of the Hebrew People* (Vol. I, 10th ed.; Vol. II, 9th ed.; New York, 1906); *A History of the Jewish People during the Babylonian, Persian, and Greek Periods* (3d ed., New York, 1927). KING, L. W., *History of Babylon from the Foundation of the Monarchy to the Persian Conquest* (New York, 1915). KNOPF, C. S., *The Old Testament Speaks* (New York, 1933). KNOTT, L. A., *Student's History of the Hebrews* (New York, 1927). OLMSTEAD, A. T. E., *History of Assyria* (New York, 1923). PRICE, I. M., *The Dramatic Story of Old Testament History* (New York, 1929). ROGERS, R. W., *History of Ancient Persia* (New York, 1929); *History of Babylonia and Assyria* (6th ed., New York, 1925). WOOLLEY, C. L., *The Sumerians* (Oxford, 1928).

B. Art and Archæology. ALBRIGHT, W. F., *The Archæology of Palestine and the Bible* (New York, 1932). BARTON, G. A., *Archæology and the Bible* (5th ed., American Sunday-School Union, Philadelphia, 1927). BELL, E., *Early Architecture in Western Asia* (London, 1924), chaps. i–iv, vii–x. CROSS, L. (Ed.), *Pre-Greek Art*. GARDNER, H., *Art through the Ages*, chap. iv. GARSTANG, J., *Foundations of Bible History: Joshua, Judges* (New York, 1931). HARCOURT-SMITH, S., *Babylonian Art* (New York, 1928). KOLDEWEY, R., *The Excavations at Babylon* (New York and London, 1914). MEISSNER, B., *Babylonien und Assyrien* (2 vols.; Heidelberg, 1920–1925) (invaluable to teachers who read German). *Museum Journal of the University of Pennsylvania* (Philadelphia), 1910– . OLMSTEAD, A. T. E., "A Visit to Babylon," in *History Teacher's Magazine*, Vol. VIII (1917), pp. 79–81. WOOLLEY, C. L., *Ur of the Chaldees; a Record of Seven Years of Excavation* (London, 1929).

C. Mythology and Religion. BARTON, G. A., *Religion of Israel* (2d ed., University of Pennsylvania Press, 1928). CHAMBERLIN, G. L., *Hebrew Prophets* (University of Chicago Press, 1911). JASTROW, M., *Aspects of Religious Belief and Practice in Babylonia and Assyria* (New York, 1911). PEDERSEN, J. P. E., *Israel: its Life and Culture* (London, 1926). SMITH, H. P., *Religion of Israel* (New York, 1928).

D. Social Life. BUDDEN, C. W., and HASTINGS, E., *Local Colour of the Bible* (3 vols.; Edinburgh, 1922–1925). HUNTING, H. B., *Hebrew Life and Times* (New York, 1921). JASTROW, M., *The Civilization of Babylonia and Assyria* (Philadelphia, 1915).

E. Literature. LEWIS, F. G., *How the Bible Grew* (University of Chicago Press, 1926). WILD, L. H., *Literary Guide to the Bible* (rev. ed., New York, 1925).

F. Original Sources in English. BOTSFORD, G. W. and L. S., *Source-book of Ancient History* (New York, 1913), chaps. iii–iv. HARPER, R. F., *The Code of Hammurabi, King of Babylon* (University of Chicago Press, 1904). JOHNS, C. H. W. (Tr.), *The Oldest Code of Laws in the World* (Edinburgh and New York, 1911). LUCKENBILL, D. D., *Ancient Records of Assyria and Babylonia* (2 vols.; University of Chicago Press, 1926–1927).

G. The Monuments as they are Today. CROSBY, R. L., *Geography of Bible Lands* (New York, 1921). HURLBUT, J. L., *Traveling in the Holy Land through the Stereoscope* (Keystone View Co., Meadville, Pennsylvania, 1900; 100 views, with guidebook and maps). The buildings surviving in Babylonia and Assyria are in a ruinous state. Photographs of sites in Mesopotamia may be obtained from the Keystone View Co., Meadville, Pennsylvania.

CHAPTER IV

A. Histories. AHL, A. W., *Outline of Persian History* (New York, 1922) (based on cuneiform inscriptions). GROUSSET, R., *Civilizations of the East* (New York, 1931), Vol. I, pp. 112–133. HALL, H. R. H., *Ancient History of the Near East* (7th ed., 1927). HOGARTH, D. G., *The Ancient East* (New York, 1915). HUART, C. I., *Ancient Persia and Iranian Civilization* (New York, 1927). ROGERS, R. W., *History of Ancient Persia* (New York, 1929). ROSS, SIR E. D., *The Persians* (Oxford University Press, 1931).

B. Art and Archæology. BELL, E., *Early Architecture in Western Asia*, chaps. v–vi, xi. WOOLLEY, C. L., *Dead Towns and Living Men* (London and New York, 1932).

C. Social Life. GLOVER, T. R., *From Pericles to Philip* (4th ed., London, 1926), chap. vii. JACKSON, A. V. W., *Zoroaster, the Prophet of Ancient Iran* (New York, 1899).

D. Exploration and Discovery. BREASTED, CHARLES, "Exploring the Secrets of Persepolis," in the *National Geographic Magazine*, Vol. 64 (1933), pp. 381–420. GARSTANG, J., *The Hittite Empire* (London, 1929) ; *The Land of the Hittites* (New York, 1910). HOGARTH, D. G., *Kings of the Hittites* (Oxford University Press, 1926). JACKSON, A. V. W., *Persia, Past and Present* (New York, 1909). STURTE-VANT, E. H., "The Hittite Tablets from Boghaz Kevi," in *Classical Weekly*, Vol. XVIII, No. 22 (April 20, 1925).

E. Original Sources in English. BOTSFORD, G. W. and L. S., *Source-book of Ancient History*, chap. v.

CHAPTERS V–XI

A. Ægean Civilization. BELL, E., *Prehellenic Architecture in the Ægean* (London, 1926). BURN, A. R., *Minoans, Philistines, and Greeks, B.C. 1400–900* (New York, 1930). EVANS, SIR A. J., *Palace of Minos* (3 vols. ; London, 1921–1928). GARDNER, H., *Art through the Ages*, chap. v. GLASGOW, G., *The Minoans* (London, 1923). GLOTZ, G., *The Ægean Civilization* (New York, 1925). HALL, H. R. H., *The Civilization of Greece in the Bronze Age* (London, 1928). HAWES, C. H. and H. B., *Crete, the Forerunner of Greece* (4th ed., New York, 1922). NILSSON, M. P., *Homer and Mycenæ* (London, 1933). TOLMAN, H. C., and SCOGGIN, G. C., *Mycenæan Troy* (New York, 1903).

B. General and Political Histories. ALLCROFT, A. H., and MASON, W. F., *History of Sicily, 491–289 B.C.* (London, 1912). BEVAN, E. R., *History of Egypt under the Ptolemaic Dynasty* (London, 1927) ; *House of Seleucus* (2 vols. ; London, 1902). BOTSFORD, G. W., *Hellenic History* (New York, 1924). BURY, J. B., *History of Greece* (2d ed., London, 1924). BURY, J. B., and KIMBALL, E., *Students' History of Greece* (New York, 1916). CARY, M., *Documentary Sources of Greek History* (Oxford, 1927) ; *The Legacy of Alexander* (New York, 1932). CURTEIS, A. M., *Rise of the Macedonian Empire* (New York, 1916). FLEMING, W. B., *History of Tyre* (Columbia University Press, 1915). GROTE, G., *History of Greece* (10 vols. ; London, 1904–1907). GRUNDY, G. B., *History of the Greek and Roman World* (London, 1926). HALL, H. R. H., *Ancient History of the Near East*. HENDERSON, B. W., *The Great War between Athens and Sparta* (London, 1927). JAMES, H. R., *Our Hellenic Heritage* (New York, 1927). MACALISTER, R. A. S., *The Philistines* (London, 1913). McCARTNEY, E. S., *Warfare by Land and Sea* (Boston, 1923). MACURDY, G. H., *Hellenistic Queens* (Johns Hopkins Press, 1932). MILLS, D., *Book of the Ancient Greeks* (New York, 1925). RAWLINSON, H. G., *Bactria* (London, 1912). SELTMAN, C. T., *Athens, its History and Coinage before the Persian Invasion* (Cambridge University Press, 1924). TARN, W. W., *Antigonos Gonatas* (Oxford, 1913).

C. Constitutional and Institutional Histories. BONNER, R. J., *Aspects of Athenian Democracy* (University of California Press, 1933). CALHOUN, G. M., *Athenian Clubs in Politics and Litigation* (University of Texas, 1913) ; *Growth of Criminal Law in Ancient Greece* (University of California Press, 1927). FOWLER, W. W., *The City-State of the Greeks and Romans* (London, 1926). GLOVER, T. R., *Democracy in the Ancient World* (New York, 1927). HALLIDAY, W. R., *The Growth of the City State* (London, 1923). URE, P. N., *The Origin of Tyranny* (Cambridge University Press, 1922). ZIMMERN, A. E., *Greek Commonwealth* (5th ed., Oxford, 1931).

D. Economic and Social Life. BRITISH MUSEUM, *A Guide to the Exhibition illustrating Greek and Roman Life* (3d ed., London, 1929). BURY, J. B., BARBER, E. A., BEVAN, E., and TARN, W. W., *The Hellenistic Age* (2d ed., Cambridge University Press, 1925). CALHOUN, G. M., *The Ancient Greeks and the Evolution of Standards in Business* (Boston, 1926) ; *Business Life of Ancient Athens* (University of Chicago Press, 1926). DAVIS, W. S., *A Day in Old Athens* (New York, 1914). DOBSON, J. F., *Ancient Education and its Meaning to Us* (New York, 1932). GARDINER, E. N., *Athletics of the Ancient World* (Oxford, 1930). GLOTZ, G., *Ancient Greece at Work* (New York, 1926). GULICK, C. B., *Life of the Ancient Greeks* (New York, 1929) ; *Modern Traits in Old Greek Life* (New York, 1927). McCLEES, H., *Daily Life of the Greeks and Romans as illustrated by the Classical Collections* (Metropolitan Museum of Art, New York, 1925). QUENNELL, M. and C. H. B., *Everyday Things in Homeric Greece* (London, 1929). ROSTOVTZEFF,

M. I., *Out of the Past of Greece and Rome* (Yale University Press, 1932), pp. 93 ff. TARN, W. W., *Hellenistic Civilization* (2d ed., London, 1930). TREVER, A. A., *A History of Greek Economic Thought* (University of Chicago Press, 1916). WRIGHT, F. A., *Greek Social Life* (New York, 1925).

   E. **Religion and Mythology.** ADAM, J., *The Religious Teachers of Greece* (Edinburgh, 1923). BULFINCH, T., *Age of Fable* (Everyman's Library, New York, 1916). GAYLEY, C. M., *The Classic Myths in English Literature and in Art* (Boston, 1911). HARRISON, J. E., *Mythology* (Boston, 1924); *Myths of Greece and Rome* (Benn's Sixpenny Library, London, 1928). HOWE, G., and HARRER, G. A., *Handbook of Classical Mythology* (New York, 1929). MOORE, C. H., *The Religious Thought of the Greeks from Homer to the Triumph of Christianity* (2d rev. ed., Harvard University Press, 1925). NILSSON, M. P., *History of Greek Religion* (Oxford, 1925).

   F. **Art and Archæology.** *American Journal of Archæology* (Baltimore), 1885– . *Art and Archæology* (Washington, D.C.), 1914– . BEAZLEY, J. D., and ASHMOLE, B., *Greek Sculpture and Painting* (New York, 1932). BELL, E., *Hellenic Architecture* (London, 1920). DICKINS, G., *Hellenistic Sculpture* (Oxford, 1920). GARDNER, E. A., *Greece and the Ægean* (London, 1933); *Handbook of Greek Sculpture* (2d ed., London, 1920). GARDNER, H., *Art through the Ages*. HOPPIN, J. C., *A Handbook of Attic Red-Figured Vases* (2 vols.; Harvard University Press, 1919); *A Handbook of Greek Black-Figured Vases* (Paris, 1924). MAGOFFIN, R. V. D., *The Lure and Lore of Archæology* (Baltimore, 1930). PFUHL, E., *Masterpieces of Greek Drawing and Painting* (New York, 1926). POLAND, F., REISINGER, E., and WAGNER, R., *The Culture of Ancient Greece and Rome* (Boston, 1926). RICHTER, G. M., *The Craft of Athenian Pottery* (Yale University Press, 1923).

   G. **Literature, Philosophy, and Science.** ALLEN, J. T., *Stage Antiquities of the Greeks and Romans* (New York, 1927). BOWRA, C. M., *Tradition and Design in the Iliad* (Oxford, 1930). BRETT, G. S., *Psychology, Ancient and Modern* (New York, 1928). BURTON, H. E., *The Discovery of the Ancient World* (Harvard University Press, 1932). CARY, M., and WARMINGTON, E. H., *The Ancient Explorers* (London, 1929). FOWLER, H. N., *History of Ancient Greek Literature* (new and rev. ed., New York, 1928). HEIBERG, J. L., *Mathematics and Physical Science in Classical Antiquity* (Oxford University Press, 1922). LANG, A., *Homer and the Epic* (New York, 1893). LEAF, W., *Homer and History* (New York, 1915). MORE, P. E., *Hellenistic Philosophies* (Princeton University Press, 1923). MURRAY, SIR G., *Aristophanes and the War Party* (London, 1919); *History of Ancient Greek Literature* (Appleton's Dollar Library, New York, 1927). NORWOOD, G., and DUFF, J. W., *Writers of Greece and Rome* (Oxford University Press, 1925). ULLMAN, B. L., *Ancient Writing and its Influence* (New York, 1932).

   H. **Source Selections and Authors in Translation.** ÆSCHYLUS, complete works (H. W. Smyth (Tr.), Loeb Classical Library, New York, 1922–1926); plays (Everyman's Library, New York, 1928; World's Classics, London, 1925). ARISTOTLE, *On the Athenian Constitution* (E. Poste (Tr.), 2d ed., New York, 1892); *Politics* (Loeb Classical Library, New York, 1932). ARRIAN, *Anabasis of Alexander* (Loeb Classical Library, New York, 1929–1933). BOTSFORD, G. W. and L. S., *Source-book of Ancient History*. BOTSFORD, G. W., and SIHLER, E. G., *Hellenic Civilization* (New York, 1924). DEMOSTHENES, *Oration on the Crown* and *Third Philippic* (A. W. Pickard-Cambridge (Tr.), *The Public Orations of Demosthenes*, Vol. II, Oxford, 1912). EURIPIDES, plays (Everyman's Library, New York, 1916; A. S. Way (Tr.), Loeb Classical Library, New York, 1925–1929). HERODOTUS, history (Everyman's Library, New York, 1930; Loeb Classical Library, New York, 1924–1929). HILL, MRS. IDA C. (THALLON), *Readings in Greek History* (Boston, 1914). HOMER, *Iliad* (Everyman's Library, New York, 1921; A. Lang, W. Leaf, and E. Meyers (Trs.), rev. ed., New York, 1929; Loeb Classical Library, New York, 1928–1929); *Odyssey* (S. H. Butcher and A. Lang (Trs.), London, 1929; Everyman's Library, New York, 1920; Loeb Classical Library, New York, 1927–1928). PLUTARCH, *Lives* (Everyman's Library, New York, n.d.). SOPHOCLES, plays (Loeb Classical Library, New York, 1928–1929; World's Classics, new ed., rev., New York, 1925). THUCYDIDES, *History of the Peloponnesian War* (Everyman's Library, New York, 1933; Loeb Classical Library, New York, 1919–1923). XENOPHON, works (Loeb Classical Library, New York, 1918–   ).

CHAPTERS XII–XIX

A. **General and Political Histories.** BAKER, G. P., *Constantine the Great and the Christian Revolution* (New York, 1930). BOAK, A. E. R., *History of Rome to A.D. 565* (rev. ed., New York, 1929). FELL, R. A. L., *Etruria and Rome* (Cambridge University Press, 1924). FERRERO, G., *Greatness and Decline of Rome* (5 vols.; New York, 1909). FERRERO, G., and BARBAGALLO, C., *Short History of Rome* (2 vols.; New York, 1918–1919). FOWLER, W. W., *Rome* (New York, 1912). FRANK, T., *History of Rome* (New York, 1923). FREEMAN, E. A., *Story of Sicily: Phœnician, Greek, and Roman* (2d ed., New York, 1894). GROUSSET, R., *The Civilizations of the East*, Vol. I, pp. 133–162. HAVELL, H. L., *Republican Rome* (London, 1923). HEITLAND, W. E., *Short History of the Roman Republic* (Cambridge University Press, 1916). HOW, W. W., and LEIGH, H. D., *History of Rome to the Death of Cæsar* (New York, 1917). MCCARTNEY. E. S., *Warfare by Land and Sea*. RANDALL-MACIVER, D., *The Etruscans* (Oxford, 1927). ROSTOVTZEFF, M. I., *History of the Ancient World* (Oxford, 1928), Vol. II.

B. **Constitutional and Institutional Histories.** ABBOTT, F. F., *History and Description of Roman Political Institutions* (3d ed., Boston, 1911); *Roman Politics* (Boston, 1923). ABBOTT, F. F., and JOHNSON, A. C., *Municipal Administration in the Roman Empire* (Princeton University Press, 1926). ARNOLD, W. T., *Roman System of Provincial Administration* (3d ed., rev. by E. S. Bouchier, Oxford, 1914). BUCKLAND, W. W., *Manual of Roman Private Law* (Cambridge University Press, 1928). FRANK, T., *Roman Imperialism* (New York, 1921). HADLEY, J., *Introduction to Roman Law* (Yale University Press, 1931). HUNTER, W. A., *Introduction to Roman Law* (new ed., rev. and enlarged by A. F. Murison, London, 1921).

C. **Economic and Social Life.** ABBOTT, F. F., *Common People of Ancient Rome* (New York, 1917). BAILEY, C. (Ed.), *The Legacy of Rome* (Oxford University Press, 1924). CHARLESWORTH, M. P., *Trade-routes and Commerce of the Roman Empire* (2d ed., rev., Cambridge University Press, 1926). DAVIS, W. S., *A Day in Old Rome* (Boston, 1925); *Influence of Wealth in Imperial Rome* (New York, 1933). DILL, SIR S., *Roman Society from Nero to Marcus Aurelius* (London, 1925). FOWLER, W. W., *Social Life at Rome in the Age of Cicero* (New York, 1926). FRANK, T., *Economic History of Rome* (2d ed., Johns Hopkins Press, 1927); *Economic Survey of Ancient Rome* (Johns Hopkins Press, 1933), Vol. I. FRIEDLANDER, L., *Roman Life and Manners under the Early Empire* (tr. of 7th ed., rev.; 4 vols.; Vol. I, 2d ed., New York, 1909–1928). GLOTZ, G., *Ancient Greece at Work*. GWYNN, A. O., *Roman Education from Cicero to Quintilian* (Oxford, 1926). HARRISON, F. (Ed.), *Roman Farm Management; the Treatises of Cato and Varro* (tr., with notes of modern instances, by a Virginia farmer, New York, 1913). HEITLAND, W. E., *Agricola, a Study in Agriculture and Rustic Life in the Greco-Roman World* (Cambridge University Press, 1921). JOHNSTON, H. W., *Private Life of the Romans* (rev. by Mary Johnston, Chicago, 1932). LOUIS, P., *Ancient Rome at Work* (New York, 1927). MCDANIEL, W. B., *Roman Private Life and its Survivals* (New York, 1929). QUENNELL, M. and C. H. B., *Everyday Life in Roman Britain* (London, 1924). ROSTOVTZEFF, M. I., *Out of the Past of Greece and Rome* and *The Social and Economic History of the Roman Empire* (Oxford, 1926). SHOWERMAN, G., *Rome and the Romans* (New York, 1931). SOTTAS, J., "The Ship of St. Paul's Last Voyage," in the *Mariner's Mirror*, Vol. VII (1921), pp. 258–266. TREBLE, H. A., and KING, K. M., *Everyday Life in Rome* (Oxford, 1930).

D. **Mythology and Religion.** CARTER, J. B., *Religion of Numa* (New York, 1906); *Religious Life of Ancient Rome* (Boston, 1911). FOWLER, W. W., *Religious Experience of the Roman People* (London, 1922). GLOVER, T. R., *Conflict of Religions in the Early Roman Empire* (11th ed., London, 1927). PAIS, E., *Ancient Legends of Roman History* (New York, 1905).

E. **Art and Archæology.** EHRENBERG, V., "Karthago," in *Morgenland*, Heft 14 (1927). ENGELMANN, W., *New Guide to Pompeii* (2d ed., rev., Leipzig, 1929). LUGLI, G., *The Classical Monuments of Rome and its Vicinity* (Rome, 1929), Vol. I; *Horace's Sabine Farm* (Rome, 1930). MAGOFFIN, R. V. D., *The Lure and Lore of Archæology* (Baltimore, 1930). POULSEN, F., *Etruscan Tomb Paintings* (Oxford 1922). STRONG, E., *Art in Ancient Rome* (Ars Una : Species Mille) (2 vols.; New York, 1928). WARSHER, T., *Pompeii in Three Hours* (Rome, 1930).

F. **Literature, Philosophy, and Science.** BOISSIER, G., *Cicero and his Friends* (New York, 1925). DUFF, J. W., *Literary History of Rome, from the Origins to the Close of the Golden Age* (7th ed., London, 1927); *Literary History of Rome in the Silver Age* (New York, 1927). FRANK, T., *Life and Literature in the Roman*

Republic (University of California Press, 1930). ROLFE, J. C., *Cicero and his Influence* (Boston, 1923). SIKES, E. E., *Roman Poetry* (London, 1923). TEUFFEL, W. S., *History of Roman Literature* (2 vols.; rev. by L. Schwabe, London, 1900).

G. **Source Selections.** BOTSFORD, G. W. and L. S., *Source-book of Ancient History*. LAING, G. J., *Masterpieces of Latin Literature* (Boston, 1903). MUNRO, D. C., *Source Book of Roman History* (Boston, 1911).

H. **Authors in Translation.** AUGUSTUS, *Monumentum Ancyranum* (W. Fairley (Tr.), *Pennsylvania Translations and Reprints*, Vol. V, No. 1; E. G. Hardy (Tr.), *Monumentum Ancyranum*, 1923); D. Robinson (Tr.), *The Deeds of Augustus as Recorded on the Monumentum Antiochenum*, 1926. AURELIUS ANTONINUS, MARCUS, Meditations (Loeb Classical Library, London, 1924; Everyman's Library, New York, 1919). CÆSAR, JULIUS, *Gallic War* (Everyman's Library, New York, 1915; Loeb Classical Library, New York, 1917). CICERO, letters (E. S. Shuckburgh (Tr.), 4 vols., London, 1915–1920; Loeb Classical Library, New York, 1912–1929); speeches (Loeb Classical Library, New York, 1923–1931). HORACE, complete works (Everyman's Library, 1911). JOSEPHUS, works (Loeb Classical Library, New York, 1926–   ). LIVY, *History of Rome* (Everyman's Library, New York, 1913–1924; Loeb Classical Library, New York, 1919–   ; D. Spillan and C. R. Edmonds (Trs.), 2 vols., New York, 1922). POLYBIUS, histories (Loeb Classical Library, New York, 1922–1927). STRABO, *Geography* (Loeb Classical Library, New York, 1917–1933). TACITUS, *Annals* (A. J. Church and W. J. Brodribb (Trs.), London, 1921; Loeb Classical Library, New York, 1925–1931).

CHAPTER XIX

A. **Guides to the Study of the Middle Ages.** An admirable syllabus and exhaustive bibliography for the study of the Middle Ages is to be found in the compilation of PAETOW, L. J., *A Guide to the Study of Medieval History* (1931). THOMPSON, J. W., *Reference Studies in Medieval History*.

B. **General Reading.** ADAMS, G. B., *Civilization during the Middle Ages*, chaps. i, ii, iv, v. BAYNES, N. H., *The Byzantine Empire*. BOISSONNADE, P., *Life and Work in Medieval Europe*, chaps. i–iii. BURY, J. B., *The Invasion of Europe by the Barbarians* and *The Later Roman Empire*. CHEYNEY, *Short History of England*. DILL, S., *Roman Society in the Last Century of the Western Empire*. *Encyclopædia of Social Sciences*, article "Migrations." GUMMERE, F. B., *Germanic Origins*. MUNRO and SONTAG, *The Middle Ages* (1928), chaps. iii–v, vii. ROBINSON, J. H., *The New History*, chap. vi (The Fall of Rome). THORNDIKE, L., *History of Medieval Europe*, chaps. iii, v, vii.

Additional works on the period are the extensive contribution in eight volumes of HODGKIN, *Italy and her Invaders*, and his small book on *Theodoric the Goth*. The well-known work of the celebrated historian GIBBON, *The Decline and Fall of the Roman Empire* (ed. by J. B. Bury), although written a century and a half ago, is still of great interest and importance and is incomparable in its style. *The Cambridge Medieval History* devotes its first volume to this period; see also Volume II.

DOROTHY MILLS's *Middle Ages* and E. M. TAPPAN's *Heroes of the Middle Ages* are written especially for young people.

C. **Source Material.** HAYES, C. J. H., *An Introduction to the Sources relating to the Germanic Invasions*. For an account of the early Germans see TACITUS, *Germania*. OGG, *A Source Book of Medieval History*, chaps. i–iv. THATCHER and McNEAL, *A Source Book for Medieval History*.

CHAPTER XX

General Reading. A. **The Christian Church.** *Cambridge Medieval History*, Vol. I, chaps. iv, vi. FLICK, A. C., *The Rise of the Medieval Church*. FOAKES-JACKSON, F. J., *History of the Christian Church to 461 A.D.* MUNRO and SONTAG, *The Middle Ages*, chaps. ii, vi, xiii. THORNDIKE, *History of Medieval Europe*, chap. vi. WALKER, W., *The History of the Christian Church*.

B. **Monasticism.** CUTTS, E. L., *Scenes and Characters of the Middle Ages*, Part I (Monks of the Middle Ages). GASQUET, F., *English Monastic Life*, chaps. i, ii, iii, v. TAYLOR, H. O., *Classical Heritage of the Middle Ages*. THOMPSON, J. W., *Economic and Social History of the Middle Ages*, chap. v. THORNDIKE, op. cit., chap. ix. WORKMAN, *Evolution of the Monastic Ideal*.

C. Mohammed and his Followers. AMEER ALI, *The Life and Teachings of Mohammed.* BECKER, C. H., *Christianity and Islam. Cambridge Medieval History,* Vol. II, chap. x. GIBBON, *Decline and Fall of the Roman Empire,* chaps. l, li. GILMAN, *The Saracens.* HOGARTH, D., *Arabia.* MARGOLIOUTH, D. S., *Mohammed and the Rise of Islam.* MUNRO and SONTAG, op. cit., chap. ix. THORNDIKE, op. cit., chap. x.

D. Source Material. AYER, J. C., *A Source Book of Ancient Church History. Life of Saint Columban (Translations and Reprints,* University of Pennsylvania, Vol. II, No. 7). GREGORY, BISHOP OF TOURS, *History of the Franks* (E. Brehaut (Tr.)). *The Rule of Saint Benedict* (F. Gasquet (Tr.)). Portions of the Rule are to be found also in HENDERSON, E. F., *Select Historical Documents of the Middle Ages,* and THATCHER and MCNEAL, *A Source Book for Medieval History. The Koran* (J. M. Rodwell (Tr.) ; Everyman's Library). There are many other translations. LANE-POOLE, S., *Speeches and Table Talk of the Prophet Mohammed.*

CHAPTER XXI

A. General Reading. ADAMS, *Civilization during the Middle Ages.* BOISSONNADE, P., *Life and Work in Medieval Europe,* Book I, chaps. viii–x ; Book II, chaps. i–iii. *Cambridge Medieval History,* Vol. II, chaps. xviii–xx. CUTTS, *Scenes and Characters of the Middle Ages,* Part II. DAVIS, H. W. C., *Charlemagne.* DAVIS, W. S., *Life on a Medieval Barony.* DU CHAILLU, *The Viking Age.* GJERSET, K., *History of the Norwegian People.* HASKINS, *The Normans in European History.* HODGKIN, *Charles the Great.* MAWER, A., *The Vikings.* MUNRO and SONTAG, *The Middle Ages,* chaps. x–xii. SALZMANN, L., *Life in the Middle Ages,* chap. ii. SEIGNOBOS, *Feudal Régime.* THOMPSON, *Economic and Social History of the Middle Ages,* chap. viii. THORNDIKE, *History of Medieval Europe,* chaps. xi–xiv.

HAAREN and POLAND, *Famous Men of the Middle Ages,* chap. ix (Charlemagne). TAPPAN, *Heroes of the Middle Ages,* chap. ix ; *In Feudal Times,* chaps. i, iii, iv, vi. Written especially for young people.

B. Source Material. DUNCALF and KREY, *Parallel Source Problems in Medieval History,* pp. 3–26. *Early Lives of Charlemagne* by EGINHARD and the MONK OF ST. GALL (A. J. Grant (Tr.)). OGG, *Source Book of Medieval History,* chap. x. THATCHER and MCNEAL, *A Source Book for Medieval History,* pp. 341–417.

CHAPTER XXII

A. General Reading. BRYCE, *The Holy Roman Empire,* chaps. viii–xi. *Cambridge Medieval History,* Vol. V, chaps. i–iii, xii–xiii. COTTERILL, H. B., *Medieval Italy,* Part IV. DAVIS, H. W. C., *Medieval Europe,* chaps. v–vii. FLICK, A. C., *The Rise of the Medieval Church.* HENDERSON, E. F., *History of Germany in the Middle Ages.* MUNRO and SONTAG, *The Middle Ages,* chaps. xiv-xv. THOMPSON, *The Middle Ages,* chaps. xv–xvii, and *Feudal Germany.* THORNDIKE, *History of Medieval Europe,* chap. xv. TOUT, *The Empire and the Papacy.*

B. Source Material. DUNCALF and KREY, *Parallel Source Problems in Medieval History* (Problem II, Canossa). HENDERSON, *Select Historical Documents of the Middle Ages.* THATCHER and MCNEAL, *A Source Book for Medieval History.*

CHAPTER XXIII

A. General Reading. ADAMS, G. B., *The Growth of the French Nation.* *Cambridge Medieval History,* Vols. v, xviii–xix. CHEYNEY, E. P., *Short History of England.* DAVIS, W. S., *History of France.* EVANS, JOAN, *Life in Medieval France.* HASSALL, *The French People,* chaps. viii–ix. HUTTON, W. H., *Philip Augustus.* LANG, A., *The Maid of France.* LOWELL, F. C., *Joan of Arc.* LUCHAIRE, *Social Life at the Time of Philip Augustus* (Krehbiel (Tr.)). MUNRO and SONTAG, *The Middle Ages,* chaps. xxiii, xxxv-xxxvi. PERRY, F., *Saint Louis the Most Christian King.* PUTNAM, RUTH, *Charles the Bold.* SEIGNOBOS, *The Evolution of the French People.* TILLEY, A. A. (Ed.), *Medieval France,* chaps. ii–iv. THORNDIKE, *History of Medieval Europe,* chaps. xiv, xxvi.

B. Source Material. FROISSART, SIR JOHN, *Chronicles of England, France and the Adjoining Countries.* See also *The Boy's Froissart* (ed. by Lanier). *Memoirs of Philip de Commines.*

CHAPTER XXIV

A. **General Reading.** ADAMS, G. B., *Constitutional History of England* (rev. ed., 1934) ; *History of England from the Norman Conquest to the Death of John.* CHEYNEY, *Social and Industrial History of England* and *Short History of England.* CROSS, *A History of England and Greater Britain.* DAVIS, H. W. C. (Ed.), *Medieval England.* GREEN, *Short History of the English People.* HASKINS, *The Normans in European History,* chap. iii. There are also the great series edited by HUNT and POOLE, on political history, and TRAIL and MANN'S *Social England.* For references on life in medieval England see under Chapter XXVI. McKECHNIE, *Magna Carta.* MUNRO and SONTAG, *The Middle Ages,* chaps. xvii, xviii, xxxv–xxxvi. NORGATE, K., *England under the Angevin Kings.* THORNDIKE, *History of Medieval Europe,* chap. xxv.

B. **Source Material.** BLAND, BROWN, and TAWNEY, *English Economic History: Select Documents.* CHEYNEY, *Readings in English History.* COLBY, *Selections from the Sources of English History.* HENDERSON, Select *Historical Documents of the Middle Ages,* Book I. KENDALL, *Source Book of English History.* LEE, *Source Book of English History.* MORGAN, R. B., *Readings in English Social History.* STUBBS, *Select Charters* (1913).

CHAPTER XXV

A. **General Reading.** ARCHER and KINGSFORD, *The Crusades.* BAYNES, N. H., *The Byzantine Empire* (Home University Series). *Cambridge Medieval History,* Vol. V, chaps. vi–ix. CUTTS, *Scenes and Characters of the Middle Ages.* DAVIS, *Medieval Europe,* chaps. vii, viii. *Encyclopædia Britannica* (14th ed.), article "Crusades," by ERNEST BARKER. JUSSERAND, *English Wayfaring Life in the Middle Ages.* KREY, A. C., *The First Crusade.* LANE-POOLE, S., *Saladin and the Fall of Jerusalem.* LANE-POOLE and GILMAN, *The Moors in Spain.* MUNRO and SONTAG, *The Middle Ages,* chaps. xx–xxi, xxv. NORGATE, K., *Richard the Lion Heart.* PAETOW, L. J. (Ed.), *The Crusades* (essays). SALZMANN, *English Life in the Middle Ages.* SCHEVILL, F., *History of the Balkan Peninsula.* THORNDIKE, *History of Medieval Europe,* chap. xvi. WEBSTER, *History of Commerce,* chaps. vi–vii. WRIGHT, J. K., *Geographical Lore in the Time of the Crusades.* See also references to knights, pilgrims, and wayfaring life under Chapter XXVII.

B. **Source Material.** THATCHER and McNEAL, *A Source Book for Medieval History,* Sect. IX. *Translations and Reprints,* University of Pennsylvania, Vol. I, Nos. 2, 4 ; Vol. III, No. 1. VILLEHARDOUIN and JOINVILLE, *Memoirs of the Crusades.*

CHAPTER XXVI

A. **General Reading.** ABBOTT, W. C., *Expansion of Europe,* Vol. I, chaps. i, iii. ABRAM, A., *English Life and Manners in the Middle Ages,* chaps. iii (town life), vii (business life), xiii–xvi. BEAZLEY, *The Dawn of Modern Geography,* Vol. III. BOISSONNADE, P., *Life and Work in the Middle Ages,* Book II, chaps. iv, vi–viii. CHEYNEY, *Social and Industrial History of England.* COTTERILL, H. B., *Medieval Italy.* COULTON, G. G., *The Medieval Village.* CRUMP and JACOBS, *The Legacy of the Middle Ages.* CUNNINGHAM, *Western Civilization in its Economic Aspects,* Vol. II. CUTTS, E. L., *Scenes and Characters of the Middle Ages,* Part VII. GIBBINS, *Industrial History of England.* JAYNE, *Vasco da Gama and his Successors.* KNIGHT, M. M., *Economic History of Europe to the End of the Middle Ages.* LIPSON, E., *An Economic Introduction to the History of England,* chaps. ii, v, vi–viii. LODGE, R., *Close of the Middle Ages.* MARTIN, *The Golden Age of Prince Henry the Navigator.* MUNRO and SONTAG, *The Middle Ages,* chaps. xxvi, xxviii, xxix. PIRENNE, *Medieval Cities.* POWER, E., *Medieval People.* SALZMANN, L., *English Life in the Middle Ages,* chaps. ii–iv (country, town, and home life), xi (industry, trade, and finance). SYNGE, *A Book of Discovery.* SYMONDS, *Age of Despots.* THORNDIKE, *History of Medieval Europe,* chaps. xvii–xix, xxi, xxxii. TICKNER, *Social and Industrial History of England.* VINOGRADOV, *Growth of the Manor.* Also references at end of Chapter XXVI.

B. **Source Material.** BLAND, BROWN, and TAWNEY, *English Economic History: Select Documents.* MARCO POLO, *Travels* (Everyman's Library). OGG, *A Source Book of Medieval History,* chap. xx. THATCHER and McNEAL, *A Source Book for Medieval History,* Sect. X. *Travels of Sir John Mandeville* (Macmillan).

Bibliography 861

CHAPTER XXVII

A. General Reading. BULFINCH, *The Age of Chivalry.* BURCKHARDT, *The Civilization of the Renaissance.* CORNISH, *Chivalry.* CRUMP and JACOB, *The Legacy of the Middle Ages.* CUTTS, *Scenes and Characters of the Middle Ages,* Part VII. DAVIS, H. W. C. (Ed.), *Medieval England,* chap. vi. (heraldry). DE VINNE, *Invention of Printing.* HASKINS, *The Renaissance of the Twelfth Century* and *The Rise of Universities.* HEARNSHAW, F. J. C., *Medieval Contributions to Modern Civilization,* chaps. iv–v. HULME, *Renaissance and Reformation.* MELLER, *A Knight's Life in the Days of Chivalry.* MUNRO and SONTAG, *The Middle Ages,* chaps. xxxi, xl. PRESTAGE (Ed.), *Chivalry,* chap. ix (the idea of a gentleman), PUTNAM, *Books and their Makers during the Middle Ages.* RAIT, *Life in the Medieval University.* RANDALL, *The Making of the Modern Mind,* Book II. RASHDALL, *History of the Universities in the Middle Ages.* SAINTSBURY, *The Flourishing of Romance.* SANDAYS, *History of Classical Scholarship.* SEDGWICK and TYLER, *History of Science.* SMITH, J. H., *The Troubadors at Home.* SMITH, P., *Erasmus.* TAYLOR, H. O., *The Medieval Mind.* TICKNER, *A Social and Industrial History of England,* chaps. ii–iv (schools, universities, and books). TILLEY, A. A. (Ed.), *Medieval France,* chaps. vi–x. THORNDIKE, *History of Magic and Experimental Science.* THORNDIKE, *History of Medieval Europe,* chaps. xx–xxi. VAN DYCK, *The History of Painting.* WALSH, *The Thirteenth the Greatest of Centuries.*

B. Source Material. STEELE, *Medieval Lore* (extracts from an encyclopedia of the thirteenth century). *The Song of Roland* (O'Hagan (Tr.)). *Aucassin and Nicolette* (tr.). MALORY, *Morte d'Arthur* (a collection of the stories of the Round Table made in the fifteenth century for English readers). ROBINSON and ROLFE, *Petrarch* (letters). WHITCOMB, *Literary Source Book of the Italian Renaissance.* SCHEVILL, F., *The First Century of Italian Humanism* (source problems). COULTON, *Life in the Middle Ages,* Vols. II and III, or *Medieval Garner* (1 vol.).

CHAPTER XXVIII

A. General Reading. ABBOTT, W. C., *The Expansion of Europe,* Vol. I. ADAMS, G. B., *Growth of the French Nation.* ARMSTRONG, E., *Charles V.* Arnold and GUILLAUME, *The Legacy of Islam.* BRYCE, *Holy Roman Empire,* chap. xiv. *Cambridge Medieval History,* Vol. VIII, chap. xv; Vol. II, chap. ii. CHAPMAN, C. E., *History of Spain.* HAYES, C. J. H., *A Political and Cultural History of Modern Europe,* Vol. I, chap. i. JOHNSON, *Europe in the Sixteenth Century.* MERRIMAN, R. B., *Rise of the Spanish Empire,* Vols. II–III. MUNRO and SONTAG, *The Middle Ages,* chaps. xxiii, xxxv–xxxvi. THOMPSON, *Middle Ages,* Vol. II, chap. xxiii (Mohammedans and Christian Spain).

B. Source Material. *Memoirs of Philip de Commines* (ed. by A. R. Scoble) (c. 1460–1500). DE MONSTRELET, *Chronicles.*

CHAPTER XXIX

A. General Reading. ROBINSON'S *Western Europe* (latest ed., 2 vols.) has a fuller account of the Church. CREIGHTON, *History of the Papacy,* Vol. III. CUTTS, *Scenes and Characters of the Middle Ages* and *Parish Priests and their People.* The works of FLICK and WALKER cited above. FOAKES-JACKSON, *Introduction to the History of Christianity.* GASQUET, *English Monastic Life.* HAYES, *Political and Cultural History,* Vol. I, chap. iv. HEATH, S., *Pilgrim Life in the Middle Ages.* JESSOPP, *The Coming of the Friars.* LEA, H. C., *A History of the Inquisition of the Middle Ages.* (Account of the medieval Church and the abuses that prevailed. Vol. I also contains chapters upon the origin of the Franciscan and Dominican orders.) MUNRO and SONTAG, *The Middle Ages,* chaps. xxxii, xxxiv, xxxviii. PASTOR, *History of the Popes.* SABATIER, *Saint Francis.* SMITH, Preserved, *Age of the Reformation,* chap. i, and *Erasmus.* TAYLOR, H. O., *The Medieval Mind.*

B. Source Material. THATCHER and MCNEAL, *A Source Book for Medieval History.* SCOTT, HYMA, and NOYES, *Readings in Medieval History.* COULTON, G. G., *Life in the Middle Ages,* Vols. I and IV.

CHAPTER XXX

A. **General Reading.** BEARD, *Martin Luther.* *Cambridge Modern History,* Vol. II. CHAMBERS, R. W., *Thomas More.* CHEYNEY, *Short History of England,* chap. xii. EMERTON, *Erasmus. Encyclopædia Britannica* (11th ed.), article "Reformation," by J. H. ROBINSON. GASQUET, *The Eve of the Reformation.* HULME, *Renaissance and Reformation.* JACKSON, S. M., *Huldreich Zwingli.* JANSSEN, *History of the German People,* Vols. I–II. LINDSAY, *History of the Reformation* (2 vols.). McGIFFERT, *Martin Luther.* PASTOR, *History of the Popes.* POLLARD, *Henry VIII.* SHAPIRO, J. S., *Social Reform and the Reformation.* SMITH, P., *The Age of the Reformation* and *The Life and Letters of Martin Luther* and *Erasmus.* TAYLOR, H. O., *Thought and Expression in the Sixteenth Century* (2 vols.). WALKER, W., *John Calvin.*
B. **Source Material.** CHEYNEY, *Readings in English History,* chap. xii. GEE and HARDY, *Documents Illustrative of English Church History.* HAZLITT, *Luther's Table Talk. Luther's Primary Works* and *The Augsburg Confession* (ed. by Wace and Buchheim). SMITH, P., *Luther's Correspondence.* WHITCOMB, *Source Book of the German Renaissance.*

CHAPTER XXXI

General Reading. ADAMS, *Growth of the French Nation,* chap. xi. *Cambridge Modern History,* Vol. II, chaps. ix, xv, xvii–xix; Vol. III, chaps. i, vi–viii, xv, xix, xx; Vol. IV, chaps. i, iii–vi, xiii–xiv. GINDELY, *History of the Thirty Years' War.* HAYES, *A Political and Cultural History of Modern Europe,* Vol. I, chaps. iv–v. JOHNSON, *Europe in the Sixteenth Century,* chaps. vii–ix. LINDSAY, *History of the Reformation,* Vol. II. MOTLEY, *Rise of the Dutch Republic.* PERKINS, J. B., *France under Mazarin,* chaps. iv, v, vi, vii, x. PUTNAM, RUTH, *William the Silent.* SMITH, P., *Age of the Reformation.* WAKEMAN, *Ascendancy of France,* chaps. i–v.
GRIFFIS'S *Brave Little Holland* and HAAREN and POLAND'S *Famous Men of the Middle Ages* (Henry IV, Gustavus Adolphus, Charles V) are written especially for young people.

CHAPTER XXXII

A. **General Reading.** ADAMS, G. B., *Constitutional History of England* (1934). BUCHAN, *Oliver Cromwell. Cambridge Modern History,* Vol. III, chap. xvii; Vol. IV, chaps. viii–xii. CHEYNEY, *Short History of England.* CROSS, *History of England.* GARDINER, *The First Two Stuarts and the Puritan Revolution.* HAYES, *A Political and Cultural History of Modern Europe,* Vol. I, chaps. ix–x. MACAULAY, *Essay on Milton* and *History of England.* POLLARD, *History of England,* chap. v. TREVELYAN, *England under the Stuarts.*
B. **Source Material.** BLAND, BROWN, and TAWNEY, *English Economic History,* Part II. CHEYNEY, *Readings in English History.* CLARENDON, *History of the Great Rebellion.* COLBY, *Selections from the Sources of English History,* Part VI (The Stuart Period). DYKES, *Source Book of Constitutional History from 1660.* GARDINER, S. R., *Constitutional Documents of the Puritan Revolution.* GEE and HARDY, *Documents Illustrative of English Church History.* LEE, *Source Book of English History.* MORGAN, R. B., *Readings in English Social History,* Book IV. PROTHERO. *Select Statutes . . . of the Reigns of Elizabeth and James I.* ROBERTSON, C. G., *Select Statutes . . . to illustrate English Constitutional History, 1660–1832.*

CHAPTER XXXIII

A. **General Reading.** ABBOTT, *Expansion of Europe,* chap. xxv. ADAMS, *Growth of the French Nation. Cambridge Modern History,* Vol. V (Age of Louis XIV). HASSALL, A., *Louis XIV.* HAYES, *A Political and Cultural History of Modern Europe,* Vol. I, chap. vi. JOHNSON, A. H., *The Age of the Enlightened Despot,* chaps. i–iii. LOWELL, *The Eve of the French Revolution.* PERKINS, *France under Louis XIV* and *France under the Regency,* chaps. i–x. TAINE, *The Ancient Régime.* WAKEMAN, *Ascendancy of France,* chaps. ix–xi, xiv–xv. WELLS, *Outline of History.* Vol. II, chap. xxxvi.
B. **Source Material.** SAINT-SIMON, *Memoirs* (English tr., 3 vols.).

CHAPTER XXXIV

General Reading. ABBOTT, *Expansion of Europe*, Vol. II. ANTHONY, K., *Catherine the Great*. ATKINSON, *History of Germany (1715–1815)*. BAIN, R. N., *The Pupils of Peter the Great* and *Slavonic Europe: A Political History of Poland and Russia from 1447 to 1796*. BRIGHT, *Maria Theresa* and *Joseph II*. *Cambridge Modern History*, Vols. V–VI. CARLYLE, *Frederick the Great*. HASSALL, *The Balance of Power*. HAYES, *A Political and Cultural History of Modern Europe*, Vol. I, chaps. vii–viii. HENDERSON, *Short History of Germany*. JOHNSON, *The Age of the Enlightened Despot*, chaps. iv, vii, ix, x. KLUCHEVSKY, *A History of Russia*. MARRIOTT and ROBERTSON, *Evolution of Prussia*. PARES, B. A., *History of Russia*. PHILLIPS, *History of Poland* (Home University Library). PLATONOV, *History of Russia*. POKROVSKY, *History of Russia*. RAMBAUD, *History of Russia*. REDDAWAY, W. F., *Frederick the Great and the Rise of Prussia*. TUTTLE, H., *History of Prussia*. WALISZEWSKI, *Life of Peter the Great*.

CHAPTER XXXV

A. General Reading. ABBOTT, *The Expansion of Europe*, Vol. II. ANDRÉ MARIUS, *Columbus*. BAKER, J. N. L., *History of Geographical Discovery and Exploration*. BEAZLEY, *The Dawn of Modern Geography*. BOLTON and MARSHALL, *Colonization of North America*. BOURNE, *Spain in America*. CHEYNEY, *European Background of America*. CUNNINGHAM, W., *Growth of Industry and Commerce*. DANVERS, *The Portuguese in India*. FISKE, *The American Revolution*. HAYES, *A Political and Cultural History of Modern Europe*, Vol. I, chaps. ix–x. HUNTER, *A Brief History of the Indian People*. JAYNE, *Vasco da Gama and his Successors*. MERRIMAN, *The Rise of the Spanish Empire*. MUZZEY, *A History of Our Country* (1936), with valuable study aids and excellent bibliography. PARKMAN, *The Struggle for a Continent*. PRESCOTT, *The Conquest of Mexico* and *The Conquest of Peru* (in one volume in Modern Library). ROBINSON, J. HOWARD, *The Development of the British Empire*. SMITH, *Oxford History of India*. SYNGE, *Book of Discovery*. VAN LOON, *Golden Book of the Dutch Navigators*. WILLIAMSON, J. A., *Short History of British Expansion*.

B. Source Material. CHEYNEY, *Readings in English History*. HART, *American History as told by Contemporaries*. *Jesuit Relations and Allied Documents* (1 vol.; ed. by Kenton). MUZZEY, *Readings in American History*. ROBINSON and BEARD, *Readings in Modern European History*, Vol. I, chaps. vi–vii.

Index